READING INSTRUCTION FOR CLASSROOM AND CLINIC

EDWARD B. FRY
READING CENTER
RUTGERS UNIVERSITY

McGRAW-HILL BOOK COMPANY

NEW YORK ST. LOUIS SAN FRANCISCO DÜSSELDORF
JOHANNESBURG KUALA LUMPUR LONDON MEXICO
MONTREAL NEW DELHI PANAMA RIO DE JANEIRO
SINGAPORE SYDNEY TORONTO

This book was set in Century Schoolbook, and was printed and bound by Kingsport Press, Inc. The designer was Edward Zytko; the drawings were done by John Cordes, J. & R. Technical Serivces, Inc. The editors were William J. Willey and David Dunham. Matt Martino supervised production.

READING INSTRUCTION FOR CLASSROOM AND CLINIC

Library of Congress Catalog Card Number
71–168461
07–022604–0

1234567890 KPKP 798765432

CONTENTS

PREFACE

I have tried to write a readable book about reading that is a little more modern and complete than the earlier how-to-do-it types of books and a little more helpful than books which cite numerous conflicting research studies.

There is certainly a place for both types of books in the broad spectrum of educating teachers, but my experience in teaching graduate reading courses leads me to believe that there is also a place for a book which tells how to teach reading in loud, clear language, gives the teacher numerous alternatives among older and newer methods, and tells him or her something of the vastness of the field of reading.

Reading materials no longer consist of only books and charts; they now consist of boxes of folded pieces of cardboard, overhead transparencies, and plastic cubes which roll out sentences. Comprehension is still taught by asking students questions after they have read a passage; but the questions can be graded by taxonomies, and the drill might even be in the form of programmed instruction or the cloze technique. Even phonics which has been around so long is no longer just the careful thinking of one person but is based on phoneme-grapheme frequency counts, similar to basic word lists; and a degree of completeness and precision has been added.

This book has a remedial reading emphasis. Hence it is aimed at a second course in reading rather than a beginning reading methods course for elementary teachers. It is entitled *Reading Instruction for Classroom and Clinic* because some teachers who take this course will wish to remain in a regular classroom and improve their own reading instruction while others will become reading specialists and handle other teachers' problem readers. I have tried not to forget the secondary school because it is an important and a growing field and because the difference between teaching reading in an elementary school and in a secondary school is often slight.

Because some secondary teachers may not be familiar with regular elementary classroom reading methods and because some upper elementary teachers may wish a quick review, a chapter on the traditional method of teaching reading, namely, basal texts, is included. This chapter also serves as a convenient point of departure when we consider linguistic and kinesthetic methods.

The first chapter is a simple overview on how to teach reading, which is amplified and expanded in the rest of the book.

Since a basic premise of *Reading Instruction for Classroom and Clinic* is to "start where the child is," the theme of "test-teach-test" runs throughout many sections, beginning with Chapter 2 on measuring reading achievement. This chapter is balanced with Chapter 11 on selecting reading materials. Here another basic premise is encountered—that of matching the child's ability to the difficulty level of the materials. These chapters, together with the chapters on phonics, basic vocabulary, and comprehension, form the basis of what is taught in reading.

The latter half of the book is a bit more clinical or diagnostic in that it discusses expectancy and IQ tests, vision, hearing, and other physical and psychological areas where problems can occur.

Nothing used to unnerve me more than to have taught what I thought was a fairly satisfactory course in remedial reading in the spring semester, only to have a student confront me in the summer, almost in a state of panic, saying: "I have just been assigned to teach remedial reading! What do I do?" After several semesters I learned that what the teacher really wanted was a little reassurance and perhaps a suggestion on what to do the first day or two; after that, her knowledge gained from the course and previous experience usually took over and she was handling the course like the professional that she really was. In order to help in solving the perennial problem of "What do I do?" I have tried to answer it in several ways—as a simple overview in the first chapter, in more detail in the chapters on phonics, basic vocabulary, and comprehension, and as a bigger package in the chapters on organization and special methods.

But reading is not always as simple as step 1, step 2, step 3, and some sections of the chapters on comprehension and varieties of special methods still rely upon individual selection and creativity on the part of the teacher. Neither will the teacher find an easy answer to the short question, "Why do some children fail?" Diagnosis might provide some insights, but basically I have concentrated on a more positive goal of just accepting the child "where he is" and then moving him toward the goal of becoming an efficient reader. Toward that end, I have included a chapter on higher reading skills.

Last but not least, this is partially a source book. The appendixes at the end of each chapter indude much useful material in such areas as testing, phonics, basic vocabularies, readability formulas. These, it is hoped, will make this book a handy reference course for teaching reading and testing in either classroom or clinic.

I would be pleased to receive comments from readers.

Edward B. Fry

1

OVERVIEW – HOW TO TEACH READING

How do you teach a child to read?

This is an easy question and a difficult question. It can be answered in a sentence. It can be answered in a paragraph. It can be answered in a chapter. If you answered it in a whole book, there would still be more to tell.

But to illustrate the first answer, here is a one-sentence description of how you teach a child to read: "You teach a child to read by helping him to learn the relationship between the printed symbols and their meanings."

You might say that that is not much of an explanation, and you would be correct. Nevertheless, this is a very fundamental concept and one which underlies almost all reading instruction. Well, perhaps a one-sentence definition is not too satisfactory. Let us try a one-paragraph answer to our opening question: "Teaching reading usually begins by presenting the child with simple, carefully controlled vocabulary arranged in short, easy sentences in a book or on a chart. The child is given help and practice in reading these sentences both aloud and silently. More words are added to the reading material, and the sentences and stories get longer. Phonic skills are taught, that is, the relationship between letters and sounds are made clear. Comprehension skills are developed, that is, the child reads silently and answers many kinds of questions. The reading matter, phonics lessons, and comprehension drills gradually increase in difficulty as the child demonstrates increasing ability. This usually takes quite a bit of reading practice and many review lessons."

Perhaps the one-paragraph explanation of teaching reading is more satisfactory. But it still does not give great insight into the reading process, nor does it tell specifically what methods are best for teaching the child to read. Let us therefore try the one-chapter explanation and follow this with the one-book explanation.

This book is written from the standpoint of the individual child. Certainly many of the methods discussed herein apply to classroom situations, but to understand the reading process we must consider what happens to *a* child, not to some vague thing called a *group*.

HOW DOES ONE TEACH A CHILD TO READ?

Let us assume that you are confronted for the first time with the task of teaching a child to read. How will you go about it?

DETERMINE THE CHILD'S READING ABILITY The first thing to determine is the present reading level of the child. Do not be influenced by his size, his age, how many years he has been in school, or any other factor which has only a general correlation with reading skills. Find out for yourself as closely as possible what level of material the child can successfully read; this can be quickly and easily done by using the oral reading paragraphs found in the Appendix to Chapter 2. In the next chapter we will discuss the limitations of oral reading tests and other methods of determining reading ability level, but for now let us state simply and firmly that the first thing to do is to find out the child's reading level.

SELECT PROPER MATERIAL After the child's reading level has been determined, choose some reading material in the appropriate level from a selection of graded materials. (Information on graded reading materials is given in Chapter 3.) In other words, one of the most important things a reading teacher does is to match the reading ability of the student with the difficulty level of the reading material. It is important to do a careful and accurate job of matching because the farther she misses the match, the more difficult her teaching job will be; and the closer the match, the easier her teaching will be.

A simple way of checking the difficulty level of a book or article for a particular child is to ask him to read aloud from several randomly selected places. If he makes about one mistake in every twenty words this book is about right for him, and the teacher (or another student) can help him with the difficult words. If he makes fewer than one mistake in twenty words, the book can be read silently for pleasure or practice. If the child makes noticeably more mistakes than one in every twenty words, that book should not be used for him.

At times this book may seem too easy or too elementary, but I have found in my experience of training teachers that many of them literally *do not know what to do first.* When they look at the child, seemingly, all sorts of vague theories of education pop into their heads. They may have been told a hundred times that you should "begin where the child is"; yet, when a real live child walks up to them, they seem to blank out with not the faintest idea of what to do. Unfortunately, in their eagerness, even experienced teachers will sometimes begin "teaching" before they know "where the child is." Some basic procedures are fundamental to the entire learning process. They could be stated in much more complex terms, but there is not much point in doing so. For the time being, let us proceed simply and clearly. Before finishing this book, however, you may appreciate that reading is a much more complex process than it appears to be.

HAVE THE CHILD READ ALOUD AND SILENTLY After you have found the child's reading ability level and matched it with the correct reading material, what do you do next? You open the book and have the child read aloud, helping him as often as necessary. You then have him practice reading silently, again helping him if he needs it. This can be done alone or in groups. Keep these practice lessons short so the child does not become bored or fatigued. Schedule the sessions regularly and frequently. For student interest, reading material is often presented on charts or cards and in filmstrips, games, and pamphlets; it does not really matter how it is presented as long as it is at the right level.

TEST AND TEACH INSTANT WORDS For children and all learners, material is usually presented in a graded order of difficulty—easiest things first. Much research has been conducted to determine the proper vocabulary and its order of presentation for the teaching of reading. This is the strong point of most major series of reading texts, which begin with very few words in the first little book (seventeen in some preprimers) and gradually increase the vocabulary load. This increase in vocabulary load can be seen on the last few pages of most children's reading texts. So, teachers using a basic reading series have a built-in graduated vocabulary. However, in remedial reading, individualized reading, and multitext reading programs, it is a good idea to supplement and cross-check on normal vocabulary development by having some systematic list of new words to be taught. A carefully graded list, which we shall call the Instant Words, can be found in the Appendix to Chapter 4.

The Instant Words, which are the commonest words in the English language, are arranged in order of frequency of occurrence in reading material and in children's writing. A child should learn to recognize them instantly in order to have ease in reading because they occur so very often. They correspond roughly to the reading difficulty level of materials. Roughly, groups marked I are first grade, groups marked II are second grade, and so on.

The same procedure used to determine the reading level of words (which is then matched with the difficulty level of material) can be followed with vocabulary. Ask the child to read the first five words at the top of each group of twenty-five Instant Words, beginning with the first group if necessary. If he has trouble pronouncing any of them aloud, ask him to read the entire column and check the words he misses. These may be taught in a variety of ways—by having him listen to them, review them, take spelling lessons on them, play card games with them, and others. Many methods of testing and teaching Instant Words will be given in Chapter 4 for both individual and group situations.

PHONICS Basically, our writing system is phonetic. "Phonetic" means that our letter symbols tend to represent speech sounds. There are many exceptions, but every good reader should know at least the basic phonic principles. Phonics are a tremendous help to older students, particularly boys, in learning to read. Use the phonics check test in Chapter 6 to determine the child's ability and the order of teaching phonetic skills. There are also a number of phonics charts with carefully chosen example words that will help you in teaching all the major phonetic rules. Further teaching suggestions are also given in Chapter 6.

Exactly when to begin the teaching of phonics is an emotionally loaded question. Research results are inconclusive; so, in the vacuum, many people have substituted hot arguments. Personally, I think it should begin in kindergarten under the guise of reading readiness activities (playing with letters, coloring them, and mentioning their sounds) and under the guise of speech improvement (reading poems and games aloud and emphasizing different speech sounds). In any event, I would have regular phonic lessons in the first grade and teach a fairly complete line by the third grade with some repetition, remedial lessons, and fine points taught throughout the elementary years. Phonics can often be taught as part of a spelling lesson, as is done in many parts of the country. It does not make any difference what you call it, as long as the child learns the relationship between letters and their sounds. In phonics, as in everything else, you start where the child is—and you test, teach, test again, and then teach some more.

Secondary teachers usually find it necessary to teach (or, at least, to review) phonic skills for slow and remedial students.

COMPREHENSION There is no point in reading if the child doesn't understand what he is reading. The purpose of reading is to communicate with the author, namely to receive his ideas. Comprehension is usually not too difficult for beginning readers because their speaking and listening vocabularies are far superior to their reading vocabulary. It is usually just a process of showing them the relationship between written and spoken language. However, within a few years after they have learned to read, comprehension becomes a major concern and usually must specifically be taught. The usual method of teaching comprehension is to have the child read a short passage then to have him answer written or oral questions. There are plenty of drill materials available. (See Chapter 10 for suggested variations of methods and materials.)

PRACTICE Children simply cannot learn to read unless they are given ample practice. This, however, should not be used as an excuse for repeated drills that are boring to the children. They do require practice to learn to read orally and silently. It takes practice to learn phonics. It takes practice to learn the Instant Words (and to recognize them instantly without phonics or context cues). Games provide excellent practice methods. In any event, keep the reading lesson moving. Go from oral reading to phonics charts to word games to silent reading comprehension drills, and so forth. I often advise teachers to have three or four different kinds of reading activities each hour. Schedule regular lesson periods and stick to them come hell or high water, PTA meetings, or Little League baseball games.

Of course, one of the best methods of practice is simply to supply a book that the child finds interesting and let him read. Usually the child's attention can be held during extended silent reading if the book is a little on the easy side and is interesting to him. For silent pleasure reading, help the child to select a book that is easier than you would use for instruction. Oftentimes it is possible to encourage the child to read on his own by supporting his visits to the library, by assigning oral or written book reports, or by other means.

TRADE SECRETS

The following are a few tricks of the teaching trade. Although they apply especially to children who have problems in learning to read (remedial readers), they also apply to most children in normal classrooms.

SUCCESS Nothing motivates like success. In the reading clinic we say that a child must be successful with every lesson; and if he is not, then *we* have given him the wrong lesson or presented it in the wrong manner. I first seek a level where he can be successful. If he cannot read a whole sentence in a primer, I teach him just one word and say "That's great. We are really getting somewhere now. Let's see if we can learn two whole words today." By building little success upon little success, it is surprising how fast you can change a sullen, reluctant truant into an eager learner.

LOVE The student who cannot read is rejected in many ways every day in school and in the world. He is set aside. He is different. He is a failure. Worse yet, it is often the teaching profession that has failed him. And it is the teacher who daily reminds him of his shortcomings in the way class assignments are made in social studies or arithmetic. The reading teacher should turn this situation around. If love is too strong a word, let's say that the teacher must care about the child and must show by both word and deed that she is human.

DISCIPLINE Just as love implies a certain warmth and allowance for personality differences, so discipline is its counterbalance, for without some structure to the teaching situation, love has little opportunity to shine. A teacher cannot love a child who is always talking or who demands recess when she says it is time to study phonics. We insist that a child get to lessons on time, have a minimum of absences, pay attention during lessons, and not be disruptive. Occasionally after a few weeks of instruction we may have to offer some children a choice between stopping the reading lesson or settling down. I have never yet had the child decide to stop, but I would quite honestly let him do so if that is what he wanted. You can lead a horse to water but you can't make him drink. The decision to learn must be the child's and not his parents' or his teacher's.

INTEREST Children are poor actors when it comes to feigning interest. Learn to recognize the signs of fatigue and lack of interest, such as losing the place in oral reading, daydreaming, fiddling with objects, and so forth.

Discipline will not make boring lessons good lessons. The teacher must be skillful enough to present lessons that are easy enough to provide success, but difficult enough to provide challenge and growth. Try to find reading materials that have a natural interest for the child. Turn some of your drills into competitive games, again keeping in mind that each child must experience some success. Boys like baseball, skin diving, cowboy adventures, and so forth, not stories about neat little children in short pants pulling wagons.

EXPECTANCY One of the things the teacher should know very early in the teaching relationship is the student's level of reading expectancy. No one expects an eight-year-old to read like a high school student, and most people do not expect a three-year-old to read at all. Most teachers do expect, and should expect, a bright student to read better than a dull student. These are broad statements, but they are intended to introduce the concept of expectancy. Well-trained teachers develop much finer gradations of expectancy, usually based on IQ tests which yield a mental age. Whereas IQ tests are not to be believed categorically, they are an aid to the teacher's subjective opinion and should be used as one method of determining expected ability levels.

A ten-year-old boy of average intelligence should be reading at a grade level of 4.8. If, however, he is a little on the dull side and has an IQ of 90, he should only be reading at the 3.8 grade level. Conversely, if he is on the bright side and has an IQ of 110, he should be reading at the 5.8 grade level.

Note that it is quite normal to have a two-year spread in reading achievement at age ten; in fact, it is normal to have a four-year spread in reading ability at age ten (fourth grade) in a class of average size. One of the sad things about most teacher training is that teachers pass courses in educational psychology and say they understand the normal distribution curve in college, but in their own classrooms, working with real children, they have not the slightest notion of how to apply ability norms or what they mean.

If you do not know how to translate IQ into mental age and you cannot translate mental age into grade level expectancy, read Chapter 13 carefully. (It will save you a lot of trouble.) Needless to say, it is not fair to use IQ tests which require reading when testing students with suspected reading problems.

Reading lessons will not cure mental retardation, and it is not fair to parents or to the teaching profession to let a common assumption go unchallenged. The assumption, if you have not heard it before, goes like this: "If Johnny could only learn to read better, he would do better in all his school subjects." Before saying yes to this statement, be sure to give Johnny a nonreading IQ test. The reading methods discussed in this book work well for mentally retarded or dull children, but, they do not cure real mental retardation. This, unfortunately, is not what many parents and classroom teachers want.

Some leaders of some minority groups claim that all testing, including both reading achievement and IQ testing, is unfair and causes minority children to score abnormally low. There is some truth in this; the answer, however, is not to eliminate testing but to use tests properly. Quite obviously it is unfair to test a Spanish-speaking child on an English test. But great wrongs have also been done to many children by not discovering their greater potential and giving them remedial attention. Children from minority or disadvantaged groups follow the normal distribution curve just as any other group of children do; some are bright and some are dull. It is just as great a mistake not to recognize this fact as to assume that all are equally bright or equally dull. Good teachers try to develop each child to his maximum capacity.

THE BALANCE OF THIS BOOK In this chapter we have looked over the broad problem of how to teach children to read and touched very lightly on some important aspects of the problem. Each of the topics mentioned thus far will be expanded and refined on a practical level and on a more theoretical or research-oriented level. In addition, it is necessary to consider such topics as vision and hearing testing, causes for reading failure, and lesson organization for individual and group instruction.

2

MEASURING READING ACHIEVEMENT

Here are four situations which demand use of some measure of reading achievement.

1. A rather interesting thing occurs every semester at most reading clinics. It is found that from 25 to 50 percent of the children who apply for admittance do not need remedial reading at all. Quite often the trouble with the child is an overeager parent. Quite a few fourth grade boys are reading at the fourth grade level. These boys have normal intelligence and apparently are not emotionally disturbed; their only trouble is that their parents want them to read seventh grade material.

2. Teachers and guidance counselors, particularly in secondary schools, sometimes make the mistake of confusing lack of attention or motivation with lack of reading ability. It is certainly true that lack of reading ability can cause poor school motivation, but there are other causes. In any event, one of the first things to do with any student who is getting generally poor grades or who is underachieving in a particular subject is to give him a good reading test to find out if reading is one of the causes.

3. On receiving a new class or a new pupil, teachers are often given only vague information such as "Joe is a poor reader" and "Mary is a good reader" or "Bill was in my middle group." Hence, the first step in selecting pupils for special help

in reading at the beginning of reading instruction is to determine their present reading levels.

4. A remedial instructor, in beginning instruction with a new student, has only been told that he is a "nonreader." Some early textbooks and some older teachers frequently refer to a child as a nonreader if his reading ability is definitely below that of his peers. The term nonreader (or its Latin translation "dyslexic") has taken on certain emotional connotations which in the minds of some people are associated with some mysterious disease, or at least with the comfortable feeling that the difficulty had been explained by using the word. First of all, nonreader is a misnomer. Most so-called nonreaders who are sent for reading help and have been in school for several years are not nonreaders. They can read something, although usually at a level somewhat lower than their classmates. Even students who have failed to learn to read with any degree of fluency after one year of instruction still can usually read something, if only a few words or a few short sentences. Hence it is especially important for remedial reading teachers to test at the beginning of instruction and at fairly frequent intervals thereafter.

INFORMAL ORAL READING TESTS

Probably the easiest and fastest way of determining a student's reading ability (below seventh grade ability, at least) is by using a set of oral reading paragraphs.

The oral reading paragraph test, which is composed of a set of short paragraphs graded from easy to difficult, is read aloud by the student while the teacher notes the mistakes. By knowing the difficulty level of the paragraphs and then determining which ones the student can read, a quick and useful measure of the student's reading ability can be obtained. Such a set of paragraphs is included in the Appendix to this chapter. They were developed to screen students at a reading clinic, but many principals and classroom teachers use them for initial placement. There are two paragraphs at the first grade level (one easy and the other hard), two paragraphs at the second grade level, and two paragraphs at the third grade level. Then there is one paragraph each for grades four through seven. If you as teacher suspect that a child is reading at the fourth grade level, ask him to read the fourth grade paragraph. If he has considerable difficulty, have him read a second grade paragraph; then, if he masters that, let him progress to the easy third grade paragraph, and then to the difficult one. If, on the other hand, a fourth grade child quickly and easily reads the fourth grade paragraph, try him on a fifth or sixth grade paragraph to determine his level. It is not necessary to begin all children with the first paragraph, as this would only waste time; any child who can read the third grade paragraphs efficiently can certainly read the first grade paragraphs.

These paragraphs have what is called curricular validity. This means that they are not standardized, even though they have been used with a large number of children; rather, they are intended to help the teacher judge the level of curriculum material on which the child can work. If the child can read the beginning second grade paragraph with only one mistake, the teacher might assume that this child could read an easy second grade book by himself, but that for reading instruction, he might work best and most efficiently in a hard or upper-second-grade book. The teacher would, of course, want to use more then just one paragraph (sometimes two or three are helpful) to determine the student's independent and instructional levels. However, it is much better and much more accurate to use these paragraphs than simply to use the information that "Joe is in the second grade." Sometimes knowing the grade in which the child is physically placed is misleading when starting reading instruction.

TEST STANDARDIZATION

In discussing how to measure reading ability and having already used such terms as curricular validity and standardization, it might be helpful to explain exactly what standardization means in a reading test. A "standardized test" is one that has been tried out on a large number of children. Let us say we have a reading test with fifty items ranging from very easy to difficult. We administer this test to 1,000 elementary school children and find on analyzing the results that the average second grader gets twenty-three items correct and the average third grader gets thirty-six items correct. If the test is given in the middle of the year, we now make up a table and say that a raw score of 23 gives us a grade placement level of 2.5 and a raw score of 36 gives us a grade placement level of 3.5.

Now along comes Johnny Jones. Since he takes the test and gets thirty-six items correct, we say that his reading ability is equivalent to that of a third grader, or that his reading grade is 3.5. Please note that we have not said anything about the kind of book that Johnny Jones can read. We have only determined how Johnny compares with the 1,000 children in this particular standardized group. It is quite possible, and often happens, that a child can score 2.3 on a standardized reading test and yet cannot read a second-grade book if his life depends upon it.

It is true that there is a rough correlation between scores on a standardized reading test and the type of curriculum material that the student can use. However, this rough correlation is not accurate enough for reading instruction, particularly since some standardized reading tests tend to give a grade placement somewhat higher than the curriculum material. To put this in another way, a second-grade textbook is usually a little too difficult for most second graders. It is certainly not too difficult for second graders in a favorable socioeconomic situation in which the average mental age is above that of the national norms for second graders, but in the "average school" (particularly in schools which have children who are a little below average), "second grade" books are often a little too advanced. This is perhaps one cause for the large number of children who are identified as needing remedial reading.

One reason for this is that superior schools tend to set the standards. An educator in a slightly below-average school does not like to admit that he must still use a first-grade book with his beginning second graders; hence, he will plow right ahead, buy the second-grade book, and proceed to use it, even though the first-grade book would be far better for the children. Sometimes it seems that the people who make the decisions to buy the books do not know what the children in a classroom are really like or what their levels of achievement are. Certainly, if their only input of information consists of the average scores on the standardized tests, they are apt to make the same mistake. Curriculum-centered tests like the oral test in the Appendix to this chapter will help to avoid this use of inappropriately graded materials.

LIMITATIONS OF ORAL READING TESTING

No single method of determining reading level is completely accurate. This is certainly true of oral reading paragraphs. One major cause of oral reading inaccuracy is that children are nervous during the testing situation. Every child is a little nervous at having to read alone before a teacher who is counting the mistakes being made. A little nervousness is normal and the test makes allowance for this. However, certain children become so tense and emotionally involved in the oral reading testing situation that they make many unnecessary mistakes, which they would not have made in a more relaxed situation. To counteract this, the teacher must use other methods of testing such as silent reading tests. She should also observe the child during reading lessons and in other reading situations.

Sometimes children actually read better in an oral situation than they do in a more normal silent reading situation. I have always enjoyed the story reputedly attributed to Horace Mann, one of the first school inspectors in the United States, who would test children in the rural schools by giving them a newspaper to read aloud. The country children, never having seen a newspaper, would read the top line all the way across the page regardless of the columns. This, of course, showed a classic lack of understanding of what they were reading. Sometimes when a child has been in a school or a classroom which places an overemphasis on oral reading ability, he will score higher on an oral reading paragraph than he really deserves. That is, his reading comprehension and general reading skills are not up to his oral reading grade level.

In defense of oral reading paragraphs it must be said that usually if a child can read the material aloud, with no mistakes or very few, he does actually comprehend the material. The reason for this is obvious. A child begins his first year in school with more than 5,000 words in his speaking vocabulary and a fairly complete knowledge of grammar, at least on a practical level. In reading on most of the primary levels, then, the initial task is to translate the visual symbol into a sound symbol which he can recognize.

As the child reaches the upper elementary grades, and especially the secondary school years, many more skills are associated with reading than the mere learning of the simple correspondence between visual and auditory symbols. But within the elementary ability ranges, oral reading is an excellent index of reading ability.

BETTS' LEVELS OF READING

An interesting conception of reading levels has been given by Emmett Betts, who postulates four levels of reading ability for each pupil.

BASAL LEVEL Basal level is the highest level at which a child can read for his own pleasure and enjoy it. At this level a child should be able to pronounce 99 percent of the words, if reading aloud, and score 90 percent on a comprehension test covering the material. In other words, he can pronounce practically all of the words and understand most of the ideas. If he has been properly trained, he can read on this level with expression and relative freedom from nervous tension symptoms.

INSTRUCTIONAL LEVEL At the instructional level, a child can read with help, as he does in a reading circle. He can pronounce 95 percent of the words and score 75 percent on an informal comprehension test. This level provides enough new words of sufficient difficulty to be challenging, yet not so difficult as to be frustrating.

FRUSTRATION LEVEL At the frustration level, the learning process breaks down and reading is poor. A child can pronounce only 90 percent of the words and would score 50 percent or less on a comprehension test. If left alone a child will not read on this level. If forced to read on the frustration level, bad habits and nervous signs will appear, i.e., a tense voice, erratic body movements, finger pointing, and other carry-overs from more juvenile habits. If forced to read silently on the frustration level, a child will try to avoid it, will be easily distracted, will read at a very slow rate, may use lip movement, loses his place, and in general does a poor job of reading.

Betts lists some of the symptons which may appear in any oral reading but which are most likely to appear when a child is reading at the frustration level:

1. Lack of rhythm, or word-by-word reading
2. Failure to interpret punctuation
3. High-pitched voice
4. Irregular breathing
5. Increased tendency to stutter

6. Meaningless word substitution
7. Repetition of words
8. Insertion of words
9. Partial and complete word reversals
10. Omission of words
11. Practically no eye-voice span (Good readers have a high eye-voice span, which means the eyes are moving ahead of the voice, and this is necessary for good comprehension and oral punctuation.)

CAPACITY LEVEL Capacity level is the highest level of material which a child can comprehend if the material is read to him. It is the goal of reading instruction to enable a child to read for himself anything which he can comprehend orally. This is seldom accomplished before seventh grade reading ability is achieved.

TABLE 2-1
BETTS' READING LEVELS

Basal level	Pronounce 99 percent of the words Comprehend 90 percent on an informal test
Child can read for himself and enjoy it. In oral reading, expression is good with few signs of nervousness. (This level also called Independent Reading Level.)	
Instructional level	Pronounce 95 percent of the words Comprehend 75 percent on an informal test
Child can read with help. Good for oral reading in group or silent reading where help with difficult words can be easily obtained from an adult or another child. This level is challenging but not frustrating – learning can occur.	
Frustration level	Pronounce 90 percent or less of words Comprehend 50 percent or less on an informal test
Child will not read on this level by himself (without real force). In oral reading many nervous symptoms appear. Material is so difficult it blocks learning and kills enthusiasm. Not to be used.	
Capacity level	Comprehend 75 percent if the material *is read to* the child
This is the theoretical level up to which a child can be taught to read. Capacity level frequently stays ahead of instructional level through the seventh grade.	

THE RULE OF 1-OUT-OF-20

Betts' three levels can also be simplified to what I call the "*1-out-of-20 rule.*" This is a quick and simple way of determining a child's reading level. Simply select a book which you hope is at the right level and ask the child to read aloud from it. If he makes about 1 mistake out of every 20 words, the book is on his instructional level. If he makes more errors than 1 out of 20 words, the book is on his frustration level. If he makes fewer errors than 1 out of 20 words, the book is on his basal level. This rule is often suggested to parents who wish to know how to help their children select books from the library. Like other simple rules related to reading, it is not infallible; but it is certainly superior to the practice followed by many parents who turn the child loose to select any book he sees, with no consideration of reading level. For example, Johnny would select a book on rockets if he is interested in rockets; the problem is that Johnny's reading ability is only at the third grade level, while the particular book happens to be written on the sixth grade level. In this case Johnny's failure at reading the book is practically assured, parents' pleas and teacher's admonitions notwithstanding. If the child insists on taking out a book that is much too hard for him because he is interested in the special subject matter, do not argue too much with him but try to interest him in taking out at least some books that are at a reading level in which success is reasonably assured.

One reason why so many children dislike or fail reading is that too much material is presented on their frustrational level. Quite frequently a child's textbooks, and this is particularly true of science books, are written on a level one or more grades higher than that in which they are used. This means that the average child must stumble along at his frustrational level in social studies, science, and arithmetic books. It is no wonder that he has to be driven to read them and that he develops a dislike for these subjects. But reading *instruction*, which gradually increases the difficulty level of material which he reads, can very definitely help a child in all of his school subjects.

STANDARDIZED ORAL READING TESTS

One of the oldest and most respected of oral reading tests is the Standardized Oral Reading Paragraphs by William S. Gray. This test consists of twelve graded paragraphs. The child reads aloud from one copy while the teacher records the time required for each paragraph and counts the number of errors on another copy of the test. The test directions instruct the teacher to note different types of errors, such as omissions, repetitions, substitutions, and grossly incorrent accents or mispronunciations. The total errors on each paragraph, combined with the time required, determine the score for each paragraph. The faster the student reads the paragraph, the more errors he is allowed. The scores for each paragraph are totaled to give a raw score, which can then be translated into a grade-level score. I have found that the grade-level score from the Gray oral reading test is usually lower that that obtained from other standardized silent reading tests and hence is more useful in selecting curriculum material. The Gray test has an added advantage in that many persons are familiar with it; and when results are reported to the schools, they are readily understood.

The recording of such specific types of oral reading errors as repetitions, omissions, reversals (saying *saw* for *was*), and substitutions is of very little help to the reading teacher. Earlier books went to great pains to suggest specific drills for correcting each type of reading error; in this book, however, the teacher is enjoined to consider all types of oral reading errors as simply symptoms of poor reading. Poor reading can be corrected by following such basic instructional procedures as helping the child to achieve success by giving him practice on material that is not frustrating, helping him to learn the phonics he needs, and improving his basic vocabulary. A more modern version of Gray's oral test was edited by Helen Robinson.

Another oral reading test which is widely used is the Gilmore Oral Reading Test. Like others, this oral test has a series of paragraphs graded in order of difficulty, which the child reads aloud; in addition a comprehension section is included. This test also provides space for the teacher to indicate the type of error (substitution, hesitation, omission, etc.). Because of the comprehension section, this test takes much longer to administer than Gray's oral or the oral reading paragraphs mentioned earlier. I prefer to measure reading comprehension on a group silent reading comprehension test. This saves time because it can be administered to large groups. Silent reading tests also give a more reliable comprehension score.

I have found that Gilmore oral norms give a grade-level score far too high, and thus are particularly bad for matching a pupil's reading level to suitable reading materials.

Another useful test involving individualized oral reading is the Diagnostic Reading Scales by George Spache. This test includes some word lists which are read aloud, and the results of these word lists guide the teacher in determining where to begin within the group of twenty-two reading passages. These scales yield three reading levels for each pupil: (1) an instructional level for all reading, (2) an independent level for silent reading, and (3) a potential level for auditory comprehension. Some phonic tests are also included in the Spache battery.

There are a number of other good oral reading tests, such as those developed by Morton Botel, Arthur Gates, and Donald Durrell. A complete list of published oral reading tests, together with critical evaluations, is contained in Buros' *Mental Measurement Yearbooks* or his new volume entitled *Reading Tests and Reviews.*

SILENT READING COMPREHENSION TEST

The most useful and the most common type of silent reading test is the paragraph comprehension test, consisting of a paragraph or two, followed by multiple-choice test questions. The paragraphs are ranked in order of difficulty and can range roughly from second grade through college graduate ability levels.

The advantage of this type of test is that it can be administered easily to a large group of students. It can be scored objectively, either by the teacher or by machine. And, because of the ease in collecting data, it is usually standardized on large groups throughout the country. The real benefit of this type of test is that it measures the child's silent reading comprehension. This, after all, is the major goal we are seeking in reading instruction. Most of a child's lifetime reading will not be oral reading; rather, it will be silent reading, during which he is expected to comprehend the material. In fact, harking back to our original definition of reading—namely, the ability to understand written symbols—we find that the paragraph comprehension test furnishes a measure of exactly that objective.

There are a number of excellent paragraph comprehension tests on the market. In Figure 2-1 are several samples of paragraph comprehension items from the Metropolitan Achievement Test, upper-primary level, which is designed for second and third grade children. The authors call this section of

TEST 3 *Reading: Stories*

SAMPLE

Talk, Polly.
You can talk, pretty bird.
Talk for the cooky.

A Polly is a —
☒ **bird** ☐ **girl** ☐ **cat**

B Polly can —
☐ **swim** ☐ **dance** ☒ **talk**

Last spring Paul and his sister Sue planted a garden. The garden was in two boxes on the roof. Daddy bought some special dirt for the garden. Mother showed them how to put the seeds just under the top dirt. Paul and Sue watered their garden every day. They made newspaper tents to shade the young plants from the hot sunlight.

41 The best name for this story is —
☐ **Some Special Seeds**
☐ **A Roof Garden**
☐ **Some Pretty Plants**
☐ **Paul and Sue**

42 The children planted the garden in the —
☐ **summer** ☐ **fall** ☐ **winter** ☐ **spring**

43 When Paul and Sue made a garden, Mother and Daddy —
☐ **were surprised** ☐ **helped**
☐ **were unhappy** ☐ **watched**

44 In this story, the word *just* means —
☐ **not far** ☐ **fair** ☐ **good** ☐ **almost**

45 The newspapers kept the plants from getting too —
☐ **hot** ☐ **wet** ☐ **cold** ☐ **dirty**

FIGURE 2-1 Sample page from Metropolitan Reading Test.

the test "Reading: Stories." In Figure 2.2 is a paragraph containing comprehension items from the California Reading Test, junior high level, designed for grades seven, eight, and nine. The authors call this section "Interpretation of Material." Thus, even though most authors use a paragraph comprehension test, they often refer to it by a different name.

TEST 2—SECTION G (Continued)

In the succeeding years, ships increased in size as well as in luxury. The Mauretania, launched in 1908, was considered a marvel because it weighed nearly 30,700 tons. It held the transatlantic speed record of five and one-half days for twenty years. Each year, however, brought changes in ships, with increased weight and speed, until the Bremen was built and crossed the Atlantic in nine hours less time than the previous record holder. Later the Queen Mary and the Normandie exceeded that record by about 24 hours. The present record is held by the S. S. United States.

✓ **Mark the number or letter of each correct answer. You may look back to find the answers.**

126. In the 19th century the Americans built the

[1] **clipper ships.**
[2] **Mayflower.**
[3] **Bremen.**
[4] **Mauretania.** ____126

127. American shipping was stimulated through competition with

[a] **Italy.**
[b] **Germany.**
[c] **Japan.**
[d] **England.** ____127

FIGURE 2-2 Sample page from the Interpretation of Material section of the California Reading Test, Junior High Level–Grades 7, 8, and 9.

Another aspect of silent reading that is measured in many different tests is a vocabulary, or word meaning, test. In this section, typically, one word or a short phrase is given and the student is asked to select one of four choices which means the same, about the same, or, in some instances, the opposite of the original work or statement. One value of this type of test is obvious in that it attempts to measure the child's knowledge of words. Sometimes vocabulary tests are more diagnostic when they divide words into several sections, such as mathematics, general science, or general reading. One of the difficulties of this type of test is that vocabulary is closely related to intelligence, e.g., the reading test really measures intelligence. While this unfortunate confusion between a so-called basic ability such as IQ and a learned ability such as reading can perhaps not be avoided, still it casts some doubt on the usefulness of this section of the test. Thus, *reading teachers should tend to rely more heavily on the paragraph comprehension section of a silent reading test for measurement of reading ability.*

Unfortunately, some group reading tests, particularly on upper-elementary or secondary levels, tend to include some relatively specific skills which have little to do with specific "general reading ability." Examples of such supplementary skills measured are "reference skills" and "advertisement reading."

Even more unfortunate is the fact that the makers of these tests insist upon adding such tangential skills into the total reading score. This means that when arriving at a "total reading score," all parts of the reading test are lumped together to yield a total score that is a sum of paragraph comprehension, vocabulary, advertisement reading, following directions, poetry comprehension, and so forth. Reading teachers are warned, therefore, to cast a wary eye on "total reading scores" and to look most carefully at the subtest scores. Usually some specific subtest such as paragraph comprehension will be much more valuable than the total score for deciding at what level a student can read or whether a particular student is in need of remedial help.

Another subtest in many group silent reading tests is sentence comprehension. This subtest consists of single sentences for the student to read, followed by a question on that sentence. This subtest is much more useful than reading advertisements and probably more useful than single-word knowledge, although somewhat less useful than paragraph comprehension.

Another danger that teachers should be warned against is the "orangutang score." This is a rather colorful name for the pure-chance guessing level. Suppose we took an orangutang and taught him to put a paw print in one of four squares. He could choose any square he wished. Next we place a typical multiple-choice item in front of him with four choices. After he has read the item he chooses one of the squares in which to place his paw print. On the average, out of 100 items he will get 25 correct by pure chance; this raw score of 25 correct can then be translated into a grade-level score.

The orangutang score for the California Reading Test is computed in Figure 2-3. The publishers caution the test-user by shading the left-hand and extreme right-hand sections of the graph. It is my feeling that this caution is not nearly strong enough. The shaded-in section should be printed solid black so that it is impossible to get a grade level score from an orangutang raw score. Unfortunately there are many teachers and school administrators who think that a score of 5.2 on the California Reading Test, junior high, means something. It does not. It is worse than useless because it is misleading. An adminis-

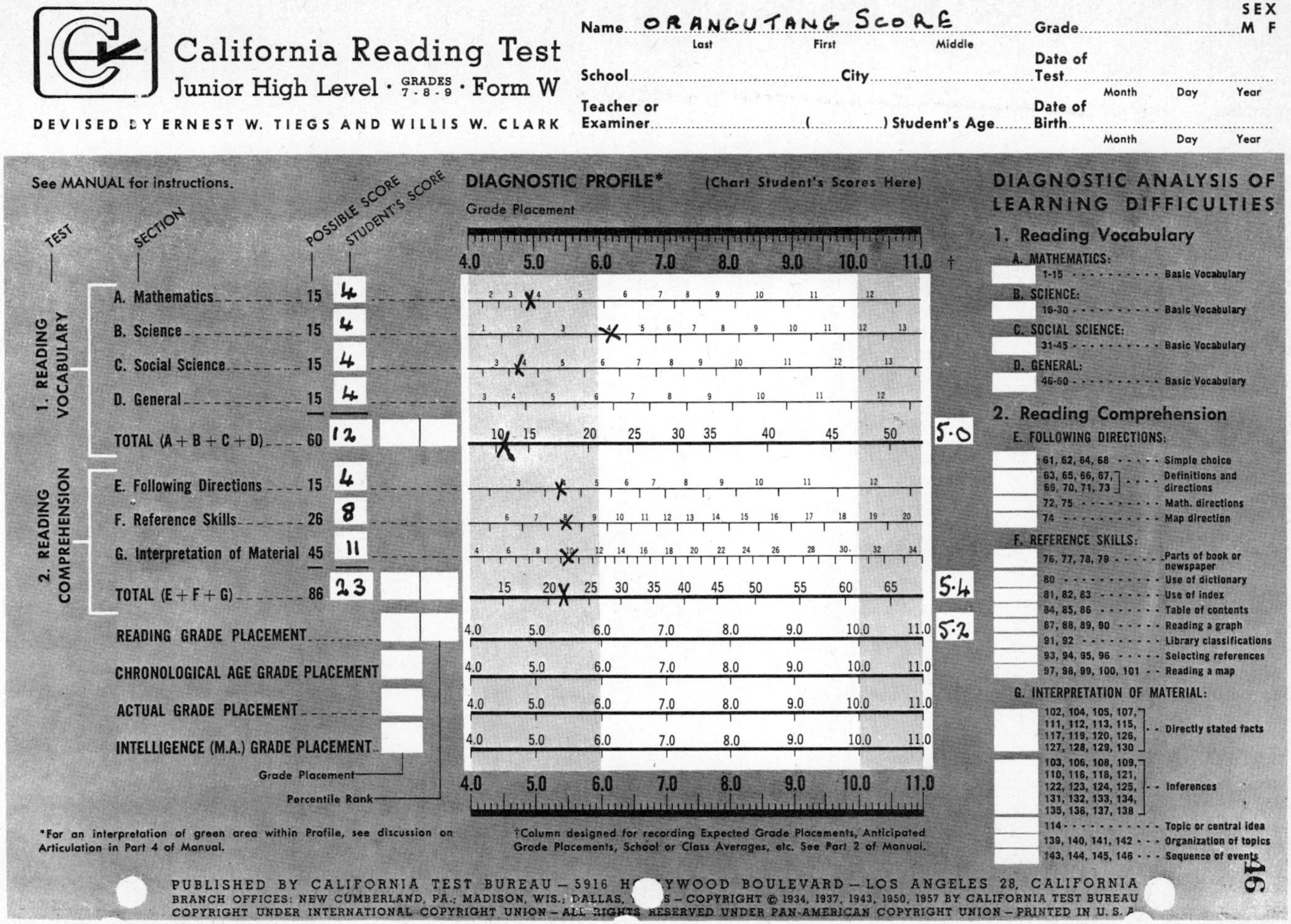

California Reading Test
Junior High Level · GRADES 7-8-9 · Form W
DEVISED BY ERNEST W. TIEGS AND WILLIS W. CLARK

Name ORANGUTANG SCORE (Last, First, Middle) Grade ____ SEX M F
School ____ City ____ Date of Test ____ (Month, Day, Year)
Teacher or Examiner ____ (____) Student's Age ____ Date of Birth ____ (Month, Day, Year)

See MANUAL for instructions.

DIAGNOSTIC PROFILE* (Chart Student's Scores Here)
Grade Placement

TEST	SECTION	POSSIBLE SCORE	STUDENT'S SCORE
1. READING VOCABULARY	A. Mathematics	15	4
	B. Science	15	4
	C. Social Science	15	4
	D. General	15	4
	TOTAL (A + B + C + D)	60	12
2. READING COMPREHENSION	E. Following Directions	15	4
	F. Reference Skills	26	8
	G. Interpretation of Material	45	11
	TOTAL (E + F + G)	86	23

READING GRADE PLACEMENT
CHRONOLOGICAL AGE GRADE PLACEMENT
ACTUAL GRADE PLACEMENT
INTELLIGENCE (M.A.) GRADE PLACEMENT
Grade Placement
Percentile Rank

Grade placements recorded: 5.0, 5.4, 5.2

*For an interpretation of green area within Profile, see discussion on Articulation in Part 4 of Manual.

†Column designed for recording Expected Grade Placements, Anticipated Grade Placements, School or Class Averages, etc. See Part 2 of Manual.

DIAGNOSTIC ANALYSIS OF LEARNING DIFFICULTIES

1. Reading Vocabulary
- A. MATHEMATICS: 1-15 — Basic Vocabulary
- B. SCIENCE: 16-30 — Basic Vocabulary
- C. SOCIAL SCIENCE: 31-45 — Basic Vocabulary
- D. GENERAL: 46-60 — Basic Vocabulary

2. Reading Comprehension
- E. FOLLOWING DIRECTIONS:
  - 61, 62, 64, 68 — Simple choice
  - 63, 65, 66, 67, 69, 70, 71, 73 — Definitions and directions
  - 72, 75 — Math. directions
  - 74 — Map direction
- F. REFERENCE SKILLS:
  - 76, 77, 78, 79 — Parts of book or newspaper
  - 80 — Use of dictionary
  - 81, 82, 83 — Use of index
  - 84, 85, 86 — Table of contents
  - 87, 88, 89, 90 — Reading a graph
  - 91, 92 — Library classifications
  - 93, 94, 95, 96 — Selecting references
  - 97, 98, 99, 100, 101 — Reading a map
- G. INTERPRETATION OF MATERIAL:
  - 102, 104, 105, 107, 111, 112, 113, 115, 117, 119, 120, 126, 127, 128, 129, 130 — Directly stated facts
  - 103, 106, 108, 109, 110, 116, 118, 121, 122, 123, 124, 125, 131, 132, 133, 134, 135, 136, 137, 138 — Inferences
  - 114 — Topic or central idea
  - 139, 140, 141, 142 — Organization of topics
  - 143, 144, 145, 146 — Sequence of events

46

PUBLISHED BY CALIFORNIA TEST BUREAU — 5916 HOLLYWOOD BOULEVARD — LOS ANGELES 28, CALIFORNIA
BRANCH OFFICES: NEW CUMBERLAND, PA.; MADISON, WIS.; DALLAS, TEXAS — COPYRIGHT © 1934, 1937, 1943, 1950, 1957 BY CALIFORNIA TEST BUREAU
COPYRIGHT UNDER INTERNATIONAL COPYRIGHT UNION — ALL RIGHTS RESERVED UNDER PAN-AMERICAN COPYRIGHT UNION — PRINTED IN U. S. A.

FIGURE 2-3 Orangutang score.

trator might be able to say, "There are no children in my junior high school reading below fifth grade level," because he uses well-recognized standardized reading tests which tell him that. However, if he only knew how to interpret tests, he would realize that the test is saying, "This test is too hard for this student and hence you should choose an easier test."

So that I will not be accused of singling out one test company, the orangutang score was computed for Metropolitan Achievement Test, Upper Primary Level, which is illustrated on page 16. We find that the orangutang score on the reading comprehension section of this test is 1.8. This means that if we measure the orangutang's ability by using this test we find he can read at the upper first grade level. There are many ways of using statistics to mislead; if we push the orangutang score into a few more refinements we find that by using the beginning second grade norms found in the testing manual, our orangutang has a percentile rank of 35, and a stanine score of 4. This places him above the lowest third of the class in reading ability.

It has already been explained how grade-placement scores are derived. Percentiles and stanines are another way of expressing how a child compares with a standardization group. For example, if a child has a percentile of 50, this gives him a stanine score of 5; it means that he stands right in the middle of the standardization group. In other words, a second grader with a percentile score of 50, or a stanine of 5, would be a very average second grader; 50 percent of the pupils would be above him and 50 percent of the pupils would be below him in reading ability. On the other hand, with a percentile score of 19, he would be above eighteen pupils and below eight-one pupils. Table 2-2 gives

TABLE 2-2
COMPARISON OF STANINE SCORES AND PERCENTILES

Stanine	*Group*	*Percentile*	*Class of 40 pupils*
9 (4%)	Superior 4%	96+	1
8 (7%)	Above	89–95	3
7 (12%)	average 19%	77–88	5
6 (17%)		60–76	7
5 (20%)	Average 54%	40–59	8
4 (17%)		23–39	7
3 (12%)	Below	11–22	5
2 (7%)	average 19%	4–10	3
1 (4%)	Poor 4%	Below 4	1

a comparison of stanines and percentiles, together with a group explanation of what they mean.

OTHER CAUTIONS ABOUT STANDARDIZED TESTS

Another difficulty with standardized silent group reading tests is encountered when they are used to measure reading ability below the third grade. Most children in the United States receive their basic reading instruction in one basic series of reading textbooks. Even though there is an overlap in the vocabulary of the various series, there is still a noticeable difference in many of the proper names and subject-matter words (for example: *swimming, cow, horse, aunt,* etc.). A standardized test using reading material for first- and second-grade pupils must use some subject-matter words, but these words are not necessarily the same ones used in the reading series of a particular child. Hence, there is a possibility that in many instances the use of nationally standardized reading tests below the end of the second grade is less than satisfactory.

Another problem with some standardized reading tests is that they may have more "top" than "bottom." In other words, they may do a good job of measuring average and above-average pupils, but perform less adequately in measuring the abilities of below-average pupils. The SRA Achievement series, which includes reading comprehension and reading vocabulary tests, illustrate this problem. In the technical manual the authors state, "Each battery has been so constructed that it does not contain easy items suitable for the seriously retarded pupil to answer correctly and only a relatively few items simple enough for the low-average learner to handle successfully." Combine such a test score with the orangutang score and it is worthless for remedial pupils. In fact, it is worse than worthless – it is positively misleading because orangutang scores make it appear that a pupil is making normal progress only a little below the group when, in fact, he may not be able to read at all.

The careful and wise teacher can still use the SRA or any similar test for useful diagnosis of silent reading ability, but she must compute the orangutang score and disregard all scores at or below this level. She should then give the next lower form of the test to those pupils whose scores were so disregarded (again paying attention to the orangutang score). Teachers with an average or below-average class should probably always select a lower form of the test whenever possible. For example, the SRA Achievement Series has forms at the following levels: second to fourth grades, fourth to sixth grades, and sixth to ninth grades. Teachers of average fourth grades should choose the 2-4 form (not the 4-6 form), and teachers of average sixth grades should choose the 4-6 form and not the 6-9 form. Using lower forms is the only hope teachers have of finding poor readers by means of group tests.

One final word of caution: Teachers should be leery of the "diagnostic" value of most group reading subtests. It has been mentioned previously that some subtests measure trivial or, at best, minor reading abilities; these are bad enough in themselves but worse if given equal weight with subtest scores which are as important as paragraph comprehension scores.

Still another subtest score problem is the fact that some subtests are too short to be consistently reliable. If a subtest contains fewer than twenty-five items, it is often questionable whether a child's score is a true enough score to be helpful. Unreliability means that the child can score high one day and low the next, not as a function of ability but simply because the test is not long enough to be reliable.

A further problem is that of overlapping measurement of the same skills. One subtest might be called reading comprehension and another reading vocabulary; on the surface it appears that they are testing different skills. However, a high coefficient of correlation between the two, and a careful examination of the individual items, might show that both subtests are really measuring much the same thing. Hence, the only thing of which the teacher can be fairly certain is that the student's general silent reading comprehension is average or low or high. To say that there is a meaningful difference between vocabulary and comprehension scores is not always accurate.

All major test publishers have technical manuals which explain how their tests were standardized. These manuals should show that the particular test was administered to at least several thousand pupils for each form and not less than 1,000 pupils at each grade level and, furthermore, that this sample was selected from all over the United States and, perhaps, that some control was made of size and socioeconomic status of schools or pupils.

Reading tests have been put out by some textbook publishers that yield grade levels and appear to be standardized tests, but for which there are neither technical manuals nor formal statements concerning the standardization group available. My recommendation is that these tests not be used. The scores are meaningless, for the standardization group may have been only 100 children, all from an upper-middle-class district. How can you compare your children with these norms when the publisher fails to describe the standardization group?

Technically, the score obtained on a standardized test is only valid if the child is from exactly the same type of group from which the standardization was made. This is most often violated with some urban children or with disadvantaged children, whether they be urban or rural. Some test-makers have included disadvantaged children in their standardization group while others have not. In other words, some reading tests are written for and standardized on middle-class, suburban, white populations. Educators who give standardized tests to disadvantaged populations should make certain that the tests items do not contain a vocabulary or assume a background knowledge that is too heavily loaded towards middle-class children. They can use the standardized scores, but they should interpret them with due caution, and, preferably, they should also have local norms which give a special standardized score for their school or region.

Now, in view of all these dire warnings about the use of standardized group reading tests, the reader may begin to wonder if he should use them at all. The answer is definitely yes. Standardized tests are helpful and should be used. Often they are much better than teacher judgment and may cause the teacher to take a new look at the child. They may support the teacher's opinion and give her courage to recommend a class change, a change in text material, or a direct recommendation to a principal or parent.

Well-constructed standardized tests, even though predominantly multiple choice in form, can test reading comprehension skills. Furthermore, good comprehension tests measure more general reading skills than simple recall of facts. Comprehension sections are valuable if they contain questions of "getting the main idea," "mood," "inference," and so forth.

Another type of analysis, sometimes performed by the computers of the scoring companies, is the number or percentage of students who missed each item in the test. If, for example, all the students in the fourth grade missed items 2, 6, and 8 and these items all required the use of inference, perhaps a little more teaching emphasis on this reading skill might be called for. Notice that this item-analysis procedure is suggested for the class as a group; when such an item analysis is done for a single child, it is not as reliable, even though it might suggest some areas of weakness to the teacher. Figure 2.4 shows a computer scoring giving a computer "right response" record of each item on a standardized achievement test. This is a good example of the type of information computer scoring can provide the teacher. If we read across the top line we see that on the reading vocabulary test the raw score was 26. The grade equivalency is 5.1 (one month into the fifth grade).

These scores place Ann at the 52d percentile in national norms which means that she is above fifty-one students and below forty-seven in a group of one hundred typical United States students. Since all scores are inexact, that is they are apt to vary somewhat, it is really more accurate to say that Ann probably falls within a band of scores and this is shown by the X's on the national percentile graph. In other words, her true score probably lies within the 40th to the 63rd percentile bands. Glancing at the percentile graph, it is easy to see that Ann is quite average in reading, good in spelling, and poor in arithmetic. The plus or minus below each item number indicates if Ann got the item right or wrong. By comparing the individual test record the teacher can see exactly the type of item the student missed.

Other important computerized scoring services include a right-response record for the entire class and the comparison of each student against local norms. Comparison with local norms might mean that the child is compared only with other children in his school or his school district for that particular testing or for some cumulation of past years. Local norms might be particularly useful in some inner-city areas where militant parent groups are sensitive about comparisons, but they are strongly recommended for every situation.

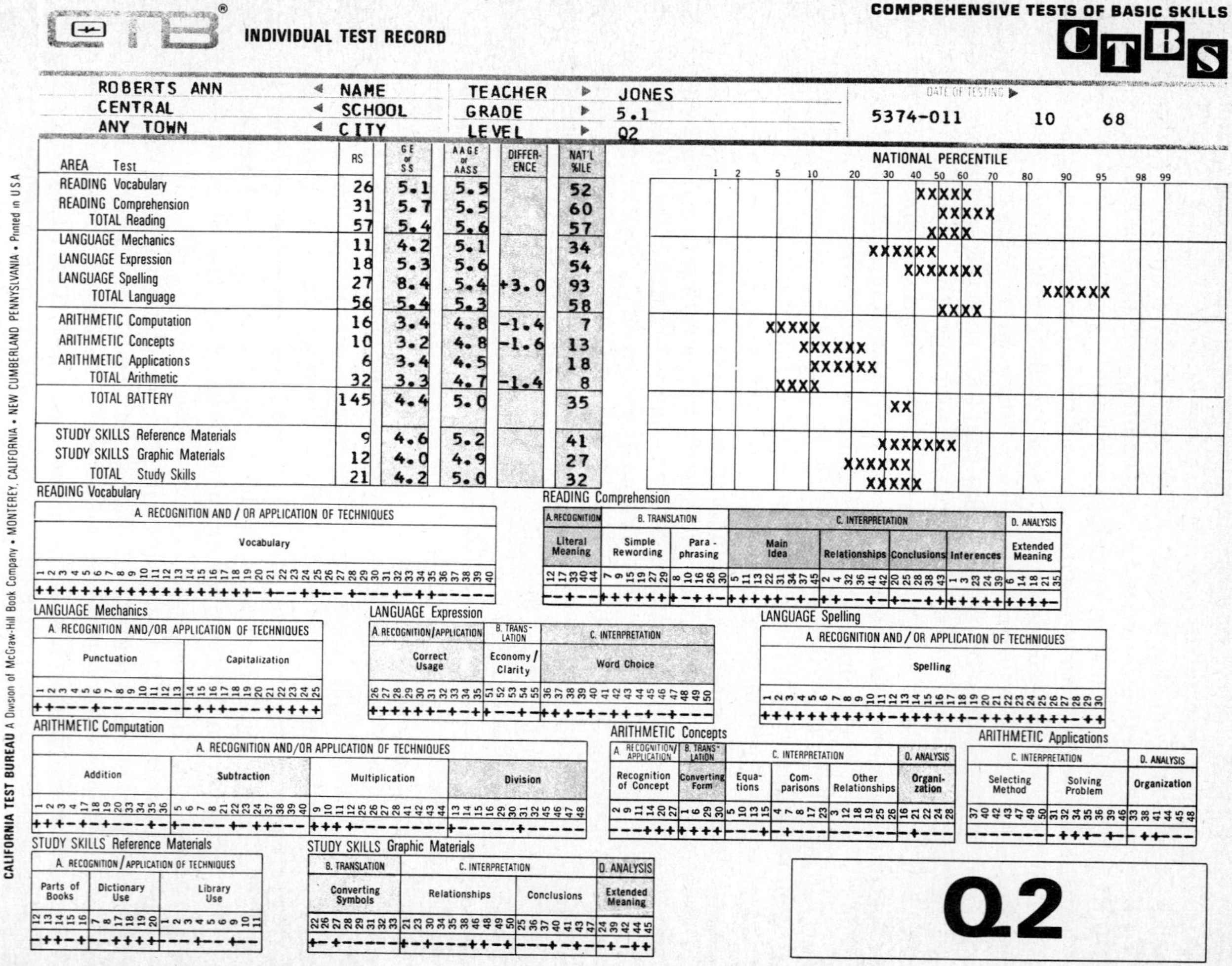

CTB INDIVIDUAL TEST RECORD

COMPREHENSIVE TESTS OF BASIC SKILLS CTBS

ROBERTS ANN	NAME	TEACHER	JONES
CENTRAL	SCHOOL	GRADE	5.1
ANY TOWN	CITY	LEVEL	Q2

DATE OF TESTING 5374-011 10 68

AREA Test	RS	GE or SS	AAGE or AASS	DIFFERENCE	NAT'L %ILE
READING Vocabulary	26	5.1	5.5		52
READING Comprehension	31	5.7	5.5		60
TOTAL Reading	57	5.4	5.6		57
LANGUAGE Mechanics	11	4.2	5.1		34
LANGUAGE Expression	18	5.3	5.6		54
LANGUAGE Spelling	27	8.4	5.4	+3.0	93
TOTAL Language	56	5.4	5.3		58
ARITHMETIC Computation	16	3.4	4.8	-1.4	7
ARITHMETIC Concepts	10	3.2	4.8	-1.6	13
ARITHMETIC Applications	6	3.4	4.5		18
TOTAL Arithmetic	32	3.3	4.7	-1.4	8
TOTAL BATTERY	145	4.4	5.0		35
STUDY SKILLS Reference Materials	9	4.6	5.2		41
STUDY SKILLS Graphic Materials	12	4.0	4.9		27
TOTAL Study Skills	21	4.2	5.0		32

NATIONAL PERCENTILE 1 2 5 10 20 30 40 50 60 70 80 90 95 98 99

READING Vocabulary — A. RECOGNITION AND / OR APPLICATION OF TECHNIQUES: Vocabulary

READING Comprehension — A. RECOGNITION: Literal Meaning; B. TRANSLATION: Simple Rewording, Para-phrasing; C. INTERPRETATION: Main Idea, Relationships, Conclusions, Inferences; D. ANALYSIS: Extended Meaning

LANGUAGE Mechanics — A. RECOGNITION AND/OR APPLICATION OF TECHNIQUES: Punctuation, Capitalization

LANGUAGE Expression — A. RECOGNITION/APPLICATION: Correct Usage; B. TRANSLATION: Economy / Clarity; C. INTERPRETATION: Word Choice

LANGUAGE Spelling — A. RECOGNITION AND / OR APPLICATION OF TECHNIQUES: Spelling

ARITHMETIC Computation — A. RECOGNITION AND/OR APPLICATION OF TECHNIQUES: Addition, Subtraction, Multiplication, Division

ARITHMETIC Concepts — A. RECOGNITION/APPLICATION: Recognition of Concept; B. TRANSLATION: Converting Form; C. INTERPRETATION: Equations, Comparisons, Other Relationships; D. ANALYSIS: Organization

ARITHMETIC Applications — C. INTERPRETATION: Selecting Method, Solving Problem; D. ANALYSIS: Organization

STUDY SKILLS Reference Materials — A. RECOGNITION / APPLICATION OF TECHNIQUES: Parts of Books, Dictionary Use, Library Use

STUDY SKILLS Graphic Materials — B. TRANSLATION: Converting Symbols; C. INTERPRETATION: Relationships, Conclusions; D. ANALYSIS: Extended Meaning

Q2

CALIFORNIA TEST BUREAU A Division of McGraw-Hill Book Company • MONTEREY, CALIFORNIA • NEW CUMBERLAND PENNSYLVANIA • Printed in U S A

FIGURE 2-4 Individual test record.

SUMMARY

In this chapter I have attempted to provide some insight into ways of measuring reading ability. The simplest and quickest individualized method of measuring reading is through informal oral paragraphs. If more accuracy is desired, a standardized set of oral paragraphs will give comparisons with the standardization group, which is useful in reporting results to other schools or in measuring gains.

In order to measure silent reading comprehension skills, silent reading comprehension tests should be used, emphasizing particularly a paragraph reading subtest. Caution should be taken not to use orangutang test scores or to use total test scores which include measures of such tangential reading skills as advertisement reading.

There are several ways of stating reading ability, the most useful for instructional purposes being reading achievement stated in terms of curricular validity. The oral paragraph test in the Appendix to this chapter and the 1-in-20 rule give this type of information. Curricular-validated tests help the teacher in the selection of reading materials for instruction.

Standardized tests are recommended for comparing the reading ability of pupils in various sections of the United States; good tests are available for both oral and silent reading comprehension. In addition to grade-level scores, standardized tests also report results in terms of percentiles and stanines, which show how a student ranks in comparison with the standardization group. Local norms are also recommended. The essence of this chapter is, "Before you begin teaching, find out where the child is."

APPENDIX 2-A ORAL READING PARAGRAPHS

(For Determining Independent and Instructional Reading Levels)*

The purpose of this test is to aid teachers in determining the independent reading level and the instructional reading level of a child by having him read aloud several paragraphs.

The independent reading level is that difficulty level of reading material at which the child can read with relative ease and independence; in other words with little or no help from the teacher. This child should be able to pronounce nearly all the words at this level.

The instructional reading level is that difficulty level of reading material at which reading instructions are most effective. The child should know most of the words but not all.

Frustration Reading Level: If reading instruction is given with material at too hard a level (i.e., too many unknown words) then the child's progress is not as rapid and symptoms of nervousness and dislike of reading may occur.

How to Use: In using this test the teacher asks the child to begin reading an easy paragraph and continue until he reaches a paragraph in which many mistakes occur. It is not necessary to start with the first paragraph. The teacher may estimate the child's reading ability and begin just below the independent level.

Speed-Time: The paragraphs are not timed but excessive rapidity or slowness may be noted in the margin as an interesting characteristic of the child's reading ability.

Mistakes: The only mistakes counted are one for each word the child is unable to pronounce or that he mispronounces *without* correcting himself. If he omits a word ask him to read the line again more carefully.

Scoring: Zero, one, or two mistakes per paragraph give independent level; three or four mistakes per paragraph indicate instructional level; five or more mistakes indicate frustration level.

Marking of Paragraphs: There are two paragraphs per grade level for grades one through three. The first paragraph is marked 1-A. This means easy first paragraph. The next is marked 1-B. This means hard first.

There is only one paragraph for each level beyond third grade.

Upper limit: The last paragraph is marked seventh-grade reading level, but actually it is indicative of all junior high reading levels. If a child can read it perfectly, he can do most junior and senior high readings satisfactorily; but for a more accurate determination of reading ability for nonremedial junior and senior high school pupils, a standardized silent reading test is recommended.

ORAL READING PARAGRAPHS TEST

Student's name__________
Date__________
Examiner__________
Class__________
Score: Independent reading level__________
Instructional reading level__________
For examiner's notations (Have the student read from another copy.)

No. 1-A

Look at the dog.

It is big.

It can run.

Run dog, run away.

0–2 Independent__________
3–4 Instructional__________
5 or more Frustration__________
Speed: Fast__________
Average__________
Slow__________
Very slow__________

No. 1-B

We saw the sun.

It made us warm.

Now it was time to go home.

It was a long way to walk.

0–2 Independent__________
3–4 Instructional__________
5 or more Frustration__________
Speed: Fast__________
Average__________
Slow__________
Very slow__________

No. 2-A

The door of the house opened and a man came out. He had a broom in his hand. He said to the boy sitting there, "Go away." The boy got up and left.

0–2 Independent__________
3–4 Instructional__________
5 or more Frustration__________
Speed: Fast__________
Average__________
Slow__________
Very slow__________

No. 2-B

The family ate their breakfast. They they gave the pig his breakfast. It was fun to watch him eat. He seemed to like it. He is eating all of it.

0–2 Independent__________
3–4 Instructional__________
5 or more Frustration__________
Speed: Fast__________
Average__________
Slow__________
Very slow__________

No. 3-A

When the man had gone, the boys were surprised to see how many boxes he had left in their little back yard. Right away they began to pile them on top of each other. They made caves and houses. It took so long that lunch time came before they knew they were hungry.

0–1 Independent ______
2–3 Instructional ______
4 or more Frustration ______
Speed: Fast ______
Average ______
Slow ______
Very slow ______

No. 3-B

The man became angry because his dog had never talked before, and besides he didn't like its voice. So he took his knife and cut a branch from a palm tree and hit his dog. Just then the palm tree said, "Put down that branch." The man was getting very upset about the way things were going and he started to throw it away.

0–1 Independent ______
2–3 Instructional ______
4 or more Frustration ______
Speed: Fast ______
Average ______
Slow ______
Very slow ______

No. 4

Three more cowboys tried their best to rope and tie a calf as quickly as Red, but none of them came within ten seconds of his time. Then came the long, thin cowboy. He was the last one to enter the contest.

0–1 Independent ______
2 Instructional ______
3 or more Frustration ______
Speed: Fast ______
Average ______
Slow ______
Very slow ______

No. 5

High in the hills they came to a wide ledge where trees grew among the rocks. Grass grew in patches and the ground was covered with bits of wood from trees blown over a long time ago and dried by the sun. Down in the valley it was already beginning to get dark.

0–1 Independent ______
2 Instructional ______
3 or more Frustration ______
Speed: Fast ______
Average ______
Slow ______
Very slow ______

No. 6

106023

Businessmen from suburban areas may travel to work in helicopters, land on the roof of an office building, and thus avoid city traffic jams. Families can spend more time at summer homes and mountain cabins through the use of this marvelous craft. People on farms can reach city centers quickly for medical service, shopping, entertainment, or sale of products.	0–1 Independent____ 2 Instructional____ 3 or more Frustration____ Speed: Fast____ Average____ Slow____ Very slow____

No. 7

The President of the United States was speaking. His audience comprised two thousand foreign-born men who had just been admitted to citizenship. They listened intently, their faces aglow with the light of a newborn patriotism, upturned to the calm, intellectual face of the first citizen of the country they now claimed as their own.	0–1 Independent____ 2 Instructional____ 3 or more Frustration____ Speed: Fast____ Average____ Slow____ Very slow____

(If the last paragraph is read at the independent level, use a silent reading test to determine advanced skills.)

APPENDIX 2-B HOW TO SELECT A READING TEST

The first step in selecting a reading test is to find out what is available. A comprehensive listing can be found in the latest edition of *Mental Measurements Yearbooks*, edited by Oscar Buros and published by Gryphon Press. These large reference works are published every several years and list most of the tests published in English throughout the world. The best-known features of the books are the critical reviews written by a wide variety of testing specialists, but the *Mental Measurements Yearbooks* also contain fairly detailed information on the contents of every test as well as its cost, number of forms available, etc. *Tests in Print*, companion volume to the *Mental Measurements Yearbooks* by the same editor and publisher, gives the factual information without the critical reviews; however, it may not have as up-to-date a listing as the yearbooks.

Other sources of information on reading tests are the various textbooks on reading such as this one. Reading texts will frequently have a list of tests, sometimes with annotations.

A practical but less systematical approach would be to look through publishers' catalogs. Since there are less than a dozen major publishers of reading tests, this is not an impossible job; but often the catalogs of all companies are not available in one convenient source.

When surveying the field of reading tests, the user will have certain criteria in mind such as a specific grade level or a desire for some particular measurement of reading skill: rate, phonics, general comprehension, etc. After locating some suitable tests, here are some of the things you might look for:

1. *Validity*: Does the test really measure what you want it to? The first step in measuring content validity would be to simply look in Buros or the publisher's catalog and find out if the subtests, or parts of the tests, measure the reading skill that you want to measure. A more advanced step would be to get an actual copy of the test and examine the test items, possibly by taking the test yourself. These steps will help you to determine whether the test is really measuring what you want it to measure.

A second type of validity known as correlational validity tells you how well the test correlates with some other standard measure. Frequently the publisher's catalog, a critical review, the test manual, or a technical manual issued with the test will have the results of a sample administration of the test along with some other well-known test. A coefficient of correlation is then reported so that you may judge how similar the test you are looking at is to the standard instrument. If you wish the test to be somewhat like the standard measure, a correlation of 0.70 or higher should be reported. However, it is not always desirable that one test measure the same things that another test measures. Hence, a low correlation of validity might simply be saying that the test measures something different than the standard test. Critical comments on the validity of a test can frequently be found in test reviews in such publications as those by Buros and in some professional journals which carry test reviews, such as *Educational Measurement.*

2. *Reliability*: If you use the test again and again, can you expect the student to get the same or nearly the same score? If, for example, a test is unreliable it will yield a different score on repeated testings due to no other influence such as learning. Hence, a test must be reliable in order to be usable. Reliabilities are determined by finding the coefficient of correlation between a test-retest situation or through a statistical technique known as split-half correlation in which half of the test is correlated with the other half of the test. In any event the user must demand that the commercially published test have a high reliability—usually a correlation of 0.90 or higher. Most publishers provide the reliability of the test in either the teacher's manual or a technical manual.

3. *Range*: You must select a test that has adequate range for the population which you are testing. Bear in mind that few group tests have adequate range for a normal class. There are usually one or two very slow pupils or one or two very bright pupils, or both, which score outside the range of the test. However, most of the pupils in the class should be inside the usable range of the test. The publisher gives suggestions concerning proper range but even these must be taken with caution, as publishers sometimes suggest that tests have wider ranges than they really accurately measure. One step in finding the bottom of the test range would be simply to compute the orangutang (chance) score. If there are 40 four-choice items, simply take a raw score of 10 and convert this into a grade-level score; this will give you the bottom of test range. The total possible correct will give you the absolute top range, though from the standpoint

of accuracy it is probably somewhat below this. It is probably a safe rule that anyone who scores within 10 percent of the top or bottom of the test should be given the next higher or lower form, as the case may be. Teachers should refuse to record or consider any score which is at or beyond the determined range. This caution is given because sometimes it is possible to get a grade-level score which is indeed beyond the range of the test.

4. *Standardization*: The usefulness of any standardized score depends on how well the population being tested compares with the standardized population. The score of one child is simply how he compares with the standardized group. Large nationally standardized tests frequently would have 300,000 students scattered in at least four geographical areas and three different-sized school districts. The test manual or the technical manual will tell you about the standardization; and if you feel that the sample is small or that it was tested on students essentially different from yours, you might wish to select another test or at least accept the scores with caution.

Many test publishers will give you local norms, which means that the score of any one child can be given a percentile or some other score based upon the population of his local school district or whatever size sample was used in determining the local norms. These local norms are oftentimes much more meaningful than the national norms. When tests are scored by the computer of the publisher, he will give you local norms at usually very little or no additional expense. If this is not possible, often a school psychologist or a local testing expert can develop local norms with very little effort.

5. *Scoring*: Most published tests can be scored either by the individual doing the purchasing or by the test publisher. Generally, for the sake of accuracy and for the teachers' convenience, it is best to have them scored by the publisher. However, some districts have a policy of having teachers score simple beginning reading tests because they feel it places the teacher in closer contact with the results and knowledge of their students' behavior. Some publishers have scoring aides which make the teachers' scoring much less difficult. There are special stencil-type scoring keys and special answer sheets which sometimes require very little effort to score. Medium-size and larger school districts sometimes purchase automatic or semiautomatic scoring equipment.

6. *Forms*: Most published tests come in two or more forms. If repeated testings are anticipated, it is sometimes good to have a test which has three or more forms. This information can be gleaned from the publisher's catalog or other sources, but care must be taken to see that the forms have a high degree of reliability with each other.

7. *Time*: An important factor in selecting a test is the time it takes to administer. You should always allow a little more time than the test manual recommends for passing out the tests, collecting them, etc. Of course you should follow the manual's directions exactly for minutes allowed the student to work on the test if it is a timed test. There is a wide range of items on different tests. Some leading tests can easily be given in a twenty-minute period and others take two one-hour sittings.

8. *Cost*: There is a wide range of cost in tests. A test booklet may cost anywhere from a few cents to 25 or 30 cents. Oftentimes the more expensive booklets can be saved and separate answer sheets can be used. Hence, the number of reuses must be calculated in the total cost. The cost of scoring should also be considered along with the cost of purchasing the test, as some tests may be relatively expensive to purchase but cheap to have scored. Hence, purchase costs and scoring costs should be calculated at the same

time. Please do not consider that they will be scored free even if they are done by teachers. Teacher time is worth real money; and any district that squanders it on mechanical clerical test-scoring, simply because they think they are saving money, may be penny-wise and pound-foolish.

9. *Critical Reviews*: The importance of critical reviews has already been mentioned, but let us consider it here again as a last as well as a first step. Testing experts often have insight into the value of a test that a classroom teacher or principal will not have. You do not always have to agree with the experts, but it is worthwhile considering what they have to say. The prime source of these critical reviews is the Buros *Mental Measurements Yearbooks*, but a few professional journals also carry test reviews.

APPENDIX 2-C AN ALPHABETICAL LIST OF READING TESTS

GROUP TESTS

American School Achievement Tests: Part I. Reading.
Willis E. Pratt, Robert V. Young, and Clara E. Cockerville. Bobbs-Merrill Co. Inc. Primary grades two to three, intermediate grades four to six.

Basic Sight Word Test.
Edward W. Dolch. Garrard Press. Grades one to two.

Botel Reading Inventory.
Morton Botel, Cora L. Hensclaw, and Gloria C. Cammarota. Follett Publishing Company. Grades one to twelve. Phonics Mastery, Word Recognition, and Word Opposites Tests.

California Phonics Survey.
Grace M. Brown and Alice B. Cottrell. California Test Bureau. Grades seven to twelve and college.

California Reading Test.
Ernest W. Tiegs and Willis W. Clark. California Test Bureau. Grades one to two, 2.5–4.5, four to six, seven to nine, and nine to fourteen. Vocabulary and Reading Comprehension.

Davis Reading Test.
Frederick B. Davis and Charlotte Croon Davis. Psychological Corporation. Grades eight to eleven and eleven to thirteen. Yields two scores: Level of Comprehension, and Speed of Comprehension.

Detroit Word Recognition Test.
Eliza F. Oglesby. Harcourt, Brace & World, Inc. Grades one to three.

Developmental Reading Tests.
Guy L. Bond, Theodore Clymer, and Cyril Hoyt. Lyons and Carnahan. Grades 1.5, 1.5 to two, three to five, four to six. Primary reading: Basic Vocabulary, General Comprehension, Specific Comprehension. Intermediate reading: Basic Vocabulary, Reading to Retain Information, Reading to Organize, Reading to Evaluate, Reading to Appreciate, and Average Comprehension.

Diagnostic Reading Tests.

Committee on Diagnostic Reading Tests, Inc. Published also by Science Research Associates. Survey section: Kindergarten to grade four. Word Recognition and Comprehension, Word Attack. Survey Section: Lower level, grades four to eight. Word Recognition and Comprehension, Word Attack, and Rate of Reading. Survey section and diagnostic battery, upper level, grades seven to college freshman year. Vocabulary, comprehension: Auditory and Silent, Rates of Reading, Word Attack.

Durrell-Sullivan Reading Capacity and Achievement Tests.

Donald D. Durrell and Helen Blair Sullivan. Harcourt, Brace & World, Inc. Grades two to five, three to six. Reading Capacity Test. Reading Achievement Test. Two parallel tests at each level reveal discrepancies between understanding of spoken language and understanding of the printed word.

Gates Advanced Primary Reading Tests.

Arthur I. Gates. Bureau of Publications. Grades 2.5 to third. Word Recognition and Paragraph Reading.

Gates Basic Reading Tests.

Arthur I. Gates. Bureau of Publications. Grades three and five to eight. Reading to Appreciate General Significance. Reading to Understand Precise Directions. Reading to Note Details. Reading Vocabulary. Level of Comprehension.

Gates-MacGinitie reading tests.

Arthur I. Gates and Walter H. MacGinitie, Teachers College, Columbia University. Vocabulary and Comprehension for grades one, two, and three, two forms for each. Speed and accuracy for grades two and three, three forms. Speed, vocabulary, and comprehension for grades four, five, and six, three forms. Speed, vocabulary, and comprehension for grades seven through twelve, three forms.

Gates-MacGinitie reading tests

Arthur I. Gates. Bureau of Publications. Grades one to three. Word Recognition. Sentence Reading. Paragraph Reading.

Gates Reading Survey.

Arthur I. Gates. Bureau of Publications. Grades 3.5 to ten. Vocabulary, Level of Comprehension, Speed and Accuracy.

Iowa Silent Reading Tests. New Edition.

H. A. Greene, A. N. Jorgansen, and V. H. Kelley. Harcourt, Brace and World, Inc. Grades four to eight and nine to fourteen. Elementary and Advanced Tests. Rate and Comprehension, Directed Reading, Word Meaning, Paragraph Comprehension, Sentence Meaning, and Location of Information.

Kelley-Greene Reading Comprehension Test.

Victor H. Kelley and Harry A. Greene. Harcourt Brace and World, Inc. Grades nine to thirteen. An overall measure of reading comprehension, and three significant reading abilities: ability to comprehend paragraphs, to find details, and to retain.

Lee-Clark Reading Test. 1958 Revision.

Murray Lee and Willis W. Clark. California Test Bureau. Grade one, primer. Auditory Stimuli, Visual Stimuli, Following directions, Total Score. Grades one to two, First Reader. Same as primer level, plus Completion and Inference.

Metropolitan Achievement Tests: Reading.

Walter N. Durost, Harold H. Bixler, Gertrude H. Hildreth, Kenneth W. Lund, and J. Wayne Wrightstone. Harcourt, Brace & World, Inc. Grade two, Upper Primary Reading Test, grades three to four, five to six, Intermediate Reading Test, grades seven to nine, Advanced Reading Test. Vocabulary and Comprehension at each level.

Nelson-Denny Reading Test.
M. J. Nelson and E. C. Denny; revision by James I. Brown. Houghton Mifflin Co. Grades nine to sixteen. Vocabulary, Comprehension, and Rate.

Nelson Reading Test. Revised Edition.
M. J. Nelson. Houghton Mifflin Co. Grades three to nine. Vocabulary and Paragraph Comprehension.

Primary Reading Profiles. 1967 Edition.
James B. Stroud, Albert N. Hieronymus, and Paul McKee. Houghton Mifflin Co. Grades one to three. Aptitude for Reading, Auditory Association, Recognition, Word Attack, and Reading Comprehension.

Reading Comprehension: Cooperative English Tests. 1960 Revision.
Clarence Derrick, David P. Harris, and Biron Walker. Educational Testing Service. Grades nine to twelve and thirteen to fourteen. Vocabulary, Level of Comprehension, and Speed of Comprehension.

SRA Reading Record.
Louis P. Thorpe, D. Welty Lefeverr, and Robert A. Naslund. Science Research Associates, Inc. Grades eight to thirteen. General Comprehension, Vocabulary, and Rate.

SRA Reading Test.
Louis P. Thorpe, D. Welty Lefeverr, and Robert A. Naslund. Science Research Associates, Inc. Grades one to two, two to four, four to six. Comprehension and Vocabulary.

Schonell Reading Tests.
Fred J. Schonell. Oliver and Boyd Ltd. Ages five to fifteen, six to nine, seven to eleven, nine to thirteen. Word Reading Test, Simple Prose Reading Test, Silent Reading Test A, Silent Reading Test B, Test of Analysis and Synthesis of Words Containing Common Phonic Units. Test of Directional Attack on Words, and Visual Word Discrimination Test.

Schrammel-Gray High School and College Reading Test. H. E. Schrammel and W. H. Gray. Public School Publishing Co. Grades seven to twelve and college. Gross comprehension, Rate, and comprehension Efficiency.

Sequential Tests of Educational Progress: Reading.
Educational Testing Service. Grades four to six, seven to nine, ten to twelve, and thirteen to fourteen. Vocabulary and Reading Comprehension.

Silent Reading Comprehension: Iowa Every-Pupil Tests of Basic Skills, Test A.
H. F. Spitzer, Ernest Horn, Maude McBroom, H. A. Greene, and E. F. Lindquist. Houghton Mifflin Co. Grades three to five and five to nine. Vocabulary and Comprehension.

Silent Reading Diagnostic Test. The developmental Reading Tests.
Guy L. Bond, Theodore Clymer, and Cyril J. Hoyt. Lyons and Carnahan. Grades three to eight. Recognition Pattern, Error analysis, Recognition Technique, and Word Synthesis.

Stanford Achievement Tests: Reading.
Truman L. Kelley, Richard Madden, Eric F. Gardener, and Herbert C. Rudman.

Harcourt, Brace & World, Inc. Primary I. Reading tests, grades 1.5–2.4. Primary II. Reading tests, grades 2.5–3.9. Intermediate I. Reading tests, grades four to 5.5. Intermediate II., grades 5.5–6.9, Vocabulary and Comprehension. Advanced test, grades seven to nine, Paragraph Meaning Test.

Stanford Diagnostic Phonics Survey.

Grace M. Brown and Alice B. Cottrell. Consulting Psychologists Press, Inc. High school and college. Measures ability to relate "written sounds" to "spoken sounds."

Stanford Diagnostic Reading Test.

Bjorn Karlsen, Richard Madden, and Eric F. Gardener. Harcourt Brace & World, Inc. Grades 2.5–8.5. Comprehension, Vocabulary, Auditory Skills and Rate of Reading.

Survey of Reading Achievement: California Survey Series.

Ernest W. Tiegs and Willis W. Clark. California Test Bureau. Junior high level, grades seven to nine; Advanced level, grades nine to twelve. Vocabulary, Ability to Follow Directions, Reference Skills, and Comprehension.

Traxler High School Reading Test, Revised 1967.

Arthur E. Traxler. Public School Publishing Co. grades ten, eleven and twelve. Rate of Continuous Reading and Ability to Locate Main Ideas.

INDIVIDUAL TESTS

Diagnostic Reading Scales.

George D. Spache. California Test Bureau. Grades one to eight and retarded readers in grades nine to twelve. Word Recognition, Oral Reading, Silent Reading, Auditory Comprehension, and Phonics Test.

Gates-McKillop Reading Diagnostic Tests.

Arthur I. Gates and Anne S. McKillop. Bureau of Publications. All grades. Oral Reading: Word Perception, Phrase Perception, Blending, Recognition of visual forms of sounds, etc.

Gilmore Oral Reading Test.

John V. Gilmore. Harcourt, Brace & World, Inc. Grades one to eight. Oral Reading. Comprehension and Rate.

Gray Oral Reading Test.

Helen M. Robinson and William S. Gray. Bobbs Merrill Co., Inc. Grades one to sixteen and adults. Oral Reading Comprehension.

Leavell Analytical Oral Reading Test.

Ullin W. Leavell. American Guidance Service, Inc. Grades one to ten.

Oral Reading Criterion Test

Edward Fry. Dreier Educational Systems. Grades one through seven. Oral Reading Paragraphs.

Phonics Knowledge Criterion Test

Edward Fry. Dreier Educational Systems. Grades one to six and remedial. Tests ninety-nine phoneme-grapheme correspondences.

Phonics Knowledge Survey.

Dolores Durkin and Leonard Meshover. Bureau of Publications. All grades.

Phonovisual Diagnostic Test.

Lucille D. Schoolfield and Josephine B. Timberlake. Phonovisual Products, Inc. Grades three to twelve.

Reading Diagnostic Record for High School and College Students.
Ruth Strang, Margaret M. Conant, Margaret G. McKim, and Mary Alice Mitchell. Bureau of Publications. High school and college. Oral Reading Passages, A, B, C, and D.

Rosewell-Chall Auditory Blending Test.
Florence G. Rosewell and Jeanne S. Chall. Essay Press. Grades one to four.

Rosewell-Chall Diagnostic Reading Test of Word Analysis Skills.
Florence G. Rosewell and Jeanne S. Chall. Essay Press. Grades two to six.

Slosson Oral Reading Test (SORT).
Richard L. Slosson. Slosson Educational Publications. Grades one to eight. and high school.

APPENDIX 2-D LIST OF TEST PUBLISHERS AND THEIR ADDRESSES

American Guidance Service, Inc.
720 Washington Avenue, S.E.
Minneapolis, Minnesota 55414

The Bobbs-Merrill Company, Inc.
4300 West 62nd Street
Indianapolis, Indiana 46206

Bureau of Publications
Teachers College
Columbia University
New York, New York 10027

California Test Bureau,
McGraw-Hill Book Company
Del Monte Research Park
Monterey, California 93940

Committee on Diagnostic Reading Tests, Inc.
Mountain Home, North Carolina 28758

Consulting Psychologists Press, Inc.
577 College Avenue
Palo Alto, California 94306

Dreier Educational Systems
320 Ratitan Ave
Highland Park, New Jersey 08904

Educational Testing Service
Princeton, New Jersey 08540

Essay Press
P. O. Box 5, Planetarium Station
New York, New York 10012

Follet Publishing Co.
1010 West Washington Boulevard
Chicago, Illinois 60607

The Garrard Press
Champaign, Illinois 61820

Harcourt, Brace & World, Inc.
757 Third Avenue
New York, New York 10017

Houghton Mifflin Company
53 West 43rd Street
New York, New York 10036

Lyons and Carnahan
407 East 25th Street
Chicago, Illinois 60616

Phonovisual Products, Inc.
Box 5625
Washington, District of Columbia 20016

The Psychological Corporation
304 East 45th Street
New York, New York 10017

Science Research Associates, Inc.
259 East Erie Street
Chicago, Illinois 60611

Slossom Educational Publications
140 Pine Street
East Aurora, New York 14052

Webster Division
McGraw-Hill Book Company
Manchester Road Manchester, Missouri 63011

Western Psychological Services
12035 Wilshire Boulevard
Los Angeles, California 90025

3

BASIC SERIES: HOW MOST CHILDREN LEARN TO READ

This chapter describes briefly the most common method of teaching developmental reading in the United States, namely, through the use of a basal reading series.

In most schools the only person who really knows how beginning reading takes place is the first grade teacher. To secondary teachers and even to upper elementary teachers, beginning reading is something of a mystery. The mystery is further compounded by the many recent magazine articles describing such special approaches as individualized reading, language-experience methods, heavy phonics, linguistic methods, and new alphabets like the ITA. While each special approach has its value for teaching reading, the fact remains that the majority of children in the United States still learn how to read from a set of basic texts. This set of books, also called a "reading series," has as its strong point the carefully controlled introduction of new words. On the first page of the first book, one or two words are introduced. On the second page another new word is introduced; on the next page another one; on the following page perhaps no new words, but the words already introduced may be used in a different fashion. The teacher's manual which accompanies the series urges the teacher to stress word and sentence meanings.

The first book, which is paperbound and contains only about thirty pages, is called a preprimer. The preprimer

TABLE 3-1
NUMBER OF WORDS USED IN A TYPICAL BASIC READING SERIES

	Total words	*New words*	*Book length (pages)*
Preprimer, first grade	17	17	44
Preprimer, second grade	38	21	60
Preprimer, third grade	58	20	88
Primer	158	90	151
First reader	335	177	190
Second grade, first book	536	213	233
Second grade, second book	882	346	241
Third grade, first book	1,234	352	263

introduces a total of fifteen or twenty words, all of which are new to the child, since this is the first formal reading instruction he receives. See Figures 3-1, 3-2, and 3-3. Sometimes wall charts made by the teacher or publisher are used for reading lessons. This may be done prior to or concurrent with the lessons in the preprimer.

Because of the extremely limited vocabulary in the preprimer, the story line is often carried by the pictures. Every page usually contains a descriptive picture which tells a story, usually about some incident in the lives of a six-year-old boy and a six-year-old girl. The ages of the children are obviously selected to be the same as those of the typical first grade student so that maximum identification with the characters in the story can occur.

Accompanying the preprimer and all the books in the reading series through the sixth or eighth grades is a teacher's manual and a set of activity books. The teacher's manual suggests lessons and methods of teaching reading skills. In a typical reading series, word and sentence meanings are stressed and repetition of words is encouraged. In fact, the repetition of the words which are taught is built into the stories. Phonics instruction is often not begun until the child has a sight vocabulary of at least fifty words, which is generally by the latter half of the first grade. Even then, phonics instruction is very light. Different series vary both in the amount of phonics included and in the time when phonics is introduced. Most series used in the United States include a fair amount of phonics in the activity books and in the teacher's manuals by the end of the third grade. However, teachers who favor a strong phonics program believe that not enough phonics instruction is given in these series and that what is given is introduced too late.

At Home pages: **3–6**
Activity Book page: **3**

PRE-PRIMER I

At Home

Come

One day Bill decides to have a parade. He is wearing a newspaper soldier's hat and carrying an American flag. When he notices Linda and Ricky watching him marching around the yard, he asks them to come and join the parade. They each run to get something for the parade. Linda comes running with a tin horn and Ricky has a toy drum. The story ends when finally Rags joins the children in their parade.

New Word
page 3: come

Review Words*
Bill, said, Linda, Ricky, Rags

Word Cards**
Bill, come, Linda, Rags, Ricky, said

Picture Cards
Bill, Linda, Ricky, Rags

PREPARATION FOR READING

Identifying Old and New Concepts Ask the children if they have ever gone to or been in a parade. Let them tell about the parades they have seen. Ask them what kinds of things they usually see in a parade. Discuss some reasons that might cause people to want to have a parade—to celebrate a national holiday, to advertise a circus coming to town, to honor a great hero, etc. Let them speculate whether there really has to be a reason other than just enjoying a parade to have one.

* The words listed here as review words were introduced in the readiness books but are treated in this lesson as new words for thorough review purposes.

** Under this heading are listed the word cards which may be used in the lesson. Each word corresponds to a card found in the Word Card Set for the first-grade program of this Series. The superior figures ("and[2]") indicate the number of cards needed for the lesson.

Come (3–6) 47

FIGURE 3-1 Sample page from a teacher's manual for the Sheldon readers published by Allyn and Bacon.

Come

3

Ask the pupils if they have ever seen or been in a parade. Encourage them to tell what it was like and why it was held. Explain that Bill is the leader of the parade in this story. Review the "said phrase" and the use of quotation marks. Review: Bill, Linda, Ricky, Rags. **Introduce:** come. **Ask: Who is in this picture? What is Bill doing? What does the title tell about the story? What do you think Linda and Ricky will do? See lesson plan.**

FIGURE 3-2 Sample first page of a basal series (Teacher's Edition).

Bill said,

"Come, Linda."

4

Ask: Who has come to join the parade? What is Linda carrying? What is Bill doing? What does Bill want Linda to do? Direct pupils to read the page to learn who is talking.

Here and Near

Basic Words: 18 *Phonic Sets Words:* 13 *Enrichment Words:* 5
Cumulative Vocabulary (Basic and Phonic Sets Words): 64

Here and Near is designed to be read after successful completion of *At Home*.

The 36 words introduced in *Here and Near* are listed below in the order of their introduction. They are of three major types:

Basic Words: Words which will appear repeatedly but which most children will be unable to identify independently. They include basic vocabulary units which will be used to develop word-analysis skills and frequently used irregular verbs which should be taught as wholes.

Phonic Sets Words (PS): A phonic set is a group of new words derived phonically from a known basic word by substitution or addition of initial or final consonants, consonant blends, or consonant digraphs. **Phonic Sets Words** in this book are limited to initial consonant substitution and one instance of initial consonant addition. Children are expected to use their developing word-analysis skills to identify these new **(PS)** words.

Enrichment Words (E): Interesting, meaningful words which have limited use at this level but are needed at times to improve readability and story comprehension. They are words often unsuited to analysis but easily recognized because they appear in obvious context and are carefully illustrated.

Variants formed by adding *'s* or *s* to known roots are not listed as new words.

3.	20.	37. for	54.
4.	21. ran (PS)	38. boat	55. doctor (E)
5.	22.	39. my	56. Hi
6. with	23. mumps (E)	40. yellow	57. sit (PS)
7. up	24.	41. blue	58.
8. want	25.	42. red	59.
9.	26. will (PS)	43. near	60. store (E)
10.	27.	44.	61.
11. down	28. set (PS)	45. that	62. balloon (E)
12.	go	46. man (PS)	63.
13. he (PS)	29.	popcorn (E)	64.
we (PS)	30.	47.	65.
14.	31.	48.	66.
15. cookies	32. let (PS)	49.	67.
16. some (PS)	33.	50. took (PS)	68.
17.	34.	51.	69. fill (PS)
18. pan (PS)	35.	52.	70. fun (PS)
19. funny	36. something	53. green	71.

FIGURE 3-3 Sample word list at back of a basal reader.

Bill ran to call the policeman.
"Can you help me ?" said Bill.
"Our dog ran away.
He is not at home."

The policeman said, "Hi, Bill.
My car is near here.
I can get it and come for you.
You can ride with me.
We can go and look for Rags."

60

Ask: What is Bill doing now? Have the pupils read the first paragraph to find out what Bill is saying. Have the rest of the page read silently. Ask: Will the policeman help Bill? Let two pupils pretend to be Bill and the policeman. Have them dramatize the page.

FIGURE 3-4 Sample page from a first reader.

At one period in the earlier years of this century a strong program of regular phonics instruction was taught in schools in the United States. Then, in the 1930s and for several decades thereafter, phonics instruction declined to such an extent that in a few reading series it was taught almost not at all. Lately, the trend is to give more regular and systematic phonics instruction. The basal reading series are beginning to include more phonics instruction, and the special "phonics systems" of teaching reading are enjoying a mild growth phase.

In the basic readers, children are often taught to learn new words by "context cues." This means that they are taught to look at the whole sentence in which the word occurs and to guess what word would fit there or would make sense in terms of the story. They are sometimes also encouraged to use some phonic skills such as the beginning sound of the word.

The strong point of most basal reading series, however, is the way in which the vocabulary is introduced on a gradual basis and repeated a sufficient number of times. Theoretically, this repetition insures mastery of the new word. In Figures 3-1 to 3-4, sample pages are displayed from a typical reading series so that the reader can see what the child and teacher sees. One sample page from the end of a book tells the teacher how many new words have been introduced in the book. Some of the worst teaching is done by teachers who do not follow the teacher's manuals. If the teacher "pushes" the children through the books and does not refer to the teacher's manual, her lessons are apt to become stereotyped and she will often neglect to teach many of the reading skills suggested by the series author. Conversely, poor teaching may occur if the teacher follows the teacher's manual too exactly. Sometimes the suggested lessons may be too easy or too hard for a particular group, or more repetition may be required than is included in the teacher's manual. Good reading instruction requires that the teacher be flexible and provide for the needs of her particular children.

A typical reading series may have three softbound, small short pre-primers. These may be followed by a hardbound primer and a hardbound first-grade book. Two somewhat larger hardbound books may be used in the second grade, and two hardbound books in the third grade. The fourth, fifth, and sixth grades may have only one reading book apiece since, in these grades, the children are reading many other types of books as well. Some series include seventh and eighth grade reading books, while others assume that the children will be reading from a literature book. A literature book is typically an anthology of classic writing supplemented by suggested drills and activities. Some schools now substitute paperbound original books for hardbound literary anthologies in the upper grades.

Some newer basal series use much greater variety in book sizes. The Scott Foresman reading system utilizes many small paperbound books rather than the traditional organization pattern described above. The content of the newer series tends to be more urban oriented and racially integrated; at least one series, Bill Martin's *Sounds of Language* (Holt, Rinehart and Winston), makes extensive use of selections of stories and illustrations from children's trade books to add variety and interest.

Many series also include a variety of supplementary materials:

A *big book*, which is a giant replication of a preprimer. The pages are large enough to be read easily 8 or 10 feet away, thus suitable for group activity use.
A series of *word or phrase cards*, which the teacher may hold up individually and explain or place in pocket charts so that she or a child can construct new sentences using the new words that are introduced.
Games and *pictures* or *word wall charts* which supplement the reading lessons.
Tests which are developed by the series author to diagnose progress in general reading ability and/or specific skills taught.

For details on how reading skills that are taught in a basal series the reader is referred to the teacher's edition or the teacher's manual of any basal reading series.

Not all first grade children learn to master all the first grade books in the first grade. In fact, in many schools, children are still struggling with their preprimers at the end of the first grade. In other schools, many of the children will have mastered the preprimers in kindergarten and be well into the second-grade books by the end of the first grade. The socioeconomic status of the community is one of the chief correlates of learning to read satisfactorily in the first grade. However, the philosophy of the school is also important. Some schools prefer to teach no reading at all in kindergarten, and delay formal reading instruction for several months at the beginning of the first grade.

In any event, once reading instruction is begun a typical teacher would divide her class into three groups: "fast," "average," and "slow." In a typical American classroom the fast group will complete all the first grade books, the middle group might complete only the primer, whereas most children in the slow group will learn to read satisfactorily through the preprimer, with a few stragglers unable to progress this far. These groups tend to maintain this relationship as they continue on through the six elementary years. Sometimes a child will shift up or down to a higher or lower group within his room. Occasionally a teacher will organize more or fewer ability groups, but three seems to be the most common number. It is difficult for teachers to work with four or more groups, and children seldom break neatly into two groups.

Needless to say, all children do not learn to read from basal reading series nor do all teachers prefer to use basal reading series.

In contrast to the basal approach are the so-called individualized reading methods in which each child proceeds at his own pace and level of difficulty. Individualized reading may sometimes include group instruction in which the whole class joins in practicing certain reading skills; or a small group may be formed temporarily when one area of weakness needs to be stressed. Most of the time, however, the teacher listens to the children read aloud, one at a time, and tries to see that each child is working at his correct difficulty level. She also listens for mistakes and looks at his written work carefully to check for skill weaknesses. (Does he know vowel sounds? Is he getting the main idea of the paragraph?) But a good amount of the individualized reading instruction revolves around the child as he reads silently to himself, often from a carefully selected library book rather than from a basic text. Individualized reading is used more in the upper elementary grades than the primary grades, although it can be used anywhere. This approach is discussed more fully in Chapter 12.

In most classrooms the total "language arts" approach is an important part of a child's learning to read. This means that spelling and writing and listening to stories and poems all contribute to reading skills. Many schools which have a weak phonics program in their basal reading series have a strong phonics program in their spelling series. Many children "catch on" to reading through their writing lessons; in fact, one major remedial reading method which will be discussed later is based on a child writing his own reading book. (This method, which is very time-consuming for the teacher, is perhaps best suited for small groups.) Even if a basal series is used, most teachers have the children read in a wide variety of books obtained from classroom, school, and community libraries.

SUMMARY

Most children in the United States learn to read from a basic reading series. Each series contains carefully graded books for each elementary grade. The greatest value of these series is the careful and gradual introduction of new words, followed by adequate repetitions for each new word. In addition, the series contains teacher's manuals and student activity books which help to augment reading skills. The teacher usually breaks her class into three groups to allow for individual differences in learning rate. Practice in all of the language arts – writing, spelling, and reading supplementary books – helps the child to learn to read.

4

BASIC VOCABULARY – THE INSTANT WORDS

As mentioned in the preceding chapter, the chief principle of reading instruction in a basic series is the controlled or gradual introduction of new words. In individualized or remedial reading, also, a major teaching strategy is to find out which basic reading vocabulary words a student knows and to teach him the words he does not know.

A basic reading vocabulary is a list of words (usually several hundred words) which is absolutely essential for reading. The basic vocabulary compiled for this book (see Appendix 4-A) is referred to as the Instant Words, because these are the words a child must recognize instantly in order to have reading facility. These words are used over and over again, like *the* and *is* and *man*. They are used so frequently that the student cannot take time to stop and sound them out or he will lose the meaning of the sentence.

The Instant Words are the commonest words of the English language. They are based on frequency counts of words used in children's reading material and in their speaking and writing. The first 300 Instant Words make up nearly one-half of all written material. If, for example, a frequency count were made of the words used in this book, the result would be that about one-half of the words come from this list of the first 300 Instant Words. In children's reading material the percentage is even higher. A study of reading material used in the first three grades revealed that the first 300 Instant Words comprised approximately 63 percent of all words used. These words, of course, have a high overlap with the vocabularies used in basal reading series. If we examine the readers for the first three grades in several basal reader series we find that the first 300 words comprise between 58 and 77 per cent of all the words.

Many studies in educational research are equivocable and difficult to reproduce. However, the word-frequency studies are quite stable and easy to verify. The Instant Words are based on such exhaustive frequency counts as the Thorndike-Lorge word list, which is derived from counting millions of words in children's and adult literature, and the Rinsland list, which is based on a frequency count of words used by children in writing themes. Other studies were also consulted, such as those by Dolch and Buckingham, and Fitzgerald.

There are 600 Instant Words in all, arranged approximately according to grade level. The first 100 words are approximately at first grade level of difficulty, the second 100 Instant Words at the second grade difficulty level, and the third 100 words at the third grade level of difficulty. The last 300 Instant Words are approximately at the fourth grade level of difficulty. By level of difficulty is meant, for example, that a child who is nearing the end of the second grade, who has made normal reading progress, and who is reading near the end of the basal series work for the second grade should be able to read most of the first 200 Instant Words.

The Instant Words were originally devised for a remedial reading situation to diagnose and teach older children who had not learned to read up to their expected grade level. For example, a remedial reading student might be a fifth grade child with normal intelligence who was reading on the second grade level or a seventh grade boy who was reading on a third grade level. These children have had a poor development of reading skills, and hence it is necessary to determine their basic vocabulary development before starting to teach them basic vocabulary without necessarily having them go through all the basal reading books.

A further problem is that many older children have learned their reading skills from different basal series. While there is a high degree of overlap of the basic words presented in different series, there is considerably less than complete agreement among them. Hence, the Instant Words are taken from the same sources as the vocabularies used in most basal reading series. By using the Instant Words as part of individualized or remedial reading instruction, the teacher can be assured that the student is progressing soundly in the area of basic vocabulary. This allows the teacher to use a wide variety of materials, such as basal readers and trade books and games.

A further advantage of using the Instant Words is the way in which they are divided into groups. They are arranged in groups of twenty-five. Groups follow in order of frequency of use. For this reason it is most important that children learn the first group of twenty-five Instant Words first, since these are the words used most frequently in the English language and also those that are used most often in all readers. The second group of twenty-five Instant Words include those used next most frequently in English.

One difficulty encountered in attempting to utilize other basic word lists is that they are not broken down into small enough teaching groups. For example, the Dolch Basic Sight Vocabulary is a list of 220 words plus 95 common nouns, but no indication is given as to which should be taught first. Richards' Basic English Vocabulary of 850 words, or the Thorndike first 500 words involves the same problem. Richards' list of 85 words suffers an additional disadvantage in that it was especially designed for the teaching of English as a second language. The words have been edited, which means that they were selected not strictly on the basis of a frequency count but rather selected by the author who was compiling a list which he felt was most useful in basic English communication for students who do not regularly speak English. On the other hand, the Thorndike list of the commonest 500 words suffers from being an unedited list which is determined strictly according to frequency principles. In this type of list we see such logical inconsistencies as inclusion of only five of the seven days of the week or failure to include several of the numbers from one to ten.

The Instant Words is an edited list based on frequency determined by several studies from different viewpoints, i.e., writing, reading, spelling. After the multiple frequency importance was established, the list was edited to insert certain logically consistent words, such as the missing days of the week. Some editing was also done to omit "babyish" words, in deference to older remedial reading students who might be using the list.

TEST AND TEACH THE INSTANT WORDS

In using the Instant Words, the solid teaching maxim of first "Finding out where the child is" should be followed before beginning instruction. To do this on an individual basis is quite simple. The teacher asks a child to read aloud the first five words in each group of twenty-five words. If the student misses any of these words he may then be asked to read the entire list. The teacher should write down the words that the student misses on a sheet of paper, preferably in neat manuscript writing, and then use the list of missed words for instruction. For example, these words might be put on individualized flash cards, or the student might merely study the list until he can read it without error. The list can be used for spelling or for any of the other teaching methods which might be used.

Strangely enough, children seem to have difficulty in learning the Instant Words. This is partly due to the fact that some of them are not subject-matter words. It is much easier to teach a child the difference between the words *dinosaur* and *cowboy* than it is to teach him the difference between *this* and *that* and *these* and *those*. Studies have shown that it takes the average six-year-old nearly a year of reading instruction to master the first 100 Instant Words and the average seven-year-old approximately a year to master the second 100 Instant Words. Adults and older children taking remedial reading instruction naturally learn these words at a much faster rate. Nevertheless, the learning of the Instant Words roughly parallels total reading development. This does not mean that at the end of the first grade a child knows only 100 words or that at the end of second grade he knows exactly 200 words. He knows many more, but these additional words usually are peculiar to the stories he has been reading. He will know quite a number of additional words such as *Jane*, *Sally*, *ranch*.

Teachers should not try to teach too many Instant Words at one time. For young children, learning no more than two or three each lesson is quite enough. Teachers of older children should be more than satisfied if a child masters an entire group of twenty-five words in a week. Most children will learn these words at a much slower rate than one group in a week. The danger is for the teacher to be in such a hurry that she rushes the child through the Instant Word list too rapidly. *Allow plenty of time for review.* The use of games and a variety of teaching methods makes the review both interesting and profitable. The teacher should not be surprised if there is a fairly high rate of forgetting of Instant Words. Instant Words are hard to retain. On a given day, a child may read quite satisfactorily a list of ten difficult Instant Words; but three or four days later he may be able to recall only five of the words. It takes patience, good teaching methods, and persistent review to remedy the difficulty.

The phonics approach may work well with some children in learning some of the Instant Words, but this approach may not give a student the instant recognition that is desired in teaching the Instant Words. Hence, the whole-word method of teaching is better for this list.

METHODS OF INSTRUCTION

Methods used in teaching the Instant Words vary with the teacher, the pupil, and the educational situation. Any approach that is successful is acceptable, and any method that works is a good method.

Good methods to use in teaching the Instant Words include card games, easy reading, flash cards, and spelling lessons augmented by lavish praise, stern talks, competition, or a play-therapy climate. The pupil can learn to read words in books, on flash cards, in his own compositions, or from a screen on which words are flashed at 1/25th of a second. Children are taught singly and in large groups, in the classroom and out under the trees. But all the while the student is also being taught three things by word and deed: (1) We care about him. (2) We want him to read. (3) These Instant Words are important.

EASY READING Easy reading is one of the best methods of teaching Instant Words. This means, simply, that if a child can read second grade level material

FIGURE 4-1 Individual flash cards and word games are excellent devices to use in teaching a basic reading vocabulary.

(whether fluently, hesitatingly, or with help) for him easy reading is reading first grade material. Betts gives an excellent definition of easy reading: A child can read easily when he can pronounce 99 percent of the words. Another Betts rule-of-thumb is that when a child averages fewer than one mistake for every twenty words, the material is "easy" for him. Easy reading is especially beneficial because it is certain to contain the Instant Words, and a child who barely knows these words gets practice in recognizing them. Easy reading gives the child a feeling of success and encourages him to try to learn more.

FILMSTRIPS Some primary children become discouraged at the sight of a whole page of print. And children in remedial reading classes have sometimes learned to hate a page of print. For these pupils it is often better to teach them reading in a completely different setting. We have had success with reputedly "hopeless cases" by having them do a fair amount of reading from filmstrips projected on the screen. There is something about a partly darkened room with its illuminated image that focuses attention, much as the television screen does for us all. We try to induce a sort of game atmosphere by flashing the word on the screen as quickly as an eye blink (tachistoscopically) and daring the child to see it. If he does catch the word he can write it down, paying attention to proper spelling. When called upon, he can tell the teacher the word and earn the reward of proving his accuracy. (Perhaps the child is being trapped into reading, but the process is painless.) In case he does not know how to read the word, the teacher or another student reads it aloud so that he can hear it and associate the visually written image with the sound. In any event, the student sees the word on the screen again and corrects his written response or writes it for the first time if he has missed it altogether.

Filmstrips are also an excellent large-group method. Inexperienced teachers with an unruly class often get excellent cooperation and attention when using filmstrips as described above. But just because this is such a good method and is interesting to the children, the teacher should not "work it to death." Do not continue tachistoscopic lessons until boredom sets in; usually ten minutes for primary children and not over twenty minutes for older students is adequate. Too frequent repetitions can also cause interest to wane; several times a week for several months at a time, followed by several months of varied activity, will help to keep interest high.

For variety, repetition, and challenge to older children the Instant Words may also be combined into Instant Word phrases (both series of filmstrips are published by Learning Through Seeing, Sunland, California). These phrase filmstrips correlate with the word filmstrips. For example, the twenty-five words on the Instant Word Filmstrip No. 1 are used on Instant Phrase Filmstrip No. 1 and no other words are used in making up the phrases. All twenty-five words are used in Part 1 of the phrase filmstrip; then the same twenty-five words are used again in new phrases in Part 2 and again in new phrases in Part 3 so that each Instant Word is repeated at least three times in three different phrases in each phrase filmstrip. In phrase filmstrips beyond No. 1, words introduced earlier may be used in making up phrases (Instant Filmstrip No. 3 may use a word from No. 1) but all new words are used at least three times, once in each part.

The Instant Word phrases are difficult to see when flashed at 1/25th of a second or faster, and they provide a challenging drill and interesting review for secondary students or adults. Elementary children who have mastered the first 300 Instant Words (Set I, a box of twelve filmstrips) have their interest renewed when meeting the same words on the phrase filmstrips. These children or older remedial readers will know most of the words; and, rather than review the words and improve their knowledge of them by using the simpler word filmstrips, the same systematic review effect can be obtained from using the phrase filmstrips.

The flashing can be accomplished easily by using any tachistoscope, which is nothing more than a filmstrip projector, plus some attachment like Learning Through Seeing's inexpensive Tachist-o-flashers (see Figure 4-2).

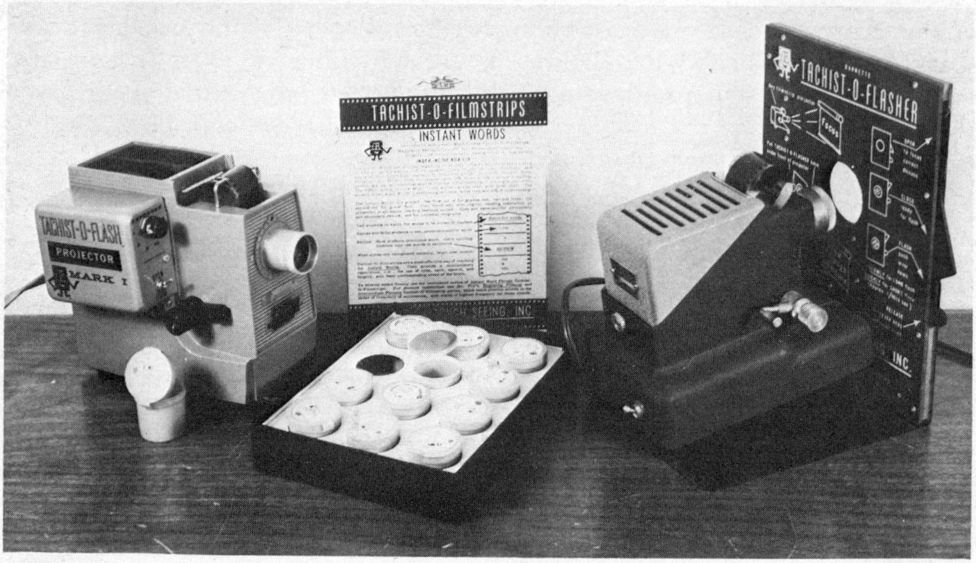

FIGURE 4-2 A common type of tachist-o-flasher: one projector has a built-in flasher; the other is a filmstrip projector with an external flasher. Filmstrips contain Instant Words.

Other more elaborate flashing devices include SVE's Speed-I-O-Scope and other camera-shutter-type devices. The more expensive devices have a time-of-exposure regulator; but it makes no difference how fast the flash is for reading training, as long as it is faster than a saccadic movement (one-fifth of a second)—and they all do that. The flashing should occur in a partially darkened room, dark enough so that the image on the screen is clear but light enough so that one can see to write. Flashing in a totally dark room may give some students retinal shock, a mildly painful but not dangerous sensation to the eyes.

PSYCHOLOGICAL PRINCIPLES Reshowing each word and pronouncing it immediately after the student has seen it and attempted to write and say it (we can assume that most students will try to say the word themselves, even if not called on) gives what the psychologist calls the *knowledge of results*, a very effective tool in learning and motivation. In addition to knowledge of results, some of the learning principles involved in the process are (1) *learning set*, i.e., paying attention to the right thing; (2) *multisensory approach*, i.e., the use of eyes, ears, speech, fingers, with their corresponding areas of the brain; (3) *learning small units* which increase the frequency of the rewarding effect of *knowledge of results*; and (4) the sheer *novelty* of the use of the screen which is unlike other reading experiences.

Another interesting aspect of using filmstrips in a partly darkened room is the lessening of distractions. This is particularly recommended with brain-damaged children who are characterized by easy distractability.

To some extent the group filmstrip procedure provides for individual differences in reading ability and learning rate in that the better students can try to write and say all the words correctly and the poorer students can merely observe the word, try to copy it, and listen carefully when they are told what it is. However, teachers may wish to divide the class group so that the more advanced students may work on harder words. Slower students who need more practice can often receive help from a better student who is assigned to work with a small group of slower students.

Hence we see how other important learning principles are involved in these suggested methods of teaching a sight vocabulary, namely that a certain amount of *practice*, or repetition, is necessary. Both experienced teachers and psychological experimenters have found that duller children need more repetition, practice, and even overlearning (practice after mastery) in order to really learn. Spacing out the practice is also desirable, since too much at one time not only causes boredom but is inefficient because a point is reached where little or no learning takes place.

FIGURE 4-3 Flash cards for teaching a basic vocabulary come in either a large size for large groups or small children or a smaller size for individual or small-group instruction.

FLASH CARDS It is not necessary to have a tachistoscope to take advantage of many of these learning principles. Flash cards such as those shown in Figure 4-3 accomplish many of the same things. Both flash cards and the tachistoscope can be used to present words to large groups or to individuals. In fact, either can be self-administered by the student, although self-administration often makes correction a problem. Flash cards are used frequently with small groups. The teacher flashes the word as quickly as possible. The student who says the word first is allowed to hold the card. The point of the game is to see who holds the most cards. Inequities in reaction time or ability can be offset partially by giving each student a turn at recognizing the word; if he misses, the next student takes his turn.

Students sometimes work alone with a small pack of flash cards, separated into two piles: (1) the cards he knows, and (2) the cards he does not know. When he is finished, the teacher or a superior student checks up on the "know" pile and then helps him with the "don't know" pile.

BINGO Bingo is an excellent game for teaching Instant Words to large groups, and it is equally useful for use with small groups. Twenty-five words can be placed on a card (five rows and five columns) in random order; each "player" is given a card. The teacher calls off the words at random or may take the precaution of drawing the word cards out of a hat. Markers can be small squares of cardboard. The first student to cover a complete row, column, or diagonal line wins. Even though there has been a winner, the class often likes to continue playing until every word is covered. If the game is played until the board is filled, the teacher can sometimes spot poor readers by the number of words which remain uncovered. In a teaching situation in which some of the students do not know all of the words, an excellent opportunity for instruction can ensue, and the teacher can show the card or write the word on the board after saying it; this presents the desirable opportunity of giving poor readers an equal chance at winning.

PAIRS CARD GAME Another game played with great success is called Pairs. This is a rummy-type of card game for two to five players. First a deck of fifty cards is purchased or made by the teacher or by an able child. The fifty-card deck contains twenty-five pairs of identical cards (using exactly one group of twenty-five Instant Words). Each player is dealt five cards. The first player asks one other player if he has a specific card (the asking player must hold the mate in his hand). If the asking player secures the card, he has a "pair" and may lay it down. If not, he draws from the deck. The object is to get as many pairs as possible. For most efficient reading instruction, the players should know some, but not all, of the words used in a given deck. If the asking player does not know how to read a card, he may show it and any player or the teacher may read it for him. Likewise, the player asked may request to see the card being asked for, so that he may compare it with the cards in his hand.

REVIEW Once in a while it is a good idea to review easy words already mastered, just for fun; but, generally, instructional games should follow the same rules as the selection of instructional reading material, i.e., they should not be too easy nor too hard.

We have suggested only a few of many possible specific methods for teaching the Instant Words. Experienced reading teachers know and use many more. In remedial reading, especially, a variety and interchange of methods is desirable.

In Appendix 4-A the 600 Instant Words are given, followed by the Instant Word recognition test that can be used in checking the word knowledge of individual students or large groups.

APPENDIX 4-A THE INSTANT WORDS*

FIRST 100 WORDS (approximately first grade)

	Group 1a	*Group 1b*	*Group 1c*	*Group 1d*
1.	the	he	go	who
2.	a	I	see	an
3.	is	they	then	their
4.	you	one	us	she
5.	to	good	no	new
6.	and	me	him	said
7.	we	about	by	did
8.	that	had	was	boy
9.	in	if	come	three
10.	not	some	get	down
11.	for	up	or	work
12.	at	her	two	put
13.	with	do	man	were
14.	it	when	little	before
15.	on	so	has	just
16.	can	my	them	long
17.	will	very	how	here
18.	are	all	like	other
19.	of	would	our	old
20.	this	any	what	take
21.	your	been	know	cat
22.	as	out	make	again
23.	but	there	which	give
24.	be	from	much	after
25.	have	day	his	many

SECOND 100 WORDS (approximately second grade)

	Group 2a	*Group 2b*	*Group 2c*	*Group 2d*
1.	saw	big	may	ran
2.	home	where	let	five
3.	soon	am	use	read
4.	stand	ball	these	over
5.	box	morning	right	such
6.	upon	live	present	way
7.	first	four	tell	too
8.	came	last	next	shall
9.	girl	color	please	own
10.	house	away	leave	most
11.	find	red	hand	sure
12.	because	friend	more	thing
13.	made	pretty	why	only
14.	could	eat	better	near
15.	book	want	under	than
16.	look	year	while	open
17.	mother	white	should	kind
18.	run	got	never	must
19.	school	play	each	high
20.	people	found	best	far
21.	night	left	another	both
22.	into	men	seem	end
23.	say	bring	tree	also
24.	think	wish	name	until
25.	back	black	dear	call

THIRD 100 WORDS (approximately third grade)

	Group 3a	*Group 3b*	*Group 3c*	*Group 3d*
1.	ask	hat	off	fire
2.	small	car	sister	ten
3.	yellow	write	happy	order
4.	show	try	once	part
5.	goes	myself	didn't	early
6.	clean	longer	set	fat
7.	buy	those	round	third
8.	thank	hold	dress	same
9.	sleep	full	fall	love
10.	letter	carry	wash	hear
11.	jump	eight	start	yesterday
12.	help	sing	always	eyes
13.	fly	warm	anything	door
14.	don't	sit	around	clothes
15.	fast	dog	close	though
16.	cold	ride	walk	o'clock
17.	today	hot	money	second
18.	does	grow	turn	water
19.	face	cut	might	town
20.	green	seven	hard	took
21.	every	woman	along	pair
22.	brown	funny	bed	now
23.	coat	yes	fine	keep
24.	six	ate	sat	head
25.	gave	stop	hope	food

FOURTH 100 WORDS (approximately fourth grade)

	Group 4a	*Group 4b*	*Group 4c*	*Group 4d*
1.	told	time	word	wear
2.	Miss	yet	almost	Mr.
3.	father	true	thought	side
4.	children	above	send	poor
5.	land	still	receive	lost
6.	interest	meet	pay	outside
7.	government	since	nothing	wind
8.	feet	number	need	Mrs.
9.	garden	state	mean	learn
10.	done	matter	late	held
11.	country	line	half	front
12.	different	remember	fight	built
13.	bad	large	enough	family
14.	across	few	feel	began
15.	yard	hit	during	air
16.	winter	cover	gone	young
17.	table	window	hundred	ago
18.	story	even	week	world
19.	sometimes	city	between	airplane
20.	I'm	together	change	without
21.	tried	sun	being	kill
22.	horse	life	care	ready
23.	something	street	answer	stay
24.	brought	party	course	won't
25.	shoes	suit	against	paper

FIFTH 100 WORDS (approximately fourth grade)

	Group 4e	*Group 4f*	*Group 4g*	*Group 4h*
1.	hour	grade	egg	spell
2.	glad	brother	ground	beautiful
3.	follow	remain	afternoon	sick
4.	company	milk	feed	became
5.	believe	several	boat	cry
6.	begin	war	plan	finish
7.	mind	able	question	catch
8.	pass	charge	fish	floor
9.	reach	either	return	stick
10.	month	less	sir	great
11.	point	train	fell	guess
12.	rest	cost	hill	bridge
13.	sent	evening	wood	church
14.	talk	note	add	lady
15.	went	past	ice	tomorrow
16.	bank	room	chair	snow
17.	ship	flew	watch	whom
18.	business	office	alone	women
19.	whole	cow	low	among
20.	short	visit	arm	road
21.	certain	wait	dinner	farm
22.	fair	teacher	hair	cousin
23.	reason	spring	service	bread
24.	summer	picture	class	wrong
25.	fill	bird	quite	age

SIXTH 100 WORDS (approximately fourth grade)

	Group 4i	*Group 4j*	*Group 4k*	*Group 4l*
1.	become	herself	demand	aunt
2.	body	idea	however	system
3.	chance	drop	figure	lie
4.	act	river	case	cause
5.	die	smile	increase	marry
6.	real	son	enjoy	possible
7.	speak	bat	rather	supply
8.	already	fact	sound	thousand
9.	doctor	sort	eleven	pen
10.	step	king	music	condition
11.	itself	dark	human	perhaps
12.	nine	themselves	court	produce
13.	baby	whose	force	twelve
14.	minute	study	plant	rode
15.	ring	fear	suppose	uncle
16.	wrote	move	law	labor
17.	happen	stood	husband	public
18.	appear	himself	moment	consider
19.	heart	strong	person	thus
20.	swim	knew	result	least
21.	felt	often	continue	power
22.	fourth	toward	price	mark
23.	I'll	wonder	serve	president
24.	kept	twenty	national	voice
25.	well	important	wife	whether

APPENDIX 4-B BRIEF INDIVIDUAL INSTANT WORD ORAL READING TEST*

HOW TO USE: Ask the student to read each word aloud. Mark each word read incorrectly with an *X* on the word. Stop the test when the student misses two complete lines.

SCORING: Count the total number of words read correctly and write the number correct in the space provided. This test does not yield a grade level but rather aids the instructor in selecting curriculum materials and planning lessons. The letters in parentheses indicate the group of Instant Words. "1a" means first 100 word group "a," "2c" means second 100 word group "c," etc. Students should know nearly all of these words when they have obtained the upper fourth-grade reading ability level. Do not use this test for teaching; use the complete list of Instant Words.

1.	(1a)	the	is	of
2.	(1b)	they	if	would
3.	(1c)	by	our	which
4.	(1d)	who	their	other
5.	(2a)	upon	because	say
6.	(2b)	where	year	found
7.	(2c)	right	leave	another
8.	(2d)	five	shall	also
9.	(3a)	don't	does	ask
10.	(3b)	myself	eight	write
11.	(3c)	off	start	close
12.	(3d)	early	eyes	though
13.	(4a)	country	tired	brought
14.	(4e)	believe	month	whole
15.	(4i)	die	minute	fourth

Total number of words read correctly (maximum 45) ____________

APPENDIX 4-C THE INSTANT WORD RECOGNITION TEST*

This is a test for individual or group administration in primary grades and remedial reading situations for:

1. Determining the starting point in teaching the Instant Words, which is a graded high-frequency reading vocabulary.

*By Edward Fry, Rutgers University Reading Center. Reproduction prohibited by copyright law. Copies of the test may be obtained from Dreier Educational Systems, Highland Park, New Jersey 08904.

2. Measuring general reading achievement, which is useful for such purposes as placing children in reading groups.

DIRECTIONS FOR THE INSTANT WORD RECOGNITION TEST

This test may be given to one child or to a whole class. However, with first graders or slow students or older remedial children the test is more valid if it is administered to small groups of ten or fewer pupils so that the teacher can observe each student and see that he follows directions properly and does not look at another child's paper–separation of seats is desirable.

Instruct the students to fill in the data at the top of their test sheets. Writing the teacher's name or group, date, and Form 1 or Form 2 on the chalkboard is helpful. For Form 1 of the test the teacher reads the directions for Form 1, and for Form 2 the teacher reads from the directions for Form 2. The child marks the same test blank. The only difference in Form 1 and Form 2 is the difference in directions.

Next, copy the example on the chalkboard:

A *it* *have* *can* *a* *with* and say:

"In this test we want to find out how many words you can read. I am going to call out one word for each line and you are to place an *X* on top of the word I call out.

"Now look at the first line of words, line A. If I call out the word *can*, you place an *X* on top of the word *can* like this (illustrate on chalkboard). You should all mark an *X* on *can*."

Check to see if all the students have the examples marked correctly.

Next read off the list of words from either Form 1 column or Form 2 column (not both). Read the line number, the word, the word used in a simple sentence or phrase, and the word once more. Do not give additional repetitions of the word or any additional hints, examples, or other help.

For example:

"Line 1, *and,* Bill *and* Mary went to town, *and.*"

INTERPRETATION

This test measures the sight recognition of the Instant Words (which is a little easier than the skill of reading them aloud).

The test is in serial order progressing from easy to hard. The column at the far right tells from which group of Instant Words the line was selected. There are two lines for each group of twenty-five Instant Words. The first line for each group is a random selection of words, while the second line of each group chooses groups of words which have similar beginning sounds. Hence, if a student gets the first line for each group correct and not the second the teacher may well suspect that the student knows beginning word *sounds* but not the Instant Words at this level.

The main value of this test is that it will suggest to the teacher which groups of Instant Words can most profitably be taught to individuals or groups.

Though this test does not have a large standardization group, it has been administered to 153 first graders in December and their mean score was 11.1.

It also has some value in predicting success in reading or when compared with the paragraph meaning subtest of the Stanford Achievement Test given in May. The correlation was 0.77. This also indicates that the Instant Word Recognition Test can also profitably be used for ranking students within the class as one of the criteria for placing them in reading groups.

Note that the same Students Test Sheet is used for both Form 1 and Form 2; the only difference is in the teachers directions.

For an individually administered oral reading test the student may be asked to read aloud from the Student Test Sheet.

TEACHERS DIRECTIONS FOR INSTANT WORD RECOGNITION TEST

FORM 1. LOWER LEVEL

1.	and	Bill *and* Mary went to the store.
2.	that	Is *that* your pencil?
3.	up	Look *up* at the airplane.
4.	so	John took his ball *so* the children could play.
5.	go	Did you *go* to school?
6.	was	He *was* the tallest boy in the class.
7.	she	Did *she* help you?
8.	were	The children *were* skating.
9.	could	Bill *could* not find his pencil.
10.	saw	We *saw* the helicopter land.
11.	eat	What shall we *eat* for lunch.
12.	white	Betty wore a *white* sweater.
13.	each	*Each* boy did his best.
14.	next	The *next* boy was named Henry.
15.	must	You *must* use a sharpened pencil.
16.	such	It was *such* a lovely day we went for a walk.
17.	buy	Please *buy* a loaf of bread.
18.	green	Janie wore a *green* dress.
19.	seven	There were *seven* boys on one team.
20.	sit	Billy wanted to *sit* in the big chair.
21.	bed	Linda went to *bed* at eight o'clock.
22.	set	Do you help Mother *set* the table?
23.	through	We went *through* a dark tunnel.
24.	town	The little *town* had pretty houses.

FORM 2. LOWER LEVEL

1.	be	I will *be* at home.
2.	as	Run *as* fast as you can.
3.	out	We went *out* to play.
4.	had	They *had* a new ball.
5.	come	Please *come* here.

6. what *What* time is it?
7. give Please *give* the book to John.
8. their Lucky is *their* dog.
9. could We *could* see everyone.
10. back Bill played in the *back* yard.
11. found Jane *found* a nickel.
12. bring Did he *bring* the fruit?
13. why *Why* did Betty stay home?
14. never We *never* went to that zoo.
15. shall I *shall* go home.
16. sure Tom was *sure* he had a pencil.
17. every *Every* house had a porch.
18. goes Jack *goes* to the store for his mother.
19. write Can you *write* your name?
20. hot The stove was *hot.*
21. wash Did you *wash* your hands?
22. along Ride *along* the sidewalk.
23. fat She held a *fat* little puppy.
24. took We *took* a lunch with us.

FORM 1. UPPER LEVEL

25. garden Mother likes her *garden.*
26. told She *told* me a secret.
27. cover *Cover* your mouth when you sneeze.
28. street Which *street* do you live on?
29. mean I *mean* what I say.
30. fight Girls don't like to *fight.*
31. side Which *side* are you on?
32. wind The *wind* howled through the trees.
33. follow Let's play "*Follow* the Leader."
34. short We will only stay a *short* time.
35. note He took a *note* home.
36. cost How much does that *cost*?
37. dinner It's time for *dinner.*
38. feed May we *feed* the monkeys?
39. sick Some people make me *sick*!
40. farm Grandpa lived on a *farm.*
41. kept Grandma *kept* cookies in a jar.
42. ring She wore a gold *ring.*
43. idea Whose *idea* was this?
44. strong How *strong* are you?
45. result What is the *result* of striking a match?
46. court The *court* fined him $15 for speeding.
47. twelve *Twelve* things make a dozen.
48. perhaps *Perhaps* you can help me.

FORM 2. UPPER LEVEL

25.	story	This is a good *story.*
26.	table	Put the dishes on the *table.*
27.	number	What *number* comes after nine?
28.	still	Hold your hand *still!*
29.	need	How many do you *need?*
30.	feel	How do you *feel?*
31.	front	Put the smaller children in *front.*
32.	wear	You should *wear* your sweater when it is cold.
33.	pass	*Pass* the ketchup, please.
34.	ship	They painted their *ship* black.
35.	less	Three is *less* than five.
36.	cow	A *cow* eats grass.
37.	egg	She had an *egg* for breakfast.
38.	fell	Jack *fell* down the stairs.
39.	great	The President is a *great* man.
40.	finish	When you *finish* the book, put it back on the shelf.
41.	well	They went to the *well* for water.
42.	wrote	I *wrote* a letter to my friend yesterday.
43.	herself	She cut *herself* on the nail.
44.	study	You need a quiet place to *study.*
45.	enjoy	Most boys *enjoy* playing football.
46.	continue	*Continue* to practice until I tell you to stop.
47.	aunt	My *aunt* is very nice.
48.	possible	We can only do something if it is *possible.*

STUDENT TEST SHEET
INSTANT WORD RECOGNITION TEST
LOWER LEVEL

Student's name____

Date____

Teacher or group____

A.	it	have	can	a	with	(Example)
1.	you	the	is	and	be	(1a)
2.	at	this	as	that	are	(1a)
3.	I	about	me	out	up	(1b)
4.	he	so	had	been	some	(1b)
5.	go	by	or	some	us	(1c)
6.	what	his	which	has	was	(1c)
7.	she	take	give	again	down	(1d)
8.	three	who	their	were	work	(1d)
9.	could	because	into	think	night	(2a)

10. box book saw say back (2a)
11. eat want four found last (2b)
12. bring white black where ball (2b)
13. use why each these let (2c)
14. tree next tall never name (2c)
15. shall thing kind call must (2d)
16. over such own only sure (2d)
17. buy every fly clean thank (3a)
18. gave sleep green goes small (3a)
19. write those myself seven eight (3b)
20. hat hot sing hold sit (3b)
21. hard bed wash fail dress (3c)
22. always sat set along ground (3c)
23. keep fat eyes only through (3d)
24. town ten took pair part (3d)

UPPER LEVEL

Student's name ______________________________

Date ______________________________

Teacher or group ______________________________

A. it have can a with (Example)
25. garden father across story brought (4a)
26. done told different table tried (4a)
27. number matter together cover hit (4b)
28. still sun city state street (4b)
29. need mean send thought half (4c)
30. enough during feel hundred fight (4c)
31. side front young kill air (4d)
32. wear wind world won't built (4d)
33. follow company pass begin reason (4e)
34. certain ship sent fair short (4e)
35. bird wait note less ever (4f)
36. past cow cost charge milk (4f)
37. egg dinner return ground hair (4g)
38. hill feed fell alone sir (4g)
39. became cry great whom sick (4h)
40. finish bread farm floor snow (4h)
41. well fourth step kept act (4i)
42. heart real swim ring wrote (4i)
43. herself idea themselves wonder twenty (rj)
44. smile stood study strong whose (4j)
45. demand figure enjoy human result (rk)
46. court case increase continue price (4k)
47. aunt lie rode twelve mark (41)
48. public president perhaps pen possible (41)

APPENDIX 4-D PAIRS: A CARD GAME FOR FUN AND READING INSTRUCTION

PAIRS is played like Rummy or Fish, except that only two cards are needed to make a book or pair. Two to five children may play. Five cards are dealt to each player, and the remainder of the deck is placed in the center of the table.

The object of the game is to get as many pairs as possible. There are only two cards alike in each deck.

The player to the right of the dealer may ask any single other player if he has a specific card. For example, "Do you have 'and'?" The player asking must hold the mate (in the example, the *and* card) in his hand. The player who is asked must give up the card if he holds it. If the first player does not get the card he asks for, he should draw one card from the pile. Then the next player has a turn at asking for a card.

If the player succeeds in getting the card he asked for, either from another player or from the pile, he gets another turn. As soon as the player gets a pair he puts the pair down in front of him. The player with the most pairs at the end of the game wins.

If the child *doing the asking* does not know how to read the word on the card, he may show the card and ask any of the other players or anyone present.

If the child *who is asked* for a card does not know how to read that word or is unsure of himself, the best thing to do is to ask to see the card of the player requesting the card or ask a nonplaying person who can read to look at his hand.

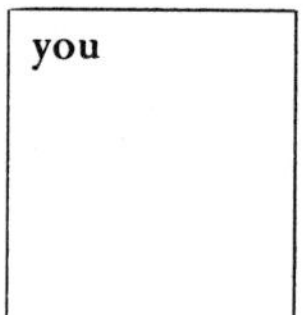

FOR READING INSTRUCTION. The children should know some but not all the words used in a particular deck. They should have help in playing until they know almost all the words and can get along by themselves. They can usually accomplish this quite rapidly as the game is highly motivating. The children should play the game on several different occasions until they can call out all the words instantly. They should then move to the next harder deck. Reviewing easier decks is also recommended.

Decks are identified on the back as to the order in which they should be played. Deck 1-a contains the most used words in the English language and should be played first. Deck 1-b contains the next most used words and should be played next. This should be followed by deck 1-c, then 1-d. Each deck of Pairs is correlated with an Instant Words Tachist-O-Filmstrip.

The cards may also be used as flash cards for small groups. For entertainment and review Pairs is often played by older children.

APPENDIX 4-E SAMPLE BINGO CARD

the	of	it	with	at
a	can	on	are	this
is	will	you	to	and
your	that	we	as	but
be	in	not	for	have

Note that by making five rows and five columns exactly one set of twenty-five Instant Words will fit on a card. Children can use bits of paper for markers, and the teacher can use a list of the words to call off each.

5

PHONICS – SOUNDS OF ENGLISH

There is hardly a word or concept associated with reading instruction that causes more emotional response than *phonics*. For some reason, this concept seems to arouse violent opinions, if not accusations and controversy. Many parents and even a few educators have maintained that phonics will cure any reading problem. Unfortunately, they are wrong, for no single panacea has been devised. It would be wonderful, though, if teaching reading were so simple that all one had to do was to administer the child a strong dose of phonics lessons.

If a parent calls me on the telephone and asks if I teach reading by using phonics, I always say "yes." I am rather certain that the parent knows little or nothing about teaching reading, and chances are that he or she is dissatisfied with whatever instruction is being given at school. I also know that there could be any number of reasons why their child's reading progress is disappointing them. Reading failure might be due to any of a number of reasons: a low IQ; or the child may be unable to profit from reading instruction for reasons such as brain damage, emotional problems, physical or emotional immaturity, vision problems, hearing problems, frequent change of schools, speech problems, or the previous teaching itself may have been poor.

Some of those parents who feel confident that phonics will cure anything from mental retardation to laziness have received this impression from articles which have appeared recently in national magazines, newspapers (particularly letters to the editor columns), or books which offer half-truths.

The interesting thing about the staunch phonics advocates is that they are partly correct. A good dose of phonics will indeed cure some remedial readers. It is also true that during the 1930s, 1940s, and 1950s there was a deemphasis of phonics in most schools in the United States. An even more disheartening fact is that many teachers themselves do not know much about phonics. Our teacher-training schools and state certification boards must both share the blame for this.

Hence, the plea is double-edged. Parents must realize that there is a good deal more to teaching reading than just phonics, and teachers must learn more about phonics and how to teach these skills effectively.

Children enter school with an oral-aural (speaking and listening) vocabulary of thousands of words, but a reading vocabulary of zero. Phonics then can be a useful tool in helping the child to "unlock" these printed symbols and translate them into the spoken words which he already knows.

ALPHABETS

Most writing, and this certainly includes English, is based on speech or oral communication. The fundamental way of transmitting an idea from one person to another person is through the medium of spoken language. Writing is a way of putting spoken language down on paper. A set of symbols called letters, which is collectively known as the alphabet, is used to do this. By definition, an alphabet is a group of symbols which represent speech sounds.

There is another method of communicating written ideas which is used in other cultures. The Chinese, for example, use a system of characters each of which stands directly for a concept or an idea. If a Chinese wishes to write house, for example, he will put down a single character which stands for the idea of a house. The character does not stand for a particular speech sound, the result being that people in north China who cannot talk to people in south China because their speech is different can read the writing of the southern Chinese (and sometimes even the Japanese) because they use the same characters. Many primitive societies also have a kind of picture writing or a less developed set of symbols which work in essentially the same way.

Completely regular phonetic writing requires a symbol to represent each speech sound. At one time, English was more like this; but after centuries of constant change and evolution and language influences from many different sources, English is not completely phonetically regular. Some letters used in writing have a half dozen or more distinctly different sounds.

How phonetically regular is our alphabet? Experts disagree. Our language is very complex and there are different ways of classifying each sound. The question is made more complicated by the wide variety of dialects used in English and by the number of rules considered regular. However, most experts agree that English is more than 50 percent regular. Those who apply a larger number of rules have even claimed that English is 90 percent or more phonetically regular.

In spoken English, there are about forty-two different *phonemes*; or speech sounds. The experts differ over the exact number: Some say thirty-nine, some say forty-four; but there is general agreement on the main speech sounds.) The disagreement over the total is partly due to combinations and fine distinctions which do not trouble the ordinary reader. To write these forty-two speech sounds, we have an alphabet of only twenty-six letters. Worse than that, at least three letters in the alphabet are of no use at all since they do not represent any speech sound; for example, the letter *c* sometimes sounds like an *s* (as in *city*) and sometimes like a *k* (as in *cat*), but there is no sound peculiar to the letter *c*. The other two worthless letters are *x* and *q*; *x* usually makes a *ks* sound as in *box*, and *q* is usually used with *u* and makes the *kw* sound as in *queen*.

Now, let us study the useful letters that we have.

Language experts have broken English letters into two major categories: vowels and consonants. There is disagreement at times (as over almost everything else in language) over what is a vowel sound and what is not. Still, we shall find this breakdown useful.

What is the difference between a vowel and a consonant? It is difficult to say exactly, but here are some of the characteristics of a vowel: It always uses the vocal cords; for example, *a* as in *ate* or *e* as in *me* cannot be made without using the vocal cords. A consonant may or may not use the vocal cords. The sounds made by *f* as in *fit* or *t* as in *top* do not use the vocal cords, but a consonant like *n* must use the vocal cords. Another distinction is that a vowel is a relatively open and flowing sound which can be sounded as long as desired. This does not apply to all consonants; for example, the *t* sound must be made short and quickly. Also, the passage of air through the speaker's mouth is often twisted and contracted in making consonants, while the mouth is relatively open in vowel sounds. Note the use of the lips in blocking the air when making the *b* sound as in *boy*. Or note the whistling of air through the teeth in making the *f* sound. Now contrast this with the sound made by *i* in the phrase "I am," or contrast it with the sound made by the vowel *a* as in *day*.

Another important difference between vowels and consonants is that a vowel must be present in every English word—in fact, every English syllable. This is the definition of a syllable: a separate vowel sound. We can have a one-syllable word; in fact, a one-letter syllable, and so a one-vowel word. *I*, for example, is a word; *A* is a word; but there is no word which is *t* or *f* or *m*. Hence, vowels can stand alone, but consonants cannot. Consonants must always be used in combination with a vowel when used in speaking English.

CONSONANTS*

A glance at Charts 1 and 3 at the end of this chapter reveals that most consonant sounds are represented by single letters. Consonants are much easier to work with than vowels because most of them have only one sound, whereas vowels have a number of different sounds.

In addition to the letter *c*, which we have already discussed, there are two consonants which have several sounds: the letters *q* and *s*. *G* sometimes makes its own sound, as in *good*, but it also makes a *j* sound, as in *general*. The rule is that *g* makes its own sound before *a*, *o*, and *u*, as in *good*, *gad*, and *gut*. It makes its *j* sound before the vowels *i*, *e*, and *y*. There are exceptions, of course, but this rule frequently applies as it stands. Incidentally, *c* breaks down into the same classification: making the *s* sound before *i*, *e*, and *y* and the *k* sound before *a*, *o*, and *u*. The other consonant which makes two sounds is *s*. *S* usually makes its own sound at the beginning of a word or syllable, but sometimes at the end of a word or syllable it makes a *z* sound, as in *is* or *has*.

In the following pages, references will frequently be made to the charts at the end of the section. Phonics rules are difficult to learn and to "see" as a unified whole. The following section presents a plain text description of the main phonics rules and subdivisions. The chart section, in the appendixes of this chapter, presents the same information in a slightly different fashion. It is hoped that the charts will serve two purposes: (1) to give the reader a unified picture, and (2) to use the charts themselves as teaching material. The next chapter deals with phonics teaching methods.

CONSONANT DIGRAPHS Some consonant sounds are represented by a combination of two letters or digraphs. The most common of these are the combinations *sh* as in *shoe*, *ch* as in *chair*, *wh* as in *wheel*, and *th* as in *the* (Chart 4). Note that a digraph is a separate speech sound. The *sh* sound as in *shoe* does not sound like a blend between an *s* sound and an *h* sound; it is completely separate and really should have its own letter; unfortunately, our written language, being imperfect, does not have it.

Just to make things more difficult, the digraph *th* has two sounds, which are called "voiced" and "voiceless" because the vocal cords are used in making the first but not the second. The two *th* sounds might be contrasted in the common words *this* (voiced) and *thing* (voiceless). Note that the mouth is held in the same position to make both sounds; the only difference between the two is the use of the vocal cords. Unfortunately, there is no rule to tell when a voiced and when a voiceless *th* sound should be used.

Although they are of minor importance, two other digraphs should be mentioned briefly. These are *ph* which makes the *f* sound as in *phone*, and *ng* which makes the sound found in *sing* (which is different from an *n* and *g* blend).

*If the reader is interested in why these particular phonics principles are listed, he will find my article, "A Frequency Approach To Phonics," published in *Elementary English* in November, 1964, most helpful. It lists and organizes five different phoneme-grapheme frequency counts.

CONSONANT BLENDS Blends such as *bl* at the beginning of the word *black* or *gr* at the beginning of the word *grass* have not been discussed because these do not present any particular problem to the reader as digraphs do. If the reader knows the sound of *b* as a single consonant and that of *l* as a single consonant, he can put them together to form the sound *bl*.

However, some teachers like to teach consonant blends and those who do find that initial consonant blends are more helpful to beginning readers than medial or final consonant blends.

The initial consonant blends fall into three families:

The *S* family—*st*, *sp*, *sc*, *sk*, *sw*, *sm*, and *sn*

The *R* family—*pr*, *tr*, *gr*, *br*, *cr*, *dr*, *fr*

The *L* family—*pl*, *cl*, *bl*, *fl*, *sl*, *gl*

These are all the beginning blends of consonants in the English language with the exception of *tw* (Chart 8). Persons not familiar with phonics sometimes think that any two letters can be blended together. This is not true with blends at the beginning of a word.

At the end of a word or in the middle of a word, some of the above blends may be used and there are about eleven more that have any degree of frequency. These are listed in Chart 9.

VOWELS

SHORT VOWELS Vowels, unfortunately, are much more complex than consonants. Each of them has several major sounds, and many of them have a number of sounds. Vowel sounds contribute more than consonants to the variations in spoken language which are known as dialects. If the reader wishes to see the real complexity of pronouncing vowels, he should consult any unabridged dictionary, which will give a dozen or more sounds for the letter *a* and nearly as many for most other vowels. These complexities have been simplified considerably because it is not necessary for reading teachers to know the many fine distinctions in vowel sounds.

To simplify, there are two major kinds of vowel sounds. The more common class contains the so-called short sounds. These sounds are seen in the words *at*, *end*, *is*, *hot*, *cup*. If a student has no other knowledge of phonic rules, and nothing else to go by, he is better off using the short sounds in attempting to read new words since they occur most frequently (Chart 2).

LONG VOWELS The other major class of vowels contains the so-called long sounds, as in the following words: *ate*, *me*, *tiny*, *go*, *use* (Chart 5).

A problem arises when the reader encounters a strange word: Which vowel sound should he use? There are three simple rules which will guide him in many instances:

1. *The final e rule* is one way of showing that a vowel is long, even though the syllable ends in a consonant. For example, in writing the word *note* we

need to show that the vowel sound of *o* is the long sound. This is done by putting an *e* immediately after the consonant. The final *e* rule states that an *e* at the end of a word makes the preceding vowel long. An *e* at the end of a word is not sounded. If the long *e* is to be sounded at the end of a word, letter *y* as in *funny* is usually used.

2. *The long vowel digraphs* are another way of showing the long vowel sound when the syllable ends in a consonant. This group includes three vowel sounds with six spellings. The long *e* sound is made by the combination *ea* and *ee* as in the words *eat* and *seem*. The long *a* sound is made by the combination *ai* and *ay* as seen in the words *fail* and *stay*. The long *o* sound is made by the combinations *oa* and *ow* as is seen in the words *coat* and *own*.

3. *The syllable-ending rule* states that if a syllable ends in a consonant the vowel sound is short and if the syllable ends in a vowel the vowel sound is long. The word *no* ends in a vowel, and hence the vowel *o* has a long sound. If, however, a syllable ends with a consonant, as in the word *not*, the vowel immediately changes to a short sound.

SCHWA Unfortunately, the vowels have other sounds besides their long and short ones. One of the most confusing sounds made by vowels is the so-called general unaccented vowel sound, or *schwa*. This sound is usually made by one of the three letters *a*, *e*, or *o* as the *a* in *about*, the *e* in *happen*, and the *o* in *other*. The *a*, *e*, and *o* all make the same sound when they are used as a schwa. There seems to be no good way of determining just when a vowel makes this schwa sound; but it only happens when the vowel is unaccented. The reader should at least be aware of this problem because the schwa sound occurs frequently; and if he does not know about it, he might think that phonic rules are even more misleading than is the case (Chart 6).

VOWEL PLUS "R" Another set of vowel sounds occurs when the vowels are followed by the letter *r*. First of all, the combinations *er*, *ir*, and *ur* all make the same sound, as in *her*, *girl*, *church*. This should be fairly easy to remember and teach.

The combination *ar*, however, has two sounds. The most common is the *ar* sound heard in *far*; but sometimes *ar* makes the *air* sound, as in *vary* or *Mary*. The combination *or* frequently makes the broad *o* plus *r* sound heard in the word *or* or *more* (Chart 6).

BROAD "O" SOUND The broad *o* sound is written in several different ways. It is written *o* as in *off*, *a* before *l* as in *all*, or *aw* as in *saw*, *au* as in *haul*, or *o* before *r* as in *or*. The *a* before *l* and *a* before *w* combinations can simply be memorized as giving the broad *o* sound (Chart 7).

DIPHTHONGS There are two common vowel diphthongs. First there is the *oi* sound as in *oil*, which is also written *oy* as in *boy*.

The other common vowel diphthong is the *ou* sound in *out*. It is written *ou* in *out* or *our*, and it is written *ow* in such words as *how* and *down*. Unfortunately, *ow* is also used by the double-vowel rule to make the long *o* sound in such words as *own*. In these instances the letter *w* acts like a vowel (Chart 7).

Language experts say that some vowel sounds such as the long *i* or the long *a* are really diphthongs, but for the sake of simplicity it is best to classify them as long vowel sounds.

THE LETTER "Y" The letter *y* deserves special mention because it is sometimes a vowel and sometimes a consonant. At the beginning of a word *y* is usually a consonant, as in *yes* and *yet*. But at the end of a word or in the middle, *y* usually makes one of two vowel sounds. If it is at the end of a short word or a syllable in the middle of a word, it usually has a long *i* sound as in *my*, *why*, or *cyclone*. (Note that in the short words there are no other vowels present.) If *y* is the only vowel in a word, it is usually at the end and has the long *i* sound.

If *y* is at the end of a longer word (two or more syllables), it usually has the long *e* sound as in *funny*.

OTHER SOUNDS OF "U" and "OO" Unfortunately, the letter *u* also makes two sounds, in addition to the short *u* (*u̇*) as in *put*. This is the same sound as the so-called short *oo* sound as in *book*. The second *u* sound is the two dot *u* (*ü*) as in *truth*; this sound is the same as the long sound in *moon*. These two *u* sounds are often not taught to beginning readers as they are easily confused with the more frequent short *u* and the long *u*. In fact, many teachers and adults who read quite well cannot often distinguish them from the long and short *u*. It is not necessary to teach these sounds to young readers, but the teacher should at least know about them. Older children who use dictionaries will come across them in word pronunciation (Chart 7).

THE SHORT "EA" There are, of course, many exceptions to these rules, but only a few occur with enough frequency to be worth mentioning. One would be the short *e* sound of *ea* found in such words as *heavy* and *head*. By the long vowel digraphs taught earlier, we would expect *ea* to make a long *e* sound as in *easy*, but it does not always do this. There are some exceptions, such as *head*, *heavy*, and *ready*, in which *ea* makes the short *e* sound.

CONSONANT EXCEPTIONS

There are a few more phonics principles that the teacher should be acquainted with. These might be used with older and brighter students.

First of all, phonetics experts tell us that we should recognize at least two more consonant phoneme sounds:

1. The *ng* sound as in *sing* which technically is not a blend of *n* and *g*. (If you doubt it make an *n* and a *g* sound, carefully noting the position of your tongue; then make the *ng* sound as in *sing*.)
2. The *zh* sound as made by the second *s* in *usual*, the *g* in *garage*, and the *si* in *vision*.

Some dictionaries point out that the *wh* digraph really makes an *hw* blend. We have seen that it is a phoneme (and voiceless) different from the *w* which is similar, but less blowing and definitely voiced. Whether *wh* is a phoneme or two phonemes (*hw* blend) is a technical point of little importance for the teaching of reading. Teachers may take their preference.

A few other exceptions are:

This letter or digraph	*sometimes makes the sound of*	*as in*
PH	F	phone
GH	F	cough
X	GZ	exam
G	J	edge
TI	SH	attention
S	SH	sure
CH	SH	machine
CH	K	echo

The reason for mentioning these exceptions is that so often a clever logician will point to one of these exceptions and try to prove that the teaching of phonics is really a hopeless task. The cold facts are that phonics principles do work a high percentage of the time. Teachers should not be dissuaded by these few exceptions, nor by some odd way of spelling *fish*, as was clearly devised as *ghoti* (*gh* as in cough, *o* as in women, and *ti* as in motion).

This is not to say that the English language does not need an alphabet reform and a spelling reform. I would readily endorse such reforms for it would greatly simplify the teaching of reading and spelling; such simplification could make teaching faster, and with fewer failures. But the hard fact is that it probably will not come in the foreseeable future. Most innovations run into the difficulty that adults have learned the present system, have already mastered it, and reject the work entailed in making any change. Hence, they oppose it and, through their representatives, vote against it. Many times in recent years, alphabet and spelling reform measures have been presented in both the United States Congress and the British House of Commons. They have all been voted down. Since for the present, we seem to be bound to our present alphabet and spelling systems, let us at least make use of the regular rules and principles, as presented here, for the teaching of reading and spelling.

SILENT LETTERS There are only a few silent consonants, and they do not occur very often. They are *w* before *r* as in *write*, *k* before *n* as in *knife*, and the so-called silent blend of *gh* as in *light*.

It is a technicality whether double consonants are also silent, at least in part. For example, the second *l* in *all* might as well not be there (except to give a unique word form that is different from *al*) but the second *d* in *middle* is there because it is really part of the last syllable.

In vowels, the main silent letter is the *e* at the end of any word such as *come*. Most other vowels standing alone are not silent. Vowels appearing as part of vowel digraphs taught earlier such as *ea* or *oa* may be viewed as having one silent letter; usually, however, they are considered to be vowel digraphs.

ACCENT AND SYLLABIFICATION

The rules for breaking words into syllables and then accenting a given syllable are complex indeed. Some dictionaries provide good explanations for those interested in the details. A few general rules may be of help to the reading teacher:

1. There are as many syllables in a word as there are separate vowel sounds. Do not be fooled by word size. For example, *polio* has three syllables (po-li-o) and *straight* is a one-syllable word.
2. If there is one consonant (or consonant digraph) between two vowels, the consonant goes with the second vowel (for example, *ago*, *meter*).
3. If there are two consonants between two vowels, the consonants are split, but do not split consonant digraphs or blends (for example, *button*).
4. The accent usually goes to the first syllable, except when the first syllable is a prefix such as *de*, *re*, etc. (for example, *debate*, *repair*).
5. Double words from natural syllables (for example, *baseball*).

TERMINOLOGY OF PHONICS

Understanding the language we speak is an important part of a good education. For this reason, teachers should use the proper terms when teaching phonics so that students will learn them in a natural setting. Because some of the terms have come into more general use recently, they are defined here.

Phoneme: A speech sound. It is a minimum sound unit which, if changed, will change meaning. For example, the difference between *pin* and *pan* or between *tin* and *pin* are phoneme changes—note, they change meaning. The word *pin* has three phonomes: *p*, *i*, and *n*.

Grapheme: The symbol or symbols used to write down a phoneme. The letter *p* in *pin* is a grapheme. Sometimes a grapheme is two or more letters. For example, the *ph* in *phone*, which makes the *f* phoneme is a grapheme, as is the *ch* in *chair*. Some linguists would define a grapheme as any written symbol which changes meaning. By this definition such things as question marks qualify as graphemes. For most reading teachers, our initial definition of a grapheme as the symbol or symbols needed to write a phoneme is accurate enough.

Phonics: The teaching of phoneme-grapheme correspondence is usually for the purpose of helping a student learn to read. Phonics generally refers to one direction of correspondence, that is to have the student look at the grapheme and say the phoneme. The reverse procedure of having the student hear or say the word and then write down the grapheme is usually called *spelling*. Therefore, phonics instruction often aids spelling and vice versa.

Phonetics: The science of speech sounds. This is the scientific study of the sounds used in studying a language. Some reading teachers say *phonetics* when they probably mean *phonics*.

APPENDIX 5-A EASY CONSONANTS

CHART 1

T top  to take not at	N nut  not no and in	R ring  run red from our
M man  me my some from	D dog  do day good and	S saw  some so this us
L letter 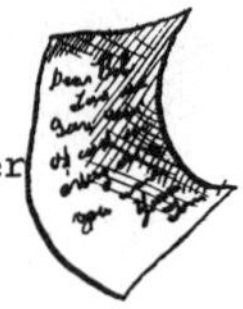 little like will girl	C cat  can come because second	P pencil  put pretty up jump
B  book but be about remember	F fish  for from if before	V valentine  very visit give leave

APPENDIX 5-B EASY VOWELS

CHART 2

I

Indian

in	with
is	will
it	little

E

elephant

end	when
egg	get
every	red

A

apple

and	can
at	bad
as	man

O

ostrich

on	not
off	box
ox	stop

U

umbrella

up	but
us	much
until	just

1. "E" at the end of a word

   The letter E is silent at the end of a word

are	some
one	like

2. "Y" at the end of a word containing another vowel sound like long E

very	many
any	pretty

APPENDIX 5-C DIFFICULT CONSONANTS

CHART 3

G

girl

good
go
get

again
dog
big

H

hat

have
he
had

her
him
has

K

king

kind
keep
kill

like
make
work

W

window

we
with
will

away
between
twenty

J

jar

just
January
jump

object
enjoy
major

X

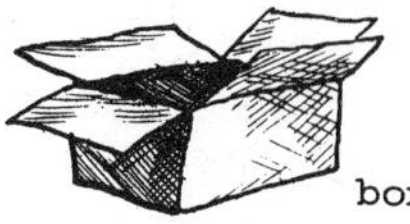

box.

six
ax
extra

box
ox
tax

QU

queen

quite
quart
quick

square
equal
squirrel

Z

zebra

zero
zoo
zone

lazy
prize
dozen

Y

yacht

you
year

lawyer
canyon

Y

at the end of a short word say the long I sound

my
why

APPENDIX 5-D CONSONANT DIGRAPHS AND SECOND SOUNDS

CHART 4

TH

mother

the	other
that	another
there	smoother

TH

three

think	with
thing	both
thank	fourth

CH

chair

child	which
change	such
church	each

SH

shoes

she	wish
should	wash
shall	fish

WH

wheel

when	which
what	where
who	why

PH

phone

physician	alphabet
phonograph	nephew
phrase	triumph

C

city

certain	face
cent	once
circle	office

S

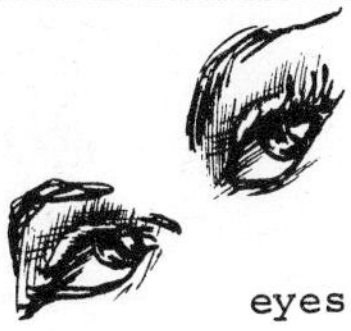

eyes *

is	use
as	present
was	please

*The z sound for s hardly ever occurs at the beginning of a word

G

general

gem	charge
gentleman	age
giant	danger

APPENDIX 5-E PHONETICS CHART: LONG VOWELS

CHART 5

Final E rule: An E at the end of a word frequently makes the vowel long.

A	I	O	U
make	white	home	use
take	while	those	produce
came	five	close	cube
made	write	hope	pure
name	ride	note	tube

Note: Long E is omitted because of its infrequency.

Open-syllable rule: When a syllable ends in a vowel that vowel frequently has the long sound.

A	E	I	O	U
table	we	I	so	duty
paper	be	idea	go	pupil
lady	he	pilot	no	music
baby	me	tiny	open	student

Long-vowel digraphs: These are known as long-vowel digraphs. There are only six common ones.

EA	EE	AI	AY	OA	OW
eat	see	fail	stay	coat	own
year	three	remain	day	boat	know
please	seem	train	gray	road	show
easy	sleep	aid	clay	oak	yellow

APPENDIX 5-F PHONICS CHART: SCHWA AND VOWEL PLUS R

CHART 6

Schwa: The unaccented vowel in a word frequently has the sound of A in *ago*.

A	E	O
about	happen	come
again	problem	other
away	bulletin	money
several	hundred	love

ER, IR, UR: They all frequently make the same sound.

ER	IR	UR
her	first	turn
were	girl	church
other	third	fur
after	sir	hurry

AR has two sounds: AR as in far, AR as in vary ("air" sound)

OR has a unique "O" sound

AR	AR	OR
are	vary	for
far	Mary	or
start	care	before
hard	January	more

APPENDIX 5-G DIPHTHONGS AND OTHER VOWEL SOUNDS

CHART 7

Broad O sound is made by O, AL, AW, AU.

O	AL	AW	AU
on	all	saw	because
long	ball	law	auto
upon	also	awful	August
off	talk	lawn	haul

Diphthongs make a sliding sound from one vowel sound to another.

OI	OY	OU	OW
OI and OY make the same sound		OU and OW make the same sound	
OI	*OY*	*OU*	*OW*
point	boy	out	how
voice	enjoy	about	down
coin	toy	our	brown
oil	royal	round	now

Double O makes the same sound as one-dot and two-dot U.

EA sometimes makes the same sound as short E.

OO	U	EA
OO long sound (same as Ü)	*Two-dot Ü*	
soon	June	ahead
school	truth	heavy
too	rule	ready
room	junior	bread
OO short sound (same as U̇)	*One-dot U̇*	
good	put	
book	full	
look	push	
took	sugar	

APPENDIX 5-H INITIAL CONSONANT BLENDS

These mainly fall into three families.

CHART 8

S family

ST	*SP*	*SC*	*SK*	*SW*	*SM*	*SN*
stand	sport	school	sky	swim	small	snake
state	space	scream	skate	sweep	smell	snow
stick	spot	scout	skin	swing	smart	snare
story	speed	scare	skirt	switch	smile	sneak
study	spend	screen	skip	sweet	smash	snap

R family

PR	*TR*	*GR*	*BR*	*CR*	*DR*	*FR*
pray	try	gray	bread	cry	dry	fry
price	tree	grade	broom	crazy	drink	from
press	trip	grow	brown	crew	dream	free
present	truck	grand	brake	cross	drum	front
pretty	trade	grass	bring	cream	drop	fruit

L family / TW

PL	*CL*	*BL*	*FL*	*SL*	*GL*	*TW*
play	club	black	fly	slow	glad	twelve
plus	clown	blue	flag	slap	globe	twice
place	clay	blood	flat	sleep	glove	twin
plane	clear	blow	flood	slide	glass	twenty
plant	class	blame	flower	slip	glow	twist

APPENDIX 5-I FINAL CONSONANT BLENDS AND SILENT CONSONANTS

CHART 9

Final blends

ND	*NT*	*CT*	*NG*	*LD*
and	ant	act	long	old
blond	bent	duct	sang	mild
grand	hunt	fact	king	told
band	can't	protect	finger	build
end	don't	subtract	young	wild

NC(E)	*NK*	*RT*	*MP*	*PT*	*LT*
once	ink	part	jump	kept	salt
since	think	smart	lamp	September	belt
dance	bank	heart	camp	slept	built
prince	trunk	hurt	bump	crept	melt
bounce	thank	art	stamp	swept	fault

Silent consonants

SILENT C BEFORE K	*SILENT K BEFORE N*	*SILENT W BEFORE R*	*SILENT GH*
back	know	write	high
luck	knife	wreck	right
rock	knee	wrist	taught
sick	knock	wrong	light
deck	knit	wrench	night

6

PHONICS TESTING AND TEACHING

All good teaching depends upon the teacher's knowing what the student knows and does not know. The teacher can then proceed to teach what the student does not know, preferably in some systematic, logical, and interesting order. In phonics, this is fairly easy to do, since the phoneme-grapheme correspondences are fairly orderly and finite.

In this chapter we will consider some of the problems of teaching phonics and then several tests that can be used in diagnosing student strengths and weaknesses.

SIZE OF UNIT TO BE TAUGHT A moderate controversy continues among phonics enthusiasts concerning the size of the phonetic unit to be taught to the child. In an earlier chapter, phonics were discussed in terms of phonemes and graphemes. These are the smallest meaningful units, and the type of units I prefer to teach in phonics. However, let us look at some of the other viewpoints first.

Some reading authorities claim that phonemes, and more especially consonants, should never be taught in isolation. That is, they should always be taught in conjunction with a vowel sound. In the very word *consonant, con* means "with" and *sonant* means "sound", this implies that this phoneme was made to go with another sound such as a vowel. Also, in actual speech a consonant never appears in isolation. However, in the teaching of reading, this leads to some interesting considerations. Try to sound out the word *cat*, for example. You have four alternatives:

1. Each phoneme can be sounded in isolation; for example: *c-a-t*
2. The consonant may be sounded only with a vowel which immediately follows it; for example: *ca-t*
3. The consonant may be sounded with the vowel immediately preceding it; for example: *c-at*
4. No attempt is made to isolate the consonant sounds from their context of a word; for example, the student would be told to listen for or emphasize the sound that he heard at the beginning or end of the word: *cat*.

Each of these systems has its benefits and its drawbacks. For example, the second system, with the vowel following the consonant, has some technical accuracy in terms of speech production but binds the phonics teacher in teaching the child to say a kind of syllable, *ca* (short *a*), which, by most standard phonics rules, would lead him to believe that it was a long *a*. However, advocates of this system, such as the Hay-Wingo series of phonetic readers, have devised drills in which the student learns to pronounce the consonant with ten or fifteen vowel sounds. Hence, the student says *ca*, *ce*, *ci*, *co*, *cu* (short vowel sounds); then adds the long vowel sound to *ca*, *ce*, *ci*, *co*, *cu*; then, if this system were to be extended logically, he would add broad *o*'s, diphthongs, etc. – all this drill for one consonant sound. It must, of course, be repeated with all the different vowel sounds as each new consonant is taught. Thus, under this system the student learns a permutation of all of the vowels and consonants. (For example, if each of twenty consonants were to be matched with fifteen vowel sounds, there would be 300 different combinations to learn, which is a considerably larger number than if the student simply learned the phonemes in isolation.)

The third method, with the vowel preceding the consonant, violates a major usage principle, namely, that the beginning consonant sound is one of the most useful rules in phonics. Since vowels are not pronounced with initial consonant sounds in this system, initial consonant sounds must be pronounced alone and then blended with the vowels. This grouping would tie in with another older teaching phonics system known as *family phonics*, in which the student learns a variety of initial consonant sounds or blends with various *phonograms*. A phonogram is any group of letters which make up one or more sounds; for example, in our example of *cat*, family phonics, or drill in this system, would have the child learn *cat*, *fat*, *rat*, *sat*, *mat*, etc. The teaching of more complex phonograms under family phonics would include such groupings as *light*, *fight*, *might*, *right*, *sight*, etc.

The concept of phonograms is enough to make a scientifically oriented linguist hold his head in anguish, for it is a rather loose description of the language. Yet, reading teachers have been using this approach for years. Part of the trouble is that the scientifically oriented psycholinguists have not yet settled on the optimum size unit for learning in word analysis. From what little research has been done, it appears that the size of unit needed to break down a word varies with the individual and his degree of maturation. For example, adults might be able to see whole words and, when attacking new words, to look for significant parts (such as prefixes, suffixes, roots) that he already knows. Or, in looking for recognizable sections, they might not always look for the prefix, suffix, and root organization but might instead look for clusters of letters which are familiar to them from other words. For example, they might arrive at an accurate pronunciation of *some* because of their familiarity with words like *come*. In analyzing a word like *psycholinguistic*, an adult would quite easily see that he knew the work *psycho* and the word *linguistic* and would easily put them together, whereas a child who is not familiar with either *psycho* or *linguistic* might have to break the word down into smaller units, that is, into individual phonemes or syllables.

Hence, the venerable third grade teachers from the country schools who have been teaching phonograms for years, if not centuries, have undoubtedly hit upon a truth of word perception which only today is beginning to be dignified by the linguistics experts who refer to the well-known family phonics drills as "consonant substitution exercises." We can only hope that in a few years more definitive research will be conducted by educational, linguistic, and psychological investigators concerning optimum size of learning unit for word analysis skills.

Finally, we come to the fourth method mentioned—that of not isolating sounds at all, but simply emphasizing them as they occur in words. Certainly, from the standpoint of speech production, this has accuracy on its side. However, from the standpoint of the student trying to learn to sound out or analyze the sounds of the word, it really begs the question. If we tell a child to pay attention to the sound that he hears at the end of *cat* and to see if it is not the same sound he hears at the beginning of *Tom*, we are simply asking him to learn that the grapheme *t* makes the phoneme *t*. In other words, we are asking the student to *abstract* the principle rather than *teaching him* the principle. Perhaps those who favor the discovery technique of teaching might prefer this system.

Most of the tests and phonics teaching materials mentioned in this book tend to emphasize the first approach, namely, that of teaching phoneme-grapheme correspondence in isolation. This has the slight drawback that a few of the consonants such as *b* and *d* cannot be pronounced without some kind of vowel sound. We circumvent this by putting a light schwa at the end of the consonant sound so that the child says *B*uh rather than b*UH*. In other words, if a schwa must be used with a consonant, emphasize the consonant, not the schwa. However, for the vast majority of consonants and all of the vowels, they can quite easily be pronounced in isolation, which allows us to use the parsimonious first method. However, should the personal preferences of a teacher dictate the use of one of the other systems, a good many of these tests and teaching materials can be modified slightly to apply to any of them.

INDIVIDUAL PHONICS ANALYSIS

In the appendixes at the end of this chapter are several individual and one group phonics tests. These tests are aimed at diagnosing specific strengths and weaknesses. They will answer such questions as: "Does the student know the short vowel sounds?" or "Does he know which combinations make the broad *o* sound?"

As in most testing, the longer the individual test, the more accurate it will be. There is no substitute for spending time with a child in order to make sure that he gains insight. This is particularly true when the interaction is patterned or structured, as it is in the testing situation.

You can learn a great deal about a child's phonics skills simply by having him read, and then noting which words he stumbles on and what he does when he stumbles. The use of tests makes it considerably easier to make systematic diagnosis.

The Individual Phonics Analysis presented here is for individualized instruction and, of course, for remedial or tutoring situations where the teacher has some time to spend with the student. Maybe there is a rare and ambitious classroom teacher who will use it, but, by and large, it is too time-consuming for large-group instruction. It has the advantage of pinpointing a large number of specific strengths and weaknesses. I will not attempt to enumerate all the phonics skills in the test. Basically, they are those taught in the preceding chapter, and for more detailed information, the reader should turn to an actual copy of the test directions which is included at the end of this chapter.

The analysis consists of three parts: (1) *the directions* to be read by the teacher while administering the test until she is familiar enough to get along without it; (2) the *student record sheet* on which the teacher records the student's strengths and weaknesses (this can be kept in his file folder and used as a plan for teaching needed phonics skills); and (3) a *student card* which may be usefully placed in front of the student, rather than allowing him to look at the more complex direction sheet. (To have him look at an answer sheet would be unsatisfactory because in some instances it gives the answers to the test questions.)

Because the test is time-consuming, it is not necessary to complete the test in one sitting, or even in two. Teachers may prefer to do a little bit each day, and when they find a weakness, to stop and test, and then to proceed with the test. Do not use the test for teaching; merely use it to find strengths and weaknesses. Then, in making up your own individualized teaching material, you will probably want to refer to the teaching suggestions in the next chapter or to the materials list at the end of it.

BRIEF INDIVIDUAL PHONICS ANALYSIS

For those teachers who do not have time to use the Individual Phonics Analysis, there is a short one-page Brief Individual Phonics Survey which is an individual test that shows the weaknesses in only six broad categories: easy consonants, hard consonants, consonant digraphs, short vowels, long vowels, and difficult vowels. This Brief Phonics Survey might be useful for teachers who wish to survey a large number of students in a short period of time or for school psychologists or others who are interested only in obtaining a more general answer to the question: "What phonics areas are weakest?"

GROUP PHONICS ANALYSIS

Finally, there is a Group Phonics Test which can be given to any number of students simultaneously. This consists of three parts (a, b, and c), graduated in difficulty level. This group test, like all group tests, lacks the specificity and accuracy of individual testing but may be useful for classroom teachers and school systems wishing to survey their student's phonics knowledge. Any part may be given separately, and, as with most tests, caution should be used in attempting to use the more difficult sections of the group test for younger or less knowledgeable students. Conversely, it would be meaningless to give the easiest parts of the test to students of more advanced knowledge. (This test is available from Dreier Educational Systems, Highland Park, N.J.)

COMMERCIALLY AVAILABLE PHONICS TESTS

A number of commercial phonics tests are available; several of them are prepared as appendages to oral reading tests. Five of these tests are listed here. Sample copies are usually available from the publisher.

Phonics Knowledge Survey
Dolores Durkin and Leonard Meshover
Published by Bureau of Publications, Teachers College

This is an individual test that has thirteen parts ranging from letter names and consonants to sounds of *x* and letters and syllabification. It is probably one of the best of the commercially available individual phonics and diagnostic tests.

Gates-McKillop Reading Diagnostic Tests
Arthur Gates and Ann McKillop
Published by Bureau of Publications, Teachers College

This is part of an individual diagnostic battery which has oral paragraphs and flashed words and phrases. The phonics section has eight parts such as Giving Letter Sounds, Naming Capital Letters, Vowels, etc.

Diagnostic Tests of Word Perception Skills
(To accompany Webster's Classroom Reading Clinic)
Published by Webster Division, McGraw-Hill

This is a useful individual phonics diagnostic test containing fourteen parts which progress from letter names in consonant sounds to prefixes, suffixes, and compound words. Not all sections are devoted to phonics; for example, there is one section on reversals and one on knowing the Dolch Basic Sight Words. Each section correlates with parts of the Webster Classroom Reading Clinic and other materials published by the same company.

California Phonics Survey
Grace Brown and Alice Cottrell
Published by California Test Bureau, McGraw-Hill

This is a group test of higher phonics skills, suitable for elementary children or remedial reading. The range is from grades seven through college.

Durrell Analysis of Reading Difficulty
Donald Durrell
Published by Harcourt, Brace World

This is an individual test appended to a set of oral reading paragraphs. Weak in its phonics section, several valuable parts deal with learning to hear sounds in words and sounds of letters (blends and digraphs).

Phonics Criterion Test
Edward Fry
Published by Dreier Educational Systems

This is an individual test of ninety-nine phoneme-grapheme correspondences. The student is asked to read two nonsense syllables for each correspondence.

More than any other reading skill, phonics needs teaching for transfer. Teachers will often do a good job of teaching phonics skills from charts and games; but when a child is confronted with an unknown word while reading, teachers fail to apply the phonics skills by refusing to tell the child an unknown word and asking him such questions as, "What is the beginning sound?" or "What is the vowel sound in that word?" Teachers can also discuss the sounds in new words that they are presenting during reading lessons, science lessons, social studies lessons, and other subjects.

APPENDIX 6-A BRIEF INDIVIDUAL PHONICS SURVEY*

Student's name____________________
Examiner____________________
Date____________________
School or class____________________

Phonics is an important and useful skill associated with reading. Poor ability in phonics does not always mean poor reading ability, but if reading ability is poor it can often be improved by having part of the instruction include phonics lessons.

How to Test: Ask the student to read the nonsense words aloud. Tell him that these are not real words. Encourage him to try to sound out the words. Do not tell him the correct answers; you might want to use this test again.

How to Score:

1. Circle each letter or digraph read incorrectly (not the whole nonsense word).
2. Mark both the consonant and the vowel areas to the right as either "Perfect," "Knew some," or "Knew None."

Section 1				*Perfect*	*Knew some*	*Knew none*
TIF	NEL	ROM	Easy consonants	☐	☐	☐
DUP	CAV	SEB	Short vowels	☐	☐	☐

Section 2						
KO	HOAB	WAJE	Hard consonants	☐	☐	☐
ZEEX	QUIDE	YAIG	Long vowels	☐	☐	☐

Section 3						
WHAW	THOIM	PHER	Consonant digraphs	☐	☐	☐
OUSH	CHAU	EANG	Difficult vowels	☐	☐	☐

*By Edward Fry, Rutgers University Reading Center.

APPENDIX 6-B DETAILED INDIVIDUAL PHONICS ANALYSIS*

An individual test of one important reading skill.

TEACHERS DIRECTIONS

The teacher follows the directions printed in lowercase letters and may read aloud the part between quotation marks. The student should look at the student card.

1. *Letter names*
   "What are the names of these letters?"
   A B M T F E Z X Q Y J a f t q m

2. *Consonant sounds*
   A. "Tell me the sounds these letters make."
      Group 1. T N R M D
      Group 2. S L C P B F
      Group 3. V G H W K J Z Y
   B. "Listen carefully. I will sound a letter and you tell me what letter it is." Read every letter in each group. You may repeat each letter only once. Use first sounds of *s*, *c*, and *g* as in the words *sat*, *cane*, *goal*.
      Group 1. d m r n t
      Group 2. f b p c l s
      Group 3. y z j r w h g v

3. *Short vowel sounds*
   A. "Tell me the short or commonest sound of these letters."
      E A I O U E I A O U
   B. "Read these nonsense syllables aloud."
      NOL DIL FAV HET JUP
      If the child has trouble reading the nonsense syllables above, read them slowly for him and give him another chance on these.
      SAK LIM FOD HEV ZUT
      This test also shows ability to blend letters together.
   C. "Listen carefully when I say these sounds and tell me which letter they represent."
      u o a i e o u i a e
   D. "Tell me what vowel sound you hear in these nonsense syllables—tud, kol, lan, mip, jev, loz, tob, muj, wid, vap, het."

4. *Long vowels—final E rule*
   A. "Read these nonsense words."
      NATE KIPE JOLE ZUNE

*By Edward Fry, Rutgers University Reading Center.

B. "Can you tell me the Final E Rule?"
Answer must include two parts: the E on the end is silent *and* it makes the preceding vowel long.

5. *Long vowels—common vowel digraphs*
   A. "Read these nonsense words."
   MAIT JEET WOAX TAY ZEAS MOAV
6. *Hearing the difference between long and short-vowel sounds*
   "Tell me which vowel you hear in each of these words and whether it is long or short."
   "nape, mod, giz, gav, lote, guk, tike, zef, bave"
   You may repeat each word only once.

7. *Syllable-ending rule*
   A. "Read each of these nonsense syllables."
   MO RET RU SIZ LI SAF TA GOP
   B. "Can you tell me when a vowel is pronounced long and when it is pronounced short according to where it is in the syllable? (What is meant by the Syllable-Ending Rule?)"

8. *Consonant digraphs*
   A. "What sounds do these letter combinations make?"
   SH CH WH TH
   B. "The combination TH makes two sounds. Can you tell me both of them?"
   C. "Tell me which letter combinations you hear when I say these sounds."
   CH TH (voiced) SH TH (voiceless)

9. *Difficult consonants*
   A. "Below are several words. Tell me what sound the C makes at the beginning of each of them."
   CITY CAT CYCLONE CENT COAT
   B. If the child correctly answers the above ask him, "Why (or under what conditions) does C make a K sound and when does it make the S sound?"
   C. "What sound does G make in the following words?"
   GO GAVE GEM GIANT
   D. "Why (or under what conditions) does it usually make each sound?"
   E. "What sound does S make in the following words?"
   SAT HAS IS WAS JUST
   F. "What other letter can make one of these sounds?"
   G. "What sound does X make?" If necessary, show the example words below.
   FOX SIXTEEN
   H. "What sound does QU make?" If needed, show examples.
   QUICK SQUARE

10. *Schwa sound*
   A. "What is the sound you hear from the letter underlined in these words?" You may read the word for the student as he looks at it. *Caution*: If you emphasize the schwa, it will not be a schwa.
   GASOLINE BALLOON OCCUR QUIET AGAIN

B. "Does each of the letters underlined have the same sound?"
"What is it called?"

11. *Vowel plus R*
   A. "What sounds do the following combinations make?"
   IR ER OR UR AR
   B. "The combination AR makes two sounds. Do you know what they are?"

12. *Sounds of Y*
   A. "What is the sound of Y in the following words?"
   YAZ PY SETY YOMP NY

13. *Consonant blends*
   A. "Can you give the sound of the following blends?"
   ST PR TR GR BR PL SP CR CL DR FR
   SC BL FL SK SL SW SM GL SN TW
   B. "The following blends are seen at the end of words. Can you give sounds for them?"
   ND NT CT LD NK RT MP PT

14. *Diphthongs*
   A. "Give the sound."
   OI OU OY

15. *Broad O*
   A. "Give the sound."
   AU AW

16. *Double O*
   A. "Two O's together (OO) make two different sounds. Can you use both of them in each of these nonsense words?"
   ZOOP VOOT

17. *Silent letters*
   A. "What are the sounds made by the letters underlined in the following words?"
   COME MAKE KNOW BLACK RIGHT WRONG

18. *Hearing sounds*
   A. "Tell me which letter or letters make the following sounds."
   oi (answer may be OI or OY)
   x (KS sound)
   r (answer may be R, ER, IR, UR)
   j (answer may be G or J)
   qu (answer may be KW sound, Q or QU)
   nt
   oo (short vowel as in "moon,"
   answer may be OO or U)
   z (answer may be Z or S)

sp
y (consonant vowel as in "Yes")
au (answer may be O, AU, AW, A;
student should explain it is broad)

19. *Syllabification*

"Divide these words into syllables." (Let student mark Student Record Sheet.)

STREET SUNSHINE BACON DIVER RABBIT CHAIR TABLECLOTH
REDSKIN PINWHEEL SAILBOAT BUTTON LESSON JUSTICE LANTERNS
DRAGON BESIDE EVIL MUSIC

STUDENT CARD FOR THE INDIVIDUAL PHONICS ANALYSIS

DO NOT USE THIS CARD FOR INSTRUCTION
(Use phonics charts)

Directions: Student holds this card and listens to directions given by teacher.

1. A B M T F E Z X Q Y J

   a f t q m

2. Group 1. T N R M D

   Group 2. S L C P B F

   Group 3. V G H W K J Z Y

3A. E A I O U E I A O U

3B. NOL DIL FAV HET JUP
SAK LIM FOD HEV ZUT

4. NATE KIPE JOLE ZUNE

5. MAIT JEET WOAX TAY ZEAS MOAV

7. MO RET RU SUZ LI SAF TA GOP

8. SH CH WH TH

9A. CITY CAT CYCLONE CENT COAT

9C. GO GAVE GEM GIANT

9E. SAT HAS IS WAS JUST

9G. FOX SIXTEEN

9H. QUICK SQUARE

10. GASOLINE BALLOON OCCUR QUIET AGAIN

11. IR ER OR UR AR

12. YAZ PY SETY YOMP NY

13A. ST PR TR GR BR PL SP CR CL DR FR SC BL FL SK SL SW SM GL SN TW

13B. ND NT CT LD NK RT MP PT

14. OI OU OY

15. AU AW

16. ZOOP VOOT

17. COME MAKE KNOW BLACK RIGHT WRONG

RECORD SHEET FOR THE INDIVIDUAL PHONICS ANALYSIS*

Student's name ______________________________
Teacher or group ______________________________
Date ______________________________

Directions: Read from the Teacher's Form. Mark each letter or syllable missed on this sheet. Check box if all are known.

1. *Letter Names*

☐ A. Student reads	A B M T F E Z X Q Y J
☐ B. Student reads	a f t q m

2. *Consonant Sounds*

☐ A. Student reads	Group 1. T N R M D
	Group 2. S L C P B F
	Group 3. V G H W K J Z Y
☐ B. Student listens	Group 1. d m r n t
	Group 2. f b p c l s
	Group 3. y z j r w h g v

3. *Short Vowel Sounds*

☐ A. Student reads	E A I O U E I A O U
☐ B. Student reads	NOL DIL FAV HET JUP
	SAK LIM FOD HEV ZUT
☐ C. Student listens	u o a i e o u i a e
☐ D. Student listens	tud kol lan mip jev loz tob muj wid vap het

4. *Long Vowels—Final E Rule*

☐ A. Student reads	NATE KIPE JOLE ZUNE
☐ B. Knows rule	1. E silent 2. preceding vowel long

5. *Long vowels—digraphs*

☐ A. Student reads	*MAIT JEET WOAX TAY ZEAS MOAV*

6. *Hearing long versus short*

☐ A. Student listens	nape mod giz gav lote guk tike zef bave

7. *Syllable-ending rule*

☐ A. Student reads	MO RET RU SIZ LI SAF TA GOP
☐ B. Knows rule	1. when long 2. when short

8. *Consonant digraphs*	
☐ A. Student reads	SH CH WH TH (either TH OK)
☐ B. Knows both TH's	1. voiced 2. voiceless
☐ C. Student listens	ch th (voiced) sh th (voiceless)
9. *Difficult consonants*	
☐ A. Knows two C sounds	CITY CAT CYCLONE CENT COAT
☐ B. Knows why change	1. why K 2. why S
☐ C. Knows 2 G sounds	GO GAVE GEM GIANT
☐ D. Knows why change	1. why G 2. why J
☐ E. Knows two S sounds	SAT HAS IS WAS JUST
☐ F. Knows second sound	1. S sometimes sounds like Z
☐ G. Knows sound of X	FOX SIXTEEN 1. sounds like KS
☐ H. Knows sound of QU	QUICK SQUARE 1. sounds like KW
10. *Schwa sound*	
☐ A. Student listens and looks at word, repeats sound	GASOLINE BALLOON OCCUR QUIET AGAIN
☐ B. Knows sound	1. all the same 2. called schwa
11. *Vowel plus R*	
☐ A. Student reads	IR ER OR UR AR (either sound)
☐ B. Knows two AR's	1. "air" sound 2. "ar" sound as in "far"
12. *Sounds of Y*	
☐ A. Student reads	YAZ PY SETY YOMP NY
☐ B. Knows why change	1. beginning 2. end one vowel word 3. end word with another vowel
13. *Consonant blends*	
☐ A. Student reads (beginning blends)	ST PR TR GR BR PL SP CR CL DR FR SC BL FL SK SL SW SM GL SN TW
☐ B. Student reads (final blends)	ND NT CT LD NK RT MP PT
14. *Diphthongs*	
☐ A. Student reads	OI OU OY
15. *Broad O sound*	
☐ A. Student reads	AU AW
16. *Double O sounds*	
☐ A. Knows both	ZOOP VOOT 1. long sound 2. short sound
17. *Silent letters*	
☐ A. Tells which are silent	COME MAKE KNOW BLACK RIGHT WRONG

18. *Hearing sounds*
☐ A. Student listens — oi x r j qu nt oo (long) z sp y (consonant) au

19. *Syllabification* (Let student mark this sheet)
☐ A. Divide words — STREET SUNSHINE BACON DIVER RABBIT CHAIR TABLECLOTH REDSKIN PINWHEEL SAILBOAT BUTTON LESSON JUSTICE LANTERNS DRAGON BESIDE EVIL MUSIC

APPENDIX 6-C GROUP PHONICS ANALYSIS*

INTRODUCTION

This is a diagnostic group test to help the classroom teacher in determining which of several basic phonics skills her pupils have mastered. It is also designed to aid the busy teacher in discovering which pupils need help in this important method of word attack.

The skills tested, such as the sounds of consonants and vowels, are presented in the same order that they are frequently introduced in reading textbooks and teachers' manuals and by reading authorities.

This test is not designed to supplant the regular reading tests now used which frequently yield grade level or percentile scores of general reading ability. Rather, it is designed to assist the teacher and curriculum specialist in determining strengths and weaknesses in one specific area of reading. Certainly not all the phonics skills found in teachers' manuals or professional books of reading methods are covered by this test but enough are covered here to give the teacher insight into each pupil's progress.

SKILLS TESTED

The ability to read numbers is only a related reading skill, but it is useful to know and serves as an introduction to harder work to follow. A child not knowing how to read at least two-digit numbers would be likely to become confused on later parts of the test.

The ability to read letters, while not necessarily a phonics skill and not even necessary for easy reading of words, is again useful information to have concerning a child's language development. Sometimes, the teacher will be surprised by the children who fail this section.

*By Edward Fry, Rutgers University Reading Center.

The ability to hear consonant sounds is the first and one of the most important of the phonics skills. Knowing consonant sounds profoundly influences "word attack" in reading and is a valuable tool for all readers to master. Nearly all teacher's manuals of reading text series begin this skill in the first grade. However, this does not mean that the skill is always mastered by the end of the first year.

The ability to alphabetize is not essential to primary reading or phonics, but some schools teach it early in the primary years while others prefer to wait. Nevertheless, it is useful information concerning a child's language development and is usually related to development in phonics ability.

The ability to recognize vowels is usually considered to come before the next two important phonics steps; i.e., knowing short word sounds and long vowel sounds.

The ability to recognize short vowel sounds is another really important phonics skill. A child not familiar with the short vowel sounds will be greatly handicapped in sounding out new words. This skill is a little difficult to test for in a group test situation. The teacher might be particularly careful in pronouncing the short *o* and short *a* (as found in such words as *hot* and *hat*).

The ability to recognize long vowel sounds is another phonics skill of major importance. Long sounds of vowels are used a little less frequently than short vowel sounds, but they are usually easier to teach because of their similarity to the letter name.

The ability to use vowel-sounding rules for long and short vowel sounds. These rules tell when to pronounce a vowel with a long sound and when to pronounce it with a short sound.

1. The digraph vowel rule holds that when certain two vowels are found together, the first vowel is pronounced long and the second is silent (Example: *main*). There are many exceptions to this and the other rules, but they are still worth knowing.
2. The final e rule states that the final *e* in a word is silent and it makes the preceding vowel long (Example: *hat, hate*).
3. The open and closed syllable rules hold that: (a) when a syllable ends in a vowel, sometimes called an open syllable, the vowel is given its long sound (Example: *go*), and (b) when a syllable ends in a consonant, sometimes called a closed syllable, the vowel is given its short sound (Example: *got*).

The *syllabification* rules are useful in determining how a new word breaks into syllables for using the above vowel sounds. The teaching of these rules is usually one of the final stages in the phonics curriculum. Like the above rules, they have plenty of exceptions, but they are still useful in attacking an unfamiliar word.

1. One-syllable words. This row tests to see if the child can find the one-syllable words, one of which has more letters than some two-syllable words. It is helpful if he knows the rule which states that there are as many syllables as there are independent vowel sounds.
2. Double words. This is the easiest step in breaking words into syllables. Almost any child who can read the words should be able to tell where the syllable division comes.
3. The double-consonant rule states that when there are two consonants between two separated vowel sounds, the consonants are divided to form the syllable division (Example: *lan-tern*).
4. The single-consonant rule states that when only one consonant is found between two separated vowel sounds, the consonant goes with the last consonant (Example: *ra-dar*, not *rad-ar*).

GENERAL DIRECTIONS

1. Instruct children to fill in name, date, etc. With young children the teacher should then check to see that this has been done properly. Placing the date, school name, etc., on the chalkboard is helpful.
2. Explain that they are to place an × over the letter or number mentioned. Illustrate this on the chalkboard by writing a row of numbers and placing an × over a number. Example:

4 3 2 1 5 6

3. Allow adequate time for the children to look over each row; younger children naturally take longer than older children. You can help prevent copying and tell how long they are taking by asking the children to look up to the front of the room as soon as they have finished a row.
4. In large groups, it is usually inadvisable to wait until the last child finishes each row before starting the next, as children who do not know the phonics skills will frequently stall for time and hold the entire group back. Hence, a teacher must use her judgment as to when to start the next row; a good rule of thumb would be to start the next row when approximately 90 percent of the children have finished.
5. Since this test is not timed and not standardized, the teacher may stop the test at any time and begin again at any time. The test might be spread out over several days for younger children. As with all tests, the results will be better if testing is done when the children are attentive and not disturbed by outside influences.
6. For children who have not been taught the more difficult phonics skills, the teacher may wish to administer only the first page of the test, saving the second page for later in the year. Generally, a child must do well on the first page or else he will do little or nothing on the second page.

SPECIFIC DIRECTIONS

Read the following directions for each line to the class after students have filled out their names, date, etc. and you have explained how to put an × on the number or letter desired.

Row

In the row with the dog, put an X on top of the numbers that I call out.
6 put an X on top of the 6

In the same row:
5 put an X on top of the 5

In the same row:
9 put an X on top of the 9

Row.

Next, on the row with the cat, put an X on top of the numbers that I call out.
81 put an X on top of 81 (be sure to say eighty-one, not eight, one)
24 put an X on top of 24
17 put an X on top of 17

Row.

In the row with the apple, put an X on top of the numbers that I call out.
721 put an X on top of 721 (be sure to say seven hundred and twenty-one, *not* seven, two, one)
925 put an X on top of 925
127 put an X on top of 127

Row.

In the row with the car, place an X on top of the letters that I *name* (say *names* of letters; for example, B is pronounced "bee").
B place an X on top of the B
Z place an X on top of the Z
P place an X on top of the P

Row.

In the row with the bicycle, place an X on top of the letters that I *name*.
F place an X on top of the F
O place an X on top of the O
N place an X on top of the N

Row.

In the row with the chair, place an X on top of the letters that I *name*.
Q place an X on top of the Q
K place an X on top of the K
D place an X on top of the D

Row 1.

Place an X over the letter that I *sound*:
B, as in BALL, B (teacher: sound this as "bh" like the beginning of the sound of ball)
C, as in CAT, C
N, as in NOSE, N

Row 2.

Place an X over the letter that I *sound*:
L, as in LINE, L
V, as in VACUUM CLEANER, V
S, as in SNAKE, S

Row 3.

Place an X over the letter that I *sound*:
G, as in GOLD, G
M, as in MOTHER, M
T, as in TREE, T

Row 4.

Place an X over the two letters (blend) which I sound:
SH, as in SHOW, SH
FR, as in FREE, FR
CL, as in CLOSE, CL

Row 5.	Place an X over the two letters (blend) which I sound: WH, as in WHITE, WH BR, as in BROWN, BR TW, as in TWENTY, TW
Row 6.	Place an X over the three letters which I *sound*: STR, as in STREET, STR THR, as in THROW, THR SPR, as in SPRING, SPR
Row 7.	(Read slowly) Put an X on top of the letter that comes *after* the letter I name, in alphabetical order. For example, if I say B ("bee") you mark C (Cee). (Stop for any question or further explanation. You may repeat once.) All right now, put an X on top of the letter that comes after I (Eye). Put an X on top of the letter that comes after V (Vee) Put an X on top of the letter that comes after E (Ee)

Row 8. Now I want you to put an X on top of the letter that comes *before* the letter that I name. For example, if I say B (Bee), you mark A. Ready now:
Mark the letter that comes before S
Mark the letter that comes before X
Mark the letter that comes before J

Row 9. In row 9, I want you to mark the three *vowels*. (Do not explain word "vowel," just tell them to mark three vowels.)

Row 10. In row 10, I want you to mark the three vowels.

Short vowels

(Teacher: Say only vowel sound.)

Row 11. Place an X over the letter that sounds like E ("eh") as in PETE ("eh"). On this side of the paper, we mark only one letter in each row.

Row 12. Place an X over the letter that sounds like I ("ih") as in SIT, I ("ih").

Row 13. Place an X over the letter that sounds like O as in HOT, O ("oh").

Row 14. Place an X over the letter that sounds like A as in MAD, A ("ah").

Row 15. Place an X over the letter that sounds like U ("uh") as in HUT, U ("uh").

Long vowels

Row 16. Mark the vowel sound you hear in the word READ. I'll repeat it only once more. READ

Row 17. Mark the vowel sound you hear in the word NAIL. (Pause) NAIL (do not repeat).

Row 18. Mark the vowel sound you hear in the word COAL. COAL

Row 19. Mark the vowel sound you hear in the word DIED. DIED

Row 20. Mark the vowel sound you hear in the word USE. USE

Long and short-vowel sounding
Rules: final E and double-vowel Rules

Row 21. The following are not real words, but read them and sound them out to yourself quietly, then mark the ones asked for. In Row 21:
Mark TWO words containing the E ("eh") sound as in the word MET, E ("eh").
(Teacher may repeat the above directions, if necessary.)

Row 22. Mark two words containing the E ("ee") sound as in MEET, E ("ee").

Row 23. Mark two words that contain I ("ih") sound as in TIN, I ("ih").

Row 24. Mark two words that contain the A (long A) sound as in MATE, A.

Row 25. Mark two words that contain the I (long I) sound as in KITE, I.

Row 26. Mark two words that contain the U (long U) sound as in USE, U.

Row 27. Mark two words that contain the sound O, as in GO, O.

Row 28. Mark two words that contain the sound U (short U, "uh") as in HUT, U.

Row 29. Mark two words that have only one syllable. (Teacher may repeat directions once, but do not explain what a syllable is. If a child does not know, tell him to leave it blank.)

Row 30. Divide the following words into two syllables by drawing a line between them. (Place example on chalkboard: MILKMAN, MILK/MAN.)

Row 31. Divide these words into two syllables by drawing a line between them as you did in Row 30.

Row 32. Divide these words into two syllables by drawing a line between them as you did in Row 30.

SCORING

Look over the paper to see that there are exactly three marks per line on the first page; if there are not place an × in the right-hand margin since the line is wrong.

There must be exactly one mark per line in the first part of page 2, lines 10 through 19, and exactly two marks per line in lines 20 to 27.

Place the scoring stencil over the paper and mark a line wrong by placing an × opposite the line in the right-hand margin if each hole does not show an ×.

You may get a total score by counting the number of lines correct, but the test is most useful if you just look over the papers and see what skills the children are weak in.

You may spread out all the test papers, side by side and overlapping so that just the errors in the margin are exposed, in order to get a bird's-eye view of weak and strong areas of phonics knowledge for the entire class.

GROUP PHONICS ANALYSIS, PART A

Name______________________________
School______________________________
Date______________________________
Grade______________________________

			Score "c" if all correct	
	2 9 6 3 1 4 8 5 7	1 digit		*Ability to read numbers*
	24 37 21 62 97 81 42 17	2 digits		
	942 127 831 925 136 721 342	3 digits		
	C M Z F X B N S P A	Capitals		*Ability to read letters*
	d s b f z p q o m z n	Lowercase		
	q z t l u x w k i p d b	Lowercase		
	1. B C M T D G Z N R S	Single		*Ability to hear consonant sounds*
	2. F H L P W V M T S K	Single		
	3. Y M T Q J L F Z G P	Single		
	4. SH TR CL WH SW CH FR DR	Blend (2)		
	5. TH PL BR FL SM WH GR TW	Blend (2)		
	6. STR CHM THR PHM SPR SCR HYP	Blend (3)		
	7. W B C F G H M N S J	Letter after		*Ability to alphabetize*
	8. R M V Y W H T I F A	Letter before		
	9. S M E U V T C B L I			*Ability to recognize vowels*
	10. B O N G T R A C I F			

Total no. lines right, p. 1______ Total no. lines right, p. 2______ Total no. lines right, entire test______

GROUP PHONICS ANALYSIS, PART B

Name ______________________________

11. E A O I U			*Ability to recognize short vowel sounds*
12. C E A I U			
13. I O E A U			
14. I U O A E			
15. U O A E I			
16. A I E O U			*Ability to recognize long vowel sounds in words*
17. E A O I O			
18. O E A U I			
19. I A E U O			
20. A E I O U			
21. PELL SEEG WEEG HEF BEAS KEEM	Vowel digraphs		*Ability to use vowel-sounding rules (for long and short vowel sounds)*
22. FEEB PETT SED FEEK NEM CREL			
23. STIED PIB DRIT HAIS NIEG RIE			
24. JATE KAM BRATE WHAL RAD LAT	Final E		
25. PIFE SRIT WID SHIG TIZ MIVE			
26. DRUB SOT BLUS MUKE SUTE CHURD			
27. MO BON STO WHOS BLONS ROP	Open and closed syllables		
28. SU BRU STRU MUN RU SLUD			
29. STREET SUNSHINE BACON DIVER RABBIT CHAIR	One syllable		*Syllabification*
30. SUNSHINE REDSKIN PINWHEEL SAILBOAT	Compound words		
31. BUTTON LESSON REPEAT LANTERNS	Single and double Consonants		
32. HOTEL BESIDE EVIL MUSIC	Between vowels		

7

PHONICS TEACHING MATERIALS

One of the most important things to know about planning phonics lessons is that good phonics materials teach specific skills. Conversely, poor phonics materials have a mishmash of specific phonics elements such as consonant sounds, blends, and digraphs all mixed in one lesson. As pointed out in the preceding chapter, it is possible to diagnose the specific phonics skills a student needs. If he already knows his beginning consonant sounds, the next thing he needs to know are the short vowels. Materials which continue to teach consonant sounds are merely a waste of time.

A variety of methods can be used in teaching most phonics skills. This is good, because the teacher is free to present the skill needed with one set of materials and can give additional practice with another set. She knows that it often takes much repetition for mastery of phonics skills but that there is no need to continue the repetition to the point of boredom. If the student is tired of trying to master a set of sounds from charts or flip cards, the same concepts can often be taught with bingo games or filmstrips. One characteristic of a good remedial teacher is that she have a variety of methods at her fingertips. We will consider some of the common methods of teaching phonics skills here, but there are as many more as the ingenuity of the teacher provides.

CHARTS

In the appendixes for Chapter 5 a set of charts was given to present the teacher with an overview of the major phonics skills. These charts are also useful for explaining the sounds to students. For an individual child or in a small group, the chart can be used as it appears in this book. For larger groups, the teacher may wish to put all or part of the chart on the chalkboard. Charts are used most often to give a visual stimulus and concentration point while the teacher is giving a verbal explanation.

The charts are also useful for use in several kinds of drills. For example, the first chart, containing twelve easy consonant sounds, can be placed in front of the child; while the teacher points to the different pictures, the child can give the sound. The sound can be made either in isolation (that is, the student gives only the phoneme or sound) or in combination (by having the student read the example word or picture), emphasizing the sound being taught while pronouncing the word. Many teachers use the charts both ways. The additional words on the chart which illustrate the sound being taught may be read by the student with the help of the teacher, again emphasizing the sound being taught.

There are a number of other charts which teach phonics skills. Some commonly used ones are the Ginn phonics charts and the Hammond phonics charts and the charts developed by Kottmeyer and published by the Webster Division of McGraw-Hill.

FIGURE 7-1 One set of Webster charts used to teach short vowel and consonant sounds.

WORD WHEELS AND FLIP CARDS

Both word wheels and flip cards provide for substitution of parts of words. For example, the word wheel might have *at* printed on the front of it and a little hole where the first letter should appear. As the face of the wheel is rotated, successive consonants or blends would appear to form such words as *cat*, *mat*, *rat*, etc. A flip card is essentially the same, but it is different mechanically. A large flip card would have *at* printed on it; then a number of smaller cards on hinges or rings could be flipped in front of the *at* to make *cat*, *mat*, *rat*, etc. Other variations of this same principle might include (1) having children play with letter boxes and try to make as many words as they can with one "family" or phonogram, or (2) using similar teacher-constructed drills on the chalkboard or on ditto sheets for the student to complete by writing.

Needless to say, any part of the word can be substituted, not just the beginning consonant sound. Substitutions might occur for vowels, terminal consonant sounds, prefixes, suffixes, phonograms, etc. Besides teaching the principle and specific facts that different consonants make different words, these devices also assist in the teaching of the blending together of sounds. It is often necessary to stress blending, especially if too much drill in isolation has been conducted or if the students have difficulty in blending phonemes.

Since blending is often difficult for disadvantaged children, or those from lower socioeconomic levels, teachers should expect to do more phonics drills with them that involve blending isolated sounds into words. Both individual and group oral drills in blending sounds are beneficial. Sometimes having the students help each other provides interesting variation and additional practice.

BINGO GAMES

A game of universal appeal to students, young and old alike, is Bingo, or Lotto. Everyone is familiar with the basic principle of the game: A number of cards are prepared with consonants arranged in different orders for each card. The teacher calls out a consonant sound, for example, "*T* (sound) as in Tom." The student places a marker (a bean, a piece of paper, etc.) on top of the square when he locates the letter. The teacher calls off the sounds in a random order by pulling labeled pieces of paper out of a hat or may structure the game clandestinely so that weaker students needing encouragement are enabled to win with a slightly higher frequency.

Bingo can also be played to teach the names of letters by naming the letter before calling it out; it can also be used to teach any of the other phoneme-grapheme correspondences, such as long vowels, diphthongs, etc.

In a teaching situation, teachers might supplement the learning by also saying the phoneme and writing it on the board. Thus, the students who do not know the grapheme for a given phoneme can learn it in an interesting gamelike atmosphere. In fact, teachers might use a series of *successive prompts*. At the most difficult extreme, the student would mark his Bingo card in response to the simple verbal clue of having the teacher say the phoneme. The next prompt would be to give an example word; and the third prompt (really a dead giveaway) would be to write the letter or digraph on the chalkboard. Even with the giveaway situation, the game atmosphere still prevails because it could be luck that determined which student would complete a row and thereby win the game.

In order to take better advantage of the learning situation, the teacher might have students continue the game until all of the spaces were filled. Theoretically, all students should complete the game at the same time, thereby removing a part of the competitive aspect. It has been my observation that students like to do this anyway. I, as a teacher, like to do it because it then gives me some diagnostic information, namely, students who do not have all of their squares filled either were not paying attention or need more help in learning the phoneme-grapheme correspondences being taught.

The teacher might make her own Bingo games based on the information presented in the charts of Chapter 5, or there are some commercially prepared phonics Bingo games from the Gerrard Publishing Company and other commercial game companies.

RUMMY

The card game of Rummy, which has a deck of approximately fifty cards, in which students are to match the cards by sounds is also an interesting way to teach phoneme-grapheme correspondences. A rummy-type game can be constructed similar to Pairs that was described in Chapter 4, again using phonics material presented in the charts. There are also some commercially prepared phonics rummy games produced by Kenworthy and other companies.

Rummy-type games are suitable for small groups of two to five students when they have acquired some skills and need repetition. Bingo games are better for initial instruction or weaker students. In using these games, and all other materials for that matter, the curriculum content should be on the "cutting edge"; in other words, do not have the students play a game for the game's sake. Let the student think that he is just having fun and relaxing, but you should know that it is either a little repetition or drill which he sincerely needs or a new skill which he is learning. Do not have students play phonics games just to kill time. This is one of the things which has given games a bad name in some school districts. There is nothing wrong with games as part of the regular instruction period. In fact, they are excellent instruction. But games, like any other teaching material, can be misused and overused. *Make every game teach a needed skill.*

TRANSPARENCIES

The overhead projector is rapidly becoming one of the most popular teaching devices. In some districts, there is one in every classroom, and there is hardly

FIGURE 7-2 Phoneme-grapheme correspondences can be taught by using a wide variety of games.

a district that does not have at least one in every school. Transparencies are clear plastic sheets approximately 8 by 10 inches which have instructional material printed or drawn on them. For phonics instruction, they can be used in much the same way as the charts described earlier. They have certain advantages over charts in that their presentation of an illuminated image attracts and holds the students' attention. They also can be used to isolate the visual stimulus to a much greater degree. For example, in the chart shown in Figure 7-1, twelve were consonants presented in the first chart. In developing a set of overhead transparencies, it is possible to present only one consonant on each transparency. (See Figure 7-3.) Thus, the teacher can zero in on only the *t* sound or the *b* sound. Even greater visual concentration can be obtained by a process of "masking," in which the teacher takes one or two pieces of paper and covers part of the slide so that, at first, only the illustration appears; then, by moving the paper downward on the page, only the illustration plus one word appears. Later, she may wish to show one column of illustrating words. Transparencies have the advantage that they can be written on with a grease pencil, enabling the teacher to underline words or circle the letters being taught. The teacher can get the students more involved in the lesson by writing her own example words right on the transparency or writing words suggested by students. Students like to see words that they have suggested for illustrating a phonics sound appear on the screen. This further dramatic proof of sounds that they make being represented by graphic symbols is an important step in the teaching of phonics.

A number of companies supply readily prepared phonics transparencies. The ones referred to above are published by Learning Through Seeing, Inc., which has some ninety-nine different transparencies. An example is shown in Figure 7-3. Other sets of prepared material are issued by Systems of Education, among other publishers. Teachers, of course, may prefer to make their own overhead transparencies. The simplest way of making a transparency is simply to write out the content on a piece of plain paper, using any soft pencil and making the letters about ½ inch high, and then to duplicate the material on a sheet of plastic on a Thermo-Fax machine or some other copying device. Transparencies can also be made by drawing directly on sheets of plastic with either grease pencils or special ink pens. Coloring can be added to any transparency by applying special inks or using certain felt-tipped pens.

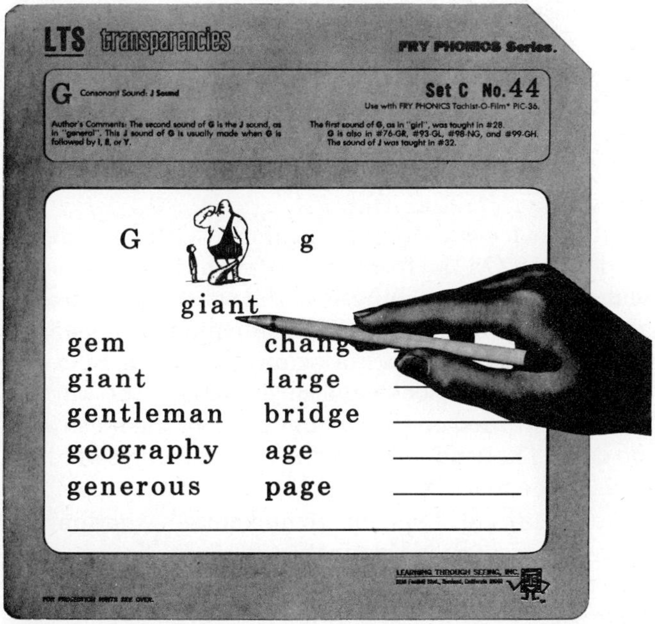

FIGURE 7-3 An overhead transparency used to teach phonics. Additional words can be written on the transparency with a grease pencil or a special marking pen.

FILMSTRIPS

A number of companies manufacture color filmstrips containing phonics materials similar to the kind which teachers place on charts and transparencies. Filmstrips have the advantage of further isolating the visual stimulus and storing a large number of charts in a very small space. They have the disadvantage of making it difficult to mask off portions, and it is impossible to write on them when the teacher wishes to add her own words. In fact, in considering the advantages and disadvantages of these similar devices, it should be pointed out that one advantage of printing charts on paper is that they can be left hanging in the room for the students to refer to at other times during the day or week, whereas overhead projectors and filmstrip projectors are usually turned off when not in direct use.

Another type of phonics filmstrip is the tachisto filmstrip. Initially it is advised to teach phonics in a manner similar to that used with charts, overhead transparencies, and regular filmstrips. But a tachisto filmstrip is made so that the example words can be flashed, thus adding the motivation of tachistoscopic drill to the sometimes inactive and less vivid phonics explanation. Tachistoscopic drills are perhaps best suited to the teaching of whole words as in teaching a basic vocabulary, but they can also be used for the follow-up and drill necessary to teach phonics skills. The phonics filmstrips which are published by Learning Through Seeing, Inc., can be used for initial instruction, but they are perhaps best suited for providing an interesting follow-up for presentations on the overhead projector. Appendix 7-B shows the correlation between my phonics filmstrips and overhead transparencies. This chart also gives some idea of the scope and detail of the transparencies and tachisto filmstrips.

CARD-READERS

A card-reader is an audio-visual device which can read aloud (with an auditory output) a card which is placed into it. On the front of the card a word may be printed; when placed in the machine, the machine says the word. The best-known card-reader, the Language Master, produced by Bell and Howell, can also record a short segment of student response. For example, the machine might be used in this manner: The student looks at a card and says the word into the machine; his response is recorded on the bottom track of the piece of tape stuck on the back of the card. The student then has the machine tell him what the word is, that is, he asks the machine to read the card. By comparing his response with that read from the card, he is able to find out whether he read it correctly, a phenomenon which teaching enthusiasts refer to as "immediate feedback." The card-reader can read the word so that it can be heard by a small group through a speaker, or it can output through a set of earphones so that just one child or as many as have connecting earphones can hear it and others will not be disturbed. Teachers have observed that when a child listens through earphones there is an additional benefit – distracting sounds in the room are cut down and it is easier for the child to pay attention to what he is trying to learn.

WORKBOOKS

Workbooks are softbound books to be written in. A number of different series are available which are designed to teach phonics skill.

A typical drill for very young children is to show the symbol *d*, then pictures of a cat, dog, mouse, and door. The student draws [illegible] symbol *d* to the pictures which begin with the *d* sound. Older studen[illegible] more writing ability and perhaps more reading ability might be asked to [illegible] write in consonants or blends in front of the phonogram *ight* to construct words.

Most of these workbooks are bound. Many of the same types of drills come on loose sheets or on ditto masters which can be run off by the teacher and distributed to students as needed.

PROGRAMMED INSTRUCTION

A new revision of the traditional workbook is the so-called programmed text which uses principles of programmed instruction to teach phonics skills. One of the best known sets of this type of material is the programmed reading series by Sullivan Associates. A student covers up one side of the paper with a mask, and then reads an item; for example, filling in a missing vowel in a word. By sliding a marker down from the side of the page cover, he can see immediately whether or not he has filled in the correct vowel. Sample pages are displayed in Figures 7-4 and 7-5. The Sullivan Programmed Readers teach more skills than phonics, but it is a series which heavily emphasizes phoneme-grapheme correspondences, especially in the booklets for the earlier grades.

RECORDS AND TAPE RECORDERS

Workbooks can also be used to relate the lessons to tape-recorded instructions so that the student can have auditory output from a tape recorder or record while he has a workbook in front of him. The voice on the record can say:

> Look at the top of your page. Do you see a letter that makes the *d* ("duh") sound? If you do, put a circle around it. Now, look at the bottom of your page. Which one of those objects also starts with the *d* ("duh") sound? Put an *x* on top of each picture that starts with a *d* ("duh") sound. (Long pause) Good. You should have put an *x* on top of the picture of the dog and the donkey. Now I want you to write down as many words as you can think of that begin with the *d* sound; or if you can't write any words beginning with *d*, draw a picture of some object or animal whose name begins with a *d* sound, and when you are finished take it to your teacher. Turn off your machine now.

In this situation, the child plus the tape recorder plus a piece of paper or a workbook page constitute an entire little learning system. The teacher need only get the system started and theoretically, at least, it will continue to completion – the desired learning taking place. It is helpful to have a little system such as this when the teacher wishes to pay attention to other students. In a sense, her students are receiving an individualized kind of instruction.

PHONIC READERS

There are a variety of reading texts which emphasize phonics instruction or the phonetic approach to the teaching of reading. A good example is the

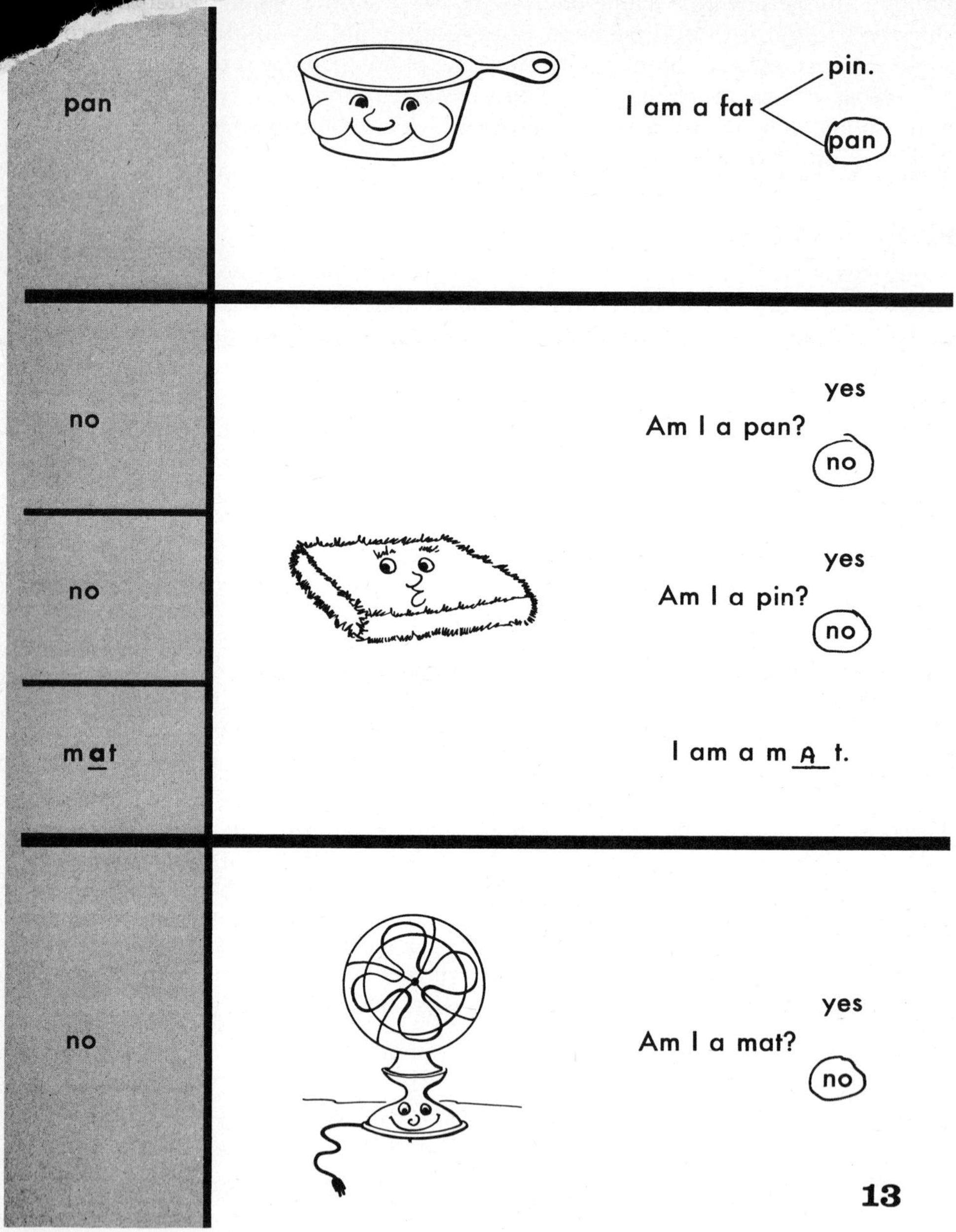

pan

I am a fat pin. / pan

no

Am I a pan? yes / no

no

Am I a pin? yes / no

mat

I am a m A t.

no

Am I a mat? yes / no

13

FIGURE 7-4 Page from the *Programmed Reading Series* (Sullivan Associates). Student covers left-hand gray section while responding to frame at right. Then he moves card down to see if his response is correct.

FIGURE 7-5 Page from the *Programmed Reading Series* (Sullivan Associates).

Lippincott Readers which start with very simple phonetically regular words and gradually teach more phoneme-grapheme correspondences. The same principle is also followed by many of the so-called linguistic series. There is much more to linguistics than phoneme-grapheme correspondences, but some of the recently marketed linguistic readers use chiefly a controlled phoneme-grapheme approach which, by any other name or in another generation, would be called just phonics. One difficulty with phonetic readers is that they are constructed, as basal readers are, to be used as the major method of instruction with a classroom full of children; thus, they are less amenable to skipping about and teaching specific skills. They have the advantage, however, of giving one more method of teaching phonics.

TEACHER-DIRECTED ACTIVITIES

Last, but not least, there is the ingenuity of the teacher in constructing her own materials. Teachers often devise materials similar to those discussed earlier in this chapter. Many teachers also exhibit great skill in creating their own games, charts, and devices (see Figure 7-6). One phonics skill which is frequently ignored in games and prepared materials is that of listening, or asking the student to hear the sound and make the grapheme. Most of the materials discussed in this chapter emphasize recognition of the sound, with the student perhaps making the sound after seeing the printed symbol.

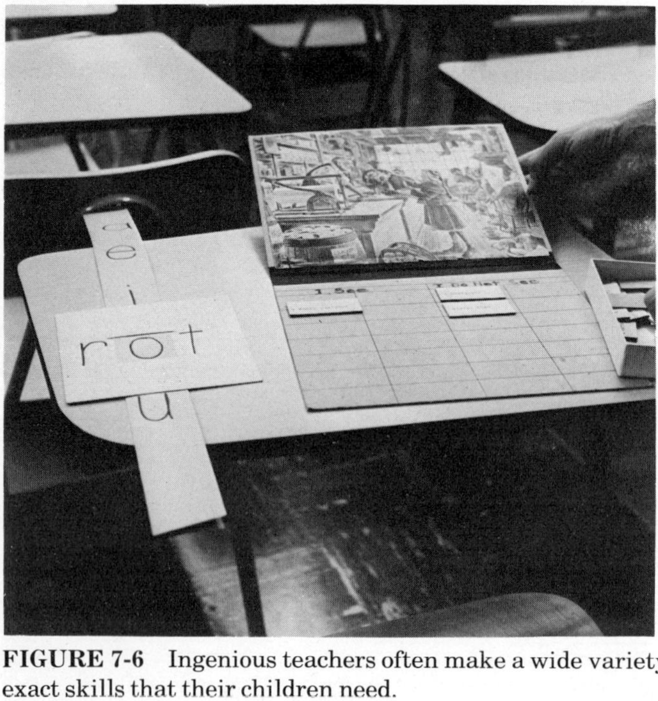

FIGURE 7-6 Ingenious teachers often make a wide variety of games to teach the exact skills that their children need.

Informal drills are perhaps the best method of teaching the phoneme-grapheme correspondence, in contrast to the grapheme-phoneme correspondence. One reason for the prevalence of the latter in all but tapes and card-reader devices is the obvious impossibility of presenting sounds by means of commercially available materials. Teachers can conduct phonics listening drills as they do spelling lessons, simply by calling off the sound and asking the child to write the corresponding symbol. The game of Bingo also teaches the correspondence in this direction.

Teachers' magazines frequently contain suggestions for making games; one of the better-known books on this subject is *Reading Aids Through the Grades* by David Russell, who has written a companion volume, *Listening Aids Through the Grades*. Both are published by Teachers College at Columbia University.

CONCLUDING COMMENT

Phonics is perhaps easier to systemize than is any other reading skill. As a consequence, it is fairly easy to apply the phonics test and to teach the basic principle. On the negative side, its very systemization makes it difficult to present in a lively way so as to avoid boring the children. In order to overcome this tendency, the use of a wide variety of instructional materials is suggested. All the materials and games mentioned here are intended to be interesting, sometimes fun, and always instructive. The cardinal sin in using phonics materials is to waste time by having the game or drill repeat some previously learned skill instead of going on to the next skill which needs initial instruction or meaningful practice to ingrain it.

APPENDIX 7-A PHONICS MATERIALS LIST

+ Bishop — Educational Division Meredith Corp. — 1–4 Remedial
Phonics With Write and See. This is a set of three self-correcting workbooks which uses a chemical marker to provide feedback to the student.

+ Breke — Charles E. Merrill — 1–6
New Phonics Skills Text. This is a well-known set of supplementary phonics workbooks which also have teacher's editions. There are tapes to accompany the first four books, if desired.

Brown and Hodes — Instructo Corp. Paoli, Pennsylvania — 1+
First Experience With Vowels and Consonants. Two kits with nineteen multisensory activities including picture cards, charts, duplicating master books, records, puzzles, tracing cards, writing materials, and teacher's manual.

Buckley and Lamb — Phono-Visual — Primary
The Phono-Visual Game Book. This book contains forty-six game suggestions.

Clymer, Barrett, and Burmeister — Ginn — 1–5
Ginn Word Enrichment Program. This set of five workbooks begins with visual discrimination and continues through syllabification.

+ Cordts — Eyegate — 1
Functional Phonics, Parts 1 and 2. This set includes twelve color filmstrips, six records, a teacher's manual, and pupil activity books.
Material by the same author and same title is put out by Benefic Press. (Workbooks).

+ Crane — Modern Curriculum Press — Primary
Phonics Is Fun. Three workbooks range from identifying consonant sounds to syllabification.

Dolch — Garrard — 1+
Dolch Games. These games are part of the famous remedial reading materials developed by Dr. Edward Dolch. The *Take* game is particularly recommended for teaching initial consonant sounds, medial vowel sounds, and ending consonant sounds, though all games teach either phonic skills or phonic readiness (listening skills). Game titles include *Consonant Lotto, Syllable Game, Vowel Lotto, Group Sounding Game,* and *Take.*

Durrell and Murphy — Harcourt, Brace & World — Primary
Speech to Print Phonics and *Phonics Practice Program.* This is a well-devised system of cards and a teacher's manual that can be used from kindergarten through the elementary grades.

Ellson, Harris Barber and Adams — Ginn — Elementary and Remedial

Ginn Tutorial. Individualized procedures to supplement Ginn Readers (100th edition). Includes *Word Analysis Book* and other materials.

Feldman — Teachers College Press — 2–4

Ways to Read Words, More Ways to Read Words, and *Learning About Words.* Three phonics workbooks, for elementary or remedial students, which contain some context cues.

Fry — Learning Through Seeing — Elementary and Remedial

Fry Phonics Series. This is a set of ninety-nine overhead transparencies that teach phonics skills by an illustrated key word followed by a group of high-frequency example words and there is space on the transparency for the teacher to add her own words. The series is grouped into the following sections:
Easy Consonants, Short and *Long Vowels, More Difficult Regular Consonants* and *Digraphs, More Vowel Sounds, More Difficult Vowel Sounds, Beginning Consonant Blends,* and *Common Exceptions.*
Similar material but with more example words is also available on filmstrips from the same publisher. The filmstrips can also be used tachistoscopically.

Glim — Harcourt, Brace & World — 1–3

Palo Alto Reading Program—Sequential Steps in Reading. This is a set of books, workpads, cards, and wall charts which can be a basic skills program used along with an individualized reading or a basal reading series.

Halvorsen, Thomas, Partts, Helkamp, Engels, and Meighen — Lyons and Carnahan — 1–6

Phonics We Use. This is a well-known set of phonics workbooks ranging from grades one to six, with one book per grade level and teacher's edition.

Hargrave and Armstrong — McCormick-Mathers — 1–6

Building Reading Skills Series. This is a set of workbooks covering the elementary years and accompanied by a set of 104 flashcards.

Harris, Krekmore, and Green — The Economy Co. — 1–3

Phonetic Keys to Reading. This is a set of books, teacher's manual and cards that can serve as a main or supplemental reading system for grades one to three.

Heggen and Villars — 3M Visual Products, St. Paul, Minnesota — Elementary

Phonics. This is a set of transparencies and duplicating masters in eight sequential units.

Heilman, Helkmap, Thomas, and Carsello — Lyons and Carnahan — 1–6

Phonics We Use—learning Games Kit. This is a set of ten separate games to supplement phonics and reading instruction:
Old Itch: Initial consonant sounds; played with deck of cards.
Spin-a-Sound: Initial consonant sounds; played with a board and spinner.

Bingobang: Final consonant sounds and symbols; played on a board with cards.
Blends Race: Initial consonant blends and symbols; played on a board with a spinner.
Digraph Wheel: Initial consonant digraph; played on a board with corresponding spinner on board.
Digraph Hopscotch: Initial and final digraphs; played on a board with dice.
Vowel dominoes: Long and short vowels; played with picture cards.
Spin Hard Spin soft: Hard and soft sounds of *c* and *g*; played with bingo-type cards.
Full House: Vowel, digraph, and diphthongs; played on bingo-type cards with matching picture word cards.
Syllable Count: Syllabification and accent; played on bingo-type cards with spinner.

Herr — Imed, Los Angeles (1415 Westward Blvd.) — 1–5
Phonics. A series of workbooks that can be used in elementary grades or on a remedial basis with older children.

Hughes — Open Court — Primary
Foundations Program. Reader and workbook series for teaching initial reading.

Johnson, Wonsavage, and Singleton — American Education Publications — 2–3
This is a series of very small workbooks:
Phonics and Word Power, Program 1, Books A, B, C
Phonics and Word Power, Program 2, Books A, B, C
Phonics and Word Power, Program 3, Books A, B, C

Kottmeyer — Webster Division, McGraw-Hill — Remedial
Word Analysis Charts. This set of five charts presents a quick and basic overview of phonics from initial consonant sounds to syllabification.

Kottmeyer and Ware — Webster Division, McGraw-Hill — 1–4
Webster Word Wheels. This set of sixty-three wheels emphasizes phonic and structural analysis skills such as beginning blends, prefixes, suffixes.

Kottmeyer, William, and Ware — Webster Division, McGraw-Hill — 2–6 and remedial
Magic World of Dr. Spello. This is a remedial reading workbook which has a spelling emphasis but is excellent for teaching most phonic skills.

Light — Creative Playthings — K–2
Turn-A-Word. This is a set of three five-sided blocks strung together with an elastic string. By turning the cubes, various CVC words can be made.

Major — Milliken Publishing Co., St. Louis — 1–3
Phonics Development. Twenty transparencies and twenty duplicating masters for each of several primary grades.

McKee, Harrison, McCowen, and Lehr — Houghton Mifflin — Primary
Learning Letter Sounds. This text workbook system is accompanied by teacher's guide and filmstrips.

Listen and Do. This set includes records, duplicating masters, teacher's guide.
Get Set. Games for beginning readers.

Mountain — Teaching Aids, Indianapolis, Indiana, (1718 Lafayette Rd.) — Elementary

Word-roll. A phonics bingo game played with wooden dice that contain word parts.

Naggi, Sullivan, and William — Fordham Publishing Co., Bronx, N.Y. — 1+

Look, Learn, and Listen. Sixteen kits, each containing eight full-color transparencies, sixteen duplicating masters, and one cassette or record. Each kit deals with a few letters.

Parker and Scannell — SRA — 1–3 and Remedial

Reading Laboratory 1 — Word Games. This reading laboratory, unlike the more familiar laboratories, consists of special games and drill cards which teach phonics sounds. A phonics survey and teacher's manual are included.

Platts — Educational Service, Inc., Stevensville, Michigan — K–6

Spice. This is a spiral-bound manual with many ideas for inexpensive teacher-made materials and games.

Rasmussen and Goldberg — SRA — 3–5

Cracking the Code. This set consists of a paperback reader and workbook and a teacher's guide. It is divided into twelve levels of sound spelling patterns.

Schoolfield and Timberlake — Phono-Visual Products — Primary

Phonics Fun — Consonants and Phonics Fun — Vowels. Twenty-six duplicating masters in each set.
Phonovisual Consonant Workbook.
Phonovisual Vowel Workbook.
Charts, records, and other materials for a complete beginning reading phonics-oriented system.

Sheldon — Allyn and Bacon — Elementary

Phonics Charts. This is a set of nineteen color charts, measuring 20″ by 25″.

Sullivan Associates — McGraw-Hill — Elementary

Programmed Reading. A series of programmed instruction workbooks with a heavy phonic (linguistic) beginning reading approach. Can be used as a basal or supplementary series.

Thompson — Allyn and Bacon — Remedial

Phonics In Action. This workbook is aimed especially at the remedial student.

Thompson — Allyn and Bacon — 1–3

Happy Times With Sounds. Three well-known workbooks used frequently in the primary grades.

Continental Press 1–3

Phonics & Word-Analysis Skills. This is a set of low-cost and widely used spirit master duplicating books. Four books each have thirty pages of various phonic skills drills.

Dennison Elementary

Dennison Phonetic Charts. Each of the following sets contain three color charts, measuring 25″ by 22″: *Consonants, Consonant Blends, Consonant and Vowel Digraphs, Vowels, Vowel Combinations*, and *Spelling and Syllabification Rules*.

Dexter & Westbrook, Ltd. 1–2

Fun with Words: Levels 1, 2, 3, 4, 5, 6 – Kits A, B, C, D, E, F.
Time for Sounds: Each kit contains fifty extra-sized cards and an answer key. Kit A has initial consonant sounds for grade one and Kit B has initial blends and digraphs for grade two.
One too Many. Levels 1 and 2 Kits A, B.
Riddle Riddle Rhyme Time. Levels 1 and 2 Kits A, B.

Harper & Row Elementary

Word Go Round. A double-wheel device to substitute initial consonant, medial vowel, or final consonant sound.

Ideal Elementary

The Ideal Company has a number of materials which are sold through school supply houses, such as: *Initial and Final Consonant Charts, Consonant Pictures for Pegboards Magic Cards – Consonants* (Magic cards have a plastic cover so they can be written on over and over again), *Blends and Digraph Charts, Magic Cards – Blends and Digraphs, Vowel Charts – Vowels*, and *Magic Cards Vowels*.

Instructo Elementary

The following are some materials to be used on flannel boards: *Initial Consonants Substitution, Toy Chest of Beginning Sounds, Final Consonant Blends*, and *Long and Short Vowels*.

Instructor Publications Elementary

Instructor Basic Phonics. Each small set contains twenty-four charts and ninety-six flash cards. The sets are entitled: *Vowels and Vowel Digraphs, Single Consonant Sounds, Digraphs, Diphthongs, Initial Consonant Blends*, and *Compound Phonograms*.

Kenworthy Primary and Elementary

The Kenworthy Company produces a number of boxes which contain letters and phonic drill cards, such as: *Picture Phonics Cards, Reading Made Easy, Word Prefixes, Phonics for Reading, ABC Game Phonic Rummy, Rainbow Word Builders, Word Family Fun* (by Mountain), *Phonetic Word Drill Cards, Word Blends, Word Suffixes, Doghouse Game, Junior Phonic Rummy, Alphabet Flashcards*, and *UNO Phonics Game*.

Milton Bradley Elementary

The following boxes of flashcards and games are sold in most school supply houses:

Giant Vowel Poster Cards, Alphabet Picture Cards, Vowel Links Poster Cards, Phonetic Drill Cards, Phonetic Word Wheel, Giant Consonant Poster Cards, Beginning Consonant Poster Cards, Phonetic Quizmo, Phonetic Word Builders and *Phonetic Word Analyzer.*

Modern Curriculum Press Cleveland, Ohio — Primary

Phonics Picture Cards. This set contains 176 picture cards grouped according to phonic skills: beginning consonants, long vowels, etc.

Systems for Education — Elementary

Adventures in Phonics. A series of overhead transparencies with a number of example words and a key word illustration.

Play Art Educational Equipment — 1–3

Phonetic Word Drill Cards. This is a set of cards on rings. Word beginnings flip on left side, and word endings flip on the right side—to make a whole word.

APPENDIX 7-B FRY PHONICS SERIES *LTS* TRANSPARENCIES TABLE OF CONTENTS

SET A EASY CONSONANTS

Transparency number	*Letters taught*	*Sound description*	*Correlates with Fry Tachist-O-Film No.*
1	T	Regular	1
2	N	Regular	2
3	R	Regular	3
4	M	Regular	4
5	D	Regular	5
6	S	Regular	6
7	L	Regular	7
8	C	Regular (K sound)	8
9	P	Regular	9
10	B	Regular	10
11	F	Regular	11
12	V	Regular	12

SET B SHORT AND LONG VOWELS

Transparency number	*Letters taught*	*Sound description*	*Correlates with Fry Tachist-O-Film No.*
13	I	Short	13
14	E	Short	14
15	A	Short	15
16	O	Short	16
17	U	Short	17
18	Y	Long E	18
19	E	Silent	18
20	A	Long final E rule	25
21	I	Long final E rule	26
22	O	Long final E rule	27
23	A	Long open syllable rule	28
24	E	Long open syllable rule	29
25	I	Long open syllable rule	30
26	O	Long open syllable rule	31
27	U	Long open syllable rule	32

SET C MORE DIFFICULT REGULAR CONSONANTS AND DIGRAPHS

Transparency number	*Letters taught*	*Sound description*	*Correlates with Fry Tachist-O-Film No.*
28	G	Regular	19
29	H	Regular	19
30	K	Regular	20
31	W	Regular	20
32	J	Regular	21
33	X	KS Sound	21
34	Q	QU makes KW sound	22
35	Z	Regular	22
36	Y	Consonant	33
37	TH	Digraph voiced	23
38	TH	Digraph voiceless	23
39	CH	Digraph	24
40	SH	Digraph	24
41	WH	Digraph (HW blend)	24
42	C	S sound	34
43	S	Z sound	35
44	G	J sound	36

SET D MORE VOWEL SOUNDS

Transparency number	*Letters taught*	*Sound description*	*Correlates with Fry Tachist-O-Film No.*
45	Y	Long I sound	33
46	A	Schwa	37
47	E	Schwa	38
48	O	Schwa	39
49	EA	Long E	40
50	EE	Long E	40
51	AI	Long A	41
52	AY	Long A	41
53	OA	Long O	42
54	OW	Long O	42
55	OR	OR sound	43
56	AR	AR sound	43
57	AR	AIR sound	43
58	ER	R sound	44
59	IR	R sound	44
60	UR	R sound	44

SET E MORE DIFFICULT VOWEL SOUNDS

Transparency number	*Letters taught*	*Sound description*	*Correlates with Fry Tachist-O-Film No.*
61	O	Broad O	45
62	AL	Broad O	45
63	AW	Broad O	45
64	AU	Broad O	45
65	OU	OU diphthong	46
66	OW	OU diphthong	46
67	OI	OI diphthong	47
68	OY	OI diphthong	47
69	OO	2-dot U or Long OO	48
70	OO	1-dot U or Short OO	48
71	U	2-dot U	48
72	U	1-dot U	48
73	EA	Short E sound	–

SET F BEGINNING CONSONANT BLENDS

Transparency number	*Sound description*	*Correlates with Phonics Practice Tachist-O-Film No.*
74	PR	17
75	TR	17
76	GR	16
77	BR	16
78	CR	17
79	DR	16
80	FR	16
81	ST	15
82	SP	15
83	SC	15
84	SK	15
85	SW	17
86	SM	17
87	SN	17
88	PL	14
89	CL	14
90	BL	14
91	FL	14
92	SL	14
93	GL	14
94	TW	18

SET G COMMON EXCEPTIONS

Transparency number	*Letters taught*	*Sound description*	*Correlates with Phonics Practice Tachist-O-Film No.*
95	PH	F sound	18
96	KN	N sound	18
97	WR	R sound	18
98	NG	NG sound	23
99	GH	Silent blend	—

8

COMPREHENSION: WHAT IS MEANING?

This chapter and Chapter 9 will provide some background on the complex subject of reading comprehension. Since it is such a very complicated topic, a wide variety of approaches will be considered. Some of the approaches are admittedly only partial explanations of a part of the comprehension process, but they should serve to stimulate readers' thinking about the topic. When we consider comprehension teaching techniques in Chapter 10, the teacher will perhaps better understand why a variety of methods are needed and why it is a difficult subject area to teach.

This chapter then will give a number of sometimes fragmentary views of comprehension, and Chapter 9 will illustrate in a more organized fashion how nearly every topic discussed in this book is related to the comprehension process. Finally, Chapter 10 presents a how-to-do-it approach with suggested teaching methods.

Comprehension involves the problem of meaning. What does the author mean? What does his writing mean to the reader?

Comprehension is a very important and an extremely difficult topic. It is the very core of the reading process. In my opening remarks about learning to read, I stated that reading is learning "the relationship between the printed symbols and their meaning."

In this chapter, we shall attempt to understand different aspects of comprehension. The topic is very complex because it involves both thought process and the nature of language. Thus, it touches on much of the entire field of psychology and of linguistics. Our study of comprehension is further complicated by the fact that there is considerably less than unanimous agreement among scholars and researchers on the nature of the process. Nearly all research undertaken so far has tackled one small aspect of the problem, and the findings have not always held up in all situations. Whenever scholars have tried to create an all-embracing theory of language learning, their theories have invariably fallen short of completely satisfactory answers and have usually been attacked by other scholars in the field. Hence, in this chapter we shall consider several models or theories of the reading-comprehension process. Hopefully, this will give some insight into the complexity of the process.

In Chapter 10 we shall consider teaching methods for increasing comprehension. Of course, these methods should be based on a thorough understanding of the comprehension process, if that were possible. But we must realize at the outset that no one has a thorough understanding of the process and that most comprehension-teaching materials work on only part of the problem.

COMMUNICATIONS MODEL

Let us begin our investigation of comprehension with a communications model. Although this model could take any of a number of forms, it is basically conceived of as the process of transmitting information through several stages, and it may be diagrammed in much the same way as radio transmitters and receivers are diagrammed. For example, Figure 8-1 shows a flow diagram of a communications model. The source might be a person talking. The sound of speech is then transmitted by a radio transmitter through the medium of the

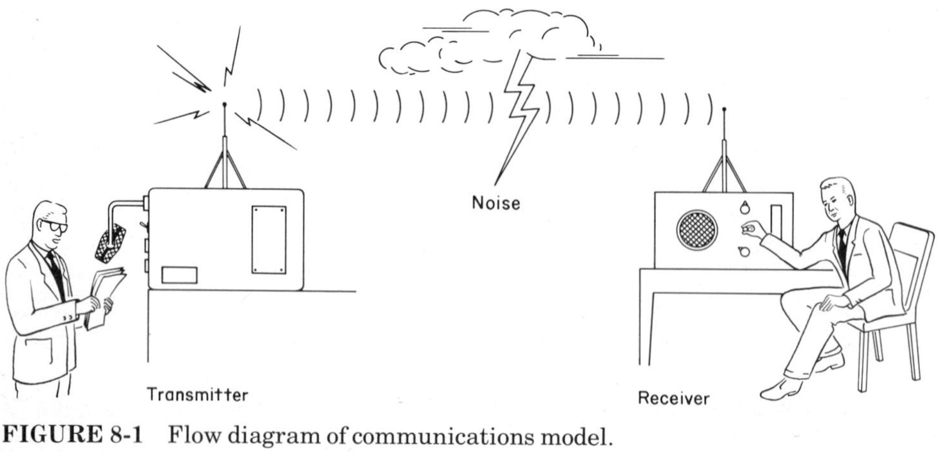

FIGURE 8-1 Flow diagram of communications model.

air; finally it is received by a radio receiver and listened to. Errors in transmission can creep in at any stage, and each stage of the communications process is subject to different sources of errors. The person at the source induces different types of errors from those of the transmitter. Likewise, errors for the medium of transmission are different from those of the receiver. Engineers might interpret the errors as sources of information loss. Some of the error sources could be called "noise." An example of noise would be the static induced by lightening as the information is passing through the air medium.

Figure 8-2 illustrates the communications model applied to the reading process. An author is the source of ideas. The method by which he transmits his ideas is that of writing. The medium through which he will transmit his writing to the reader is publication, and this may involve many steps, such as editing, rewriting, and retyping. From this emerges a book, which is then sold and distributed and finally arrives in the hands of the reader.

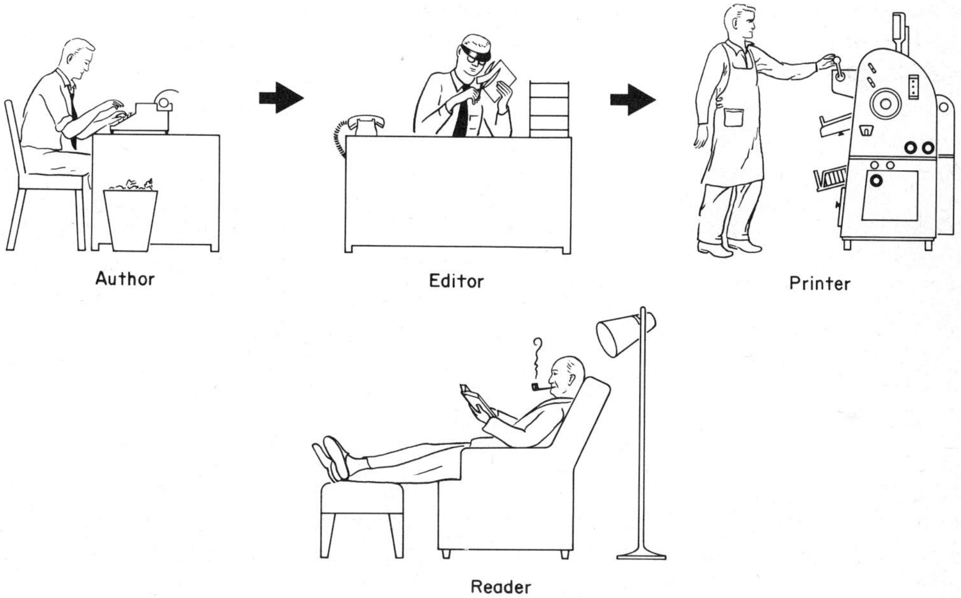

FIGURE 8-2 Communications model applied to the reading process.

If we look at that type of communication process known as reading, we see that it is quite possible to have a number of errors in the transmission of ideas between the author and the reader. To the extent that these errors occur we can say that the communication process breaks down. We are particularly concerned, of course, with the last stage; namely, the process which the reader goes through in order to obtain the information. But it helps to understand that there are other stages in the communication process.

READING AS SPEECH SYMBOLS Another aspect of the communication process is illustrated in the insight experienced by the little boy who said, "Readin' ain't nothin' but talkin' writ down." English writing does tend to be very similar to English speech, although the grammatical forms of written and spoken English are significantly different. Anyone who has ever had his conversation or an impromptu speech recorded and then transcribed is immediately aware of the fact that he does not speak in sentences and in paragraphs. In other languages (Greek, for example), grammatical forms for speaking and writing are very different. English, however, is predominantly written speech. As mentioned earlier, an alphabet is, by definition, a set of symbols which represent speech sounds.

One problem with reading is that we are using a "double abstraction." One level of abstraction is the sound level. If a person says the word *dog*, he is making a sound symbol which represents the concept of a dog. The sound symbol does not smell, taste, or sound like a dog. Very young children who use the sound symbol "bow-wow" for the concept "dog" are really using a much more direct symbolization. However, in reading we use a symbol which stands for a symbol. The letters *d-o-g*, when perceived as a unit, form a symbol which stands for the sound symbol, and thus, in turn, stands for the concept. When one stops to consider the complexity of the reading process, it is truly amazing that so many children ever learn how to read.

Efficient readers do not always go through this stage of recognizing the words as sound symbols. When children or adults learn to read they frequently learn how to read aloud. In other words, they learn the relationship between the printed symbol and the sound symbol. Since they usually already know what the sound symbol means, it is easy to make the connection. However, mature readers can read at least twice as fast as they can listen. In other words, a normal reading rate is usually twice as fast as a speaking rate. Many efficient readers can read several times the normal speech rate (the normal speech rate is about 125 words per minute). As we shall see in a later chapter, trying to read aloud or trying to read while subvocalizing the words is an undesirable habit, for it inhibits efficient silent reading. Hence, even though there is a direct conceptual link between speaking and writing, efficient readers can often omit or largely subdue the vocalization process while reading.

THE SPOKEN VERSUS THE WRITTEN WORD One difficulty with writing is that it does not and cannot contain as much information as speech. The personal presence of the speaker enables the listener to gain meaning from a fairly large number of body gestures and speech inflections, all of which convey nonverbal meaning. Very few of these can be recorded graphically. We have a few punctuation marks such as the question mark or the exclamation mark which attempt to give some of the basic intonation patterns, but most of the subtleties of personal communication cannot be written down. For example, the tone of a person's voice might indicate that he is not at all sure that what he's saying is correct. Another tone might suggest that what he says is completely ridiculous. Yet another tone might indicate the depth of great sincerity.

Body gestures, while more commonly attributed to those who speak certain foreign languages, are also present when the English language is spoken. A wink of the eye might completely change the meaning of the paragraph; a coy look might change a perfectly straightforward sentence into a provocative one. A shrug of the shoulders might contain more meaning than the ten lines of prose which accompany it. The absence of bodily posture and vocal intonation can cause a student to say, "I understand it if I hear it, but not if I read it." The fact is that much more information is transmitted through spoken communication than is contained in the sequence of words he uses.

An interesting illustration of how meaning can be changed by intonation is given in Lefevre's book *Linguistics and the Teaching of Reading.* Figure 8-3 illustrates how a sentence, when given different intonations, can take on a number of different meanings. Even though the sentence was especially selected, it does illustrate what differences in inflection can do to alter the meanings of words and sentences. For those reading teachers interested in the topic of linguistics, Lefevre's book is a good place to start. Other references on linguistics can be found in the bibliography at the end of this book.

Directions: Emphasize italicized word to change meaning.

I did not say you stole my red bandana.	(Someone else said it)
I *did* not say you stole my red bandana.	(Disputatious denial)
I did *not* say you stole my red bandana	(Disputatious denial)
I did not *say* you stole my red bandana.	(I implied or suspected)
I did not say *you* stole my red bandana.	(Someone else stole it)
I did not say you *stole* my red bandana.	(You did something else with it)
I did not say you stole *my* red bandana.	(You stole someone else's)
I did not say you stole my *red* bandana.	(You stole one of another color)
I did not say you stole my red *bandana.*	(You stole something else red)

FIGURE 8-3 An illustration of how changing the stress on different words in the same sentence can change the meaning. Linguists also refer to this as a change in intonation or melody. Part of the stress would be to use a rising pitch on the stressed word followed by a pause.

GESTALT

In the communications model we saw one way of visualizing the reading process. Let us consider the problem from another angle, that of gestalt psychology. The term "gestalt" refers to a meaningful whole or organizational pattern. It has some interesting implications for the reading process. In an earlier section we considered reading comprehension as part of the process of communicating an idea from the author's mind to the reader's mind. In this section we shall endeavor to understand reading from the standpoint of the reader's perception of meaningful units. Some readers will recognize this as an application of gestalt psychology.

LETTERS AS UNITS OF MEANING The reader is presented with a page of printed matter, such as that at which you are now looking. How does he perceive it so that he gets the ideas from it? Surely he does not look at the page as a whole to see if the margins are neat and the words arranged in straight lines. No, obviously he must look at some smaller unit. For example, let us assume that the reader is presented with this sample sentence: "The old black dog ran and bit the boy."

If we examine this sentence in its smallest units we see that it is composed of letters of the alphabet. By definition, an alphabetical letter is a symbol which stands for a speech-sound. If our language were perfectly phonetic, which it is not, each letter would stand for a speech-sound and each speech-sound would have a letter. If we take the first word, *the*, and examine the first letter of the word, *t*, we might remember that *t* stands for the *t* sound as seen in the beginning of *top* or *toy*. This might be a useful bit of information, but unfortunately in this case it is incomplete, because the two letters *th* are a digraph and must be seen as one unit in order to get the proper speech-sound. This is usually the *th* sound as heard at the beginning of the word *this*. To get the right speech-sound we must sometimes see letters in combinations and not as single letters.

WORDS AS UNITS OF MEANING Since it is obviously senseless to look for meaning, or the idea in the author's mind, by examining individual letters, there is no point in studying it further. Let us then take a slightly larger meaningful unit, namely, the entire first word *the*. If we see the letters *t, h, e* placed together in that particular order they form a meaningful unit, a word. If we then ask, "What is the meaning of the word *the*?" we have a relevant question but unfortunately one that is not easy to answer. *The* is an article; more than that, it is a definite article; "the dog" is different from "a dog." The word *the* contributes to the transmission of meaning but, by itself, *the* has almost no meaning.

---

the
t = t sound in "top"
but
th = th sound in "this"
(So do not always stop at individual letters.)
the = a word, but of little meaning
the dog = a particular dog, different from "a dog"
Hence meaning is in larger group, not smallest unit.

FIGURE 8-4 Analysis of a word

Perhaps it is not fair to study a word like *the*; we should take a more basic word such as *dog*. Here again, we look closely at *dog*; we see that *d* by itself means nothing but a speech-sound, but when *d*, *o*, and *g* are placed in that particular relationship, one understands the concept of *dog*. If the same letters are arranged in any other order (for example, *god*) they give us quite a different meaning. Hence, not only are the particular letters of the alphabet important but also the order in which they are arranged.

PHRASE AS A UNIT OF MEANING Now back to our analysis of the sentence, "The old black dog ran and bit the boy."

We have seen that the idea that the author is trying to convey to the reader is certainly not contained in individual letters; neither is the meaning conveyed, always, in the single whole word. We have seen that some words (*dog*) have more meaning than other words (*the*). If we look at some of the other words in the sentence (*old* and *black*), we sense that these are interesting words, but by themselves they hardly convey complete meanings. The word *black* is a vague concept. It is true that black is a color, but the author is not trying to give us the idea of "blackness." He is simply trying to tell us about an animal which is not just "a dog" but a particular dog, namely, "the dog." Furthermore, this dog is not to be confused with other dogs because he is "black" and he is "old." The reader cannot derive meaning, then, from any of the four words by themselves. *The* and *old* and *black* by themselves have little meaning, and the word *dog*, even though it conveys some meaning and can stand alone, is still not as meaningful as when it is seen in context with "the old black." Hence, in order to understand what the author wanted to say, the reader must perceive "the old black dog" as one unit.

"Perception" is not the same thing as eye movements. Perception here is a mental or psychological phenomenon, and whether the reader sees the four words in one fixation, or two or three, is not as important as his mental process, which would perceive them as a meaningful group.

A SENTENCE AS A UNIT OF MEANING What is the author trying to say to the reader? Is he simply trying to convey the notion that "the old black dog" exists? No, he is trying to tell a much larger and more complex idea, namely, that "the old black dog is *running* and he is *biting* the boy." The author wishes to tell us that a particular action took place between this dog and a certain boy. He is trying to give us a "complete thought." English teachers sometimes explain a sentence as being composed of a subject and a predicate. But a psychologist would be happier with the teacher's definition of a sentence as a complete thought. Psychologists sometimes refer to these units of meaning as "gestalts." Gestalt is a German word which means "organization" or "whole" or "pattern." Thus a word is a gestalt; a phrase such as "the old black dog" is a larger unit of meaning or a larger gestalt. The whole sentence, "The old black dog ran and bit the boy," is an even larger meaning-unit or gestalt. The teacher will be able to extend this idea quickly to a definition of a paragraph as simply a larger unit of meaning or a larger gestalt.

The gestalt psychologist tells us that man's mind works in terms of meaning-units. Psychologists certainly did not invent the idea that man writes in words or sentences or paragraphs; rather, they observed that words and sentences and paragraphs are organized in written and oral communication because this is the way in which man's mind works. If the reader understands this, he will know where to look for the meaning in a written work. He will not look at the individual letter for meaning. He will not look at the individual word for meaning. He will look at the combinations of interrelated words in such units as phrases and sentences and paragraphs. By themselves, very few words contain enough meaning to be worthwhile. It is the way words are used in relationship to each other that expresses the meaning.

LOOK FOR LARGER UNITS Slow readers who read one word at a time often have great difficulty in understanding a printed page. They perceive single words as single words, and meaning is simply not contained in individual words. Fast readers are often superior readers because they perceive words as groups. Their minds are set upon understanding the interrelationship of words. If students insist upon reading slowly and saying each word to themselves, they are placing their mental emphasis in the wrong place.

Subvocalization is a distraction because, as explained previously, meaning is not contained in the sound-symbol. Pronouncing words aloud while reading is only a crutch to help the very immature who have a better speaking than reading knowledge of the language.

Some readers get "too close" to the material. They insist on carefully scrutinizing and pronouncing each word in a sentence. If it is a long sentence, by the time they have reached the end they have forgotten the beginning. Better is the reader who tries to perceive the sentence as a whole so that he sees the interrelationships among all the words and phrases. The important thing in reading is for the reader to place his attention where it should be: on trying to comprehend the ideas.

LARGER UNITS REQUIRE MATURITY The younger or less mature the reader, the smaller the gestalt he can handle. In other words, young children and beginning readers have difficulty in perceiving or understanding larger patterns as wholes. Therefore, materials suitable for beginning reading contain short sentences. It is easier for a beginning reader to combine four or five words into a meaningful whole, as in a short, simple sentence, than to see the overall pattern of a twenty-five- to fifty-word sentence. College textbooks frequently contain fifty-word sentences, and many sentences in some secondary reading texts contain more than twenty-five words. Sentences this long comprise many subordinate clauses and prepositional phrases (small gestalts which add up to a larger gestalt). The ability of the student to handle such large and complex sentence patterns depends upon two things: his innate intelligence and his past learning. While the teacher can do little about the former, it is the teacher's primary purpose to deal with the latter. The best way for a student to learn to handle larger and larger sentence-patterns is to do as much easy reading as possible, for it is through experience that he becomes familiar with the complex sentence-patterns used in English writing. It is only when the simple or fairly simple patterns have been mastered that the student should be exposed to the more complex sentences which are used in adult material.

Figure 8-5 presents an example of a one-sentence large gestalt, which, subsequently, can be broken down into a number of smaller gestalts. The first sentence is fairly complex, with a number of clauses similar to those found in adult reading materials. Beneath this sentence the same ideas have been broken down into short sentences similar to those which might be found in a beginning reader's book.

The large grey house the farmer lived in has been
sold to the soldier who was here last summer.
There is a large grey house.
A farmer lived in it.
The house has been sold.
A soldier bought it.
The soldier was here last summer.

FIGURE 8-5 Large and small gestalts in sentences.

The mature reader has the ability to form larger gestalts. He is familiar with the handling of the phrases, and it is not necessary for the author to break them down into simple gestalts for him. The large sentences also contain subtle interrelationships which are difficult to express in short, choppy sentences. The large sentence has a certain flow and unity which short choppy sentences have not. In teaching reading comprehension, the teacher should take large sentences and explain what information they contain. Then the student should be given adequate practice in reading both small and large sentences in order to gain facility in handling the larger gestalts which characterize more mature reading.

GRAMMAR It is interesting to note that English grammar is largely in harmony with the gestalt idea. If you ask an English teacher, "What is a sentence?" the answer will probably be, "A complete thought." The teacher may not be aware that she is telling you that a sentence is a gestalt. If you ask the same teacher, "What is a paragraph?" the answer will doubtless be "A number of sentences which convey a main idea or concept." The teacher says that a paragraph is really a larger gestalt. Figure 8-6 illustrates the progression of grammatical units from word to phrase to sentence to paragraph to chapter to volume

Word (word part)
Phrase
Sentence
Paragraph
Chapter (article)
Volume (book)
Series

FIGURE 8-6 Grammar units are expanding gestalts.

to series. Words might be broken down further into roots, prefixes, suffixes, and so on. It is interesting to consider our language as a series of expanding gestalts. It is also interesting to observe that a student may gain an understanding on one level and yet have none on another level. A student, for example, may be able to tell you what a sentence means but be utterly stumped when asked to explain a paragraph. Or, conversely, an adult may have difficulty in explaining a page or a chapter of a book, yet may be able to give a good account of what the whole book is about. Teachers should probably stress reading comprehension at each of these levels.

In many respects the teaching of formal grammar is an excellent method of teaching reading comprehension. The old-fashioned diagramming of sentences reveals many of the subtle interrelationships of words and phrases; this type of knowledge can help the reader every bit as much as it helps the writer. Many English and reading teachers teach vocabulary improvement, or word knowledge. Some teachers break down words further into roots, prefixes, and suffixes so that when students learn parts of words they can apply them readily to an entire family or class of words. It is to be hoped that word knowledge is taught by all teachers, regardless of the approach employed. For example, the chemistry teacher should teach terms specifically related to chemistry and the shop teacher the technical terms in his field. Teachers of English at secondary and elementary levels also spend a moderate amount of time explaining what constitutes a sentence and a paragraph. While this is often done from the standpoint of writing, the student has but to turn it around to gain fresh insight into the reading process.

CULTURAL CONTEXT AND IMPLIED STANDARD

Another way of approaching reading comprehension is to understand it in terms of its total contextual setting. Many of our words, phrases, and sentences change with the cultural context. Used in one setting or context they will mean one thing, and in another setting they will mean something quite different.

First of all we must consider the problem of implied relative standards. For example, if father is having a cup of coffee and says, "That's hot!" he means that the temperature of the coffee is about 150 degrees Fahrenheit.

Later in the day he shows a visitor around his steel mill and points to a chunk of glowing red metal and says, "That's hot!" He means that the temperature is about 4,000 degrees.

If the visitor asks, "That's hot?" He means that in his mill they regularly work with metal at 6,000 degrees.

Of course, *hot*, like many other words and phrases, can have an unlimited number of meanings and shades of meanings. If father later in the day hears that the value of a certain stock has risen, he might say, "That's hot!" meaning "That's amusing," or "It should rise even higher" or, perhaps, "Old Jones should have followed my advice and bought when I did."

For lunch at a Mexican restaurant, he might bite into a chili pepper and exclaim, "That's hot!" meaning it is piquant.

A colleague comes in and asks which item is selling best. Father points to Widget 603 and says, "That's hot!"

In another cultural group, teenagers, for example, "hot" might mean stolen. But even here the more narrow context must be understood—a "hot car" might be a stolen car or it might be a fast car.

All adverbs and adjectives suffer from the relative standard problem. Running a hundred yards in 10 seconds might be "excellent" for a high school athlete but only "good" for a college athlete. Standards differ, and the use of a descriptive word often implies some standard which is familiar to the reader.

Another problem is the purely subjective standard of the author. Perhaps this might be expressed as the "Beauty is in the eyes of the beholder" problem. A character in a story may describe another by saying, "She's pretty." The mature reader, however, knowing that animosity exists between the two characters, may fully realize that she is not really pretty but grossly underweight, with stringy hair and poor posture; or the author might wish to convey the impression that the character thinks that she is pretty, and that that is all that is needed for telling the story.

READING SIMULTANEOUSLY AT MULTIPLE LEVELS Some stories are written purposely to appeal to several types of audiences, or to several levels of sophistication. *Alice in Wonderland* is an excellent example of what purports to be a simple narrative for children, the fantastic adventures of Alice making a fine story in themselves. At the same time, parents can easily recognize character traits of their friends or of nationally known figures. Other adults may perceive caustic or penetrating commentaries on social problems which are quite beyond the grasp of children.

Classics, poems, the Bible—in fact, many forms of writing from ancient proverbs to modern novels—can convey varied meanings to different people. To comprehend the depth of some writings requires not only a good formal education but a breadth of experience in reading and in living.

I have sometimes been tempted to tell my students that the real purpose of a college education is to learn how to read, and the remark would be made only half-facetiously. Take the word *fault* as an example: it conveys much more meaning to one who has taken a geology course than it does to one who has never taken such a course or never acquired equivalent knowledge from wide reading or experience.

Critical reading requires a multiple type of comprehension in that it asks the student to do several things simultaneously. On one level the student must understand what he is reading; at the same time, on a higher level he is asked to evaluate what he reads against his own background of knowledge. He might try to discern whether what he reads is logically consistent with earlier parts or whether these concepts agree with some other philosophy. He may read a newspaper article and weigh the happenings against his knowledge of propaganda techniques. Critical reading usually implies the use of some preestablished standards, or criteria, and the ability to read at several levels simultaneously; or, at least, the mental ability to evaluate what he has just read.

CONCRETE TO ABSTRACT CONTINUUM

A simple and useful definition of reading comprehension divides the process into two parts: objective and subjective. Objective comprehension is the understanding of directly stated facts, numbers, names, and so on. Subjective comprehension is the understanding of such things as tone, mood, inference, evaluation. The objective-subjective differentiation is more a continuum than a dichotomy. Matters of fact shade almost imperceptibly into matters of inference, opinion, and evaluation. It is difficult to draw a sharp line between the two. It is also difficult to make a smooth continuum. Nevertheless, the concept of such a continuum can be a valuable aid to the reading teacher.

VARIATION OF WORD ABSTRACTNESS Sometimes the variation along the concrete to abstract continuum can be made by changing a single word in the sentence. Figure 8-7 outlines a continuum beginning with a very simple concept that even a child can understand, "The man is *tall*." The use of the action word *running* is also easy to comprehend. When the term "happy" is inserted the interpretation begins to be subjective. The man may show that he is happy by smiling, but, still, the state of happiness is at least a level of abstraction somewhat more subjective than the concept "tall" or "running."

1. The man is tall.
2. The man is running.
3. The man is happy.
4. The man is thinking.
5. The man is perverse.

FIGURE 8-7 Concrete to abstract continuum changing one word.

On the next level we see that the man is "thinking," which often would have no observable action. Older children could probably understand this fairly easily, but not the youngest. Finally we come to the term "perverse" which has rather a difficult meaning. The word is probably not in the vocabulary of most elementary children. Hence we see that by changing only one word in a sentence we can change its degree of abstractness. This is an excellent illustration of the importance of vocabulary in reading.

CONCEPT DIFFICULTY Difficulty in degree of abstractness can increase by the very nature of the concept. Figure 8-8 illustrates growth in this type of abstraction.

The first sentence, a straightforward concept of possession, is not difficult to grasp. The next sentence, "They are good to eat," brings in the slightly higher but still elementary level of their value to people; this function might be considered a higher level of abstraction than being or possessing.

1. I have two beans.
2. They are good to eat.
3. They are lima beans.
4. They contain some protein.
5. Bean growing affects the economy.
6. Beans are an enigma.

FIGURE 8-8 Concrete to abstract continuum changing conceptual difficulty.

The statement, "They are lima beans," classifies them according to type. This sentence infers that the reader is familiar with more than one type of bean. He may know string beans, navy beans, or jelly beans, and the classification "lima" serves as a distinguishing characteristic. The next sentence, "They contain some protein," is a qualified statement of analysis. The knowledge of the existence of protein and perhaps of its importance presupposes a higher level of knowledge or degree of abstract conceptualization than earlier statements of existence, function, or classification. In the next sentence, "Bean growing affects the economy," a much higher degree of knowledge on the part of the reader is presumed. The relationship between a basic foodstuff and the economy of a community or nation is again a reasonably advanced type of thinking which implies that our simple subject of beans affects such things as the kind of houses some people live in, corner groceries, and wholesale markets.

Probably at the extreme end of the abstractness continuum are the ambiguous statements that are used more often by poets and artists than by prose writers. Depending upon its setting, "Beans are an enigma," may have connotations that are so mystical, inferential, or far-reaching as to defy clear interpretation.

GRAMMATICAL ABSTRACTNESS CONTINUUM Readability formulas, as we shall see in a later chapter, use as one of their main inputs the length of sentences in determining difficulty of reading material – the longer the sentence, the harder the reading material.

Grammatical complexity also increases reading difficulty. Some studies of the numbers of such grammatical convolutions as prepositional phrases, and conditional clauses show a direct relationship between numbers of prepositional phrases and sentence length. The more phrases and clauses, the harder it is to comprehend the sentence.

There are some promising developments in the field of modern grammar which lead to the expectation of innovations in reading comprehension. Both linguists and psychologists have turned their attention to such problems as the traditional grammar breakdown of words into nouns, verbs, articles, and so on, and of sentences into clauses and phrases. They have freed themselves from traditional patterns of thinking in grammar and are beginning to adopt new terminologies. They have also devised new analytical tools in the form of mathematics techniques and digital computers. It appears that in the future we will know a good deal more than we do now about the structure of our language. Ultimately this should lead to real insights into reading comprehension.

In Figure 8-9 we see a few of the ways in which grammar can modify a simple statement. Beginning with the straightforward statement, "I like you," we see some of the forms commonly used in English to interpose conditions of abstractness of relationship on the fundamental statement.

I like you.
I should like you.
I may like you.
I like you but . . .
If I like you, will you . . .
Liking you could be interesting.
To like you is similar to . . .
I might have liked you if . . .

FIGURE 8-9 Varying complexity by changing grammatical conditions.

BLOOM'S TAXONOMY OF EDUCATIONAL OBJECTIVES APPLIED TO READING COMPREHENSION A committee of educational psychologists headed by Benjamin Bloom and David Krathwohl have prepared a list of objectives or goals that might be used in achievement testing. Many of their achievement goals can be applied directly to reading comprehension. While this taxonomy follows in general a concrete-to-abstract continuum, it has the advantage of listing a number of specific and useful skills.

The taxonomy consists of six major divisions, the first of which is "knowledge." Basically, knowledge covers objective comprehension. When applied to reading comprehension, this would mean that the student is able to gather from the printed page such things as specific facts, terminology, and ways and means of dealing with these specific facts or terms. On a slightly higher level, but still within the framework of knowledge, the reader would be able to extract facts about such things as trends, criteria, and theories if these were specifically stated.

The next level of the taxonomy is "comprehension." Since in this chapter our interest is in applying the taxonomy to the problem of reading, this implies that the reader is able to translate the ideas, as stated in the material he is reading, into his own words or into some other words which have equivalent meaning. He might write his own translation or merely pick out one of three paragraphs and present it as the best translation of the original passage. Higher skills in the comprehension section are interpretation and extrapolation of the material. In other words, the student perceives the written material clearly enough so that he is able to make a logical extension ("it would follow that—").

The next section of the taxonomy refers to "application." Here such comprehension skills as following directions and solving written problems are classified. Many teachers of arithmetic or wood shop or sewing have wished that their students could follow written directions they receive. It is one thing to give a verbal report on what words mean, but quite another to translate written material into action.

"Analysis" is the next level of classification. In reading comprehension this refers to the student's ability to identify the various elements that were contained in a paragraph or a passage. It also refers to the student's ability to see relationships between the various elements he has isolated. Finally, it might refer to the student's ability to reduce an organizational principle inherent in the writing.

The fourth taxonomical category is "synthesis." Originally, in achievement testing, this referred to the production of an original plan or a set of abstract relationships. This category does not pertain directly to the topic of comprehension, and we shall, therefore, consider a higher-level extension of some previously mentioned skills such as seeing relationships and organization principles or extending a trend found in the written material (extrapolation).

The highest category in the classification is "evaluation." This category has definite implications for reading and would probably have implications for what is known as "critical reading." Here the taxonomy urges the use of judgment in terms of internal evidence and external criteria. Judging on the basis of internal evidence would be one of logical consistency and cohesiveness. The student might be able to answer such questions as "Would the character really have done that?" or "Does this story hang together?" The evaluation in terms

1.00 Knowledge
  1.10 Knowledge of specifics
  1.11 Knowledge of terminology
  1.12 Knowledge of specific facts
  1.20 Knowledge of ways and means of dealing with specifics
  1.21 Knowledge of conventions
  1.22 Knowledge of trends and sequences
  1.23 Knowledge of classifications and categories
  1.24 Knowledge of criteria
  1.25 Knowledge of methodology
  1.30 Knowledge of the universals and abstractions in the field
  1.31 Knowledge of principles and generalizations
  1.32 Knowledge of theories and structures

INTELLECTUAL ABILITIES AND SKILLS

2.00 Comprehension
  2.10 Translation
  2.20 Interpretation
  2.30 Extrapolation
3.00 Application
4.00 Analysis
  4.10 Analysis of elements
  4.20 Analysis of relationships
  4.30 Analysis of organizational principles
5.00 Synthesis
  5.10 Production of a unique communication
  5.20 Production of a plan or proposed set of operations
  5.30 Derivation of a set of abstract relations
6.00 Evaluation
  6.10 Judgment in terms of internal evidence
  6.20 Judgment in terms of external criteria

Source: B. S. Bloom and D. R. Krathwohl, *Taxonomy of Educational Objectives*, Longmans, Green & Co., Inc., New York, 1956.

FIGURE 8-10 Outline of the taxonomy of educational objectives: cognitive domain.

of external criteria may bring in the ideas discussed under cultural context and implied standards. It would also draw on the breadth of the student's knowledge in all fields.

A more detailed discussion of the taxonomy and its application to reading comprehension can be found in the appendix to this chapter.

COMPREHENSION SUBDIVISIONS IN READING TESTS

Even though Bloom's taxonomy was designed specifically for achievement test-makers, none of them seems to have followed it in measuring reading comprehension. The maker of each different standardized reading comprehension test seems to follow his own plan. While there is some overlap, there is no consistent agreement as on which skills make up "reading comprehension." Some test-makers include vocabulary or word knowledge as part of comprehension; others consider reading comprehension a separate skill.

One of the most detailed organizational patterns for a reading test is found in the California Reading Test (see Figure 8-11). It has two major subdivisions: reading comprehension and reading vocabulary. Reading vocabulary is measured in four fields: mathematics, science, social science, and general. The reading comprehension area is broken down into three sections: following directions, reference skills, and interpretation of material. The "interpretation of material" section is closely related to what other test-makers have called "paragraph comprehension." Each of the reading comprehension sections can be broken down further (see organizational chart, Figure 8-11). In the "interpretation of material" section, the largest number of items pertain to directly stated facts and inferences. Statistically, it is a questionable procedure to show the large number of subdivisions because sometimes only one item may be given to a particular subskill, as indicated in Figure 8-11. However, this figure does give some idea as to the type of thinking that the test authors had in developing a reading comprehension test.

Other test authors tend to use the following rough grammatical breakdown:

1. Word knowledge (vocabulary), usually consisting of multiple-choice items and sometimes involving antonyms or synonyms
2. Sentence meaning
3. Paragraph meaning or paragraph comprehension
(Sometimes several paragraphs or a short passage)

Some investigators have found that a child who scores well on one of these tests usually does well on others. This undoubtedly means that different tests tend to measure the same skill. If so, this indicates one fallacy inherent in the models for comprehension, namely, they may appear in a conceptualized system as representing different skills but, when various tests that purport to measure these skills are actually administered to children, there is sometimes such a high overlap among skills that there is no point in testing them separately.

The measurement of reading comprehension under timed conditions is another influencing factor. Most reading tests discussed here might be classed as "power tests." This means that the student is allowed as much time to use the test as he really needs, e.g., the test is not highly speeded or timed. However, there are a few tests that may measure comprehension under timed conditions. Speed-of-reading tests usually allow only one reading of a passage which is timed; the comprehension section is then a power test.

The California Reading Test has four subdivisions under the vocabulary

Following Directions
Simple choice (4)[a]
Definitions and directions (8)
Mathematics directions (2)
Map directions (1)
Reference Skills
Parts of book or newspaper (3)
Use of dictionary (1)
Use of Index (3)
Table of contents (3)
Reading a graph (4)
Library classifications (2)
Selecting references (4)
Reading a map (5)
Interpretation of Material
Directly stated facts (16)
Inferences (20)
Topic or central idea (1)
Organization of topics (4)
Sequence of events (4)

[a]Number within parentheses indicates the number of items in each category.

FIGURE 8-11 Outline of the reading comprehension section of the California Reading Test.

section: mathematics, science, social sciences, and general. Other reading tests might have different types of paragraphs or reading passages which would roughly follow the same four subject-matter categories.

Another type of comprehension test frequently included in a reading battery (especially for primary children) is a test of auditory comprehension. While this is not a true measure of *reading* comprehension, it is closely related, the object being to find out how much the child understands by listening.

Most reading tests require that the student read a passage and then answer questions which reveal his actual comprehension of the content. A quite different type of procedure is followed in the "cloze" technique. This is a measure of language ability which is highly correlated with reading comprehension, in which the student reads a passage of some 250 words from which every fifth word has been deleted. The student tries to fill in or select from a multiple-choice list the word that fits in every fifth blank. The cloze procedure may be used in varying frequencies of omissions (sometimes it may be every tenth word or every verb). This technique is presently being used mostly in reading research but is finding its way into the more widely used classroom reading comprehension tests. A somewhat similar earlier technique was used with the Minnesota Speed of Reading Test in which the student was asked to strike out absurd words as he read.

OTHER COMPREHENSION MODELS

I have tried to avoid giving an exhaustive discussion of the many models which can be applied to the reading process. The English language is a much-studied and much-analyzed phenomenon. Likewise, human thinking and human learning have been subjected to a great deal of research and theorization. It is quite probable that many of the leading learning theories found in psychology texts could be applied to the comprehension process. The same is true of many of the linguistics analyses. And, when the two areas come together to form the field of psycholinguistics, the process of reading comprehension assumes special relevance.

One interesting attack on the comprehension problem has been made by Jack Holmes and Harry Singer who have been working on a Substrata Factor Theory.* By using a number of reading and related language arts tests, plus a statistical factor-analysis technique, they have developed a rather elaborate structure of what they feel contributes to Power of Reading. Without going into the numerous details, their broad outlines find that the main contributing factors are "word recognition, word meaning, and reasoning-in-context."

Dr. George Spache has also developed a theoretical model of reading behaviors related to comprehension. He has patterned his model partially after the work of J. P. Guilford and it has five main categories: Cognition, Memory, Divergent Production, Convergent Production, and Evaluation.† Each of these main categories is seen in its relationship to another set of categories, such as Units (word), Class (sentence), Relations (paragraph), Systems (structure), Transformations, and Implications.

CONCLUSION

The difficulty of understanding the process by which children gain reading comprehension is undoubtedly due to the complexity of the process itself. We have viewed it from several different aspects, each one of which affords some new insights and perhaps a partial answer to the truth we seek. In an effort to increase our understanding, several models and systems were examined to learn whether, singly or together, they could help to provide an answer to the innocent question, "What is reading comprehension?"

*For further information see Harry Singer, "Substrata—Factor Theory of Reading: Theoretical Design for Teaching Reading," in *Challenge and Experiment in Reading,* International Reading Association, Conference Proceedings, vol. 7, 1962; and Jack Holmes, "Factors Underlying Major Reading Disabilities at the College Level," *Genetic Psychology Monographs,* vol. 49, 1954.

†For further information see George D. Spache, *Toward Better Reading,* Garrard Publishing Co., Champaign, Ill., 1963.

APPENDIX 8-A READING COMPREHENSION SUGGESTIONS*

1.00 KNOWLEDGE

Knowledge involves the recall of specifics, universals, methods, processes, patterns, structures, and settings. The recall involves little more than remembering the appropriate materials. Relating and judging is used too insofar as the student has to answer questions which are in a little different form in a test situation than in the learning situation.

1.10 Knowledge of Specifics

(The recall of specific bits of information with the emphasis on symbols with concrete referents.)

1.11 Knowledge of Terminology

Knowledge of definitions. Either the generally accepted definition, the different words usable for one definition, or the knowledge of the meaning most appropriate for a word.

Example:

Underline the correct definition:

Pact: a. bundle b. agreement c. group

1.12 Knowledge of Specific Facts

(Knowledge of dates, events, persons, places, etc. This may be very exact information such as naming an exact person or date. It also includes approximate or relative information such as an approximate date.)

Example: (Refer to B)†

The diameter of Clavius is ________ miles.

1.20 Knowledge of Ways and Means of Dealing with Specifics

(Knowledge of the methods of organizing, chronological sequence, and the principles for judging and criticizing.)

1.21 Knowledge of Conventions

(Knowledge of the characteristic ways of treating and presenting ideas and phenomena. For purposes of communication, people agree on the meaning given to different symbols.)

Example: (Refer to B)

The dark areas on the surface of the moon are called seas or ________.

1.22 Knowledge of Trends and Sequences

(Understanding the relationship of events to time.)

Example:

Number these events in correct sequel.

________ Spain transferred Louisiana back to France.
________ Napoleon sold Louisiana for $15,000,000.
________ Louisiana was explored and claimed by France.
________ Louisiana was ceded to Spain.

*Based on the *Taxonomy of Educational Objectives* by B. S. Bloom and D. R. Krothwohl, Longmans, Green & Co., New York, 1956.

†"Refer to B" or "Refer to A," etc., means see the indicated paragraph on page 158 or 159.

1.23 Knowledge of Classification and Categories
(Knowledge of fundamental classes or divisions of a topic.)
Example: (Refer to B)
The moon's volcanic craters, mountains, and dark areas are
________ called seas.
its most noticeable features
________ range from twenty to fifty miles.

1.24 Knowledge of Criteria
(Knowledge of the standards by which facts or opinions are judged.)
Example:
The best way to discover the speed limit in a school zone is
________ to ask a pedestrian.
________ check the traffic code.
________ watch the other cars.

1.25 Knowledge of Methodology
(Knowledge of the different procedures used in solving particular problems.)
Example:
Salk Vaccine was proved effective by
________ studying effects of polio in the victim.
________ experimentation with the germ.
________ comparing the percent of those who were injected with the vaccine and contracted the disease with the percent of those who did not take the vaccine.

1.30 Knowledge of the Universals and Abstractions in a Field.
(Knowledge of the main ideas and abstract ideas in a selection.)

1.31 Knowledge of Principles and Generalizations.
(Knowledge of summarizing information and connecting the correct principle with a situation.)
Example: (Refer to A)
1. Give the main idea of paragraph A.
2. The heat reaching the moon from the sun is absorbed at the surface because
   ________ the moon has little or no atmosphere.
   ________ a part of the moon is exposed to the sun for a period of two weeks.
   ________ only a small amount is reflected back into space.

1.32 Knowledge of Theories and Structures
(Knowledge of a group of principles forming one theory.)
Example:
The craters on the moon were probably caused by
________ tidal action when the moon was in a molten state.
________ explosions.
________ impacts of meteorites.

2.00 COMPREHENSION
(Knowing what is being communicated and being able to make use of the idea.)

2.10 Translation
(Changing the idea from one form of communication to another form and keeping the same meaning. This is understanding each part of a selection.)

Example: (Refer to E)
"Shoulder high" as used here means
________ he was carried on shoulders.
________ he was as high as a man's shoulders.
________ he had broad shoulders.

2.20 Interpretation
(The explanation or summarization of a communication. Whereas translation involves an objective part-for-part knowledge, interpretation involves a reordering, rearrangement, or a new view of the material. The ability to interpret various types of social data.)
Example: (Refer to D)
What idea is the writer trying to get across?
________ Russia has a better educational system than America.
________ America should step up her space progress.
________ The American educational system needs improving.

2.30 Extrapolation
(Determining implications, effects, consequences, and conclusions from the facts given in a statement.)
Example: (Refer to A)
Since there is little or no atmosphere, could there be human life on the moon? Explain your answer.

3.00 APPLICATION
(Using the knowledge one has in a particular situation. This involves following directions, generalized methods, and technical principles.)
Example:

1. Only words of more than one syllable can be divided. Underline the words below that can be divided.
   COME NED PRETTY BOOK PAPER
2. Any number can play. The first player holds the sticks upright, opens his hand, and lets them fall. He then tries to pick them up one by one without moving any others. If a stick moves he loses his turn. The black stick can be picked up only after picking up a yellow, red, blue, and green in that order. The black may then be used to lift other sticks.
   Answer Yes or No.
   ________ May a player pick up the black stick after picking up a red, yellow, blue, then green?
   ________ Is the black the only stick that is able to be used to help pick up other sticks?
   ________ Does the player lose his turn if he would move a red stick while trying to pick up the black one?
3. Sift together two cups of flour, a teaspoon of baking powder, and one-fourth of a teaspoon of salt. Cream one-half cup of shortening, one cup of sugar, two eggs, and three-fourths of a cup of milk. Add flour mixture and blend well with one teaspoon of vanilla. Pour into a 9 by 9 inch cake pan. Bake in a preheated oven at 235 degrees for forty-five minutes.
   Answer Yes or No.
   ________ Would the sugar be sifted?

________ Should you add the vanilla at the same time you add the milk?
________ Do you turn the oven on at the same time you put the cake in the oven?

4. From the barber shop you went down Perry Street for three blocks and turned right at the post office. At the first light two blocks down you took a left on Maple. After one block on Maple you saw a drug store and turned right. Going one block you came to the school and turned right on West Main. You took a right after traveling four blocks on West Main and went straight for three blocks. Where did you stop?
   Barber shop   Drug store   School   Post office

4.00 ANALYSIS
(The breakdown of the material into its different parts and recognizing the relationships of the different parts to each other and the underlying organization.)

4.10 Analysis of Elements
(Identification of ideas in a passage that are assumed but not stated.)
Example:
At a minimum there are about 1 billion suns in our galaxy with planets. Each of these can be expected to have at least two planets of the type of Earth and Mars. It is possible that
________ only Earth and Mars have life existing there.
________ only Earth has life.
________ many planets have life possibly in some form.

4.20 Analysis of Relationships
(Understanding the connections that different ideas in a selection have to each other.)
Example: (Refer to C)
President Jefferson sent James Monroe and Robert Livingston to purchase West Florida and New Orleans because
________ France now owned the territory.
________ free use of the Mississippi River was important to Americans.
________ Napoleon was trying to revive the French empire in North America.

4.30 Analysis of Organizational Principles
(Recognizing the organization of the selection as well as the purpose for which it has been written and the mood and attitude of the writer.)
Example: (Refer to D)
1. Which propaganda tricks have been used?
   Bad names   Glad names   Transfer   Testimonial
2. What is the mood of this stanza?
   Proud   Lonely   Defeated

5.00 SYNTHESIS
(Putting together information from many different sources and producing something original and concrete. Skill in taking facts and seeing their relationship.)

5.10 Production of a Unique Communication
(Getting ideas, feelings, and experiences across to others taking into con-

sideration the kinds of effects to be achieved, the kind of audience, and the medium to be used.)

1. Which would be a catchy title?
   ________ Features of the Man in the Moon
   ________ Surface Features of the Moon
   ________ What You See on the Moon
2. Make up a last line for this poem:
   There was a little boy
   Who lived all alone
   Wishing he could have one toy

   ____

5.20 Production of a Plan or Proposed Set of Operation
(Planning something while taking into consideration certain requirements.)
Example: (Refer to B)

1. Check the best outline.
   I. Surface features
   II. Craters
   III. Mountain chains
   I. Surface features
   II. Clavius
   III. Appenines
   I. Volcanic craters
   II. Mountains
   III. Dark areas
2. After reading paragraph D choose what you think would be the best solution.
   ________ Improve the math departments.
   ________ Stop all "life adjustment" courses.
   ________ Put good educators in administrative positions.

5.30 Derivation of a Set of Abstract Relations
(Producing a set of abstract relations from either concrete data or abstract symbols.)
Example:

1. The following is the average height and weight of boys and girls in three sixth-grade classrooms. Study them and check the best conclusion.

Girls		Boys	
Height	Weight	Height	Weight
5′ 0″	98 lbs.	4′ 5″	90 lbs.
5′ 1″	102 lbs.	4′ 8″	97 lbs.
5′ 3″	110 lbs.	5′ 0″	100 lbs.

   ________ All sixth-grade girls are taller and weigh more than all sixth-grade boys.
   ________ A few sixth-grade girls are taller and weigh more than sixth-grade boys.
   ________ The average weight and height of sixth-grade girls is more than sixth-grade boys.

6.00 EVALUATION

(Critical reading of material. Quantitative and qualitative judgments about the extent to which material and methods satisfy criteria. This may involve use of standards either determined by the individual or given to him.)

6.10 Judgments in Terms of Internal Evidence

(Judging the accuracy of a selection by taking into consideration consistency, exactness of statement, and documentation given in the selection.)

Example: (Refer to D)

Does this paragraph give good arguments for a change in our educational system?

________ Yes ________ No

Check possible reasons for your answer.

________ Russia is leading us in progress in space.
________ People in the education field have not had good training.
________ There are not any definite facts given.
________ Money is spent on unnecessary things.
________ The paragraph appeals to feeling more than to reason.

6.20 Judgment in Terms of External Criteria

(Judging the accuracy of a selection by taking into consideration standards by which such things are judged.)

Example: (Refer to D)

1. This paragraph fits the definition of propaganda because
   ________ it is an attempt to influence the thoughts of others.
   ________ it is criticizing our educational system.
   ________ it states that Russia is leading the progress in space.
2. According to our Christian culture, which is the best motto for a doctor?
   ________ An apple a day keeps the doctor away.
   ________ Dead men tell no tales.
   ________ Life is precious; preserve it at all costs.

Note: The following paragraphs are used as examples in some of the preceeding questions.

A

Since the moon has little or no atmosphere, most of the heat reaching it from the sun would be absorbed at the surface and but a small amount reflected back into space. The portion of the moon's surface exposed to the sun's rays continuously for a period of two weeks and then divested of sunlight for an equal period must experience great extremes in temperature. Recent measurements of the heat which the moon radiates to the earth have revealed for the sunlight side a temperature near absolute zero, or −460°F. in round numbers.

B

The most conspicuous surface features of the moon are its volcanic craters, mountains, and dark areas called maria or seas. The craters of most of the volcanoes are more or less round. Some are immense—for example, Clavius, 142 miles in diameter—but many range from twenty to fifty miles. The mountain chains are, with the exception of the appenines, very short and irregular but reach to great heights.

C

West of the Mississippi lay the vast area of Louisiana. First explored and claimed by France, Louisiana had been ceded to Spain in 1763. In 1800, Spain transferred it back to France, and Napoleon sought to use it to revive the once-great French empire in North America. To the increasing number of American settlers in the region beyond the Appalachian Mountains, the right to unrestricted navigation of the Mississippi River had become a problem of life or death. Spain had for several years agreed to permit free use of the Mississippi River by Americans. The ceding of Louisiana to France caused fears on the part of the United States. President Jefferson sent James Monroe and Robert Livingston to Paris, with instructions to purchase West Florida and New Orleans. Congress appropriated $2,000,000 for this purpose.

D

The lead the Russians have over us in the Sputnik race can be laid at the door of so-called progressive education in American schools. For years self-appointed experts and "soft" educators have been undermining our schools. Our curriculum has been watered down by substituting "life adjustment" courses and trivialities for intellectual discipline. Money has been wasted on costly fads and frills instead of the three R's. Instead of being taught to study, our ablest pupils have had their brains put to sleep by assembly-line methods that level them to the lowest common denominator.

E

The day you won your town the race
We chaired you through the market place;
Man and boy stood cheering by,
And home we brought you shoulder-high.

(A. E. Housman)

9

COMPREHENSION – TASK ANALYSIS

INTRODUCTION

Chapter 8 dealt with some of the complexities of understanding what is read. Comprehension might be the most important part of the reading act, but it is only one part of the act. This chapter proposes a task analysis of the factors involved in teaching reading.

A task analysis is an extremely detailed procedure and is intended to give some insights into the complex job of teaching reading. This chapter is not easy to read and may be omitted by those teachers who simply want a little practical assistance in helping their students learn how to read.

Far more questions may be raised than will be answered. The most significant question, possibly, will be: "Why is it so difficult to teach reading?" and we shall try very hard to find a satisfactory answer. It might also help to explain why research done in one area is not applicable in another area. The problem of nontransferability of research results is an inevitable outcome when research is undertaken in a field so complex that it is practically impossible to control all variables involved.

Many of the variables are interdependent. Take just a few, such as readability, rate, and response; it is quite obvious that if we hold the readability constant and change the response from reading aloud to reading silently, we should get a much faster reading rate. If, however, at the same time that we change the response we also shift the readability level, we might bring the rate back down to where it was while reading aloud. Hence, reading research assumes that all interdependent variables are held constant while only one is varied. (In advanced statistical procedures, it is possible to vary more than one dependent variable and hold the others constant by mathematical manipulation; but, even so, the philosophy of holding all variables constant except one remains.)

Since I am interested in practicing what I preach about individual differences, I suggest that advanced or serious students of reading read this task analysis fairly carefully for the insights it will yield and the research it suggests. Intermediate students might wish simply to skim the task analysis and read the sections which are of particular interest.

Research has been done on many parts of the task analysis and much more will surely be done in the near future. It is not the purpose here to cite all the relevant research but rather to make the student aware of the general problem and to familiarize him with some research studies that bear importantly on the reading act.

Since we are dealing with a new approach to the reading act, this chapter is being written in a new style or at least one that is somewhat different from that of preceding chapters. A task analysis is often reported first in outline form so that the structure of its major points and supplementary parts may be seen in broad perspective. Therefore, a section of the outline will be presented and then discussed. This method of discussion, or "glossing," is an interesting presentation technique that teachers find helpful in teaching reading comprehension and many other subjects. If teachers were to present the entire task analysis outline in one section, students would find it both formidable and boring. My purpose here is to breathe a bit of interest and insight into what might be otherwise just a lifeless skeleton of listed details.

TASK ANALYSIS

A. Sensory input

1. Visual
   a. Opaque
   b. Projected
2. Tactual
3. Kinesthetic

It seems logical to start on a task analysis with a discussion of the sensory input. One of the obvious facts about the reading act is that some sensory input must be received by the reader. In reading, this input is received usually through the visual sense, since almost by definition reading requires use of the eyes; however, there are exceptions, notably the reading done by blind persons, who use their tactual sense. Occasionally in a remedial reading or special reading situation, the tactual sense (sense of touch) is used by having students feel raised letters or trace words in sand.

One rather famous method, developed by Fernald, emphasizes the kinesthetic sense in which sensory input is carried to the brain by the movement or position of the muscles. Fernald's method is really a multisensory approach in which the child traces letters with his finger so that tactual, visual, and kinesthetic senses are usually employed simultaneously.

Some of the problems in the reading act that would fall under the sensory input category relate to the validity of visual perception training. Research reports certainly are not clear on the value of this type of training, but neither do they state clearly that it should be disregarded. A number of reading teachers have used tachistoscopes and some of the reading-readiness activities involve so-called perceptual training.

Another type of problem that might be included in this area is the question of whether there is any difference in reading comprehension or reading efficiency if the material is presented by an opaque or projected image. An ordinary printed page is an opaque image, and a page or word projected on a screen is an illuminated projected image. Research is needed to determine whether there is a different stimulus value in terms of reading comprehension. Some comparison studies have used colored ink or paper.

B. Mediating activity

1. Vocalization
2. Subvocalization
3. Thinking about
4. Phonics
5. Word-part recognition

Between the time when the reader sees the reading material and makes a response, some type of mediating activity usually occurs. This activity may be overt or covert, that is, it may be an activity which can be seen or heard by someone else or it may go on solely within the reader's mind. Vocalization, for example, is quite obviously an overt task: the student, while reading for himself, will say the words so that someone sitting near him can hear him say them. This is generally not advisable for silent reading, but it often occurs with poor or beginning readers. Subvocalization cannot be observed or heard by someone else; the reader says the words to himself so that he may "read" or comprehend. Some research has shown that during most so-called silent reading there are very minute muscle movements in the tongue or vocal chords. Other observations show that some reading comprehension can occur with virtually no subvocalization.

Elementary children are often told to think about the material, both in oral and in silent reading. It is difficult to give the proper intonation of the sentence if the student does not understand it and does not think about what it means. This point touches on a problem of major concern to teachers and researchers, i.e., the nature of internal processes involved in reading. Undoubtedly, the reader is testing what he is perceiving against a mass of background information. For example, when he perceives the word *dog* it calls up some memory of a dog or a concept of a dog in his mind. Exactly what goes on in the brain during the reading act is not known; but physiologists are beginning to pinpoint with some precision various areas of the brain, and it is hoped that some insights will be forthcoming as they are able to map out in greater detail the brain areas which deal with speech, memory for colors, arousal of emotional feelings, visual imagery, word knowledge, and others.

Very poor readers may need phonics to help them unlock certain words. If a student looks at a word, has to think of how the letters sound, translates this into a word which he knows by listening, and then acts upon the word or fits it into his comprehension scheme, all of this is mediating activity. Instead of using phonics in the initial step, many students use word parts for difficult words. They may know the parts of a word separately and be able to put them together, or they may know one part and be able to guess the others using context cues.

It is probably quite safe to say that at all levels of reading, from beginning to the most advanced, a good deal of mediating activity takes place, although the type of mediating activity probably changes as the reader matures.

C. Response

1. Observable behavior
   a. Read aloud
   b. Perform act
   c. Answer questions in writing
   d. Answer questions orally
   e. Emotional response (cry, laugh)
   f. General attitude or behavioral change
2. Content of response
   a. Repeat verbatim
   b. Paraphrase
   c. Criticism (see Bloom's Taxonomy, Chapter 7)
3. Delay of response
   a. Immediate
   b. After varying delay

The response is generally what might be called "doing something." It is the type of behavior that can be observed by someone else. This is in contrast to mediating activity discussed above, which can be internalized and is not directly observable by another person. Perhaps one of the most common observations of reading behavior in the elementary school is reading aloud. However, there are numerous other ways of responding to written material; the reader may perform an act or answer questions either in writing or orally.

Another type of very meaningful response is an emotional response which is observed in such reader reactions as laughing, crying, or exhibiting other evidence of feeling. Somewhat less direct, although perhaps of greater importance, is a general change in attitude or behavior which persists over a longer period of time.

The form of response may display considerable variability. In Bloom's Taxonomy as applied to the reading act (see Chapter 7), it was seen that responses to reading can vary all the way from giving simple facts or practical applications to critical analysis.

The response to reading need not always occur during the reading act or immediately following it. The delay of response may be extended for as long as a lifetime. The most usual measure of comprehension is to have a student make responses to questions immediately after the reading; but frequently, as in tests of various subject-matter courses, he may be expected to respond some hours or months after he has read the chapter. Delay of response brings in the factor of memory and other factors of learning.

D. Reward and/or motivation

1. Primary
2. Secondary
3. Knowledge of results
4. Subjective
5. Punishment
6. None (incidental)
7. Set

Some psychologists state that people do not do anything without expectation of a reward, whether the reward be money, food, or a feeling of pleasure. In any event, nearly every act has some kind of consequence. The kind of consequence that the act produces helps to determine whether the act will be continued or repeated and, if repeated, whether it will be modified.

The topic of reward is almost indistinguishable from the topic of motivation. Why does a person do something? He does it because he will be rewarded or because if he does not do it he will be punished, and the absence of punishment is, in itself, a type of reward.

Knowledge of results is a type of reward. Knowing that we have done something correctly tends to encourage us, to make us feel good. If we find out that we did not do something correctly, we know that we must modify our behavior in order to be rewarded in the future.

Psychologists have broken rewards down into two categories: primary and secondary. Primary rewards are those which satisfy body needs directly. For example, a person without air is rewarded by being given air; a person without water is rewarded by being given water, and so on. Secondary rewards are those which lead to primary rewards. For example, money is a good secondary reward because it can be used to buy food or warmth or satisfy various other primary needs.

Man has in common with animals a variety of primary needs, such as food and warmth; but he is distinguished from animals by his more elaborate and often highly subjective needs. Although ego satisfaction, which drives some men so far in life, or curiosity about the stars, which motivates others, is difficult to equate with the primary need structure, they nevertheless have real motivating power. These subjective needs can cause students to want to learn how to read and can motivate them to read book after book.

Punishment should also be classed with rewards because it does act as a motivating force. It is sometimes called a "negative reward." Whereas corporal punishment has all but vanished from our schools, its subtler forms (teacher's scorn or extra work assignments) are still factors in many learning situations.

There are times when students learn for no apparent reason. This is called incidental learning. It can sometimes be accounted for if we simply say that a person is naturally curious and wants to learn just because there is something to be learned. Another variable is the student's "learning set," in which case the learning is greatly enhanced when the student intends to learn. Any teacher can testify to the importance to the student of wanting to learn how to read.

Motivation, it is seen, is closely interrelated to many other factors. If a student is highly motivated, he can read material on a high difficulty level, can learn with less practice, or can learn faster. Most of the variables in the task analysis are highly interdependent.

E. Knowledge of results

1. Type
   a. Simple (right or wrong)
   b. Correct response (shown if wrong)
   c. Explanation given
2. Method of presentation
   a. Teacher
   b. Answer key
3. Teaching machine
4. Life situation

We have already mentioned that "knowledge of results" is one of the important factors affecting the reward. Since it is also an important part of the teaching situation, and is usually controlled by the teacher, it should be given attention again at this point. The simplest type of knowledge of results in the teaching situation can be illustrated by the teacher who says, "That's wrong." A slightly better teaching situation might occur when the teacher says, "The word was *cog* not *dog*." A superior situation would occur when the teacher says, "The word was *cog*—don't you notice that the beginning letter is *c* not *d*?" Hence these three examples show the three main types of knowledge of results: (1) simple (right or wrong); (2) correct response; and (3) explanation given.

In addition to the teacher, such reading materials as games, workbooks, and teaching machines can also give all three types of knowledge of results. While the teacher's explanation might appear on the surface to be the best type of knowledge of results, it is probable that it is the best type only in certain situations.

It is the most difficult and time-consuming to give, and from the standpoint of economy, the teacher or reading material might not always be able to do this. Sometimes the simple type of knowledge of results can be so quickly and easily administered that it is administered with a high degree of frequency and is equally effective. In any event, teachers and learning psychologists concur that knowledge of results is extremely important for learning.

The method by which the knowledge of results is presented may affect the reader's comprehension. He may consider the knowledge of results more important if the teacher tells it to him. Many workbooks and other training materials such as reading laboratories have answer keys for the student to check answers following various comprehension drills. A newer learning technique, that of teaching machines and programmed instruction, places heavy emphasis on the immediate and complete giving of knowledge of results. Programmed learning would give the student knowledge of results immediately following each question or small segment of material.

Out of school, in real-life reading situations (as opposed to training situations), the reader frequently gets knowledge of results. If he is trying to follow a set of printed directions, his inability to assemble a machine might quickly tell him that his reading comprehension is lacking.

F. Reward variations

1. Amount
   a. Fixed amount per unit
   b. Variable amount per unit
2. Frequency
   a. Every unit
   b. Not every unit (partial; fixed ratio; variable ratio; fixed interval; variable interval)
3. Relation to response
   a. Indiscriminate (occurs whether response is right or wrong)
   b. Discriminating (only right answers rewarded)
   c. Shaping
4. Timing
   a. Immediate
   b. Delayed

This category is a rather technical one, but it has some interesting teaching applications. The first section deals simply with the question of whether a constant or variable amount influences the rate of learning. For example, some teachers might always say "That's good" if a student answers a question correctly or reads orally satisfactorily. At other times the teacher might go into brief periods of ecstasy about the superlative performance of a child. Some parents have the questionable practice of paying children for bringing home

"A's," and sometimes the amount of reward can vary considerably from the elementary school child who gets 25 cents for an "A" to the high school student who receives an automobile. There can be little doubt that the amount of reward has some effect on the student's performance.

The section on frequency uses many terms derived from B. F. Skinner's work with animal performance. However, it has some interesting implications for the teaching of humans. A *fixed* ratio would provide a student with a reward every time he answered a question or every fifth time he answered a question, while a *variable* ratio might mean that he would be rewarded *on the average* of every fifth question. Likewise, the variations in interval have to do with the time elapsed; for example, the teacher would tell the student he was doing good work every five minutes exactly or would reward him on the average of every five minutes. Incidentally, experiments with animals have shown that much more continuation of the activity will occur under a variable type reinforcement. Since this highly irregular spacing of intervals is the type of reinforcement which occurs in most classrooms, it is likely that this also tends to promote greater continuation of the performance after the rewarding has stopped.

Only a very poor teacher would use indiscriminate rewarding or tell a student he was doing well, regardless of the merit of his performance. However, some teachers who do not grade properly may be doing this.

An interesting notion related to this area is that of shaping or rewarding the student only as he comes closer and closer to the desired goal. In this situation, the teacher gives a reward for very simple and even for only partially accurate responses at the beginning of training; but as training progresses and the student matures, rewards are given only for increasingly better responses.

Most studies in psychology agree that the more immediate the reward after the act, the better the learning. Teachers should set up lessons which allow the student to know as quickly as possible after he has performed an act whether or not it was correct. This is one reason why tutoring is more effective than large-class teaching. Immediacy of knowledge of results is one of the strong points of programmed learning and teaching machines. Workbook and teaching materials which are self-correcting or can be corrected by the student in a group immediately after he has responded also take advantage of this principle.

G. Rate of reading

1. Student-controlled versus other control
2. Speed set
3. Relaxed
4. Study set
5. Skimming

The rate of reading is usually controlled by the student, but there are some special circumstances in which other controls can be applied; for example, a pacing device has a shutter which slowly covers the page, forcing the student to read at a certain rate. The rate of reading can also be greatly varied by the student's intention. If, for example, he has a speed set and tries to read as fast as he can, his reading speed will definitely be faster than when he is relaxed. The purpose of his reading will sometimes affect his rate of reading. Sometimes he will wish to study slowly enough so that he can remember every detail; at other times he will merely skim to glean the main ideas or to pick out certain kinds of information.

H. Practice and review

1. Practice or review
2. Planned practice or review
3. Only as needed
4. Amount learned or read before practice
5. Massed versus distributed

Let us look at the practice and review section from the standpoint of reading comprehension, even though all of these categories could be applied to practically every kind of reading lesson. In the first instance, different types of reading comprehension will ensue for the student who is allowed to reread the materials as he wishes. This review may be planned; for example, the teacher may say, "Be sure to read this page twice"; or the student may simply go back and read a paragraph he did not understand clearly.

The amount of material that a student reads before reviewing also can affect his comprehension. The student who reads an entire book before going back may have better comprehension than the student who rereads each page after he has read it once.

The topic of mass versus distributed practice has been studied by psychologists for some time. This refers to whether the training or reading is done all at once or at spaced intervals. A student who reads a topic for a half hour a day might comprehend more fully than the student who spends eight hours in one day reading the material.

I. Readability

1. Legibility
2. Word difficulty
3. Sentence difficulty
4. Style difficulty
5. Picture or graph cues

Readability and readability formulas are discussed in some detail in a later chapter. At this point, we will consider two aspects of most readability formulas – word difficulty and sentence difficulty.

One would expect such things as legibility and spacing to affect readability. Anyone who has tried to read an old book printed in very small type with little space between lines has probably been impressed with the difficulty and laboriousness of reading this type of material.

The writer's style also affects readability. Some authors express themselves in a crystal-clear fashion, while others, writing on the same subject, seem to do their best to confuse the issue. It is quite possible that part of the difficulty could be due to differences in the reader. The first writer may be able to communicate with a certain type of reader because he has amassed a similar background, vocabulary load, mode of expression, and other traits.

Beginning reading books frequently rely heavily on pictures to provide clues to the meaning of the reading material. Other books, particularly texts, use pictures and graphs for further elucidation of the ideas expounded in the text. The difficulty of the subject matter is also related to the readability of written material.

J. Reading content

1. Scientific
2. Social science
3. Artistic and poetic (literary)
4. Mechanical
5. Language style and variations
6. Mathematical
7. Philosophical

Some persons can read about political science with ease but have difficulty reading about biology.

This section is intended to enumerate some of the different types of reading materials which are interdependent variables in the task of teaching reading comprehensibly. These subject categories are particularly related to the student's individual experience, interest, and learning. No attempt is made here to give an exhaustive list of content areas. Melville Dewey and the Library of Congress have devised detailed systems for classifying reading matter.

K. Subject-matter organization

1. Chronologic (historical)
2. Unit (natural unit in subject matter)
3. Problem-centered
4. Descriptive
5. Sequential (steps 1, 2, 3, etc.)
6. Theoretical
7. Practical
8. Analytic (whole to part)
9. Synthetic (part to whole)

These categories are fairly self-explanatory. The thing to keep in mind here is that a change in the type of organization can affect comprehension, rate of reading, and the amount of practice needed. In short, each category is a dependent variable.

L. Supplementary presentations

1. Visual
   a. Pictures
   b. Graphic material
   c. Filmstrips
   d. Motion pictures
   e. Written (charts, outlines)
2. Audio
   a. Verbal
   b. Music
3. Laboratory experience (realia)
4. Instructors (to answer questions)
5. Discussion group
6. Reference materials or text
7. Traditional class or lecture
8. None

Elementary texts frequently provide aids to comprehension, in addition to the written material. The pictures in preprimers are a familiar supplement. They almost carry the story. In many textbooks and in most other types of books, pictures and graphs often provide valuable aids for understanding the written text. The pictures and graphs are not always printed in the book but may be presented by the teacher or made available to the student elsewhere. Some teachers, for example, make excellent use of filmstrips and motion pictures to stimulate interest in reading and to motivate students to read stories or books.

The supplements are not all visual; frequently a talk by the teacher or a recording serves much the same purpose. Some experimental use has been made of having students read while music is being played.

There are numerous ways of supplementing reading experiences. Laboratory experiences and realism (for example, seeing a *real* fire engine) are two of these ways. Merely having the instructor around to answer the students' questions can be another important form of supplemental help, as are discussion groups, reference material, and traditional lessons on the subject being read about.

No supplements may be involved in the reading of novels, in taking reading tests, or in many other situations.

M. Classroom environment

1. Teacher personality (dynamic, bright, etc.)
2. Teacher training
3. Peer-group pressure

4. Physical conditions (temperature, ventilation, noise, etc.)
5. Classroom emotional climate
   a. Autocratic – unstructured
   b. Hawthorne effect
6. Size of class or group

In the classroom many things affect learning. A teacher who is bright and dynamic may be better for most children than a slow and dull teacher.

Students pick up many of their attitudes and aspirations from the peer group or other students. In some communities, some groups would highly value reading and learning to read, while others might place less emphasis on it.

The physical conditions of the classroom affect reading or learning to read. It would be quite hard to concentrate on reading if the temperature were a constant 99 degrees and the ventilation poor. Numerous physical distractions can detract from reading comprehension–noise, movements, and other sorts of distracting stimuli.

Classrooms or learning groups also acquire various emotional climates. Some students, it has been observed, perform better under a relatively authoritarian teacher and others under a moderately permissive teacher. Another factor which affects the emotional climate of the classroom and has limited many research studies is the "Hawthorne effect," which occurs when the student and teacher know that they are in an experiment and try harder than they normally would, thereby giving the experimental group falsely high results.

While it is by no means clear that poorer instruction is always done in larger groups, the class size or reading group size can affect learning. Some students pay attention better in smaller groups than they do in larger groups.

N. The lesson

1. Length of lesson
2. Variety in the lesson
3. Variety of different lessons
4. Frequency of lessons
5. Time of day
6. Time of year
7. Individual's activity

If a lesson is too long, learning will cease. The problem of how long is "too long" is often solved by experienced teachers who notice when children grow restless and cease to pay attention. Sometimes a number of short lessons is superior to one long lesson. Variety within the lesson can sustain interest and prolong the effective training time. Teachers who interchange the different types of activity can lengthen the interest span. Varieties in the types of lessons can also help to sustain interest and increase learning.

The frequency of lesson periods also affects overall learning. Whether lessons are held twice a day or once a week can make a difference, even though the total training time remains the same. The time of day and time of year also make a difference. Trying to teach reading during the last hour of the day or during the last week of the school year is a difficult and trying task.

The amount of activity engaged in by each pupil also affects his interest and learning. Donald Durrell offers an interesting learning concept which he calls "density of response." An example of a very low "density of response" lesson (and hence a poor lesson) is the typical situation in which the teacher says, "Johnnie, come up to the board and point out the long *a*." Much time is wasted while Johnnie walks from his seat to the chalkboard. Moreover, only one student is active in pointing out the *a*. With this type of instructional situation, the average student could make very few responses each hour and each day. In contrast, under a programmed learning situation, each student responds to a large number of small bits of information, perhaps two or three per minute.

O. Individual differences

1. Learning ability
   a. General intelligence (e.g., Binet IQ)
   b. Simple factoral systems (e.g., Wechsler Intelligence Scale for Children, Primary Mental Abilities Test)
   c. Complex factor system (e.g., Guilford)
   d. Extrasensory perception
2. Biological factors
   a. Age-maturity
   b. Health (general, eyes, ears, etc.)
   c. Fatigue (initial and terminal)
   d. Sex differences
   e. Body chemistry
3. Personality characteristics
   a. Personality types and factors (e.g., Thematic Apperception Test; Minnesota Multiphasic Personality Inventory; introversion-extraversion needs; achievement motive; the work of analysts Freud, Adler, Jung)
   b. Mental health

Intelligence is undoubtedly the chief factor in reading comprehension. Measures of intelligence seem to proliferate with the years. They range from Binet's original concept of general intelligence through the well-known Wechsler test (which tests some ten abilities) to more modern models, like Guilford's structure of the intellect comprising 125 different categories. Certain factors, such as memory for symbols or ability to synthesize, might have much greater bearing on the reading act than other intellect factors. There are also special types of differences in learning abilities. Some children prefer to learn from a visual rather than an auditory stimulus. The extreme example of this is "idetic imagery," in which the person with this ability can close his eyes and yet retain visually the entire page.

Another factor which may affect learning or reading comprehension is ESP, or extrasensory perception phenomenon. While ESP research is not accepted by all behavioral sciences, it is slowly growing in acceptance as a research variable. If, for example, it does exist in certain students, these students could be facilitated in learning to read, if other students were also reading the same passage at the same time, even though the other students were reading it silently.

No one doubts that there are solid biological factors affecting learning and comprehension. In most cases it would be difficult to teach a two-year-old or a ninety-two-year-old to learn how to read. Determination of the ideal starting age is still a highly controversial matter, but most western nations seem to have settled on an age somewhere between five and eight. Poor health can affect learning as well as fatigue. There is a distinct sex difference in learning to read; girls are superior to boys. Finally, there are a number of other physiological differences, such as body chemistry, alterations of which can facilitate or impede learning or comprehension. Some common examples of changes in body chemistry would be endocrine dysfunctions or the use of drugs.

The study of human personality is itself worthy of many books. Much work has been done in this field; two widely known tests listing personality characteristics are Murray's Thematic Apperception Test and the Minnesota Multiphasic Inventory (MMPI). Other ways of classifying personality, or aspects of a personality, are the introversion-extraversion extreme, the various needs classification, and achievement motive, among others. Some of the research on personality has been conducted from the standpoint of the healthy personality, but much more of it has attempted to understand and cure the abnormal or mentally unhealthy personality.

Mental health, of course, can have an overriding influence on learning or reading and, as a factor in a task analysis, cannot be ignored. Children with emotional problems have long been a concern of educators.

P. Environmental influence and previous learning

1. Social class
2. Knowledge
   a. Basic skills (particularly language and writing)
   b. Subject matter
3. Childhood
   a. Rearing practices
   b. Home influence
4. Emotional learning
   a. Pleasant associations
   b. Unpleasant associations

If we do not know anything about 100 children except that they come from lower-income homes, and we have another group of children that we know nothing about except that they come from upper-income homes, we can immediately predict that there will be much greater reading achievement in the children from the upper-income homes. There are many reasons for this, but research has shown that children from upper-income homes learn more easily, have fewer failures, and read more. Part of this has to do with such factors as the education of their parents, the sets of values of their parents and friends, and the types of occupations the children are expected to enter. Hence, family income is a variable in children learning how to read or in the amount of reading they do.

The student's previous learning also affects his reading comprehension and future learning. Whether or not he is accomplished in the basic skills of writing and spelling, or whether or not he knows about a tractor, a switch-blade, a bank, an iguana—all make a difference in his reading comprehension and learning ability.

Many psychologists believe that childhood rearing practices have definite influences on the school behavior of children. Whether or not the child has received adequate amounts of his mother's attention may affect his reading. Whether the child is punished with a razor strap or verbal chastisement for bad behavior can affect his school performance. Likewise, a child picks up many pleasant and unpleasant associations at home and learns to love, fear, or dislike reading.

Q. Measurement of reading ability

1. When measured
   a. During learning
   b. Immediate posttest
   c. Delayed posttest
2. What measured (see also other sections)
   a. Rote memory for facts
   b. Generalization of concepts
   c. Transfer of performance context
3. How measured
   a. Recall (unaided memory, for example essay test)
   b. Recognition (memory with stimulus support, for example multiple-choice test)
   c. Relearning (savings score)
   d. Performance test
   e. Cloze test
   f. Speed
   g. Attitude scale or inventory
4. Type of scoring
   a. Number right

b. Number wrong
c. Rights minus wrongs
d. Probability of responding correctly
e. Subjective rating
f. Derived indicators (acquisition curves, retention curves)
5. Reading subskills
   a. Phonics
   b. Context clues
   c. Word analysis (roots, etc.)
6. Related reading skills
   a. Reference skills
b. Reading poetry
c. Detecting propaganda

This review of ways of measuring reading ability is intended to give some suggestions for the measurement of reading skill and comprehension. "How well does a student read?" is not a simple question. Nearly every factor listed in this section bears on the answer, and most of the factors in the total task analysis have direct implications.

R. Training efficiency

1. Cost of materials
   a. Initial investment
   b. Long-term investment
2. Training time required
3. Quality of students required
   a. Aptitude level
   b. Prior experience
4. Quality of instructor required (cost)
   a. None required
   b. Formal qualifications (e.g., degrees)
   c. Other qualifications (e.g., personality)
5. Logistics
   a. Space requirements for training
   b. Space requirements of material
   c. Maintenance required for material
   d. Reusability
6. Percentage of students reaching criterion
7. Amount of learning
   a. In comparison with other methods
   b. In comparison with objectives
8. Acceptance of training method
   a. By students
   b. By instructors
   c. By administration and others
   d. By parents

This category is really intended more for the administrator than for the teacher or student, although it can effect them all.

The task-analysis concept frequently comes from military or industrial training situations, and the ultimate factor that the administrator searches for is efficiency. Cost is an ever-present factor and must be taken into account in all educational situations. Even though one particular system may be twice as good as another, if it costs 200 times as much as the other system it probably will not be used. If the cost is the same and yet the program takes four times the amount of training time, it also probably will not be used. Likewise, if the system works only on very high-IQ children or if it works but there is a fairly high percentage of failures, one must expect that it will be readily discarded. Finally, if the training method is rejected by parents or teachers, or children, or administrators, it will undoubtedly be discarded. Hence teachers as well as administrators must take these training efficiency factors into consideration before and during the teaching of reading.

CONCLUSION

This task analysis, while far from complete, is intended to give an overview of the complexity of the reading act, both from the standpoint of teaching reading and from the standpoint of the learner, and the many factors which affect them. It is hoped that this task analysis may stimulate an interest in research into the problem and facilitate understanding of research already done. It is also hoped that teachers may be helped to gain insight into some of the factors involved in the use of various teaching methods and materials.

The purpose of this task analysis is to help the reader understand that if one research study finds that increasing the amount of practice increases speed and another study finds that increasing the amount of practice does not affect speed, then there could be all sorts of explanations or further questions to ask such as "Was the reward the same?" or "Was the classroom emotional climate the same?"

Hence this task analysis might be used as a checklist in designing and evaluating reading research studies.

It can also be used in developing ideas for an infinite number of term papers, masters theses, doctoral dissertations, or major research projects. The investigator simply selects one factor to vary and then attempts to hold all other factors constant. It might be difficult, but that is one important way the field of reading will progress.

APPENDIX 9-A A TASK ANALYSIS OF THE READING ACT

Sensory input
- Visual
- Tactual
- Kinesthetic

Mediating activity
- Vocalization
- Subvocalization
- Thinking about
- Phonics
- Word-part recognition

Response
- Observable behavior
- Content of response
- Delay of response

Reward and/or motivation
- Primary
- Secondary
- Knowledge of results
- Subjective
- Punishment
- None (incidental)
- Set

Knowledge of results
- Type
- Method of presentation
- Teaching machine
- Life situation

Reward variations
- Amount
- Frequency
- Relation to response
- Timing

Rate of reading
- Student-controlled versus other control
- Speed set
- Relaxed
- Study set
- Skimming

Practice and review
- Practice or review
- Planned practice or review

Only as needed
Amount learned or read before practice
Massed versus distributed

Readability

- Legibility
- Word difficulty
- Sentence difficulty
- Style difficulty
- Picture or graph cues

Reading content

- Scientific
- Social science
- Artistic and poetic (literary)
- Mechanical
- Language style and variations
- Mathematical
- Philosophical

Subject-matter organization

- Chronologic (historical)
- Unit (natural unit in subject matter)
- Problem-centered
- Descriptive
- Sequential (steps 1, 2, 3, etc.)
- Theoretical
- Practical
- Analytic (whole to part)
- Synthetic (part to whole)

Supplementary presentations

- Visual
- Audio
- Laboratory experience (realia)
- Instructors (to answer questions)
- Discussion group
- Reference materials or text
- Traditional class or lecture
- None

Classroom environment

- Teacher personality (dynamic, bright, etc.)
- Teacher training
- Peer-group pressure
- Physical conditions (temperature, ventilation, noise, etc.)
- Classroom emotional climate
- Size of class or group

The lesson

- Length of lesson
- Variety in the lesson
- Variety of different lessons
- Frequency of lessons

Time of day
Time of year
Individual's activity

Individual differences

Learning ability
Biological factors
Personality characteristics

Environmental influence and previous learning

Social class
Knowledge
Childhood
Emotional learning

Measurement of reading ability

When measured
What measured
How measured
Type of scoring
Reading subskills
Related reading skills

Training efficiency

Cost of materials
Training time required
Quality of students required
Quality of instructor required (cost)
Logistics
Percentage of students reaching criterion
Amount of learning
Acceptance of training method

10

TEACHING COMPREHENSION

The last two chapters have mentioned some of the rudimentary concepts basic to a theoretical orientation toward reading comprehension. This chapter proposes to be more practical and to direct its attention to the classroom teacher who may be thinking: "Yes. All that stuff about Bloom's taxonomy and other theories is interesting, but what do I do tomorrow morning?" Here, then, are some specific things to do which will help improve the student's reading comprehension.

PRACTICAL STEPS IN IMPROVING READING COMPREHENSION

The easiest way to teach a child to read with comprehension is to start him reading and keep him reading.

EASY READING If you can get a child or a whole class to be quiet and read for half an hour, one hour, or six hours, you are already doing a very effective job of teaching comprehension. This is not as easy as it may sound because you may have to pay attention to matching reading level with book difficulty. You must also pay attention to the students' interests and other things mentioned in earlier chapters; but if you can do it, simply getting a child to read is excellent instruction.

If a child learns to enjoy a book or a short story, this is a valuable lesson in itself. Good reading teachers, of course, have an improvement goal in mind. When they are at first successful in getting a child to read a very easy book, they will attempt to interest him in a slightly more difficult book; and after that, one a little further advanced. It is a basic principle that any kind of reading helps all types of reading. The student who reads ten Hardy Boy books during the summer is much better prepared to read social studies and science books during the fall than the student who has read nothing during the summer. Teachers in all subject areas should encourage students to read books that are easy and interesting.

Students will usually not voluntarily read books which they do not comprehend. It can be assumed that if a student reads books or short stories without too much prodding, he comprehends them. Little informal checks by the reading teacher on reading comprehension are always in order. The teacher might say, "Tell me about that last story you read." A teacher might ask to see a book that a student is reading and read a page or two that the student has just read and discuss it with him. A teacher might also encourage students to ask for definitions of difficult words, phrases, or passages. If a student reads at home, he might be encouraged to put a slip of paper in the book so that he can later ask the teacher about some term or passage which he may not understand. The teacher might tell him about the difficult word and suggest that he use some reference book, such as the dictionary.

If a teacher has been successful in urging students to ask questions about their reading, she has an excellent feedback concerning the difficulty of a particular book for a particular child. If a teacher invariably says, "Look it up in the dictionary," she may so effectively discourage children from asking questions about their reading that she will no longer get the feedback.

Free reading, or just allowing students to read in class, like any other teaching method, can be overused. A teacher who uses the method of free reading too often probably omits the teaching of other important reading skills. On the other hand, the teacher who never allows for any free reading in class may be neglecting an important type of lesson. It is to be hoped that she encourages students to ask questions. There is an important difference in atmosphere and class attitude between a teacher who remains actively interested in the students' reading and readily available for their questions and the one who busies herself elsewhere during the free reading period.

VARIATION IN TYPES OF READING There is always a danger that students will get "stuck" on one type of reading: one boy will select nothing but science fiction; one girl reads nothing but mystery stories; while another boy's reading diet consists mostly of sport stories. It is part of the teacher's job to see that the students have a variety of types of reading material. Fiction is fairly easy for many students, but it may take a bit of guidance to show them that they can and will enjoy reading plays. Poetry can be funny, moving, and thought-provoking, but many students would never turn to a poem without some encouragement. Comprehension must include all types of reading. If we are to teach comprehension of poetry, drama, news stories, job applications, and cooking recipes, students should be given practice in reading all of these types of materials.

COMPREHENSION DRILLS One of the standard methods of teaching reading comprehension is through "comprehension drills." These are short passages several paragraphs in length, followed by some comprehension questions. Good examples of this type of material are the McCall Crabb *Standard Test Lessons in Reading* which have been used by reading teachers since 1926. These little books, ranging in difficulty from third through twelfth grade, contain drills of a paragraph or two of interesting material, followed by ten multiple-choice questions. The paragraph and questions may be used under timed conditions (three minutes to read and answer questions) or under untimed conditions. The students may be given an answer key so that they can score their own answers, or the teacher can score them, or at the end of an instruction period the students can trade papers and score each other's papers while the teacher reads the answers. After the students' answers have been corrected, it is a very helpful follow-up procedure for the student to check on his wrong answers by reading the paragraph again. See Appendix 10-D for a McCall Crabb sample page.

On the secondary level, I have developed a workbook containing 400 or 500 word passages, each of which is followed by ten multiple-choice questions. The workbook was designed primarily for speed and comprehension drills for older and superior secondary students but can be used with benefit for below-average secondary pupils under untimed conditions, if the stress is placed on comprehension. The questions are divided roughly in half: the first five questions are chiefly objective questions (matters of fact); the second five questions are chiefly of a subjective nature (inference, mood, tone, and other areas, such as those found in the upper levels of Bloom's taxonomy). Figure 10-1 shows several ways in which studying wrong answers can be used to aid reading comprehension.

Reading comprehension materials come in graded series. The McCall Crabb books, ranging from third grade through twelfth grade, have already been mentioned. Other booklets in approximately the same range are Gates-Peardon, *Practice Exercises in Reading,* and Guliver-Coleman (see example in Appendix 10-E), *Reading for Meaning* (grades four through twelve). There are also materials which start at the first and second grade level, such as the *Reader's Digest Skill Builders, Diagnostic Reading Workbooks,* and *Reading Skill Texts.* In a different format, but with the same basic idea, are the various reading laboratories, such as those put out by Science Research Associates. The reading laboratories consist chiefly of a boxful of pamphlets, each pamphlet containing a short reading passage followed by comprehension questions that the student can score himself. A boxful contains a number of reading selections at several grade levels; by using a reading test in the workbook, the student is

A. Study the question carefully. You may not have read it correctly.
Example:
5. The island monkeys served the doctor by:
(a) bringing him tea,
(b) allowing themselves to be caught,
(c) catching other monkeys, or
(d) sitting in wire cages in trees.
The correct answer is (d) but the student's answer was (b). On rereading the question carefully after knowing that his choice was wrong, he might see that while it is true that the monkeys were caught it is highly doubtful that they would allow themselves to be caught. The other two answers, (a) and (c), are also obviously wrong.
B. Look for the correct answer in the story for objective questions.
Example:
I. Dr. Causey's reputation as a monkey catcher was:
(a) poor,
(b) average,
(c) good, or
(d) the best in the world.
The student chose (b) which was wrong. By looking back in the story the student found the sentence in the middle of a paragraph: "Dr. Causey was very good at catching these animals." Hence the student can see that (c) was the best answer choice and also that the answer was specifically given in the middle of a paragraph. Hence, he must read a little more carefully in the future.
C. Glance over the entire story and think about it for subjective questions.
Example:
9. From reading this article you would judge that Dr. Causey is really interested in:
(a) monkeys
(b) world health
(c) jungles
(d) adventure
The student chose (a) because most of the article was about monkeys. While it is true that the doctor did work with monkeys and probably had some interest in them, was this really his main interest? Probably each of the answers was partly correct. The student might have to reason that the doctor used monkeys to expose them to disease, to get blood samples, to analyze these blood samples, to find viruses, to advance medical science, to help people's health everywhere. Hence the answer is (b) "world health," even though nowhere in the story does it say, "The doctor is really interested in world health."

Source: Edward Fry, *Teaching Faster Reading*, Cambridge University Press, Cambridge, England, 1963.

FIGURE 10-1 Improvement of low comprehension by study of wrong answers.

guided to the correct reading level and encouraged to work at his proper level, gradually proceeding to the next higher one.

GLOSSING A method of teaching reading comprehension that has come down to us from the middle ages is that of "glossing." Many teachers use it instinctively. In glossing, the teacher reads a bit of the text, then stops to make an explanation of it, point out an interesting term, a subtle interrelationship, or a hidden meaning. The French refer to this method as "explication de texte." The method is a good one because it can be used with any type of material: fiction, poetry, history, science, etc. Sometimes it is a good idea to provide the student with his own copy of the passage being read and let him follow along while the teacher reads aloud. The teacher can often make the printed word come alive and seem vibrant with meaning. Perhaps the student has tried reading the same passage and has gotten almost nothing out of it. When the teacher reads it aloud with expression and a few side comments, the whole passage suddenly becomes clear and meaningful.

Glossing, like any other teaching method, can, of course, be ruined by an unskillful teacher. At worst, the teacher simply stands up in front of the class and reads the textbook to the students. Instead of making the meaning leap from the page, the passage goes limp and the students are bored to death. Herein is seen that indefinable and sometimes ephemeral difference between a good teacher and a boring one. Glossing is a method which requires that a good teacher be able to draw upon the breadth of her education and previous reading experience.

A minor form of glossing is employed in the "guided reading activities," the traditional reading lesson in which a teacher sits with a group of students while one of them reads aloud from the text. During pauses in the reading, or while changing readers, the teacher comments about the story or asks questions about interesting points that might have been missed.

Sometimes subject-matter teachers (such as high school chemistry or history teachers) are at a loss as to how they can teach children to read with understanding. Glossing the text for a supplementary book in their subject is an excellent way. Elementary teachers who teach all subjects have found interesting ways of combining reading instruction with various subject matters.

SUBJECT-MATTER TEXTS The authors of various subject-matter texts, such as science and social studies books, often combine a good deal of reading comprehension instruction with the teaching of their subject matter. A frequent device is to include a series of questions to be answered at the end of each chapter of the textbook. In order to be able to answer these questions correctly, a student must have comprehended the chapter fairly well. The teacher should correct the student's answers as soon as possible (preferably immediately) and return them to him so that he will have some knowledge of his comprehension skills. Class discussions of the questions while the students are correcting their own papers, or while papers are being exchanged among students, are also helpful in the teaching of comprehension.

Working the so-called "word problems" in arithmetic and mathematics books are also excellent ways of teaching reading comprehension. The student must be able to read and understand the written material in order to solve the problem. By using this type of problem, the teacher can easily teach reading comprehension and valuable mathematic skills at the same time. Group explanations of sample word problems are often very effective in helping the student to comprehend this type of writing. Sometimes it is necessary for the teacher to go through the work problem, phrase by phrase, and explain it to the students. Once the student has been guided carefully through a sample problem, he should then try to do some work on his own and secure help only when it is absolutely necessary.

Science workbooks also have a very valuable type of feedback to help the student in evaluating his reading comprehension. If the student tries to mix several chemicals together and does not get the desired result, one of the things he may well question is his understanding of the directions. Seeing the empirical verification of reading comprehension is often much more meaningful than simply looking up an answer in a drill book which tells the student that his answer is or is not correct. Writers of vocational texts also provide many excellent ways of teaching reading comprehension by demonstrating the practical outcomes of following written directions.

Some textbooks also do an excellent job of teaching the vocabulary of their discipline. In some instances, new terms are underlined when they are first used. In others, the new terms are formally defined, either in context or in a separate definition or glossary section. Whether or not the textbook does a specific job of teaching new terms, the teacher should make a point of emphasizing the subject-matter terminology by means of explanations, exercises (filling in the correct blank in the sentence), and quizzes which require the students to comprehend the new terms.

Teachers should use questions at the end of chapters with some discretion; occasionally authors include a large number of activities and questions with the intention that the teacher select only some of them. If assignments based on questions at the end of the chapter are too long and dreary, students can acquire an active dislike for the book, the subject, and the teacher. There are also some texts that, although they contain questions, do not have a good variety of questions; the teacher might well add some of her own that are more interesting or probing.

PROGRAMMED INSTRUCTION One of the newer educational methods is the presentation of curriculum material by teaching machine, or programmed instruction. This is a self-instructional procedure in which a small bit of information requires some type of response from the student. For example, a sentence or two of information might be presented and then followed by a question, which the student answers by writing a word or phrase (constructed response) or by selecting one of several answers (multiple choice). Immediately after the student has responded, the machine or a specially arranged book tells the student the correct answer. He is then given a further bit of information which requires another response, and he proceeds from question to question. One of the characteristics of programmed instruction is that the bits of information, or "frames" as they are sometimes called, are carefully sequenced so that one frame leads to the next with continuity of thought. Programs, if skillfully designed, allow the student to make a fairly high percentage of correct responses. According to many learning theories, the immediacy of the response promotes better learning; and the fact that the student receives many correct responses is rewarding and motivating. Another characteristic of programmed instruction is that it has been through a careful tryout procedure and used on a specific population. Thus the material has been tried out and revised, based on use with students similar to those for whom it is intended. Unfortunately, this is not always true of published curriculum material.

Since programmed instruction frequently relies heavily on the student's ability to read and comprehend, each response and each bit of feedback tends to make every frame a reading comprehension item. Thus, programmed instruction in almost any subject matter area is also an effective method of teaching reading comprehension.

However, there are a number of "programs" which are intended to teach specific reading comprehension skills. Appendix 10-B illustrates a section of a program designed to teach a student how to follow directions. This particular program is one of the type known as a "scrambled book." The student reads a passage, is presented with a question, and then is given three possible answers. If he chooses the first answer, he turns to page 123; if he chooses the second answer he turns to page 128; if he chooses the third answer he turns to page 133. If he simply turns to the next page, he will be lost; therefore, he must select one of the three answers and turn to one of the pages. If he does this and the answer is incorrect, he will be told that it was the wrong choice because he did not understand such and such and that he must go back and try again. When he chooses the right answer, the page to which he turns will give the answer, the explanation why it is correct, and a further direction. Telling the student *why he was right or why he was wrong* is another powerful learning principle, and it is easily handled in the "scrambled book" type of programmed instruction.

This sample, incidentally, is from a series of programs called "Lessons for Self-Instruction" containing a number of programmed units which tie in with the California Achievement Tests. If, for example, a teacher gives the California Reading Test and finds that a student is low in following directions or in reading comprehension (called "Reading Interpretation" on this test), she then can select a programmed unit from the "Lessons for Self-Instruction" that will give him the help he needs in the area of specific weakness.

Another interesting and important point of programmed instruction is that diagnosis of the student's educational needs precedes instruction. Some programs are tied in with achievement tests ("Lessons for Self-Instruction"); whereas other programs have small pretests at the front of the program that determine whether the student needs the skills which will be taught. If, for example, the student is able to pass the pretest with a high score, there is no need to give him the program. It might be helpful if more curriculum material followed this practice. Some programs also tell the teacher what reading ability level is needed before the student is ready to go through the programs successfully.

Quite a bit of programming has been done in the area of vocabulary improvement. Figure 10-2 shows a constructed response program for the teaching of vocabulary improvement. This program is of the small-step constructed response type which is a major type corresponding to the scrambled books.

An example of small-step or linear program was seen in Chapter 7 in the figure illustrating the Sullivan Programmed Reading. This type of programming differs from the scrambled book in that the student follows a "linear" progression; namely, one item directly follows the other. No switching of pages is necessary. With a teaching machine, the machine simply presents the next item; and in a programmed text, the student usually masks the correct answers and reads down the page, exposing the answers after he has read and responded to the questions.

Individual differences are usually handled in programmed instruction by allowing each student to proceed at his own pace. One of the advantages of programmed instruction is that good students may proceed as rapidly as they wish without disturbing others; they, therefore, can cover much more material. Conversely, slower students may take all the time they need without holding back the class. Since programmed materials are individual by nature, a teacher can provide faster students with additional work in reading comprehension while other students are moving more slowly in studying whatever the subject field (perhaps science or foreign language). Programmed instruction is ideal for homework and study periods and for reading groups which are working without the teacher.

Branching is another method of allowing for individual differences. Branching allows the student to skip ahead, to review a section, or to receive supplementary instruction not given to all students. Branching is most easily handled by a multiple-choice or scrambled-book type of program in which the student's choice of an answer leads him directly to an item well advanced in the program, an item earlier covered so that he is forced to review a section, or an item that is part of a subsystem or supplementary instruction.

Programmed instruction has created a number of terms of its own, making use of such words as "branching" and "scrambled book" and many rather specialized words chosen from related fields, such as "feedback" which comes

104. yes	104. The definition of the parts of ADVERTISE is "make turn toward." Is this definition close to the real meaning of the word? ________
105. not (*It's in front of another prefix.*) toward turn	105. See whether you can go from the definition of ADVERTISE to the definition of INADVERTENT. IN- means "________"; AD- means "________"; VERT means "________"; -ENT is a sufix which is about the same as -ING.
106. (*If you said "yes," skip to Item 111. If you said "no," go on to Item 107.*)	106. INADVERTENT = "not turning toward." Here are some sentences containing the word: "That was an inadvertent hint." "Inadvertently, we left her name off the list of people to be invited." "His remark was an inadvertent slap in the face, but I was hurt by it anyway." ("Slap in the face" means "insult.") From the definition of the parts and from the examples of how the word is used, can you give the real meaning of INADVERTENT? __________ (yes or no)
107. second (*The second ones all have "not" in them.*)	107. INADVERTENT = "not turning toward." "That was an *inadvertent* hint." We are looking for something that a hint can be. What can a hint be? It can be *helpful* or *not helpful*, *big* or *small* (*not big*), given by someone *meaning to help* or given by someone *not meaning to help*. Because INADVERTENT begins with IN- we would have to choose the [first, second] one in any of the pairs of possible meanings.
108. Your opinion. (*We hope it doesn't seem that way.*)	108. INADVERTENT = "not turning toward." An *inadvertent* hint: hints can be small (*not big*). Does it seem to you that a word with the definition "not turning toward" could have anything to do with size? ________

109. yes yes	109. Could we say that a *helpful* hint "turns you toward" the right answer? _______ Could we say that someone who *means to help* is "turned toward" the job of helping (paying attention to what he is doing)? _______
110. a	110. We can't choose between "not helpful" and "not meaning to" by knowing that INADVERTENT = "not turning toward" and knowing that hints can be inadvertent. Look at another sentence: "Inadvertently, we left her name off the list of people to be invited." Which of the following makes more sense? **a.** "Without meaning to, we left her name off the list." **b.** "Not helpfully, we left her name off the list." Sentence _______ makes more sense.

Source: Sample items from Susan Meyer Markle, *Words—A Programmed Course in Vocabulary* (High School Level), Science Research Associates, Chicago, 1963.

FIGURE 10-2 Constructed response program for the teaching of vocabulary improvement.

from a branch of learning theory known as information theory (probably borrowed originally from electronic engineering or cybernetics). Those readers interested in programmed instruction per se may refer to my book on the topic (*Teaching Machines and Programmed Instruction*, McGraw-Hill, 1963).

SYSTEMS APPROACH An area somewhat related to programmed instruction is known as "systems approach." It is a broader term than programmed instruction in that part of a "system" for teaching some desired goal might be to have part of the topic taught by programmed instruction. Other parts of the system might include reading books, taking tests, viewing motion pictures, listening to tapes, performing laboratory experiments, etc. To some extent, a basal reading series which utilizes text, workbook, teacher charts, and sometimes tests, charts, or records, is a kind of systems approach. But modern proponents of the systems approach would place greater emphasis on specifying instructional goals (the exact behavior that the student is expected to learn), greater emphasis on individualization, and greater emphasis on new media, such as programmed instruction, single concept films (short and individually viewed), language-laboratory type of listening experiences, and others.

GAMES AND OTHER MATERIALS A number of activities other than those already mentioned are valuable for the teaching of reading comprehension.

Comprehension-building games come in a variety of types at many levels.

For beginning readers there are matching games in which the student matches a word with an object. This can be done on a workbook page by drawing a line from the word or phrase to the object or by placing words (on cut-out pieces of cardboard) next to the appropriate picture. Older children sometimes like crossword-puzzle type games which require a good understanding of vocabulary. Another type of seatwork (i.e., work which can be done at the desk) aimed at building sentence comprehension is the "true-false" evaluation of nonsense sentences, such as:

1. Cats can fly.
2. Some birds can swim.

Teachers can make or purchase pocket charts or flannel boards which the students manipulate by cards, building sentences or answering questions. Even in some relatively ordinary commercial games (Monopoly, for example) students must comprehend such phrases as "Go to jail" or "Pay the bank $100."

The teacher's manuals for many basic texts contain excellent suggestions on comprehension-building activities, and teachers are well advised to keep on hand a collection of teacher's manuals other than those which accompany the series they are using at the time. These manuals contain many excellent teaching suggestions. In addition, a small booklet aimed at activity-type projects has been very useful to teachers (*Reading Aids Through the Grades* by David Russell, Bureau of Publications, Teachers College, Columbia University, New York).

VARIETY IS IMPORTANT FOR TEACHING READING COMPREHENSION

In teaching reading comprehension, *variety* is the key word. Variety will add interest to lessons and will prevent practice from becoming boring drill.

VARY THE SUBJECT MATTER The subject matter is one of the most obvious things that can be varied. It takes quite a different approach to comprehend a set of directions on how to build a model airplane or how to bake a cake compared with that to read a story from history. Yes, both are reading, but one would be read much more slowly and carefully than the other. What the author intends a reader to get from a short story is different from what the author intends him to get from a set of directions. The reading teacher should point this out to the student. And the best way to point it out is not by lecturing, but by giving the student some sample questions following the reading.

Here are a few suggestions of different types of subject matter or types of stories that teachers might select for comprehension drills and reading practice:

Adventure stories—space, animals, war disaster, frontiers.
Bibliography—lives of heroes, journals of explorers, autobiographies.

Sports — baseball, auto racing, football, basketball (newspaper accounts of current sports events are sometimes especially useful with older students).
How to do it — get a job, repair a car, build a model, make money.
Romance and family situations — liked more by girls.
Strange and interesting — how people lived long ago, ancestors, causes of death, great inventions, humor, science.

VARY THE LENGTH The length of the reading selection should be varied. In the beginning, getting the student to read one word or one sentence is often a feat of great success. But even after learning to read a whole paragraph, a student should sometimes return to reading one word or one sentence. As a student's ability advances, the standard technique of using comprehension drills based on reading a paragraph or several paragraphs should be used. However, he should sometimes read a whole story and a whole book. Some students take real pride in having accomplished the feat of reading a whole book.

Comprehension questions should likewise point out that sometimes the important thing to derive from reading is the main idea of a paragraph or that the whole chapter is really discussing just one main idea.

Teachers should look at length on variations like this:

One word: Getting the meaning of one word is often called vocabulary-building, but it is a kind of comprehension skill. Teachers should occasionally discuss and ask questions about one word.
A phrase: Several words together often take on a meaning not contained in one word alone. The phrase "under the weather" does not have much to do with weather.
A sentence: Sentences can be short and sweet with a simple noun-verb-object pattern, or they can be very complex with conditionals, subordinate clauses, etc. Pick out some long and short sentences from the material you are using, discuss them, and ask comprehension questions about them.
A paragraph: The paragraph is a traditional unit of teaching comprehension; it is good and should be used, but not exclusively.
A chapter or story: Many paragraphs form a larger unit. Teach your students to read these larger units. Show that sometimes you have to see several paragraphs in relation to each other to get meaning. Ask questions which can only be answered by reading many paragraphs or the whole story.
The book: Even younger students like long stories. Guide them into reading easy whole books, and then slightly harder ones.

VARY THE TYPE OF QUESTION The type of questions can be very important in teaching comprehension. The easiest type of questions is simply to ask for details of simple matters of fact, such as "What was the color of the boy's hair?" It is good to get the facts straight, but here are some more interesting types of questions that you can use:

Time sequence: What happened first? What will happen if things continue like they are going?

Traits: Is the hero happy? Honest? (These questions may not be answered directly in the story.)
Comparison: Which is bigger? Is this better than the last story? Which story was written longer ago?

The type of response that the student is asked to make is also dependent on the type of question. Quite obviously a true-false or a multiple-choice question merely requires recognition of the correct answer whereas a completion or short-answer essay question is more difficult because it requires recall.

The cloze technique is an interesting and important type of comprehension drill because it is easy for the teacher to construct and score and it tests the student's knowledge of language patterns and recall with context clues. To make a cloze technique comprehension drill, the teacher simply selects several paragraphs and types them up on a ditto sheet with a blank for every tenth word. The student attempts to fill in the missing words. Variety can even be introduced in using the cloze technique (and other comprehension drills) in the following ways:

1. Vary the type of answer from demanding the exact word omitted to accepting a reasonable substitute.
2. Vary the means of correction from self-correction, to teacher correction, to other student correction.
3. Vary self-correction from allowing the student to check himself against the undeleted passage to a class discussion of acceptable answers.
4. Vary the frequency of words omitted from every tenth word to every fifth word or twentieth word.
5. Vary the type of omissions from a mechanical deletion, such as omitting every tenth word, to a subjective deletion such as omitting only nouns and verbs that would test for story comprehension, to a subjective deletion that would omit structure words and really test language knowledge more than subject matter.
6. Vary the kind of subject matter from short stories, to history, to physical education, and (for the daring) to poetry.
7. Vary the time allowed for the drill from unlimited to three minutes for a short passage. Speeding up sometimes introduces a little excitement.
8. Vary who makes up the cloze passage. It does not always have to be the teacher; let the students sometimes make them up for each other.
9. Vary the reward to the student from public recognition to a silent pat on the back. Gold stars, marks in grade books, or extra privileges for notable improvement are also good.

VARY THE DIFFICULTY LEVEL AND STYLE The difficulty level of reading material should be varied. Most teachers like to give a lot of practice on easy material because it helps the children feel successful, and this is very important. However, it is not good teaching if the teacher does not try to move students ahead to more difficult material. This is the right idea—but they should not be too hasty. They should try comprehension drills on easy material and then on slightly harder material. If students experience too much failure or frustration, they should return to the easy material for a while. But attempting to vary the difficulty level can add interest. Sometimes students will enjoy doing a comprehension drill or reading a book that is very simple for them.

A readability graph, found in the next chapter, will help a teacher to determine quickly the grade level difficulty of any passage.

The difficulty level of the questions can also be varied. Sometimes a teacher will give an easy set of questions and sometimes a difficult set, or she can mix some easy and some difficult questions within one drill. A standard rule of thumb might be to try to follow a kind of normal distribution curve with a few very easy questions, a few very difficult questions, and most of the questions in the medium difficulty range.

Varieties in style do not always mean varieties in difficulty. A modern black author may use quite a different style and vocabulary from Mark Twain, but both authors are important for the reader to understand. Newspapers and fairy tales are not written the same way (hopefully), yet a readability formula might show them both to be on the same grade level of difficulty.

CONCLUSION

Improving comprehension is the most difficult and the most important part of teaching reading. There are no firm rules on how to do it; in fact, the teacher's personality and the characteristics of the class may have a good deal to do with the methods selected. Although this chapter has presented a number of ways to vary the teaching of comprehension, the teacher might consider one last variety; not to vary the instruction much at all—simply find a way she likes and that suits the students and stick with it. But this ultimate variety has its dangers.

APPENDIX 10-A SELECTED BIBLIOGRAPHY OF MATERIALS FOR THE TEACHING OF COMPREHENSION

Fry, Edward. *Reading Faster—A Drill Book.* New York: Cambridge University Press, 1963. (Easy high school)

Gates, Arthur I., and Celeste Peardon. *Practice Exercises in Reading.* New York: Bureau of Publications, Teachers College, Columbia University, 1933. (Grades three to six; four different books for each level)

Guiler, W. S., and J. H. Coleman. *Reading for Meaning.* Chicago: J. B. Lippincott Co., 1955. (Grades four to twelve)

Johnson, Eleanor. *Diagnostic Reading Workbook.* Columbus, Ohio: Charles E. Merrill Books, Inc., 1937. (Grades one to six)

Lessons for Self Instruction in Basic Skills. Monterey, Calif.: California Test Bureau, McGraw-Hill Book Company, 1963. (Grades three through high school; programmed scrambled books in reading and language)

McCall, W. A., and L. M. Crabb. *Standard Test Lessons in Reading.* New York: Bureau of Publications, Teachers College, Columbia University, 1926, 1950. (Grades three to seven)

Parker, Don. *SRA Reading Laboratories.* Chicago: Science Research Associates, 1957 and later. (Grades one through high school)

Reader's Digest Reading Skill Builders. Pleasantville, N. Y.: Reader's Digest Services, Inc., 1958. (Grades two to six)

Reading Improvement for Junior High Schools. Chicago: Scott Foresman and Company, 1955. (Remedial, five and six)

Reading Skilltexts (by the editors of *My Weekly Reader*). Columbus, Ohio: Charles E. Merrill Books, Inc., 1956. (Grades one to nine)

Simpson, Elizabeth. *The SRA Better Reading Books.* Chicago: Science Research Associates, 1951. (Grades six, eight, and ten)

Smith, Nila B. *Be a Better Reader.* Englewood Cliffs, N. J.: Prentice-Hall, Inc., 1958. (Grades seven to nine)

Stone, Clarence, and Charles Grover. *Practice Readers.* St. Louis: Webster Publishing Company, 1947.

APPENDIX 10-B SAMPLE PROGRAMMED PAGES FROM *LESSONS FOR SELF-INSTRUCTION—BASIC SKILLS IN FOLLOWING DIRECTIONS*

117

(1) Undress, (2) dry with a towel, (3) bathe.

No! It seems that you did not read the question.

Go again to No. 107. Read the question and the two other answers.

118

Below are a few steps seen from the side:

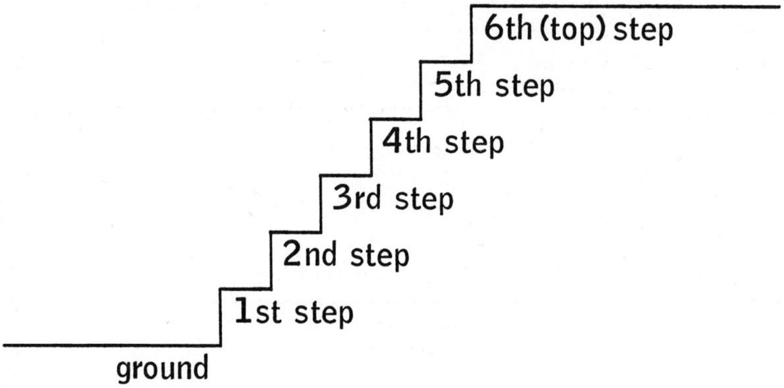

In your mind, take a walk up the steps to the top. Then turn around and walk down three steps.

On what step did you stop?

I am on the fourth step. (No. 123)

I am on the third step. (No. 128)

I am on the second step. (No. 133)

123

I am on the fourth step.

Sorry, you are wrong. Repeat the exercise. Think: How many steps are there in all? How many steps did you walk down from the top?

Return to No. 118. Try again.

128

I am on the third step.

Yes, you are. You walked up six steps. (On the drawing they are marked 1st, 2nd, 3rd, 4th, 5th, and 6th, the "top.")

Then you walked down three steps. You went from the sixth step to the fifth; from the fifth to the fourth; and from the fourth to the third step.

Go to No. 116.

133

I am on the second step.

No! If you followed directions, you cannot be on the second step.

To start with, you walked from the ground to the top. Did you count the steps? From the top you went down three steps. Where did you stop?

Return to No. 118. Try once more.

APPENDIX 10-C SAMPLE PAGES FROM *READER'S DIGEST SKILL BUILDER*

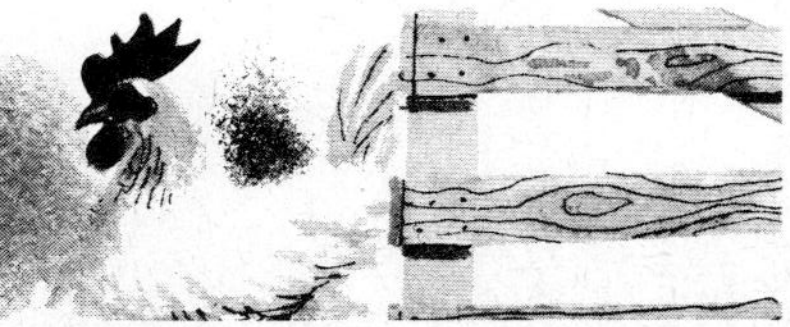

54

JOE KELLER'S FARM

Key Words: raccoon, animal trainer, different, pecks

Joe Keller has a farm. It is not much like any farm you have ever seen.

Have you ever seen a turkey that can run a toy train?

Have you ever seen a rabbit that can drop money into a bank?

Have you ever seen a

THINK THIS OVER

In what ways is Joe Keller's farm different from other farms you have seen?

YOU NAME IT

This story could have another title. Read the names below. Which one would make the best title for this story? Draw a line under it.

The Turkey Farm

The Pig That Played Ball

The Animal Trainer and His Farm

The Cow That Smiled

WRITE THE MISSING WORD

One word is missing in each sentence. Choose the correct word. Write it on the line.

1. Mr. Keller can train a pig to do ....

   tricks ticks sticks

2. The .... wants to go where Joe goes.

   sleep peep sheep

3. The rabbit can .... money into a bank.

   drip drop hop

Best Score: 3 **My Score:......**

APPENDIX 10-D SAMPLE PAGE FROM *STANDARD TEST LESSONS IN READING* (McCALL-CRABBS)

41

A Persian ruler owned a rare and beautiful pearl. He had three sons. He decided to give the jewel to the one who had shown the greatest nobility of character. He called his sons to him and asked each to tell what had been his most worthy act during the past year.

The eldest son said, "Last week a merchant entrusted me with some precious jewels. I could have taken a few of them and he never would have known it. But I chose to be honest and deliver them all."

"Well done," the father said, "but you could hardly have done otherwise. It would have been shameful to rob a man who had placed such confidence in you."

The second son said, "As I walked by the lake the other day, I saw a child drowning. I jumped into the lake and rescued him."

"Your heroism is certainly to be commended," said the father, "but it would have been cowardly and ignoble to allow the child to drown."

Then the third son spoke. He said: "Recently, as I was crossing the mountains, I saw that one of my worst enemies had rolled, while sleeping, near the edge of a precipice. I felt that it was my duty to waken him, and thus probably save his life. I knew that he would not thank me for my kindness. Indeed, I felt sure that he would not understand it, and would be angry with me. Nevertheless, I awakened him and my only reward was his wrath."

"That was indeed a noble act," said the father. "Take the pearl, my son. It is yours."

1. This story is about (a) an Egyptian ruler (b) a Persian (c) a British nobleman (d) an African pearl
2. The ruler owned a (a) pearl (b) diamond (c) ruby (d) topaz
3. The jewel was (a) large (b) a noble one (c) transparent (d) an unusual one
4. The father planned to give the jewel to the (a) eldest son (b) youngest son (c) ablest son (d) noblest son
5. The eldest son was (a) dishonest (b) truthful (c) honest (d) brave
6. The father stated that the eldest son had (a) been dishonest (b) acted noblest (c) done well (d) fallen below expectations
7. The second son saw (a) a man (b) a child (c) a woman (d) no one mentioned
8. The child in the lake was (a) swimming (b) screaming (c) wading (d) drowning
9. The third son felt he could avoid harsh words by (a) awakening the man (b) letting the man sleep (c) doing the man a kindness (d) removing the man from danger
10. The prize was awarded to the (a) one who returned good for evil (b) eldest (c) youngest (d) bravest

No. right	0	1	2	3	4	5	6	7	8	9	10
G score	3.7	4.0	4.4	4.9	5.5	6.1	6.8	7.8	9.2	10.4	12.2

43

Every evening Farmer Brown walked around his big farm to make sure that things were all right. One night he found the bars to the pasture down and his horse Ned eating outside along the road. Farmer Brown thought some boys had left the bars down for a joke. The next night Ned was out again, and this time Farmer Brown became angry. The following evening he watched from his garden to find out who the boys were. He waited an hour. Then he saw Ned, who had eaten his supper, walk up to the bars, take them down one by one with his nose, and walk through. Farmer Brown laughed and decided he would have to scold his horse instead of the boys.

1. The farmer first found the bars to the pasture down (a) in the morning (b) one afternoon (c) one night (d) last week
2. Farmer Brown walked around the pasture (a) every evening (b) every morning (c) twice a day (d) all day
3. Farmer Brown thought the bars were taken down by (a) Ned (b) Mrs. Brown (c) his brother (d) some boys
4. The second time he found the bars down Mr. Brown was (a) cold (b) happy (c) angry (d) hungry
5. He watched from the (a) house (b) road (c) window (d) garden
6. The story says Ned ate his (a) supper (b) breakfast (c) corn (d) oats
7. Farmer Brown waited (a) all day (b) an hour (c) five minutes (d) all evening
8. Ned walked to the (a) house (b) garden (c) bars (d) pasture
9. At first Farmer Brown thought he would have to scold (a) the boys (b) his neighbor (c) the girls (d) Ned
10. Ned ate his supper (a) in the house (b) in the pasture (c) in the garden (d) near the house

No. right	0	1	2	3	4	5	6	7	8	9	10
G score	**2.5**	**2.8**	**3.1**	**3.4**	**3.7**	**4.0**	**4.4**	**4.8**	**5.2**	**5.7**	**6.3**

APPENDIX 10-E SAMPLE LESSON FROM *READING FOR MEANING*

UNIT 19

About seventy years ago lovers of canaries were astonished to see in the hands of a few breeders birds of a beautiful deep-orange color. They were products of a process called "color feeding." For years those who had this secret guarded it carefully, but finally it became known that the intensified color was the result of adding red pepper to the diet during the period of molt.

Color feeding is simple. Birds of good natural hue are selected and, at the very beginning of the molt, in addition to the regular diet of seed and greens, they are given a food prepared by mixing one part of finely ground sweet red pepper to two parts of egg food (made from equal parts of hard-boiled egg, chopped fine or grated, and dry bread crumbs, unsalted cracker crumbs, or ground zwieback). Some fanciers add to this a drop or two of olive oil and a little sugar. A teaspoonful of the color food is fed each day through the entire period of molt until all the body feathers are fully grown, and then it is gradually discontinued. Care is taken to feed only freshly prepared food in which the egg is not stale.

As the new feathers come in, they are noticeably deeper and richer in color than the old ones. The enhanced color is due to the element taken from the pepper and remains until the next change of feathers. Most birds eat the color food greedily and those that do not seem to care for it at first are usually quick to acquire a taste for it if the ordinary food supply is cut down for a day or two.

---

breeders. Bird breeders are persons who raise birds.
canary, a small singing bird with yellow feathers.
diet, the kind and amount of food that is eaten.
discontinued, stopped.
enhanced, made better; increased.
fanciers, people who are especially interested in something, such as flowers, dogs, or birds.
greedily, hungrily.
hue, color.
intensified, made greater or stronger.
molt, shedding of feathers.
noticeably, can be noticed easily; strikingly.
zwieback, a kind of bread or cake cut into slices and toasted crisp in a closed oven.

General Directions for Unit 19

Write your answers in the spaces provided. Under *GETTING WORD MEANINGS,* you will write words as answers; under *GETTING THE FACTS,* you will write A, D, or N as answers; under the other headings, you will write numbers as answers.

GETTING WORD MEANINGS. In the space at the right, write the underlined word which means:

1. a quantity or amount of something ready for use . . . . ______ 1
2. get or obtain as one's own; attain . . . . ______ 2
3. surprised; amazed; astounded . . . . ______ 3
4. essential part of a substance; ingredient; constituent . . . . ______ 4
5. step by step; proceeding little by little . . . . ______ 5
6. usual; common; regular; normal . . . . ______ 6
7. way; method; procedure . . . . ______ 7
8. broken off; dropped; given up; suspended . . . . ______ 8
9. increased; heightened; augmented . . . . ______ 9
10. greatly; markedly; prominently; conspicuously . . . . ______10

44

CHOOSING THE BEST TITLE. The best title for this selection is . . . .

1. Regular Diet of Birds
2. Natural Color of Birds
3. Feeding and Care of Birds
4. Enhancing the Color of Canaries

GETTING THE MAIN IDEA. The main idea in this selection is that . . . .

1. The diet of birds requires constant care.
2. Some canaries have a beautiful deep-orange color.
3. Birds require careful feeding and handling.
4. The color of canaries can be changed by means of diet.

GETTING THE FACTS. For your answer write A (agrees), D (disagrees), or N (not included).

1. Dieting is good for birds. 1
2. Birds molt just once a year. 2
3. Most birds can be made to like color food. 3
4. The molting period lasts only a short time. 4
5. The color in boiled eggs changes the color of the feathers. 5
6. The color food is fed only at the beginning of the molting period. 6
7. The color food is discontinued when the body feathers start to grow.. 7
8. During their molt the birds are fed color food instead of their regular diet. 8

MAKING AN OUTLINE. Make a partial outline of the selection by writing the numbers of four of the following items in the proper spaces.

1. Bread crumbs
2. Seed and greens
3. Hard-boiled egg
4. Sweet red pepper
5. Teaspoonful of salt
6. Salted cracker crumbs
7. At the very beginning of the molt
8. Throughout the entire period of molt

I. When color food is fed

A. ....

II. What the color food contains

A. ....

B. ....

C. ....

DRAWING CONCLUSIONS. The best conclusion to draw from this selection is that . . . .

1. Birds can be made to like any type of diet.
2. The color of all birds is due to their diet.
3. It is possible to change the color of some birds.
4. Canaries have been color-fed for more than seventy years.

Pupil's Score ....

GRADE	6	7	8	9	10	11	12	13
SCORE	12	16	18	20	22	23	24	25

45

11

SELECTING BOOKS

The two primary rules in selecting reading material for remedial reading students and beginning readers, whether they are children or adults, are

1. Keep it short.
2. Keep it easy.

For more advanced students, from upper second grade ability on through adulthood, interest in the subject material becomes a predominant factor. However, interest will not entirely overcome the difficulty level of the material. Therefore, for the slightly advanced readers a new set of selection rules must be used:

3. Keep it interesting.
4. Select the correct level of difficulty.
5. Vary the difficulty level and length.

These simple rules need some explanation, particularly with respect to "easy" material and "relative difficulty" levels. Chapter 2 mentioned a number of tests and methods for determining a child's reading ability level. It is not difficult to find a child's level of reading achievement. It is a little more difficult to apply tests to the reading material to determine with accuracy its difficulty level, but it can be done. The good teacher then matches the child's reading ability with the difficulty level of the material.

The producers of reading materials (authors of reading books and the publishing industry) and the consumers (teachers and librarians) have developed some standards of reading difficulty based on average children's reading ability in each grade level. There is a rough consensus of teachers, librarians, and publishers as to what constitutes first-grade level of difficulty, second-grade level of difficulty, etc. These levels have some correspondence with how children progress through school, in terms of growth of reading ability levels. It has been charged, particularly by teachers in schools serving slightly below-average socioeconomic-level communities, that the established readability levels are too optimistic. This means, for example, that most of the third-grade students in a slightly below-average school cannot read third-grade difficulty level of material. However, the gradual progression concept can be very useful in the teaching of reading and in the selection of books for children, if teachers do not become bound by the grade-level concept.

WHAT MAKES A BOOK DIFFICULT? Some of the more prominent factors in increasing reading difficulty are the following:

1. Vocabulary difficulty (word frequency, use level, or length)
2. Grammatical complexity (sentence length)
3. Concept complexity (concrete-to-abstract continuum)
4. Specialized subject matter (history, physics)
5. Format (type size, white space surrounding word, margins)
6. Illustrations (graphs, charts, figures, or lack thereof)
7. Writer's style and organization
8. Mechanical aids (underlining, subheads, italics)

All of these factors can contribute to the difficulty level of reading material. One of the best and more professional methods of judging the difficulty of reading material is the application of readability formulas which take into account chiefly the two factors of vocabulary and sentence length. Among the poorest criteria of difficulty level—and these criteria are frequently applied by both publishers and parents—are type size and subject matter. For example, some children's books, which are intended primarily to be read to children, contain passages such as this:

The gorgeous white rabbit hopped across the road to Peter's grandfather's ranch. Timidly he perked up his ears and looked for some carrots because it was nearly his supper time.

This passage may be set in very large, bold type; and the page may be beautifully illustrated in four-color plates. The subject matter is obviously intended for three-to-six-year-olds. However, a readability formula would probably peg this passage at about the seventh-grade reading difficulty level. This means that it could be read only by a child of seventh-grade reading ability who is about twelve years old.

INTEREST LEVEL The preceding passage about the white rabbit illustrates a classic case of the disparity between interest level and readability level. Many times a day in most libraries, children interested in rocket ships or similar topics select books totally unsuitable to their reading levels and then cannot read them. Teenagers with below-normal reading ability want to read about dating and cars but find that these normally fascinating topics are not interesting when written at a reduced readability level.

Hence, in helping to select reading materials, teachers and librarians must be certain that children are not frustrated in their reading desires. Teachers and librarians must know the difficulty level of the book as well as the reading achievement skills of the student. A child who has met with failure on two or three trips to the library is not likely to try again.

For some reason, librarians have been reluctant to adopt the readability concept or to use readability formulas in judging books. One suspects that because they see more bright children than other segments of the population, they tend to feel that third- or fourth-grade standards for a book are rather meaningless. Having recently observed a fourth-grade child who had eighth-grade reading ability and who mastered *Tom Sawyer* without any trouble, thenceforth a librarian is likely to regard it as suitable for children from the third to the tenth grades. While it is true that the book can be read and enjoyed by some children in third, fourth, fifth, and sixth grades, the fact is that the average sixth grader in the United States cannot enjoy Mark Twain's *Tom Sawyer* in its original form. Librarians, who ordinarily see only high-IQ children, often fail to realize this.

High interest and motivation, of course, can cause the child to read books or material of a more difficult level than he normally would. A teenage boy with ninth-grade reading ability who wants to know how to repair his car may gladly spend an hour reading material of twelfth-grade difficulty level, but when given a history book of eleventh-grade difficulty finds that he tires easily and has difficulty comprehending it after the first few minutes.

READABILITY FORMULAS The most widely used formulas for judging readability of children's materials are based only on two factors: vocabulary difficulty and grammatical complexity as reflected in sentence length.

Two of the best and most widely used readability formulas are the (1) Spache, for grades one through four (technically 1.5 to 3.9), and (2) Dale-Chall, for grades four through sixteen.* Both of these formulas, in their original form, use fairly complicated procedures involving mathematical computations and the use of constants. (In the appendix to this chapter these formulas are presented in a short form in which most of the mathematical computation has been eliminated through the use of charts.) Both formulas have detailed sets of

*Edgar Dale and Jeanne Chall, "A Formula for Predicting Readability Instructions," *Educational Research Bulletin*, Ohio State University, vol. 17, Feb. 17, 1948, pp. 37–54; and George D. Spache, "The Spache Readability Formula," *Good Reading for Poor Readers*, The Garrard Press, Champaign, Ill., 1958.

rules for word counts. (Is a hyphenated word two words? Is *coming* different from *comes*?) In addition, both formulas determine vocabulary difficulty by first presenting a set vocabulary (in Spache's formula, some 700 words; and in the Dale-Chall, 3,000 words), then declare that any word not appearing on this vocabulary is unfamiliar. It is the percentage of "unfamiliar" words which determines the difficulty level of the passage. Both formulas use sentence length as the simplest measure of grammatical complexity. Grammatical studies of difficulty level, counting prepositional phrases, adverbial clauses, and all of the various grammatical segments, tend to rank the difficulty of the passage in the same manner that average sentence length would.

In an effort to find a short and quick method of determining readability, I have developed a Readability Graph which, like the two formulas described, uses vocabulary difficulty and sentence length as parameters. However, by using a graph, many arithmetic computations required by the original forms of the Spache and Dale-Chall formulas are avoided. The Readability Graph is simple because it determines word difficulty level by using an *average* word length (average syllables per 100 words) instead of a vocabulary of 700 or 3,000 words. A further simplification lies in its coverage of a single range (from first grade through adult reading materials) without necessitating the use of two different formulas.

The Readability Graph is presented in the appendix.

ADULT READABILITY The Employee Research Section of General Motors Corporation has studied readability in connection with communication research (General Motors publishes thirty-five house organs and much other material).* It has developed a simple plastic analog device in which are inserted only two bits of information: average sentence length and number of syllables per 100 words. The calculator gives readability in four levels (see Table 11-1).

Levels of Reading ability of the United States population is one of the more interesting subjects considered in this study. The fact is that only 40 percent of the population can read material that is of high-school level of difficulty.

The United States has a low rate of complete literacy but not the lowest in the world. Although reliable figures are not readily available, we might accept third-grade reading ability as a standard; on this basis, about 7 or 8 percent of the total population is illiterate. These figures might serve to challenge our government, our educational system, and particularly our reading teachers.

FORMAT Format, which includes page layout and type size, does contribute to readability but not as much as one might think. Readability studies which vary the type size have generally shown that adults can easily and rapidly read materials set in anything from 9-point to 12-point type. Newspapers are usually

*General Motors Corporation, *The Reading Ease Calculator,* Science Research Associates, Chicago, 1950.

TABLE 11-1
READING ABILITY LEVELS OF THE UNITED STATES ADULT POPULATION

Reading-ease calculator score	*Easily read by % of U.S. adult population*[a]	*Estimated education completed*	*Number of words in typical vocabulary*	*Typical magazines read*
Very easy	90.0	4–5th grade	10,000 to 12,000	All pulps[b]
Easy	80.0	6th–8th grade[c]	13,000 to 16,000	*Reader's Digest*
Hard	40.0	High school	19,000 to 21,000	*Time Magazine*
Very hard	4.5	College	25,000 and over	*Atlantic Monthly*

[a]Percentages based on 1948 Bureau of Census estimate of United States population of twenty-one years of age.
[b]*True Story*, *True Detective*, etc.
[c]Educational level of average United States adult.

set in 9-point type. This book is set in 10-point type. Books for young children, such as primers, are frequently set in 14-point type. There is a slight tendency to use larger type in books for younger children. There is also a tendency to print modern books in larger type. Fifty years ago it was not uncommon for publishers to set books and magazines in 8-point or even smaller type.

In addition to the size of the type, the white space surrounding each word

TABLE 11-2
A SAMPLE OF TYPE SIZES, STYLES, AND LEADING

4-point type	This line is set in a reader face type
6-point type	This line is set in a sanseriph type
8-point type	**This line is set in a Bodoni type**
9-point type	This line is set in Old English type
10-point type	This line is set in a Gothic type
11-point type	This line is set in 11-point type
12-point type	This line is set in 12-point type

Both leading and line length contribute toward readability. This paragraph is set in 9-point type, the lines are 80 mm. long, and the leading between the lines is 3 points.

can be increased by using larger spaces between words and larger spaces between lines (called leading). Books are considered a little more readable if there is an adequate amount of white space around words and in the page margins, as well as adequate leading. Publishers of children's books, especially texts, are generally concerned with this problem.

The length of the line is also a factor in readability, shorter lines tending generally to be more readable. Eighty millimeters is generally considered to be an optimum line length. Some modern textbooks are set in two columns per page in order to shorten the length of lines in the interest of readability. Newspapers also take advantage of this by setting type in columns. It is interesting to note that tabloids which appeal to people of lower reading ability tend to have narrower columns.

Readability studies have looked into the relative readability of different type styles. With the exception of very fancy types, such as Old English, adults seem to be able to read most type styles with equal ease. Children's book publishers tend to use a "reader typeface," which is certainly one of the easiest type faces to read. A typeface class known as Bodoni (with exaggerated thickness and thinness of the lines) is thought to be more difficult for children to read.

Other experimentation on type variations centers on the difference be tween serif and sans-serif types. Reader typefaces, such as that in which this book is set, have small hairlines at the base of the *l*, *d*, etc. These little lines are called serifs and tend to give style and shape to the letters. The so-called modern typefaces tend to omit the serifs, and some adults feel that this is more tiring to read over a long period of time.

Margins around the page contribute to reading ease. Generally, the wider the margins, the easier the reading. The eye is attracted to any contrast, such as the difference between the edge of the page and the table, wide margins tending to keep the eye centered on the contrast between the type and the whiteness of the page.

The kind of paper used is also a factor in readability. A pure white paper with a high rag content and a dull finish is generally considered best. Expensive editions are frequently printed on this type of paper. Pages with a high gloss have the disadvantage of reflecting light, causing a distraction to the eye of the reader. Frequently, some coating is used to make the paper glossy; this is often done in the "slick" magazines or in textbooks which want a high quality of photographic reproduction. Impurities in cheaper papers, as in newspapers, tend to detract from the clearness of the type.

The tinting of papers and inks to add different colors has been studied, but results have been inconclusive. Most readers prefer black ink on white paper. Perhaps this is because they are used to this combination, but research has failed to show the superiority of other tints. Sight-saving classes (for nearly blind students) have at times emphasized the use of a green tinted paper, but this is admittedly for a very small and special segment of the population.

WHERE BOOK LISTS CAN BE FOUND Once you start looking for them, you will find that there are nearly as many book lists as there are books. Any librarian can quickly supply you with a half dozen book lists with titles such as "The Ten Best Children's Books of Last Year," "One Hundred Children's Classics," "Mystery Stories for Teenage Girls," "Books on Africa for Young Readers," etc.

Basal reading series frequently contain book lists as well as references to sections of book lists that accompany teacher's manuals.

Experienced teachers, principals, librarians, and supervisors at the local, county, and state levels invariably have a few book lists at hand. Teachers can find book lists published nearly every month in professional journals. *The Reader's Guide to Perodical Literature* and the *Education Index* can help in locating them.

Even though there is no shortage of book lists, here are a few that might be of particular interest to readers of this book. Spache has published a very interesting book entitled *Good Reading for Poor Readers* (Garrard Press, 1964), which contains a large book list which is classified according to interest area. Each of the titles is annotated, the interest level (the age of a child who might be interested in the book) is given, as well as the readability level according to the Spache or Dale-Chall readability formulas. It also has six pages of book lists.

A comprehensive list of materials can be found in *El-Hi Textbooks in Print* published annually by R. R. Bowker. This reference book includes all basal readers and many supplementary materials, including such related materials as a separate listing for programmed-instruction materials. They are classified by subject with a title and author index for elementary, junior, and senior high school texts and pedagogical books.

Another excellent source which annually lists 8,000 books, many with readability formula scores reported, is *The Elementary School Library Collection: A Guide to Books and Other Media* edited by Mary Gaver (Newark, N.J., Bro-Dart Foundation, 5th ed., 1970).

Most colleges and universities offer courses entitled "Children's Literature" for both the elementary and secondary levels; these can be very helpful and useful to reading teachers. The courses generally cover children's classics, modern literature, and materials for remedial readers. Even though teachers may not be able to take the course, the textbooks for these courses can be very useful.

DIFFERENT TYPES OF READING MATERIAL Though it comes as no surprise to teachers that reading material appears in many other forms than books, some discussion of these forms might be helpful. I served as a consultant to a high school that was having difficulty with its remedial reading program. The teacher complained that she had absolutely no material easy enough for her poorest students and no money to purchase anything. I suggested that she simply walk across the street to the elementary school and ask for old copies of student newspapers used in the lower grades. By using a little discrimination, childish stories were eliminated and both the budget and problems of reading material shortage were temporarily solved. While remedial reading programs are certainly not supposed to operate on no-budget, we all know that sometimes it happens.

Here are some of the standard kinds of children's reading material:

1. *Basal reading texts* were discussed in Chapter 4, but it should be pointed out that reading texts can also be used on a supplementary basis. Some books (in particular, those from a reading series not currently being used as the main text in a class) should always be in the classroom library or available in the school library. Many texts, especially those which emphasize the children's literature or classic stories approach, make very interesting supplementary reading. In some school districts, previously used texts provide a very low-cost source of reading material for a classroom or remedial reading situation. Care should be taken that the stories are not too childish for the poor readers who are older. Texts in such special areas as social studies or science can make interesting supplementary reading also.

2. *Trade books* are books which are sold in bookstores (such as novels or other book-length stories). Each year there are hundreds of titles of trade books published for children and adolescents, and these, together with the established classics, form the bulk of the fiction section of most school libraries.

3. *Series books* form a special class of trade books. While often not of high literary merit, they are often very interesting for children and motivate them to extend their reading experience. Some of the famous series titles are *The Hardy Boys, The Bobsey Twins*, etc. Sometimes a poor reader will begin with one book in a series, become interested and then will proceed to read the next half dozen. By the time he has done this, his reading is invariably improved. Other series of books are more oriented toward school use, for example, the *Childhood of Famous Americans* (a biography series), or the Row Peterson science booklets. Other series that are equally popular in the classroom and in the home are the Landmark *All About Books* and similar series designed to combine entertainment and education.

4. *Adapted classics* are a special type of book used in schools and are particularly suitable for remedial reading instruction. These books include such classics as *Huckleberry Finn* and *Lorna Doone*, which have been simplified by removing some of the long descriptive passages and difficult vocabulary. Sometimes the sentence lengths are shortened and passages are rewritten. English teachers are often horrified to see some of their favorite stories cut and simplified, but what they fail to appreciate is that these books are not intended for good readers; they are intended for students who are unable to read the original version. A student who reads an adapted classic at an early age will often tackle the original version as he grows older. Other students in remedial classes might never be able to read the original version and the well-adapted version is certainly better than nothing or an inferior story.

List of publishers of adapted classics

American Book Company, 55 Fifth Avenue, New York, New York 10003.
Appleton-Century-Crofts, Inc., 35 West 32nd Street, New York, New York 10017.
Globe Book Company, Inc., 175 Fifth Avenue, New York, New York 10010.
C. S. Hammond & Company, Maplewood, New Jersey 07040 New York.
Harper & Row Publishers (Wheeler), 2500 Crawford Avenue, Evanston, Illinois 60201.
Julian Messner, Publishers, Inc., 8 West 40th Street, New York, New York 10018.
Laidlaw Brothers, Thatcher and Madison Streets, River Forest, Illinois 60305.
Longmans, Green & Company, Ltd. 119 West 40th Street, New York, New York 10018.
McGraw-Hill Book Company (Webster Division), Manchester Road, Manchester, Missouri 63011.
Regents Publishing Company, 200 Park Avenue S., New York, New York 10003.
Scott, Foresman and Company, 1900 East Lake Avenue, Glenview, Illinois 60025.
Singer (Sanborn) Company, 249 West Erie Boulevard, Syracuse, New York 13200.
Steck-Vaughn Company, Box 16, Austin, Texas 78700.

5. *Drill books, pamphlets, workbooks, and charts* are some of the numerous media which contain interesting shorter bits of reading material. The Literature Sampler* is a boxful of pamphlets, each containing a section from some well-known book of children's literature. The pamphlet is interesting reading material in itself, but it also encourages the student to continue to read the full book. The cards are graded, and a number of different types of literature are presented for each difficulty level. Secondary schools have used anthologies of short stories and various reading selections for a long time. Anthologies are also becoming more prevalent in the elementary schools. Some workbooks and "reading laboratories" contain a number of short reading selections, which are designed primarily for use with comprehension drills but make interesting shorter passages in themselves.

6. *Student newspapers and magazines* are now being sold by the hundreds of thousands in American schools. Many student newspapers (for example, *My Weekly Reader** and *Young America Reader*†) are designed to help the student to develop reading skills. Even though student newspapers and magazines are published with a specific grade level in mind, there is no reason why a teacher cannot use easier newspapers with poorer reading students and vice versa, if she does so with discretion. Secondary schools seem to favor magazines over student newspapers. One worthy of particular mention is *Practical English*‡ which is intended for the mildly remedial secondary student who needs some reading and writing improvement. Another student magazine, *Read*,* is intended primarily for junior high school students.

7. A *special reading series* designed for remedial reading is very helpful.

**Literature Sampler*, Encyclopedia Britannica, Inc. Chicago, 1964.
*American Education Publications, Columbus, Ohio.
†Young America Magazines, Silver Springs, Md.
‡Scholastic Magazines, 33 West 42nd St., New York, N.Y.
*Young America Magazines, Silver Springs, Md.

Teachers who use individualized reading techniques in the regular classroom also find them very helpful. While reaching to very low reading levels, these books strive to maintain high interest value for older children. Frequently they are built around some exciting topic (such as diving in the *Deep Sea Adventure Series* by Harr Wagner) or center on exciting characters from history (as in the *American Adventure Series* by Wheeler) or cowboys (as in the *Cowboy Sam Series* by Beckly Cardy).

List of children's literature materials

Arbuthnot, Mary Hill. *Children and Books.* 3d ed. Glenview, Ill.: Scott, Foresman and Company, 1964.

Burton, Dwight L. *Literature Study in the High School.* New York: Holt, Rinehart and Winston, Inc., 1964.

Carlsen, G. Robert. *Books and the Teen-age Reader.* Evanston, Ill.: Harper & Row, Publishers, Incorporated, 1967.

Larrick, Nancy. *Parents' Guide to Children's Reading.* Revised edition. New York: Pocket Books, Inc., 1964.

Larrick, Nancy. *Teacher's Guide to Children's Books.* Columbus, Ohio: Charles E. Merrill Books, Inc., 1960.

Fader, D., and McNeill, E. B. *Hooked on Books.* New York: G. P. Putnam's Sons, 1968.

Viguers, Ruth Hill. *Margin for Surprise.* Boston: Little, Brown and Company, 1964.

HIGH-INTEREST MATERIALS Reading teachers should be continually on the alert for books and materials that students really want to read. I recall, from my remedial reading teaching days in a secondary school, the great success of *Hot Rod* by Gregor Felson, a book which was particularly popular with boys who had never before read a book. It was a great joy to hear a student, who had been struggling with phonics and other special materials, demand to read a full book, to see him sit down and become so engrossed that he asked not to be disturbed until he had finished the book. *Hot Rod* became so popular that six copies were stolen from the library in one semester and students were recommending it to one another. On the upper elementary level, I had the same kind of success with *Boxcar Children* by Gertrude Warner (Scott, Foresman, Chicago, 1950). These are only two of the dozens of books which "catch on" with students, and the reading teacher can find out about them by talking to students, teachers, school and children's librarians, and supervisors.

Teachers of minority groups have found that articles or books written by authors of the same minority group as the student often have great appeal. Black students often take a special interest in the writings of black authors, and students of Puerto Rican or Mexican-American descent like authors of a similar or at least a Spanish-flavored background. In fact all children in integrated schools often enjoy reading the writings of minority group authors, and these writings help to explain and provide intergroup understanding. The writings must not always be books or articles; sometimes even poetry or songs can appeal to the toughest adolescent.

TABLE 11-3
READING INTERESTS OF AMERICAN SECONDARY-SCHOOL STUDENTS (GRADES SEVEN TO TWELVE)

Boys	*Girls*
Adventure (outdoor, war)	Adventure (not grim)
Outdoor games	Humour
School life	Animals
Mystery	Romance
Humour	Family life
Stories about men (including biographies)	Stories about men and women (including biographies of women)
Science (how to make things)	Domestic arts (how to cook, etc.)

A number of studies have investigated the reading interests of children. Table 11-3 lists some of the reading interests of secondary school boys and girls. You will note that there is a marked sex difference. Boys tend to like outdoor adventures, which are a little rough, and stories about men. Girls like some adventure (although not too rough), and they are willing to read stories about men or women. Girls are interested in stories about family life and domestic arts, but boys would not be caught dead reading them. Boys, on the other hand, are more interested in science, how to do things, and outdoor games.

Teachers can also find out a great deal about children's reading interests simply by asking them what they like or having them fill out questionnaires. After a few students in the class start reading books, they can keep a record of the books they especially liked and then pass on the suggestions to other students in the class. Teachers who teach the same level for several years can collect these records and have a good idea about what types of reading appeal to that age level.

Books sometimes receive a great interest impetus from their theoretical enemies – television and movies. If a story has been televised or made into a feature film, many students who have seen and liked the showing are well disposed to read the book in full.

Recently a number of materials for beginning readers have been developed by trade book publishers. High on the success list have been the famous Dr. Seuss books which, while using a controlled vocabulary suitable for beginning readers or first-grade reading level, manage to have good rhyme, meter, humor, and interesting situations.

CONCLUSION

The importance of knowing what materials make good reading for students can hardly be underestimated. Librarians can be very helpful, as can such library-type courses as "Children's Literature." Teachers who specialize in remedial reading, however, must have additional sources of books and reading materials especially suited to their particular students. A number of these materials have been mentioned in this chapter and more are mentioned in Chapter 12.

Whenever materials are to be selected, the primary rule is to match the student's reading ability with the difficulty level of the material. In this chapter were also presented some information about judging the difficulty of reading materials and the use of readability formulas.

APPENDIX 11-A AN ANNOTATED LIST OF REMEDIAL READING MATERIALS

Much of the following list of materials was developed by Joseph Zelnick in cooperation with Edward Fry for a Job Corps Center. Since Job Corps boys range in age from sixteen to twenty-one, the materials are a little slanted towards secondary and adult poor readers, but many of the references are equally useful at all age levels. Some purely elementary materials have been added.

MATERIALS FOR BEGINNING READERS LEVELS 1–2

Adair, U.B., and R. L. Curry. *Reading for a Purpose.* Chicago: Follett Publishing Co., 1965. Basic literacy text for young adults and adults, emphasizing a sight-word approach. Includes exercises in writing and language usage.

Alesi, Gladys, and Dora Pantell. *Family Life in the U.S.A.* New York: Regents Publishing Co., 1962. The story of an Americanized family with school-age children. For beginning English classes. Emphasis is on oral communication.

______. *First Book in American English.* New York: Oxford Book Co., 1962. Written as a language book for the foreign-born, but suitable for adult literacy classes. Includes exercises in reading, writing, and English usage.

Bamman, Henry, and Robert Whitehead. The *Checkered Flag Series.* San Francisco: Harr Wagner Publishing Co., 1967. A high-interest, low-readability series for upper elementary boys with second grade reading ability. Contains comprehension checks.

Basic Reading Skills. Detroit: Division of Improvement of Instruction, Adult Basic Education Skills Training Center, Board of Education of the City of Detroit, 1965. A workbook designed for adult nonreaders. The approach in this book, which aims to build a knowledge of thirty basic words and simple sentence structure, is audial, visual, and kinesthetic.

Betts, Emmett (ed.). *The American Adventure Series.* Chicago: Wheeler Publishing Company, 1951. An old standby, long a favorite of remedial and classroom teachers. Books range from 2 to 6.

Boning, Richard A. *Specific Skill Series.* Rockville Center, N.Y.: Darnell Loft, Ltd., 1962–1965. A multilevel program of five reading skills: Locating the Answer, Following Directions, Using the Context, Getting the Facts, Working with Sounds. These workbooks are available in reading levels 1 through 6.

Bright, Emma L., and Eva C. Mitchell. *Home and Family Life Series.* New London, Conn.: Arthur C. Croft Co., 1949. Set of four beginning adult readers. Carefully controlled vocabulary. Accompanying workbook contains exercises for building sight vocabulary, word recognition, and basic reading skills. Titles include: *A Day with the Brown Family, Making a Good Living, The Browns at School, The Browns and Their Neighbors.*

Buchanan, Cynthia D. *Programmed Reading for Adults.* New York: McGraw-Hill Book Co., 1966. Basic literacy program for adult illiterates. This linear program begins with number identification and formation and proceeds to capital letters, small letters, phonetically regular words. Books 1 to 5 (now available) enable the student to reach the upper-primary reading level.

Case, Angelica. *Everyday English and Basic Word List for Adults.* New York: Noble and Noble, 1964. List of 1,000 essential words arranged thematically in units or lessons. Suitable for beginning and intermediate readers.

______. *How We Live.* New York: Noble and Noble, 1949. Basic literacy text for beginning adult readers.

______. *Your Family and Your Job.* New York: Noble and Noble, 1948. Basic literacy text for adults.

Chandler, Edna W. *The Cowboy Sam Series.* Chicago: Benefic Press, 1960. An excellent beginning series for young or upper elementary children.

Chapman, Byron E., and Louis Schulz. *Mott Basic Language Skills Program.* Chicago: Allied Education Council, 1965. A full language-arts program for adults with an emphasis on reading skills. The four basic texts range from beginning reading through secondary reading level. Supplemental materials are available which include books of general interest as well as vocational reading materials. Teacher's manual includes sections on how to teach reading and diagnose reading difficulties, in addition to word lists and a graded reading bibliography.

Engelmann, Siegfried, and Elaine Bruner. *Distar Reading.* Chicago: Science Research Associates, Inc., 1969. A kit of materials used to teach beginning reading by the author's unique approach (heavy language use), which is favored by many educators of the disadvantaged.

English for Today. New York: McGraw-Hill Book Company, 1961. A series of six books which present a complete course in English as a second language. From Book I, which starts with a picture vocabulary of common nouns and one verb, graded lessons are presented in sequence through Book VI, which is an anthology of contemporary writers. Some stories are shortened, but none are simplified. Book I, *At Home and at School*; Book II, *The World We Live In*; Book III, *The Way We Live*; Book IV, *Our Changing World*; Book V, *Life in English-Speaking Countries*; Book VI, *Literature in English.*

______. *First Steps in Reading English.* New York: Washington Square Press, 1957. Basic literacy text. Begins with words and sentences composed of only seven letters. Words with new letters are introduced gradually. Picture clues accompany all lessons.

Gates, Arthur I., and Celeste C. Peardon. *Gates-Peardon Reading Exercises.* New York: Bureau of Publications, Teachers College, Columbia University, 1963. Series of ten reading booklets designed to improve basic reading skills, such as reading for details, reading for ideas, and following directions. Introductory level, suitable for beginning readers.

Geake, Robert, and Donald Smith. *Visual Tracking.* Ann Arbor, Mich.: Ann Arbor Publishers, 1962. A self-instruction workbook designed to aid in the development of perceptual skills. Using the alphabet as a model, exercises emphasize discrimination among letters of decreasing size. Can be used with child or adult beginners in remedial work.

Goldberg, Herman R., and Winifred T. Drumber (eds.). *New Rochester Occupational Reading Series—The Job Ahead.* Chicago: Science Research Associates, 1963. Identical stories about the problems of youth written on three reading ability levels: second grade, third and fourth grades, and fourth and fifth grades. Accompanying workbooks provide practice in basic skills.

Guyton, Mary L., and Margaret E. Kielty. *From Words to Stories*. New York: Noble and Noble, 1951. Basic literacy text for adults. Short selections about everyday experiences. Utilizes a sight-word approach. Total vocabulary is 144 words.

Harding, Lowry W., and James B. Burr, *Men in the Armed Forces*. Madison, Wis.: United States Armed Forces Institute, 1950. A beginning adult reader. The subject matter is geared to life in the armed forces, although selections include common everyday experiences.

———. *Servicemen Learn to Read*. Madison, Wis.: United States Armed Forces Institute, 1956. A workbook which accompanies the beginning reader, *Men in the Armed Forces*.

Helson, Lida G. *A First Course in Remedial Reading*. Cambridge, Mass.: Educators Publishing Service, 1964. A workbook with a strong phonics approach to remedial reading. In addition to the sound elements which are presented, this book contains lists of nonphonetic words, homonyms, and rules of syllabification and spelling.

Henderson, Ellen C., and Twila S. Henderson. *Learning to Read and Write*. New York: Holt, Rinehart and Winston, 1964. This book represents a linguistic approach to teaching beginning reading to adults.

Henney, R. Lee. *System for Success*. Chicago: Follett Publishing Co., 1964. Multiple skills programs (reading, writing, arithmetic, grammar) consisting of two books. Book 1 for beginning readers (reading levels 0–4) utilizes a family phonics approach. Book 2, reading levels 5–8, contains factual reading selections on different topics. The exercises which follow each selection emphasize reading comprehension and vocabulary development.

Laubach, Frank C. *Building Your Language Power*. Programmed by William C. Wolf. Morristown, N. J.: Silver Burdett Co., 1965. Adult literacy program consisting of six graded books. Based on the "Each One Teach One" system originally developed by Frank Laubach. Like the earlier Laubach program, the current materials use a strong phonics approach.

———. *Streamlined English*, rev. ed. New York: The Macmillan Co., 1955. A basic adult literacy text for those beginning to learn to read and write. Has a strong phonics approach.

Mitchell, Eva C. Revised by Marion M. Murphy. *Language Workbook*. New London: Arthur C. Croft Co., 1964. Designed to help beginning adult readers to learn daily communications skills which are used socially and at work. Accompanies reading books in *Home and Family Life Series*.

Mountain, Lee, and Edward Fry. *Storybooks for Beginners*. Highland Park, N.J.: Dreier Educational Systems, 1971.

New Reading Skill Builders. Pleasantville, N.Y.: Reader's Digest Services, Educational Division, 1967. Contain short stories and articles adapted to a wide range of reading levels. Selections are illustrated and accompanied by comprehension and word-building exercises. For grades one through six.

Pollack, Cecelia, and Patrick R. Lane. *Hip Reader*. Brooklyn, New York: Book-Lab Inc. (1499 37th St.), 1969.

Rambeau, John and Nancy. *The Forest Jim Readers*. San Francisco: Harr Wagner Publishing Co., 1959. A supplementary primary reading series with an outdoor flavor.

Reader's Digest Adult Readers. Pleasantville, N. Y.: Reader's Digest Services, Educational Division, 1964. Twelve different titles in three reading levels, grades one through four. *Second Chance*, *Mystery of the Mountains*, *Send for Red*, and *Workers in the Sky* suitable for beginning readers.

Richards, I. A., and C. M. Gibson. *English through Pictures*. New York: Pocket Books, 1946. Designed for teaching reading to adult beginning readers and the foreign-born. Presents about 500 words, simply illustrated.

Robertson, M. S. *Adult Reader*. Austin, Texas: Steck-Vaughn Co., 1964. A reading work-textbook for teaching adult beginners to read. A variety of topics are presented in short selections. Sight-word approach is utilized in presenting new words. Exercises include word recognition, handwriting, and comprehension. The total vocabulary consists of approximately 450 words most frequently used by adults.

Smith, Edwin, and Florence Lutz. *My Country*. Austin, Texas: The Steck Co., 1956. Basic reading text for adolescent and adult beginning readers. Total vocabulary of 206 words. Exercises designed to develop sight-word vocabulary as well as word analysis skills.

Smith, Harley A., and Ida Lee King. *I Want to Read and Write*. Austin, Texas: The Steck Co., 1950. A word-text for teaching adult beginners to read and write. Exercises in reading and writing provide practice with about 300 basic words.

Smith, Harley, and Ida Lee King. *I Want to Learn English*. Austin, Texas: The Steck Co., 1956. Work-text in reading and writing for adult beginners. Slightly higher level than *I Want to Read and Write*.

Steps to Learning. Books 1 and 2. Austin, Texas: Steck-Vaughn Co., 1965. Work-texts for adults in beginning reading and writing. Reading exercises start with auditory and visual discrimination. Sight words, phonics, and structural analysis are integrated with short, illustrated reading selections, simple writing exercises, and lessons in beginning arithmetic. Book 1 contains a total vocabulary of 302 words. In Book 2, 276 new words are added.

Sullivan, M. W. *Reading*. Palo Alto, Calif.: Behavioral Research Laboratories, 1966. Programmed reading materials for beginning adult readers. In this linear program the student first learns letter-sound associations through pictures and phonetically regular words. The format is similar to the materials previously developed by the Sullivan Associates. Series I, which is now available, consists of four books which reach the upper-primary reading level. An accompanying placement test indicates the book in which a student may start the program.

Weinhold, Clyde. *Adult Basic Education Series: English*. New York: Holt, Rinehart Winston, 1963. An elementary text in basic English. Common patterns in structure and usage are presented in simple terms for adults.

What Is It Series. Chicago: Benefic Press, 1960. A series of science readers written on a 1–4 reading level. The program presents basic science facts in more than forty areas of science. Each book is forty-eight pages long and contains many illustrations in color. Titles in the series are: *What is the Earth*; *What is Electricity*; *What is Heat*; *What is a Magnet*; *What is a Machine*; and others.

Woolman, Myron. *Reading in High Gear*. Chicago: Science Research Associates, 1964. The "Accelerated Progressive Choice" reading program designed for culturally disadvantaged learners or slower learners. Since it starts with beginning reading, it can be used with nonreaders. The program, divided into three parts, progresses to eighth-grade reading level in Word Attack Skills. Perceptual training receives emphasis in the first part of the program.

MATERIALS FOR INTERMEDIATE READERS
LEVELS 3–6

Alesi, Gladys, and Dora Pantell. *Second Book in American English.* New York: Oxford Book Co., 1962. Continues program presented in *First Book in American English.* Selections are dialogues accompanied by comprehension and language practice exercises.

Allen, Virginia F. *People in Livingston.* New York: Thomas Y. Crowell Co., 1953. An intermediate reader for adults who are learning English. The stories center around the fictional town of Livingston where the people are typical of Americans all over the United States.

Bamman, Henry (program director). *Kaleidoscope Readers,* (Three O'Clock Courage, One Thing at Once, etc.). San Francisco: Field Education Publications, 1969. Paperbound story and workbook type exercises that span the elementary range.

Benner, Patricia Ann. *Troubleshooter. A Program of Basic English Skills.* Boston: Houghton Mifflin, 1969. A series of workbooks for writing basic English.

Boning, Richard A. *Specific Skill Series.* Rockville Center, N. Y.: Barnell Loft, Ltd., 1962–1965. A multilevel program of five reading skills: Locating the Answer, Following Directions, Using the Context, Getting the Facts, Working with Sounds. These workbooks are available in reading levels 1 through 6.

Burton, Ardis E., et al. *Stories for Teen-Agers.* New York: Globe Book Co., 1960. Collections of short stories of interest to adolescents, written by popular modern writers. These books deal with problems faced by modern youth. Book A, 3–4 reading level. Books I and II, 5–6 reading level.

Carson, Esther O. *Campus Work Experience.* Castro Valley, Calif.: Esther O. Carson, 1962. A work-text for slow learning students. It contains a collection of readings and exercises centered around student accounts of work experiences.

______. *Teen-Agers Prepare for Work.* Castro Valley, Calif.: Esther O. Carson, 1962. Books I and II. These work-texts are designed for slow learners of high-school age who are potential dropouts or dropouts. They consist of short selections which provide information about jobs and everyday problems which confront youth and adults.

Cass, Angelica. *Everyday English and Basic Word List for Adults.* New York: Noble and Noble, 1964. List of 1,000 essential words arranged thematically in units or lessons. Suitable for beginning and intermediate readers.

______. *How to Become a U. S. Citizen.* New York: Noble and Noble, 1959. Basic literacy text which gives information for those seeking citizenship.

Crosher, G. R. *Pacemaker Story Books* (A Bomb on the Submarine, The Fire on the First Floor, etc.). Palo Alto: Fearon Publishers, 1955–1956. A paperback series of small books (forty pages) with high adventure titles.

Coleman, James, et al. *The Deep Sea Adventure Series.* San Francisco: Harr Wagner Publishing Co., 1962. Eight books ranging in reading levels from second to fifth grades. Each story is a different adventure of Don and his diving-boat crew. These Books have been used successfully with young adults as well as with children.

Dixson, Robert. *American Classics.* New York: Regents Publishing Co., 1953, 1964. Books 1–10. Simplified and adapted classics of American literature. Vocabulary ranges from 750 words (Book 1) to 2,600 words (Book 10). Titles include *Moby Dick, Red Badge of Courage, Huckleberry Finn,* and others.

Elfert and Weinstein. *Achieving Reading Skills.* New York: Globe Book Co., 1958. A book of readings drawn from well-known stories and graded in readability levels from third to seventh grades. Accompanying exercises are designed to aid in building basic reading skills.

Federal Textbook for Citizenship. Washington, D. C.: Superintendent of Documents, Government Printing Office, 1964. Simple reading materials which deal with citizenship. Can be used for literacy training classes. Available free to schools and adult citizenship classes. Series of three titles includes *Our United States, Our American Way of Life, Our Government.*

Feigenbaum, Lawrence H. *Successful Reading.* New York: Globe Book Co., 1958. A basic reading text which contains reading selections, readings on reading skills, and exercises designed to aid in building reading skills.

Gates, Arthur I., and Celeste C. Peardon. *Gates-Peardon Reading Exercises.* New York: Bureau of Publications, Teachers College, Columbia University, 1963. Series of ten booklets designed to improve such basic skills as reading for details, reading for ideas, and following directions. Preparatory level, elementary level, and intermediate level are suitable for intermediate readers.

Gilford, Henry. *Plays for Today.* New York: Walker Educational Book Corp. Kit of sets of short plays. Excellent for oral reading practice.

Globe Adapted Classics. New York: Globe Book Co., 1945–1955. Graded adaptations of famous stories ranging from fourth- to tenth-grade reading levels. Exercises and questions are included in the texts. A few of the more than fifty titles are published in paperback as well as hard-bound editions. Titles include *From Earth to Moon, Treasure Island, The Count of Monte Cristo, 20,000 Leagues under the Sea,* and others.

Goldberg, Herman R., and Winifred T. Brumber (eds.). *New Rochester Occupational Reading Series—The Job Ahead.* Chicago: Science Research Associates, 1963. Identical stories about the problems of youth written on three reading levels: second grade, third and fourth grades, and fourth and fifth grades. Accompanying workbooks provide practice in basic skills.

Gray, William S., Marion Monroe, and A. Sterl. *Basic Reading Skills for Junior High School Use.* Glenview, Ill.: Scott, Foresman and Company, 1957. This work-textbook presents a balanced program of reading skills which include comprehension, phonics, structural analysis, and using reference materials. It is written on about a fourth-grade level.

Guiler, Walter S., and John H. Coleman. *Reading for Meaning,* rev. ed. Philadelphia: J. B. Lippincott Company, 1955–1965. Nine graded workbooks, designed for fourth- through twelfth-grade reading levels, consist of short selections with exercises which give practice in six basic reading skills. Books 4, 5, and 6 suitable for intermediate readers.

Henderson, Ellen C., and M. Edwards. *Reading for Pleasure.* New York: Holt, Rinehart & Winston, 1965. Low-reading level, high-interest anthology of biography, adventure, and humor.

How and Why Wonder Books. Columbus, Ohio: Charles E. Merrill Publishing Company, 1960–1964. Colorful, profusely illustrated books on many areas of science. These books, written on an elementary reading level, present a mature approach.

Interesting Reading Series, rev. ed. Chicago: Follet Publishing Co., 1961. Nine small books which contain fictional and nonfictional stories and accounts of a variety of topics. These high-interest books are on about a third-grade reading level.

Kottmeyer, William, and Kay Ware. *Conquests in Reading.* St. Louis: Webster Division, McGraw-Hill Book Company, 1962. Workbook for remedial instruction in reading and spelling skills. It contains many exercises in phonics, structural analysis, and sight-word recognition.

Kottmeyer, William, et al. *The Everyreader Series.* St. Louis: Webster Division, McGraw-Hill Book Company, 1947–1962. Adapted classics and other low-level high-interest stories, each written at about a fourth-grade reading level. Some titles are available in paperback editions, others in clothbound or paperback.

Kottmeyer, William. *Junior Everyreader Series.* St. Louis: Webster Division, McGraw-Hill Book Company, 1947–1962. Adapted classics and other stories. Published in paperback and hardcover. Ten books in the series. Written on approximately a third-grade reading level.

———. *The Magic World of Dr. Spello.* St. Louis: Webster Division, McGraw-Hill Book Company, 1963. Remedial work-textbook for improving spelling and word-analysis skills. Exercises include generalization in phonics, structural analysis, diacritical markings, and sight-word development.

Laubach, Frank C., and Pauline J. Hord. *A Door Opens.* New York: The Macmillan Company, 1963. True life stories for adults. The characters face real problems. Stories contain a basic adult vocabulary. Written on about a fourth-grade reading level.

———. *Going Forward.* New York: The Macmillan Company, 1963. A continuation of stories from *A Door Opens.* Progresses to sixth-grade reading level.

Lerner, Lillian, and Margaret Moller. *Vocational Reading Series.* Chicago: Follett Publishing Company, 1965. Vocationally oriented stories of interest to teenagers. While dealing with problems of young adults, each story brings out general and technical information about a vocation. Titles include *Marie Perrone, Practical Nurse*; *The Delso Sisters, Beauticians*; *John Leverson, Auto Mechanic*; *The Millers and Willie B.—Butcher, Baker, Chef.* Reading levels 4–6.

Lessons for Self-Instruction in Basic Skills. Monterey, Calif.: California Test Bureau, McGraw-Hill Book Company, 1963, 1965. Multilevel programs utilizing the branching principles of programmed instruction. Published in booklets about 120 pages in length, each booklet focusing upon a particular aspect of reading comprehension, reference skills, mechanics of English, and arithmetic skills. Programs range from third- to ninth-grade levels in difficulty.

Liddle, William. *Reading for Concepts.* St. Louis: Webster Division, McGraw Hill Book Co., 1970. Paperbound books A through H teach comprehension by a short story followed by comprehension. Reading levels 1.9 through 6.4.

McCall, William A., and Lelah M. Crabbs. *McCall-Crabbs Standard Test Lessons in Reading.* New York: Bureau of Publications, Teachers College, Columbia University, 1961. Series of five booklets, seventy-eight lessons in each, containing short reading selections. Exercises contain multiple-choice questions which help develop reading comprehension. Although the lower-level books are designed for elementary grades, they have been used successfully with poor readers on the secondary level and in opportunity programs. They range in reading levels from 2 through 12.

Monroe, Marion, Gwen Horsman, and William S. Gray. *Basic Reading Skills for High School Use.* Glenview, Ill.: Scott, Foresman and Company, 1958. A skills work-textbook written on about the sixth-grade reading level. Suitable for intermediate and advanced readers.

Our United States. Syracuse: The New Readers Press, 1965. Collection of articles which first appeared in *News for You.* Maps and illustrations. Written on about the sixth-grade level.

Rasmussen, Donald, and Lyn Goldberg. *Cracking the Code.* Chicago: Science Research Associates, Inc., 1968. Story book and workbook with a phonetic emphasis.

Reader's Digest Adult Readers. Pleasantville, N. Y.: Reader's Digest Services, Educational Division, 1964. Twelve different titles in three reading levels, 1 through 4, suitable for intermediate readers. *Men Who Dare the Sea, Santa Fe Traders, Valley of 10,000 Smokes, A Race to Remember, I Fell 18,000 Feet, What's on the Moon, First at the Finish, Guides to High Adventure.*

Reading Skill Builders. Pleasantville, N. Y.: Reader's Digest Services, Educational Division, 1958-1966. Short stories and articles adapted to a wide range of reading levels. Selections are illustrated and accompanied by comprehension and word-building exercises. Levels IV, V, VI, suitable for intermediate readers.

Roberts, Clyde. *Word Attack.* New York: Harcourt, Brace & World, Inc., 1956. A remedial text designed to improve word-analysis skills. Five word attack approaches are developed: contextual, auditory, structural, visual, and kinesthetic.

Schleyen, George. *Stories for Today's Youth.* New York: Globe Book Company, 1963. A collection of original short stories which deal with real problems faced by modern youth. This text is written on a fourth- to fifth-grade reading level.

Science Readers. Pleasantville, N. Y.: Reader's Digest Services, Educational Division, 1963. Four books. Low reading level, high-interest articles and stories about science and the world around us. Exercises and simple experiments follow most stories. Available at reading levels 3, 4, 5, 6. Titles: *The Earth, Living Things, Matter and Energy, Astronomy and Space.*

Simonson, Bengt, and Earl Roe. *Good Manners in the U. S. A.* Syracuse: The New Readers Press, 1963. This booklet gives information on American customs and manners in various situations. Written on a fifth- to sixth-grade reading level.

Simpson, Elizabeth A. *Better Reading Books.* Chicago: Science Research Associates, 1962. Three reading books that start at fifth-grade reading level and gradually increase in difficulty. Each book contains articles of uniform length followed by exercises in reading comprehension and vocabulary. The articles cover a wide variety of subjects generally of interest to youth and adults. The selections are suitable for those who have mastered the basic word-recognition skills but who need to improve in vocabulary and reading comprehension. Book I, reading levels 5.0–6.9; Book II, reading levels 7.0–8.9; Book III, reading levels 9.0–10.0. Individual progress folders are available at additional cost.

Smith, Harley A., and Ida Lee Wilbert. *How to Read Better.* Austin, Texas: Steck-Vaughn Co., 1964. Series of two reading work-textbooks for adults who are on at least a fourth-grade reading level but who need more practice in developing basic skills. Contents consist of stories and short articles on a variety of topics accompanied by practice exercises and check tests. Book II continues the skills development program which is started in Book I.

Smith, Nila B. *Be a Better Reader.* Englewood Cliffs, N. J.: Prentice-Hall, Inc., 1959–1963. A series of six books on different reading levels. The first part of each book is skills-centered; the second part is subject-centered. Selections are designed to develop basic reading needed by high-school students. Practice is given in reading materials related to science, mathematics, literature, and social studies. Books I and II are suitable for intermediate readers.

Spectrum of Skills. New York: The Macmillan Company, 1964. A series of eighteen booklets which provide multilevel instruction in comprehension, word analysis, and vocabulary development. The six booklets in each skill are designed for readers on fourth-, fifth-, and sixth-grade reading levels. The complete *package* contains four copies of each of the eighteen booklets, a teacher's guide, and a student record book.

Springboards. East Norwich, N.Y.: The Great Society Press, 1965. Low interest, high-level supplementary reading materials. Each story is a self-contained four-page pamphlet complete with exercises. The series contains about forty titles written on a third- to sixth-grade reading level. Each pamphlet is priced at 10 cents.

Stone, Clarence, et al. *New Practice Readers.* St. Louis: Webster Division, McGraw-Hill Book Company, 1960–1961. Seven readers for reading levels of grades two through eight. Each book contains short reading selections on a variety of topics. Exercises which follow each selection help to build important reading skills. A vocabulary exercise precedes each selection. Suitable for intermediate and advanced readers.

Teen-age Tales. Boston: D. C. Heath and Company, 1959–1966. Series of nine books designed for reluctant readers of high-school age. Books A, B, and C written on third- to fourth-grade reading levels. Books 1, 2, 3, 4, and 5 are written on fifth- and sixth-grade reading levels.

Titus, Nicholas, and Negash Gehremariam. *Trouble and the Police.* Syracuse: The New Reader Press, 1963. Booklet. Explains police functions and defines legal terms. Written in dialogue on about a sixth-grade reading level.

Turner, Richard H. *Turner-Livingston Reading Series.* Chicago: Follett Publishing Company, 1962. Series of booklets which contain stories about problems common to young adults. Each story is followed by exercises aimed to develop reading skills and vocabulary improvement. Titles include *The Person You Are, The Money You Spend, The Family You Belong To, The Jobs You Get, The Friends You Make, The Town You Live In.* Reading levels 5–6.

We Are Black. Chicago: Science Research Associates, Inc., 1969. A kit of short reading selections and skill cards, ranging from grade levels two to six, about black people but suitable for all students.

We Honor Them. Syracuse: The New Reader Press, 1963. A booklet which contains short selections about twenty black Americans. Approximately sixth-grade reading level.

Woolman, Myron. *Reading in High Gear.* Chicago: Science Research Associates, 1964. Basic reading program, divided into three parts, for teenagers. Second part for intermediate readers.

MATERIALS FOR ADVANCED READERS LEVELS 7–12

Abramowitz, Jack. *Follett Basic Learning Program.* Chicago: Follett Publishing Company, 1964. A program for the development of basic communications skills, presented in content areas as well as language arts. The program comprises sets of booklets in the different areas. Titles include *World History Study Lessons, American History Study Lessons, Study Lessons in Our Nation's History, Learning Your Language, Success in Language, Study Lessons on Documents of Free-*

dom. Comprehension check workbooks, teacher's guides, and test pads are available.

Advanced Reading Skill Builders. Pleasantville, N. Y.: Reader's Digest Services, Educational Division, 1958. Books I, II, III, and IV. Selections adapted from regular editions of *Reader's Digest*, written on seventh- and eighth-grade reading levels. Accompanied by comprehension checks and vocabulary-building exercises.

Bushman, John C., Marvin Laser, and Cherry O. Tom. *Scope*: *Reading 1*. New York: Harper & Row, Publishers, Incorporated, 1965. Stories, articles, and poems covering a variety of topics and ethnic backgrounds. Teacher's guide contains comprehension exercises.

———. *Scope: Reading 2*. New York: Harper and Row, Publishers, Incorporated, 1965. Second book in the Scope reading series.

Caughran, Alex M., and Lee Harrison Mountain. *Reading Book 1*; *Reading Book 2*. New York: American Book Company, 1965. Two developmental reading texts for high-school level readers. A skills development program is integrated with the stories and articles in each book.

Caughran, Alex M., and Lee Harrison Mountain. *Reading Skillbook*. New York: American Book Company, 1962. Books 1 and 2. Work-textbooks which aid in the development and refinement of word recognition, comprehension, interpretation, faster reading, and using reference materials. Book 1 is skill-centered and Book 2 is selection-centered.

Coronet Learning Programs. Chicago: Coronet Instructional Films, 1962–1964. These reusable programmed-instruction booklets are available in language arts, guidance, science, mathematics, health, and social studies. They are for use primarily on junior-high and high-school levels. Titles include *How to Improve Your Reading*, *Your Study Skills*, *Vocabulary Growth*.

Drachman. *Making Friends with Words*. New York: Globe Book Company, 1956. A functional approach to usage and vocabulary improvement. Exercises designed to appeal to adolescents and youth.

Feigenbaum, Lawrence H. *Effective Reading*. New York: Globe Book Company, 1953. A reading skills text which contains three sections. Part One, Reading to Learn, contains selections on different topics of common interest. Part Two, Reading for Social Living, deals with vocational and recreational reading. Part Three, Reading Tests, Drills, and Word Games, provides practice in reading skills.

Fry, Edward B. *Reading Faster*. New York: Cambridge University Press, 1963. A drill book designed to improve reading speed and comprehension. All the selections have been simplified to the 2,000-word vocabulary list and have wide appeal for teenagers and young adults.

Gainsburg, Joseph C. *Advanced Skills in Reading*. New York: The Macmillan Company, 1962. A series of three books designed to reinforce and build basic reading skills. These skills-centered texts present a sequential program in the basic reading skills, along with many practice exercises. These are suitable for junior-high and senior-high school readers.

———, and Samuel J. Spector. *Better Reading*. New York: Globe Book Company, 1962. Reading-improvement text for junior-high and high-school level readers. The book is skills-centered.

Glassman, Jerrold R. *Programmed Reading*. New York: Globe Book Company, 1966. Programmed reading textbook for teenagers. Each chapter presents or continues a reading skill and has a supplementary "branching" unit for reinforcement or review, if needed. The "branching" unit reteaches the skills in the original chapter utilizing a different approach and a different context.

Granite, Harvey, Millard Black, Virginia Lewis, and Jo Stanchfield. *Houghton Mifflin Action Series* (Encounter, Challenger, etc.) Boston: Houghton Mifflin Co., 1970.

Guiler, Walter S., and John H. Coleman. *Reading for Meaning,* rev. ed. Philadelphia: J. B. Lippincott Company, 1955–1965. Nine graded workbooks designed for fourth-through twelfth-grade reading levels. They consist of short selections with exercises which give practice in six basic reading skills. Books 7–12 are suitable for advanced readers.

Herin, Ruth B., and Gertrude Stearns. *Help Yourself to Improve Your Reading.* Part I and Part II. Pleasantville, N. Y.: Reader's Digest Services, 1962. Paperbound book with a collection of adapted and condensed articles on junior-high reading level. Similar in format to *Reader's Digest Skill Builders.*

Johnson, Eleanor M., et al. *Reading Improvement Skilltext Series.* Columbus, Ohio: Charles E. Merrill Publishing Company: 1964. Modern Reading Books I, II, III (revised). An illustrated series which presents a reading and study improvement program for students on the junior-high and high-school levels. The reading selections cover a wide variety of topics which are interesting to adolescents and youth. A reading placement test is included in each book.

Lessons for Self-instruction in Basic Skills. Monterey, Calif.: California Test Bureau, McGraw-Hill Book Company, 1963, 1965. Multilevel programs utilizing the branching principles of programmed instruction. Published in booklets about 120 pages in length, each booklet focusing on a particular aspect of reading comprehension, reference skills, mechanics of English, and arithmetic skills. Programs range from third- to ninth-grade levels in difficulty.

Literature Sampler. Secondary ed. Chicago: Learning Materials, Inc., 1963. Excerpts from more than 100 books on a variety of topics; reading levels from grades five to eleven. Includes questions for discussion, student record forms, and teacher's guide. *Sampler Library,* paperback editions of fifty of these titles, is also available.

McCall, William A., and Lelah M. Crabbs. *McCall-Crabbs Standard Test Lessons in Reading.* New York: Bureau of Publications, Teachers College, Columbia University, 1961. Series of five booklets, seventy-eight lessons in each, containing short reading selections. Exercises contain multiple-choice questions which help develop reading comprehension. Although the lower-level books are designed for elementary grades, they have been used successfully with poor readers on the secondary level and in opportunity programs. They range in reading levels from grade two through twelve.

Markle, Susan M. *Words.* Chicago: Science Research Associates, 1963. A linear self-teaching vocabulary program on the junior-high level. Attention is given to roots, prefixes, and suffixes as well as etymological aspects of our language. The "branching" principle is utilized intermittently in this text-workbook.

Pooley, Robert C., et al. *Accent: U.S.A.* Glenview, Ill.: Scott, Foresman and Company, 1965. Third book in the Galaxy program. Contains high-interest selections accompanied by a skills-development program.

———. *Perspectives.* Glenview, Ill.: Scott, Foresman and Company, 1963. Second book in the Galaxy program. Contains high-interest selections accompanied by a skills-development program.

______. *Vanguard.* Glenview, Ill.: Scott, Foresman and Company, 1961. First book in the Galaxy program for reluctant readers of high-school age. Contains high-interest selections accompanied by a skills-development program which is integrated with the selections.

Reader's Digest Readings: English as a Second Language. Pleasantville, N. Y.: Reader's Digest Services, Educational Division, 1964. Articles and stories adapted from the regular editions of *Reader's Digest.* Selections include comprehension and vocabulary exercises. Suitable for intermediate and advanced readers.

Robbins, Allen. *Word Study for Improved Reading.* New York: Globe Book Company, 1954. A work-textbook which contains a variety of exercises for vocabulary building. Emphasis is on structural analysis.

Rudd, Josephine. *Word Attack Manual.* Cambridge, Mass.: Educators Publishing Service, 1961. Workbook containing lessons in word recognition, structural analysis, and dictionary skills.

Scholastic Literature Units. New York: Scholastic Book Services, 1960-1964. A series of paperback books which contain stories, articles, and poems on a variety of topics which appeal to youth. Titles include *Animals, High Adventure, Small World, Moments of Decision, The Lighter Side.*

Sheldon, William D., George Mason, Nicholas Silveroli, Warren Wheelock. *Breakthrough.* Boston: Allyn & Bacon, 1969. A series of paperbound readers ideal for junior high or remedial secondary pupils.

Simpson, Elizabeth A. *Better Reading Books.* Chicago: Science Research Associates, 1962. Three reading books starting at fifth-grade reading level and increasing gradually to tenth-grade reading level. Selections are uniform in length and contain comprehension and vocabulary exercises. Book I is for intermediate and advanced readers; Books II and III for advanced readers.

Smith, Nila B. *Be a Better Reader.* Englewood Cliffs, N. J.: Prentice-Hall, Inc., 1959-1963. A series of six books on different reading levels. The first part of each book is skills-centered; the second part is subject-centered. Selections are designed to develop basic reading needed by high-school students. Practice is given in reading materials related to science, mathematics, literature, and social studies. Books III to VI for advanced readers.

Stone, Clarence, et al. *New Practice Readers.* St. Louis: Webster Division, McGraw-Hill Book Company, 1960-1961. Seven readers for reading levels from grades two through eight. Each book contains short reading selections on a variety of topics. Exercises which follow each selection help to build important reading skills. A vocabulary exercise precedes each selection. Books F and G are suitable for advanced readers.

Summers, Edward G. (general editor). *Reading Incentive Series.* St. Louis: Webster Division, McGraw-Hill Book Co., 1968. A high-interest set of readers for junior and senior high school.

Turner, Richard H. *Turner-Livingston Communications Series.* Chicago: Follett Publishing Company, 1964. Stories about young adults. Each story deals with a phase of communication. Exercises which accompany stories aim at developing reading skills and vocabulary improvement. Titles include *The Television You Watch, The Language You Speak, The Newspaper Your Read, The Letters You Write, The Movies You See, The Phone Calls You Make.* Reading levels 6–7.

Woolman, Myron. *Reading in High Gear.* Chicago: Science Research Associates, 1964.

Basic reading program for reading levels from grades one to eight, divided into three parts. The third part is for advanced readers.

Works, Austin M. *Vocabulary Builder Series.* Cambridge, Mass.: Educator's Publishing Service, 1964. A graded vocabulary workbook which introduces ten words in each lesson. New words are used in meaningful sentences.

MULTILEVEL MATERIALS, AUDIO-VISUAL AIDS, PERIODICALS, AND GAMES

American Education Publications. Columbus, Ohio: *Weekly Reader,* reading level 1–5; *Senior Weekly Reader*, reading level 6; *Current Events*, reading level 7–8; *Every Week*, reading level 9–10; *Our Times*, reading level 11–12; *Science and Math Weekly*, reading level 9–12; *How to Study Workshop*, reading level 7–9; *Reading Treasure Chest,* reading level 7–9. Low-priced periodicals and supplementary materials which cover a wide range of topics of interest to adolescents and youths.

Anderson, Norena, and Emerald Dechant. *Listen and Read Program.* Huntington, N. Y.: Educational Development Laboratories, 1963. Series of thirty tapes emphasizing relationships among reading, listening, and other language skills. Accompanying workbook contains exercises in listening skills.

Basic Dictionary of American English. New York: Holt, Rinehart and Winston, Inc., 1962. Comprehensive dictionary designed for grades four and five. Applicable in reading-improvement programs, remedial programs, and adult basic education programs.

Bauer, Josephine. *Communications: One, Two and Three.* Chicago: Follett Publishing Company, 1965. These booklets use a linguistics approach to reading with Number 1 at beginning and second-grade levels, Number 2, grade levels two to four, and Number 3, grade levels five to six.

Brooks, Charlotte. *Impact Series.* New York: Holt, Reinhart and Winston, Inc. This series has three levels from 7 to 9, and each level has four units which contain a student text, preview cards, and records. It is aimed at disadvantaged students.

City's Schools Reading Program, The. Chicago: Follett Publishing Company. This set of basal readers is especially designed for the multicultural nature of big cities. It ranges from a readiness book through third grade and was developed by the writer's committee of the Great City Schools Improvement Program of the Detroit Public Schools with Gertrude Whipple as chairman.

Classics Illustrated. New York: Gilberton Co., 1965–1966. Adapted versions of many classics in comic-book form. The colorful illustrations and simplified writing appear to reluctant readers. Titles include *Moby Dick, Crime and Punishment, Robinson Crusoe, The Sea Wolf, The Iliad, Cyrano de Bergerac.*

Controlled Reader. Huntington, New York: Educational Development Laboratories, 1963. This is a reading-pacer type of device that projects lines of print on a screen. The machine automatically advances the filmstrips so that the line of print is shown for a fixed period of time and then the next line is automatically shown. By turning a knob, only part of the line, which progresses from left to right, can be shown. The regular controlled reader is a 500-watt projector for classroom use, and there is a small 50-watt version for individual or small group use. A number of stories ranging from first-grade through high-school levels are available, and there are comprehension workbooks to accompany the stories.

Curry, R. L. and Adair, J. B. *Reading For a Purpose*. Chicago: Follett Publishing Company, 1967. This is a basic reading skills workbook utilizing the sight-word and phonics approach. Beginning reading levels.

______. *Reading For a Viewpoint*. Chicago: Follett Publishing Company. This is an advanced basic reading skills workbook utilizing the sight word and phonics approach at approximately grade levels five to eight.

Darby, Jean. *The Time Machine Series*. Chicago: Field Publications, 1968. This set of stories with an emphasis on science is designed for young children but could be used with intermediate children. In reading levels, it ranges from preprimer through grade 2.5.

Educational Design. *Reading Attainment Series*. New York: Grolier Educational Corporation. This kit, which contains 120 reading selections, skill arts, and answer keys, is aimed largely at teenage dropouts. Multilevel.

Henney, R. Lee. *Systems For Success*. Chicago: Follett Publishing Company. This set of two workbooks, the first one extending to the fourth-grade level and the second one covering approximately grade levels five to eight, has a primary emphasis on the phonics approach to reading.

Invitations to Personal Reading. Chicago: Scott Foresman and Company. This set of books for younger children contains folk tales, factual and fanciful stories, with set A at about first-grade level and Set B at about the second-grade level.

Jewett, A. (ed.). *B. Riverside Reading Series*. Boston: Houghton Mifflan Company, 1968. This set of six cloth or paperback titles appeal to average or reluctant readers and have accompanying study aids in vocabulary growth and reading skills. Intermediate level.

Junior Scholastic and *Senior Scholastic*. New York: Scholastic Magazines, Inc. Weekly news magazine, published on elementary and high-school reading levels, includes articles on current affairs, short stories, and special features.

Kottmeyer, William, and Kay Ware. *Classroom Reading Clinic*. St. Louis: Webster Division, McGraw-Hill Book Company, 1962. A flexible reading program in kit form, designed to deal with a wide range of reading difficulties. Materials include skills cards (multilevel reading comprehension exercises), word wheels (phonetic and structural analysis skills), basic sight vocabulary cards, a group word game, ten books (adapted classics), record sheets for pupils, and teacher aids.

Learning One Hundred, Communications Skills System. Huntington, New York: Educational Development Laboratories, 1968. This is an advanced audio-visual system utilizing filmstrips, tapes, and special machines, with provisions for student's responses. It teaches developmental reading from readiness through fifth grade.

Loretan, John O., and Shelley Uman. *Building Reading Power*. Columbus, Ohio: Charles E. Merrill Publishing Company, 1964. This laboratory-type kit is a programmed course in reading skills. The lesson units are in reusable booklets which are divided into three areas: context clues, structural analysis, and comprehension skills. The material is written on about a fifth-grade reading level.

Martin, Bill. *The Owl Program*. New York: Holt, Reinhart and Winston, Inc. This is an individualized learning series in four areas: science, math, literature, and social studies. Its readability and interest range levels are beginning and primary for the twenty books.

Mott Basic Language Skills Program. Galien, Michigan.: Allied Educational Council,

1967. This is a semi-programmed instruction series of sequential skill development for approximately grades two to nine.

News for You. Syracuse, N. Y.: Robert S. Laubach, Publisher. Weekly newspaper for adults written on primary and elementary-grade reading levels. Exercises for building word skills and reading skills accompany the news articles. Available October through May. Level AA–second-grade reading level; Level A–third- to fourth-grade reading levels; Level B–fifth- to sixth-grade reading levels.

Niles, Olive S., et al. *Tactics in Reading, I*. Chicago: Scott, Foresman and Company, 1961. These kits contain 124 exercises and tests for improvement and practice in basic reading skills. Each kit consists of fifty different cards, thirty-five reusable copies of each card. Tactics kits are a part of the Galaxy program and can be used with Vanguard or independently.

Pacemakers. New York: Random House, Inc. This individualized reading program of fifty children's books includes cards and self-checking exercises plus supplementary skills worksheets. It is aimed at the elementary and junior-high level reader.

Parker, Don H., et al. *Spelling Word Power Laboratory*. Chicago: Science Research Associates, 1961. A multilevel spelling improvement program which permits each individual to advance at his own rate. Lessons are printed on separate "Learning Wheels" which may be removed individually from the kit. Diagnostic tests, achievement tests, and check tests are included. Individual student progress folders available at additional cost. Laboratory II-b, fifth-grade level; II-c, sixth-grade level; III-a, seventh-grade level.

Parker, Don H., et al. *Reading Laboratory*. Chicago: Science Research Associates, 1956–1964. Self-contained kits of reading materials which contain selections on a wide range of reading levels; first grade through college. Each selection and its accompanying exercises may be removed separately for individual use. The materials in each laboratory progresses gradually in difficulty. The exercises provide practice in reading comprehension, reading speed, word recognition, vocabulary development, and listening comprehension. Student Record Books for the laboratories may be purchased at additional cost.

Pathfinder Series. New York: Bantam Books, Inc. This series of commercial paperback books has a wide variety of interesting subjects, including sports, adventure, biography, adapted classics, cars, drama, poetry, historical novels, science fiction, and short stories with reading levels from third to twelfth grades.

Rambeau, J. F. *Better Reading*. Oklahoma City: The Economy Company. This remedial reading program is especially for teenagers and adults. It includes a diagnostic test, thirty structured lessons on phonics, skill building, comprehension, vocabulary, review exercises, and an evaluation test. There is a laboratory book and six supplemental readers.

Read. Columbus, Ohio: American Education Publications. Written for junior-high readers. Contains stories and articles on sports, science, current events, and other topics. Special features include jokes, crossword puzzles, etc. Published weekly.

Scope. New York: Scholastic Magazines, Inc. Weekly magazine for reluctant readers of high-school age. Contains stories, articles, and plays on many different topics. Crossword puzzles and other special features offer practice in vocabulary improvement, reading, and language arts.

Sheldon, W. D., G. E. Mason, W. Wheelock, N. J. Silvaroli, N. Woessner. *Breakthrough*

Series. Boston: Allyn and Bacon, Inc. This series of paperback titles is designed for dropouts in inner-city schools who have failed in previous remedial reading programs. Each book is a collection of short stories which range from third- to sixth-grade difficulty level.

Smith, Edwin, Robert Geesing, and Carol Geesing. *Reading Development*. Reading, Mass.: Addison-Wesley Publishing Company, Inc., 1968. This set of high-interest essays on cards packaged in kits A, B, and C emphasizes critical reading for adults with reading levels roughly 2–10.

Stanchfield, Jo et al. *Learning To Read While Reading To Learn*. Chicago: Century Consultants, 1968. This individualized reading program consists of five copies each of eighteen different titles plus a teacher's guide.

Study Skills Library. Huntington, N. Y.: Educational Development Laboratories, 1962. A series of kits containing graded exercises for reading levels 3 through 9. There are puzzles and other features. Three kits on each reading level, one each in science, social studies, and reference skills.

Sullivan, M., and C. Buchanan. *Programmed Reading For Adults*. New York: McGraw-Hill Book Company. These workbooks are in a linear programmed instruction format; the eight books have a linguistics approach and range to the sixth-grade level.

Thurstone, Thelma G. *Reading for Understanding*. Chicago: Science Research Associates, 1958. Laboratory type materials on exercise cards. Each card has ten short statements on a variety of subjects. The student picks the best possible conclusion from four that follow each statement. Two separate laboratories provide a reading range from third- to twelfth-grade levels. Junior Edition – levels 3–8; General Edition – levels 5–12.

Wilson, Hazel, and Don H. Parker. *Pilot Library*. Chicago: Science Research Associates, 1963. Kits which accompany the SRA Reading Laboratories but are for independent reading. Each Pilot Library corresponds to the Reading Laboratory on the same level and contains expanded excerpts of the selections in that laboratory. Pilot Libraries available are II-a, II-c, and III-b.

World Events. Morristown, N. J.: Silver Burdett Co. Weekly newsletter summarizing important news events. Includes special updated map issues.

World News of the Week. Chicago: News Map of the Week, Inc. Weekly magazine for young adults and teenagers. Contents include news of the week and personalities in the news. Controlled vocabulary.

Zenith Series. Garden City, N. Y.: Doubleday & Company, Inc. This series of hardcover and paperback books about minority groups is designed to stimulate the interests of slow readers. At grade levels five and six.

APPENDIX 11-B READABILITY FORMULA THAT SAVES TIME*

The purpose of this article is to present a revision of the Readability Graph together with directions for its use and to present some validity data which compare readability scores on several different formulas.

*Edward Fry, *Journal of Reading*. April, 1968, pages 513–516, 575–578.

Readability formulas have been around for many years, and a good deal has been written about them. For the reader who wants a more detailed overview of the topic, books by Klare,[9] Chall,[2] and Dale[3] are recommended. Yet, the topic seems to hold fresh interest for each semester's load of graduate students and some serious researchers. Though readability formulas are used by some teachers, librarians, and publishers, their number is all too few. Perhaps the sheer time consumption and difficulty are factors which cause the formulas mostly to languish in term papers and occasional magazine articles.

The Readability Graph was first developed when I was in Uganda and simplicity was a prime prerequisite. The original version appeared in print that was read mostly by British readers[6,7] and hence it is not too well known in the United States. Perhaps the fact that it was originally geared partly to an African set of readers has caused it to be accepted more by the emerging nations.

The Readability Graph in this article is aimed at the United States educational scene. The grade-level designations are for America; the simplicity is a need I find universal. As much as I admire the many works of Edgar Dale and Jeannie Chall, I confess that I find their readability formula loaded with fussy rules, a tedious vocabulary, and decimal figures carried to the fourth place, a bit overly precise, when it only yields some score such as "9–10 grade".[4]

Perhaps simplicity may best be measured in printed pages. The Dale-Chall formula takes about eighteen printed pages while the Readability Graph takes only about one and one-half. The SRA formula is relatively simple, but it requires a plastic gadget costing several dollars and has only four difficulty designations.

DIRECTIONS FOR USING THE READABILITY GRAPH

1. Select three 100-word passages from near the beginning, middle, and end of the book. Skip all proper nouns.

2. Count the total number of sentences in each hundred word passage (estimating to nearest tenth of a sentence). Average these three numbers (add together and divide by 3).

3. Count the total number of syllables in each hundred word sample. There is a syllable for each vowel sound; for example: *cat* (1), *blackbird* (2), *continental* (4). Do not be fooled by word size, for example: *polio* (3), *through* (1). Endings such as *-y*, *-ed*, *-el*, or *-le* usually make a syllable, for example: *ready* (2), *stopped* (2), *bottle* (2). I find it convenient to count every syllable over one in each word and add 100. Average the total number of syllables for the three samples.

4. Plot on the graph the average number of sentences per 100 words and the average number of syllables per 100 words. Most plot points fall near the heavy curved line. Perpendicular lines mark off approximate grade-level areas.

Example	Sentences per 100 words	Syllables per 100 words
100-word sample page 5	9.1	122
100-word sample page 89	8.5	140
100-word sample page 150	7.0	129
Divide total by 3	3)24.6	3)391
Average	8.2	130

Plotting these averages on the graph we find they fall in the fifth-grade area, hence the book is about fifth-grade difficulty level. If great variability is encountered either in sentence length or in the syllable count for the three selections, then randomly select several more passages and average them in before plotting.

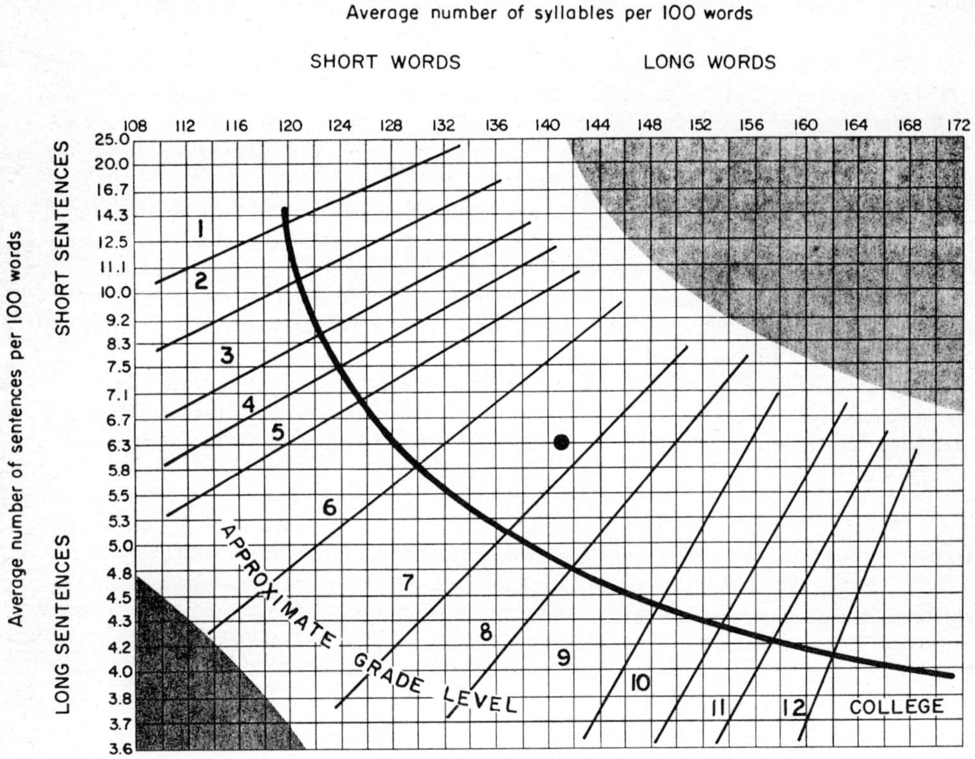

DIRECTIONS: Randomly select 3 one hundred word passages from a book or an article. Plot average number of syllables and average number of sentences per 100 words on graph to determine the grade level of the material. Choose more passages per book if great variability is observed and conclude that the book has uneven readability. Few books will fall in gray area but when they do grade level scores are invalid.

EXAMPLE:

	SYLLABLES	SENTENCES
1st Hundred Words	124	6.6
2nd Hundred Words	141	5.5
3rd Hundred Words	158	6.8
AVERAGE	141	6.3

READABILITY 7th GRADE (see dot plotted on graph)

HOW ACCURATE IS THE SCORE?

If you want a nice, simple answer on accuracy, I'll shoot from the hip and say "probably within a grade level." If you want a more technical answer, read on.

The problem of validity is difficult. First of all there are no rigorous standards of just what is fourth-grade difficulty as opposed to fifth-grade difficulty. There seems to be some loose sort of agreement between publishers and educators which is based a little on experience and perhaps a little on test data as to what grade-level designations mean. But anybody who has used an old reading test, say the 1957 California Reading Test, on a class and then used the 1965 Stanford Reading Test on the same class at nearly the same time can tell you that the class mean reading score expressed in grade level is quite different. In general, newer tests are more difficult, or in other words a ninth-grade student today reads better than a ninth-grade student of former years.

The Dale-Chall is partly validated by teacher and librarian judgments of material difficulty and partly by correlation with other formulas.[2]

Hence, the problem of validity is complicated by trying to determine grade level when grade level will not stand still and when subjective "judgments" are about as good a standard as can be found. There is a partial way out of this dilemma, however, and that is by using relative ranking. For example, if the formula continually ranks a number of reading passages in the same order as, say, a comprehension test taken on the same passages by one group of students. Or you can compare one formula with another by rank order correlations. This will answer such problems as: "Does the formula consistently rank some books hard and others easy?"

I am reasonably satisfied that my formula ranks books on a hard-to-easy continuum about as well as Dale-Chall and Flesch and SRA formulas. (See Tables 11-A1 and 11-A2. It also seems to give about the same grade level designations. (See Table 11-A3. The Dale-Chall ranks several books a little harder than the Readability Graph but perhaps the fact that it was developed about twenty years ago accounts for this. At least it is hopeful to think that present sixth- and ninth-graders can read a little better.

For those interested in how I obtained my grade-level designations (I always wondered how others did it): I simply plotted many books which publishers said were third-grade readers, fifth-grade readers, etc. I then looked for clusters and "smoothed the curve". After some use and correlational studies, the grade-level areas were adjusted. The grade-level areas did not come out too even, but that is part of the trouble with working with real data. The fact that there is much less graph space for grades four and five than for grades six and seven is interesting. It may be an inaccuracy in our data, or it may mean that fourth- and fifth-grade materials do not change in difficulty as much as sixth- and seventh-grade materials and/or students reading abilities. In any event, other formulas such as Dale-Chall and SRA do not attempt to differentiate between just one grade (Dale-Chall gives two grade designations such as 5–6 or 7–8 and SRA gives even bigger chunks).

The data in Tables 11-A1, 11-A2, and 11-A3 were obtained from the masters thesis of Andrew Kistulentz who was one of my advisees at Rutgers University Graduate School of Education.[8] The ten books were used in his tenth-grade English classes, and he constructed comprehension tests with three parts: true-false, multiple-choice, and short paragraph essay. He then ranked order correlations between the readability formulas and the comprehension tests. Most of the formulas correlated quite highly among themselves and with the comprehension tests.

The Dale-Chall formula correlated quite highly with the Readability Graph (.94). The high correlation with the Flesch formula (.96) was expected as the inputs are basically the same, only instead of mathematical computations the Graph has plotting to yield levels .5. The SRA formula also has the same inputs of syllables and sentence length but uses a plastic wheel for an analogue (slide-rule type) device to compute level (correlation .98) that yields four gross levels only.[12] The Graph yields thirteen grade levels. My only explanation as to why the Botel formula did not correlate better (.78) is that it takes into account only vocabulary difficulty and completely ignores structure complexity (as is usually reflected in sentence length).

On a lower level the Readability Graph has been compared with the Spache formula in a study done by Martin Kling and Clement Haimowitz for the Boy Scouts of America.[10,11] They concluded that, "There was a very close agreement between the readability level according to both formulas . . . It is probably more efficient to use the Fry Readability Formula at the primary grade level".[10]

CONCLUSION

Readability formulas have had a widespread, long-term interest among professionals in the reading business. However, the lack of their use in broader educational circles may be due to excessive working time and difficulty in computing some existing formulas. The Readability Graph is presented as a faster and simpler method of determining readability. It correlates highly with the Dale-Chall, SRA, Flesch, and Spache formulas. My only hope now is that it be widely used by teachers, librarians, and publishers as one important and objective method of determining readability.

Note: The Readability Graph is not copyrighted. Anyone may reproduce it in any quantity, but the author and the editor would be pleased if this source were cited.

TABLE 11-AI
RELATIVE RANKINGS OF TEN BOOKS BY READABILITY METHODS AND STUDENT COMPREHENSION SCORES

	Ranking Method					
Book title	*Fry*	*SRA*	*Botel*	*Dale-Chall*	*Flesch*	*Stud. comp.*
Light in Forest	2.5	2.5	1.0	1.5	2.5	1.5
Mice and Men	2.5	2.5	7.0	3.5	2.5	1.5
The Pearl	2.5	2.5	2.5	1.5	2.5	3.0
Shane	2.5	2.5	2.5	3.5	2.5	4.0
Death Be Not Proud	6.5	7.0	7.0	6.0	6.0	5.0
Moon Is Down	5.0	5.5	4.5	6.0	6.0	6.0
To Kill A Mockingbird	6.5	5.5	4.5	6.0	6.0	7.0
Tale of Two Cities	8.0	9.0	9.0	10.0	9.0	8.0
Silas Marner	9.5	9.0	10.0	8.5	8.0	9.0
Act One	9.5	9.0	7.0	8.5	10.0	10.0

TABLE 11-A2
INTERCORRELATIONS OF FIVE READABILITY METHODS' RATINGS AND STUDENT COMPREHENSION ON TEN BOOKS*

Readability method	*Fry*	*SRA*	*Botel*	*Dale-Chall*	*Flesch*	*Student comp.*
Fry	—	0.98	0.78	0.94	0.96	0.93
SRA	0.98	—	0.81	0.95	0.98	0.90
Botel	0.78	0.81	—	0.82	0.73	0.64
Dale	0.94	0.95	0.82	—	0.95	0.90
Flesch	0.96	0.98	0.73	0.95	—	0.94
Student Comp.	0.93	0.90	0.64	0.90	0.94	—

*A correlation of 0.5 is significant at the 0.05 level and 0.75 is significant at the 0.01 level.

TABLE 11-A3
MEAN GRADE PLACEMENTS AND MEAN STUDENT COMPREHENSION SCORES ON TEN BOOKS

Book title	*Mean Comprehension Scores and Mean Grade Placements by Method*					
	Fry	*SRA*	*Botel*	*Dale-Chall*	*Flesch*	*Student comp.*
Light in Forest	5	5	4	5	6	92
Mice and Men	5	5	8	6	6	92
The Pearl	5	5	5	5	6	90
Shane	5	5	5	6	6	89
Death Be Not Proud	7	7	8	7	8	88
Moon is Down	6	6	7	7	8	87
To Kill A Mockingbird	7	6	7	7	8	86
Tale of Two Cities	9	10	9	11	11	82
Silas Marner	10	10	10	10	10	79
Act One	10	10	8	10	12	75

REFERENCES

[1]Botel, M. *Botel Predicting Readability Levels.* Chicago: Follett Publishing Company, 1962.

[2]Chall, Jeanne S. *Readability: An Appraisal of Research and Application.* Ohio: Ohio State University, The Bureau of Educational Research, 1958.

[3]Dale, E. *Readability.* An Official Publication of the National Council of Teachers of English. Illinois, 1949.

[4]Dale, E. and Chall, Jeanne S. "A Formula for Predicting Readability," *Educational Research Bulletin*, 27, (1948), 11–20.
[5]Flesch, R. F. "A New Readability Yardstick," *Journal of Applied Psychology*, 32, (1948), 221–233.
[6]Fry, E. "Judging Readability of Books," *Teacher Education*, 5, 1964, 34–39.
[7]Fry, E. *Teaching Faster Reading*. London, England: Cambridge Press, 1963, 135–140.
[8]Kistulentz, A. C. "Five Readability Ratings Compared to Comprehension Test Scores on Ten High School Literature Books," Master Thesis. New Brunswick, New Jersey: Rutgers, The State University, 1967.
[9]Klare, G. R. *The Measurement of Readability*. Iowa: Iowa State University Press, 1963.
[10]Kling, M. and Haimowitz, C. "Application of Readability Formulas for Non-School Reading Materials at the Primary Grade Level," Mimeo. New Brunswick, New Jersey: Rutgers, The State University, 1966.
[11]Spache, G. R. "A New Readability Formula for Primary Grade Reading Materials," *Elementary School Journal*, 53, (1953), 410–413.
[12]SRA, *Reading-Ease Calculator*. Chicago: Science Research Associates, Inc., 1950.

12

ORGANIZING FOR REMEDIAL READING

Virtually everything in this book applies to the teaching of remedial reading. However, teachers sometimes need help in putting all the various components into a package or system. As mentioned in Chapter 3, typical reading lessons using a basic text are extremely well organized by the authors of the series. Of course, a teacher does not find it quite as easy as this, but it does seem at times that the only choice left is: "Which series shall I use?" Even so, this choice is often made by the school district.

Once the series is selected, a teacher merely has to follow the teacher's manual, some of which have such ridiculously detailed instructions as: "Tell the students to open the book to page 14. Now point to the picture and ask . . ."

In remedial reading, no such detailed set of instructions is available. The remedial reading teacher is usually an experienced teacher who has had superior training. She is able to take a new child and quickly find his reading level, his knowledge of phonics, his basic vocabulary, and to build lessons to suit him or to place him in a small group of children with similar needs.

ELEMENTARY REMEDIAL PROGRAMS

In an earlier day there were no remedial programs because schools used a quick and easy solution. After a few years of failure they simply persuaded the child to drop out of school. This solved the school's problems very nicely but was a little difficult for the child and his family. At the present time, compulsory school attendance laws and a general change in educational philosophy have removed this quick-and-easy solution and required the schools to face the problem of helping children to reach their highest possible level of reading ability.

There are still many schools in the United States that have no regular remedial reading instruction. Since all schools are burdened with at least *some* pupils who cannot read, these schools usually try one of two diversionary tactics: (1) the "ostrich" technique, which consists of a principal burying his head in his reports and refusing to recognize the problem, or (2) the district office adopting some glorious policy such as, "Every teacher handles her own remedial problems." The only trouble with this policy is that if every teacher *could* handle her own remedial problems there would not be any poor readers or any problem.

The great fallacy of "every teacher handling her own problems" is that teaching remedial reading takes a tremendous amount of time and effort, and for the regular classroom teacher to divert her teaching time and effort away from the regular studies and away from her normal and superior students is to jeopardize the success of her teaching. To try to incorporate remedial reading into the regular classroom work is a physical impossibility. When this is attempted, it is the superior student who suffers most because the teacher does not have time for the enrichment he needs. And it is the superior student and not the poor reader who will contribute to society as tomorrow's doctors, teachers, and cultural leaders. No, the short-sighted philosophy which tries to "economize" by refusing to provide needed remedial reading services is really providing the most expensive possible educational program; moreover, it is literally stealing the teacher's time, crippling the educational program, and putting the average and superior students under an educational handicap.

Not being able to handle reading problems as they arise by referral to remedial specialists can in a minor way be disastrous to other aspects of the school situation. A high percentage of discipline problems and dropouts results from remedial reading cases.

ORGANIZING REMEDIAL READING SERVICES Some good remedial reading programs employ one specially trained remedial reading teacher for every two elementary schools, each of which has ten to fifteen classrooms. This remedial teacher might spend mornings in one school and afternoons in another, or a couple of days a week in one school and the remaining days in another. She would usually spend most of her day teaching children in small groups of from three to ten students, depending on their reading level. Severely retarded readers or students just beginning to learn to read would be put in smaller groups. The students generally meet several times a week for periods lasting from thirty minutes to an hour. Some districts prefer to have the students meet every day for a short period, while others like longer periods and fewer sessions.

The remedial teacher usually has a special room where she can keep remedial reading books, games, audio-visual equipment, files, tests, and the other materials she needs. Even though this room may sometimes be little more than an oversized broom closet, it is usually better to have a special room than to require the teacher to lug materials from room to room, wherever one is temporarily free because of a physical education or library schedule.

DUTIES OF THE REMEDIAL TEACHER The remedial reading teacher must also have some free time, usually the equivalent of one day a week for seeing students individually, testing students who are candidates for remedial reading instruction, holding parent conferences, and coordinating reading activities with classroom teachers. The remedial teacher must frequently work very closely with the school psychologist or other counseling personnel on potential dropout and behavior problems, particularly where a reading problem is expected.

In many districts the remedial teacher is also a helping teacher or an assistant supervisor. Some districts, especially those in lower socioeconomic districts, have many more remedial reading cases than the remedial teacher can possibly handle. Much of her work, then, becomes that of assisting classroom teachers by diagnosing reading levels, phonics knowledge, etc. and giving special materials to the classroom teacher based on the diagnosis. The remedial teacher then returns to the classroom teacher the following week to check on the student and exchange special teaching materials.

Remedial teachers are extremely valuable as helping teachers. They can sometimes take over the reading group in a new teacher's room for a demonstration lesson. For example, a classroom teacher having difficulty in presenting certain phonics concepts may ask the remedial teacher to conduct a group lesson for the entire class, using special charts and filmstrips. A teacher who might hesitate to go to the principal or supervisor for help will approach the remedial teacher and ask, "Where can I get some easy interesting books on horses?" or "How do you operate a tachistoscope?" or "Do you have any games that will teach a basic vocabulary?" Remedial teachers generally have a superior knowledge of reading materials ranging from special drill books to audio-visual aids. They know where to find them, how to use them, and what the materials teach.

Remedial teachers sometimes assume responsibility for administering and interpreting reading tests. As mentioned in earlier chapters of this book, remedial teachers know which subtest scores are most valuable and can interpret them for the classroom teachers so that they may understand exactly why Johnny is doing so poorly in his reading and other studies or why Ezekiel who could and should be doing superior work in reading is only in the average group.

Remedial teachers are often able to explain and interpret intelligence scores. Classroom teachers may overlook the basic fact that in interpreting the

IQ scores of students with reading problems, only the nonlanguage section should be considered. The International Reading Association in its recommendations for the training of remedial reading teachers includes as mandatory a graduate course in Tests and Measurements.

Superior remedial reading teachers may be called upon to perform a number of related functions: (1) they are often heavily involved in the selection of textbooks and reading materials for all classrooms, as well as for the remedial reading room; and (2) besides teaching the most difficult children, they may also assume many of the responsibilities of a supervisor and a guidance counselor.

REMEDIAL READING IN SECONDARY SCHOOLS

The organization of remedial reading classes and the duties of the remedial reading teacher are often much the same in secondary as in elementary schools. Secondary schools are frequently organized on a "period system" in which the students spend one hour in history, one hour in English, etc. In this type of scheduling, students are frequently assigned to a remedial reading class for one entire period; hence, they meet with their remedial teacher every day. In most schools, remedial reading is given *in addition* to the required English course, but in some remedial reading is given *in lieu* of required English.

In secondary schools, it often happens that no one else on the staff will have had any formal training in reading instruction. Even English teachers frequently have had all of their training in English literature and composition. Because of this, the remedial reading teacher is frequently given a free hand and very little supervision. While this has its pleasant aspects, it also has its drawbacks in that the remedial teacher can expect little help from anyone else.

Some secondary teachers, when they observe the relatively small class loads of the remedial teacher, are inclined to view hers as a "soft job"; worse yet, they see a fine opportunity to remedy this "soft spot" by trying to refer all of their behavior problems to the remedial reading class. The remedial teacher might expect to receive more than the normal share of behavior problems; but if she is wise, she will firmly insist that no children be admitted to remedial reading who do not have a genuine reading problem in addition to reasonable normal learning ability.

Good remedial programs in secondary schools have been ruined by misguided and soft-hearted persons in guidance offices who have scheduled children for remedial reading with no more information than a teacher's recommendation. The remedial teacher is the one who should have the right to accept or reject each candidate. She should have access to test scores and should reserve the right to reject those who she feels are not suitable candidates. At this point, top administrative support of the program is essential. A secondary school remedial program might survive a skimpy budget, but an improper selection of students spells disaster. Mentally retarded children are indeed a problem, but they are not a remedial reading problem. Students of normal learning ability who need help in reading naturally resent being mixed with mentally retarded students.

Secondary school remedial teachers must often run two levels of remediation. Frequently they will have a period or two of seriously retarded readers, possibly those reading at third-grade level or below. These classes should be kept small—certainly not over ten, and preferably five or seven. For the less seriously retarded readers (say, those of fifth- or sixth-grade ability), larger groups can be handled as the students are capable of doing more independent work. They also yield to group-type activities better. In some schools, classes for the seriously retarded readers would be called Remedial Reading, while those for the less seriously retarded would be called Developmental Reading. Unfortunately, developmental reading is an even more ambiguous term than remedial reading, and in some schools developmental reading means reading for students with normal reading ability.

In some secondary schools the remedial reading teacher will be called upon to teach or establish classes for students who are slightly below normal reading ability (for example, seventh-grade ability) and classes for those desiring superior reading ability such as college prep seniors who wish a course in the improvement of reading speed and comprehension. A discussion of some of these classes for superior readers will be given in Chapter 20, but for more detailed directions the reader is referred to my book, *Teaching Faster Reading*, Cambridge University Press, New York, 1963.

LESSON CONTENT

Remedial teachers often have to build their own lesson plans starting from scratch and without help from a teacher's manual. They should keep five basic areas of instructional approach and lesson content in mind:

1. Oral reading
2. Silent reading
3. Phonics
4. Basic vocabulary
5. Comprehension.

Not every lesson will cover every one of these areas, but all five areas should be covered in at least every two lessons. Remedial reading instruction should be varied and spiced with as much variety as the teacher can devise. Remedial students frequently have poor study habits and short attention spans. As a general rule, remedial teachers should carry on at least three different activities per hour. For younger or more retarded students, an even greater variety may be necessary. In order to keep some semblance of balance in the curriculum, she might cover three of the content areas in one lesson and the remaining two plus a repeat from the first three on the second day. As students approach fifth-grade reading ability and high school age, it may be desirable to concentrate on just one or two areas.

ORAL READING Some teachers almost equate the teaching of reading with oral reading. In the last century good oral reading was the goal of all reading instruction, and the best "reader" in the family was often expected to read aloud for entertainment. Today oral reading is a means of instruction and diagnosis.

The basic theory behind oral reading is that it teaches the child the relationship between the printed symbol and the spoken symbol. Since students enter school with reasonable competency in spoken language, the initial task in reading is to get them to see the relationship between the printed symbol and the spoken symbol.

Oral reading also has the excellent diagnostic feature of giving the teacher immediate feedback on the child's reading ability and his skill needs. Oral reading is sometimes called guided reading for the reason that the teacher can instantly help the student exactly where he needs it. A student who stumbles or hesitates on a word should usually be told that word immediately. The teacher might occasionally have a different type of lesson in which the student is asked to try to sound out unknown words, but, basically, the task in oral reading is teaching him the rote written word/oral word relationship.

One of the most frequent errors in oral reading instruction is the teacher's lack of insistence on strict attention from the members of the group who are not reading. Excellent reading instruction can accrue to the silent student in the group whose eyes are carefully following along in the text while he hears the spoken word. Again this is teaching the sight-sound relationship. The non-reading students should be active, mentally participating in the reading process and not looking out the window waiting for their turns.

In a remedial reading class, a teacher will occasionally find a student who becomes exceedingly nervous in an oral reading situation. This may have been caused by numerous experiences of failure in a regular classroom. Whatever the reason, this student should not be forced to participate in group oral reading. The teacher should help the student build confidence by giving him simple silent reading exercises, and then by having him read aloud only to the teacher from short, easy passages. After some level of confidence has been established in the student, he might again be tried in group oral reading; however, if signs of extreme nervousness appear, all oral reading for this child should be stopped. There are other ways of teaching reading.

Older boys may sometimes feel that oral reading lessons are babyish, an attitude that can be offset by having all students take part in the reading of radio scripts or plays, with each student reading a part. Other excellent oral reading activities are choral reading and singing. Some choral reading activities alternate groups of students who read sections of poems. Older boys who might be prone to think of poetry as "sissy stuff" quickly change when the reading is from Robert Service or Rudyard Kipling. Songs, too, come in all gradations, from dainty to lusty. The most masculine student could hardly look askance at being asked to learn to read his high-school football song.

The fact that songs and poems can be memorized with relative ease makes them ideal for use in reading instruction. If a teacher suspects a student has momorized the material rather than reading it, all she has to do is select a few words out of context and put them on the chalkboard. Students also find the memorization of limericks a pleasant way of building their slight vocabularies.

Remedial reading students who have difficulty in concentrating on reading material often find that oral reading holds their interest. If they suspect that they may be called on next, this is incentive enough for them to keep the place. The teacher should occasionally encourage other members of the group to supply a word with which the oral reader is having trouble. This may be the first time that any member of the group has had the experience of helping another poor reader.

Oral reading should not be overused. It easily becomes a very boring experience. Good teachers learn to read the signs of loss of interest: students who lose their places, students raising their eyes from their books, students who drop things on the floor, or the tone of voice of the one who is reading. Reading clinics frequently have students for two hours at a time; and it is possible to keep the students reading every minute of the time, much to the amazement of their parents and classroom teachers. The secret is in the variety of reading activities and the recognition of when to change.

SILENT READING The goal of modern reading instruction is to enable the child to do silent reading efficiently. For maximum transfer of training, it is essential that he be given much practice in silent reading. Earlier chapters have stressed the importance of silent reading for comprehension and general reading improvement. At this point, the teacher is reminded to include definite periods for silent reading in her lesson plans.

Silent reading has a further advantage in allowing the teacher to work individually with other students or with other groups.

Since silent reading can be done as easily at home as in class, the remedial teacher should encourage the student to continue this type of activity in study hall or at home. She must remember, though, that remedial reading students frequently have such poor study habits or home conditions that silent reading outside of class cannot be relied upon. Parent cooperation can sometimes be obtained in helping the student to read silently at home for ten or fifteen minutes a day. Sometimes, however, students have such poor emotional relationships with their parents that it would be unwise to try to get the parents' participation. However, if the parents can cooperate, the teacher's assistance in selecting the right book and suggesting definite home assignments can be of great help. Further suggestions for parents are given in Chapter 17.

Silent reading can be done just for pleasure, but in a teaching situation it frequently is related to some type of comprehension building activity. Hence, a good bit of the earlier section on reading comprehension really applies to the silent-reading situation.

A reading teacher will often want to work personally with a student's teacher in selecting silent-reading materials that fit in with the regular classroom programs. English teachers who assign book reports might be requested to accept a report on an adapted classic. Together, the reading teacher and the subject-matter teacher can usually make good selections of supplementary reading materials that are on the right level for the child.

PHONICS It takes a beginning reader a long time to learn the relationship between all of the speech sounds (phonemes) and the way they are written (graphemes). If too much emphasis or too much teaching time is placed on phonics to the exclusion of other methods, the student can lose interest very quickly. On the other hand, the beauty of phonics is that by learning a small set of rules, the student can "unlock" a large number of words. If short and interesting periods of phonics instruction are included in every lesson or in nearly every lesson, the process becomes painless and the student's reading skills are greatly improved.

The processes of diagnosing and teaching phonics skills have been discussed in earlier chapters. At this point, the teacher is reminded that it is very important to use skill in working these phonics processes into the lesson plan. An interesting aspect of phonics is that a child who is growing "tired of reading" is always happy to play a game which teaches consonant and vowel sounds. The wide variety of phonics teaching methods offers interesting contrast to such activities as oral reading, silent reading, or comprehension drills.

A teacher must let children see how useful the phonics skills are in sounding out unknown words during silent reading, looking up words in dictionaries, and remembering how to spell words.

BASIC VOCABULARY The simple statistic that almost 50 percent of all reading material is made up of just 300 Instant Words highlights how essential it is for children to master the basic vocabulary. The fact that a number of these words are hard words for children to learn makes it imperative that some instruction in basic vocabulary be included in most reading lesson plans.

It will take the equivalent of three years of reading instruction, or third-grade reading ability, before a child really knows all 300 Instant Words. This entails a great deal of teaching and repetition before he will be thoroughly familiar with them. Word drills, like phonics, can be dull and boring or they can be interesting variations of other reading activities. Word study through teacher explanations, games, and spelling tests all help to do this.

Students who have progressed normally through one set of basic texts will have received systematic instruction in a basic vocabulary. But remedial reading students, or students who have shifted from text to text or from school to school, frequently exhibit a very poor reading vocabulary development. Systematic review of a basic vocabulary will help to fill these gaps in development. If a student already knows a word, or if he almost knows it, the review will proceed rapidly. If he is encountering the word for the first time, then the rate of introducing words should be slowed down until mastery occurs. In Chapter 4 a number of methods were given for diagnosing and teaching a basic vocabulary.

For older students, or for those with at least fourth-grade reading ability, the teaching of basic vocabulary will strive for "vocabulary improvement." All students continue to increase their reading vocabularies throughout their academic lives, and teachers can help this development by teaching vocabulary-building skills right from the start. The teaching of roots, prefixes, and suffixes is one way to do this. The study of word origins and varieties of word meanings is an interesting and life-long process. As testimony to its pure entertainment value, observe how interested students become in finding word origins and playing games like crossword puzzles.

COMPREHENSION The purpose of reading is to understand, and many lessons and quizzes will be devoted to building comprehension in reading. In fact, every time a teacher asks a question based on the student's reading, she is sharpening the student's comprehension. More formal are the numerous workbooks, special drill books, and other materials for teaching comprehension, many of which were discussed in Chapter 11.

Some beginning remedial teachers have had unhappy experiences by taking just one comprehension-building method (such as a reading laboratory) and using it day after day until the students rebel. Reading laboratories are an excellent method of teaching comprehension, but they are only one of many techniques.

Comprehension drills have the advantage that they are often largely self-instructive. Once a proper drill has been selected for a student, he can work silently on his own for a considerable period of time. In remedial reading lessons, this method should be used with caution. The student easily becomes frustrated at being left alone with an incomprehensible task. It often takes no more than the personal interest of the teacher to give him the support he needs to make comprehension drills effective in a remedial reading situation.

LESSON CONSIDERATIONS

In addition to the subject-matter content of the remedial reading lesson, there is another dimension of basic considerations. This is the need to strike a balance between diagnosis and instruction, review and progress, fun and work, and individual versus group procedures. These matters definitely affect the organization of the lesson plan and the success of the teaching process.

DIAGNOSIS AND INSTRUCTION By its very definition, remedial reading would be expected to include intensive and frequent diagnosis. The student enters the class with an irregular skill development; moreover, during remedial reading instruction he will often make erratic progress. He may make very rapid progress at first in acquiring a basic sight vocabulary, only to slow down to a snail's pace in acquiring phonics skills. This erratic curve may characterize most of his progress throughout the course.

Other learning patterns appear in students' general reading development. Results of reading tests often show that reading clinics and remedial reading teachers are frequently able to bring a student's progress up to about twice the normal rate. This means that a child will make a year's progress in four months (one semester) of reading instruction. This rapid progress necessitates changing the curriculum material much more frequently than would be done in the ordinary large classroom.

In a typical classroom, formal achievement testing is seldom done more frequently than on one or two days a year. In remedial reading, however, testing can be almost a constant procedure, and definite parts of the lesson plans are set aside for it. To use the individual inventories in knowledge of Instant Words and phonics skills (discussed in Chapter 4) requires a good deal of time. Lesson time is consumed both by initial testing and by continuing reevaluation of individual inventories. Some remedial teachers set aside regularly scheduled diagnostic days. Possibly on one Friday they diagnose phonics; on the next Friday they diagnose basic vocabulary; and on the third Friday they diagnose comprehension. This testing cycle may be repeated every three weeks so that a certain day of the week becomes the regular testing day and the skill to be tested rotates from week to week.

Naturally, this constant diagnostic procedure increases a teacher's record-keeping tasks. Most remedial teachers keep a file folder for each student. In addition to the initial tests and case history, a summary of progress in the various skill areas is maintained. Since a remedial teacher frequently sees thirty or more students a week for regular instruction, she cannot expect to memorize the details of the progress of each student. Summary cards showing the progress of each student are very helpful and can quickly be reviewed prior to each meeting with the child. Teachers with heavy class loads should probably plan for a few quiet minutes during each lesson in which they can look at file folders and keep them up-to-date. Other districts prefer that the remedial teacher have a definite time outside of class (possibly a free period) for the maintenance of progress records.

Testing and the maintenance of file folders can become an overburdening task and actually detract from instruction. The purpose of testing and record-keeping is to make instruction flow more smoothly and efficiently and to make it easier for teachers to fit instruction to the needs of the children. But teachers should guard against getting carried away by neat file folders. It does not help the child to write voluminous descriptions of each child's reaction to each lesson.

This may be of help in the case of a special problem child when the school psychologist and others are involved in his progress and behavior. Generally, however, fat file folders are a waste of time; nobody reads them and nobody wants to store them.

Diagnosis, when done in an interested and kindly manner, can often be a satisfying experience for both student and teacher. The student likes the individual attention and frequently is greatly encouraged to see progress in his own reading skills. Teachers find that a student is motivated when he is allowed to see his record of reading achievements. Remedial students are often surprisingly mature in accepting information about their faults or lack of specific skills. Whereas good teachers correctly emphasize progress rather than lack of skills, realistic appraisals are frequently helpful, too.

An interesting evaluation procedure is to tape record a student's oral reading and file it away for several months; then have the student read the same passage into the tape recorder again, but without further instruction this time. The student and teacher then listen to both tapes and compare progress and any continuing errors. Students like to do this and get a real increase in motivation, particularly when progress has been made. Short reels of tape can be purchased inexpensively, and one short tape can be kept for each student. Tapes can be reused after the student is transferred back to his regular class.

Instruction time must be balanced with diagnosis time. Remedial teachers will allow more time for diagnosis than is done in the regular classroom situation. A remedial teacher will determine just how much diagnosis she should schedule so as not to detract from instruction.

REVIEW AND PROGRESS Learning to read requires practice and review. Good teaching dictates that only enough review be done to ensure mastery. Then gentle pressure is exerted and progress is made toward the next higher goal.

Review may take many forms, and a variety of forms should be used. The student who has practiced with short vowels on a workbook page, then practiced with short vowels in a game, and finally used a number of short-vowel words learned in a spelling lesson may not be aware of the great amount of repetition he is getting. Repetition should be made interesting; it can easily be disguised when varieties of teaching methods are used. Nevertheless, a teacher need not be afraid to use straight repetition when asking a student to reread a story, for students do not find this offensive in the least. Sometimes rereading a story gives greater ease in second or third reading; it seems to build a feeling of confidence and success.

The teacher's judgment is the best guide in determining how much review and how much new material should be included in planning lessons. One fault of beginning teachers is their overeagerness to push ahead and finish the book before students are ready for new material. Most remedial reading students have already had too much of this type of teaching. In fact, their failure to progress at a normal rate was often the result of failing to receive just that little bit of repetition which they needed.

Lesson plans that do not provide for some repetition should be questioned, as should lesson plans that provide too much, for students will be bored and will make abnormally slow progress.

WORK AND FUN All work and no play might not always make Johnnie a dull boy, but it can sometimes cause dull reading lessons. Remedial students who associate reading with drudgery and frustration can sometimes be given a new appreciation of this valuable skill if a little humor and levity is injected.

In one secondary remedial reading class a football star was asked, "What bothers you most about not being able to read?" He replied that his worst difficulty was social embarrassment among his peers, particularly when they would pass a cartoon around the group, each boy reading the caption and laughing. A few reading lessons were planned using cartoons as source material. Once he joined in the laughter, this boy found that reading was made to order for him.

Boys in a junior-high remedial reading class could talk of nothing but racing and the Indianapolis Five Hundred. Newspaper clippings and magazine articles about race cars and drivers were brought to class and the students eagerly applied their phonics skills to such terms as "cam shaft" and "checkered flag." Elementary remedial readers frequently show great interest in the "jokes" section of the weekly student newspapers. If students can find both fun and enjoyment in the reading task, the teacher's task is immeasurably lightened.

Games that teach phonics and basic vocabulary can also be fun for the students. Some teachers encourage this attitude by such statements as, "As soon as we finish our oral reading we will relax and play a bingo game." The bingo game, of course, teaches a basic skill, but as far as the students are concerned it is relaxation. Some teachers include a bit of fun in every lesson.

On the other hand, so-called work is not always detested by students. Many students who hated reading in their regular classroom will work like Trojans in a remedial class on such tasks as comprehension drills because the materials are on the right level for them and they are getting the thrill of real accomplishment.

INDIVIDUAL VERSUS GROUP ACTIVITY Even in a remedial reading setting, a good bit of instruction must be given by group procedures. Explaining the difference between long and short vowels can frequently be done as easily with five students as with one. Having a small group of students all working on the same reading comprehension drill can sometimes provide an interesting contest when papers are corrected to see who gets the most questions right. Flashing words with a tachistoscope provides just as good instruction for thirty-five students as for one. On the other hand, one of the chief values of remedial reading is that it provides for greater individual attention and instruction. A teacher with seven students working quietly in a room can easily take one student aside for individual instruction, but the teacher who must keep thirty-five students working cannot do this.

Lesson plans for remedial reading should provide some balance and variety between group and individual instruction. Lesson plans which mark out large blocks of time for "individual instruction" are undoubtedly designed so that the teacher will supply whatever instruction the student needs at the time. The danger of this type of planning is that hit-or-miss plans so often lack systematic development and different content areas frequently get out of balance. At the other extreme are the rigid lesson plans which account for every minute of the student's day in specified individual or group activities, thus losing many of the benefits of small-group instructional procedures.

VARIETY Throughout this chapter the need for variety in lesson planning has been emphasized and many ways of achieving it have been suggested. Generally speaking, younger children need more variety and shorter periods of time allotment than do older children. Children who have "emotional problems" also tend to have shorter attention spans than regular students. Concentration for long periods of time usually requires some academic maturity which is frequently lacking among children who need remedial reading.

Even though many methods for including variety in lessons have already been mentioned, it might be helpful in this planning section to list very briefly some of the materials which help the teacher to build good variety:

1. *Textbooks.* Remember that there are more than one series of texts; variety can be attained by switching series from time to time. There are also a number of excellent supplementary reading text series.

2. *Tradebooks* and books from special series for remedial reading are often a good change of fare from the steady diet of texts.

3. *Games* can be used, especially for phonics and basic vocabulary instruction; there are also some good ones aimed at developing reading comprehension.

4. *Tachistoscopes* provide good variety of reading experience and contain materials in all of the skill areas at different grade levels.

6. *Programmed-instruction materials* are sometimes highly motivating and aimed at specific skill development.

7. *Drillbooks and workbooks* may both accompany basic texts and be used independently. Separate pages from drillbooks may be torn out if a full book seems too foreboding or contains irrelevant drills.

8. *Audio devices* such as record players and tape recorders add a change of pace so that the student may listen while someone else reads, or he may record a sample of his own aural reading. A card reader can read aloud the words on a stack of cards.

9. *Charts* for both phonics skills and short stories give a different and semipermanent exposure of reading materials.

10. *An overhead projector* adds variety to lessons with its large projected image, often in color. The films can be written on for temporary emphasis. Both commercially prepared transparencies, which teach phonics skills by pictures and example-words, and teacher-prepared transparencies are interesting. Students love to see their own stories projected for others to read.

REMEDIAL READING IN THE REGULAR CLASSROOM The regular classroom teacher is the backbone of the entire educational system. If she does not do her job, nobody else can. She may be maligned, parodied, and overworked. She may be berated on one side for not doing enough in sex education, while on the other she may be told that she has no choice but to master modern mathematics and teach it. At some time between milk-money time and playground duty the district may require her to handle the problems of her own children who need remedial reading instruction. Lucky the teacher who can call on the services of a reading specialist to perform this time-consuming task! The diagnostic procedures and the methods and materials discussed in this book would certainly work splendidly in most classrooms, but only if all students need remediation in reading. Exactly how much they can and should be used is wholly up to the teacher.

No outsider without similar pressures would dare to suggest an optimum organizational plan for remedial reading instruction. However, some teachers might use many of these techniques with a low group or with the children who do not even qualify for membership in the low group.

The tailoring of reading expectancies in other subjects is something that should be done only by the regular elementary classroom teacher or by the secondary teacher. It would make little sense to encourage a student in remedial reading by giving him successful reading experiences using a second grade reading book, only to have him return to his regular class where he has to read from a fifth-grade science book or a ninth-grade social studies text. The regular teacher can greatly aid both the remedial reading teacher and the child by lowering the amount and the level of reading required of the child. Alternate assignments involving maps, diagrams, easy reading selections, etc. should be substituted for masses of difficult required reading.

APPENDIX 12-A SAMPLE REMEDIAL LESSONS

BEGINNING READING (FIRST-GRADE LEVEL) FOR FOURTH-GRADE-AGE STUDENTS

Class size: five

15 minutes Rummy-type card game teaching initial consonants, with four students playing; teacher oversees game while giving individual phonics analysis to another student.

15 minutes Oral reading from primer *Cowboy Sam*; teacher also takes a turn reading, discusses story, and supplies words that students do not know.

10 minutes Flash cards from Instant Words, Group 2; teacher flashes a card, and the first student to call it out correctly may hold the card; if he cannot say it, another student gets a turn – all students must watch flash card because it will not be flashed again.

15 minutes Silent rereading of same *Cowboy Sam* story. A student asks teacher any unknown word; she tells him what it is and writes it on a slip of paper for him to take home and study; teacher also adds word to her list for for later review with the student next day.

45 minutes Total time.

Next day

5 minutes Review words on list; each student reads his own words.

15 minutes Workbook, page on beginning consonant; teacher gives a student an individual Instant Word Test.

10 minutes Students correct their own workbook pages and take turns reading sentences aloud.

15 minutes Instant Word Bingo, Group 2; teacher discusses meaning and sounds of some words while calling them out.

45 minutes Total time.

INTERMEDIATE READING (THIRD-GRADE LEVEL) FOR SIXTH- OR SEVENTH-GRADE-AGE STUDENTS

Class size: nine

10 minutes Flip cards teaching consonant blends; teacher flips new blends before them, card by card, and students take turns calling them out.

15 minutes Oral reading from *Deep Sea Diver* series, teacher helping.

15 minutes Students silently answer comprehension questions contained in book; teacher gives Individual Phonics Analysis to a student.

10 minutes Students trade papers and correct them as teacher reads answers; some wrong answers are discussed and looked up in text.

50 minutes Total time.

Next day

15 minutes Tachistoscope drill using Instant Words, group 14. Teacher flashes a word on the screen; students try to write the word on a sheet of paper or in a notebook; teacher calls on student to say it aloud; teacher shows word on screen to prove student was correct (or incorrect); and all students correct their spelling of the word or copy it for the first time if they missed it.

7 minutes Students read silently from page of McCall-Crabbs (comprehension drill), Book A, and answer ten multiple-choice questions in notebook. Teacher helps individual students with hard words.
13 minutes Students take turns reading questions aloud; discuss right answer, and mark their papers.
15 minutes Phonics Bingo. Teacher stresses the sound and spellings of broad *o* sound.
50 minutes Total time

UPPER REMEDIAL READING (FIFTH-GRADE LEVEL) FOR HIGH-SCHOOL STUDENTS

Class size: fifteen
(The school also has a lower remedial reading class at second- and third-grade level for eight students.)

15 minutes The teacher explains the meaning and roots of some words taken from Chapter 2 in an adapted classic, *Lorna Doone*. Teacher shows the same root in other familiar words.
25 minutes Students read Chapter 2 in *Lorna Doone* after teacher helps a student with a brief summary of Chapter 1. Teacher helps students individually and gives one Individual Phonics Analysis (including a few items at upper level).
15 minutes Tachistoscopic drill using Phonics Intermediate Level. Teacher explains sounds of "O" and slowly shows a few examples. Teacher then flashes examples; students write them and take turns giving first the sound, then the example word; then all students correct written response when word is shown again.
55 minutes Total time.

Next day

25 minutes Students work in reading laboratory (comprehension drill), each at his own level. Teacher sees that workbooks are being filled in properly and supplies help with difficult words. Teacher completes one more Individual Phonics Analysis.
10 minutes Teacher explains syllabification rules with help of Webster Word Analysis Chart, adding her own example words.
20 minutes Students divide into three groups and play Dolch Syllable Game. Teacher supervises and writes a few notes in her file on attitude development of "problem boy."
55 minutes Total time.

Next day

25 minutes The upper half of the class reads a radio script into a tape recorder (tape time is only ten minutes but it takes twenty-five minutes to complete the production). Teacher helps slower half of class in review of vowel sounds, using phonics transparencies on the overhead projector.
15 minutes Whole class listens to playback of tape. All students have copy of script and follow along.
15 minutes Teacher writes a selected spelling list on the board (words taken from preceding day's phonics filmstrip); students are given a few minutes to study them and then take practice test. Each student corrects his own paper.
55 minutes Total time.

13

EXPECTANCY – DETERMINING MENTAL ABILITY

The problem of determining mental ability through the use of intelligence tests or, indeed, through any type of evaluation procedure has come under much criticism in recent years. Much of the criticism has come from parents and some educators of urban disadvantaged students who feel with some justification that traditional methods such as standardized IQ tests unfairly penalize their children because of cultural bias.

It is true that the vocabulary and often even the pictures of many standardized tests contain words and present situations more oriented towards middle-class and even suburban children rather than lower-class inner-city children. The same problem exists with many minority-group children and with rural lower socioeconomic children.

However, even in a ghetto where all children are of one race and of the same cultural economic level, there are wide differences in individual learning ability. Good teachers should and do expect to give a greater quantity and sometimes a higher quality of work to brighter students. The problem, therefore, is to find out which are the brighter students. Often this can be accomplished by informal means, such as observation and work samples; but informal evaluations, which sometimes overlook some students, are heavily dependent on a good, experienced teacher. Good, experienced teachers are in very short supply in inner-city or rural disadvantaged schools; hence, some type of intelligence test or more or less formal method of evaluating the potential learning capacity of the children in these schools is often beneficial.

In all the furor about IQ tests, teachers are sometimes wrong and sometimes unfairly penalize certain children; they might lose sight of the fact that IQ tests are not instruments of torture used to harm children or devices designed to perpetuate the status quo of certain classes or races, but, rather, IQ tests are a tool, admittedly not perfect, to aid educators, teachers, principals, and school psychologists. The fact that IQ tests can be misused is not a unique characteristic. A bread knife can kill someone if it is misused in a certain way, and certainly the wrong textbook can provide less than no learning – it can make a child hate a certain subject.

This chapter, then, deals mainly with IQ tests – not implying that the reading teacher must use them but that she should at least understand them and, furthermore, that in understanding them, there is less chance of misusing them. All teachers should use IQ tests with caution and certainly should not let continuous observations of classroom performance outweigh test scores, but teachers of disadvantaged and minority groups should use extra caution and make due allowances for local conditions.

Educators in certain situations may decide not to use intelligence tests at all because they fear the wrath of the community or they fear that some teachers may misuse the results. When they do this, however, they run certain other risks, such as holding the whole class back by mixing several retarded children in with normal learners and then expecting uniform results (for example, expecting all second graders to read at second-grade level) or having bright children go undetected and get by with just average achievement. A good teacher never has enough time to spend with individual students, just as a school district never has enough well-trained teachers; hence, the teacher must budget her time and the district must carefully allot its teachers. If a teacher or a district spends an inordinate amount of time and effort on dull pupils in trying to bring them up to average achievement, the bright pupils who should be working above average are being neglected. If a remedial reading teacher spends her time working with many dull or mentally retarded pupils, she will be neglecting these pupils of normal learning ability who are underachieving in reading.

The problem of how much reading ability to expect from a child confronts a teacher at every lesson. When working with children of normal learning ability, who have all been exposed successfully to the standard amount of reading instruction, a teacher ordinarily knows what to expect and has only to look at a chart which converts chronological age into grade placement. She knows that the average child enters the first grade at six years and three months of age; therefore, two years later, at age eight years and three months, she would expect him to be reading like a beginning third grader. Expressed in grade placement numbers, this would be grade 3.0. Four months later he should be reading at a grade placement of 3.4, and so on throughout his school life.

If only all children were normal automatons, the teacher's life could run so smoothly! Unfortunately, children suffer from all the frailties, unpredictable growth rates, and erratic behavior which beset the human race, and the teacher must adjust to innumerable exceptions. Some children are bright and should read ahead of their age group; some are dull and should read below it; at times, whole classrooms of children from very low socioeconomic areas read even more poorly than would be expected. The determination of what to expect of a child, or of a group, is extremely tenuous, at best.

GAUGING EXPECTANCY

Because reading is a task requiring mental ability, perhaps the best way to gauge expectancy is to use a test of mental ability that has been standardized adequately. This is certainly superior to the method used by many school systems which gauge their expectations on children's birth dates. Age as a predictor is little better than nothing, and that is a fine description of its merit—"better than nothing." Anyone who has ever watched several children grow up together, or who has taught a class of youngsters, can tell you that they differ vastly in mental ability and in rate of growth, even though their age may be the same.

NORMAL DISTRIBUTION OF MENTAL ABILITY In a school that only uses the "birthday system" of placing children in grades (as many do), and this school serves a normal cross-section of children in the United States, toward the end of the fourth grade, when the average child's chronological age is ten, we could expect to find the spread of mental ages listed in Table 13-1.

TABLE 13-1
THE NORMAL DISTRIBUTION OF MENTAL ABILITY IN A CLASSROOM OF TEN-YEAR-OLD FOURTH GRADERS

Number of children	*Mental age*	*Grade of mental ability expected*
1	Seven	(upper first-grade ability)
3	Eight	(upper second-grade ability)
7	Nine	(upper third-grade ability)
10	Ten	(upper fourth-grade ability)
7	Eleven	(upper fifth-grade ability)
3	Twelve	(upper sixth-grade ability)
1	Thirteen	(upper seventh-grade ability)
32 Total		

In more graphic terms, we might diagram the class of thirty-two fourth graders as illustrated in Figure 13-1.

FIGURE 13-1 The normal distribution of mental ability and expected reading ability for an average fourth grade class.

Implications of this simple fact of normal distribution of abilities, so familiar in educational psychology classes, are often not perceived by teachers (or, perhaps teachers did not believe what they learned). Proof of this is seen in their lesson assignments or in their grouping of children for reading or in their selection of reading material.

This is not to suggest that the normal distribution of mental ages tells the whole story, because it does not. Like most other things in reading and education, it is not that neat and simple. A ten-year-old with the mental age of a thirteen-year-old is not emotionally, socially, physically, or even academically

TABLE 13-2
TABLE FOR CONVERTING MENTAL AGE INTO MENTAL-AGE GRADE PLACEMENT[a]

MA (or XA) yrs.-mos.	*MAGP grade*	*MA yrs.-mos.*	*MAGP grade*	*MA yrs.-mos.*	*MAGP grade*	*MA yrs.-mos.*	*MAGP grade*
7- 0	1.8	9- 6	4.2	12- 0	6.7	14- 6	9.0
1	1.9	7	4.3	1	6.8	7	9.1
2	2.0	8	4.4	2	6.8	8	9.2
3	2.1	9	4.5	3	6.9	9	9.3
4	2.2	10	4.6	4	7.0	10	9.3
5	2.2	11	4.7	5	7.1	11	9.4
6	2.3	10- 0	4.8	6	7.2	15- 0	9.5
7	2.4	1	4.8	7	7.2	1	9.6
8	2.5	2	4.9	8	7.3	2	9.6
9	2.6	3	5.0	9	7.4	3	9.7
10	2.6	4	5.1	10	7.5	4	9.8
11	2.7	5	5.2	11	7.6	5	9.8
8- 0	2.8	6	5.2	13- 0	7.7	6	9.9
1	2.9	7	5.3	1	7.7	7	10.0
2	3.0	8	5.4	2	7.8	8	10.0
3	3.0	9	5.5	3	7.9	9	10.1
4	3.1	10	5.6	4	8.0	10	10.2
5	3.2	11	5.7	5	8.1	11	10.2
6	3.2	11- 0	5.7	6	8.1	16.0	10.3
7	3.3	1	5.8	7	8.2		
8	3.4	2	5.8	8	8.3		
9	3.5	3	5.9	9	8.4		
10	3.6	4	6.0	10	8.5		
11	3.7	5	6.1	11	8.6		
9- 0	3.8	6	6.2	14- 0	8.7		
1	3.8	7	6.2	1	8.7		
2	3.9	8	6.3	2	8.8		
3	4.0	9	6.4	3	8.9		
4	4.1	10	6.5	4	8.9		
5	4.2	11	6.6	5	9.0		

[a]Based on the *California Test of Mental Maturity Manual* (1957).

Note: Different IQ tests would have slightly different MAGP conversions. This table is within about one month of Grade Placement for the TOGA in elementary years. There is a rise in MA in relation to Grade Placement toward secondary school because of dropouts and other factors which make the average IQ in secondary school slightly over 100.

on a par with other thirteen-year-olds in the seventh grade. So, there are valid reasons for having him in the fourth- (or perhaps fifth-) grade classroom. The solution of his problem will be found elsewhere – in the validity of *expecting him to read more proficiently* than the average fourth-grade student.

MENTAL AGE To review the concept of mental age, here is a brief explanation of how it is determined. First, we find some mental task which can be objectively graded in terms of difficulty (possibly the ability to repeat a series of digits when they are called out at one-second intervals). For example, the examiner says, "6–4–8–5–2" and the child attempts to repeat, "6–4–8–5–2." But first he starts with two digits and then proceeds to three digits, four digits, and so on until the child is no longer able to repeat the series accurately. We must now "standardize" the test by giving the test to hundreds of children of a particular age. From this "standardization" we find that the average seven-year-old can repeat five digits. (This, by the way, is one of the tasks included in the Stanford-Binet tests of intelligence.)

Now along comes Johnny; since his teacher wants to find out how bright he is, she asks him to repeat digits after her (in a particular order prescribed in the test). If Johnny can repeat five digits and no more, she says that he has the mental ability of the average seven-year-old or, to put it more formally, that he mas a mental age of seven. Of course, in determining mental age, a variety of tasks is actually used, not just this one of repeating digits.

Please note that Johnny's mental age was determined without ever asking him how old he is. Johnny might be seven or he might be nine or six.

MENTAL-AGE GRADE PLACEMENT (MAGP) Johnny's mental age can now be entered on a table for grade-placement norms. Such a table, to be used with the California Test of Mental Maturity, is presented in Table 13-2, which tells us that if Johnny has a mental age of seven, he can be expected to read at a grade placement of 1.8. In other words, Johnny has a mental-age grade placement (MAGP) of 1.8. If only the nonlanguage part of the IQ test is being used, a nonlanguage mental-age grade placement, or NLMAGP, is computed.

EXPECTANCY AGE Some educators use a straight MAGP based on an IQ test such as that described above. However, others prefer to modify the MAGP with CA (chronological age), that is, to take into account the child's chronological age as part of determining his expected achievement. Probably the most common way of doing this is to use the Horn formula, which is expressed as XA (expectancy age). The formula is:

$$\text{XA} = \frac{\text{2 MA plus CA}}{3}$$

for elementary years. This is how it works: In the case of Johnny, let us say that he is nine years old (MA 7 + CA 9). His XA will be 7 plus 7 plus 9 divided by 3, which gives us an XA of 7.7. Note that because Johnny is nine years old and has been on the earth two years longer than the average seven-year-old (and he has probably been in school longer), we expect a little more from him than from an average seven-year-old (who, of course, by definition, would have an MA of 7 and an XA of 7). Let us take another boy, Ezekiel; although he is nine years old, he has an MA of 11. We find that his XA is 10.3, a little less than an MA of straight 11. To get expectancy terms of grade placement, we again use Table 13-2 and see that the XA's indicate that Johnny should be reading at a level of 2.4, while Ezekiel should be reading at 5.0, even though they are both in the fourth grade.

INTELLIGENCE QUOTIENT Thus far I have been discussing mental ages and have avoided mentioning the well-known index of "brightness" or "dullness" known as the intelligence quotient (IQ). The IQ is used to determine something (although not everything) about a child's learning ability.

An IQ is a ratio of mental age to chronological age, expressed in the simple formula:

$$IQ = \frac{MA}{CA} \times 100$$

In the case of Johnny, who is nine years old (CA = 9) but has the mental abilities of only an average seven-year-old (MA = 7), we can say that he has an IQ of 77. On the other hand, Ezekiel, who is also nine years old, is able to do the mental tasks of an eleven-year-old; he is said to have an IQ of 122. Assuming that these IQ's are accurate, we can predict that, given reasonable motivation and environment, Ezekiel will go on to college while Johnny will have an increasingly difficult time in school and might never get a high-school diploma.

A further distinction should be made between high-IQ children and low-IQ children in terms of their ability to learn and to use abstract skills, like reading and writing. Children with low IQ's have smaller vocabularies and are less creative in using them, both in writing and speaking. Low-IQ children do not learn to associate symbols (words) with meanings nearly as well as high-IQ children do. There are many exceptions, but, by and large, high-IQ children and adults enjoy reading books for pleasure, while low-IQ children and adults do not.

In other words, the IQ ratio gives us more information than the simple MA does. It gives a prediction of future school success—success particularly in tasks or skills which require mental ability; reading is one of these skills. To put it bluntly, Johnny is going to have a difficult time ever learning to read, while Ezekiel will learn to read fairly easily by almost any method of reading instruction.

Another interesting difference between high-IQ and low-IQ children (and this is important to the reading teacher) is that the "dull" child requires much more repetition and practice to learn new words. Arthur Gates found that children who have an IQ in the 120s need twenty repetitions to learn new words, while children with IQ's in the 70s need forty-five repetitions. Conditions of learning and study vary so widely that these numbers of repetitions are not cited to show that a child must have twenty repetitions, but rather that "dull" children do need more repetition and practice to learn to read new words.*

Many teachers, unaware of differences in learning abilities, will tell you how marvelously their methods worked with Ezekiel and may gloss over how poorly the methods worked with Johnny. They may even claim that there cannot be anything wrong with the way they teach reading because: "Just look how well little Ezekiel and his counterparts are doing." What this teacher does not know is that any second-rate novice teacher using the most antiquated of methods and haphazard organization can teach Ezekiel to read. If you want to find out if a teacher can teach reading, let her try it on Johnny.

Fortunately, most children fall somewhere between Johnny and Ezekiel in learning ability. Likewise, the methods of reading instruction used by most teachers are not antiquated and haphazard. There is a wide range of teaching abilities, and the better the teacher the greater her success in teaching reading to a larger percentage of children. To express it another way, a better teacher can move the class average upward a little faster. Any teacher who claims that she has been completely successful in teaching reading to every child in her class is either not telling the truth or has not taught many children. Even the most successful of teachers will fail sometimes. An aim of this book is to help teachers to cut down on their failures and to help raise the class average a little faster.

An IQ test tells the teacher something about a child's present rate of learning, in addition to the valuable information it gives about future learning possibilities. Children like Johnny take more hours of instruction to get the same amount of learning. They require more drill in order to remember. They are more apt to slip backward in reading ability during summer vacations. In "the good old days," Johnny would have just sat around in first and second grades for a few years until he got embarrassed because his knees would no longer fit under the desk. Ordinarily, he would have quit school when he realized that he could not read much and would have gone out to milk cows and plow the field, thereby becoming a useful member of society. But today, machines milk the cows, and fields are plowed by machines operated by men who know how to read a tractor manual. Since it does not take too many men, either, Johnny must stay on in school; and the school must try to teach him. And because the public schools are not equipped to individualize his instruction, the school must try to teach him the same things that it tries to teach Ezekiel. But even Johnny knows that he and Ezekiel should not be learning the same things.

*Arthur Gates, *The Improvement of Reading*. New York: The Macmillan Co., 1950.

His school and society (and this includes Johnny's parents and his future employers) demand that Johnny be able to read, even though nearly everybody knows that he is not especially suited to the task and that he will probably never regularly use the public library. Nevertheless, to get and hold a job, he must have at least a modicum of reading ability.

What all this amounts to is that somebody in the school system is going to have to spend some time trying to teach Johnny to read. The methods discussed in this book will work for children with below-average learning ability (like Johnny's) but they will work much better if the teacher has expectations that are reasonable. A realistic perception of Johnny's needs will keep her from hopping from one reading method to another looking for a panacea.

Teachers, especially those who specialize in remedial reading, should have a good background in guidance and in the administration and interpretation of intelligence tests. Every reading teacher should have a course in Tests and Measurements. A teacher will quite often be presented with a child whose reading tests show that he cannot read up to grade level. The first thing is to determine his expectancy. Perhaps, as is often the case, the child is reading as well as can be reasonably expected. What is really needed for this child is vocational and/or educational guidance. And the guidance should be offered to his teacher and parents as often as to the child himself.

IQ tests are not always accurate, but they are much more accurate than the subjective judgments of teachers and parents. A parent will say, "I know he is bright. He combs his hair so neatly. He is polite. He used such a big word the other day . . ." Such comments are all very nice, but IQ tests do not inquire about hair combing and manners. Schools which must economize are forced to use efficient procedures, and IQ tests are a valuable economy. A teacher has only so much time and effort. The problem is: "Where can she be most effective?" The use of IQ tests and an understanding of expectancy procedures can help her judge where her effort can be placed most effectively.

CUT-OFF POINT FOR REMEDIAL READING Many school districts have a program of remedial reading to supplement classroom reading instruction. These programs are discussed more fully in Chapter 12. For the present, let us consider the cut-off point since it relates closely to IQ and expectancy.

Many districts admit only children with IQ's of 90 or above into the remedial reading program. The argument for this is that it would be prohibitively expensive to put every poor reader into remedial reading. Therefore, they choose to select only those students who have the most probability of success, and success with a reasonable amount of teaching time.

Children with very low IQ's (below 75 or 80) are often placed in a special training class with a teacher who has been educated to teach the mentally retarded child. This solves the problem for very low-IQ pupils in some districts but not for the child who has an IQ in the 80s who is too bright for special training and too slow for remedial reading classes. This is an unmet problem in many schools. Some possible solutions are: (1) retaining the child a year or more, (2) grouping classes by reading ability, where possible, (3) providing the classroom teacher with assistance in the form of diagnostic services, special materials, and suggestions on teaching methods from the remedial reading teacher, a principal or a supervisor, and (4) the more expensive way of providing enough special services so that no child is neglected.

TEST USAGE

What intelligence tests should you use? This is not a book on guidance nor is it a book on testing, although these two fields are closely related to our discussion. There is no shortage of books on guidance and testing, and many are helpful in selecting suitable tests. A good list, with evaluations of all major intelligence tests, is contained in Buros' *Mental Measurement Yearbooks.*

If you suspect that a child has a reading problem, do not use a test which requires reading ability. Examine a copy of the test. If a high level of reading comprehension is required or if considerable reading ability is involved, do not use this test for children with possible reading problems. Not all tests require reading ability. Look at the sample items from the TOGA (Test for General Ability) in Figure 13-2. In this test no reading is involved.

Some tests have parts which require reading and others which do not. For example, look at the junior-high level of the CTMM (California Test of Mental Maturity) in Figure 13-3. Test 2 of Figure 13-3 is called Manipulation of Areas and is part of a section of the CTMM known as Non-Language. No reading is involved and very little culture differentiation is involved, although there is admittedly some. Test 4 is called Inference and is part of the Language section. Here it is apparent that good reading skill is involved and, of course, thinking or reasoning ability.

These samples of well-known IQ tests enable the teacher to appreciate that reading skill is not always involved in an IQ test. The reading teacher must take this into consideration in selecting tests and interpreting IQ scores, especially when they are to be used for reading expectancy or in determining a "cut-off" point for referral to remedial reading classes.

Even though school systems may be using some tests that involve reading (for example, the CTMM), it is still possible for the reading teacher to isolate the subtests that require reading simply by glancing at the Diagnostic Profile (illustrated in Figure 13-4). Here it is seen that if one looks only at the total IQ of 76, one might feel that Robert quite possibly belongs in a special training class. But if we look at Robert's nonlanguage IQ we see that it is 93, which is definitely within the normal learning ability range. In other words, on the tests requiring reading, Robert does poorly, but he does quite acceptably where reading is not a factor. Most states, aware of this test limitation, require an individual intelligence test administered by a qualified psychologist or counselor before special placement is made.

S2

In the Verbal part of the test the teacher reads the following directions from the manual: "When you find the picture that answers the question, put a large X over it . . . In the first row are pictures of a cat, a dog, a bird, a turtle, and a fish. Find the one that moves slowly."

30

Later on in this same section of the test (Information) a more difficult item would look like this: "Find the one that is most important in the work of an electrician . . ."

1

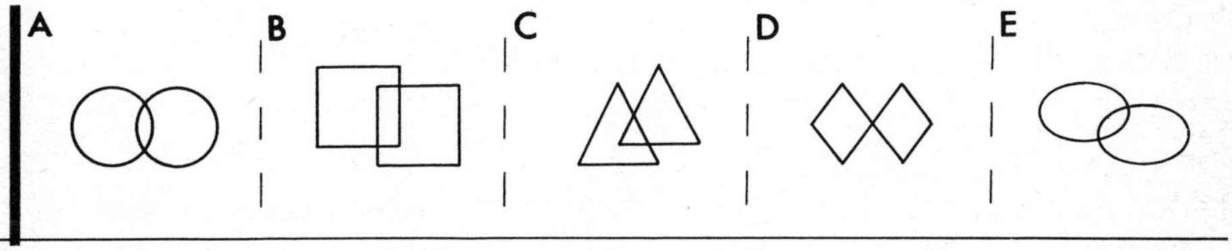

24

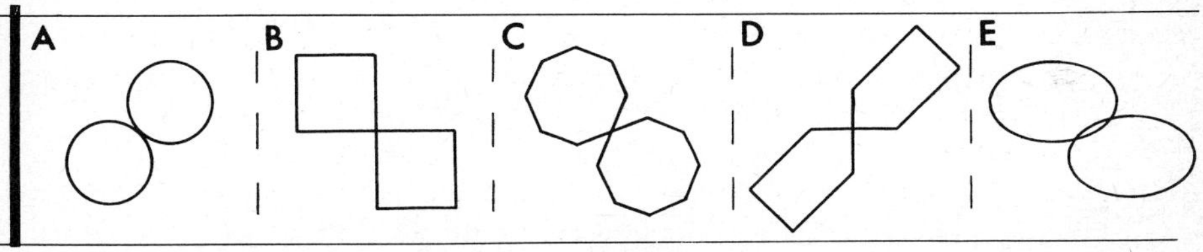

Approximately half of the items in the TOGA are in the section called Reasoning. The directions for doing all these items are: "Four of the pictures in each row follow the same rule. One picture does not . . . mark the one that does not follow the rule with an X."

FIGURE 13-2 Sample items from the TOGA (Test of General Ability, Grades 2-4).

DIRECTIONS: In each row find the drawing that is a different view of the first drawing. Mark its number as you are told.

TEST 2

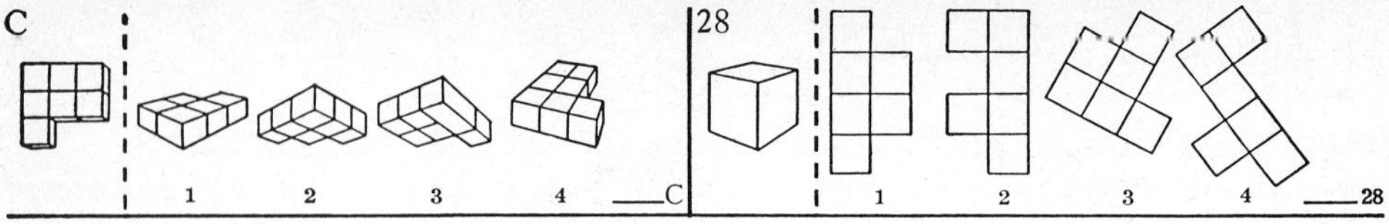

DIRECTIONS: Read each group of statements below and the conclusions which follow. Then mark as you are told the number of each answer you have decided is correct.

TEST 4

E. All four-footed creatures are animals.

All horses are four-footed.

Therefore

1 **Creatures other than horses can walk**

2 **All horses can walk**

3 **All horses are animals** ——E

54. If he remains with his friend he will suffer loss, and if he leaves his friend he will suffer loss.

But, he must remain with his friend or leave him.

Therefore

1 **He should remain with his friend**

2 **It takes courage to leave a friend**

3 **He will suffer loss** ——54

FIGURE 13-3 Sample items from the California Test of Mental Maturity, junior high level.

The moral of this study is: "Look at the nonlanguage IQ whenever a reading problem is suspected." The IQ test shown in Figure 13-4 is not a hypothetical one; Robert is a real child admitted to a reading clinic. His Gray's oral reading score was grade 3.9. You can imagine the kind of time he was having in his ninth-grade classroom. Unfortunately, there are many Roberts in our schools. But it is my hope that if more teachers, with the backing of their administrators, will follow the reading instruction principles set forth here, there will be fewer Roberts.

INDIVIDUAL INTELLIGENCE TESTS Up to this point, we have been considering group intelligence tests, which are paper-and-pencil tests that can be given to a whole class at one time. They may be administered by the class-

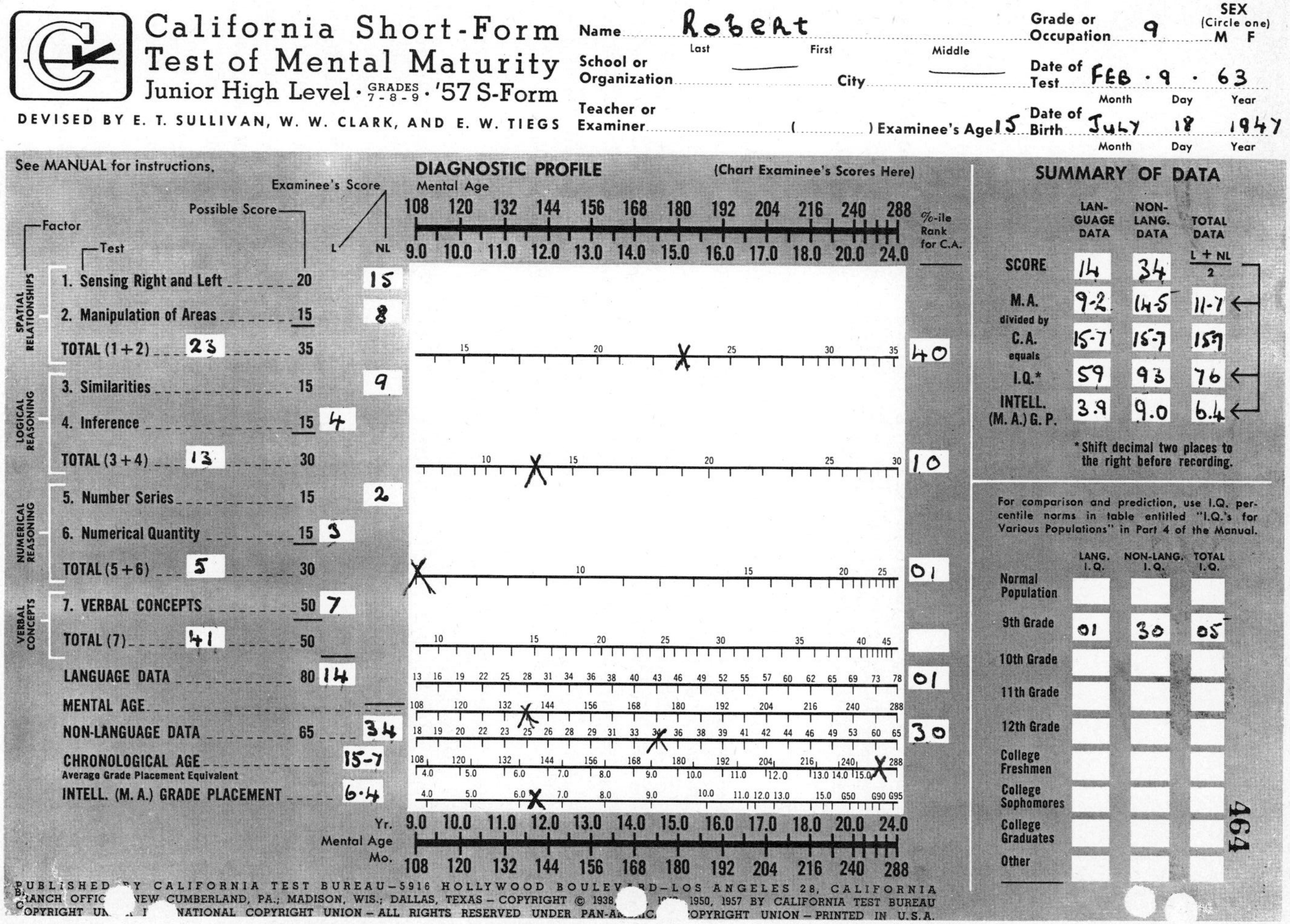

California Short-Form Test of Mental Maturity
Junior High Level · GRADES 7-8-9 · '57 S-Form
DEVISED BY E. T. SULLIVAN, W. W. CLARK, AND E. W. TIEGS

Name: Robert (Last / First / Middle)
School or Organization: — City: —
Teacher or Examiner: ( ) Examinee's Age 15
Grade or Occupation: 9
SEX (Circle one) M F
Date of Test: FEB · 9 · 63 (Month / Day / Year)
Date of Birth: JULY 18 1947 (Month / Day / Year)

See MANUAL for instructions.

Factor	Test	Possible Score	Examinee's Score L	Examinee's Score NL	%-ile Rank for C.A.
SPATIAL RELATIONSHIPS	1. Sensing Right and Left	20		15	
	2. Manipulation of Areas	15		8	
	TOTAL (1 + 2) 23	35			40
LOGICAL REASONING	3. Similarities	15		9	
	4. Inference	15	4		
	TOTAL (3 + 4) 13	30			10
NUMERICAL REASONING	5. Number Series	15		2	
	6. Numerical Quantity	15	3		
	TOTAL (5 + 6) 5	30			01
VERBAL CONCEPTS	7. VERBAL CONCEPTS	50	7		
	TOTAL (7) 41	50			
	LANGUAGE DATA	80	14		01
	MENTAL AGE				
	NON-LANGUAGE DATA	65		34	30
	CHRONOLOGICAL AGE		15-7		
	Average Grade Placement Equivalent				
	INTELL. (M. A.) GRADE PLACEMENT		6.4		

DIAGNOSTIC PROFILE (Chart Examinee's Scores Here)
Mental Age
108 120 132 144 156 168 180 192 204 216 240 288
9.0 10.0 11.0 12.0 13.0 14.0 15.0 16.0 17.0 18.0 20.0 24.0
Yr. Mental Age Mo.

SUMMARY OF DATA

	LANGUAGE DATA	NON-LANG. DATA	TOTAL DATA ($\frac{L + NL}{2}$)
SCORE	14	34	
M.A.	9-2	14-5	11-7
divided by C.A.	15-7	15-7	157
equals I.Q.*	59	93	76
INTELL. (M. A.) G. P.	3.9	9.0	6.4

*Shift decimal two places to the right before recording.

For comparison and prediction, use I.Q. percentile norms in table entitled "I.Q.'s for Various Populations" in Part 4 of the Manual.

	LANG. I.Q.	NON-LANG. I.Q.	TOTAL I.Q.
Normal Population			
9th Grade	01	30	05
10th Grade			
11th Grade			
12th Grade			
College Freshmen			
College Sophomores			
College Graduates			
Other			

464

PUBLISHED BY CALIFORNIA TEST BUREAU—5916 HOLLYWOOD BOULEVARD—LOS ANGELES 28, CALIFORNIA
BRANCH OFFICES: NEW CUMBERLAND, PA.; MADISON, WIS.; DALLAS, TEXAS – COPYRIGHT © 1938, 1950, 1957 BY CALIFORNIA TEST BUREAU
COPYRIGHT UNDER INTERNATIONAL COPYRIGHT UNION – ALL RIGHTS RESERVED UNDER PAN-AMERICAN COPYRIGHT UNION – PRINTED IN U.S.A.

FIGURE 13-4 Diagnostic Profile, California Short-form Test of Mental Maturity, junior high level.

room teacher or a special teacher or a guidance person assigned to test administration. Each test takes about one hour to administer and can sometimes be scored in a second or two by a computer or in ten minutes by hand. The scoring involves counting correct multiple-choice answers and checking the expected grade level, MA, or IQ in a scoring manual.

While group tests are useful when large numbers of children are to be tested, they are not as accurate or useful as individual intelligence tests. Individual tests should be administered by a psychologist or a person specially trained in individual test administration. It takes the examiner an hour or an hour and a half to administer the test to one child and additional time to score and interpret it. In terms of time (which in any public school is synonymous with money), they are much more expensive than group intelligence tests. Depending upon district policy and the money allotted to special services, they may be given to a large or small percentage of children who have learning problems. Thus, children with reading problems may or may not have the advantage of individual IQ testing. All teachers should know something about individual tests and their use.

By far the most widely used individual intelligence test is the Wechsler Intelligence Scale for Children (WISC). It has a verbal and a nonverbal section but does not require any reading ability because all verbal items are read to the student by the examiner.

Many research studies have reported on the kinds of patterns, or profiles, of subtest scores with children who have reading problems. Although the results of these studies are often conflicting and confusing, one thing seems fairly certain – the wider the spread between verbal and nonverbal IQ, the greater the possibility that there is some kind of underlying emotional or physical problem, even though the total IQ score may be normal. For example, it is not unusual for a child with a verbal IQ of 96 to have a nonverbal IQ of 102, giving him a total score of 98. However, another child with a total score of 98 may have a verbal IQ of 87 and a performance score of 112. This child would have a much higher probability of some emotional disturbance or physical problem such as brain damage.

Subtest scores tend to indicate abnormality when they vary three or more points from the expected norm for a child. A child's norm for subtests can be found by dividing the total IQ by 10. A child with a total IQ of 100, for example, would be expected to score 10 on every subtest. Of course no child is that normal; all score a point or two up or down from the norm on various subtests.

Reading teachers should accept children for remedial reading even if they have known emotional or physical problems, just as long as they are working below expectancy. This discussion of problems as evidenced by the WISC scatter is given so that reading teachers may understand the basis of referral of the children with whom they work and so that they may know how to interpret and apply the reports on children that they receive from school psychologists.

WISC RECORD FORM

NAME BILL SMITH AGE 11-8 SEX M

ADDRESS ANYPLACE, U.S.A.

PARENT'S NAME TIN SMITH

SCHOOL LINCOLN GRADE 5

REFERRED BY MISS JONES - TEACHER

	Year	Month	Day
Date Tested	64	9	28
Date of Birth	53	1	23
Age	11	8	5

	Scaled Score	IQ
Verbal Scale	45 *	94
Performance Scale	31 *	74
Full Scale	76	83

*Prorated if necessary

	Raw Score	Scaled Score
VERBAL TESTS		
Information	10	6
Comprehension	15	12
Arithmetic	9	9
Similarities	10	10
Vocabulary	43	12
(Digit Span)	7	5
Sum of Verbal Tests		54
PERFORMANCE TESTS		
Picture Completion	7	5
Picture Arrangement	23	7
Block Design	11	7
Object Assembly	19	8
Coding	23	4
(Mazes)		
Sum of Performance Tests		31

NOTES

MA = 10.1 FS

MA = 11.0 VS

MA = 11.9 VS — WITH DIGIT SPAN

ORAL READING - LOW 3RD

VISION — OK

GOOD ORAL VERBAL ABILITIES

MOST TROUBLE WITH SHORT TERM MEMORY (DIGITS & CODE)

RELATIVELY HIGH VERBAL & LOW PERFORMANCE SUGGEST
" GOOD ENVIRONMENT & POSSIBLE MILD BRAIN DAMAGE

RECOMMEND
REMEDIAL READING

V Bennett
Examiner

FIGURE 13-5 First page from a WISC (Wechsler Intelligence Scale for Children) individual intelligence test.

Perhaps a word of caution is in order: Reading teachers should not be bowled over by the terminology used by the psychologist who may feel the need of leaning on medical or psychological terminology. A teacher should simply look at the results of her own reading tests and at the scores made on the IQ test used; then, if she accepts a child, all she has to do is to start teaching him reading. Let the school psychologist worry about psychotherapy, perception training, neurological development, or anything else that he is concerned about.

CONVERTING IQ TO MA AND MAGP Most teachers have had courses in testing as part of their teacher training. It is often quite another matter to apply what they have learned to the classroom. I find that many of them cannot remember how to do the relatively simple calculation of converting a child's IQ into an MA. This is necessary when they want to find a child's mental age when all they have is his IQ and chronological age.

If we know the child's IQ and his age (CA), all we have to do is multiply the IQ by the CA and move the decimal point two places to the left.

$$\text{MA} = \frac{\text{CA} \times \text{IQ}}{100}$$

For example, if Gaspar is ten years old and has an IQ of 90, he will have an MA of 9 years (10 × 90 equals 9.00, with the decimal point moved two places to the left).

In order to convert MA to grade placement (giving a measure called MAGP for mental age grade placement, or grade expectancy), we subtract 5.4 from the MA. Expressed in a formula, it reads:

$$\text{MAGP} = \text{MA} - 5.4$$

The reason for subtracting 5.4 is that children enter kindergarten at an average age (CA) of 5.4; thus they are 6.4 when they enter first grade. Figure 13-6 provides some simple illustrations of converting IQ into MAGP. If you are not familiar with the concept, study it carefully. Then try working out some examples from children in your class. It seems to be much easier to read an example in a book than to apply the concepts to real children.

The MAGP can sometimes be determined directly from scales given in the IQ test manual, thus saving the work of calculating it. However, since test manuals are not as readily available as IQ scores, teachers should know how to make their own grade-expectancy calculations.

The MAGP concept works well for children in the elementary and junior-high grades but not for high-school students because most IQ tests place a "stop" or leveling off of annual MA growth at about age fifteen. MAGP can still be calculated for ages sixteen, seventeen, and eighteen and for adults; but the MA of fifteen should be used for all ages over fifteen. Perhaps less reliance

Three ten-year-olds. The CAGP for ten-year-olds is 4.6 (CAGP = CA − 5.4). Hence all would usually be placed in a fourth-grade classroom.

Gaspar (IQ 90)

$$\frac{90(\text{IQ}) \times 10(\text{CA})}{100} - 5.4 = \text{MAGP}$$

$$9.0(\text{MA}) - 5.4 = 3.6 \text{ MAGP}$$

Bert (IQ 100)

$$\frac{100 \times 10}{100} - 5.4 = \text{MAGP}$$

$$10 - 5.4 = 4.6 \text{ MAGP}$$

Gladys (IQ 110):

$$\frac{110 \times 10}{100} - 5.4 = \text{MAGP}$$

$$11 - 5.4 = 6.6 \text{ MAGP}$$

Note that these three fourth graders whose IQ's are in the normal range have expected reading abilities of mid-third grade, mid-fourth grade, and mid-fifth grade, respectively. Almost every class has a wider range than IQ 90 and IQ 110.

Now let us look at some wider deviations in IQ that are regularly found in normal classrooms.

Bill, ninth-grader (*IQ 83*)

$$\frac{83 \times 14.9}{100} - 5.4 = \text{MAGP}$$

$$12.2 - 5.4 = 6.8 \text{ MAGP}$$

Hence we expect him to have upper-sixth-grade reading ability.

Sammy, second-grader (*IQ 125*)

$$\frac{125 \times 7.5}{100} - 5.4 = \text{MAGP}$$

$$9.4 - 5.4 = 4.0 \text{ MAGP}$$

Hence we expect this second grader to read like a beginning fourth grader.

FIGURE 13-6 Examples of IQ and CA converted to MAGP and CAGP.

should be placed on MA for teenagers and adults and more reliance on such things as cultural factors and the student's degree of motivation.

In most schools, Gaspar and Gladys (IQ 90 and 110) of Figure 13-6, who are both ten years old, would both be in the same fourth-grade room. The teacher would give the same homework assignments to both of them, and they would be expected to use the same social studies book and the same science book. Let us hope that the teacher gives them different books to read. (When this kind of education occurs, it is small wonder that children like Johnny wind up in a Reading Clinic.)

However, there are hopeful signs on the horizon for American children. The "Chronological Age Lock Step" is being broken in many places; in some good schools it has been in operation for some time. Schools that have broken the barrier are admitting children to kindergarten and first grade when they can demonstrate their readiness. Here is evidence of application of the concept of MA. Once children are enrolled on this basis, improved grouping can be accomplished: They can be divided into fast and slow classes, and a more liberal policy of retentions and accelerations (holding back or skipping a year) can be established. "Ungraded" primary classrooms are another promising solution. Newer curriculum materials also help to provide for the individual differences of both fast and slow pupils. Such things as "reading laboratories," "multitext" adoption within a classroom, "individualized reading," "language experience approach," and numerous other plans to be discussed later all help to alleviate the problem of Gaspar and Gladys.

CHRONOLOGICAL AGE GRADE PLACEMENT—CAGP We should not overlook one other calculation—the chronological age grade placement (CAGP), which is the simplest and most widely used system of grade placement in the United States. It is a useful calculation to obtain for all children referred for remedial reading and aids in making admission and expectancy judgments. IQ tests can be wrong, but birth certificates seldom are. CAGP provides one more aid to prediction and requires very little effort.

CAGP is calculated by deducting the average age upon entrance to kindergarten from a child's chronological age. For example, the average child in the United States enters kindergarten at age 5.4. Hence, if he is eleven years old, he should be in grade 5.6. It is surprising how many children get placed in classes a whole year or more above or below their CAGP. Finding the CAGP helps to determine expectancy, particularly when used in conjunction with MAGP.

READING READINESS Reading readiness is a rather confusing term because it often refers to two different things. In one sense, it refers to the body of materials and teaching methods designed to "get a child ready for reading." In its other usage, readiness refers to that state of mental development which should be attained before regular reading instruction should be begun. The first is an external-stimulus concept, the second a subjective state on the part of the child. It is true that there is some overlapping—that perhaps certain teaching methods can aid the child in attaining the necessary state of mind or stage of mental development; but for now, let us consider only the mental or physical state necessary for the initiation of reading instruction.

To the extent that reading readiness is a state of mental development, it can probably be measured. This is what reading readiness tests purport to do. Many of the items on some reading readiness tests are very similar to IQ test items. In fact, some educators maintain that the two types of tests measure almost the same thing. Certainly anyone who has ever given a

Stanford Binet individual intelligence test is impressed by the fact that a normal five-year-old, with an IQ of 100, can copy a square but not a diamond. (If you do not believe this, try it out on a few five-year-olds.) At the age of seven, though, the normal child can copy a diamond. It is a little difficult to see how a child that cannot correctly copy a diamond can write all the letters in the alphabet.

Draw-a-man tests are equally dramatic with five-year-old children (see Goodenough reference in the bibliography). Of course reading and drawing are not exactly the same, but they yield an MA which is useful in determining when reading instruction may profitably be started.

In most schools, the average child has an MA of six years at about the beginning of the first grade, where reading instruction is begun. Some dramatic experiments have been performed in teaching younger children to read. Dr. O. K. Moore has had some success in teaching bright three-year-olds to do some reading by using electric typewriters and a special "responsive environment" situation. There are many school districts that use preprimers in kindergarten, and many of their children can read about fifty words before entering first grade.

In England, formal reading instruction is begun about a full year earlier than in the United States, using preprimers in many instances identical to those used in the United States. English children for the first few years of elementary school are ahead of United States children, a difference which for some reason disappears in the upper elementary grades, at which time there is very little difference. In other words, children start reading later in the United States, but soon catch up to English children. Incidentally, remedial reading is as big a problem in England as it is in the United States and in all other places where attempts are made to teach English reading to school children.

In Denver, where large-scale experiments have been conducted comparing children who start reading instruction in kindergarten with those who start reading instruction in first grade, it was found that the early starters tended to maintain a slight reading advantage throughout elementary years if classes were geared to the head start they had received. No deleterious side effects such as increase in vision problems were noted. This would appear to refute the pronouncements of specialists in various fields that children who start to read at too early an age develop vision problems, emotional problems, muscle-motor problems, and others.

An increasing number of parents are teaching their preschool children how to read prior to school entrance, and there does not seem to be any harm in this as long as the parents do not push too hard or give the child an emotional set against reading.*

*Lee Mountain, *How To Teach Reading Before First Grade.* Highland Park, N.Y.: Dreier Educational Systems, 1970.

CONCLUSION

This chapter has discussed the problem of differences in mental ability and the importance for the reading teacher of understanding these differences. Formal intelligence tests have come under some criticism, particularly by parents and educators involved with disadvantaged children or those from minority groups. Teachers and school administrators should exercise due caution in using and interpreting any IQ test results, but particularly if they are being applied to children with diverse cultural backgrounds.

Most people who have taught children will readily admit that there are individual differences in learning ability. These differences can be judged informally as well as by using formal measures, such as standardized tests. Informal methods work best when the teacher is both good and experienced. Unfortunately, it is the disadvantaged areas which seem to have the greatest shortage of teachers that are both good and experienced.

There are some dangers in using IQ tests and other dangers in not using them. However, the dangers of misuse are lessened as the educator better understands formal tests. It should be remembered that the purpose of using intelligence tests is to help make the school system more efficient in general and to help underachieving pupils in particular.

No discussion was presented on whether intelligence, or even the score on an intelligence test, is more closely related to heredity or environment. That discussion can be found in textbooks on child development and current journal articles. IQ scores can and do change, sometimes due to special conditions and at other times for no apparent reason. But at the time of testing, IQ scores do give some indication of learning potential, not an absolute indication but one significant enough that it should not be totally ignored.

APPENDIX 13-A A LIST OF INTELLIGENCE TESTS

INDIVIDUAL TESTS

Pictorial Test of Intelligence
    Joseph L. French. Houghton Mifflin Company
    Range: Age three to eight years.
    Suitable for use with physically handicapped (e.g., cerebral palsied children.)
    Administration requires a qualified examiner.

Stanford-Binet Intelligence Scale. Revised, 3d edition.
    Lewis M. Terman and Maud Merrill. Houghton Mifflin Company.
    Range Age two years to adult
    Administration requires a qualified examiner.

WAIS – Wechsler Adult Intelligence Scale
    David Wechsler. Psychological Corporation.
    Range: Sixteen years to over seventy-five years.
    Six Verbal and five Performance Tests
    Administration requires a qualified examiner.

WISC – Wechsler Intelligence Scale for Children
    David Wechsler. Psychological Corporation.
    Range: Five to fifteen years.
    Five verbal and five Performance Tests
    Administration requires a qualified examiner.

GROUP TESTS

California Short-Form Test of Mental Maturity.
    Elizabeth T. Sullivan, Willis W. Clark, and Ernest W. Tiegs. California Test Bureau.
    Level O, K, and entering grade one; Level 1, High 1 and Low 3; Level 1 H, grades three to four; Level 2, grades four to six; Level 2H, grade six to seven; Level 3, grades seven to eight; Level 4, grades nine to twelve; and Level 5, grades twelve to college and adult.
    Language and Non-Language Sections.

Cattell Culture Fair Intelligence Series
    Raymond B. Cattell, A. K. S. Cattell. Bobbs Merrill Company.
    Scale 2: Eight to fourteen years, and unselected adults.
    Scale 3: Fourteen years through college and adults.
    Non-Verbal.

D.A.T. Differential Aptitude Tests
    G. K. Bennett, H. G. Seashore, and A. G. Wesman. Psychological Corporation.
    Range: Junior-high school through college and adult.
    The Verbal Reasoning Test
    The Numerical Ability Test
    The Abstract Reasoning Test

Detroit Intelligence Tests.
    Harry J. Baker and others. Bobbs Merrill Company

Public School Primary Intelligence Test, grades two, three, four.
Detroit Intelligence Tests, Alpha, grades four to eight
Advanced, grades nine to twelve and college.
Verbal and Non-Verbal Sections.

Goodenough–Harris Drawing Test
F. Goodenough and D. B. Harris.
Psychological Corporation.
Revision and restandardization of the original Goodenough "Draw-a-Man" Test, plus a similar, newly standardized Draw-a-Woman Scale, and an experimental Self-Drawing Scale.
Range: Ages five to fifteen.
Individual or Group Test.

Henmon–Nelson Tests of Mental Ability. Revised Edition.
Tom A. Lamke, and M. J. Nelson. Houghton Mifflin Company.
Range: Grades three to six, six to nine, and nine to twelve.
College Level

Kuhlman–Anderson Intelligence Tests 7th Edition.
Psychological Corporation
Separate booklets for grades: kindergarten, one, two, three to four, four to five, five to seven, seven to nine, nine to twelve.
Yields separate Verbal and Quantitative Scores, and a Total Score.

Lorge–Thorndike Intelligence Tests
Irving Lorge, Robert L. Thorndike, and Elizabeth P. Hagen. Houghton Mifflin Company.
Levels 1 and 2 (Primary Battery)
Multi-Level and Separate Level Editions 3, 4, and 5.
College Edition, Level H.
Verbal and Non-Verbal.

Otis Quick–Scoring Mental Ability Tests, Revised.
A. S. Otis. Psychological Corporation.
Alpha Tests, grades one to four.
Beta Tests, grades four to nine.
Gamma Test, high school and college.

Pintner General Ability Tests. Revised Edition.
Rudolf Pintner, Bess V. Cunningham, and Walter N. Durost.
Grades kindergarten through nine.
Kindergarten to two, entirely pictorial and administered orally.
Intermediate, grades four to nine.

Tests of General Ability.
John C. Flanagan. Science Research Associates.
Grades kindergarten to two, two to four, four to six, six to nine, nine to twelve.
Non-Verbal. Also available in Spanish Edition.

APPENDIX 13-B SAMPLE TEST REVIEW FROM SIXTH MENTAL MEASUREMENTS YEARBOOK*

JOHN E. HORROCKS, *Professor of Psychology, The Ohio State University, Columbus, Ohio.*

Equating general ability, general intelligence, and "basic ability to learn" as the same thing, the TOGA series provides a scale of equal units for five consecutive grade levels. That intelligence and ability to learn, if not exactly interchangeable concepts, are at least so closely related that an individual's ability to learn offers a good approach to the measurement of his intelligence is nothing new to ability testing. Numerous measures of intelligence have been described by their authors as well as by others as measures of learning ability—their difference consists in the kinds of learning experiences stressed and the kinds of items selected as most likely to offer adequate measures of that learning. TOGA represents a relatively new departure by attempting to eliminate, or at least place less stress upon, school learned skills such as reading, writing, and arithmetic. For that reason TOGA should offer a fairer testing context for those who, for one reason or another, have had limited or atypical opportunities to learn.

All TOGA test items at all levels are multiple choice and are pictorial in form. Two classes of items are represented: those which require reasoning on the part of the examinee and those which require information, vocabulary, and concepts. Information required, particularly at the younger levels, is of the kind ordinarily gained outside of the classroom, and stress is placed upon application rather than upon knowledge accumulation. Eight kinds of information items are included: (*a*) recognition of a picture object when it is named, (*b*) recognition of an object from its classification, (*c*) recognition of an object on the basis of its similarity to another object, (*d*) recognition of an object's symbolic status, (*d*) selection of a picture as representative of an abstract concept, (*f*) selection of an object which involves a concept determining its use, (*g*) selection of an object as representative of the application of a principle, and (*h*) selection of an object depicting an element basic to an idea or a social institution. Content settings for information items include home, community, nature and recreation, science, and social science. Reasoning items present five line drawings, four of which are constructed on the basis of a specific rule, the fifth being different in that the rule does not apply. Speed has been eliminated in determining information performance and has been minimized

[496]

[SRA] Tests of General Ability. Grades kgn–2, 2–4, 4–6, 6–9, 9–12; 1959–60,© 1957–60; 3 scores: information, noncultural reasoning, total; IBM for grades 4–12; Form A ('59, except for tests for grades 4–12 which are copyrighted 1957); 5 levels; $1 per technical report ('60, 39 pages); $2.50 per complete specimen set; postage extra; tests for grades 4–12 may be rented; fee (45¢ per student) includes scoring service; Spanish edition available; (35–45) minutes; John C. Flanagan; Science Research Associates, Inc.

a) GRADES KGN-2. 12 pages; manual ('59, 19 pages); $3.20 per 20 tests; 50¢ per specimen set.

b) GRADES 2–4. Details same as for grades kgn–2.

c) GRADES 4–6. 15 pages; manual ('59, 21 pages); separate answer sheets must be used; $4.25 per 20 tests; $5 per 100 IBM scorable answer sheets; 50¢ per scoring stencil; 75¢ per specimen set.

d) GRADES 6–9. Details same as for grades 4–6 except: manual ('59, 25 pages).

e) GRADES 9–12. Details same as for grades 4–6 except: manual ('59, 19 pages).

for the reasoning section as a *way*, according to the author, of providing "'purer' measures of information depth and reasoning power." The question here is the advisability of de-emphasizing speed as an aspect of intellectual functioning. In life, behavior takes place under time conditions and an individual's effectiveness is often judged in terms of his "alertness" or ability to respond quickly. Insofar as speed is actually an aspect of real life effective functioning it would appear to beg the issue to eliminate it under the excuse of "power" in a measure designed to assess an individual's capacity to function in the cognitive domain.

Preliminary tryouts of TOGA items took place in 22 public and parochial schools in the Pittsburgh area and items included at the various levels in the final forms had to meet three criteria: (*a*) internal consistency as demonstrated by a correlation of "about" .40 or better with other items of the same type at all levels, (*b*) item difficulty figures which showed a trend of increase with respondents' age, and (*c*) a difficulty range between 30 and 70 percent for the middle grade of the level at which the item was placed. Norms are based on 8,041 students enrolled in 40 schools in 20 school systems located in 12 different states. With the exception of Texas (Austin and Bryan) southern and southwestern states are not included in the normative sample, nor are the states in New England and the northwest. A more complete normative picture is needed if TOGA is to find defensible use as a nationally applicable test, although its normative background is already superior to some measures of intelligence which have been on the market considerably longer.

Since TOGA is a relatively new test (1957) potential users will have to depend upon reliability and validity information supplied by the very adequate technical report provided for users of the test. The report cites 20 reliability studies of TOGA total scores, with coefficients ranging for the various levels from .77 to .90. Correlations cited (19 studies) between TOGA total scores and those of other intelligence tests vary with the level being tested but range from a low of .41 (TOGA 6–9 level and Kuhlmann-Anderson) to a high of .80 (TOGA 6–9 and Kuhlmann-Anderson). Correlations with various measures of achievement tend to cluster between .50 and .60 and range from .38 to .81. Correlations between TOGA part scores (10 studies) ranged from .25 to .67, and part score split-half reliabilities (20 studies) ranged from .69 to .83. Part score correlations with other intelligence and achievement measures present about the same picture as that provided by the total score. In general TOGA Part 1 (information) scores appear to relate most closely to Thurstone's verbal comprehension factor, and Part 2 (reasoning) scores to his reasoning factor.

TOGA is a promising, carefully constructed general measure of verbal intelligence whose author has provided excellent quantitative background information for prospective users. Further and more representative normative data are needed as well as independent data on reliability and validity. The attempt to eliminate school centered information in writing test items is a particularly strong feature, but this reviewer would question the de-emphasis of the speed factor in a general line intelligence test. Such de-emphasis, insofar as it is tenable at all, would appear more appropriate in a school learning centered academic aptitude measure.

14

VISION

We really do not know much about what takes place as the child first learns to read, despite all that has been researched and written about it. About the best we can hope to do is to gain some insight into the reading process by considering it from various viewpoints and see what the specialists in linguistics, grammar, phonics, basic word studies, comprehension models, psychology, and sociology have to say.

Vision, too, can help to give some understanding of the reading process. The anatomy of the eye is fairly well known as is the function of the eye, at least up to the point where we can trace the process through the nerves and into the brain. Physiologists are still working on basic problems of neural transmission, and much work remains to be done in brain functions and areas used in the wonderful process of seeing.

This chapter is written, in part, to give the teacher some of the general knowledge which is essential to understanding the role of vision in reading instruction; and, in part, to provide a background for understanding reading methods. There is every indication that reading methods of the future will be based in part on what we know today about vision. Teachers, and especially remedial teachers, must have a good knowledge of visual screening procedures, whether they expect to do the screening themselves or whether they will call on the school nurse to use appropriate vision tests.

I once received a letter from an optometrist which informed me that one of my students had emmetropia in each eye. My first thought was, "Good Lord, not in both eyes!" I rushed to the dictionary, and with great relief found that emmetropia means "normal acuity." In other words, the child could see clearly with both eyes. Since remedial reading teachers must exchange information with nurses, physicians, and optometrists, understanding is facilitated if both use the proper terminology. It is hoped that after reading this chapter, teachers will be more familiar with some of the common vision problems, will know how to recognize them informally and be able to use screening tests, and will be able to make proper referrals to specialists.

EYE MOVEMENTS IN READING

We occasionally hear someone remark that the way to read faster is to "make the eye move smoothly and rapidly across the line." This person has never really looked at anybody's eyes while they were reading, for the eyes never move smoothly in reading. They jerk, they stop, they jump ahead with incredible speed, and stop. This move-and-stop, move-and-stop jerkiness which characterizes reading is referred to as "saccadic movements." The term "saccadic" comes from the Greek and means "little jerk."

Normally, the eye while reading *fixates* on a word (stops and looks at it) for about one-fifth of a second; it then makes a saccadic movement to the next word, and so on across the line. The saccadic movement is five times faster than a fixation and normally takes about one-twenty-fifth of a second. Thus if we look at a person's eyes as he reads, we will see him fixate on a word, make a saccadic movement, fixate, and so on. The average person sees a little more than one word during a fixation. The amount that he sees during a fixation is known as the "span of recognition" and averages about a word and a quarter for high-school students and adults.

When the eyes get to the end of the line of print they make a large *return sweep* to the beginning of the next line. Occasionally, the eyes will make a backward movement, or *regression*, when the reader wishes to go back over a word or phrase. Regressions are common among beginning readers, but in older readers they are considered a fault or a bad habit. Everyone makes regressions occasionally when they come across a strange word or phrase, but poor readers make them habitually. Problem readers and very slow adult readers sometimes acquire the habit of making regressions even when they do not need them. The regression habit can be alleviated by reminding the student not to regress and giving him plenty of easy reading.

If you have never done so before, you should stop now and observe someone's eyes while reading. Have the person hold a book up high and read from the top half of the page while you stand in front of him and watch his eyes just over the top of the book. You should be able to see fixations, saccadic movements, return sweeps, and possibly a regression or two.

Accurate methods of seeing and recording eye movements require instrumentation. The simplest and commonest device is an eye-movement camera which shines a tiny beam of light into each eyeball and records the reflection of this light on a moving strip of film (see Figure 14-1). As the eyes move from side to side or up and down, the reflected light traces a path on the film in much the same way as a child moves a mirror to make a dot of sunlight move across a wall. In Figure 14-2 is a sample of eye movements recorded on a strip of film. There are two lines, one for each eye. If the eyes remain steady, looking at one point, then parallel, vertical lines will appear on the film because the film is continually moving past a slot and the reflected beam of light is not moving. When the eyes move from side to side, to move on to the next word, a horizontal line is made on the film. Then while the eye fixates (remains steady) on a word, two short vertical lines are made on the film. The stair step design is caused by the eyes fixating on one word, then the next, and the next across the line of print. At the end of the line, a large movement to the left is made as the return sweep is made to the next line. Regressions show up clearly, as do certain visual abnormalities—perhaps one eye that does not track.

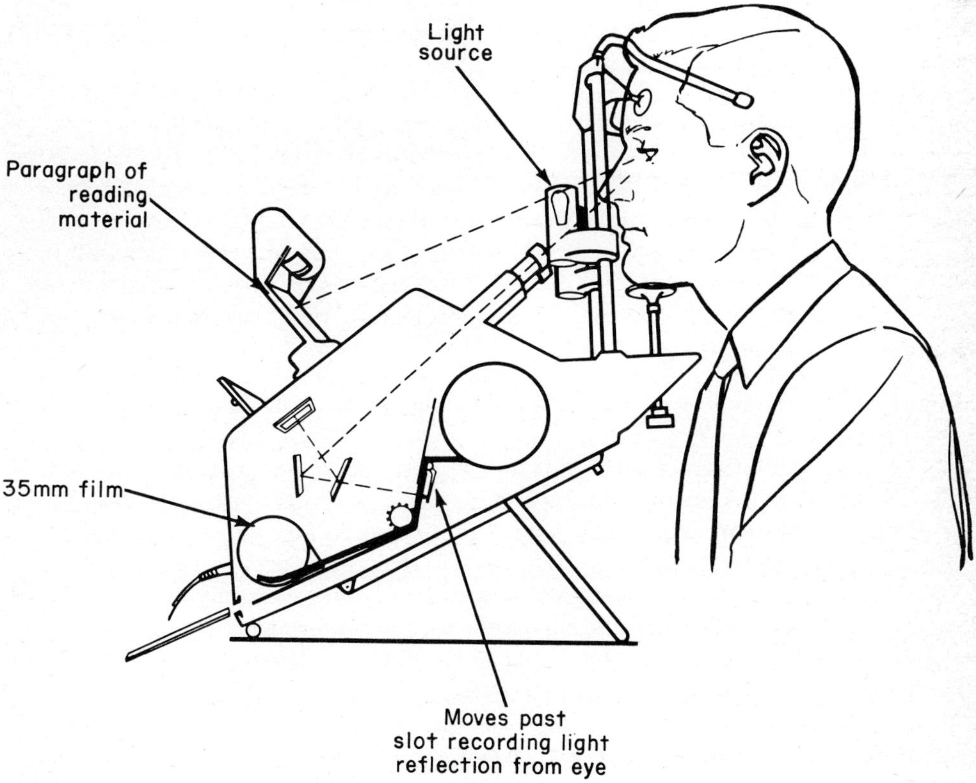

FIGURE 14-1 Photographing eye movements.

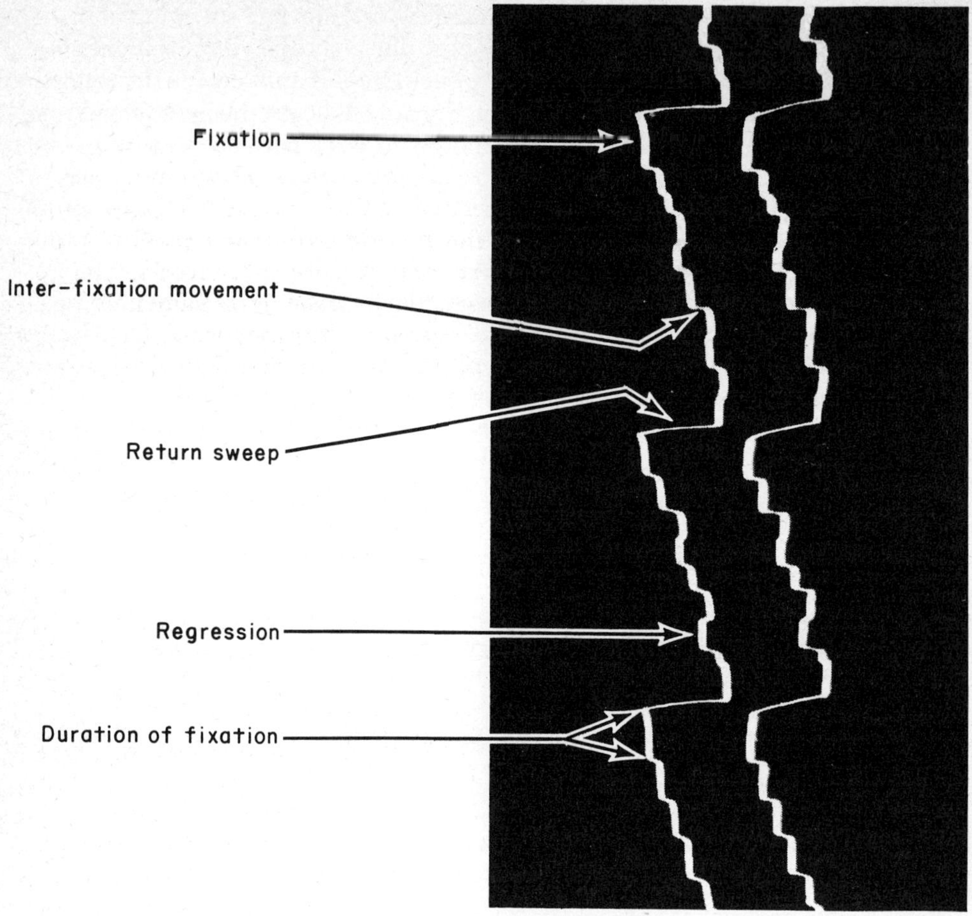

FIGURE 14-2 Sample of developed film showing eye movements.

As the reader matures there is a very noticeable maturation in the pattern of his saccadic movements. As one matures he tends to make fewer fixations per line of print. The first-grade student makes tiny movements per line, almost as if he were studying each letter. By the time he reaches high school and college, his saccadic movements become much more clearly defined and regular. The research specialist has other methods of measuring and recording eye movements – devices which measure the exterior eye muscular movements by placing tiny electrodes around the eye.

TRAINING EYE MOVEMENTS In the 1930s some reading experts attempted to improve eye movements by means of a training device known as the Metronoscope. This machine, by means of shutters operating over a role of paper tape, exposed the first third of a line of print, then the second third, then the final third. The speed of exposures could be gradually increased by turning a knob, and the difficulty level of the material could be changed by using different rolls of paper tape. The device did have some success in increasing the speed of reading, but eye-movement photography revealed no significant changes in fixations or saccadic movements.

Similar devices still used in some college and adult training programs are the Harvard and Iowa films which simulate a fuzzy printed page with only one bright, clear spot which highlights a word or phrase. The bright, clear spot jumps along in simulated saccadic movements. The films come in a series which gradually increases the speed and span of recognition. Courses using these films have consistently reported speed increases, but research data on eye movements are lacking.

Another device which some authorities claim increases span of recognition is the tachistoscope which flashes words, phrases, and symbols on the screen for less than one-fifth of a second. By keeping the flash speed faster than the time needed for one fixation, the student finds it physiologically impossible to make two fixations. The amount of material and/or the span of recognition is then gradually increased. While the tachistoscope is advocated by some for perceptual or visual training ranging in level from reading readiness through adult reading improvement, research evidence is not conclusive regarding its effectiveness or desirability. I, for one, have used tachistoscopic training quite a bit, but the only thing about which I am sure is that the tachistoscope is excellent for maintaining student interest in the subject matter. This is especially true of remedial students who often start with an active dislike for reading material in any traditional form. Tachistoscopic drill also seems to help some students overcome excessive slowness caused by word-by-word reading. The possibility of perceptual training still exists, and it is hoped that research will one day soon give us more definite information.

ANATOMY OF VISION

The eye is a small, round ball that is mostly white with a clear area in front. The white part, known as the sclerotic coat, is reasonably tough for protection and is white probably so that it will reflect light away from the interior of the eye and allow light to enter through the cornea, or clear outer covering in front.

In the act of seeing, a beam of light passes through the cornea; then through the aqueous humor which is a clear watery fluid just behind the cornea; and then through the lens which is a tough but flexible crystalline structure used to focus the rays of light on the sensitive nerves at the back part of the eyeball, known as the retina. The center part of the eye is also filled with a clear, jelly like mass known as the vitreous humor.

The nerve endings in the retina then change the light rays into electrochemical impulses which are transmitted through the optic nerve to the brain. The nerve impulses enter the brain at the occipital lobe where the vision process continues, becoming at this point very complex and diffuse as the different areas of the brain are involved in recognition, memory, and interrelationships, often resulting in some sort of thought process, learning, or physical action.

The retina is interesting in that it contains two different types of light-sensitive nerve endings, the rods and cones. The cones are used only in the daytime or for reasonably bright light and yield both sharp and color images. The rods, which see only in shades of grey, are used at night and where the light is extremely dim. The center part of the retina, the "fovea centralis," is composed almost entirely of cones. This area and the area immediately surrounding it gives the sharpest visual acuity. As we move out from the fovea centralis, acuity becomes less and less until at 90 degrees on either side very little can be seen but movement.

Try looking straight ahead and hold your fingers directly in front of your eyes. You should be able to see such marvelous details as the dirt under your fingernails, little hairs, etc. Now keep your eyes fixed on a point straight ahead and move your hand 15 or 20 degrees to the side, and you will notice that your fingernails become less distinct but that you can still tell how many fingers you are holding up. If you continue moving your hand out past 45 degrees, you can no longer tell how many fingers are being held up but may possibly be able

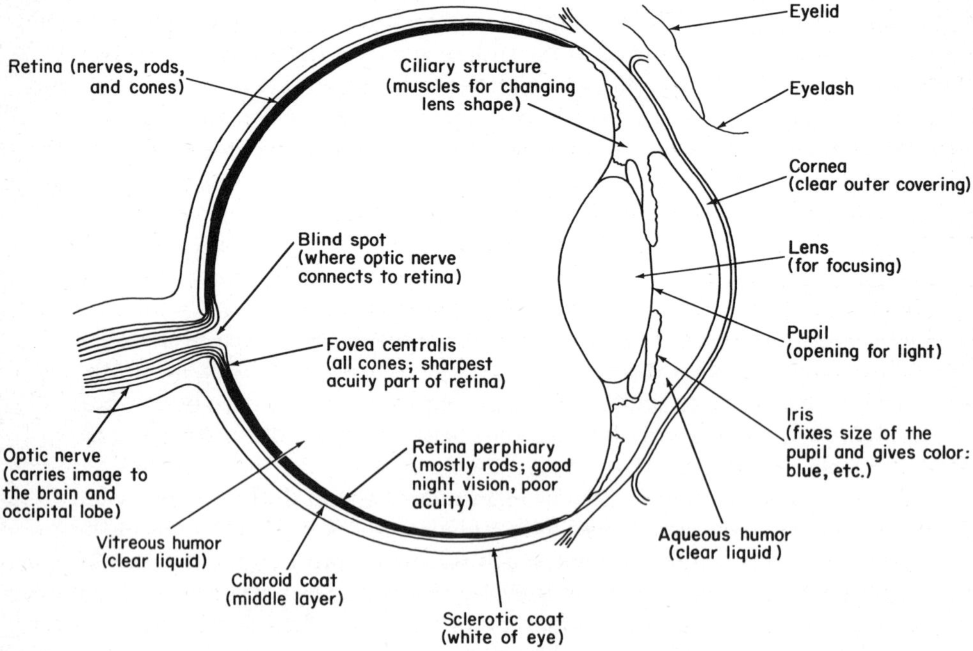

FIGURE 14-3 Anatomy of the eye.

to distinguish that it is a hand. With your arm extended almost directly out to the side you might have great difficulty knowing that your hand were there if you were not moving it. In this little experiment you are using various parts of your retina, beginning with the fovea centralis and moving outward to the periphery where acuity is very poor. Some people have abnormally poor peripheral vision, a limitation called "tunnel vision." It is best to avoid riding in a car when this person is driving in traffic.

When the normal person's eyes are relaxed, they focus on infinity, which for all practical purposes is any distance of more than 20 feet away. If a person wishes to look clearly at objects nearer than 20 feet, he must change the shape of his lens by using the "ciliary muscles" attached to the side of the lens. This process of changing the shape of the lens in order to see clearly is called "accommodation." Accommodation is interesting in that it gradually weakens as a person gets older. Young children can look at objects a few inches away from their eyes and accommodate with little strain. This sometimes horrifies mothers who have heard that the eyes might get "stuck" in a near-point (or cross-eyed) position, a rumor that has no basis in fact. You can quickly find your nearest point of accommodation simply by taking a book printed in small type and moving it slowly toward the eyeball. The point at which the type blurs is called the "nearest point of accommodation." The nearest point of accommodation increases (gets farther from the eyeball) each year that we live. When the nearest point of accommodation reaches 16 or 18 inches, reading glasses or bifocals are needed for near-point vision tasks such as reading. This usually occurs around the age of forty-five, but there is a wide range varying from the early thirties to mid-fifties.

BINOCULAR COORDINATION Up to this point, vision from the standpoint of one eye, or monocular vision, has been considered. From the standpoint of reading, only one eye is necessary, and persons blind in one eye can read quite as well as anyone else. However, two eyes are necessary if we are to get true "stereopsis," or depth perception ("3D" or third-dimensional vision). When looking off into infinity, both eyes are looking parallel. As objects approach closer than infinity, the eyes tend to turn in, or to "converge." It is this feeling of convergence caused by the pulling of the external eye muscles, together with the slightly different image in each eye, which gives the true stereopsis sensation. Persons with one eye should bump into doors because they lack this perception; they do not do so because they have learned depth perception; in other words, they have memorized that doors and people are big when close and small when far away.

The eyeballs are turned upwards and downwards, in and out, by six external muscles attached to the exterior of the eyeball. When the eyes are functioning normally, both eyes are looking at the same object; this process of the image of one eye merging with the image of the other eye is called *fusion*. If it does not occur, diplopia or double vision results.

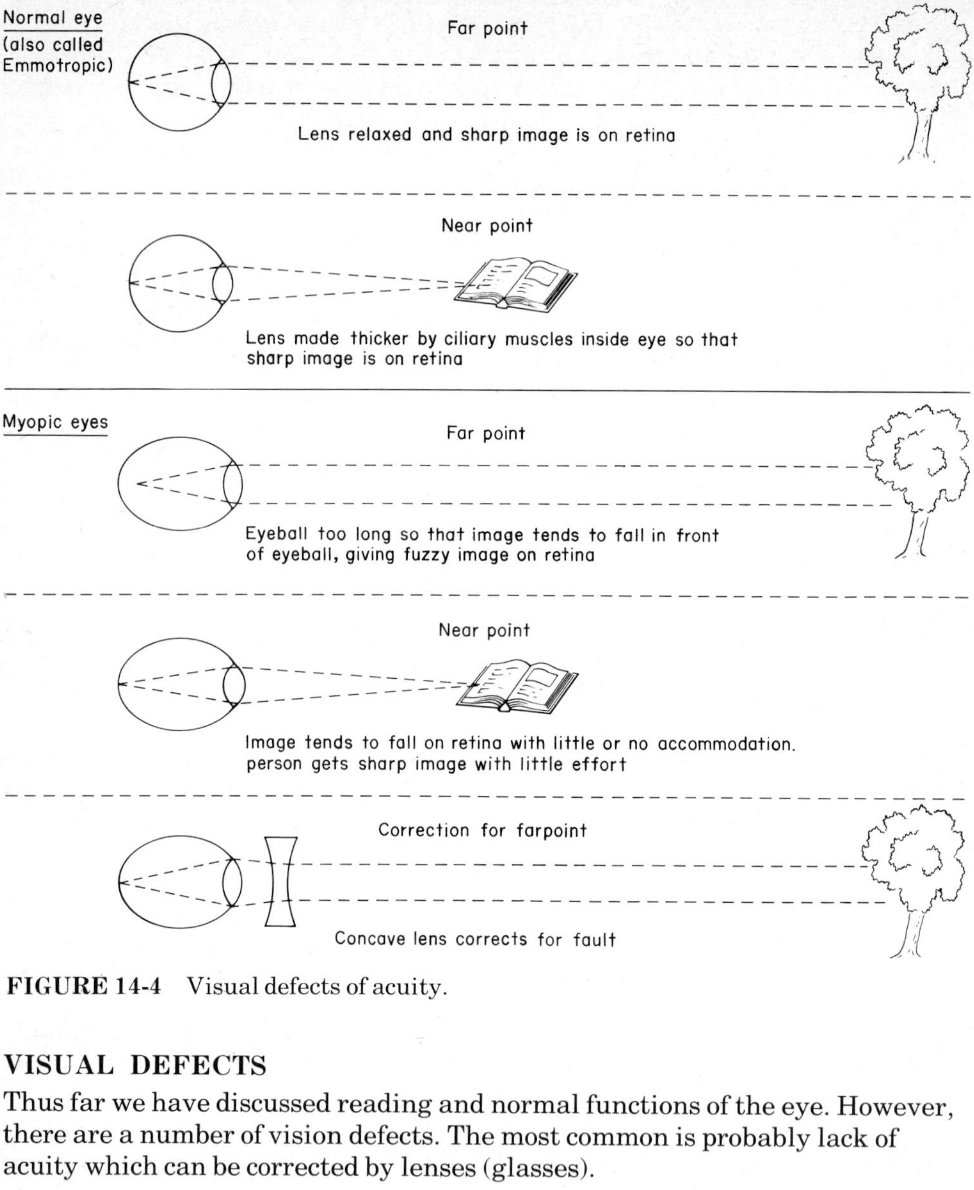

FIGURE 14-4 Visual defects of acuity.

VISUAL DEFECTS

Thus far we have discussed reading and normal functions of the eye. However, there are a number of vision defects. The most common is probably lack of acuity which can be corrected by lenses (glasses).

MYOPIA One of the commonest and most easily detected visual fault is near-sightedness, or *myopia*. In this condition, the eyeball is a little too long and the lens tends to focus the image in front of the retina, giving a slightly blurred image on the retina for transmission to the brain. The myopic person usually sees clearly at close range, such as reading distance, but cannot see clearly at a distance. The child with myopia should be sent to a specialist for correc-

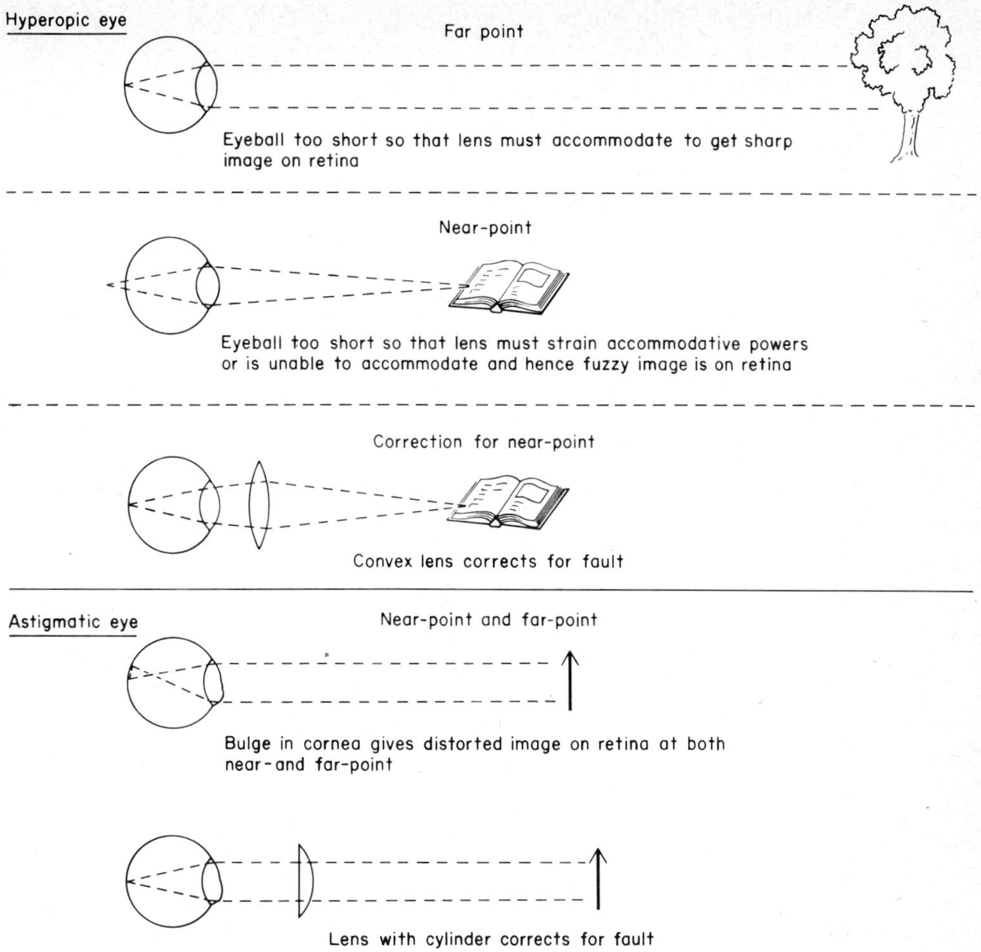

tion as soon as it is detected. In the meantime, he should be seated at the front of the classroom. Myopia is easy to correct in most cases simply by putting a concave lens in front of the eye for seeing beyond the reading distance.

HYPEROPIA Farsightedness, or "hyperopia," is another common vision fault. In this case the eyeball is too short, that is, the focal length of the lens is too long, and this gives a fuzzy image on the retina for transmission to the brain. The hyperopic person can usually see clearly in the distance by accommodating, but it causes real strain to see well at near-point. This condition is especially dangerous for students because, while they see perfectly well on the baseball field or across a large room, the letters on a printed page come in various degrees of fuzziness. This student believes that his eyesight is excellent and will prove it to you by pointing out some tiny object in the distance. Hyperopia can be easily corrected by putting convex lenses in front of the eye(s) for reading on any near-point seeing.

ASTIGMATISM A distortion in the image upon the retina can also be caused by lack of sphericity (roundness) of the cornea. This condition is known as "astigmatism." It causes blurred vision along one axis at both near-point and far-point. The cornea tends to have a bulge in it which usually runs horizontally but can be inclined at any plane. Astigmatism can usually be easily corrected by placing a cylindrical corrective lens in front of the eye. It is possible for a person to have both myopia and astigmatism, or both hyperopia and astigmatism. Both corrections can be ground into the same lens.

Interestingly enough, the new contact lenses (tiny bits of plastic that fit directly on the eyeball) do not need astigmatic corrections because they are ground with perfect sphericity (roundness); when placed on the cornea, they provide an optically perfect spherical surface, thereby automatically correcting the astigmatism.

LACK OF BINOCULAR COORDINATION Extreme lack of binocular coordination is an easily detected fault which is called "essotropia" (cross-eyedness) when the eyes turn in and "exotropia" (wall-eyedness) when the eyes turn out. These extremes of lack of binocular coordination are problems that are more cosmetic than visual in seriousness. A cross-eyed child can usually learn to read quite as easily as a normal child. For the benefit of the child's appearance, however, and possibly to aid binocular coordination, it is a good idea to have these extreme conditions corrected. This is done most frequently with surgery which, while admittedly delicate, is neither uncommon nor dangerous.

Minor faults of binocular coordination can cause trouble in the reading process. In "exophoria," for example, the student does not look wall-eyed and only occasionally, when he is very tired, might you see an eye turn out. However, when the child is asleep or when his eyes are in a rest position the eyes assume a divergent (turning out) position. Since the reading process requires convergence, or turning in of the eyes, this exophoric child must use enough additional muscle power to cause a strain on his eyes for converging at near-point for reading. This child might tend to tire of reading much more quickly than other children. He might get headaches while reading, his eyes might become red, or he might occasionally see double. He should, of course, be sent to a vision specialist. Serious tropias and phorias can often be alleviated by surgery, by special lenses (prisms), or by eye-muscle exercises (orthoptics). This condition is given special mention here because it is so often overlooked in the informal type of visual screening tests done in some schools. A teacher might send a child to the school nurse for a "vision test," and the school nurse might send him back after testing him for acuity with the remark that there is nothing wrong with him. The teacher, it is hoped, will check into the school's visual screening procedures to see that they are adequate.

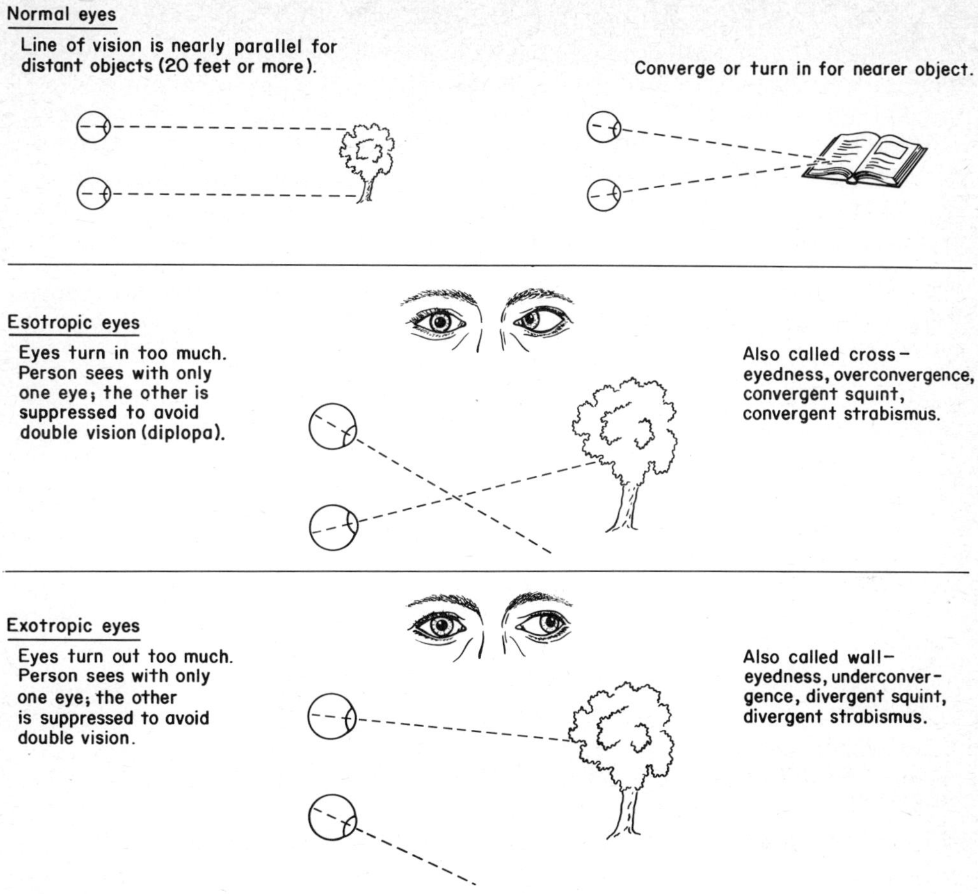

FIGURE 14-5 Binocular coordination.

OTHER EYE DISORDERS "Cataract" is a form of poor vision caused by the lens changing from clear to a milky-white opacity. This occurs often in older persons but can occur in childhood. Surgery and lenses can often help this condition. The cornea can also become cloudy in some cases.

"Glaucoma" is an abnormal increase in fluid pressure in the eyeball which, if serious, can do permanent damage. A warning symptom is the change in acuity.

Brain damage can also cause temporary or permanent visual distortion or blindness. Since vision involves the brain (eyes are mere receptors), anything which damages the brain can also damage vision if that damage occurs in an area used in the vision process. Rapid changes in vision are always cause for immediate referral to a physician.

Retinal damage can be caused by some serious illnesses, accidents involving blows to the eyeball, or looking at an extremely brilliant light (the sun or a welding arc) with unprotected eyes. These can result in temporary or permanent damage. Retinal damage can result in such symptoms as change in vision or blind spots, which should be referred to a physician.

Everyone has a blind spot in each eye where the optic nerve enters the eyeball, but this is natural and is not noticed except under special conditions. If you wish to notice your own blind spot, here is a simple demonstration:

Close your left eye. Look at the X, below, and move the page in and out slowly. Y should disappear at a point about 8 inches from the eye, and yet be visible both closer and farther away.

X Y

To notice the blind spot in your left eye, look at Y and repeat the procedure; the X will disappear.

Color blindness occurs, to at least a mild degree, in about 10 percent of males and with considerably less frequency in females. It does not affect reading and nothing can be done about it, except possibly some good vocational counseling. To determine who is color blind, the Pseudo-Isochromatic Plates (numbers in colored dots) are easy and quick to use, but this knowledge is of no help to the reading teacher.

VISION-SCREENING TESTS

Vision testing, or vision screening, although it is required by law in many states, is often done inadequately. A good visual-screening procedure would test all children who have myopia, hyperopia, astigmatism, or lack of binocular coordination. Furthermore, it should be so thorough that few overreferrals (sending children to eye specialists who do not need correction) or underreferrals (not finding students who do need correction) would occur. Probably the most accurate and least costly procedure is to have a vision specialist do the screening. Using a modified clinical technique, an opthamologist or optometrist requires only about five minutes per child for reasonably accurate screening. Such a procedure was used in the Orinda study in California, the result being relatively few underreferrals and overreferrals. Whatever its cost, it saved the parents thousands of dollars in the savings on elimination of overreferrals, to say nothing of the value of elimination of parental anxiety. Good screening procedures also result in increased learning efficiency from students who would have not otherwise been identified as needing visual remediation.

MECHANICAL AIDS TO VISION SCREENING Probably the best-known vision-screening test used by reading specialists and school nurses is the Telebinocular, a stereoscopic device that measures acuity in each eye at both near-point and far-point, as well as binocular coordination at both near and far points. Similar devices covering the same areas are the Ortho-Rater and the Sightscreener. (See Figure 14-6.)

In Figure 14-7 is a record sheet from the Telebinocular test. Note that the test can be given to a student either with or without glasses on. If the student normally wears glasses, he takes the screening with his glasses on. Many schools assume that if a student has been to a vision specialist within the past twelve months that he has received adequate eye care and does not need to be given a visual-screening test. A complaint of some schools is that the Telebinocular overrefers (sends too many students for a professional eye examination when it is not needed). If the Telebinocular manual is followed, any mark outside the heavy black line is cause for referral; but some schools, after consultation with a vision specialist, have established more lenient referral criteria.

Note that the record blank has a column for "Left [eye] Only" and "Right [eye] Only"; this means that the child sees only the left-eye target or only the right-eye target. This can be caused by extreme lack of binocular coordination;

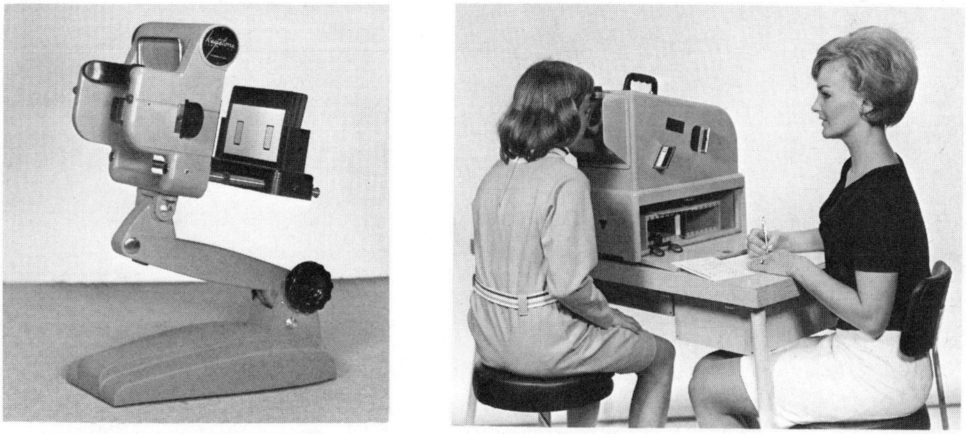

FIGURE 14-6 Visual screening with stereoscope devices. Left: Telebinocular; right: Ortho-Rater.

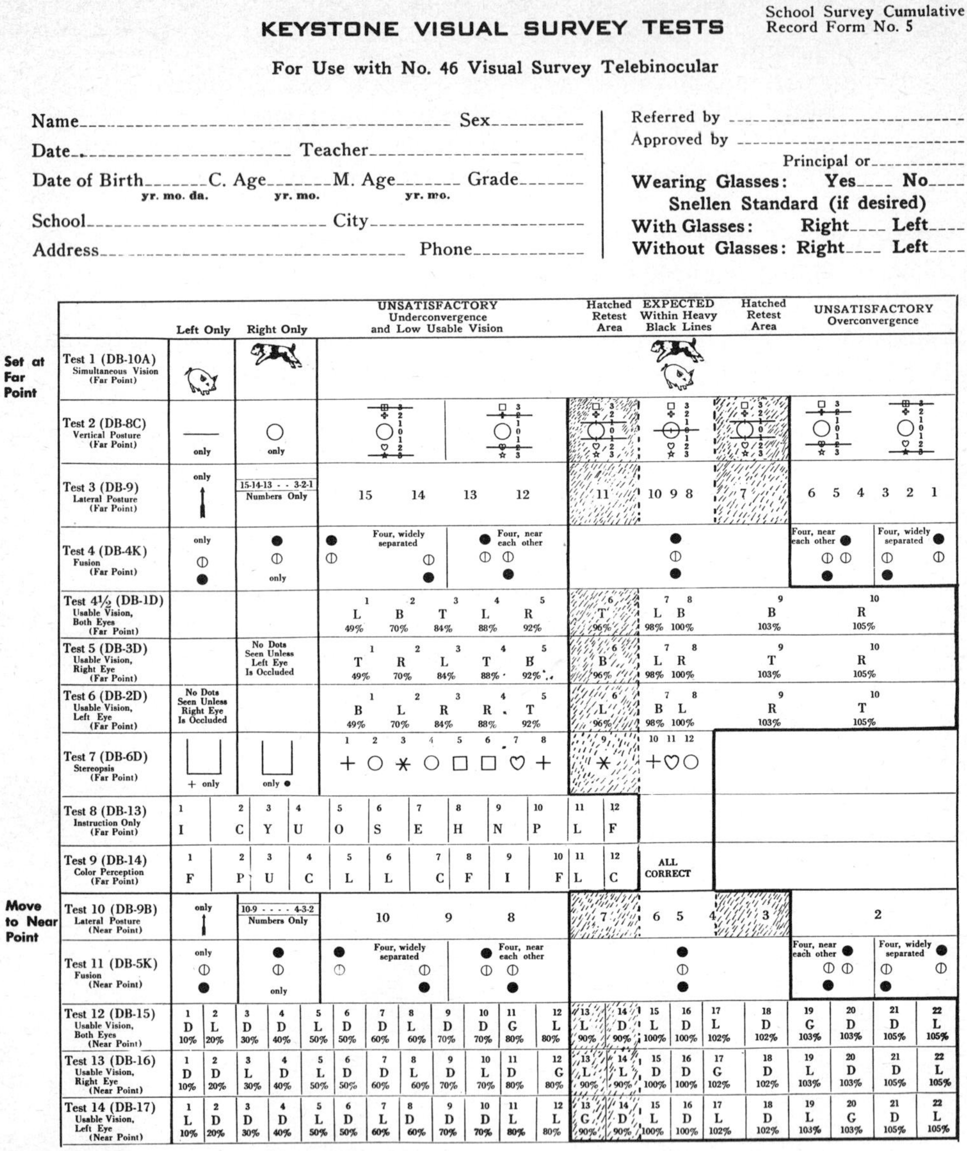

School Survey Cumulative Record Form No. 5

KEYSTONE VISUAL SURVEY TESTS

For Use with No. 46 Visual Survey Telebinocular

Name________________ Sex________
Date________________ Teacher________________
Date of Birth________ (yr. mo. da.) C. Age______ (yr. mo.) M. Age______ (yr. mo.) Grade______
School________________ City________________
Address________________ Phone________

Referred by ________________
Approved by ________________
Principal or________
Wearing Glasses: Yes____ No____
Snellen Standard (if desired)
With Glasses: Right____ Left____
Without Glasses: Right____ Left____

	Left Only	Right Only	UNSATISFACTORY Underconvergence and Low Usable Vision	Hatched Retest Area	EXPECTED Within Heavy Black Lines	Hatched Retest Area	UNSATISFACTORY Overconvergence
Set at Far Point — Test 1 (DB-10A) Simultaneous Vision (Far Point)							
Test 2 (DB-8C) Vertical Posture (Far Point)	only	only					
Test 3 (DB-9) Lateral Posture (Far Point)	only	15-14-13 - - 3-2-1 Numbers Only	15 14 13 12	11	10 9 8	7	6 5 4 3 2 1
Test 4 (DB-4K) Fusion (Far Point)	only	only	Four, widely separated / Four, near each other				Four, near each other / Four, widely separated
Test 4½ (DB-1D) Usable Vision, Both Eyes (Far Point)			1 L 49% · 2 B 70% · 3 T 84% · 4 L 88% · 5 R 92%	6 T 96%	7 L 98% · 8 B 100%	9 B 103%	10 R 105%
Test 5 (DB-3D) Usable Vision, Right Eye (Far Point)		No Dots Seen Unless Left Eye Is Occluded	1 T 49% · 2 R 70% · 3 L 84% · 4 T 88% · 5 B 92%	6 B 96%	7 L 98% · 8 R 100%	9 T 103%	10 R 105%
Test 6 (DB-2D) Usable Vision, Left Eye (Far Point)	No Dots Seen Unless Right Eye Is Occluded		1 B 49% · 2 L 70% · 3 R 84% · 4 R 88% · 5 T 92%	6 L 96%	7 B 98% · 8 L 100%	9 R 103%	10 T 105%
Test 7 (DB-6D) Stereopsis (Far Point)	+ only	only ●	1 + · 2 ○ · 3 ✱ · 4 ○ · 5 □ · 6 □ · 7 ♡ · 8 +	9 ✱	10 + · 11 ♡ · 12 ○		
Test 8 (DB-13) Instruction Only (Far Point)	1 I · 2 C	3 Y · 4 U	5 O · 6 S · 7 E · 8 H · 9 N · 10 P	11 L · 12 F			
Test 9 (DB-14) Color Perception (Far Point)	1 F · 2 P	3 U · 4 C	5 L · 6 L · 7 C · 8 F · 9 I · 10 F	11 L · 12 C	ALL CORRECT		
Move to Near Point — Test 10 (DB-9B) Lateral Posture (Near Point)	only	10-9 - - - - 4-3-2 Numbers Only	10 9 8	7	6 5	4 3	2
Test 11 (DB-5K) Fusion (Near Point)	only	only	Four, widely separated / Four, near each other				Four, near each other / Four, widely separated

Test	1	2	3	4	5	6	7	8	9	10	11	12	13	14	15	16	17	18	19	20	21	22
Test 12 (DB-15) Usable Vision, Both Eyes (Near Point)	D 10%	L 20%	D 30%	D 40%	L 50%	D 50%	D 60%	L 60%	D 70%	D 70%	G 80%	L 80%	L 90%	D 90%	L 100%	D 100%	L 102%	D 102%	G 103%	D 103%	D 105%	L 105%
Test 13 (DB-16) Usable Vision, Right Eye (Near Point)	D 10%	D 20%	L 30%	D 40%	L 50%	D 50%	D 60%	L 60%	D 70%	L 70%	D 80%	G 80%	L 90%	L 90%	D 100%	D 100%	G 102%	D 102%	L 103%	D 103%	D 105%	L 105%
Test 14 (DB-17) Usable Vision, Left Eye (Near Point)	L 10%	D 20%	D 30%	D 40%	L 50%	D 50%	L 60%	D 60%	D 70%	D 70%	L 80%	L 80%	G 90%	D 90%	L 100%	D 100%	L 102%	D 102%	L 103%	G 103%	D 105%	L 105%

FIGURE 14-7 Keystone Visual Survey Tests.

more commonly, however, it is caused by "suppression," which is the psychological shutting off of vision in one eye. A child may suppress vision in one eye if the eye has inferior acuity or if strain is caused by a tropia or another defect. Suppression can quickly be detected by covering the seeing eye (on a Telebinocular, put a card in front of one eye's line of vision) and the suppressed eye will immediately see. School personnel should take the advice of their school physician or vision specialist about this, but many schools do not refer pupils who suppress if acuity and binocular coordination are within acceptable limits.

Other devices which screen in the same areas but do not use a stereoscope are the Massachusetts Vision Test and the Atlantic City Eye Test. These devices require a semidark room in which an eye chart can be set up 20 feet away from the child. Myopia and astigmatism are screened using well-lighted Snellen letters (the typical eye chart). Hyperopia is screened by putting a lens in front of the eye. Binocular coordination is screened by using either Maddox rods (a special type of lens) or colored lenses.

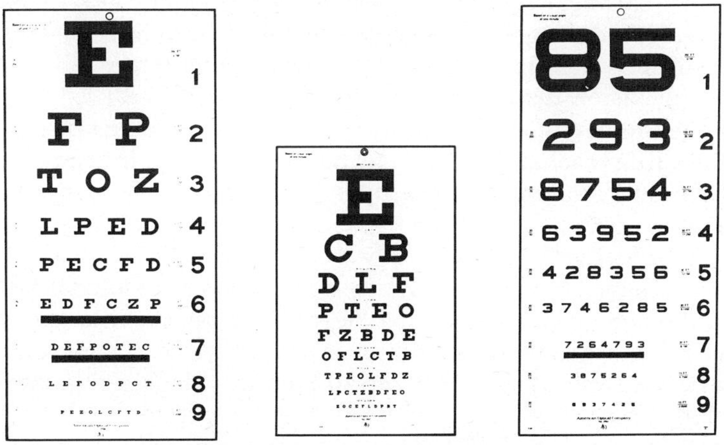

Snellen test charts for literates

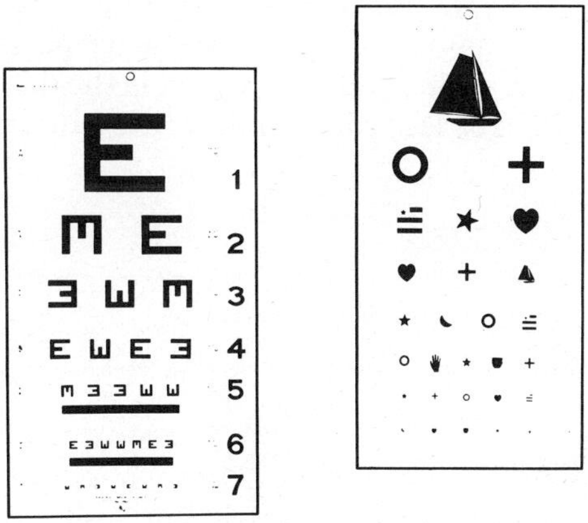

Snellen test charts for illiterates

FIGURE 14-8 Vision screening devices.

None of these mechanical devices requires specially trained personnel, and they are frequently administered by a school nurse or teacher. The cost of the two stereoscopic testing devices is several hundred dollars, that of the non-stereoscopic devices about $100. A much cheaper test that uses similar procedures is the Eames Eye Test which costs only about $12, but the user must furnish his own stereoscope.

SNELLEN TEST Back in 1862, Professor H. Snellen of Utrecht, Holland, developed a test card with standard-sized letters that is still the most widely used visual-screening test today. This test, which requires nothing more than a piece of white cardboard containing standard-sized black letters, is remarkably effective, considering its simplicity. Despite this, some school districts that spend millions of dollars for school buildings sometimes will not spend the 50 cents for this vision-testing equipment. (See Figure 14-8.)

Since the Snellen test is so widely used for testing some types of vision errors, the reading teacher should know how to use it and interpret it.

The Snellen standard of normality is the 20/20 line. Since the first number (the numerator) never changes, the test is administered at 20 feet. Hence, the denominator indicates the distance at which a person with normal vision should be able to read the particular line. When we say that a person has 20/20 vision, it means that when he is standing at 20 feet he can see the line (size of letters) which a normal person can see standing at that distance. If a person is slightly myopic, he may be able to read only the 20/30 line—meaning that a normal person is able to read this line standing 30 feet away from the chart. A child with poor eyesight such as 20/70 would see what a normal person standing 70 feet away from the chart could see. Table 14-1 shows the percentage of vision for each Snellen line. Hence the 20/70 line gives 64 percent of normal vision. The 20/70 line, incidentally, is significant for reading teachers for it is often the referral point for sight-saving classes, where such classes exist. Another interesting Snellen designation is 20/200, which is the definition of legal blindness. A person with 20/200 or less can carry a white cane, use a seeing-eye dog

TABLE 14-1
SNELLEN TEST CATEGORIES

Snellen line seen with less than three errors	Percentage of visual application
20/20 Normal	100
20/30 High-standard referral	91.5
20/40 Low-standard referral	83
20/50	76
20/70 Sight-saving class	64
20/100	48
20/200 Legally blind	20

in restaurants, take an extra deduction on his income tax, among other legal benefits. These designations refer to corrected vision; in other words, even with glasses the child cannot see better than 20/70 or 20/200.

The Snellen chart, to be effective, must be used under the proper conditions. It must be well lighted, and the student must stand exactly 20 feet away from it. Each eye should be tested separately; both eyes should remain open, but a card is placed in front of the untested eye, not touching it. A student should not be allowed to squint or turn his head sideways.

The Snellen test identifies (fails) students who are myopic and students who have astigmatism so badly that acuity is impaired. The usual school referral point is 20/30, which is slightly less than normal vision. This means that a student who misses more than two letters on the 20/30 line is referred to a specialist for further examination.

The Snellen test, of course, does not detect hyperopic (farsighted) children. These children will be able to see the 20/20 line with ease, and sometimes they can do even better and see the 20/15 line. By the addition of a + 1.5 diopter corrective lens to the test equipment, farsighted children can be detected. This test is fairly simple and all it requires of the examiner is to place the lens in front of the student's and find out whether he can still read the 20/20 line. If he can, he fails. Moderate caution might be exercised to keep this vital bit of information from being circulated among the students. The essential point is that if he can still see reasonably normally through a+1.5 diopter lens, he is farsighted and should be referred for additional vision examination.

Snellen charts for illiterates or for young children usually have lines of *E* symbols turned in different directions. The child, using three fingers, points in the direction of the *E* opening for each symbol.

Snellen charts can be obtained from the American Optical Company, Bausch and Lomb Company, or the Institute for Better Vision. They can frequently be obtained through the school physician or a local optician or vision specialist. Plus 1.5 diopter lenses can be obtained from any optician or vision specialist.

NONMECHANICAL BINOCULAR COORDINATION TESTS The most accurate way to test binocular coordination is to have a vision specialist do it. The next most accurate way is to use one of the mechanical vision-screening tests mentioned here.

The nonmechanical tests, however, are in the "better than nothing" category. One of the best nonmechanical tests is the Nearest-Point-of-Convergence Test which sometimes detects students who have exophoria (a tendency toward wall-eyedness). To administer this test, face the student and have him look at a pencil or some other object being held about 18 inches in front of his face. Gradually move the pencil toward the bridge of his nose and watch his eyes. He should be able to keep both eyes focused on the pencil until it is at least 3 inches away from the bridge of his nose. Failure occurs when one eye turns out or is no longer able to look at the pencil.

Ocular Motility is another test which examines the exterior eye muscles. To give this test, face the student and have him look at the tip of a pencil which is slowly rotated 360 degrees around his face at a distance of about 12 inches. Both his eyes should follow the pencil smoothly — down, to the side, up, to the other side, etc.

---

1. Stand a student exactly 20 feet away from this page. Light it well. Have him keep both eyes open and look at the following letters. Cover one eye by placing a cardboard in front of it (eye remains open) and ask him to read each letter. Then cover the other eye and have him read the letters in reverse order. If he misses more than two letters with either eye, stop the test and refer him to a specialist for further examination. (This is a 20/30 line; this screening is for myopia and astigmatism.)

N T O L

A E H C

2. Repeat the procedure above, but hold a +1.50 diopter lens in front of the eye that is not covered. If the student can still read the letters, stop the test and refer him to a specialist. (This screening is for hyperopia.)
3. Give the Nearest-Point-of-Convergence Test and Ocular Motility Test. (This screening is for lack of binocular coordination.)

FIGURE 14-9 A quick way to test vision.

CORRECTION OF VISUAL PROBLEMS

Teachers should be aware that controversies exist among vision specialists regarding the proper methodology for correcting visual problems. The reading field has strong adherents to this or that system, and sometimes even the type of personnel who should administer the remediation is a matter of debate. The vision field, too, has its controversies.

WHAT KIND OF SPECIALIST? The term "vision specialist" has been used frequently in this chapter, without specifying the type of specialist. This is to avoid the controversy between the medically trained (M.D.) opthamologist or oculist and the nonmedically trained optometrist (O.D.). Some people (including many medical doctors) believe that a person with a medical degree should give all vision examinations and make corrections. If one wishes to be exceedingly pure in this respect, the examination and correction should be done by a member of the Board of Opthalmology which requires several years of specialized training, in addition to the M.D. degree. However, medical doctors may legally examine eyes and prescribe glasses, although most of them do not because of the nature of the specialization. Another name for a medically trained doctor who specializes in the eye is oculist.

In another area of specialization is the optometrist who is specially trained in the measurement of vision and the prescribing of corrective lenses. Optometrists, of course, do not perform surgery, prescribe drugs, or treat eye diseases. Like medical doctors, optometrists must have state licenses in order to practice their profession.

A further category is the optician, who is a technician who grinds lenses to the prescription of an ophthalmologist or an optometrist. An optician is a highly skilled craftsman, but he may not examine patients or prescribe glasses.

Sometimes in matters of "clinical judgment" there may not be complete agreement among all specialists as to whether a patient is in need of glasses. According to his philosophy, one may believe that the patient should have a full correction (bring his acuity up to 20/20, for example) or a minimum correction which would give him just enough vision for comfort, but a little short of completely normal vision.

The question of correction of binocular coordination is also beset by differences of opinion, or "clinical judgments," among specialists—whether surgery is the best remedy for serious lack of binocular coordination and for such faults as cross-eyedness or wall-eyedness; whether the best correction is to put a prism lens before the eye; whether eye exercises or "orthoptics" are the best procedure; or, since there is an innerrelationship between acuity corrections and binocular coordination, whether minor binocular coordination problems could be aided through plus or minus sphere corrections. Eye exercises to improve acuity have fallen into disrepute among eye specialists because it cannot be proven that exercises do improve acuity.

REFERRAL PROCEDURES Schools must be cautious about referrals made on the basis of vision tests. Because of the controversy between ophthalmologists and optometrists, referral forms should leave this choice up to the parents. Eye specialists are concerned that the results of the school's screening test not be made known to the parents and ask that the teacher or nurse refrain from making such remarks as, "We think your child has myopia." Instead, they prefer that a comment such as the following be given:

A routine vision test was given to Johnny Jones. The results indicate that further visual examination should be given. The school does not provide this service. Signed, School Nurse or Remedial Teacher.

Note that the suggested referral form does not say that Johnny needs glasses, only that he needs further visual examination. This is indeed what the child does need. Let the vision specialist decide whether or not glasses are needed.

The number of children who can be expected to be referred is surprisingly high. The Orinda study which used screening procedures administered by specialists referred some 20 percent of all children tested.* Helen Robinson found in a typical Chicago school, which included grades two through eight, that about 10 percent of the children were receiving visual care but that an additional 30 percent needed it.†Kephart found significantly more under-achievers among students who needed visual care and a significant increase in learning rate once the visual care had been provided.‡

The studies of the relationship between poor vision and reading failure are not clear-cut. There is some evidence that children who are poor readers have a higher incidence of far-sightedness, astigmatism, and/or binocular-coordination problems. Note that near-sightedness (myopia) is not on this list—as a group, myopic children read as well or better than normal children, perhaps because they are more at home with a near-point task such as reading. It is also interesting that the cheapest and simplest form of visual screening, the Snellen chart, tends to detect only myopic children and, hence, is least useful in cases of reading failure. Children who are poor readers, therefore, should always be given a good visual-screening test.

*Henry B. Peters, Henrick Blum, Jerome Bettman, Frank Johnson, and Victor Fellows, "The Orinda Vision Study," *American Journal of Optometry and Archives of Optometry*, September, 1959.

†Helen M. Robinson, "Schools Need Visual Screening Tests," *The Bausch and Lomb Magazine*, vol. 30, no. 1.

‡Marguerite Eberl, "Visual Training and Reading," *Supplementary Educational Monograph No. 77*, Chicago University Press, January 1953; and Newell Kephart, "Visual Skills and Their Relation to School Achievement," *American Journal of Ophthalmology*, June 1953.

APPENDIX 14-A THIRTEEN RULES FOR HEALTHY VISION

1. *Always have adequate light for reading*

Man's eyes were originally developed for outdoor use. Good light makes it easier to see and cuts down eyestrain where there are minor defects of vision. Artificial light can seldom be too strong, but reading from a white page in direct sunlight may cause slight eyestrain. It may be difficult for teachers to judge the proper amount of light, but a rough guideline would be to have a 100-watt bulb placed from 3 to 7 feet from the printed page, supplemented by other bulbs to give the room general illumination. Utility companies will usually send a serviceman without charge to measure illumination in school or home reading areas. Present standards require 50 to 100 kilowatt candles of illumination.

2. *Avoid glare*

Glare can distract a student from reading and cause some eyestrain. Shiny desk tops and slick book pages (just as mirrors) can produce glare, which is caused when the main source of illumination (a light bulb or an open window) is in the wrong position. For example, a study light placed directly in front of a student may cause a glare on the desk or printed page. A student should not read facing a window or a light bulb, but should have the light coming from the side, the top, or over his shoulder.

3. *Avoid a dark background*

Books are usually printed with margins around the type, making it easier to read the printed words. Better books have wider margins, which aid in reading ease. However, even beyond the margins of the book, there should be a light or neutral background. Light wood for desks is much better than dark wood, and light-colored desk blotters are better than dark ones. It is better for a student to read in a room which is generally lighted than to have a light strike the page in a darkened room.

4. *Look at infinity to rest*

The eyes were made mainly for distance vision; it is easier to look at objects that are at least 20 feet away. Students who try to study in too small a room with no windows may get a confined feeling. This could be caused by the need to relax the eyes and look into the distance occasionally. Students are usually happier studying in a large room than in a small cubicle, unless the latter has windows. After a student has been reading or studying for awhile, it is restful for him to look up at some object 20 feet or more away. Closing the eyes for a minute may also help them return to a state of rest.

5. *Change body position*

While reading or studying, students often sit in one fixed position for long periods of time. It is relaxing to the eyes as well as to the rest of the body to change the body position. After studying for awhile, a student should get up and stretch and walk around. He might also shift his sitting position now and then.

6. *Watch for symptoms of eyestrain*

Some of the common symptoms of eyestrain are: redness of the eye; inflamed eyelids; headaches in the temples, the back of the head, or other parts of the head; noticeable uneasiness while reading or looking at a distant object for a long time; or holding a book much nearer or farther away from the eyes than is normal (see Appendix 14-B for a list of symptoms).

7. *Watch for diseases of the eye*

A common disease of the eye is conjunctivities or "pinkeye," a common ailment in schoolchildren. One or both eyeballs may turn quite red and feel irritated. A white discharge may appear at the corner of the eye and form a crust, which is often seen in the morning after the eyes have been shut all night. This disease spreads rapidly among school children, usually because they touch their irritated eyes and then touch another child who, in turn, touches his eyes. Students with this condition should be sent to the doctor and then told to stay home to avoid spreading the disease. It can be cured fairly easily with drugs, but, if left unattended, could become serious. Sties or other forms of inflammation of the eyelids are sometimes related to eyestrain; in any event, they should be examined by a doctor. There are many other diseases of the eyes, some of which are serious and can cause blindness. At any sign of eye infection, a student should be sent to a doctor.

8. *Remove foreign objects carefully*

Children, and sometimes adults, get bits of sand, dirt, or other foreign matter in their eyes. A small object can sometimes be removed by a student's keeping his eye closed and allowing the tears to wash the object to the corner of the eye. A larger object sometimes gets stuck; the eyelid should be pulled back and the object removed with the aid of a matchstick covered with clean, soft cotton or cotton-wool. Sometimes a foreign object can be rinsed from the eye by pouring in a small amount of clean water or by using an eyecup. If difficulty is encountered in getting an object out of the eye, or if the object is dangerous (broken glass or a fragment of metal), it should be removed by a doctor. In any event, a student should never rub his eye when something gets into it. If he gets something in his eye, he should first close his eyes for a minute or two; and if this does not give relief, seek help in the removal of the object.

9. *Avoid abnormal brightness*

Students should also be warned against looking at extremely bright lights such as a welding torch or the sun, without wearing specially made dark glasses. Looking at bright lights can cause permanent damage to the eyes.

10. *Use glasses if needed*

If a student needs glasses, it is foolish for him not to use them. Struggling with imperfect vision only consumes energy which could be put to better use and usually causes a strong disinclination to study or read – and this can sometimes be disastrous.

If glasses are not needed, they will not help. Some students think that magic accrues from wearing glasses, but if they have normal vision, glasses will do nothing. The wearing of uncorrected dark glasses will not relieve eyestrain if corrective glasses are needed.

11. *Have regular eye-screening tests*

Students are usually unaware that they need glasses. Eye-screening tests should be given to every student and teacher, upon school entrance and every three years thereafter.

12. *Watch eye balance*

It is easy for a student to think that his eyes are satisfactory if he can see accurately both at a distance and near at hand. But minor difficulties in binocular coordination frequently go undetected and may cause symptoms of eyestrain.

13. *Sudden changes in vision may mean trouble*

Any sudden change in vision (for example, vision getting noticeably worse in the course of a few weeks) means that the student should see a medical doctor, for this could be a sign of serious illness. Seeing spots before the eyes, dizziness during some seeing tasks, and blind spots also call for medical attention.

APPENDIX 14-B SIGNS OF EYE TROUBLE IN CHILDREN

Complaints

1. Inability to see well; letters of line run together or jump.
2. Headaches, dizziness, tiredness, or even nausea following close work.
3. Blurred vision.
4. Double vision.
5. Fatigue and listlessness after close work.
6. Inability to see chalkboard or television picture except when close-by.

Appearance of Eyes

1. Red-rimmed, encrusted, or swollen eyelids.
2. Recurring sties or lid inflammation.
3. Eyes or pupils unequal in size.
4. Drooping of one eyelid or both eyelids.
5. Eyes crossing inward or turning outward constantly or wandering occasionally.
6. Eyes "shaking" or oscillating.

Behavior of Child

1. Has difficulty in reading or in work requiring close vision; skips words or lines, rereads, loses place, or reads too slowly.
2. Frowns, blinks excessively, scowls, squints, or uses other facial distortions in reading.
3. Either holds books too close, or objects to and avoids close work whenever possible.
4. Rubs eyes frequently or attempts to brush away the blur.
5. Shuts or covers one eye or tilts or thrusts head forward when looking at close or distant objects.
6. Is inattentive and often uninterested.
7. Is generally fatigued or drowsy after prolonged use of the eyes or after reading or doing close work.
8. Stumbles or trips over small objects.
9. Does not do well in games requiring distant vision.
10. May be unduly sensitive to light or poor in color-detection.
11. Fails in school work.

Note: Many of these signs and systems may occur transiently during colds and other illnesses, but any persistence of any of these complaints indicates the need for an eye examination.

Source: Samuel Dirkan, "Eye Problems in Children," *Postgraduate Medicine*, vol. 34, no. 2, August 1963.

APPENDIX 14-C GLOSSARY OF VISION TERMS

Accommodation. The change in lens shape in the eye to keep a clear image on the retina as an object approaches the eye; probably starts at a distance of 20 feet and definitely must be in operation for near-point or reading distance.

Acuity. A clear image on the retina, normal vision for an eye; has nothing to do with good or bad binocular coordination.

Aqueous humor. The liquid inside the eyeball between the cornea and lens.

Astigmatism. Poor acuity from cornea not being spheroid.

Atlantic City Eye Test. A visual screening device using a lighted Snellen chart, lens test, and colored lenses for binocular-coordination testing.

Binocular. Two-eyed; using two eyes.

Binocular coordination. The way both eyes work together.

Cataract. An abnormal opacity of lens or cornea (white coating that will not allow light to come through) causing partial or complete vision loss.

Choroid coat. The middle layer of the eyeball covering.

Ciliary structure. Muscles inside the eye used in changing the lens shape for accommodation.

Color blindness. Lack of ability to see colors. Partial color blindness is common in males (some say one out of ten). Complete color blindness is rare. It does not affect reading.

Concave lens. Is thinner in the middle than edges; also see minus sphere.

Cones. A type of nerve cell found in the retina that is used in brighter or daylight vision; gives sharp acuity and colored images; is found more in the center of the retina.

Convergence. The turning in of each eye in order to see an object at some point nearer than infinity (where the eyes would be parallel and have no convergence); theoretically begins at a distance of 20 feet.

Convex lens. Is thinner on the edges than in the middle; also see plus sphere.

Cornea. The clear outer covering in front of the eyeball.

Cylindrical lens. Part of a cylindrical shape ground into a lens for astigmatic correction.

Depth perception. Same as stereopsis, three-dimension vision.

Diopter. Unit of measurement for curvature of a lens.

Diplopia. Double vision, or seeing two images at once. The brain will usually not tolerate this for long and suppresses one eye. See suppression.

Eames Eye Test. A visual screening test, using Snellen chart, lens test, and a stereoscope.

Emmotropia. Normal acuity.

Essophoria. Eyes have a tendency to turn in; See phoria.

Essotropia. Eyes turn in; see tropia.

Exophoria. Eyes have a tendency to turn out; See phoria.

Exotropia. Eyes turn out; see tropia.

Eye-movement camera. Same as opthalmograph.

Far-point. Seeing in the distance, usually at a distance over 20 feet.

Fixation. A brief stop, usually one-third to one-fifth of a second, while the eye looks at a word or phrase.

Fovea, or Fovea centralis. An area in the center of the retina composed only of cones that give sharpest acuity.

Fusion. Both eyes looking at the same image so that the image from one eye is fused with the image of the other eye in the brain.

Glaucoma. A disorder of the eye resulting in a disturbance of the circulation of the aqueous so that pressure builds up within the eye and eventually destroys the retina and optic nerve and results in partial or complete blindness.

Hyperopia. Far-sightedness; one can see well at far-point but not at near-point.

Iris. The colored part of the eye (blue, etc.) that opens to let in more light if needed.

Keystone Visual Survey. Same as Telebinocular.

Lateral posture. Binocular coordination on a horizontal plane.

Lens test. The use of a plus convex lens (usually 1.25 to 2.00 diopters) with a Snellen chart for screening for hyperopia.

Macula. Same as fovea.

Maddox rods. A special type of lens that makes a point of light look like a line; used in binocular-coordination testing.

Massachusetts Eye Test. A visual-screening device using Snellen letters, lens test, and maddox rods.

Minus lens or sphere. A concave lens used in correcting myopia.

Monocular. One-eyed; using one eye.

Myopia. Near-sightedness; one can see well at near-point but not at far-point.

Nearest Point of Convergence Test. A test for convergence conducted by moving an object toward the nose.

Ocular motility (test). The ability to move the eyes together on all planes.

Ophthalmograph. An eye-movement camera used to make a photographic record of eye movements, usually when reading.

Ophthalmologist. A medical doctor who specializes in eye diseases and vision and who usually has specific postgraduate work and is certified by a special Board of Ophthalmology.

Optic nerve. A bundle of nerve fibers connecting the retina to the brain (occipital lobe).

Optician. A skilled craftsman who grinds lenses.

Optometrist. A specially trained and licensed person who examines vision and prescribes corrective measures such as glasses. Is not an M.D. and does not treat diseases.

Orthoptics. The practice of giving eye muscle exercises to improve binocular coordination and possibly suppression.

Orthoptist. A person who gives orthoptics, or eye exercises, to improve binocular coordination. May be a trained medical technician working under a doctor's supervision or an optometrist.

Orthorater. A special stereoscope used in visual screening; a type of vision-screening test.

Overconvergence. Another term for essotropia or essophoria.

Peripheral vision. Vision using the periphery of the retina or "seeing out of the corner of the eye."

Phoreas. Less serious faults of binocular coordination in which one eye has a tendency to look away from the point of fusion but can be controlled with additional muscle effort. One may relax the muscle strain when tired or under such drugs as alcohol and suppress or have diplopia (double vision). Essophoria, where the eyes tend to turn in, and exophoria, where the eyes tend to turn out, are the most common causes of suppression.

Plus lens or sphere. A convex lens used in correcting hyperopia and in reading glasses.

Presbyopia. Lack of ability to accommodate, especially at near-point.
Prism. A lens thicker on one side, sometimes used in correcting essophoria or exophoria.
Reading Eye. Trade name for an opthalmograph.
Recognition span. Same as visual span.
Regression. A backward saccadic movement while reading.
Retina. The inner surface of the back and sides of the eyeball, composed of nerves (rods, cones, and connecting neurons).
Return sweep. An eye movement made from the end of a line to the beginning of the next line.
Rods. Nerve cells in the retina used for very dim light or night vision; gives only fuzzy black-and-white images and is found more toward the periphery of the retina.
Saccadic movement. A quick movement, about one-twenty-fifth of a second, between fixations while reading.
Sclerotic coat. The white outer covering of the eyeball.
Sight-saving class. A special class for children with partial vision, usually having between 20/70 and 20/200 corrected vision. Uses special reading materials with large type.
Snellen chart (test). A card with lines of different-sized letters used at 20 feet for testing acuity.
Squint. Another term for tropia, or serious lack of coordination.
Stereopsis. Depth perception, or 3D (third-dimension). True depth perception requires that each eye transmit a slightly different image to the brain plus a slight muscle pull from convergence. Monocular persons have a learned, or false, depth perception caused by learning that bigger objects are closer and they have more details.
Stereoscope. Device which uses lenses and shows a separate image to each eye and can simulate distance and stereopsis; is used in some vision tests.
Strabismus. Another term for lack of binocular coordination, or squint.
Suppression. Psychological blocking out of vision in an eye to avoid diplopia, which is often caused by a tropia or a phoria. It is more common than generally realized and may be commonly detected by giving a stereoscopic vision-screening test when the examinee reports seeing nothing with one eye; proof of the suppression can then be confirmed by covering the seeing eye at which time the suppressed eye immediately starts seeing things.
Telebinocular. A special stereoscope used in visual screening.
Triangulation. Same as convergence.
Tropias. Serious lack of binocular coordination resulting in one eye being more or less permanently and uncontrollably aimed away from the point of fusion. In exotropia (wall-eyedness) one eye looks outward, and in essotropia (cross-eyedness) one eye looks inward.
Tunic. Latin word meaning "cloak"; sometimes used as sclerotic tunic, etc.
Tunnel vision. Lack of normal peripheral vision; an inability to "see out of the corner of the eye."
Underconvergence. Another term for exotropia or exophoria.
Vertical posture. Binocular coordination in a vertical plane.
Visual screening. Testing for lack of normal vision without specific diagnosis.
Visual span. The amount of material (words) seen in a fixation; averages about 1.25 words.
Vitreous humor. The jellylike mass inside the main part of the eyeball.

APPENDIX 14-D LIST OF DEVICES USED IN TESTING VISION

Atlantic City Eye Test (developed by Samuel M. Diskan), Freund Brothers, 1514 Pacific Ave., Atlantic City, N. J.

Ortho-Rater, Bausch and Lomb Optical Co., Rochester, N. Y.

Visual Survey Telebinocular, Keystone View Co., Meadville, Pa.

Massachusetts Vision Test, Welch Allyn, Inc., Skaneateles Falls, N. Y.

Eames Eye Test (by Thomas H. Eames, M.D.), Harcourt, Brace & World, New York, N.Y.

Sightscreener, American Optical Co., Southbridge, Mass.

Dvorine Pseudo-Isochromatic Plates, Scientific Publishing Co., Baltimore, Md. (For testing color vision.)

15

HEARING

INTRODUCTION

There are not nearly as many school children with hearing defects as with vision defects. Estimates of significant hearing impairment vary from 1.5 percent to 5 percent. Significant hearing loss is defined as that loss which will lead to the deterioration of speech, hinder learning, or affect communication.

There is a well-known connection between hearing loss and speech. In extreme cases, years ago, deaf persons were also speechless, that is, literally "deaf and dumb." Speech is a learned phenomenon. If a person has never heard speech, he cannot naturally learn to speak. Fortunately there are special methods for teaching deaf children so that very few are unable to speak, even though born totally deaf.

But even minor degrees of hearing loss usually result in some degree of speech deterioration. This is not surprising, for all of the communication arts (speaking, hearing, writing, and reading) are interrelated. Many studies have found a close relationship between hearing loss and reading problems. It may be more important to test hearing than vision when looking for causes of reading failure.

Reading teachers should pay particular attention to a child's hearing if he has difficulty with reading. In schools that assume responsibility for testing students' hearing, the remedial reading teacher will work closely with the school nurse or audiologist in selecting hearing tests and establishing criteria for referral. Much of the process of learning to read involves a student's learning also to listen. The more she understands about the hearing (listening) process, the more a teacher may be able to use it to students' advantage. A hearing loss is often difficult to detect without some standardized hearing test, yet it may be responsible for many of the seemingly unrelated symptoms that teachers encounter, such as inattention, poor speech, bad spelling, unsatisfactory reading, or minor behavior problems.

STRUCTURE AND FUNCTION OF HEARING

The outer or visible part of the ear is probably the least important part of the hearing structure. If the outer ear is cut off by accident or is deformed at birth, it is usually restored not because it is essential to the hearing function but because its absence is an esthetic and social handicap. Only a part of the outer ear, the lower cartilege which protects the ear canal, is of some use in hearing.

EAR STRUCTURE As diagrammed in Figure 15-1, the ear consists of three parts: (1) the outer ear, which includes the ear canal and ends at the eardrum (tympanic membrane); (2) the middle ear, which contains the tiny transmission bones (ossicles); and (3) the inner ear, which consists of a spiral labyrinth (cochlea) and the auditory nerve endings.

A sound, say that emanating from the vocal chords or a bell, sets air molecules into a wavelike motion consisting of alternate patterns of condensation and rarification of the molecules. A stone dropped into a quiet pool will set up similar wavelike motions on the surface. These molecular motions in the air which produce sound are made up of extremely small movements. They

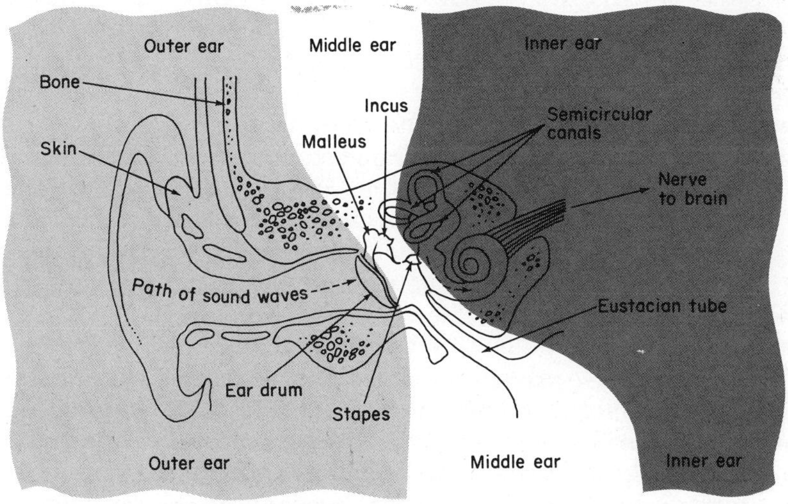

FIGURE 15-1 Schematic drawing of the ear.

are too small to be received as sound until they are amplified by a mechanical action of the ear.

The sound waves pass through the air and into the ear canal. At the end of the ear canal, the thin layer of skin known as the eardrum, or tympanic membrane, vibrates just as you may have felt a piece of tissue paper vibrate when you hum on it. Adjacent to the inner side of the tympanic membrane is a tiny bone called the hammer, or malleus, which picks up the vibration, transmits it to a middle bone called the anvil, or incus, which then transmits the vibration to a third tiny bone called the stirrup, or stapes. The stapes, in turn, transmit the vibration to a thin membrane covering, a small opening known as the oval window, or cochlear fenestra. On the other side of this oval window is the cochlea, a spiral-shaped canal coiled much like a snail shell. The cochlea is filled with a liquid, and vibrations at the oval window are then transmitted to the liquid which, in turn, vibrates small hairs along the cochlea canal. These hairs are connected with the auditory nerve and it is here that the mechanical transmissions of vibration are changed into nerve impulses for transmission to the temporal lobe of the brain. The frequency of vibration determines which hairs in the cochlea will respond by vibrating. The frequency of vibration also determines the pitch (highness or lowness) of the sound which is heard.

The ossicles, or tiny bones in the middle of the ear, play a part in the amplification of vibrations as the ratio of size between the ear drum or tympanic membrane and the oval window are in a ratio of 20 to 1. Furthermore, the ossicles have a 3-to-2 ratio. This gives a total mechanical intensification of 30 to 1.

FAILURE IN THE HEARING PROCESS Again, if we start with the outer ear and follow the structure through to the brain, looking for possible sources of hearing difficulty, we find that those of the outer ear cause the least trouble. Occasionally, the ear canal can become blocked with wax or dirt and thus inhibit the entrance of sound waves to the eardrum, but this is relatively rare and easily corrected. Because of the arrangement of wax glands and hair follicles, the ear canal is largely self-cleaning. Far more harm can be done by amateurs who attempt to clean it than by the small amount of dirt that sometimes collects there. It might be fine advice to tell a boy to wash his ears or behind his ears, but to suggest that he stick anything smaller than his elbow into his ear canal can lead to trouble. If on rare occasions the ear canal does become clogged, a child should be taken to a doctor or nurse for proper cleaning—a far less expensive procedure than sticking a hairpin through the ear drum. In temperate climates, as in the United States, outer ear infections are rare. An apparent infection or discharge of pus from the ear canal may often mean a serious infection in the middle ear or a ruptured eardrum. The person should be taken immediately to a doctor to prevent possible permanent hearing damage.

Ruptures, or breaks in the eardrum, if small are usually self-healing. Ruptures can result from the insertion of sharp objects in the ear canal, infection in the middle ear, or extremely loud noises. Ruptured eardrums can cause hearing loss and occasionally can result in a permanent rupture or scarring, with a permanent hearing loss.

The middle ear with its ossicles is interesting because it is connected to the nasal cavity (pharynx) by the Eustachian tubes. If a person has a cold or an infection in the sinus, this can cause the Eustachian tube to become infected and the infection can spread up into the middle ear. If the infection is serious enough, the Eustachian tube can close, and this sometimes results in a collection of infected matter in the middle ear which can cause temporary deafness or rupture of the eardrum. This is the reason why children should be taught to blow their noses gently and without undue pressure, because the pressure of air can force infected matter into the middle ear. This nose-ear connection is also the reason why children should not jump into water without holding their noses or using a noseclamp as the upward force of the water into the nostrils can also send foreign matter into the middle ear and cause infection. It should be noted that ear plugs do no good at all; water is kept out of the middle ear by the eardrum. An exception to this is the person who has a perforated eardrum.

A more serious difficulty causing hearing loss in the middle ear is ossification, or excessive calcium deposits on the ossicles or over the oval window. This is a relatively common phenomenon in old age and undoubtedly accounts for the gradual hearing loss in many older persons. It can also be a factor in children's hearing loss. If serious enough, this ossification can be removed by a delicate but usually successful surgical operation called fenestration.

Damage to the inner ear, which is fairly well protected and inaccessible to outside influences, is usually caused by disease or birth defects. Infections can occur in the cochlea, and these can temporarily or permanently damage the delicate receptor cells of the auditory nerve. If the nerves are damaged only in one area, a person would have a hearing loss along only a part of the sound scale – at the high, middle, or low register. Nerve damage is probably the most frequent cause of serious and permanent hearing loss.

The precise spot where "hearing" takes place is rather like the mythical place where "vision" takes place. After the nerve impulses are transmitted to the brain, a number of cerebral areas are involved in the process called hearing. Any damage either to the auditory nerve or to the involved areas of the brain can also cause hearing loss or distortions. Thus anything that damages the brain (an infection or an abnormal growth like cancer, the breaking of blood vessels and subsequent clotting as in a stroke, or direct rupture caused from outside, as from a bullet) can cause hearing loss. Hearing loss caused by brain damage is called "auditory aphasia." "Aphasia" is a general term for loss of function in any of the language areas.

Since aphasias can result from damage to just one area of the brain, they have provided some interesting insights into some of the functional areas of the brain. For example, it is possible for "verbal aphasics" to "hear" or respond to minimum pure tones at every spot in the auditory frequency spectrum and yet not be able to repeat a word. "Nominal aphasics" can repeat words but cannot connect them to meaning. "Semantic aphasics" know the meaning of isolated words but do not have the power to understand phrases or connected discourse.

HEARING TESTS

BASIC CONCEPTS Before beginning this discussion of hearing tests, several terms must be clarified. Sound is measured along two dimensions: (1) loudness or intensity, and (2) pitch or frequency. Physicists are inclined to measure sound in terms of intensity, which means the amount of air in motion – a small amount emitting a weak sound and a large amount emitting a loud sound. They also measure sound according to the frequency of the sound waves, measuring it in cycles per second (CPS). A high number of cycles per second, such as a shrill piccolo note, would be recorded as about 4,000 CPS, whereas the lowest note on a tuba would be about 60 CPS (overtones extend this range).

The commonest and best type of hearing test uses a small electronic device called a pure tone-audiometer. This machine emits sounds of different frequencies and different intensities by simply adjusting two dials. A normal sound threshold has been established for different frequencies much the same as normal visual acuity has been established in vision testing. A threshold has been defined as the minimum intensity required for perception. For example, a person's threshold for hearing would be the faintest sound he could hear at a given frequency.

It is not necessary to test a person's hearing at every cycle, for there are over 20,000 of them. Rather, six or eight points are usually selected, such as 64, 128, 256, 512, 1024, 2,048, 4,096, and 8,192 CPS. Mathematics students might be interested to note that hearing perception differences vary along a geometric rather than arithmetic scale.

A child with superior hearing ability might be able to hear normal threshold sounds from 25 to 20,000 CPS. Such a wide range is not necessary for speech and communication, which usually covers a range of from 125 to 8,000 CPS; even less is actually needed for minimum intelligibility. A person who can hear from 50 to 10,000 CPS would have all the hearing acuity needed for full enjoyment of a symphony orchestra. As a point of reference, middle C has a 256 CPS.

Intensity is measured in units called decibels. The reference point for intensity is normal hearing or zero decibel loss. A 20-decibel loss is about the spot where hearing loss first begins to be noticed and is the usual reference point in screening tests. A person with a 30-decibel loss might occasionally need a hearing aid. If he did not make use of a hearing aid by the time he had a 40-decibel loss he would begin to get distorted speech. At a 50-decibel loss within speech frequencies, the hearing aid would be needed or the person could not carry on normal activities. Between a 60- and 90-decibel loss, powerful hearing aids are required; and beyond a 100-decibel loss, only partial help is possible with any aid. For most practical purposes, absolute deafness would occur at about a 120-decibel loss. These losses refer to frequencies within each range, and absolute loss of hearing at 10,000 CPS or 50 CPS can occur without affecting the speech range of frequencies.

ADMINISTERING AUDIOMETER TESTS An audiometer test is administered by having a student hold an earphone up to one ear and use the other hand for signalling when he hears a sound. A typical instruction is to have the student raise his index finger when he hears the sound and to put it down when the sound stops. The student should face away from the examiner and the audiometric device lest he be fooled into thinking he hears the sound when he sees the examiner pressing down on the sound button. Students are frequently so eager to cooperate with the examiner or to make themselves "look good" that they will use any cue available, whereas the examiner wishes the only cue to be the pure tone coming from the earphone. It is necessary that the test be given in as quiet a room as possible. There should be no talking during the test, either on the part of the examiner or the student being tested. Hand signals are all that are necessary.

In screening large groups, the examiner usually does the "sweep test" because it is both fast and accurate. To administer the sweep test, set the intensity down at a 10-decibel loss. This means that the audiometer will make a sound just loud enough so that a person with a 10-decibel loss can hear it. This sound should be fairly distinct for a person with normal hearing. The examiner then sweeps across the frequencies—in other words, gives a sound at 125 CPS until the student raises a finger, then gives a sound at 250 CPS until the student raises a finger, etc. If the student fails to signify that he hears any frequency, he is asked to take a more extensive retest.

The retest is usually given a week or two later. This interval will correct for any hearing loss that may have been caused by a cold or other minor infection. The sweep test is repeated during the retest; and if the student fails at any one frequency, the examiner then increases the intensity to a 30- or 40-decibel loss or whatever intensity is necessary for the student to hear at that frequency. The referral criterion varies slightly in school districts depending on the school physician or consulting otologist (a physician who specializes in hearing). A conservative referral criterion which would give a maximum number of referrals to the specialist would be a 20-decibel loss at any frequency. A more lenient referral criterion, and one which is used by some districts which desire a minimum number of referrals, is a 20-decibel loss at any two frequencies or more than a 20-decibel loss at any one frequency.

AUDIOMETER (MA-2B) HEARING TEST
Rutgers Reading Center

Name *Bill Smith* Date *June 15, 1971*

Examiner *V. Bennett*

Set up Audiometer with:
- Power Switch 'on'
- Masking Switch 'off'
- Tone-mic. switch 'rev'
- Selector Switch 'red' for right ear, 'blue' for left ear

Procedure
- Student puts on earphones with red on right ear.
- Student faces away from audiometer.
- Student indicates he hears a sound by holding up one finger. Finger is put down when no sound is heard.

Sweep Test (Use first unless hearing loss is suspected)
- Set hearing loss control at 10 DB
- Text each frequency on chart below.
- If student can't hear at any frequency increase volume of sound until he can.
- It may be necessary to use a louder sound until student gets used to listening carefully.
- Indicate sound heard with an X on graph below.

LEFT EAR - BLUE EARPHONE

Frequency in Cycles per second

Loss in Decibels	125	250	750	1,000	2,000	4,000	6,000
0							
5							
10	X	X	X	X	X	X	X
15							
20							
25							
30							
35							
40							
45							
50							

RIGHT EAR - RED EARPHONE

	125	250	750	1,000	2,000	4,000	6,000
0							
5							
10	X	X	X				
15				X			
20					X		
25						X	
30							X
35							
40							
45							
50							

Results *Left ear normal; high frequency loss in right ear. Re test in one week; refer if not improved.*

FIGURE 15-2 Sample audiogram (report of audiometric test).

An audiometric test may be given by a teacher, the school nurse, the school psychologist, or an audiometrist hired for the purpose. Speech correction teachers frequently have special training in audiometry.

THE WHISPER TESTS Some impoverished school districts may not have audiometers. In this case, a "better than nothing" test is the whisper test. The examiner stands 20 feet away from the student in a quiet room. The student stands at right angles to the examiner so that he cannot see the examiner's lips. The examiner then whispers three or four words or numbers very softly. (The whisper will be softer if most of the air is first expelled from the examiner's lungs.) The student then faces in the opposite direction, and the examiner again whispers three or more words or numbers.

The secret of this test is for the examiner to establish good "local norms." She whispers as softly as she can and observes when most children can hear it. A student repeats the sound as he hears it. When a child cannot hear the whisper at the same level of intensity that most other children can, then hearing loss is suspected and referral made. The whisper test is probably not good for screening the first few children; but after the examiner has tested a few children and learned the sound level at which most children are able to hear, the test can then be repeated with the first children tested.

The whisper test can be made slightly more effective by adding *low voice*. In addition to whispering some words or numbers, the examiner can then, in the softest and lowest pitch possible, say a few words or numbers. Whispers and some consonant sounds tend to have a much higher frequency than low-voice sounds. The "th" digraphs have a high frequency sound. In contrast, lone vowel sounds are relatively low. A slight improvement on the whisper test can be made if the examiner selects such high-frequency-sound words as *six*, *thistle*, *seventeen* and some low-voice words such as *no*, *mine*, *eye*.

PHONOGRAPHIC GROUP HEARING TESTS Some schools may still use another type of group hearing test. This consists of a phonograph record and record player with a number of earphone outlets. A voice on the record says numbers in various degrees of loudness, and the student writes them down on a form. This test is probably slightly more reliable than a whisper test but inferior to an audiometer. It was usually purchased by schools before electronic audiometers were made available at sharp reductions in cost. There would be little reason, however, for a school to purchase a phonograph, now that pure tone audiometers are available.

CORRECTION OF HEARING LOSS

Many minor hearing losses discovered by audiometer tests are frequently transitory and will disappear in a few days, even if unattended, because they may be caused by a cold or some other minor nasal passage infection. However, if the hearing loss lasts over a few days and is repeated several times, a physician should be notified.

Middle and inner ear infections can usually be cured by a physician with the use of antibiotics. Years ago it was fairly common for children to have mastoid infections which were located in the spongy bone surrounding the ear. These infections resulted in pain, swelling, sometimes a discharge through the eardrum, and sometimes in temporary or permanent hearing loss. Fortunately most of these infections can now be cured by drugs without resorting to surgery as formerly was necessary. And there is the previously mentioned operation for decalcification of the ossicles, or oval window, which can restore hearing if calcification was the cause of loss. This delicate operation is performed by opening the eardrum, removing the stapes, scraping the window, and replacing the stapes with an artificial stapes. Near-normal hearing can usually be restored.

Hearing aids are usually prescribed if a loss of 35 decibels or more in the speech frequencies is found in the best ear. Hearing aids which amplify the sound come in two main types: (1) air conduction, and (2) bone conduction. The first type fits over or inside the entrance to the ear canal and amplifies the sound waves before they reach the eardrum. The other type, which usually fits just behind the ear and amplifies the sound for transmission through the bone, enables the sound vibrations to go directly to the oval window and the cochlea, thus bypassing the middle ear to some extent. In addition, there are a number of varieties, which selectively amplify certain frequencies. Hearing aids should be fitted by a specially trained physician known as an otologist rather than by a hearing aid salesman whose main interest is selling his brand of hearing aid.

For some reason or other, hearing aids are not accepted socially as well as vision aids are. An interesting solution is the tiny hearing aid which fits onto the sidebar of glasses, even worn by people with no visual defect who wish to disguise the hearing aid as a pair of glasses. Children are quick to sense the social prejudice against hearing aids, and it is part of the teacher's task to set the classroom climate for acceptance of the hearing aid. The teacher's foresight can stop any ridicule or teasing. When skillfully handled, a child with a hearing aid can enjoy both status and popularity by allowing other children to use his hearing aid occasionally.

Most hearing aids are made as small as possible for cosmetic reasons, but a higher quality of reception can be obtained if a slightly larger instrument is used. Some classes for the hard-of-hearing have special school-model hearing aids which are small boxes that are attached to the desk and coupled with a high-fidelity earphone or earphones. These superior but bulkier hearing aids could probably be used more frequently in regular classroom by hard-of-hearing students if the social climate were right. Transistor types are also available with no wires.

For minimum hearing losses such as a 20- or 30-decibel loss in the speech frequencies, hearing aids may not be required; but such special seating as placing the child near the front of the room or near the teacher's desk can overcome much of the handicap. Students with minimum hearing loss are accused of not paying attention. This is often true because they must put in so much more effort than the normal child just to hear that they fatigue easily. Bright children with hearing losses sometimes learn to "read lips," partially without any instruction. If they can look directly at the speaker, they can "hear" much better. Children with good motivation and good IQ's can cover up a minor hearing loss much better than an average or dull child. The teacher who says, "If he would pay attention he would hear all right," may be describing a child with a minor hearing loss.

SYMPTOMS OF HEARING LOSS

In many schools, screening tests for hearing are given only every three years, and in others only on a teacher's request. Thus the teacher is expected to have some informal methods of "suspecting" hearing loss. A number of the symptoms have already been mentioned, but it might be helpful to list them briefly. Some of the commonest symptoms are these:

1. Exhibiting inattention.
2. Asking to have words or phrases repeated.
3. Hearing "head noises," such as buzzing or dullness.
4. Having feelings of dizziness or nausea.
5. Pronouncing of words is poor; leaving off "s's" or omits "th's."
6. Speaking in a monotone or slurring letters.
7. Discharging from the ear or having frequent earaches.
8. Rubbing or picking at the ear.
9. Tilting the head or turning one ear toward the speaker.
10. Having frequent colds, sinus infection, or breathing difficulties.
11. Having difficulty reading or spelling.

HEARING HYGIENE

Many principles of hygiene or precautionary procedures have been mentioned in the discussion of the normal functions and defects in the hearing process. It might be helpful, too, to list briefly these principles for the teacher to review or to use in planning a lesson. These, then, are some helpful do's and don'ts for hearing hygiene:

1. Do not put objects into the outer ear canal.
2. Blow the nose gently.
3. Do not jump into water without holding your nose or using a nose clip.
4. Do not dive or swim when you have a cold.
5. Seek early treatment at any sign of pain or infection in the ear.
6. Have regular hearing tests—at least once every three years.
7. Seat a child who has a minor hearing loss at the front of the room or near the teacher's desk.
8. See that a child with a serious hearing loss obtains and wears a hearing aid. (Both his education and social development will be threatened otherwise.)
9. Avoid extremely loud noises such as being too near fire arms, firewords, or noisy machinery. High sound amplification used by some musical groups can also cause damage. (Industries now recognize the permanent damage that loud noises can cause and provide ear protectors for men working near jet aircraft and extremely noisy machinery.)

TRAINING FOR LISTENING OR AUDING

In the past decade or so, educators have expressed great concern over the training of listening skills or "auding," as this field is now being called. They reason that since a good deal of learning takes place when the child just *listens*, proper training in listening may improve this type of learning ability. Some experiments have shown that children trained in listening skills do better on listening tests.

Listening tests are similar to reading comprehension tests. A paragraph or passage is read aloud by the teacher, who then questions the students on the material read. The students may also ask questions or read prepared questions. Training in this skill consists of regular short sessions in which the teacher reads different types of passages, of different lengths, followed by a variety of questions.

Just as vision is more than the mechanical aspect of light rays striking nerve endings, so hearing involves much more of the brain than the mechanics of sound waves passing through the outer and middle ear to stimulate nerve cells in the inner ear. An Indian guide can certainly hear things in the forest that no city-dweller can. Students trained in a foreign language can hear sounds that students not trained in that language cannot hear. A good bit of "hearing" is based on learning and intelligence.

Some of the best parts of the so-called reading-readiness activities are really listening activities. For example, just listening to stories and then discussing them has long been a standard home, preschool, and primary school activity. In fact, to some extent, this activity can be used with any age group; there are many successful lessons of this type taught in upper-elementary school, high school, and even in university classes. Much of the discussion on reading comprehension can also apply to listening comprehension.

Another specific type of listening lesson aimed directly at one specific type of reading lesson is a drill aimed at hearing phoneme distinctions. For example, a teacher might say, "I am going to say two words. If they are both exactly the same, hold up your hand immediately after I say them." She then might give some of the following pairs of words:

1. *pin–pen*	(short-vowel change)
2. *bin–bin*	(no change; to see if they are listening)
3. *sam–some*	(long vowel; short vowel)
4. *can–ran*	(initial-consonant change)
5. *lan–land*	(ending addition)

The teacher can make the drill a little more challenging by holding a book or a piece of paper in front of her mouth. This muddles the sound a little and also reduces any clue the children might get from watching her mouth, thus making it more of a true listening exercise. Another variation is to have students close their eyes while listening. This type of drill ties in very closely with phonics lessons; in fact, it sometimes is a regular part of reading phonics lessons. But there is no reason it cannot be used with preschool children. It is also very good for students of disadvantaged or foreign language backgrounds.

Listening activities are quite easy to automate with a tape recorder or record player. A number of companies produce records that read stories from children's books and on all other levels, but especially adult. There are talking books developed for the blind or partially sighted, but equally useful as listening drills with or without the student reading the text along with the recorded voice.

Teachers often like to tape record their own lessons. These lessons might consist of reading some pages from a reading test, reading a background story, giving directions for some exercise or workbook assignment. There are even commercially prepared materials which do the same thing, such as the Primary Reading Program (tapes and workbooks) produced by Imperial Productions, Kanakee, Illinois. At the upper-elementary level there is the Listen and Think Program developed by Educational Development Laboratories, which has fifteen tapes and accompanying workbook at each grade level. Each lesson contains stories and a discussion of some specific listening skill. After listening, the student answers questions in his workbook, and then the tape gives him the correct workbook answers. The lesson ends with a compressed speech story.

Compressed speech is a development of research workers who wanted to find out how fast a person can listen. It was first necessary to produce very rapid speech without distortion. If you simply speed up a record or tape you get the "Donald Duck" effect of distortion. However, it was found that by clipping small segments out of a tape (at first by hand and later electromechanically) a tape could be played with varying rates of speaking without distortion. Further research showed that compressed speech, besides saving time, sometimes improved comprehension. The timesaving factor also was enough to press it into immediate use in recording for the blind and in some courses by telephone where faster listening was a great saving. Using a 33 percent compression, a forty-five-minute lecture could be played and understood in thirty minutes.

Normal speaking and listening rates in English vary between 100 and 175 words per minute; but by compressing a tape-recorded speech, it can easily be listened to at 250 words per minute; and, with training, some students obtain fairly good listening comprehension at 400 words per minute. Rate-training in listening may someday become a parallel to rate-training in reading as listening is auditory verbal information input to the human system and reading is visual verbal information input. We know that there is some relationship between normal speech and listening development and ability to learn to read, but we are not yet sure that training to improve listening rate will affect reading rate or vice versa.

Though listening training might be thought of by some as an activity for preschool or, at highest, elementary-school pupils, this is not true. Listening training is being used in high schools and even in many college study-skills courses. After all, much of the instruction in colleges and universities consists of the professor lecturing and the students listening. A good example of the type of commercially developed program for junior- and senior-high schools is the *Listen and Read* series of thirty recordings and workbooks produced by Educational Development Laboratories.

One interesting factor in using a recorded presentation is the effect of putting earphones on students. This often seems to increase concentration, perhaps by eliminating outside noises or making conversation more difficult. But in any event, putting earphones on students seems to give them a degree of isolation and concentration which is very desirable during listening drills.

For the teacher who wants further information, there are a large number of journal articles on listening. Several of the standard works in the area are David Russell's little classroom-oriented book, *Listening Aids Through the Grades*, published by Teachers College Press, Columbia University, and Sam Duker's two books, *Listening Bibliography*, an annotated bibliography, and *Listening: Readings*, a collection of articles about listening. Both are published by Scarecrow Press.

Listening training and listening activities have always been close to reading training, and they are being used more and more each year, especially as reading and the preparation for it is increasingly being emphasized for the very young child and the disadvantaged student.

APPENDIX 15-A AUDIOMETER MANUFACTURERS

Ambco Audiometers
  Ambco Electronics
  1222 Washington Blvd.
  Los Angeles, California 90007

Audivox Audiometers
  Audivox, Inc.
  123 Worcester Street
  Boston, Massachusetts 02118

Beltone Audiometers
  Beltone Electronics Corporation
  Special Instruments Division
  4201 W. Victoria Street
  Chicago, Illinois 60640

Maico Audiometers
  Maico Electronics, Inc.
  21 North Third Street
  Minneapolis, Minnesota 55401

Sonotone Pure-Tone Audiometers
  Sonotone Corporation
  Elmsford, New York 10523

Zenith Audiometers
  Zenith Hearing Aid Sales Corporation
  6501 West Grand Avenue
  Chicago, Illinois 60635

16
PHYSICAL PROBLEMS

Chapters 14 and 15 dealt with two of the major physical problems that affect children's progress in learning to read. There are problems that also detract from children's reading ability – such as abnormal growth rate and brain damage. Some school districts place a great deal of responsibility for the screening and referral of children with physical defects directly on the teachers. Other school districts place much of this responsibility on the school nurse, working with a school physician and other health specialists. Regardless of where the responsibility lies, all teachers have a duty to understand the nature and importance of children's physical problems, the various criteria or standards of normality that apply, and the referral resources available and the proper procedures for making use of the health services.

A Joint Committee on Health Problems and Education of the National Education Association and the American Medical Association have produced a booklet entitled *Health Appraisal of School Children* which mentions only three screening tests of definite and proven value: vision screening, hearing screening, and teacher-nurse conferences or teacher referral on the basis of observations. The discussions, recommendations, and standards for hearing and vision of the joint committee is largely in harmony with Chapters 14 and 15.

TEACHER-NURSE CONFERENCE AND REFERRALS

The school nurse can often be very helpful when children fail to learn to read at a normal rate. In some school districts the child is routinely sent to the nurse for a health conference whenever the child is being considered for placement in remedial reading.

Conferences between teacher and nurse are helpful both before and after the nurse sees the child. The teacher's description of the child's classroom behavior and absences, and her general observations can help the nurse do a much more effective health-counseling job. The nurse, then, working with the physician and other health services, is able to make a thorough screening and referral.

Interestingly, children will often take health suggestions from the school nurse or physician which they would ignore if given by a parent or teacher. Directions on proper eating and sleeping habits, or suggestions to see the family physician frequently, have much more force if they come from the school's medical personnel.

Observant teachers who refer children who "do not look quite right" or who "do not seem to be acting normally" are doing the child as well as the school a favor. Besides being observant of such symptoms, good teachers tend to establish an "acceptance climate" in which the students feel free to confide major or minor health problems. This confidence can contribute to understanding the student and a more accurate referral when that becomes necessary.

GROWTH

Studies of learning difficulty have shown that there are more abnormal growth patterns among underachievers than among normal achievers. Being too short for a given age or being underweight may not seem to be sufficient reasons, in and of themselves, to cause reading failure; but in combination with other symptoms, each can help to explain why normal learning did not take place. The term "multiple causation," which is almost a byword in remedial education circles, means that very frequently there is not a single cause, but usually several, of underachievement. Normal height and weight charts for the school years are illustrated in Appendixes 16-C and 16-D. They will be of help in determining the present status of a child's growth.

Early childhood development in motor skills and speech are also useful in diagnosing growth. For example, if a child is suspected of mental retardation, it is always well to get confirmation by obtaining an individual intelligence test score, especially if the parent says, "He was two years old before he started walking," or, "He didn't talk until he was almost three." Table 16-1 gives some normal developmental stages for motor and speech based on the findings of Gesell and others.

TABLE 16-1
NORMAL EARLY CHILDHOOD BEHAVIOR*

MOTOR DEVELOPMENT	
6 months	Sits momentarily without support if placed in balanced leaning position.
12 months	Walks with help.
15 months	Walks alone.
21 months	Walks backward.
2 years	Runs.
2½ years	Goes up and down stairs alone.
3 years	Draws a circle from copy.
5 years	Draws triangle from copy.
SPEECH DEVELOPMENT	
3 months	Babbling begins (vowel consonant sounds; repeated).
4 months	Shouts.
12 months	Responds to simple commands.
12–14 months	Vocabulary five or six words, mostly nouns.
18 months	Verbs and adjectives added; "good," "give ball."
24 months	Simple sentence including article and pronouns.

*Based on studies summarized in Bernard Berelson and Gary T. Steiner, *Human Behavior*, Harcourt, Brace and World, New York, 1964.

ABSENTEEISM

While it is obvious that children do not always learn at a normal rate if they are not in school, absenteeism may be further diagnostic in that it may point to a chronic health problem or to a problem in the home situation.

The attendance records of all children with reading problems should be routinely checked. If absences are excessive (over 5 percent, or approximately nine days per year), a teacher, nurse, or school counselor should endeavor to find out why and remedy the situation.

BRAIN DAMAGE

The human brain is incredibly complex. There are some 12 billion nerve cells, some of which may have as many as 10,000 different connections. Current research is giving us much insight into the function of the brain. Such factors as neural transmission and areas which are responsible for various motor and psychological functions are becoming better understood, but science still has a long way to go before it will be able to provide us with adequate descriptions and explanations.

Even though our knowledge of normal brain function is inadequate, we still must do our best to deal with abnormal functions. Mental illness and mental retardation have been the subjects of some of man's earliest recorded history, and their direct connection with physiology has been recognized. A blow to the head, a difficult birth, a serious illness have often been recorded as the probable causes of psychological abnormalities. As medical and psychological techniques improve, and as the basic sciences provide tools and insights, we are beginning to recognize more subtle variations of psychological functions and their dependency on physiology.

In this section we will consider the school child who has a mild type of brain damage or neurological malfunction that could be a cause of failure to learn to read normally.

Unfortunately, there are almost as many different terms for this condition as there are investigators. Psychiatrists have contributed much to a clarification of the problem of terminology, but special education experts have made valuable contributions as well. Table 16-2 lists some forty terms that have been used by authorities. In order to facilitate further clarification of terms, and to poke a little fun at those who pompously use big words, I have developed an easy "terminology generator" (Table 16-3) which, with only a little effort, can yield 1,000 different terms with considerable specificity of meaning and degree of involvement. Of course, this does not exhaust the possibilities as additional terms such as Strauss' syndrome, developmental lag, neurophrenia, specific dyslexia, and dozens more could be included.

TABLE 16-2
FORTY WAYS OF SAYING ABOUT THE SAME THING

MINIMAL BRAIN DYSFUNCTION
Association deficit pathology
Organic brain disease
Organic brain damage
Organic brain dysfunction
Minimal brain damage
Diffuse brain damage
Neurophrenia
Organic drivenness
Cerebral dysfunction
Organic behavior disorder
Choreiform syndrome
Minor brain damage
Minimal brain injury
Minimal cerebral injury
Minimal chronic brain syndromes
Minimal cerebral damage
Minimal cerebral palsy
Cerebral dys-synchronization syndrome

Hyperkinetic behavior syndrome
Character impulse disorder
Hyperkinetic impulse disorder
Aggressive behavior disorder
Psychoneurological learning disorders
Hyperkinetic syndrome
Dyslexia
Hyperexcitability syndrome
Perceptual cripple
Primary reading retardation
Specific reading disability
Clumsy child syndrome
Hypokinetic syndrome
Perceptually handicapped
Aphasoid syndrome
Learning disabilities
Conceptually handicapped
Attention disorders
Interjacent child

TABLE 16-3
DO-IT-YOURSELF TERMINOLOGY GENERATOR

Directions: Select any word from Column 1. Add any word from column 2; then add any word from Column 3. If you do not like the result, try again, It will mean about the same thing.

1 Qualifier	2 Area of involvement	3 Problem
Minimal	Brain	Dysfunction
Mild	Cerebral	Damage
Minor	Neurological	Disorder
Chronic	Neurologic	Dissynchronization
Diffuse	C.N.S. (Central Nervous System)	Handicap
Specific	Language	Disability
Primary	Reading	Retardation
Disorganized	Perceptual	Impairment
Organic	Impulse	Pathology
Clumsy	Behavior	Syndrome

The above system will yield 1,000 terms, but if that is not enough you could use specific dyslexia, aphasoid, neurophrenia, or developmental lag.

Personally, I prefer MBD because it could stand for minor brain dysfunction, minimal brain damage, mild brain disorder, or a number of other combinations. Generally, investigators would say that MBD is characterized by:

1. The condition is mild, generalized, and long-standing (chronic). This excludes the more serious forms of dysfunction such as mental retardation, cerebral palsy, and clear-cut aphasia.
2. The condition has a physical cause, and hence it is not primarily an emotional or environmental problem. The exact location of the physical problem is vague; sometimes there is evidence of an actual lesion in the brain or a definite chemical irregularity, but this cannot always be established.

Now consider more serious brain damage; it, too, has a whole host of possible descriptive terms and counterparts which may be related to the symptomotology or cause. For example, "cerebral palsy" is a type of brain damage resulting in poor motor-coordination. "Hemiplegia" describes the symptom when half of the body is paralyzed, whereas a "stroke" describes brain damage caused by the breaking of a blood vessel. Practically all bodily behavior and functions are controlled by the brain, and damage to the brain can be disruptive to any of them.

Brain damage may or may not result in mental retardation, but we shall consider these problems outside our present field of interest. What we wish to understand is what can be done about children whose brain damage is so slight that they have reasonably normal learning ability but who still fail to learn how to read. (Many of the symptoms, causes, and teaching techniques mentioned in this chapter apply also to the brain-damage type [exogenous] of mentally retarded child, since he differs only in degree from the mildly brain-damaged child.)

Not many years ago, most mildly brain-damaged children were thought to be "emotional behavior problems." The term "emotional problem" was bandied about, and many a parent came home from conferences with teachers or counselors or analysts worrying about what she had done wrong in raising her child. Long-suffering parents were advised to examine their own childhood rearing practices, drinking habits, sexual patterns, or sibling rivalries to get at the causes of the child's reading failure. Now that many of the physiological factors are better understood (and this is not to deny that learning failure can be caused by faulty environment), we know that a small percentage of children who have reading difficulties and "emotional problems" are suffering from minimal brain damage. Furthermore, the percentage is growing as recognition techniques improve. Though it is difficult to estimate how many children who fail to learn to read up to expectancy in a regular classroom have MBD, it is probably less than 5 percent, that is, less than one child out of twenty remedial readers.

Teacher's are warned to avoid extremes and to consider each child's problem as an individual case. There is a distinct danger that, once freed from perceiving all behavior problems as outgrowths of emotional problems, teachers may be tempted to diagnose every behavior problem as a symptom of mild brain damage. Maturity in working with children will develop a more knowledgeable, cautious, and sophisticated approach, and a teacher should learn how to avoid bandwagons.

A child with MBD also has the further problem of an "emotional overlay"; that is, his slightly abnormal behavior resulting from physical causes also causes reactions from parents, teachers, and other children; and this, in turn, reacts on him and engenders real emotional disorders.

In other words, reasonable discipline standards should be applied. He should be encouraged, but not forced, to participate in all physical and learning activities, within reasonable limits. Of course, poor mental health results when any child is placed into a situation where he could only fail.

BEHAVIORAL SYMPTOMS The child who is mildly brain damaged (referred to as MBD, which can also stand for "minimal brain damage") exhibits a number of behavioral symptoms which have been reported by various investigators. Not every MBD child has all these symptoms, but they are so common as to merit recognition. In fact, a teacher's recognition of the symptoms is often the first professional awareness of MBD in a child. Parents may have noticed some behavior as being a little strange; unless they report it to a very astute physician, they may be told that "He'll grow out of it." Accurate diagnosis can help the parents' understanding and peace of mind; sometimes medication or specific handling can effectively reduce the symptoms before they become pathological.

1. *Hyperactivity.* Many MBD children are hyperactive, which means that frequently they cannot sit still in the classroom. They are "always into something." The activity will frequently be purposeless or only ephemerally reasonable. Psychologists refer to this symptom as "motor driven" because there seems to be a need for physical motion.

2. *Short attention span.* Associated with or possibly an outgrowth of the child's hyperactivity is his short span of attention to classroom activities (listening, reading, etc.). Short attention span is, of course, characteristic of all younger children. Therefore, this symptom must be judged in relationship to other children of similar mental and chronological age.

3. *Catastrophic reaction.* Catastrophic reaction refers to the MBD child's propensity for overreacting to a situation. For example, if a child does not win a point in a game, he may dissolve in a flood of tears.

4. *Violent mood swings.* Fluctuation in extremes of mood is also a symptom of MBD. For example, a child can go from happy to sad in a relatively short period of time, with very little apparent cause; or he may be calm and peaceful at the beginning of the day and become hostile and belligerent by lunchtime.

5. *Poor coordination.* Poor coordination is another symptom which shows up in games, handwriting, art, or any motor task. MBD children tend to fall

down more often, bump into things and break things more often. Being more clumsy in both gross acts (swinging a baseball bat) and refined motor acts (speaking), they are poor at games and tend to have more speech disorders than normal children.

6. *Overreaction to stimuli.* This is one of the teacher's most disturbing experiences in working with an MBD child. If a fire engine goes past the classroom window or a new person enters the room, an MBD child becomes so excited that he may be literally unable to concentrate the rest of the period. In exciting group games, he sometimes becomes emotionally uncontrollable.

7. *Learning difficulties.* An MBD child may have difficulty in learning, even though his total intelligence score is in the normal range. Reading, almost more than any other subject, seems difficult for him to learn. This could be related to difficulties of perception, as has been shown by some psychological tests. These children are also poor in such other test functions as memory and dealing with abstract symbols, both of which are important factors in reading.

TABLE 16-4
SAMPLE WISC PATTERNS (IQ SUBTEST SCORES) OF ONE NORMAL AND ONE MBD FIFTH-GRADE BOY[a]

WISC PATTERNS			
Subtest		*Wesley*	*Dwight*
Verbal	Information	11	15
	Comprehension	12	18
	Arithmetic	10	5
	Similarities	11	16
	Digit span	10	12
Performance	Picture completion	11	11
	Picture arrangement	10	10
	Block design	11	6
	Object assembly	10	4
	Coding	12	5
	Verbal IQ	105	120
	Performance IQ	106	80
	Full scale IQ (total)	106	104

[a]The same students were tested on the Bender Gestalt (see Figure 16-1). Note that the total IQ scores are nearly the same.

DIAGNOSTIC TESTS The informal observation of a child's classroom behavior, while furnishing important clues, can be greatly improved through the use of more formal inventories. An inventory to assist the teacher in a more systematic evaluation of possible minimum brain damage is presented in Appendix 16-B. Part of it is to be filled out in consultation with a parent, and part from the teacher's own observations. It is to be completed with due caution and with realization that it takes a neurologist to diagnose brain damage. However, the MBD inventory can contribute some insights, especially when it is suspected that referral to a physician or psychologist is indicated.

In addition to behavior-rating scales, school psychologists have a number of techniques to assist them in the diagnosis of MBD. For example, the commonly administered WISC (Wechsler Intelligence Scale for Children) can be helpful if a psychologist looks at the scatter of subtest scores (see Table 16-4). Whenever a number of significant deviations occur on subtest scores, this in itself is reason for suspicion, particularly if the deviate scores are on such subtests as block design and digit span, in which case further examination might be in order.

In general, the greater the deviation, the greater the possibility of brain damage. For example, a theoretically normal child with an IQ of 90 on the total score of the WISC would have an IQ of 90 on the Verbal section and an IQ of 90 on the Performance section, with a subtest score of 9 on each subtest. This almost never happens—there are always some deviations, as was seen in Chapter 14. Subtest deviations of more than 3 points, either above or below the expected level (level expected from the total IQ score) are indications of possible trouble. A spread between Verbal and Performance IQ of more than 20 points is also a possible indication.

For further examination, psychologists frequently use a perception test such as the Bender Gestalt in which the child is shown drawings of abstract figures and asked to copy them. This type of test has an interesting in-out function; namely, a figure such as a rectangle goes into the brain through the eyes and comes out in the form of a drawing. Distortions in perception, memory, and motor skill show up in the drawing. See Figure 16-1 for results from a normal and an MBD Bender Gestalt test. Note that these Benders are for the same children whose WISC scores are reported in Table 16-4.

Another interesting type of test is the Critical Flicker Fusion test in which a light is flashed off and on at a gradually increasing rate. The point at which the flashing light becomes steady is the critical point. MBD children will frequently have a different critical flicker fusion point than normal children. A similar type of test with sound is the Auditory Flicker Fusion. Another interesting sensation test is the Spiral Aftereffects Test in which an Archimedes spiral is rotated while the child looks at it for a minute; then the spiral is stopped. Normal children will usually see an apparent reverse motion of the spiral, whereas some MBD children get no such effect.

Physicians and neurologists have many tests at their disposal. Commonly used is the EEG, or electroencephlograph, which measures tiny electrical currents emitting from the brain; this is a useful diagnostic tool but is not always accurate. A more complicated medical diagnostic test is the pneumoencephlograph, in which the fluid surrounding the brain is altered and an x-ray taken. This test is painful for a child, sometimes requiring several very

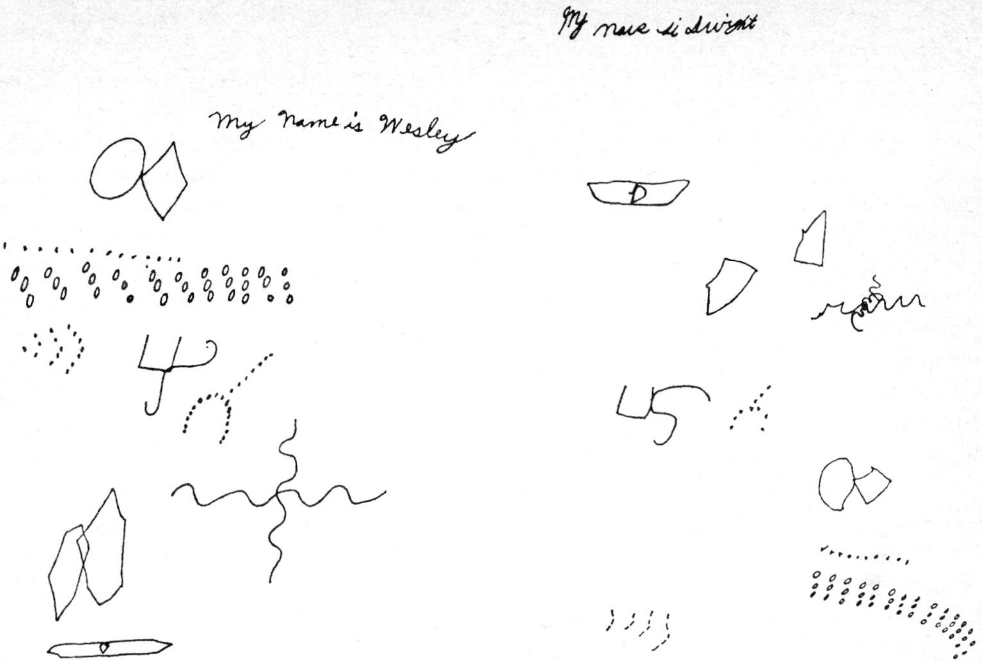

FIGURE 16-1 Bender Gestalt Tests of one normal and one MBD group of fifth grade boys.*

uncomfortable days in the hospital; for this reason it is not used except in serious cases. A newer technique is the echoencephlograph in which high-frequency sound waves are passed through the head so as to reveal a shadowy outline of the brain. All these techniques are difficult to interpret and sometimes do not show evidence of damage even though all the characteristic behavioral symptoms exist.

CAUSES OF BRAIN DAMAGE Interestingly, the cause of some kinds of brain damage may occur long before birth. It is well established that German measles in about the third month of pregnancy can hinder foetal brain development which, if serious, may cause learning difficulties or mental retardation later in life. Any number of serious illnesses or toxins in the mother's system can hinder normal development. Alcoholism, drug addiction, or toxicity caused by drugs can all affect foetal development. The mother can occasionally have serious heart condition which inhibits the flow of oxygen to the foetus; and nearly any serious pathological condition in the mother (pneumonia, tuberculosis, or anemia) can hinder normal development. Less proven but suspected in

*Taken from *Children with Minimal Brain Injury* by Sam Clements, Laura Lihtenen, and Jean Lukens, published by National Society for Crippled Children and Adults, Chicago, 1963. Both boys have the same IQ and are the same age. The task is simply to copy a neat set of drawings from separate cards on a blank piece of paper.

some cases are serious abnormal emotional states of the mother during pregnancy.

Birth is an extremely precarious time for the child. At this time he is very susceptible to minimal brain damage. Prolonged labor (more than fifteen hours) or unusually shortened labor (less than one hour) both tend to result in brain damage. Some authorities feel that a majority of babies are born with some slight brain damage, but slight damage in many areas does not hinder essentially normal development. At the time of birth, a child's skull is not solidly formed and must conform to the shape of the birth canal, at least to some extent. Extremely long labor may mean that the head is having great difficulty in fitting through a small canal, whereas extremely short labor may mean that the head has had to change shape too rapidly. Breach births (the child born in other than a head-first position) tend to contribute to a higher percentage of brain-damaged children. Twin births are also a complicating factor.

Anoxia (lack of oxygen) is another serious cause of brain damage at birth. Brain cells are among the first parts of the body to deteriorate from lack of oxygen. Most authorities are fairly certain that some amount of brain damage occurs within five minutes of being deprived of oxygen; and the longer after that that the brain cells go without oxygen, the more serious and more permanent the damage will be. In the placenta, a child receives oxygen through his umbilical cord which in turn receives it from the mother's blood supply. The blood of mother and baby do not interchange, but there is an oxygen transfer at the point of attachment in the placenta. In a normal birth, a baby continues to receive oxygen from the mother until the umbilical cord is severed; then he must start receiving it through his own lungs. Oxygen flow is stopped or decreased in some abnormal births when the umbilical cord is tangled or when other complications arise which delay the baby's ability to use his own lungs. Anoxia can also be caused at any time in later life from smothering, drowning, temporary heart stoppage, or anything which stops breathing or blood circulation.

Children born prematurely also tend to suffer a higher rate of brain damage. To be on the conservative side, teachers and counselors might consider any child as premature who weighed less than four and one-half pounds at birth or was delivered at the eight month or earlier.

Childhood diseases can also cause brain damage. Most serious of these are various viruses, meningitis (inflammation of the meninges or covering of the spinal cord), or encephalitis (an inflammation of the brain covering). In addition, there are such common diseases as measles or mumps. In general, any fever higher than 103 degrees which lasts for several days and is accompanied by such symptoms as delirium or unconsciousness can affect brain function, either temporarily or permanently.

Uncommon among school children is the type of brain damage that is caused by trauma or severe head blows, as in an automobile or other severe accident. (When a baby crawls off a table and lands head-first on the floor, it is not generally considered a serious accident.) Severe burns or poisons may also cause damage; and some specialists have seen a relationship between severe allergies and abnormal brain function.

There is also a possibility that some brain disorders are hereditary, although this is now thought to be much less common that it was formerly thought to be. Still, in some cases of mental retardation, heredity seems to be the most plausible cause.

Far more boys than girls suffer from MBD. Some studies place the ratio of boys to girls with MBD at 4 to 1 and others as high as 7 to 1. This may be because boys' heads are larger at birth and therefore receive more damage from a small birth canal or quick delivery. Boys are also more prone to inherit such abnormalities as baldness, color blindness, and hemophelia. Boys also have a higher accident rate, a higher rate of mental retardation and insanity, a higher prison rate, and, just to top it all off, higher death rates all through life: at birth, during childhood, and as adults.

ASSOCIATION AREAS OF THE CORTEX An interesting area of physiological research deals with the attempt to identify the specific areas of the brain which are "associated" with the various functions. Many neurologists believe that the cortex functions in some way such as is diagrammed in Figure 16-2. The scheme is of value merely to indicate that research is being undertaken which promises to help in determining the role of the cortex in learning and memory.

TREATMENT AND SPECIAL INSTRUCTION

For most cases of brain damage, especially minor brain damage, there is no cure. Some serious types of brain damage which are caused by blood clots or tumors can be definitely improved by surgery, but these are a small percentage of the cases. There is often some improvement with maturation, and special training can elevate some symptoms.

Some symptoms of MBD can be aided by medication; but most of the real improvement occurs through special teaching, improved environment, and the passage of time (maturation). Small and continuing doses of drugs are sometimes given to improve hyperactivity or hypoactivity. It might be helpful for teachers of MBD children to know that "logical" drugs are not always the best. For example, the behavior of some hyperactive MBD children can be improved by giving them stimulants (amphetimines such as benzedrine). Drugs to increase learning ability have not been successful with humans, but some promising experiments have been conducted on animals.

Classroom or remedial reading teachers will wish to follow all (or, at least, some) of these recommendations for helping the MBD child.

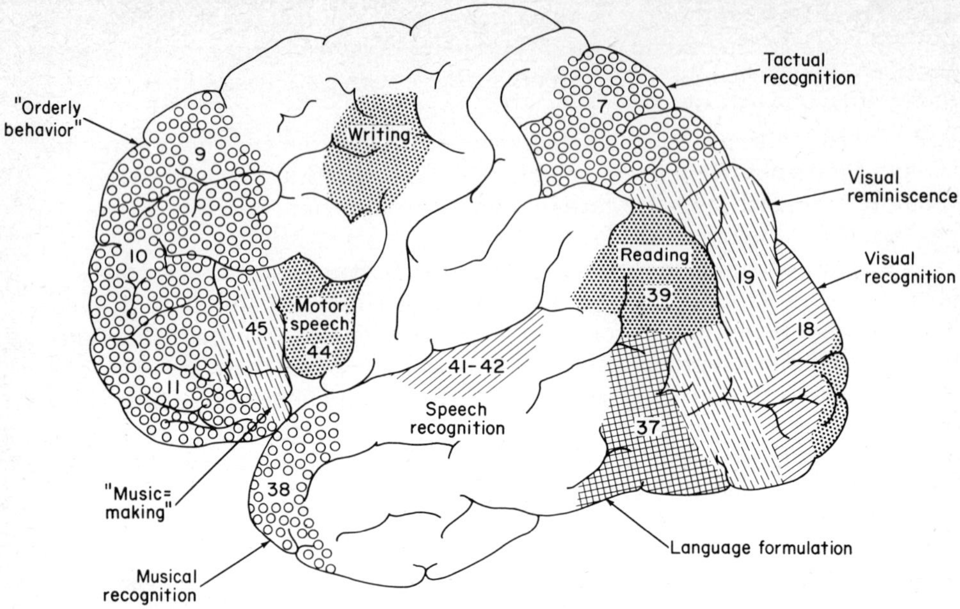

FIGURE 16-2 Diagram of possible association areas of the cerebral cortex. Note. Composite diagram of the supposed "association" areas of the human cerebral cortex. Many neurologists believe that the cortex functions in some such way as indicated; some do not. The scheme is worth while mainly to provide hypotheses for further research and to help in thinking about the role of the cortex in learning and memory.

1. *Improved environment*. Because MBD children are easily distracted, calm rooms and small classes are recommended. Sometimes an MBD child will be provided with an individual work booth, as well as with access to an individual resting place. MBD children tire easily. When they are fatigued they easily become hyperactive. Sending them to a place where they can rest quietly is good both for them and the rest of the class. However, it has been found that "special classes" are not always the best place for "special children." Often better social and academic progress can be made when the child is placed in a regular classroom. Placement should be a matter of careful judgment on the part of the teacher, the principal, the school psychologist, and others involved. Sometimes moving the child from one regular classroom into another is a solution to learning and behavior problems.

2. *Increased individual instruction*. The individualizing of instruction is desirable for several reasons. MBD children frequently do not react well to competition, especially if they are frequently the loser. They also are more inclined to display an irregular pattern of educational development, a situation which individualized instruction helps to correct. Remedial reading instruction is often beneficial.

3. *Increased counseling.* An MBD child needs a greater amount of counseling to help him to adjust socially and to respond maximally to instruction. He frequently gets great consolation from simply being shown that there are other children with similar handicaps and that he is not completely alone or different from everyone else in the class. Counseling with the parent is often just as important as counseling with the child. MBD children also require much more liaison with other special service personnel—the school psychologist, the nurse, the physician; his parents should also be included in this liaison chain.

4. *Special instruction techniques in reading.* Instructional techniques used in teaching the MBD child to read should rely heavily on such special devices as use of the tachistoscope, as described earlier, and frequent use of word cards. Some authorities recommend a phonetic approach to reading, believing that these children do better in part-to-whole learning. Some teachers who specialize with MBD children like to use color emphasis, underlining such details as often-missed short *e* in red. Kinesthetic techniques, too, have been found to be helpful. As a general rule, MBD children profit from almost all educational techniques which are ordinarily used by good remedial reading teachers.

5. *Concrete teaching materials.* Use of concrete (tangible) teaching materials is especially recommended. MBD children like to see real things and touch them. While they are often not skilled at working with wood, clay, and paint, the training in handling these materials is desirable.

6. *A teacher who is carefully selected.* The teacher's understanding of MBD children, their problems, and their needs is important. She must also be cautioned against allowing the child to "perseverate"; that is, a child will repeat an act or a partially correct answer over and over if the teacher does not stop him. The teacher's understanding of a child's catastrophic or other abnormal behavior can help the child and his classmates to accept and to overcome these symptoms. It is amazing how tolerant other children can be if their teacher shows them how.

BODY CHEMISTRY

Closely related to MBD and its many symptoms, including reading failure, are the different types of abnormalities of body chemistry. Body chemistry is a rapidly growing area of knowledge which is of great importance in understanding learning failure. Some types of chemical abnormalities are so closely related to MBD that they can be classified in the same category. Indeed the brain itself is completely dependent on the endocrine system for its normal functioning. The thyroid gland has long been known to be a factor in intelligence and activity. Extreme hypothyroidism results in mental retardation as well as in body deformation. The old saying, "The only difference between a normal child and an idiot is a nickel's worth of iodine," is at least partially true.

Hyperinsulinism is another endocrine glandular dysfunction which results in too much of the body's blood sugar being stored, with the result that the child lacks sufficient energy for learning. This disease, which is the opposite of diabetes, can be detected by means of a six-hour glucose tolerance test and can frequently be cured or largely alleviated by an appropriate diet.

Hans Selye has been investigating for years the "emergency reaction" which is a generalized reaction of the body normally occurring in emergency situations such as preparing for a fight. The emergency reaction is precipitated by a chemical from the adrenal cortex which, in turn, causes an increase in blood sugar, constriction of the blood vessels, dilation of the pupils, slight lessening of reaction to pain, increased alertness, and a number of other symptoms. This condition can be brought on either by an abnormal pathology, a drug (ACTH), or an emotional condition (getting mad). It is a good example of how a state of mind can affect body chemistry, and vice versa.

Though still in a fairly early stage of development, the science of endocrinology may one day be of great assistance to children with learning problems.

Some of those studying body chemistry are also interested in neural-transmission research. When an impulse is sent through a nerve, an electrochemical reaction takes place. Nerve impulses can be measured electrically; but they travel much more slowly than the speed of light, which is the normal electrical transmission rate. A slight chemical change occurs all along the neural pathway, causing a change, part of which is known as the acetylcholine-cholinesterase cycle. Some reading specialists (Smith and Carrigan) have attributed a large number of reading failures and even some specific reading disabilities such as word callers, etc., to a malfunctioning along this chemical cycle. While their research and theories have been criticized by some authorities, they are at least among the first reading specialists bold enough to step into the potentially important field of chemicals involved in neural transmission.

CONCLUDING REMARKS

Much of this chapter is devoted to a discussion of some of the more controversial and pioneering aspects of children's reading problems, for example, those associated with physical problems other than vision and hearing. Numerous serious accidents and illnesses can affect learning; and, as we depart from these into the less certain areas of MBD, hard facts and research agreement become less conclusive. An appendix includes a brief and cogent listing of MBD symptoms (which Shirley calls Chronic Brain Syndromes in his well-known book, *Pediatric Psychiatry*). A more detailed list of symptoms is also presented from a Public Health Service document which synthesizes more than 100 publications and clinically based opinions.

Authorities are not as yet in agreement concerning the treatment and special education needs of MBD children. My opinion is that, whenever possible, they should be left in the regular classroom. When such procedures are needed, children should be given regular remedial reading supplemental instruction. If because of behavior or academic problems, a MBD child cannot fit into a regular classroom, a second regular classroom placement should be tried before assigning him to a small special class.

"Perceptual training" or "directional training" or "physical coordination training" has not been mentioned. This is because I am not convinced, nor has research shown, that these special procedures have much to do with reading improvement. From the standpoint of perceptual training, what is the difference if a child traces or copies a word or a design? When he copies a word, he is at least familiarizing himself with a word and not just some strange geometric design. Left-to-right progression must be made by the eyes when he reads a line of print, so why waste time with left-to-right training procedures that involve arrows or dots? I am certainly not opposed to coordination training, as long as the teacher realizes that it belongs in the physical education period and not in the reading lesson.

A repeated warning: The MBD inventories in Appendixes 16-A and 16-B should be used with great caution. Even well-trained psychologists and neurologists are having difficulty making accurate diagnoses in this area. The teacher should be very, very cautious in voicing an opinion, especially to a parent. This does not mean that a teacher does not have the right to her opinion. Many schools have better vision tests because a remedial teacher, armed with knowledge, demanded better screening procedures. Many have better textbook-ordering procedures and better supplemental reading instruction because a reading teacher, armed with knowledge, helped to get an order through. It just might be that, armed with some knowledge about MBD, a reading teacher may affect some improvement in understanding, diagnosis, and procedural effectiveness. At the very least, some of the knowledge gained from this chapter may help to explain one additional cause of reading failure that is not explainable as "bad teaching" or "emotional problems."

Finally, the Do-It-Yourself Terminology Generator may help the teacher to find her way rationally through the maze of imposing "new" terminology and lingo, which threatens to confound and bewilder us as we seek answers to our very real reading problems.

APPENDIX 16-A MBD PARENT INVENTORY*

Student's name____________________
Date____________________
Informant____________________
Relationship____________________
Examiner____________________
Position____________________

(Abnormal indications are suggestions, not proof, of MBD.)
Place an X under one of these three columns.

	Normal	Moderate	Abnormal
1. Speech defect? Articulatory?_____ Stutter?_____ Present now?_____ Age stopped_____			
2. Age talking began? few words phrases sentences	 12–14 mo. 16–19 mo. 22–26 mo.	 14–15 mo. 20–21 mo. 27–30 mo.	 16 mo. + 23 mo. + 3 yrs.
3. Age walking began?	11–15 mo.	16–18 mo.	19 mo.
4. Length of labor?	2–8 hr.	9–15 hr.	under 1 hr. over 15 hr.
5. Delivery problems?	none	twin Caesarian breech	blue baby high forceps
6. Head misshapen at birth?	slight	some	gross
7. Birth weight?	$5\frac{1}{2}$–10	$4\frac{1}{2}$–$5\frac{1}{2}$ 10–11	under $4\frac{1}{2}$ over 12
8. Gestation period	within 3 weeks	off 3–4 weeks	off 1 mo. + or −

*By Edward Fry, Reading Center, Rutgers University.

	Normal	Moderate	Abnormal
9. Infant behavior: indicate degree of unusualness for sleep pattern, feeding, vomiting, crying, head banging, slow weight gain, apathy. (underline symptom)			
10. Childhood health? High fever: cause______ ____________________			over 103° for 3 days
11. Childhood behavior? Rapid or violent mood swings			
Restlessness (never still)			
Ride a bike and/or skate			
Memory (very bad or spotty)			
Sleep	$8\frac{1}{2}$ hrs. seldom waking at night		
Age bed wetting stopped completely	$1\frac{1}{2}$–3 yrs.	3–5 yrs.	over 5
Unhappy	seldom	often	always
Friends		very few	none
Irritable			
Logical: gets confused			
Discipline acceptance		often complains	can't accept
Coordination in sports			

	Normal	Moderate	Abnormal
12. Vision? Rapid change in acuity		1 yr.	instant or mos.
Double vision	never	fleeting	sustained or often
13. Hearing? Perception (misunderstands)	seldom	frequent	usually

APPENDIX 16-B MBD TEACHER OBSERVATIONS

Student's name____________________
Date____________________
Student's class____________________
School____________________
Age____________________
Teacher____________________

Directions: If you are not too familiar with the child, read this observation sheet carefully; then observe child. Compare his behavior with a number of other children. It will be more accurate if you do only a few sections at a time.

Place an X under one of these three columns.

	Normal for age (CA)	Like a younger child	Moderately abnormal	Definitely abnormal
1. SPEECH General development and vocabulary size				
Articulation problems: Slurring?_____ Omits sounds?_____ Can't pronounce some sounds?_____	almost none	almost none		
Stuttering?_____ Stammering?_____	almost none	almost none		
2. MOTOR COORDINATION Walking coordination				
Running coordination				
Throwing ball				
Handwriting (put sample in file)				
Drawing				
3. ACADEMIC Reading ability – general				
oral reading				

	Normal for age (CA)	Like a younger child	Moder-ately abnormal	Defi-nitely abnormal
phonics				
comprehension				
Arithmetic				
Can hold logical discussion				
Can learn abstract concepts				
Can learn new motor skills				
Uses words correctly				
Story writing				
4. BEHAVIOR Attention span				
Work habits over several weeks (reasonably constant or erratic)				
Mood swings (from tranquil to happy, sad, excited)				
Perseverance (repeats a task over and over with-out good reason)				
Destructive: His own things?______ Others' property?______				
Fights: physical aggression?______ Verbal?______				
Friends				
Will follow directions				

APPENDIX 16-C PHYSICAL GROWTH RECORD FOR GIRLS*

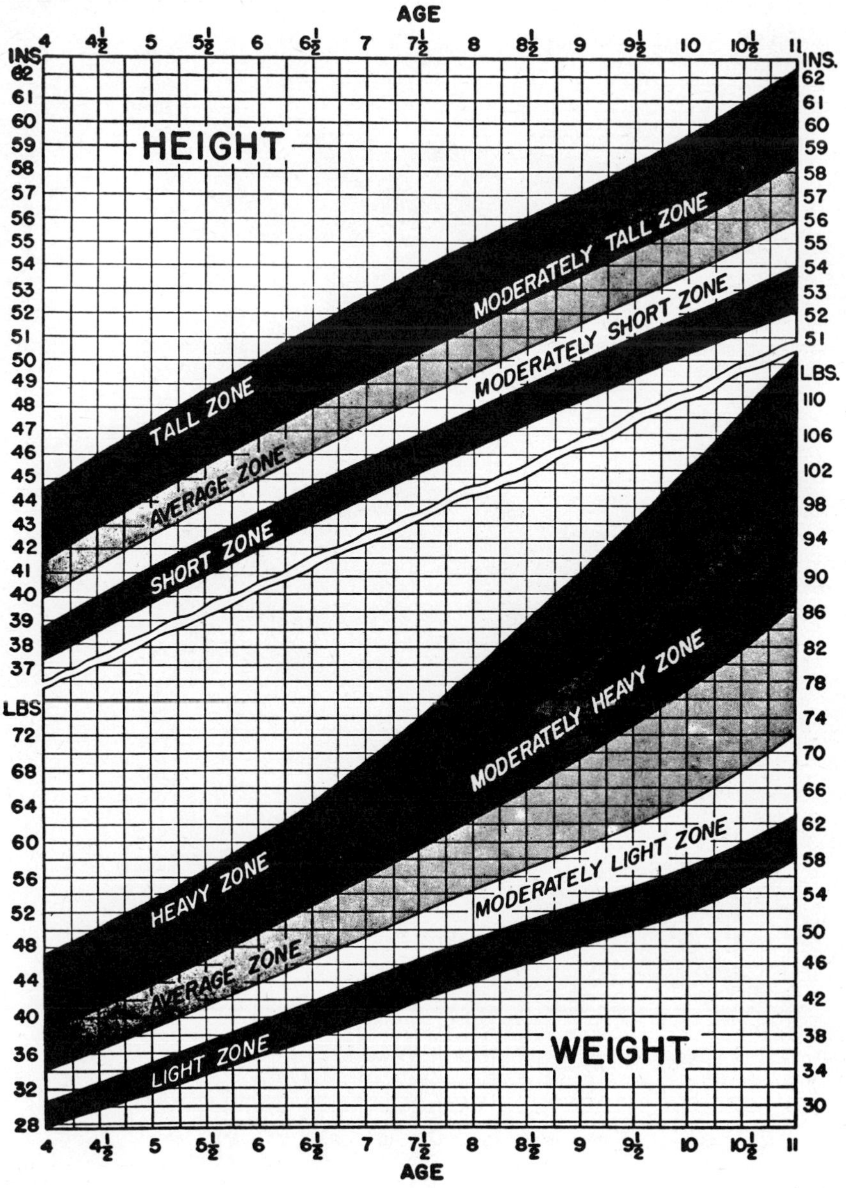

*Prepared by the Joint Committee on Health Problems in Education of the NEA and AMA, using data prepared by Howard V. Meredith, State University of Iowa.

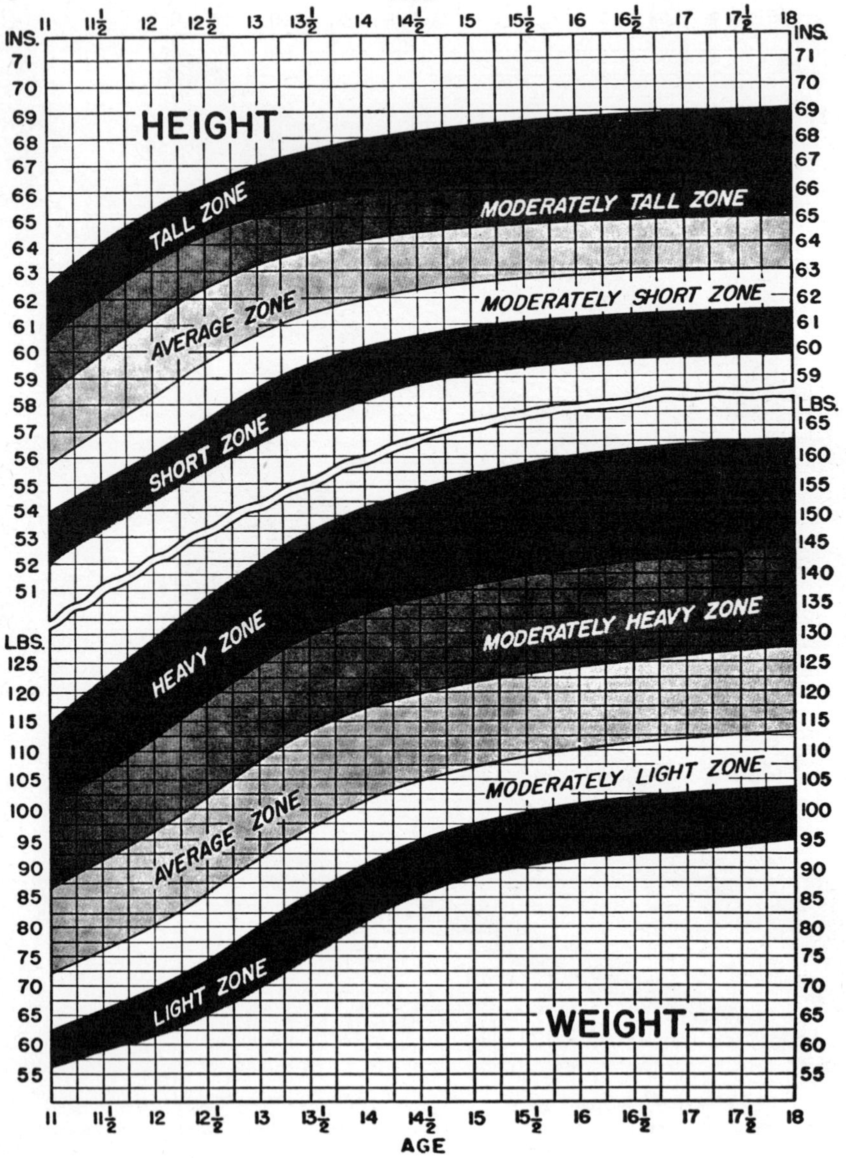
AGE
11 11½ 12 12½ 13 13½ 14 14½ 15 15½ 16 16½ 17 17½ 18
INS.
71 70 69 68 67 66 65 64 63 62 61 60 59 58 57 56 55 54 53 52 51
HEIGHT
TALL ZONE
MODERATELY TALL ZONE
AVERAGE ZONE
MODERATELY SHORT ZONE
SHORT ZONE
LBS.
165 160 155 150 145 140 135 130 125 120 115 110 105 100 95 90 85 80 75 70 65 60 55
HEAVY ZONE
MODERATELY HEAVY ZONE
AVERAGE ZONE
MODERATELY LIGHT ZONE
LIGHT ZONE
WEIGHT
11 11½ 12 12½ 13 13½ 14 14½ 15 15½ 16 16½ 17 17½ 18
AGE

APPENDIX 16-D PHYSICAL GROWTH RECORD FOR BOYS*

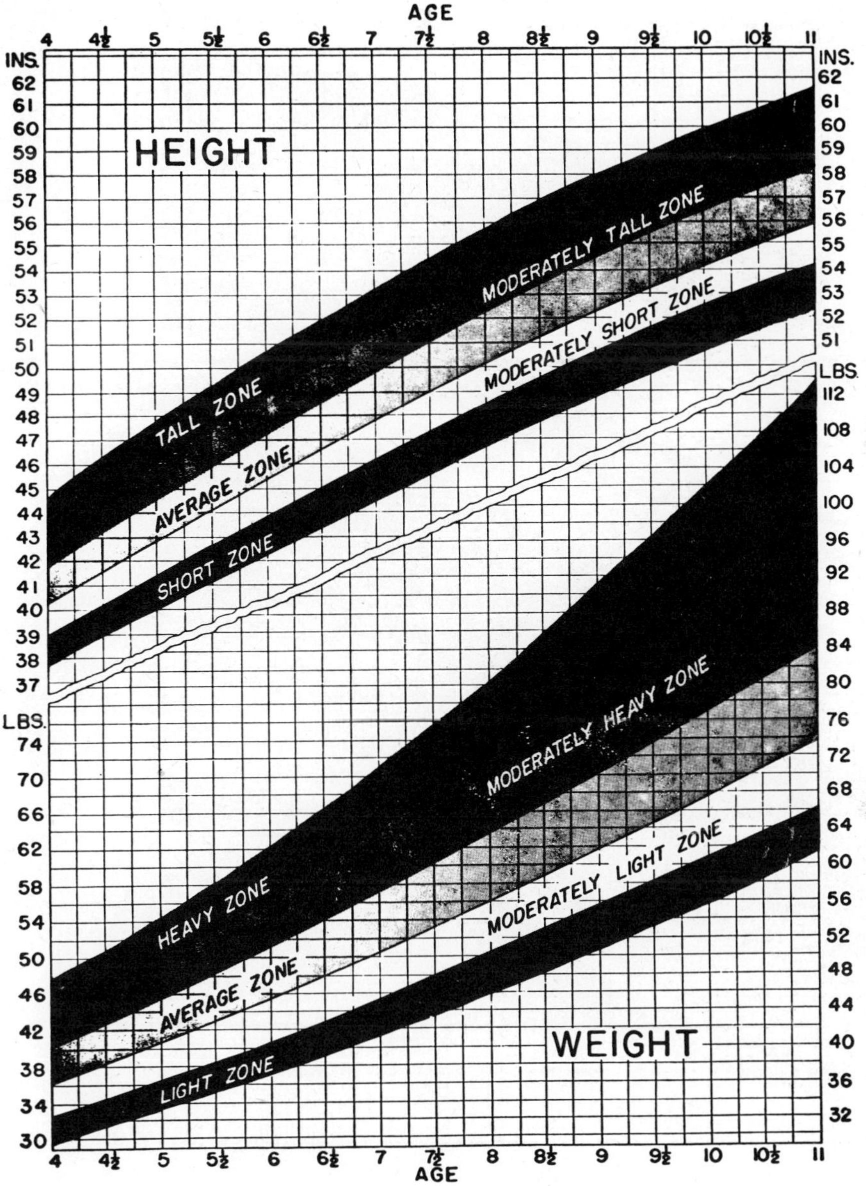

*Prepared by the Joint Committee on Health Problems in Education of the NEA and AMA, using data prepared by Howard V. Meredith, State University of Iowa.

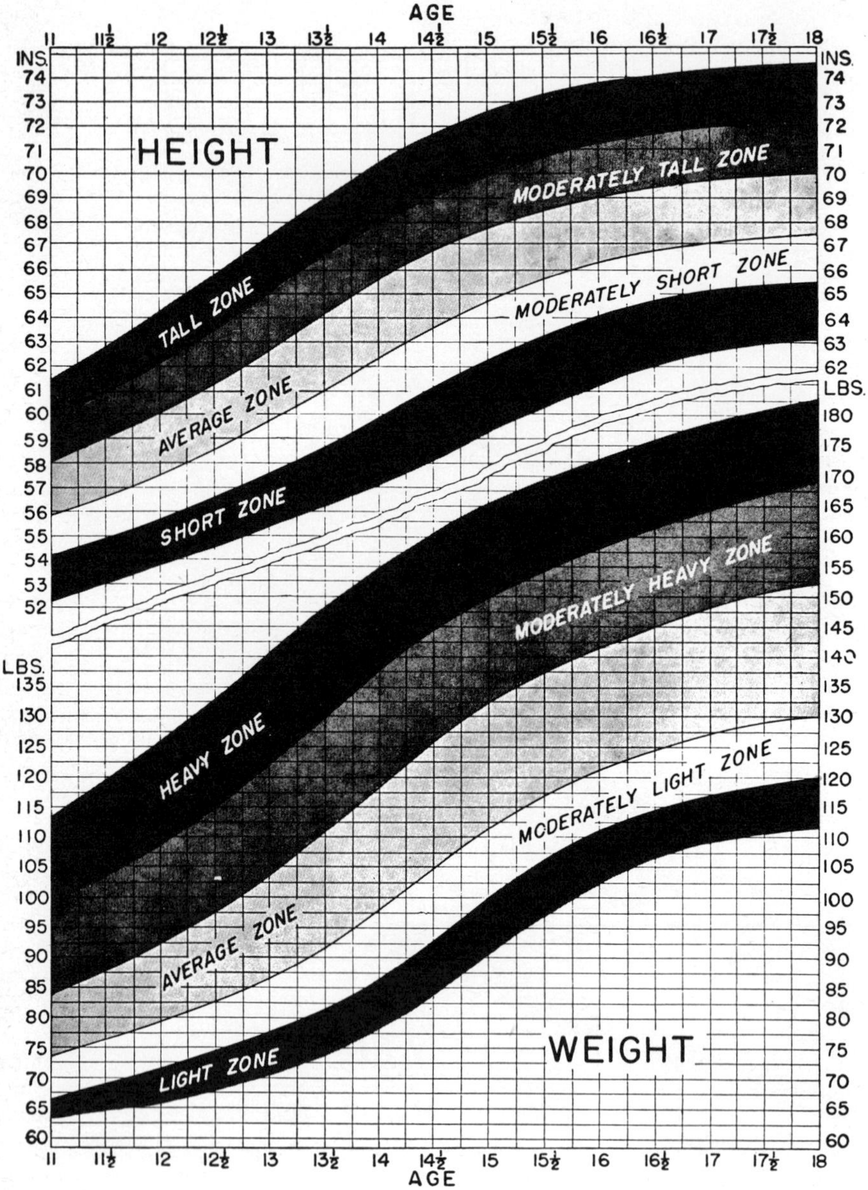
AGE
HEIGHT
TALL ZONE
MODERATELY TALL ZONE
AVERAGE ZONE
MODERATELY SHORT ZONE
SHORT ZONE
INS.
LBS.
HEAVY ZONE
MODERATELY HEAVY ZONE
AVERAGE ZONE
MODERATELY LIGHT ZONE
LIGHT ZONE
WEIGHT

APPENDIX 16-E CHRONIC BRAIN SYNDROMES*

Chronic brain syndromes result from permanent, more or less irreversible, diffuse impairment of cerebral tissue function. They may be mild, moderate, or severe, and the severity of the syndrome is generally parallel to the severity of the impairment of brain-tissue function. The type of symptomatology depends upon the location and extensiveness as well as upon the severity of the brain damage. Superimposed upon the basic syndrome may be behavioral, personality, neurotic, and psychotic disorders.

The basic syndromes may be characterized by any degree and combination of the following functional impairments:

1. Any degree of mental retardation or deficiency
2. Impairment of intellectual functions
   a. Perception
   b. Comprehension
   c. Orientation
   d. Memory
   e. Learning
   f. Thinking
   g. Judgment
3. Impairment of ability to persist in effort toward a goal
   a. Short attention span
   b. Distractibility
   c. Impulsiveness
   d. Lack of impulse control
4. Impairment of emotional reactions
   a. Inability to respond appropriately
   b. Emotional lability
   c. Lack of emotional control
5. Sensory defects
   a. Visual
   b. Auditory
   c. Tactile
   d. Kinesthetic
6. Motor disabilities
   a. Spastic paralysis
   b. Athetosis
   c. Dystonia
   d. Choreiform movements
   e. Myoclonic movements
   f. Tremors
   g. Hyperkinesis
   h. Hypokinesis
7. Convulsive states

*From Hale F. Shirley, M.D., *Pediatric Psychiatry*, Harvard University Press, Cambridge, Mass., 1963.

BEHAVIORAL SYNDROME ASSOCIATED WITH BRAIN DAMAGE IN CHILDREN

The behavior of a child with brain damage is the result not only of the structural changes or deficits and the consequent disordered physiological action of the damaged cerebral areas themselves but also of (1) the disorganizing effect of the lesion upon the functioning of the brain as a whole; (2) the endowment of the child and the level of development he has achieved at the time of the injury; (3) the way the child comes to feel about himself and the defenses or compensations he learns to use in response to his handicaps; and (4) the social influences which come to bear upon him, particularly the reactions of his parents and teachers to his handicaps and to him as a handicapped child and his reactions to their management of him. The biological defect influences the child's maturational development, his personality structure, and his relationship to his environment. To understand the child's behavior, therefore, we must always take into consideration the reciprocal interaction of the biological, psychological, and environmental forces.

APPENDIX 16-F IDENTIFYING THE MBD CHILD*

In a search for symptoms attributed to children with minimal brain dysfunctioning, over 100 recent publications were reviewed.

Many different terms were used to describe the same symptom, e.g., excessive motor activity for age might be referred to as any one of the following: hyperactivity, hyperkinesis, organic drivenness, restlessness, motor obsessiveness, fidgetiness, motor disinhibition, or nervousness. . . .

The following represents an attempt to classify some of the descriptive elements culled from the literature.

PRELIMINARY CATEGORIES OF SIGNS AND SYMPTOMS

A. *Test Performance Indicators*

1. Spotty or patchy intellectual deficits. Achievement low in some areas; high in others.
2. Below mental-age level on drawing tests (man, house, etc.).
3. Geometric figure drawings poor for age and measured intelligence.
4. Poor performance on block-design and marble-board tests.
5. Poor showing on group tests (intelligence and achievement) and daily classroom examinations which require reading.
6. Characteristic subtest patterns on the Wechsler Intelligence Scale for Children, including "scatter" within both Verbal and Performance Scales; high Verbal-low Performance; low Verbal–high Performance.

*From Sam D. Clements, *Minimal Brain Dysfunction in Children*, Public Health Service Publication No. 1415, U.S. Government Printing Office, Washington, D.C., 1966.

B. *Impairments of Perception and Concept-formation*

1. Impaired discrimination of size.
2. Impaired discrimination of right-left and up-down.
3. Impaired tactile discriminations.
4. Poor spatial orientation.
5. Impaired judgment of distance.
8. Impaired discrimination of figure-ground.
9. Impaired discrimination of part-whole.
10. Frequent perceptual reversals in reading and in writing letters and numbers.
11. Poor perceptual integration. Child cannot fuse sensory impressions into meaningful entities.

C. *Specific Neurologic Indicators*

1. Few, if any, apparent gross abnormalities.
2. Many "soft," equivocal, or borderline findings.
3. Reflex assymetry frequent.
4. Frequency of mild visual or hearing impairments.
5. Strabismus (poor eye balance or cross-eyed).
6. Nystagmus (eyeballs twitch).
7. High incidence of left and mixed laterality and confused perception of laterality.
8. Hyperkinesis (overactive).
9. Hypokinesis (underactive).
10. General awkwardness.
11. Poor fine visual-motor coordination.

D. *Disorders of Speech and Communication*

1. Impaired discrimination of auditory stimuli.
2. Various categories of aphasia.
3. Slow language development.
4. Frequent mild hearing loss.
5. Frequent mild speech irregularities.

E. *Disorders of Motor Function*

1. Frequent athetoid, choreiform, tremulous, or rigid movements of hands.
2. Frequent delayed motor milestones.
3. General clumsiness or awkwardness.
4. Frequent tics and grimaces.
5. Poor fine or gross visual-motor coordination.
6. Hyperactivity.
7. Hypoactivity.

F. *Academic Achievement and Adjustment* (Chief complaints about the child by his parents and teachers)

1. Reading disabilities.
2. Arithmetic disabilities.
3. Spelling disabilities.
4. Poor printing, writing, or drawing ability.

5. Variability in performance from day to day or even hour to hour.
6. Poor ability to organize work.
7. Slowness in finishing work.
8. Frequent confusion about instructions, yet success with verbal tasks.

G. *Disorders of Thinking Processes*

1. Poor ability for abstract reasoning.
2. Thinking generally concrete
3. Difficulties in concept-formation.
4. Thinking frequently disorganized.
5. Poor short-term and long-term memory.
6. Thinking sometimes autistic.
7. Frequent thought perseveration.

H. *Physical Characteristics*

1. Excessive drooling in the young child.
2. Thumb-sucking, nail-biting, head-banging, and teeth-grinding in the young child.
3. Food habits often peculiar.
4. Slow to toilet train.
5. Easy fatigability.
6. High frequency of enuresis.
7. Encopresis.

I. *Emotional Characteristics*

1. Impulsive.
2. Explosive.
3. Poor emotional and impulse control.
4. Low tolerance for frustration.
5. Reckless and uninhibited; impulsive, then remorseful.

J. *Sleep Characteristics*

1. Body- or head-rocking before falling asleep.
2. Irregular sleep patterns in the young child.
3. Excessive movement during sleep.
4. Sleep abnormally light or deep.
5. Resistance to naps and early bedtime, e.g., seems to require less sleep than average child.

K. *Relationship Capacities*

1. Peer-group relationship generally poor.
2. Overexcitable in normal play with other children.
3. Better adjustment when playmates are limited to one or two.
4. Frequently poor judgment in social and interpersonal situations.
5. Socially bold and aggressive.
6. Inappropriate, unselective, and often excessive displays of affection.
7. Easy acceptance of others alternating with withdrawal and shyness.
8. Excessive need to touch, cling, and hold on to others.

L. *Variations of Physical Development*

1. Frequent lags in developmental milestones, e.g., motor, language, etc.
2. Generalized maturational lag during early school years.
3. Physically immature; or
4. Physical development normal or advanced for age.

M. *Characteristics of Social Behavior*

1. Social competence frequently below average for age and measured intelligence.
2. Behavior often inappropriate for situation, and consequences apparently not foreseen.
3. Possibly negative and aggressive to authority.
4. Possibly antisocial behavior.

N. *Variations of Personality*

1. Overly gullible and easily led by peers and older youngsters.
2. Frequent rage reactions and tantrums when crossed.
3. Very sensitive to others.
4. Excessive variation in mood and responsiveness from day to day and even hour to hour.
5. Poor adjustment to environmental changes.
6. Sweet and even-tempered, cooperative, and friendly (most commonly the so-called hypokinetic child).

O. *Disorders of Attention and Concentration*

1. Short attention span for age.
2. Overly distractible for age.
3. Impaired concentration ability.
4. Motor or verbal perseveration.
5. Impaired ability to make decisions, particularly from many choices.

17

EMOTIONAL PROBLEMS AND COUNSELING

During the 1930s and 1940s many teachers were prone to see a psychological problem lurking behind every reading failure. The unsuspecting parent who called at the school to find out why his child was not reading well was told, either directly or in carefully guarded jargon, that the child undoubtedly had some deep-seated psychological problem. A reputable psychologist or psychiatrist would have blushed at the rapidity with which diagnoses of psychological or family ills were handed out by teachers and counselors who, with the best of intentions, were unaware of the damage they may have perpetrated.

Since those decades, praise be, counselors have learned when and how to refer children who have emotional problems to the appropriate specialists; and reading teachers have learned that if they stick to the teaching of reading and let the school psychologist or psychiatrist worry about emotional problems, both children and parents will benefit. Most children who demonstrate normal learning ability on any standard intelligence test can learn to read, whether they have emotional problems or not.

This chapter, then, is not intended to qualify the reading teacher as a junior-grade psychiatrist. Its concern is that the teacher gain an understanding of emotional problems and their relationship to remedial programs.

Remedial reading teachers should not usually reject a

child because of known or suspected psychological problems. The major valid reasons for excluding a child from remedial reading are that his intelligence is too low or he already knows how to read up to or close to his expected level. Once admitted to remedial reading, a child should be treated with kindness and respect, whether or not he has an emotional problem.

There are, of course, seriously mentally disturbed children who are psychotic (insane) or nearly psychotic who cannot learn anything, but these children usually have other behavioral symptoms which exclude them from the public schools; or if they are in school, they have been brought to the attention of a psychologist or physician. However, even psychotic children can often benefit from good remedial reading instruction. In fact in most mental hospitals remedial reading is considered a very important part of therapy.

All learning is more efficient if a child begins at a level where he can experience success. Hence the reading teacher's chief diagnostic tool should be a reading test, not a personality test. If a child's behavior is normal enough so that he can attend school, he can usually learn to read, at least a little, in a remedial reading situation.

Remedial teachers must be extremely careful that the reading classroom does not become a dumping ground for all the emotional problems in the school. They should accept children only if they have reading problems. Unfortunately, some classroom teachers will claim that a child has a reading problem on no other grounds than that he is a disturbing element in the room. Remedial teachers should accept disruptive children only if they otherwise qualify for remedial reading. If once they accept children who can read normally but who are behavior problems, the effectiveness of the teaching situation is greatly diminished for all the other children. It is quite important that the school administrator understands this and is willing to support the reading teacher in her insistence that the classroom teacher not refer a troublesome child merely to get rid of him.

Reading teachers should also be careful not to confuse kindness and psychotherapy with lack of discipline. Some children simply need to be told firmly to be quiet and pay attention to their work. It is true that if the work is interesting and at the right level, it will be much easier to get a child's attention; but some children simply have bad work habits and need the exterior discipline of the teacher in order to settle down. Reading instruction should be thought of as a privilege. Students who do not want to cooperate with the teacher should have the privilege withdrawn. However, in dealing with children, there are no absolutes; hence, the teacher who is continually demanding discipline or asking children to leave is probably doing a bad job of teaching.

STANDARDS OF NORMALITY

One real advantage that a teacher gains with experience is the knowledge of what is normal child behavior for a given age. Parents suffer from the usual situation of having one child at a time or, at the most, only several in one age group. Parents do not have adequate standards of comparison for their children's behavior, and often the memory of their own childhood is clouded or colored with wishful thinking. Teachers, on the other hand, see a number of children at the same developmental stage and get a better picture of normal behavior. Even with children whose behavior is slightly abnormal, a teacher learns with experience what abnormalities fall within the usual range. Hence, what may appear to a parent or an inexperienced teacher as abnormal behavior, falls into perspective to a more experienced teacher as only a slight irregularity. Parents or teachers who themselves may have some emotional problems may notice some distortion of behavior, and they may suspect that children's slight behavior deviations are more serious emotional problems.

Standardized reading and intelligence tests are all based on mean behavior for a given chronological age. They are simply more formal ways of stating normal behavior for a child of a certain age. While there are behavior-rating scales for general and emotional behavior, they are frequently so vague and generalized that they are not useful to teachers.

PARENT COUNSELING

There are at least two fundamental rules in parent counseling. The first is that a teacher should probably listen more than she talks; the second is that she should always say something good about the child.

In amplification of the listen-more-and-talk-less rule, it is based on the simple fact that a teacher will make fewer misstatements if she talks less. Moreover, an important part of every parent-counseling session is the opportunity for a teacher to get to learn more about the child than she is able to find out by direct observation in the classroom. A parent can often explain things that the teacher is unable to discover.

A teacher will sometimes feel compelled to do all or most of the talking, perhaps due to nervousness or to unfamiliarity with the parent-counseling situation. She should cultivate the art of encouraging parents to talk. Several standard techniques for doing this are:

1. Allow lapses in the conversation – some parents are slow to respond, and allowing them time to reply or even change the subject is important.
2. End the interview with, "Is there anything else you would like to tell me about Johnny?"
3. Some parents can use up more than their allotted time; and in these situations, an ending time can be announced, such as, "I have only two minutes before my next appointment."

If parents are having a conference because of a problem situation, it is also well to let them discuss briefly the fact that "their other child never had this problem." All parents like to save face and show that they are not doing such a bad job of raising children. One way they do this is to show that the brother or sister of this particular child does not have a problem. While it is certainly the better part of valor to have parents establish this fact, a teacher should not let too much of the valuable counseling time be wasted by parents who simply want the warmth and security of talking about their other child. Parents sometimes wish to avoid discussing the painful problem of their failing child; a teacher must sometimes say something like, "Yes, I am glad Mary is doing so well, but we are really here to talk about Johnny and see if we can help him."

In a parent interview, it is often helpful to learn about the family constellation. It is sometimes very revealing to find out how many people are living in the home, what their ages are, and what interests they have.

Teachers should use caution in inserting statements in a child's file about home conditions, particularly since in many states the courts have held that a child's folder is public information or, at least, available to parents on demand. Likewise, in transmitting information to psychologists or clinics, particularly if they are outside of the school system, extreme caution should be exercised in voicing any opinions about home conditions. Fact is one thing, but conjecture is another. For example, it is appropriate to say, "Mother reports that father is only home one night a week," but it is dangerous to say, "Home conditions seem very bad and there is a possibility of divorce."

Teachers should also be cautious in giving test results. Our culture has placed a strange emphasis on IQ test scores; and because they are variable from day-to-day and test-to-test, as well as difficult to interpret, exact IQ scores should usually not be given. For example, one parent may report to another at a PTA meeting that her child has an IQ of 103, and the other parent is depressed because her poor child only has an IQ of 99. A teacher knows that, had these tests been given on another day, statistical chance might have reversed the scores. All teachers should know that IQ tests vary considerably from test to test. A child who receives a score of 118 on one test might very possibly receive a score of 127 on another test. It is very difficult to explain this to parents, especially when the blunt fact is that the measurement of intelligence is something less than an exact science. On the other hand, teachers are justified in making statements that a child seems "a little above normal" or "a little below normal"; but if a child is "way above" or "way below" normal, this report should be given only on the basis of several tests, preferably one of which is an individually administered test.

Even though it is not wise to give exact IQ scores, neither is it honest to give misleading information nor to withhold information that could be useful to parents in planning for their child's future. For example, it frequently happens than an interview is scheduled with a parent whose child is simply a little below normal intelligence. Let us say that the child has an IQ of 90. A glance at the test shows that it seems reasonably regular; for example, the child seems to have answered questions up to his level of difficulty, and there is not too great a spread between language and nonlanguage sections of the test. And, just to make the situation a little more difficult, the parent is insisting that the child must try harder in school to get better grades so that he can get into a university. The teacher is being less than professional if she does not say something like, "our tests and the child's performance in school indicate that he is not suited to the type of academic work required of university students." For, even if the child did succeed in getting into the university, which is doubtful, the chances are that he would not complete his work. The teacher could honestly and safely advise, "Perhaps you should consider some alternate career or educational plan." In doubtful situations it is best to qualify the statement by saying something like, "Of course this was only one test and I only have his grades for one year, and this might not be a true indication of his potential. We will test him again next year and watch his academic work; but, in the meantime, there are the facts, and it is better to tell them to you than to keep them from you."

Probably the most dishonest thing a teacher can do is to give parents false hopes by handing out some old placebo: "He'll grow out of it," or "If we would only try harder he could make the university." Such statements as these can sometimes cause eager parents to put real pressure on a child to achieve academically; in fact, sometimes they apply so much pressure that a normal, happy child with an IQ of 90 becomes a very unhappy child with a real emotional problem – and an IQ of 90.

The problem of low IQ becomes more critical as the IQ gets lower. With IQ's below 90 on group tests, the group test should be backed up with an individual intelligence test, possibly the WISC (Wechsler Intelligence Scale for Children) or the Stanford-Binet. These tests are usually given by the school psychologist who often follows it up with a parent-counseling session. It is important that a teacher support whatever the psychologist reports and that she not try to comfort the parent with remarks such as: "Those IQ tests don't mean much. I had a boy in my class last year who . . ." Yes, IQ tests are sometimes wrong, but they are not wrong nearly as often as a parent or an uninformed teacher who thinks, or hopes, that a child will "grow out of" his low IQ. He will not. And this need not be a cause for alarm or unhappiness if he and his parents are given counseling help in planning for realizable goals.

Hence, report the results of IQ tests to parents. Report them with caution, but do report them. Never report them in exact numbers but, rather, in general terms. This is the way that IQ tests are designed to be used, namely, as good indicators of possible future academic progress.

Reading scores are not as socially sensitive as IQ scores, and some school districts adopt the policy of telling parents the exact reading grade-placement scores. Other districts prefer that the teacher make a more general statement, such as "The child is a little above where we expect him to be," or "The child is reading below his expected level." A more middle-course style of reading grade-placement reporting would be, "The child is two years below where we expect him to be."

Some parents are very hard to convince. Few are satisfied when their children are achieving "normally." Most think that their little darling should be doing much better than average and that the school is remiss for not teaching him better or placing him in a class where he can get special help. This type of parents can sometimes be mollified by being invited to sit in on a class during a regular reading session and letting them listen to their child read with his peers. If the case involves a child who is below normal in intelligence, allowing the parents to observe samples of their child's writing or arithmetic, speech, and other behaviors in comparison with other children of the same age may help to convince them that their child is not on a par with some of the others.

Although school districts differ on the policy of encouraging parents to help their children at home, most now lean toward encouraging parents to assist their children – unless, of course, it is obvious that too much pressure is already being put on a child. With some parents, a teacher may find it helpful to duplicate Appendix 17-A, Reading Suggestions for Parents, and hand it to them as part of the counseling interview.

Finally it is a good idea to end the parent conference on an "upbeat." Say something good about the child. Perhaps the child is well liked by other children, perhaps he is excellent in baseball or art. Maybe he contributed something excellent in social studies recently or was helpful in a student activity. Any teacher who cannot find something good about a child – no matter how obstreperous – probably should not be teaching. Get into the habit of looking for something good in every child, even if you do not expect his parents to show up for an interview.

Parents sometimes simply need information about reading. For example, they might be informed that phonics will not cure every remedial problem or that there is no evidence that ITA causes reading failure. Even straightforward normative information is often very helpful: Since most magazines and newspapers are written at an eighth grade or slightly higher level, most sixth graders could be expected to have difficulty in reading most articles. The suggestions for parents in Appendix 17-A of this chapter can provide further counseling help.

EMOTIONAL PROBLEMS

A number of causes for reading failure have been mentioned: poor teaching, poor home environment, poor vision, poor hearing, and MBD. It is time now to stop avoiding the issue of emotional problems and state that they, too, can cause reading failure. The chief difficulty is that in young children it is almost impossible to classify emotional problems clearly. Usually the adult mental-illness categories of neurotic, paranoid, schizophrenic, etc. either do not apply or are not usable in a school situation. One should be very careful about saying that a child who is misbehaving and has failed to learn to read is a neurotic.

But a teacher can state that a child's behavior pattern is definitely not normal. She will have the psychologist and psychiatrist decide to classify him. There is some possibility that it will not make too much difference however a child is classified, as anyone who has struggled through the verbiage and hypothecations of some psychological reports would agree. However, there are times when a psychologist's report gives excellent insight into past and present actions of the child and indicates what to expect in the future. However, it is often found that two reports on one child from two different psychologists may disagree on what type of therapy or remediation procedures should be pursued. Some of the therapy techniques currently being used on children include: play therapy, both individually and group, crisis counseling, activity therapy, behavior modification therapy (use of rewards), filial therapy (family) life-space interviewing, child study teams, interaction analysis, as well as more traditional talk therapies as advocated by such varied authorities as Freud, Horni, Rodgers, and others.

A major problem has been the inability to assess with any degree of accuracy the therapeutic value of the therapy. That is, if we were to divide a group of 100 children who need "therapy" into two groups and then give therapy to one group and none to the other, it would be very difficult to detect an observable difference between the two groups. Therapists, on the other hand, offer individual cases that have shown remarkable improvement as evidence. Hence, remedial reading programs in most schools do not include psychotherapy except on a referral basis for a few special cases.

With adults, one type of therapy that has definitely lowered the population of mental hospitals is chemotherapy, using various types of tranquilizers and energizers. Drugs are used to control or modify behavior of children with purely emotional problems as well as MBD cases. Drugs, of course, can only be used upon advice of a medical doctor.

An emotional problem may be related to reading problems in any of three different ways:

1. *An emotional problem can be caused by the reading problem.* Because a child cannot read, he may exhibit any of a number of symptoms of emotional problems, such as bed-wetting, temper tantrums, lack of interest in anything.

2. *An emotional problem can be concurrent with reading problems.* In other words, it is not at all uncommon for counselors to see children who have multiple problems; a drunken father, poor vision, a reading problem, a discipline problem, and a tendency toward frequent colds. Perhaps all these problems are interrelated so that it is difficult to tell which came first. Without trying too hard to determine first causes, let us at least recognize that concurrence occurs frequently—that some children just seem to have all the bad luck.

3. *Emotional problems can cause reading problems.* This statement is put last in this series of three, and it is intentionally inserted late in the book because it has been so misunderstood and misapplied by teachers. It is believed that teachers will make fewer mistakes if they first rule out such possible

factors as mental retardation, minimum brain damage, hearing, vision and other physical problems, poor environment, and poor education before seeking a solution in the concept that an emotional problem probably caused a reading problem.

Personally, I think that great strides will be made in improving or curing emotional problems in the next few decades. I would expect the most promising results to come from endocrinology and learning theory (backed by experimental evidence). However, there is a possibility that some of the other personality or "talk therapy" schools will also make significant contributions.

Endocrinology, a subtle and delicate science, has already verified that an extremely small amount of a chemical secreted from one of the endocrine glands can cause very definite behavioral and learning changes. Malfunction of the thyroid can certainly cause mental retardation and serious concomitant learning problems. Secretions of the pancreas can certainly cause serious decreases in the energy level. Other endocrine malfunctions and very tiny amounts of foreign substances can cause definite changes in perception of reality (under LSD, for example, still pictures may appear to be moving pictures). We have every reason to believe that with the help of radioactive trace elements, computer analysis of results, improved knowledge of cell structure, and other approaches, there will be significant advances in both real cures and substantial symptom improvement of emotional problems. And, since our interest is in reading, we may expect real help from many sciences and technologies with children who have remedial reading problems.

Learning theory thus far has not contributed a great deal to the teaching or the psychotherapeutic professions, but learning researchers are slowly amassing valuable data and are developing research techniques that some day will contribute to our understanding of behavior, whether or not the behavior is emotional in character.

In a less formal way some of the other therapy practitioners maintain that a child learns his behavior difficulties in infancy. Some practitioners frankly discuss their therapy as a learning or relearning process. Hence the more we learn about how learning occurs, under what conditions, etc., the more we will be able to control it. Even now some learning psychologists can make some rather shrewd observations about what occurs in some psychotherapeutic situations; so convincing have been their results that it is hoped that within the next few decades psychotherapists will get some real help from learning research.

READING INSTRUCTION VERSUS PSYCHOTHERAPY

There is no doubt about the fact that remedial reading makes a difference in reading behavior. If we take a group of poor readers, randomly divide it in half, and give remedial reading to one group and nothing to the other, the first group will be able to read better. This is not always true if psychotherapy is used in the same type of controlled experiment. Reading clinics and remedial reading situations in schools regularly report that children who have stopped progress in reading or who are moving at half speed are enabled to move at double speed with the help of remedial instruction. In other words, normal progress for a child in remedial reading is two years' growth in reading age for one chronological year. Furthermore, psychiatrists and school psychologists have often found that a child with a reading problem and an emotional problem, if given remedial reading, often achieves some success in reading and at the same time reduces the emotional problem. Of course, in some cases it does not, and a child still has an emotional problem – but at least he can read.

Economically it is much less expensive for a school system or parent to give a child remedial reading than to give him psychotherapy. The psychotherapist may charge from $15 to $25 or more per session, whereas a fairly good remedial reading tutor will charge from $5 to $10 a session. A school psychologist, if he does have time for psychotherapy, can see one or two children an hour, whereas the remedial reading teacher can see five to ten pupils an hour in some instances.

School districts, too, are more comfortable providing remedial reading services than psychotherapeutic services. Hardly any parent or school-board member will disagree that teaching reading is a function of the school. But some people, for various philosophical, religious, or other reasons, will hotly dispute the school's right to engage in psychotherapy.

Reading teachers should be extremely cautious in suggesting to parents that a child would be helped by psychotherapy. In fact, many school districts have a definite and established referral policy on this. Frequently, it is the parent rather than the child who needs psychotherapy, but to say so even indirectly and with the kindest motivation in the world is enough to bring the wrath of a screaming parent down upon the teacher, principal, superintendent, or anyone connected with the school. Recommendations for psychotherapy are best made in consultation with the principal, school psychologist, and the school physician. In short, let the medical and psychological profession take a good share of the responsibility for psychotherapy recommendations. A teacher has enough problems trying to teach reading without risking involvement with a sick parent.

REMEDIAL READING AS PSYCHOTHERAPY

Let us first consider psychotherapy and then remedial reading to see what similarities exist. If we observe what is actually being done during psychotherapy, we would see that most of the activity is of two sorts – talking and playing. For an older child, the therapist is more likely to spend a good bit of the time talking or listening while the child talks. For a younger child the therapy is more likely to involve toys – dolls, puppets, balls, clay, and other art materials. Depending on the psychotherapist's orientation, a child's talk or play will have an expressive emotional content which in some instances may be cathartic—that is, he talks or acts out emotional problem situations. Part of the ability of getting a child to do this lies in the attitude of the therapist and the direction in which he leads the child.

The amount of lead given by the therapist differs with his professional orientation. Most "schools" of psychotherapy believe that direct questions are usually undesirable for two reasons: (1) the client (he is no longer a child) will not tell the truth, and (2) the client cannot tell the truth until he is ready. Nevertheless, some psychotherapists feel that some direct questioning is appropriate. Whether direct questioning is used or not, the therapist can definitely lead a child into areas which he considers desirable. For example, the therapist can grunt "unh" pleasantly or harshly, depending on the direction taken by the client's conversation or activities.

A strong factor in most psychotherapy is the attitude of acceptance given by the therapist. A client can often tell the therapist things that he cannot tell anyone else, not even a parent, teacher, principal, brother, or a best friend. A client's fears or notions are frequently reasonably normal for anyone under the same circumstances; and it is only in the client's mind that these feelings or fears seem to be terribly wrong or abnormal or sinful or harmful.

A relationship of trust and friendship often develops between a client and therapist that is the only relationship that a client has with any other human. The therapist, by telling the client directly or indirectly what is normal, can help to shape his behavior. After a relationship has been established, the client frequently brings in a bit of news about what has happened to him since the preceding session. It is a rare therapist who can give the same neutral grunt when a client informs him that he has just succeeded in a difficult school subject as he gives when a client tells him that he has just committed an antisocial act. In short, neutral acceptance is not neutral. There is and should be an acceptance of a client's abnormal acts; yet this is not the same type of acceptance that is displayed toward normal acts that represent a client's growth in psychological maturity.

Hence two of the basic components of psychotherapy are an acceptance of the person, no matter what the past or present conditions are, and an education process in terms of what is normal and what is desirable for this particular person.

Now, having examined the psychotherapeutic process shorn of most of its often concomitant mystical or theoretical underpinnings, let us see whether some part of the psychotherapeutic relationship is present in the remedial reading situation.

As far as reading skills are concerned, a teacher accepts a child as he is. In taking an oral reading test, a child cannot bluff or pretend or even wildly guess his way very far. In short, in a very few minutes, both the child and the teacher know exactly how good his reading is. There is no point in pretending or covering up. The teacher's attitude is, "Let's accept the situation and start from there." The skillful teacher also does this in terms of phonics and other reading skills.

Accepting the child as he is in terms of reading is a must, a *sine qua non*, of remedial reading. And many teachers learn from this to accept all or most other aspects of the child. They accept him black or white, clean or dirty, "discipline problem" or no "discipline problem," bright or dull (if he is really too dull, he would not be in remedial reading in the first place). In fact, it is common and rather pathetic to see children enter a reading clinic thinking that they are just "dumb" and that is why they cannot learn to read.

The remedial teacher, through essays, informal conversation with a child, and parent conferences will sometimes learn a good deal about poor home conditions, and a little sympathetic understanding of this knowledge will often help a child to accept his situation. This is by no means a plea for reading teachers to probe systematically into emotional conditions of the home or to lavish sympathy on situations which are not particularly any of her business.

The remedial teacher helps a child with emotional problems by, first of all, accepting him and, second, helping him succeed in the act of reading. Every worker has his tools: mechanics have wrenches, doctors their hypodermic needles, play therapists their finger paint, and reading teachers their graded reading matter and phonics. Some reading teachers confuse their role with that of the psychotherapist and try to use the psychotherapist's tools, namely, large doses of free play or conversation about the child's problems. Maybe a little free play or a little conversation about problems is permissible, but the reading teacher's main function is to teach reading. Even when she must help an emotionally disturbed child, she should do so by using the tools of her trade.

The thing that the reading teacher can do better than anyone else is to teach reading. Psychotherapy, while important, should be a secondary task for her. And, even if psychotherapy were first, one of her big contributions to emotional development would be to produce success in the reading act. To take a child who has continually failed in learning to read and show him that he *can* learn to read is an extremely important function. This can sometimes change a child's whole self image. It is not uncommon for a child who is a constant disturbance in class (sometimes doing any annoying thing to get attention) to become a polite and helpful member of the class when he has learned to read.

Many psychologists have reported cases of bed-wetting or nail-biting or extreme sibling rivalry that were virtually cured by remedial reading. When a child is relieved of the pressure of reading failure, the undesirable, often regressive, symptoms may disappear.*

Pressures on a child because of reading failure can often be much more serious than adults imagine. As a child progresses in school, the need for reading increases. No longer is he just failing in reading; he is soon failing in social

*"Regressive" means that when a child is blocked in some type of important development such as academic development, he sometimes exhibits traits of a much younger child, such as bed-wetting or thumb-sucking or clinging to the mother figure.

studies and arithmetic and a host of other subjects. It is no chance coincidence that there is a huge incidence of very poor reading skills among juvenile delinquents and school dropouts. Failure in school subjects is no small matter. In today's culture, school is the main work of the child. To fail in school is to fail in the main task of life. Beyond this there is the often cruel pressure from parents who are ego-involved and do not want to admit to themselves or their neighbors that they have a failing child. This cruel pressure from parents is usually compounded by cruel pressures from other children: "Gee, you can't read that? What is the matter with you? I could read that when I was in second grade." A secondary student was asked what he disliked most about not being able to read. One would suspect that he feared failing so many courses that he could no longer play football or that he could not get a job if he could not read. But no. His reply was that he was embarrassed in front of his friends when they asked him to read a joke or an item from the sports page. As students get older they are subjected to the pressures of the economic world—if they cannot read, they cannot get a good job, or sometimes any job at all. Any student who says that he does not want to read is probably lying. This fabrication often leads him into a spiral of negative self-punishment, that is, protesting against society, his parents, or any control.

A reading teacher who can relieve pressures like that is performing genuine psychotherapy of the utmost value.

Even small successes in reading can have a marked effect. This is why it is important for the remedial teacher to structure lessons so that they bring about a constant string of little successes. This does not mean that each part of the lesson should be insultingly simple; rather, the steps should be small enough and presented so clearly that they can be mastered without too great a chance of failure. The same success principle applies equally to the teaching of illiterate adults. In fact, the same success principle can be extended to all teaching. If a teacher can have all her pupils succeed in many little tasks and can order these tasks so that eventually they add up to big successes, she will eliminate the destructive experience of failure for many students. More importantly, she will have eliminated a host of other problems, from lack of motivation to that type of failure we call emotional problems.

THE TEACHER'S MENTAL HEALTH

Since teachers are human beings and must interact with others, it is not inappropriate to discuss a few points of mental health for the teacher.

First of all, a teacher cannot have success with every child. Any teacher or system that claims to be able to teach every child to read either has not taught many children, has rather low standards of success in reading, or is not reporting the truth. It is undoubtedly true that the better the teacher or the better the method, the lower the percentage of failure; but even so, every teacher is going to have a few failures. A teacher will be much happier if she just admits it, let someone else have a crack at the children she has failed with, and continues doing the best job she can. Most teachers get so much glowing evidence of real growth in their children that they can accept a few failures. If they cannot accept a few failures, they are in the wrong business.

Next comes the problem of discipline or emotional problems in the class or reading group. Every teacher has one or two particularly difficult children. After all, emotional problems probably follow something like a normal distribution curve. Therefore, having a few problem children in every class, and occasionally a really serious one, is a normal expectation. However, if a teacher continually has the worst children in school, or if she has more problem children than any other teacher year after year, something is wrong. The first place she should go for help is to her principal and supervisor, who could possibly suggest some teaching methods, ways of organizing the class, or proper levels of work expectancy that may help. Other teachers can often make valuable suggestions. Even school psychologists sometimes give teachers a helping hand, although they generally do a better job with children than with teachers.

Last but not least, if "good" educational procedures do not help alleviate the emotional problems in her class, perhaps some of the problem is within the teacher herself and she should either seek some counseling for herself or consider changing professions. People who have the training and ability to be teachers usually also have the ability for many other professions. There is a continuing need for good people in most fields: social work, libraries, occupational therapy, and many others.

Beginning teachers might expect to encounter a relatively large number of discipline problems. One of the hardest jobs in the world is the first year of teaching; after that it becomes easier as a teacher develops skills, insights, and confidence.

One reason for the relatively long school vacations is the emotional strain of teaching. Most teachers take advantage of these vacations by getting away from the classroom situation, and this is an important factor in their mental health and attitude.

Changing the age level of the children she teaches or changing the subject will occasionally lower a teacher's percentage of emotional problems. Some teachers seem to adapt better to young children, whereas others prefer older ones. There is a common fallacy among beginning teachers that the older the children they teach, the easier it is, the more interesting it is, or the more prestige they have in the school system. A few years of teaching usually dispels this notion, and it is often a measure of a teacher's growth in maturity to ask to teach younger children.

A change in subject matter is also sometimes desirable for the teacher. Some teachers prefer a precise subject such as mathematics or science, whereas others prefer a less precise area such as literature interpretation or historical insights. In reading, there is some variation in skills from the more precise phonics to the vaguer subjective area of comprehension. Within reason, a teacher can emphasize the subject or area of a subject that best suits her personality. But, of course, emphasizing one subject too much and another not at all has its dangers.

Possibly the real key to much of this topic of emotional problems for both the teacher and the child is to be aware of some kind of normal standard and the deviations from that norm that are acceptable in a given situation.

APPENDIX 17-A READING SUGGESTIONS FOR PARENTS

EASY READING

Help your child select an easy book. If it is not easy, either he will not read it or he will read it under pressure and hate reading. Sometimes an extreme interest in a particular subject will cause him to go through a hard book, but not as a rule.

An easy way to find out if a book is easy enough is to have him read a page of it aloud. Excluding new names, if the child stumbles over more than one word of every twenty, it is too hard. For real ease in reading he should have 99 out of 100 words.

Do not worry about a book being too easy. A lot of easy reading builds confidence and makes him want to go on. The only problem is to find easy reading that has a *high interest* level. Get your child's teacher or a librarian to help you.

ENCOURAGEMENT

All of us work better when we are praised and are successful. Encourage the slightest progress. "Good, you learned a whole new word today."

If you infer that your child is just hopelessly dumb, he might believe you and stop trying or he might think you are hopelessly dumb for not understanding him.

Do not place him in situations that make him look bad. If you show grandmother that little sister can read so much better, he is likely to show that he is a better fighter. We all like to save face. He might never be as good as little sister, but this is no reason for him to suffer ridicule. Maybe he will learn to lay bricks or manage a business and become the richest man in the family.

Most children realize the need for learning to read. If they do not, they may be protesting against something that is not reading.

The need to read might sometimes be made into a rewarding experience by writing him a note telling him that "a ticket to the show is hidden in a red box in the garage." Do not let anybody read the note to him, and do not give him the ticket if he does not read the note (hide it somewhere else the next day with a new note).

ORAL READING

Silent reading (the child reads silently to himself) with high interest is the best type of reading for any child. However, oral reading (the child reads aloud to someone) might be encouraged, particularly with young children. Here are some do's and don'ts.

1. Follow knowing-the-19-out-of-20-words rule.
2. Do not get excited. If you have to tell him the same word ten times – tell him.
3. Phonics is sometimes difficult for parents to teach because they get confused or they make a reading lesson boring. One fairly safe and dependable rule in phonics is the beginning letter sound. Say, "What sound does it begin with?"
4. Encourage your child to guess at a word by reading the whole sentence.
5. If the child knows more phonics rules, encourage him to use them but be careful not to emphasize it so much that meaning of the story is lost.

GAMES TEACH READING

Some reading games are excellent for children to play at home. Your teacher might suggest some like Pairs, Go Fish, Word Bingo, Grab, or Anagrams.

DISTRACTIONS

Turn off the TV when it is reading time—this applies to other distractions. If you are listening to him read, then listen. It is not easy to learn to read, and it certainly cannot be taught by royal command from a distant part of the kitchen.

Bedtime should not be determined by TV programs.

See that your child goes to school each morning well fortified with a good breakfast. Balanced and adequate meals help promote learning growth as well as physical growth.

Hearing, vision, and speech problems can all hinder learning to read. If you suspect trouble in these areas consult a specialist.

Not all parents are able to help their own children. Some parents get too emotionally involved or too excited by their child's difficulty in learning. If this happens get some help from the school or a reading specialist.

Emotional turmoil does not help learning. If possible send the child off to school on a happy, even keel. A bawling out or a strong admonition is not preferable to a kiss on the cheek.

PRACTICE

Last but not least, learning to read well takes practice. Parents can help a great deal if they will provide the conditions for practice. There should always be several books available in the child's room—preferably easy or at the right level and preferably interesting. Encourage the use of the school library or take the child to the public library once a week. Good children's paperback books are available in some bookstores and sometimes at schools for relatively little expense. Seeing that there is good children's reading material in the home is the parents' responsibility. Change the books often or have new ones around. Just because the child did not like last week's books is no assurance that he will not like next week's books.

If a boy is interested in football or automobiles or a girl is interested in horses or clothes, get a book on the subject, read a little of it and discuss it with the child. Find out what the child is studying in school for social studies and get a book on some phase of the subject. (If the class is studying early America, get a book on Jefferson's boyhood for example.) This might help the child get a better grade in social studies besides giving him some stature in the class.

Parents can also encourage reading practice time. Let the child read in bed just before going to sleep or on awakening. Have a reading light in his room. Subscribe to an interesting popular or children's magazine in his name. Teaching reading is not just the school's job. Parents can help a great deal.

18

SPEECH PROBLEMS

Because of the many interesting parallels between reading failure and failure to learn to speak properly, a reading teacher should have at least a passing acquaintance with problems of speech. Both types of problems, reading and speech, fall within the language area. Many of the causes of problems are similar, and both seriously affect learning in other subject areas.

It is not easy to define speech problems precisely, but a commonly used definition is the one developed by Van Riper:

> Speech is defective when it deviates so far from the speech of other people that it (1) causes attention to itself; (2) interferes with communication; or (3) causes its possessor to be maladjusted.*

No one knows exactly how many speech problems there are, or how prevalent they are. At the mid-century White House Conference, it was estimated that about 5 percent of the school population has defective speech. This is probably a considerably lower percentage than the proportion of the population that suffers from reading problems. A conservative estimate is that about 10 percent of school-age children have reading problems; some estimates (those from Great Britain, for example) run as high as 25 percent of the school-age population. Part of the disparity in estimates is, of course, a matter of definition of the degree of retardation in reading that would be called "a problem."

*Van Riper, Charles, *Speech Correction: Principles and Methods*. Englewood Cliffs, N.J.: Prentice-Hall, 1956.

ARTICULATION

By far the commonest speech problems occur in the area of articulation. These problems include distortions in phoneme or sound production and substitutions or omissions of speech sounds. These defects occur in approximately 3 percent of the school-age population. They would include speech problems that are commonly called lisping and baby talk. For example, if a child says "bubber," he may mean "brother" or "butter."

Articulatory speech disorders are those that are easiest to cure. Speech therapists have many techniques for working with children, for example, using toys, poems, etc., which train them to make the desired sounds. These techniques also help to educate them to hear the sound in other words and to produce the sound. A common technique is to have a child watch himself and the therapist in a mirror, so that the child can see the actual position of some of the speech mechanisms, such as the lips and tongue. Remedial reading teachers and classroom teachers can often help to correct articulation problems by having the child listen carefully to words as they pronounce them correctly and by making the child aware of his incorrect pronounciation of the words. A teacher should take care never to do this in a way that will embarrass the child, especially in front of other children. A tape recorder is often helpful as another kind of "sound mirror."

It is normal for young children not to be able to pronounce all the phonemes in English. While most vowel sounds can be pronounced by the fourth year, all the consonant sounds are not completely mastered by some normal girls until the age of six and one-half and by some normal boys until the age of seven and one-half. Some of the last sounds to be mastered are "s," "z," "r," "th," and "wh." (See Appendix 18-C.) Generally, brighter children master speech sounds somewhat earlier and dull or retarded children somewhat later.

DEFECTS OF RHYTHM

The next most common type of speech problem is related to defects in rhythm. The most common of these is stuttering, which is defined as the interruption of speech rhythm by excessive repetitions, blocks or spasms, or the prolongation of sounds. These rhythm distortions are sometimes accompanied by contortions of the face or body. Speech people do not usually use the word *stammer* as it means about the same as *stutter* but is not as rigorously or comprehensively defined.

The other major rhythm disorder is known as "cluttering," which refers to distortions of sound and phrasing from speech that is too rapid and inexact.

Both stuttering and cluttering are more difficult to cure than articulation problems. Both tend to occur normally in young children. Children below the age of four and one-half, particularly boys, tend to have some speech rhythm problems. The best thing that a parent can do is "not to make a big thing of it." If a parent tends to ignore the problem and not call attention to it, particularly to siblings or to other adults, the problem will often disappear with normal development. However, a second important thing that a parent can do is to give the child time to speak. If the child is not interrupted and is given a sympathetic hearing, his verbal communication will often improve. Parents sometimes thoughtlessly interrupt young children or pay little attention to their communications, and this hinders normal development. In more psychological parlance, we would say that the parent should be neither overprotective or rejecting. Some speech therapists also feel that stuttering is increased when a parent tries to set standards too high or to push the child too rapidly into verbal or academic-type situations. The classroom teacher as a parent surrogate should also follow the same general principles as the parent in dealing with a stuttering child in a classroom.

Defects in rhythm occur in fewer than 1 percent of school-age children. For some reason, stuttering seems to be more pronounced in certain periods of a child's development. The peak periods occur between the ages of five and seven and between the ages of twelve and fourteen. Stuttering also occurs much more frequently in boys than in girls. It does not seem to be related to intelligence. Many theories have been offered concerning why children stutter, ranging from heredity to all manner of psychological situations and even extending to such physical correlates as lateral dominance. However, no clear-cut evidence has been produced in support of hereditary, neurological, environmental, handedness, or any other single cause. There is fairly wide agreement, however, that a child who stutters can develop some sort of personality problem because of his stuttering. This is all the more reason for the classroom teacher to give serious attention to a child's stuttering.

Therapy for the stuttering child is difficult and should not be attempted by a teacher untrained in speech correction.

In the first place, the principles of good mental health apply to this type of child. The teacher's primary effort should be to establish a climate of acceptance for the child as a person and to avoid calling attention to his defects. The stutterer should be given as many successful experiences as possible in related areas. For example, he might edit a newspaper, be captain of a baseball team, have his art work exhibited, or do extremely successful work in various subject areas. It has frequently been observed that children, even those with serious stuttering problems, often sing very well and without a trace of stuttering.

Professional therapy with stutterers varies with the background of the therapist. Some believe in a psychotherapeutic approach which, as was mentioned earlier, encompasses a wide range of theories and applications. Others believe in a more direct speech approach of concentrating on the problem rather than ignoring it. For example, they might have students practice repeating the words with which they have difficulty or have them appear in situations which are most likely to cause them to stutter. A few therapists even believe in "negative practice" in which the student practices trying to stutter, a device intended to help him gain control over the symptom.

OTHER SPEECH PROBLEMS

The next most common speech problem is a speech defect resulting from a hearing loss. A generation ago, the world had a number of "deaf and dumb" people, and it was thought that for some strange reason deafness and dumbness were concomitant afflictions. Better diagnostic methods have shown that few deaf persons are dumb (unable to speak), but rather, they have never learned to speak because they have never heard words. It is now possible for even a totally deaf child to learn to speak quite well with the help of extensive speech training from both a professional therapist and his mother.

Even partial hearing losses can affect speech. If a child has a high-frequency hearing loss, his speech may omit the high-frequency sounds; for example, the "s" sound has a much higher frequency than the vowels and many consonants. If the "s" is consistently omitted, this is an indication of a hearing loss. Speech therapy, together with a hearing aid, can often remedy this type of problem.

Speech defects associated with defective hearing occur in about one-half of 1 percent of school-age children. This might not sound like a great many children, but in an elementary school with 600 children, this would be an average of three children. Besides defective speech, these children would also have much greater difficulty in learning to read and in learning other subject matter that is presented orally. This is yet another reason why all children (and especially those in remedial reading) must be given a hearing test. A loss of 25 decibels between the frequencies of 512 to 2,048 can result in defective speech.

Defects in voice production are much less common among school children (.2 percent). This type of defect refers to significant deviations in quality, loudness, pitch, etc. An example of these would be a harsh or a nasal quality to the speech which is so unpleasant or uncommon that it could cause rejection or ridicule or subsequent personality problems. Such a defect can interfere with learning.

Delayed speech development can occur in otherwise normal children. There is a small minority of children who do not speak at the same age as other children and are behind in their development up to school years. Since delayed speech is also an indication of mental retardation, care must be taken, with the help of a competent psychological examination, to differentiate mental retardation from normal intelligence in a child with delayed speech.

A number of different physical problems can affect voice production, the most common of which is a "cleft-palate," which means that the roof of the mouth is open to the nasal passages. It can usually be completely cured or greatly improved through surgery. However, even after surgery, speech therapy is often indicated. Harelip (opening or scar tissue between the nose and upper lip) and other abnormalities of mouth and throat development can also affect speech production. A combination of surgery and speech therapy often greatly improves all these cases.

As in reading problems, any type of MBD (minimal brain dysfunction) or aphasia can affect speech. Though there is still some controversy concerning the exact location of the speech centers of the brain, there is some evidence that at least many of the major speech functions are located in the left cerebral hemisphere. In the event of damage to these speech areas, compensation can often take place in corresponding areas of the right cerebral hemisphere. Hence, even in cases of known brain damage, retraining can be effective because other areas can be taught to compensate for the damaged areas. A number of children with such obvious brain damage as cerebral palsy also have defective speech.

CAUSES OF DEFECTIVE SPEECH

The causes of defective speech are very similar to those for reading failure. In fact, one could almost substitute "failure to learn to read" for "speech problems" in most discussions of causality. First of all, speech specialists find that many more boys than girls have speech problems, just as reading clinics have consistently found.

Speech pathologists have also found many more defects in children with low IQ's. These defects are in addition to the lowered level of speech development expected because of mental age.

We have already considered physical defects in the mechanism in the area of the mouth and throat; but in reading, there are also problems that result from damage to the central nervous system that cause aphasias and all the learning problems. Speech pathologists have also noted difficulties in endocrine balance and general ill health as causes.

Environment is also closely related to speech problems. As in reading, these problems occur less frequently in higher socioeconomic groups than in lower groups.

Speech people find fewer problems when there is a good mother-child relationship than when there is overprotectiveness or rejection. A normal mother-child relationship is associated with much fewer speech problems than when a child is raised in an institution for all or part of his early developmental stages. Higher incidences of poor speech occur when children are raised in a silent or nonverbal environment in which speech is seldom used and its quality is poor. In all school learning, motivation to achieve is important for speech development. Exactly how this motivation is accomplished is not too clear, but at least part of it involves parent attitudes and the aspiration levels which they succeed in instilling in their children. A child also seems to *need* to identify with a parent; and the better the identification model, the better the speech development.

Information on the effect on speech of sibling order is not too conclusive. There is some evidence that first-born children are superior. There is a higher incidence of speech problems in twins.

Speech clinicians seem uncertain about the effects of bilingualism. Some feel that it hinders a child to speak two languages from early childhood on, and others feel that it makes no difference. Part of the difficulty is that bilingualism is frequently associated with lower economic status in American cities, the possibility being that it is the lower economic status that causes the speech problems rather than the bilingualism. Most, however, would agree that bilingualism does not hinder a bright child from a good socioeconomic background.

Speech people have found that speech problems are associated with lower academic achievement, especially with respect to reading. One might expect lower oral-reading achievement, but lower silent-reading comprehension is also correlated with problems in speech. It has long been known that speech therapy or improvement in speech definitely helps reading achievement. Now, perhaps, we might consider that the converse is also true, that improvement in reading can help speech problems.

Speech and reading specialists have both found that no single condition seems to be sufficient to cause a serious problem. For example, we know that more boys than girls have speech problems, but there are plenty of boys without speech problems. The same could be said for IQ, brain damage, poor environment, etc. And, while it is important to understand the causes for the speech problems the therapist encounters, his primary job is getting the child to speak better through direct training on the speech problem, regardless of the cause. The majority of speech people, therefore, know that their chief function is to spend most of their time teaching speech.

Incidentally, most speech experts have rejected the theory that mixed dominance of lateral confusion is a cause of speech problems.

SPEECH THERAPY

Here again there are a number of parallels between the correction of speech problems and the correction of reading problems. As in reading, a speech therapist usually begins with a diagnostic test, using the most suitable of the number of excellent diagnostic tests of articulatory disorders which systematically go through the phonemes used in English in the initial, medial, and final position of a word or syllable. The articulation test is often given with the aid of a series of pictures and might be considered as basic to speech therapy as the oral paragraphs are to remedial reading.

Speech therapists usually like to have a measure of intelligence and usually prefer that an individual intelligence test be given by a psychologist. When the services of a psychologist cannot be secured, they may give a less exact group intelligence test themselves. A parent questionnaire, either filled out by the parent at home or during an interview at school, often gives the speech therapist useful information on the background development of a child. Additional diagnostic evaluation in the area of MBD is also sometimes secured.

A hearing test is given routinely and is mandatory in any type of articulatory disorder.

A speech therapist is not finished with the initial test battery; she will usually continue to test and teach, and then test again and modify her future teaching on the basis of cumulative test results.

An attitude of acceptance is encouraged. The speech therapist is enjoined to use individual standards for individual children and to set up individual standards that are reasonable and proper for a child to try to achieve. As before, the therapist must plan a child's work so that he may achieve a logical sequence of successes during training. This means the establishment of short-term, easily reachable goals accompanied by praise and encouragement.

The speech therapist also recognizes a general developmental pattern which starts with babbling and progresses to imitating sounds, then single words, and longer phrases and sentences. A developmental curve is also evident in the types of phonemes that can be made, recognizing that vowel sounds are easier than the more difficult consonant sounds. As in reading, speech therapy also recognizes the existence of uneven development and plateaus in the learning curve; thus, a child is expected to make steady or rapid reading progress for a time and then reach a plateau when nothing seems to happen even though lessons are continued. Plateaus are usually followed by further growth. Hence unevenness of development occurs so often as to be considered normal; even regression at times comes within normal limits. Sometimes the cause for a plateau or regression is a parent; it may be an emotional disturbance at home or at school or a period of ill health. At other times, there may be no apparent cause for lack of progress.

Speech therapists have found that regular and definitely scheduled lesson times are important. Like all teachers, they prefer optimum learning time, such as mid-morning rather than late afternoon. One can see that correction of speech problems, like the correction of learning problems, takes practice, time, work.

There are interesting curriculum parallels between teaching reading and teaching speech. In addition to the various developmental sequences, speech therapists are also concerned with teaching the high-frequency or most-used sounds first. They also like to teach the initial sound of a word first. With younger children, they attempt to appeal to the interest level in the selection of subject matter in poems and stories as well as in the use of toys and games. With older students, the subject is attacked a little more directly with word lists, phoneme drills, contrasting exercises, and prose passages using more adult subject matter. In the use of audio-visual materials; the tape recorder is a hands-down favorite, but many speech therapists also use such other audio-visual materials as charts and filmstrips. Some experimental use has been made of programmed instruction and conditioning approaches.

Another interesting similarity between speech training and reading training is the instructor's difficulty in choosing between analytic and synthetic methods. Should the teacher try to analyze the specific phoneme which is causing difficulty and drill on just this specific phoneme, or should the training be aimed at a broader segment of language development: teaching only the pronunciation of phrases and sentences which bear directly on the problem phoneme? A similar conflict occurs when reading teachers must decide whether to use phonics in isolation or whole words, phrases or sentences. Among speech teachers, opinions vary as to degrees of emphasis on parts or wholes, the result being that they use a little of both.

CONCLUSION

It is important for a remedial reading teacher to know something about speech problems as they are related in many ways to reading problems. First of all there is a higher percentage of children with speech problems in remedial reading than in normal classrooms. Second, there are many common causes for both reading and speech problems, and it may help a reading teacher to understand "why" reading failure occurs if she knows some of the causes for speech failure. Finally, remedial reading teachers and speech correction teachers often work together in the same department and with the same children; it helps if they know a little about each other's work.

I am not advocating that by reading this chapter one will become a speech correctionist or that reading teachers should engage in speech correction, but there are times and situations when there is no speech correctionist available and a little knowledge of how to handle a speech problem, especially if it is of the articulatory type, is desirable.

The best solution then is to send the student to a speech correctionist if a teacher suspects a problem; but if no correctionist is available, here are a few do's and dont's:

1. Make sure there is a problem. Read the definition of a problem at the beginning of this chapter and look at the normal development scales in Appendix 18-B.

2. If it is an articulatory problem, provide a little regular instruction and drill after testing to see which sounds are problems. See appendix 18-A. Be sure to give an audiometer test. Instruction might include the use of a mirror and tape recorder for visual and auditory feedback from a child's own efforts and to help call attention to the teacher's speech production. Phonics materials often provide good drill suggestions.

3. For other types of speech disorders, it is probably best to leave them alone, except that with any type of speech disorder good mental-health practices are highly recommended (for example, do not embarrass the child, provide successful experiences, etc.).

APPENDIX 18-A TESTING FOR SPEECH PROBLEMS

A number of speech tests are available for speech therapists. They tend to fall into two major categories: (1) language-development scales and (2) articulation inventories.

The language-development scales test the overall development of a child's use of language. An example of this type of test is the Verbal Language Development Scale (American Guidance Service, Circle Pines, Minnesota, 1959). These scales are based upon developmental observations such as the Language Development Chart described in the Appendix 18-B.

Articulation tests frequently contain a series of pictures; a child calls the name of the object in the picture, and the examiner notes his pronunciation. The pictures are so graded that all the phonemes in English are systematically tested. An example of this type of test is the Photo Articulation Test (King Company, Chicago). If a reading teacher is interested in a rough type of articulation test she might use the phonics charts in Appendix 5-A-D. Test a child by pointing to the picture and see if he can say the sound. The phonics charts have the limitation of testing only the sound in the initial position, but they give a fairly complete listing of most regularly used English phonemes. A quicker, less specific articulation test is to have a child count slowly to twenty.

Every articulation test should be accompanied by a brief continuous discourse test. This test is accomplished by showing a child a picture or getting him to tell a short story – listening for his phrasing and flow of speech. The continuous discourse test sometimes reveals disorders of speech rhythm (stuttering and cluttering) as well as articulation problems in a more normal speech situation.

APPENDIX 18-B CHILD LANGUAGE DEVELOPMENT CHART: BIRTH THROUGH AGE FIVE*

0–4 weeks: Neonate: Birth cry
Crying without purpose
Whining, whimpering
3 weeks: Clucking sounds
Differentiated types of crying – pain, hunger, pleasure
4 weeks: Throaty sounds
Listening to noises

4–8 weeks: Babbling stage – child coos and gurgles random sounds
Groaning sounds
Wails, squeals, laughs
Facial responses – smiles

*Compiled by Speech and Hearing Center, Rutgers University.

8–16 weeks:	Continued babbling stage
	Gutteral sounds
	Clucking
	Vocalizes expressions of pleasure
	Responds to speaking voice
	Blowing bubbles
16–20 weeks:	Vocal play
	By this time says all the vowel sounds
	Syllable repetition
	Vocalizes eagerness and displeasure
	Begins to imitate sounds
6 months:	Lalling stage begins – repetition of sounds and sound combinations without comprehension
	Imitates sounds
	Crows happily
	Expresses recognition of familiar objects and people
	Laughs when offered toys
7 months:	Continued lalling stage
	Polysyllabic vowel sounds
	Spontaneous vocalizations
	Shouts for joy
	Clicks tongue
	Vocalizes satisfaction in attaining objects
	Laughs at hearing words
8 months:	Advanced babbling and lalling
	Continues imitation
	Vocalizes interjectional matter
	Responds to his name
	Inner language development
9 months:	Stage of imitation, inflection, and intonation
	Makes expressive sounds
	Says "da-da" or equivalent
	Listens with selective interest to familiar words
	Differentiates words
10 months:	One-word vocabulary, at least
	Trends toward actual speaking becoming more pronounced
	Rudimentary imitation of sounds
	Makes adjustments to response to certain words
11 months:	Says two or more words
	Says more consonants than vowels
	Understands simple commands
12 months:	Repeats familiar words
(1 year)	Vocabulary of four or more words
	Echolalia stage – automatic involuntary repetition of heard phrases and sentences
	Puts words and gestures together to be understood
	Uses sounds of an object or animal for its name
	Points out pictures upon request
	Performs simple commands

15 months:	Vocabulary of up to ten words One-word sentences Fluent expressive jargon – communication by words and gestures Responds to "no" and "don't"
18 months:	Vocabulary between five and twenty-two words Sentences consisting of noun and verb "Naming stage" – proper nouns given to everything Uses jargon conversationally Voice has wide range of pitch, intensity, and tonal quality; pitch is high and strained Recognizes environmental noises
24 months: (2 years)	Vocabulary of 200 words or more (50 to 60 percent Nouns). Two-thirds intelligible Three-word sentences – sing-song Produces twenty-five phonemes – eleven vowels and fourteen consonants Uncertain and inconsistent pronunciation – omits beginnings and endings of sentences Articulated speech is beginning Is able to carry on a conversation Refers to self by own name Starts using pronouns "me," "mine" and "you" Uses phrases – no past tense or plurals Can name objects and pictures Asks a number of questions Better control over pitch Final consonant is often present but medial consonants often omitted Proportion of fricatives decreases as proportion of nasal consonants increases Post dentals, dentals, and labial sounds become more frequent Formulates negative judgments
30 months:	Vocabulary of about 300 words Development increases in same areas as for two years Three- or four-word sentences Begins using plurals Pronunciation shows telescoping Uses words to designate concepts and relationships Long monologues Pitch variation continues
3 years:	Vocabulary of about 900 words Four- or five-word sentences 90 percent is intelligible Substitution errors are common Has mastered vowels and diphthongs Uses more verbs and pronouns Begins using prepositions Answers simple questions Begins to whisper

	Can say full name
	Tells simple stories
	May have frequent nonfluencies
	Voice is well controlled
42 months:	Yelling is normal speaking tone
	Rate of speech more rapid
	Omissions and substitutions of medial consonant is frequent
4 years:	Vocabulary of about 1,540 words
	Six- to eight-word sentences
	Uses compound and complex sentences
	Uses slang
	Uses conjunctions
	Uses many more plurals
	Asks innumerable questions
	Carries on long and involved conversations
	Marked inflection
	Understands prepositions
	Repetition reduced

Common difficulties at age four

	Omissions of essential words
	Wrong use of verbs
	Incorrect use of auxiliary verbs
	Wrong number and case of pronouns
	Omissions of articles
	Omissions of or wrong use of prepositions
5 years:	Vocabulary of about 2,000 to 2,500 words
	Six- to eight-word sentences
	100 percent intelligibility
	Asks "Why?"
	Well-modulated voice
	Asks meanings of words
	Defines words
	Knows some colors
	Counts to 10

APPENDIX 18-C EARLIEST AGES AT WHICH SOUNDS WERE CORRECTLY PRODUCED, IN POSITIONS INDICATED, BY 75 PERCENT of 204 CHILDREN

		Consonants Syllable position: Initial	Medial	Final	Vowels and diphthongs				Consonant blends			
IPA*	Conventional	Age	Age	Age	IPA	Conventional		Age	Blend	Age	Blend	Age
m		2	2	3	i	Long E	Me	2	pr-	5		
n		2	2	3	ɪ	Short I	Is	4	br-	5		
ŋ	(ng)	—	3	nt**	ɛ	Short E	Met	3	tr-	5		
p		2	2	4	æ	Short A	At	4	dr-	5	sl-	6
b		2	2	3	ʌ	Short U	Up	2	kr-	5	sw-	5
t		2	5	3	ə	Schwa	Alone	2	gr-	5	tw-	5
d		2	3	4	ɑ	Broad A	Father	2	fr-	5	kw-	5
k		3	3	4	ɔ	Broad O	Off	3	θr-	6	-ŋk	4
g		3	3	4	ν	Short OO	Look	4	pl-	5	-ŋg	5
r		5	4	4	u	Long OO	Moon	2	bl-	5	-mp	3
l		4	4	4	ʒ	Zh	Garage	2	kl-	5	-nt	4
f		3	3	3					gl-	5	-nd	6
v		5	5	4					fl-	5	spr-	5
θ	(th voiceless)	5	nt	nt	ju	Long U	Use	3	-ld	6	spl-	5
ɤ	(th voiced)	5	5	nt					-lk	5	str-	5
s		5	5	5					-lf	5	skr-	5
z		5	3	3	ou	Long O	Go	2	-lv	5	skw-	5
ʃ	(sh)	5	5	5	au	Ou	Out	3	-lz	5	-ns	5
ʒ	(zh)	nt	5	nt	eɪ	Long A	May	4	sm-	5	-ps	5
h		2	nt	—	aɪ	Long I	Ice	3	sn-	5	-ts	5
		5	nt	—	ɔɪ	Oi	Boy	3	sp-	5	-mz	5
w		2	2	—					st-	5	-nz	5
j	(y)	4	4	—					-st	6	-ŋz	5
tʃ	(ch)	5	5	4					sk-	5	-dz	5
dʒ	(j)	4	4	6					-ks	5	-gz	5

*IPA stands for International Phonetic Alphabet.

**Not tested.

Source: Based on information in Johnson, Wendel, et al., *Diagnostic Methods in Speech Pathology*, Harper & Row, New York, 1963.

19
SPECIAL READING METHODS

The methods of reading instruction in this chapter are called "special" primarily to distinguish them from the methods ordinarily used in teaching children to read—that is, with a basal reading series, as mentioned in Chapter 3. Other methods are discussed in other chapters—programmed instruction and comprehension drill books in Chapter 10, games in Chapters 4 and 8, among others, all of which could also be called "special" methods by this definition.

The methods considered in this chapter vary in the intention of their developer and in professional opinion as to their specific applicability to regular classroom or remedial reading. The Fernald kinesthetic technique was developed for use with rather serious remedial reading cases, while linguistic methods are advocated for all children. But if pushed, most of the methods developers or advocated would say that any of the methods discussed are appropriate for both remedial and normal classrooms. Some classroom teachers are notorious followers of directions; and, if the directions for a particular method do not specifically state "for a normal classroom," then they look no further and set it aside. However, teachers today are better trained and more resourceful in incorporating diverse methods into an organizational pattern suitable for either a small group or an entire classroom of children.

The modern concept is that a *teacher* is a "director of learning," not a performer in front of a group or a vocal mechanism for dispensing knowledge. The modern teacher's job is to see that children are given the experience of learning by a variety of methods, to evaluate the learning, and then to provide new approaches. No longer is it the teacher's job just to know her subject and to present it clearly by lecture and textbook. Of course, the teacher must know her subject, but she is also a specialist in finding out how much the child knows at each stage of learning and in using such a wide variety of methods that the child cannot help learning.

THE FERNALD KELLER KINESTHETIC TECHNIQUE

The late Dr. Grace Fernald was a school psychologist who founded the Clinic School, the main remedial training branch of the School of Education at the University of California at Los Angeles. With her associate, Helen Keller (not the famous blind person), she developed a kinesthetic method which is described in her book, *Remedial Techniques for Basic School Subjects* (McGraw-Hill Book Company, 1943). The name of the method, "kinesthetic," refers to the involvement of the kinesthetic sense which is the sensation occasioned when a muscle is moved. For example, if you put your hand behind your back and move a finger, the reason you know a finger has moved is because your kinesthetic sense has so informed you. This kinesthetic sense is used mostly in the tracing of large word forms with a finger. If a finger is touching a surface, the movement also involves the tactual sense.

This method tends to be used with children who have more serious reading problems or when other remedial procedures have failed.

STAGE 1 Fernald delineates four stages of development. In the beginning the child is started out with the motivation to write a story, which may consist of no more than two words, perhaps just the title of a picture. The vocabulary is completely unrestricted. For example, the child may wish to call a nice-looking picture of a father figure "The Lousy Bum." Whereas *lousy* and *bum* are not exactly the words found in most preprimers, the *the* just happens to be the commonest word in the English language. So the child not only learns to read words which interest or somehow amuse him but also learns a good basic vocabulary. Some psychotherapists are pleased at the possibilities for catharsis and acceptance inherent in freely allowing the child to create his own reading matter. The child is encouraged, but not forced, to write more than a title. In the beginning of instruction, stories are usually quite short, usually only a sentence or two; as instruction progresses, the stories lengthen.

When a beginning reader (regardless of age) wants to know a word to write in his story, the teacher writes the word on a large slip of heavy paper (3 by 8 inches). The child traces the word with his finger, saying the word slowly and aloud, sometimes dragged out syllable by syllable (*go-ing*, *ta-ble*), while his finger moves over the letters. For reasons of continuity, Fernald prefers cursive script but manuscript writing may be used.

After the child has traced the word several times and feels that he knows it, he turns the slip of paper with the word written on it face down and tries to write the word correctly on a sheet of scratch paper. He then compares his written word with the word the teacher has written. If they are the same, he returns to the tracing of the word and repeats the process of writing it first on scratch paper and seeing if he can do it correctly. Sometimes for additional practice he may try tracing the word with his eyes closed or in a pan of sand. The latter method, tracing a word in a pan of sand, is sometimes recommended for very difficult remedial cases which may involve mental retardation or brain damage.

After the child has written the word correctly in his story, he takes the slip of paper on which the teacher has written the word and files it alphabetically in a little file box. In this way the child begins to build his own personal spelling dictionary. In later stories he may then refer back to words he has previously used, saving the teacher the trouble of writing the word again. This is particularly important if the teacher is working with more than one child.

At the end of the day the teacher takes the child's story and types it on a primary typewriter (large-sized letters). In addition to typing the story neatly, she may first go over the story with the child and clean up glaring faults of grammar. Minor points of grammar are overlooked at first in order to encourage the child to produce longer stories; haggling about numerous details of grammar can be inhibiting to creative writing, as some of our best-selling modern authors so amply demonstrate. When the teacher types the story, she also makes a special list at the bottom of the page of the words that she has supplied that day.

When the child comes to class the next day, the first thing he is asked to do is to read his own story. He is then asked to read the list of words at the bottom of the page. He is also asked to read the "new" words for each of the preceding three days. If he reads the words correctly for three days, it is presumed that he knows them, and they are no longer repeated. But until he knows the new words, he must be able to say them correctly three days in a row. The teacher keeps a record by putting a check mark after each word that is pronounced correctly for the day or an *X* if the child is not able to say it correctly.

These typed stories are then kept in a special notebook so that the child literally writes his own book. Children are often encouraged to draw pictures to illustrate their own stories. Users of this method tell interesting stories of how much some of the children come to value "their book." One parent of a child who hated reading found him in a closet late one night well after bedtime reading "his book" with a flashlight. (See Figure 19-1.)

STAGE 2 The first stage, which involves the tracing and all the methods just described, may last from several months to several years depending upon

Trouble in Outer Space
by John

In outer space the rocket ship had trouble. A meteor hit the rocket ship.

The red light went on then the man put his space helmet on.

rocket ship
outer space
trouble
meteor

I Hate School
by John

I hate school and teachers.

One of these days if I get mad enough I will kill one and run away. And I will not come back to see he or her buried *ha ha*!

The End

buried
enough
school
mad
kill
hate
ha ha
teacher

FIGURE 19-1 Sample stories generated by an eleven-year-old student with second-grade reading ability. Words at the bottom are the words that were supplied by the teacher.

the child's rate of growth. After this a second stage is entered in which the tracing of large words is discontinued and the teacher writes the words needed for the child's story on a slip of paper. The child looks carefully at the word, turns the slip of paper over, and tries to write it on a sheet of scratch paper. The rest of the procedure is the same. One difficulty that the teacher must guard against is that the child, in his eagerness to get on with the story, will simply take the slip of paper bearing the word and copy it directly into his story. This defeats many of the special features of the method. Fernald claims that one of the reasons why children have trouble in learning to read is that they have never really paid attention to a word.

STAGE 3 In a later stage of reading development, books are introduced. The child reads silently. If he does not know a word, he asks the teacher to read it. He then writes the word from memory. Note that at this stage the teacher no longer writes the word, but the child studies the printed word in the book. The child always reads silently from the book before attempting oral reading; he learns any unknown words by asking the teacher what they are and then writes them from memory.

STAGE 4 Finally the stage arrives when all writing is discontinued. The child reads from a book. If he does not know a word, the teacher tells it to him; he studies it a moment carefully, and then goes on reading. Fernald would admonish most reading teachers, telling them that they are trying to teach most beginning remedial cases as if they are in the final stage rather than by treating them as if they are in the beginning stage.

Now let us look back over this method and recapitulate the many interesting points of instruction involved.

1. *Interest.* The child writes about what interests him. This point may involve some aspects of psychotherapy, namely, emotional catharsis and acceptance. The motivation to read his own story, typed by the teacher, is high.
2. *Self-selection of vocabulary.* No basic vocabulary is needed; the child builds his own.
3. *Kinesthetic and tactual sensory involvement.* Involvement of these two senses is sometimes found in writing or spelling lessons, but not always in reading lessons.
4. *Phonics instruction.* The slow pronouncing of words, often by syllables, is a form of phonics instruction that shows the child the relationship between the written symbol and the speech sound. This approach can be as effective as formal phonics drill.
5. *No books are used at first.* In the beginning stages, this not only saves on the cost of books but also solves the problems of having to use "middle class" books with disadvantaged children or "babyish" books with older pupils.
6. *Many language arts skills are involved and related.* The child simultaneously learns many language skills—not only reading but also spelling, handwriting, grammar, and creative writing. Grammar, spelling, and the rest are not isolated subjects, but come alive.

Like all methods, the kinesthetic method has some disadvantages. First of all, it takes a teacher with a great deal of ability and tolerance for ambiguity. There is no teacher's manual to tell her what to do, day by day. The "next day's story" must come out of the child's head, and there are some days when it takes some subtle teasing. Second, it requires much work on the part of the teacher: typing the stories, preparing the slips of paper and file boxes, and sometimes developing interest units around which social studies can also be related to the children's creative stories. When children start reading books, the teacher must select them carefully to be sure that they are on an easy level and about topics which interest the children.

In using the kinesthetic method in a reading clinic with older children, it is modified somewhat in that small slips of paper are used by the teacher in writing the words for the child's story. The child then traces the word with his pencil over the teacher's writing. The rest of the procedure for the early stages is the same. This modified method may also be included as part of a remedial lesson. It works well, but again the teacher should be cautioned about simply allowing the child to copy the word supplied by her in his story—he must go through the tracing and trial writing of the word on a sheet of scratch paper in order to get maximum benefit out of the method.

When a teacher tries the method at first with too large a group of children, the results can be disastrous – some children will not write, and those that do write need so many words that she cannot get around to them all. Students unfamiliar with the method need careful individual guidance. The teacher would do better to start out with one or a few children; then work up to using the kinesthetic method with a group, say the size of a reading group (one-third of a normal-sized class). The larger the group, the more overwhelming will loom the retyping chores. Hence, this method is feasible mostly with a smaller group. It is possible, though, that retyping does not require any more time than is required for good preparation of most types of lessons.

READING LABORATORIES

The best-known "reading laboratories" are boxes full of graded short reading selections followed by comprehension questions, with each story printed on a seperate heavy piece of paper. They were originally developed by Don Parker and published by Science Research Associates (see Figure 19-2). The value of these "labs" is that a child works at his own level and corrects his own work, leaving the teacher free to supervise and help one or a few children at a time.

The children start by taking a simple reading comprehension test in a workbook. The results of this test determine which level a student will work

FIGURE 19-2 Photograph of a typical SRA reading laboratory and a list of the grade-level ranges of various reading laboratory kits.

on. Each level has a different color so that a student is not embarrassed in case he has to work on a lower grade level. The teacher's manual gives the grade level for the teacher's information.

An extremely important feature of the labs is that they allow each child to work on his own level. Thus, in a normal fifth grade where the range of student abilities can often be from second- to eighth-grade levels of reading ability, there is something appropriate for everyone. Since students work individually, they can also change levels as often as necessary, either up or down.

The labs have basically two types of drill materials. The power builders are the main selections. These are two- or three-page selections on a variety of interesting topics, such as adventure stories or popular science. The selections are then followed by ten multiple-choice comprehension sections and an optional additional phonics drill consisting of questions and simple tasks designed to teach the sound of various letters and letter combinations. When a student has read his selection, he brings it back to the lab box and exchanges it for an answer card. He returns to his seat and corrects the page in his workbook where he has written his answers. He keeps a record of the number of questions answered correctly on a graph provided in the workbook. If he has a number of perfect or near-perfect sets of answers, his teacher will usually suggest that he move up and start taking drills on the next higher level.

The labs also contain another type of drill called the rate builders. These are short, rigidly timed selections with all the questions printed on one side of the card. The goal here is to encourage the student to read and respond rapidly. These drills are similarly scored and graphed.

The SRA Reading Laboratories were originally intended as wide-range supplementary materials. For example, one of the first kits was aimed at about junior-high grade levels with reading selections varying from third through twelfth grades. The newer labs are aimed at a specific grade level and have a narrower range. The publishers suggest that they approach a basal reading method, but most schools use them as supplemental to a basal series of reading texts. Reading laboratories are widely used in remedial reading programs. Their interesting graded selections are useful in comprehension drills, but most remedial teachers prefer a more systematic and diagnostic method of teaching phonics and increasing vocabulary.

Another laboratory-type set of materials is the *Literature Sampler* published by Encyclopedia Britannica Press. This, again, is a boxful of folded pieces of cardboard with graded stories printed on them. The *Literature Sampler* provides somewhat longer reading selections, many of which are taken from classic or widely acclaimed modern children's books. Each selection is a reasonably self-contained unit, but it ends with the suggestion that the child may like to continue reading the book, whereupon the title and publisher are given.

Somewhat in the same vein, but with different emphasis, is *Reading Clinic*, published by Webster Division, McGraw-Hill Book Company. This boxful of materials consists of some paperbound graded adopted classics, a rather complete set of phonic word wheels, the Dolch Basic Sight Word cards, and a copy of William Kottmeyer's textbook on remedial reading to help the teacher know what to do with all the material and comprehension drill cards.

Scott, Foresman and Company also has a graded boxful of materials called *Tactics in Reading* for secondary students who need help in reading skills. Educational Design, Inc., has an interesting kit of reading and comprehension selections, the *Reading Attainment System*, which was originally developed for the Job Corps and has a range of reading difficulty at the third and fourth grade level. The *Reading Development* kits by Edwin Smith (Addison-Wesley) are intended for illiterate or semiliterate adults and have a difficulty range from 1.7 through tenth grade.

LINGUISTICS

In the 1930s Leonard Bloomfield, one of the giants of American linguistics, the "scientific" study of language, was confronted with the practical problem of how to teach his son to read. Bloomfield reasoned that since his son already knew how to speak and hence knew both the vocabulary and structure of the English language, the main thing that he did not know was the relationship between the graphic symbols (printed words) and phonic symbols (spoken sounds). Therefore, his reading instruction, initially at least, consisted of teaching the gradually increasing complexity of the relationship between letters and their sounds. In other words, he used a largely phonics approach.

Bloomfield developed a set of reading materials which first introduced only very simple, phonetically regular words, using short vowels. He built his son's reading vocabulary by introducing new words with minimal changes in graphemic structure (not by adding words loaded with meaning and perhaps selected with an eye on frequency tables, as is done in most of our modern reading series). To oversimplify the difference between the two approaches, Bloomfield would say that the proper word to teach after *bat* is *cat* because it changes only one grapheme, whereas authors of most basal series would say that the word to introduce after *bat* would be *flew* because both words can now be used in a meaningful sentence. Bloomfield would retort that *flew* is ridiculous; the *ew* grapheme is a rather uncommon method of making the two-dot *u* phoneme; it is better to teach the short and long vowels first. A child certainly knows enough language to have no difficulty in understanding the words *bat flew*—what he has trouble with is looking at that particular combination of seven letters and translating them into a sound which he does know. Authors of modern basal series would retort that by teaching a child merely to grunt out letter sounds, we are back fifty years into the area of strong phonics emphasis which yielded not only boring reading lessons but caused slow reading and "word callers"—children who could read the words aloud without understanding them. And so the phonics-antiphonics argument goes.

Bloomfield's original materials were given a few apparently successful school tryouts in the 1930s but then seemed to have been forgotten until they were exhumed by admirer and dictionary author Clarence Barnhart. These dusted-off "linguistic materials for teaching reading" were published in 1960 (Leonard Bloomfield and Clarence Barnhart, *Let's Read*, Wayne State University Press, Detroit, 1960) and have created a renewed interest among educators. Barnhart and other authors interested in linguistics, such as Charles Fries, have continued to develop materials in this vein (vocabulary selection by gradually increasing the complexity of the phoneme-grapheme relationship).

Figure 19-3 shows a sample page from Bloomfield and Barnharts' new linguistic approach.

can Dan fan man Nan pan ran tan an
ban van

a can a fan a pan a man a van
a tan van a tan fan

Dan ran. Nan ran.
Van ran. A man ran.

Nan can fan Dan.
Can Dan fan Nan?
Dan can fan Nan.
Nan, fan Dan.
Dan, fan Nan.

Dan ran a van.
Dan ran a tan van.
A man ran a tan van.

FIGURE 19-3 Sample page from *Let's Read* by Leonard Bloomfield and Clarence L. Barnhart (C. L. Barnhart, Inc., Bronxville, N.Y., 1963). Note the absence of pictures and the use of only phonetically regular words and one vowel sound.

For an interesting contrast, a page is also reproduced in Figure 19-4 from a McGuffey Reader from the middle of the nineteenth century.

LESSON III.

Năt hăt făn căn

f

a fan a hat

Ann and Nat.
Ann has a fan.
Nat has a hat.
Ann can fan Nat.

FIGURE 19-4 Sample page from *McGuffey's Eclectic Primer*. This is from the 1881 edition still in print (American Book Company). The first McGuffey Readers appeared in the 1840s. Note the similarity of phonetically regular words in the third lesson with the third lesson of Bloomfield and Barnhart's "modern" linguistic approach.

Some other modern linguists are moderately horrified that the term "linguistic approach" to reading is applied to systems which use only one aspect of linguistics, that is, emphasis on a more systematic phoneme-grapheme correspondence development. While not disagreeing that this is important, they say there is much more to linguistics which has important implications for reading teaching. Look again, for example, at Figure 8-10 in Chapter 8 in which the meaning of a sentence changes radically with the change in accent on different words. This aspect of linguistics is either not taught or not emphasized properly in Bloomfield's system or in most other "linguistic" systems. Interestingly enough, quite a bit of emphasis was given to sentence "tunes," as some linguists call them, in the readers of the last century.

Another important concern of linguists is the structure of the language; loosely defined this might be called grammar, or how words can be put together in meaningful combinations. For example, we can say, "The bird flies," but we cannot say, "Bird the flies." Why not? Because *the* is a noun signaler. *The* before a word makes it a noun. Hence, by shifting the place of *The* from before *bird* to before *flies* we have reversed the function of the words from noun to verb and vice versa. So the "pattern," another good linguistic word, connotes meaning and must follow certain rules. This, of course, has important implications for the teaching of comprehension. A much-used practical application of this type of thinking is in the teaching of English to foreigners in which many substitution sentences are used. A substitution sentence is a type of drill in which a teacher first shows and then tries to elicit from the student what words can be substituted in various parts of the sentence. For example, in the sentence:

The dog runs quickly.

For the first word we can substitute *A* but not much else. For the second word we can substitute a large number of words such as *cat*, *boy*, etc. For the third word we can substitute a large number of another type of word; for example, *walks*, *swims*, etc., but we cannot substitute words like *cat* or *boy*, hence we have defined *dog*, *cat*, and *boy* as being words of one class. Of course, teachers will immediately recognize this as similar to the traditional grammar of teaching parts of speech; but, like the difference between phonics and phoneme-grapheme, it is a little more precise with a somewhat unique and sharper definition.

Substitution sentences also have some interesting implications for the teaching of reading. At least one publisher, Scott, Foresman and Company, has developed a teaching device called a "Rolling Reader" which consists of a set of cubes the size of large dice with words printed on each side. One cube in the set has only articles, one cube has only nouns, one cube only verbs, etc. A child rolls out the cubes and always has a sentence face up if he puts them in the correct "pattern."

Substitution sentences and other features of structural linguistics (such as varieties of sentence patterns) are also built into the teaching methods of at least one basal reading series, *The Sounds of Language Readers* by Bill Martin, Jr. (Holt, Rinehart and Winston, New York, 1966). (See Figure 19-5.)

Learning sequence: **a) Silent reading, b) exploring meanings, c) oral reading, d) language analysis.**

* My Little Brother

by H. R. Wittram,
pictures by Carole Kofod Butterfield

Transforming sentences:

older / younger / big — friend. / cousin. / sister.

This is my little brother.

My / Her / **His** **name is Timmy.**

I / She / **He** **is** / am **three years old.**

FIGURE 19-5 Sample page from *Sounds Around the Clock,* Sounds of Language Readers by Bill Martin, Jr., Holt, Rinehart and Winston, New York, 1966.

Modern linguists have so closely identified their work with the structure of languages that the whole area is sometimes referred to as *structural linguistics*. However, not all linguists would be happy with such a limiting definition, since a science of language has many other facets. Linguistics, in its broadest sense, would include such more or less separate fields as:

1. *Semantics and philology*, which study word meanings, frequently by tracing their development through languages.
2. *Phonetics*, the science of speech sounds, which was a well-developed field before the modern structural linguists got under way. Besides furnishing a great aid to speech therapy, the phoneticists have contributed to the teaching of foreign languages and have worked in such areas as the type of dialect placement made popular by Bernard Shaw in *Pygmalion* (or its musical version, *My Fair Lady*), which is sometimes called dialect-mapping.
3. *Comparative languages*, perhaps a branch of philology, but with current emphasis on modern languages. In its ancient or primitive setting, it is related to the field of anthropology or archeology.
4. The *traditional grammarian* has been largely superseded by the *structural linguist* working in an area he calls syntax.
5. A new field, that of psychology, is making some advances in the area known as *psycholonguistics*, which treats language as a part of the thinking process.
6. *Writing systems* cover the many varied ways of recording language graphically.

These and other branches of linguistics promise to make significant contributions to the teaching of reading in the coming decades. Controlled experiments using the linguistic approach of phoneme regularity do not show these methods to be superior or inferior to traditional basal reading series methods.

NEW ALPHABETS

Some of the "new" reading methods for beginning readers have devised "new" alphabets. Probably the best known of these is the ITA which attempts to give greater phoneme-grapheme regularity by adding new letters to the alphabet and by changing spelling rules. The notion of new alphabets (or augmented alphabets) is not at all new nor is the notion of changing spelling rules for greater regularity. Figure 19-6 shows some examples of "new alphabets" dating back to the seventeenth century; but in reality, improved alphabets have been proposed and sometimes adopted throughout recorded history. This trend still continues, although most recently in English the new alphabets have been aimed at beginning reading instruction. The proponents often recommend their new alphabets for remedial reading instruction as well. Here are a few that have appeared on the current American reading scene.

ITA The Initial Teaching Alphabet is a forty-three-character alphabet developed by Sir James Pitman. It includes twenty-four Roman or Latin

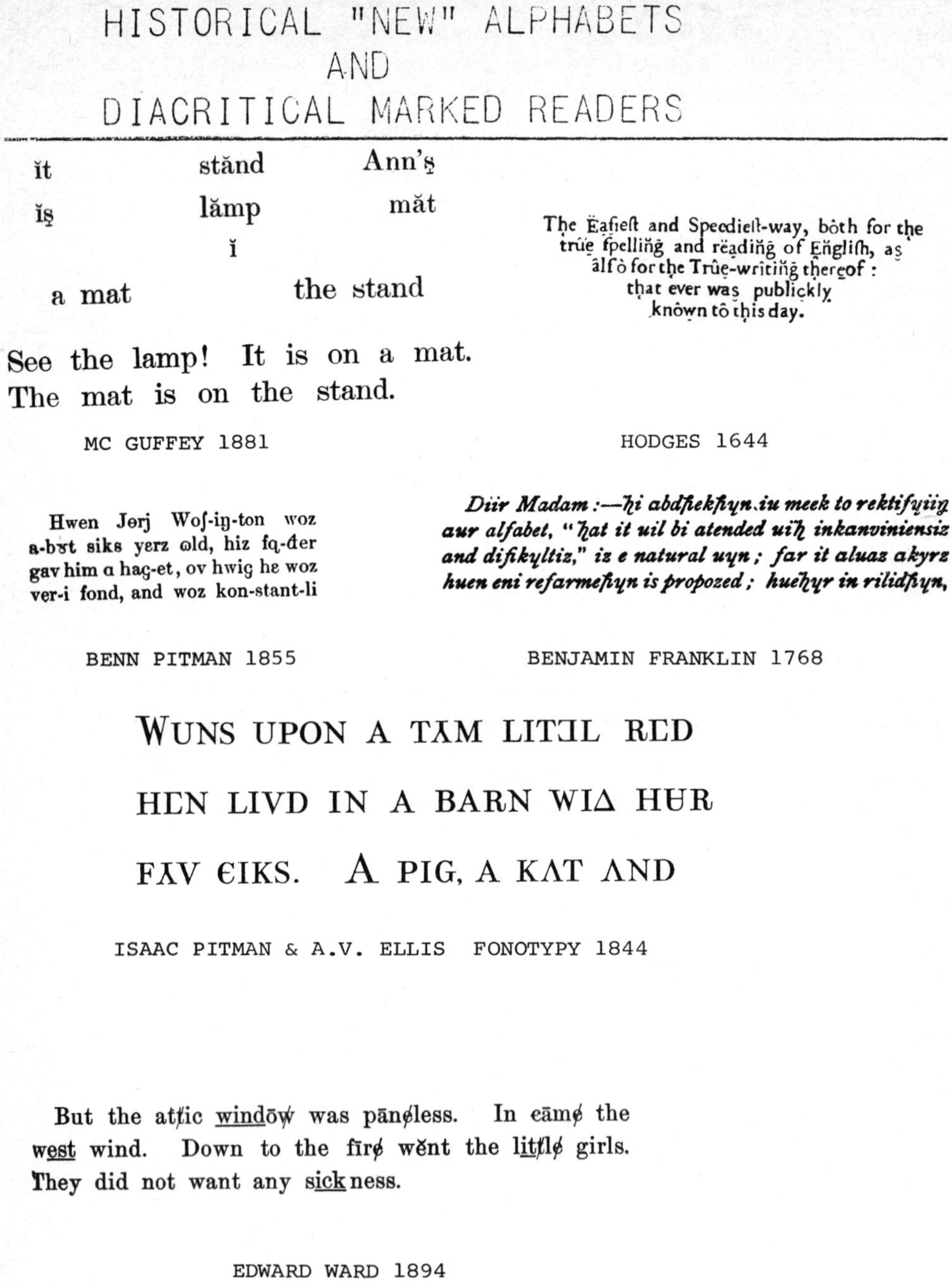

FIGURE 19-6 Examples of "new" alphabets dating back to the seventeenth century.

CURRENTLY USED NEW ALPHABET AND DIACRITICALLY MARKED FIRST GRADE MATERIALS

Sample of Primer Printed in ITA

"dœn't run awæ," ben sed tω hiz cat.
"dœn't fiet," miek sed tω hiz cat.
"wæt heer," sed ben and miek.
"wee will bee at scωl."

Sample of Primer Printed with DMS

"Lo̊øk, Bill," sa̸id Lindå.
"Hēr̸e co̊me̸s Ri̸cky.
Hē is̲ âll rea̸dy fôr sc̸hööl.
Lo̊øk up and sē̸e funny Ri̸cky."

Sample of Primer Printed in Unifon

⅃EN M+CTƎR H+PO TRΔD. HI
P+KT UP BΔBI HɯBƎRT, HELD
H+M +N H+Z B+G ORMZ AND CAИ
U LULUBΔ.

Sample from first drill book for use with Words in Color

t

a̲t	*ta*	*ut*	*tu*
i̲t	*ti*	*et*	*te*
	ot	*to*	

characters that are used in traditional English (*x* and *q* are missing), plus nineteen augmented or additional letters. Most of the new letters are formed by a fusion of two lowercase Roman letters. Five of these new letters, the long vowels, are made by placing a lowercase *e* immediately adjacent to the preceding vowel. Diphthongs, other vowel sounds, and consonant digraphs are frequently formed in a similar way by placing two letters in close juxtaposition. Writing in the ITA is also constrained by a special set of spelling rules. Hence, some words with no letters look different because of the spelling rules only. Both the new letters and the spelling rules add a further constraint in that the traditional word form is preserved so that in a later stage of training the students may transfer to the traditional orthography with a minimum of difficulty.

In an early paper, Pitman estimated that 39.25 percent of words were radically changed when written in ITA, 10.50 percent were moderately changed, 23.75 percent had minor modifications, and 26.50 percent were unchanged. The goal of ITA is to establish a consistent phoneme-grapheme relationship so that one letter will always make the same sound, and vice versa. This goal is not always achieved, partially because of concessions made to word form, but it is a tremendous improvement over the traditional orthography.

Despite the lack of conclusive research results, the Initial Teaching Alphabet has been used in a number of American and British schools. The first regular use of the ITA in a public school occurred in Britain in September of 1960.

WORDS IN COLOR Another British-based system aimed at taking advantage of some phonetic regularity principles is the Words in Color system devised by Caleb Gattegno. This system which has been commercially available longer than the ITA is used by fewer schools than is the ITA. Proponents of the Gattegno system also make some interesting statements such as, "Words in Color makes the English language phonetic through the use of color, enabling the learner to master the mechanics of reading in eight weeks or less." Forty-seven different sounds of English are taught by using different colors for each sound. Since it is difficult for children, or even adults, to distinguish forty-seven different colors, some of Gattegno's symbols are split in half so that they are really two-colored rather than a unique color. This system does not have the color printed in children's workbook material, but rather there are twenty-one drill charts containing 270 letters or letter groups that make a phoneme and some phonetically regular words. The teacher drills the student to make the sounds in isolation, then blends them together. For example, the first page of the first book simply contains a number of *a*'s of various sizes. The second page consists of a number of *u*'s. The third page consists of groups of *a*'s and *u*'s together which the student would blend as a word. After the five vowels are introduced (short sounds), consonants are introduced; and the student can now begin to blend vowels and consonants to form short meaningful and meaningless words. The teacher is also instructed to get a large selection of colored chalk so that she can write letters and words on the board for drill.

The memorization of the forty-seven different sounds with their corresponding colors, as well as the 270 letter combinations which are commonly used in writing these sounds, would appear to be a totally mechanical memorization approach to beginning reading. Demonstrations by the publisher, Encyclopedia Britannica, have been interesting and lively. Nevertheless, research proof is lacking as yet for the superiority of this method over any other.

DIACRITICAL MARKS The Diacritical Marking System (DMS) that I have developed has over 99 percent phoneme-grapheme regularity and aims at

FIGURE 19-7 These beginning readers are learning the Diacritical Marking System.

achieving essentially the same goals as the Initial Teaching Alphabet without distortion in word form or change in spelling.

The DMS is somewhat simpler than the diacritical marking systems found in most dictionaries, since the intention is to aid beginning readers rather than to give extreme accuracy. Regular consonants and short vowels are not marked, since these are the most common usages of the letters. Long vowels have a bar over them. Regular two-letter combinations, which make unique sounds such as the consonant digraphs and diphthongs, have a bar under both letters. Silent letters have a slash mark through them. These marks plus a few others, such as those used for the broad *a* and other sounds of *u*, constitute the bulk of the marks used. Nearly every word used in first-grade reading books is marked; likewise, all work that a teacher duplicates or puts on the board contains the DMS marks. In writing, children have the option of using or not using the marks.

UNIPHON Another new phonetically regular alphabet that has been used with some experiments in the Chicago area is Uniphon, developed by John Malone. This forty-letter alphabet, which the author calls "a single sound alphabet," uses block letters which have an additional interesting characteristic of being specially designed so that they can be read by computers for automatic translating purposes.

Research has not conclusively shown the superiority of any of the new alphabets over traditional approaches to beginning reading and remedial reading.

PHONIC EMPHASIS READERS

As was said of the new alphabets, it is difficult to come up with a totally new concept. Even the linguistic and phonetic readers are scarcely new. Look at the sample first few pages from the McGuffey readers of 1887 and compare them with the first few pages of the Bloomfield and Barnhart's readers (Figures 19-4 and 19-3).

A number of phonics teaching methods are presented in Chapter 5 and 6. Likewise much of the section in this chapter on Linguistics could just as easily appear in this section; but this section will be confined to a brief description of several sets of readers used mostly for beginning reading instruction. They are also used as supplemental or remedial reading series by some teachers.

The Lippincott Readers, more formally known as *Basic Reading* by Glenn McCracken and Charles Walcutt (J. B. Lippincott Company, Philadelphia, 1963), are a good example of a reading series which uses a development of phonics rules for its underlying structure (see Fig. 19-8). In most basal readers (Chapter 2) a "word ladder" or gradual introduction of whole words is the core of the structure. In a basic series the words already introduced are printed in the back of the book. Their repetitions are often controlled, and new words are selected with a view to their being added to this list. Phonics principles are a secondary consideration. In the phonic readers, new phonics principles are gradually introduced and the words used to illustrate them are secondary. Typically, a phonics series introduces more words, but the words fall within categories, that is, illustrating a rule—*bat, cat, mat, nat.* There is no proof that either method (basal or phonics) is superior for beginning or remedial reading instruction. Look at Figure 19-8, which gives the sound-spelling sequence for the Lippincott readers, and contrast this with the figures in Chapter 2 which show the gradual introduction of words in a traditional reading series.

There are a number of different types of phonetic readers. Figures 19-9 and 19-10 show sample pages from the Cordits series and the Hay-Wingo series. Note that the Hay-Wingo series when teaching a consonant sound such as *f* does not teach the sound in isolation. Rather, the consonant is used only with a vowel sound.

PROGRAMMED INSTRUCTION AND TEACHING MACHINES

Programmed instruction, with particular reference to its use in teaching reading comprehension, was discussed in Chapter 10. There are a number of programs other than those specifically designed for reading comprehension. Programming can be used for such diverse reading tasks as teaching discrimination of forms, phonics, and vocabulary building.

An interesting set of materials that takes advantage of some of the features of programmed instruction, linguistics, and kits is the Macmillan Reading Spectrum which is a group of partly programmed booklets in three curriculum areas: Reading Comprehension, Vocabulary Development, and Word Analysis for grades four, five, and six (see Figure 19-11). The booklets are boxed for permanent classroom display so that there are four each for six levels in each curriculum area, besides some sets of graded supplementary reading books. The blending of straight prose with programmed material is an interesting and potentially valuable development.

Teaching machines (those devices which visually present an item to a student, require his response, then tell him the correctness of his response before proceeding to the next carefully sequenced item) do not usually do anything that the same program in book form (scrambled book or programmed book) cannot do. However, at least in experiments, there are now some teaching machines which add the dimension of sound, and this is something that a book cannot do. For example, the machine can both show and read aloud a statement and question. Some teaching machines can also receive a vocal response by the child and this, too, is something that a book cannot do. Language laboratories can sometimes be programmed to operate like an oral-aural teaching machine for reading.

ar

arm	darn	tar	dart	tart	cart
art	card	mar	hard	harm	part
are	star	car	farm	far	scarf

FIGURE 19-8 Sample pages from *Basic Reading* by Glenn McCracken and Charles C. Walcutt (J. B. Lippincott Co., Philadelphia, 1963).

Sound-spelling Sequence in Grade 1

Pre-Primer

Sound	Page	Sound	Page	Sound	Page
short a	1	r	8	p	20
short e	2	s	10	dr,gr	22
short i	3	d	11	sp,mp	24
short o	4	nd	12	hard c	26
short u	5	t	14	h	28
m	6	st,nt	16	f	30
n	7	hard g	18		

Primer

Sound	Page	Sound	Page	Sound	Page
ar	1	le	22	ai	44
er	5	k	24	long i,ie	50
ed	6	ck	26	ir	51
w	7	magic e	31	long o	57
ow(cow)	12	a(care)	31	ore,or	58
l	14	long a	32	oa,oe	64
ll	15	long e,ee	36	j	68
b	21	ea	40	v	73

Reader 1-1

Sound	Page	Sound	Page	Sound	Page
sh	1	-ing	33–38	dg,dge	89
ch,tch	5	-ed	44–47	-tion,-sion	97
th	8	er as er	52	oo(cook)	101
wh	14	ar as er	53	oo(food)	102
qu	17	ir,or,ur as er	54	ow(snow)	115
x	18	-y,-ay	64	ow(cow)	118
y	19	-ey	64	ou	119
z	20	soft c	75	oi,oy	130
ng	26	soft g	88		

Reader 1-2

Sound	Page	Sound	Page	Sound	Page
long u	1	wr,kn	26	ea as long a	62
long ue	1	silent b	36	ear	62
long ui	1	silent l	36	ie as long e	72
ew,eau	8	silent g	48	ei as long e	72
aw,au	14	silent h	48	ei as long a	78
ph as f	18	silent gh	48	eigh as long a	78
hard ch	18	gh as f	48	ey as long a	78
ch as sh	18	ea as short e	62	ough	101

AUDIO-VISUAL DEVICES

An audio-visual device, in contrast to a teaching machine, is any device which presents an audio or visual output usually with the aid of electricity. Most of

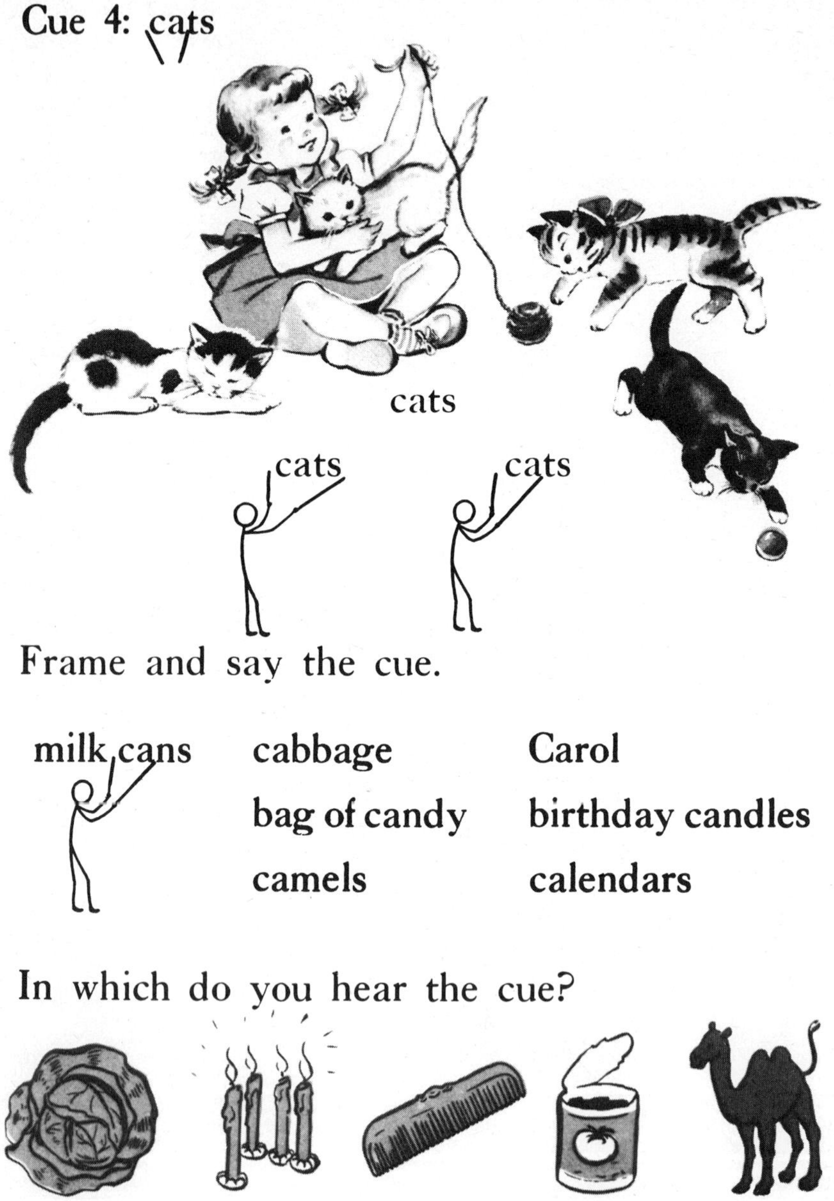

FIGURE 19-9 Sample page from *I Can Read, Functional Phonics for Power in Reading* by Anna D. Cordits (Beckley-Cardy Co., Chicago, 1953).

a e i o u

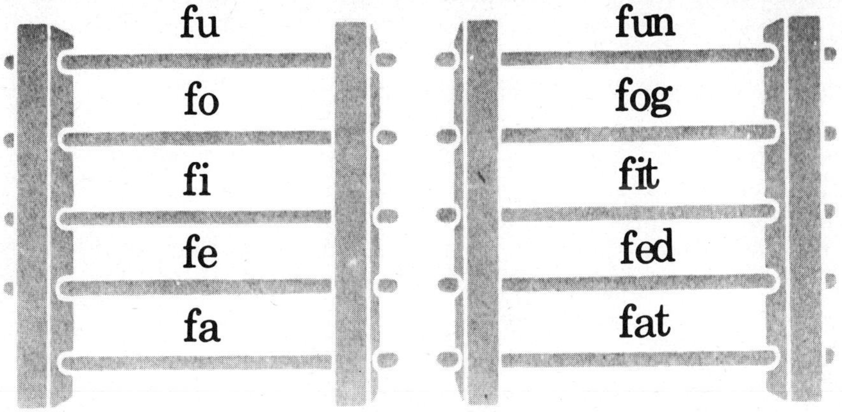

fun	fit	fig	fed
fan	fat	fog	fad

fat	fin	fun
fan	fit	fuss

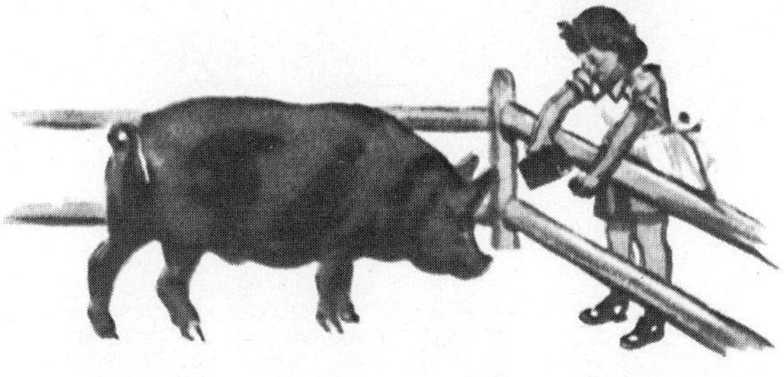

Peg said, "Funny fat pig,

Do you want a fig?"

Peg fed four figs to the pig.

FIGURE 19-10 Sample page from *Reading with Phonics* by Julie Hay and Charles Wingo (revised; J. B. Lippincott Co., Philadelphia, 1960).

them work just as well for a classroom-sized group as for an individual. Common audio-visual devices are phonographs, motion picture projectors, tape recorders, filmstrip projectors, overhead projectors, and various types of still-picture projecting devices. A few such as tachistoscopes and pacers are used primarily for reading instruction. At one time or another most of the audio-visual devices have been used in some way to teach reading.

MOTION PICTURE FILMS Motion picture films have moderately wide usage in teacher training and in introducing and motivating secondary students for reading-improvement courses. On the adult level of speed improvement, there have been a number of series of films of the "Harvard Film" type which show a silent fuzzy page of printed matter. Suddenly, the first word or

FIGURE 19-11 Sample material from the Macmillan Reading Spectrum materials. In the programmed (Practice) section the student covers the answer to a question until he has responded to it on a separate sheet of scratch paper.

PRACTICE

A. Read this article. Look for words and phrases that stand for other words and ideas.

Herbs

[1]Herbs are the leaves of plants which we use to season our food. [2]Oregano gives pizza and spaghetti their special flavors. [3]For this reason oregano is a popular herb. Basil and thyme are two other herbs, used to flavor salads and soups.

Fresh herbs may be used in cooking, but dried herbs are also used by cooks. [4]The bottled herbs which you find in grocery stores have been dried. Often the dried leaves have been crushed. [5]Some of these are then ground into powders.

[6]Herbs grow best in places that have mild climates; however, in colonial days New England housewives grew their own. [7]And the New England climate is not mild. Even today cooks in many different parts of the United States plant and tend their own herb gardens. [8]Why don't you try planting one in your backyard?

Answer the questions about the numbered sentences in the article about herbs.

1. In Sentence 1, what do we use to season our food?
   a. which **b.** leaves **c.** plants — 1. b

2. In Sentence 1, the word *which* stands for ________.
   a. food **b.** leaves **c.** plants — 2. b

phrase lights up and becomes clear, then the next word or phrase—the idea being to guide the student's eyes along the line at a given rate. The next day a film with a slightly faster rate (say, twenty-five words per minute faster) will be shown, and each day a progressively faster rate is used. These films are used primarily for speed improvement at upper secondary, college, and adult levels.

Basal reading series often recommend motion picture films to stimulate interest and add meaning to the stories or accompanying literature books.

TACHISTOSCOPE Tachistoscopes are a common audio-visual aid used in reading instruction. They frequently consist of a filmstrip projector with a shutter attachment so that a frame can be shown at one or more speeds faster than a fixation (see Chapter 14 for a description of eye movements). The important feature of the tachistoscope is not the speed with which the shutter can flash (actually, any speed which is faster than a fixation, one-fifth of a second, is satisfactory) but the content of what is flashed. The content of material used in tachistoscopic training may include: discrimination-training forms, words illustrating phonics principles, basic vocabulary, phrases, and vocabulary building materials. For example, both the Instant Words mentioned in Chapter 4 and the phonics principles materials in Chapters 6 and 7 with numerous example words are available on tachistoscopic filmstrips (Learning Through Seeing, Inc.). For some suggested teaching procedures in using tachistoscopic filmstrips, see pages 51–54, Chapter 4.

Tachistoscopes do not always use filmstrips. The Keystone View Company tachistoscope, one of the earliest and best known, uses $3\frac{1}{4}$- by $4\frac{1}{4}$-inch glass slides with a mask that can expose just one word or phrase at a time. Other small individual tachistoscopes are simple spring-loaded devices which expose a word on a card. Most tachistoscopes operate by a shutter that briefly exposes the word to view (hence the derivation of the word: *tachistos*, "speediest," and *scope*, "to view"); but one well-known tachistoscope, the Tach X, moves the lens in and out of focus so that the word is in focus for only a brief instant. This has the advantage of giving the student a clue as to where the word will appear, but it also has a disadvantage in that some people find the sensation of reading words going rapidly in and out of focus slightly nauseating. No tachistoscope should be used in a completely darkened room, as the relatively bright flash can cause retinal shock, an experience which, while only temporary and not damaging, can sometimes cause an unpleasant sensation in the eyes. In addition, since writing may be required in response to tachistoscopic flashes, some lighting in the room is desirable. Better quality filmstrips and projectors can be used in a normally lighted room if there is not too much direct light on the screen.

Tachistoscopes, like many other devices for teaching reading, are somewhat controversial. The controversy centers mostly around the value of perception training. There is no controversy about whether a tachistoscope interests students; it most assuredly does. Furthermore, a tachistoscope can be a very good way of getting restless children to pay attention to basic words or whatever skill is being presented; and paying attention is the first step in learning.

Filmstrip-type tachistoscopes may be operated by the student for the benefit of himself and/or a group ot students.

The only book devoted solely to the use of this device is *Tachistoscopic Teaching Techniques* by Gaspar Barnette (William C. Brown Company, Dubuque, Iowa, 1951).

PACERS (ACCELERATORS) Pacers, or accelerators, are devices which project or expose reading material at a controlled rate. Their usual aim is to increase reading speed by gradually increasing the speed at which the reading material is displayed.

A typical pacer is a device which lets a shutter slowly come down over the page of reading matter. A student can set the rate at which the shutter descends, and he tries to have it come down as rapidly as possible while still reading ahead of it. This type of shutter is also excellent for discouraging regressions—once the shutter descends, there is no looking back. Other pacers use a thin bar or a band of light which moves down the page at a controlled rate. (See Figure 19-12.)

Among the several projected group-type pacers on the market, the best known is probably the Controlled Reader (Educational Development Laboratories, shown in Figure 19-13), which projects a line of print on a screen from

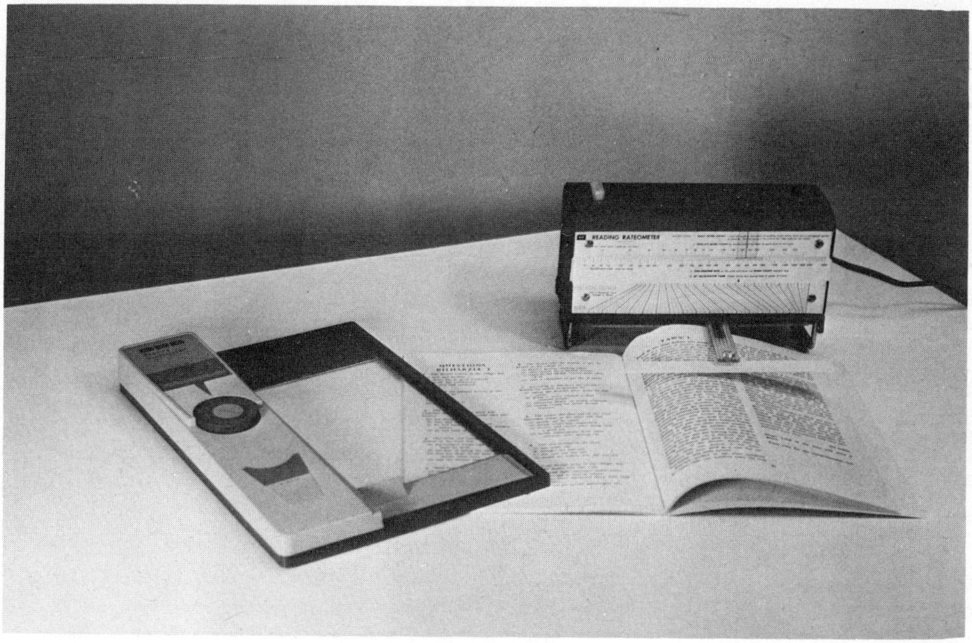

FIGURE 19-12 Accelerator and/or pacer.

FIGURE 19-13 Controlled Reader on special film strips that project one line at a time. Automatic advance.

a special type of filmstrip. After allowing a set amount of time for the line to be read, the next line is shown. The teacher can advance or retard the rate at which the new lines of print are exposed. This device also has an attachment which permits only part of the line to be shown as a moving band of light steadily exposes the balance of the line. The band of light moves from left to right, and the manufacturer claims that this aids in the training of left-to-right eye movement.

FILMSTRIPS Filmstrips used in the traditional sense (still-frame projection, not flashed) are used mostly for reading enrichment. Several publishers have illustrated filmstrips with some written material that can be used for reading enrichment. These filmstrips may accompany specific reading materials but more often are designed for literature enrichment or social studies. In any event, the novelty of having the reading material projected on the screen has a certain motivating value. Glenn McCracken, in a well-publicized experiment, conducted a beginning basal reading program largely by showing the material on the screen rather than having the children read from books.

OVERHEAD PROJECTORS Overhead projectors may be used in a fashion similar to filmstrips. Those which use large plastic slides or transparencies are more popular because of the ease with which transparencies can be prepared. A Thermo-Fax or other copying machines can quickly make any drawn or printed material into a slide. Since transparencies can be made from anything written in pencil or ink, a teacher may sit at home and make any kind of chart, which can be converted into a transparency in a matter of seconds with a copying machine. For typed copy, primary typewriters are best for making transparencies because of their large type.

Handmade slides can also be made by drawing directly on sheets of clear plastic with a grease pencil or special inks. Some inks and some felt-tip pens can also be used to make colored images.

Copying pages from books presents several problems. First is the legal problem of copyright violation. Generally, teachers who make a single copy for classroom use are not prosecuted, since the law is unclear about permissions needed. On the other hand, a school system that makes multiple copies is definitely subject to legal penalties. Copying something and then selling it is a definite violation, and the courts have dealt harshly with such violations over the years.

The second problem in copying material from books for overhead projection is that letter size for most overhead projectors must be at least $\frac{1}{4}$ inch high (preferably $\frac{1}{2}$ inch high) for easy readability, and few books are printed in this size type. Some copying machines cannot copy a page in a book (the page must be cut out), although others can copy a page while it is still in the book.

Commercially prepared overhead projector transparencies are gaining in popularity because of their ease of use and technical excellence. Regularly published overhead transparencies have several advantages over copying book pages and teacher-made materials. They are "laid out" in order to look best and teach best on a screen using the correct size of type, sometimes in color. Some use "overlays" in which several sheets of plastic may be used on top of each other, adding successively greater amounts of material to be projected. Commercially prepared transparencies cover a wide variety of subjects, and a teacher may examine them carefully to see that they meet her needs. Commercially published transparencies may seem to cost more than those made by the teacher, but, this does not take into account the value of the teacher's time.

A transparency can be used in a variety of ways. A teacher can mask off part of the material with a sheet of paper when she wishes to call attention to a part of the transparency, or she can write with a grease pencil or in ink directly on the transparency, underlining a word or letter or circling a word. Grease-pencil marks can be erased, but some inks are permanent.

Some of the commercial transparencies provide space for a teacher to write in extra words or letters. Some teachers add to the projected lesson by writing down the answers to questions while the students watch. This is excellent for reading instruction, as the students see the written words being formed as the teacher says them.

TAPE RECORDERS Tape recorders using prerecorded tape can be used in the same manner as phonographs, but their real advantage is the ease with which a child's voice can be recorded and immediately played back. The chief advantage of a tape recorder in reading instruction is the motivation it provides to students and the incentive for students to read aloud clearly and accurately. Especially with older children, a tape recorder serves almost as a supplementary teacher. A small group of children can work in a corner or a small room and take turns reading aloud into the recorder. When they are finished, they listen to each other read, following along in the book to check for mispronunciations and omissions. This activity will interest the children for a surprisingly long time and accomplishes many of the benefits of a reading group, namely, child interaction is excellent; each child receives practice reading aloud and then has practice in associating the spoken word with the printed word. In most small groups, at least one child will know the correct pronunciation of a word another child mispronounces, so that part of the function of the

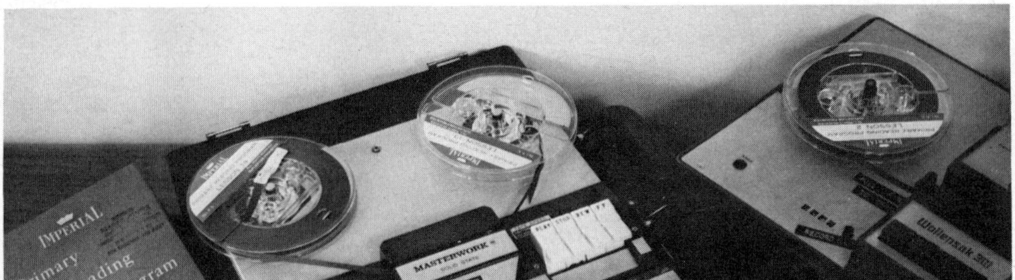

FIGURE 19-14 Two tape recorders and printed material, stories, and workbooks. In the foreground is the jack for multiple headphones.

teacher is fulfilled by the group. In this fashion, the tape recorder can almost take the place of a teacher's aide by "extending" the amount of reading instruction given in a single day. Like all other methods, however, this type of lesson must not be overused or the children will lose interest.

Tape recorders fulfill another useful function by providing an important type of feedback to a child. In oral reading when the teacher corrects a child, the child will often not have been conscious that he had made the mistake; in fact he will often say when corrected, "That's the way I read it." The tape recorder, with its objective recording, shows the child clearly what he did say.

A similar function of tape recorders as used by some teachers is to provide a permanent record of a child's progress. The teacher will record samples of each child's reading aloud at the beginning of the year and at several other times. The child may read either the same or a different passage. The two readings are then placed for the child so that he may see the progress he has made. Parents are also very much interested in this type of progress report on their children.

Tape recorders have long been a very important tool of the speech correctionist. Reading teachers, while not confusing themselves with speech correctionists, will also find great value at times in using this tool for instructional and remedial purposes. They will find it especially useful for some milder forms of speech therapy, particularly if the difficulty is of an articulatory character. Students who omit or consistently mispronounce certain sounds can often correct themselves or be helped to self-correction by simply becoming aware of the fault. Recorded test sentences or oral reading are excellent ways of making the child aware of his speech faults.

A tape recorder may be used as a substitute teacher for individual or group instruction. For example, a teacher can read a text story to which the children listen over earphones as they follow the story in their own reading books. At the end of the story the teacher asks questions to which the children respond by writing their answers on scratch paper. At the end of the lesson the teacher (still on tape) tells the students to exchange papers while she reads the answers for correction.

Many programmed instruction principles can also be used on tape by having the student listen to a small bit of information, perhaps phonics sounds, then respond by writing a word or symbol. The tape can then tell him if his response was correct or if visual feedback is necessary. It might ask the student to refer to a code sheet, for example: "The word you should have written should look just like the word opposite number 24 on your code sheet." The tape recorder can even ask the student to turn off the machine while he reads a portion of prose or does a worksheet and then to resume listening when the task has been completed.

A few publishers sell prerecorded tapes which contain reading lessons with accompanying printed material such as worksheets.

Listening instruction may also be taught by means of the tape recorder.

Listening instruction is one of the language arts closely allied to reading, writing, and speaking. A common form of listening instruction is the oral presentation of a passage followed by comprehension questions.

CARD READERS Card readers such as the Language Master (Figure 19-15), the EFI Audio Flashcard Reader, or the Bio Dynamics Instructacasette (a casette recorder with special adaption for card reading), are special audio-visual devices which read cards (audio output) and may allow for the recording of a brief oral response. It is usually used by one student. One way of using a card reader is to have the student look at a card and try to read the word or phrase printed on it. The student then puts the card in the machine, and the machine reads the card aloud to him. The student may then hold the "talk lever," reinsert the card in the machine, and say the word or phrase correctly. He can then listen and compare his voice with that of the teacher as she repeats the word or phrase printed on the card; or the teacher may later take the stack of cards that the child has been working with and spot-check his work by listening to a few cards.

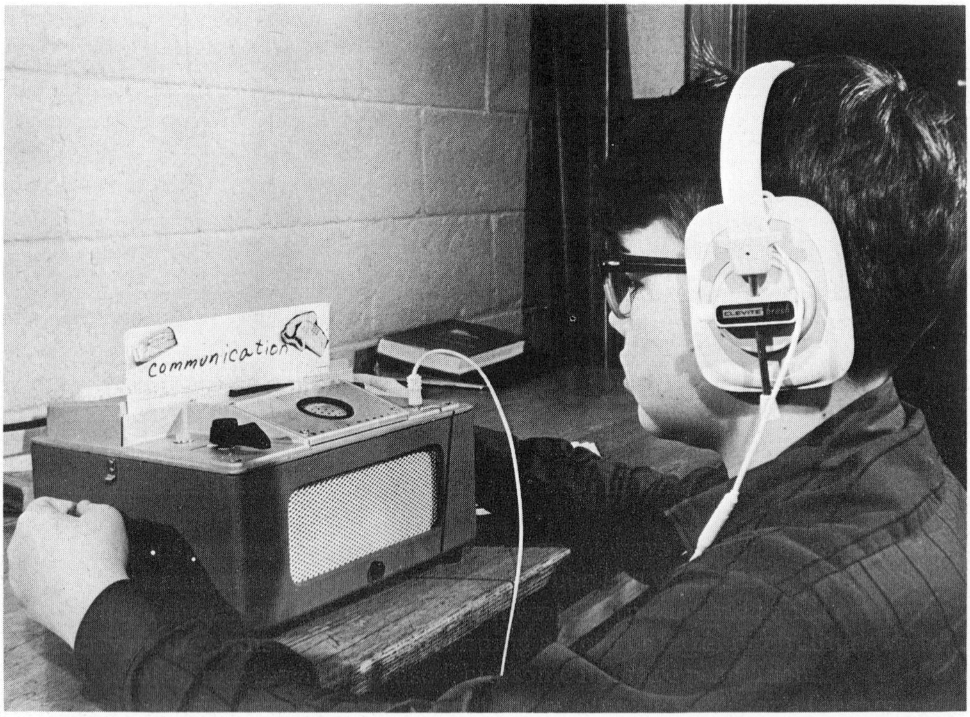

FIGURE 19-15 Illustration of the Language Master, a type of card reader which will "say" (audio output) a word or phrase printed on a card. Both preprinted-prerecorded cards and blank cards for writing and recording students' own words or phrases are available.

Mechanically, a card reader is a type of two-track tape recorder. Along the bottom of the card is a strip of magnetic tape. When the card is inserted into the machine it is moved past a magnetic recording head which can play back the teacher's voice on the top track or record or play back the student's voice on the bottom track. The student cannot accidentally erase or record over the teacher's voice on the top track, because in order to record on the top track a special switch in the back of the machine must be turned on. Prerecorded and preprinted audio cards can be purchased from several companies with the reading phrases and some phonics material, or the teacher can purchase blank cards and make her own. The cards come in various sizes from 3 by 5 inches (suitable for one word) to about 14 inches in length (suitable for a moderately long sentence). Card readers are also excellent for instruction in speech correction or for foreign language instruction.

Earphones are also available so that the machine can be used in a classroom without causing too much disturbance. Earphones also have the desirable side effect of increasing a child's concentration by isolating him somewhat from the environment.

One desirable feature of card readers, as is true of the tachistoscope, the tape recorder, and other audio-visual devices, is the high degree of student interest it engenders. Possibly its greatest benefit is its ability to act as a kind of substitute teacher for the extension of instruction to individual students or small groups while the teacher is engaged elsewhere. These audio-visual devices tend to emphasize the teacher's role as a "director of learning" who sees that each child has the right learning aid at the right time, without herself being the sole source of instruction.

CHARTS AND GAMES

Specific charts and games have been discussed in connection with phonics and basic vocabulary. Most games seem to be especially valuable for phonics teaching and word teaching. It is well to mention them here in this chapter on special methods because they do constitute a special method of teaching reading; and although the method is used more often in a remedial situation than a regular classroom, it is potentially an important source of instruction for every child. Only a few publishers of basal reading series incorporate games to any extent, even into suggested supplemental activities; it is hoped that in the near future, games will be much more widely used as a high-motivation teaching medium. Interestingly enough, a well constructed game has many of the qualities of programmed instruction—isolated small stimulus requiring student response, and with immediate feedback on correctness of response. The curriculum content of the games is very important. In fact, it is probably the poor curriculum content of some games now on the market that has caused games to be banned by some school districts. Games, just like textbooks and audio-visual materials, should be carefully evaluated by such standard criteria as (1) assessing their content and possible curricular value, (2) looking them over carefully (not just the title), (3) considering the reputation of the publisher and the author, and (4) trying them out on a number of children before ordering large quantities.

Charts used for reading instruction (other than those included in some series to be used with preprimer instruction) are usually intended for the teaching of phonics. Charts have the advantage over most audio-visual materials of being relatively easy to leave up for a semipermanent display. After a teacher has explained the chart and used it in a lesson, she can leave it hanging in front of the class for a few days with the beneficial effect of having the children refer again and again to it at different times during the day.

Key word charts (those charts that teach one sound and illustrate the sound by a key word that can also be illustrated) are often left on display in the room to form a kind of sound dictionary (see Figure 19-16). Then, when the

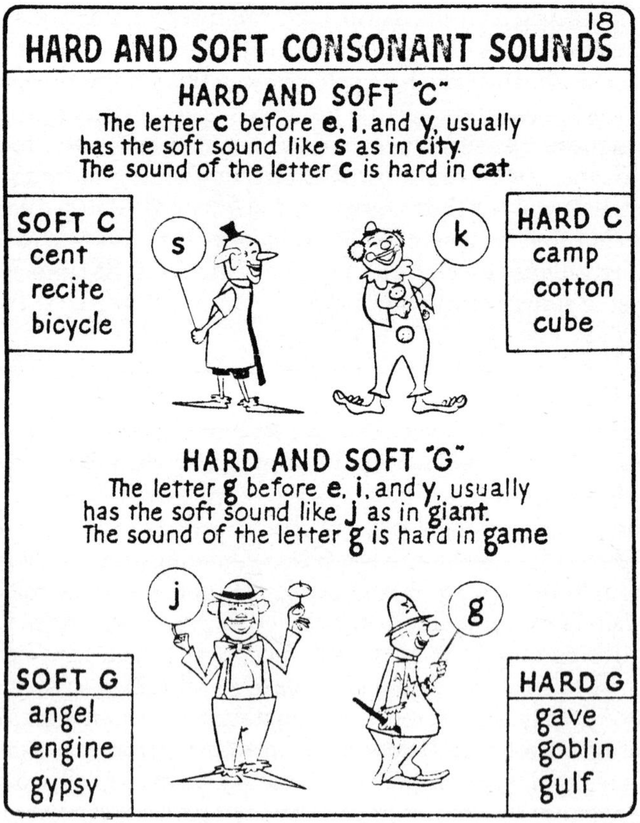

FIGURE 19-16 Sample *Word Study Chart* from a chart series by Edna Horrocks and Terese Norwick (Ginn and Co., Boston, 1958).

child needs to know a particular sound of a letter, he looks up at the chart with the key picture or key word that he knows and is able to recall the sound that the letter or grapheme makes.

THE LANGUAGE EXPERIENCE APPROACH

The language experience approach to reading is essentially a total language arts approach with heavy emphasis on children's writing and a consequent deemphasis on basal series. In fact, some teachers who use the language experience approach do not use any basal series. This does not mean that the children do not read books. Quite the contrary. There is a strong emphasis on use of children's literature books, and these classrooms are usually well stocked with library books on a wide variety of subjects and difficulty levels.

At the lower levels, teachers make many "experience charts." These are stories dictated to them by the children, frequently in a group, with each child taking turns telling about some common experience – the weather, a new item, a social studies project, etc. The teacher edits the children's dictation a little so that the vocabulary is somewhat suitable to their level, and the story comes out in a more or less proper arrangement of sentences and paragraphs. The teacher frequently writes the story on a large sheet of paper with a felt-tip pen so that the words can be read at a distance. If the children produce a story or two a day, within a short time the class library of chart stories is quite large, and often impressive. The teacher saves the stories for review by the whole class or a subgroup, and children are allowed to come up individually or in small groups to read the current and previous day's stories.

Encouraging children to write their own stories is an important element in this method. After writing stories, the children may be called on to read them to the class. At times children are encouraged to read each other's stories by trading them. The teacher may also keep a bulletin board upon which are posted some of the better stories for other children and class visitors to read. Stories are changed frequently.

Teachers vary in the amount of systematic teaching they give to such skills as phonics and spelling. Some teachers merely try to help each child as he demonstrates difficulty, occasionally giving some more or less formal instruction when they notice a number of common needs such as a list of words frequently misspelled or difficulty with short vowel sounds. Other teachers prefer to supplement individual help by using a standard spelling list or a series of workbooks to teach spelling or phonics skills or handwriting skills. But the core of the language arts approach is that all the language arts skills (reading, handwriting, spelling, grammar, speaking, etc.) are as well integrated as it is possible to make them. The chief reading emphasis is on stories written either by the children or by the teacher for the children and on "trade," or nontext, books.

This method has many points in common with the Fernald Keller Kinesthetic Method and with the methods used in many of the schools which are building a more progressive type of curriculum.

An interesting variation on this method is suggested by novelist-teacher Sylvia Ashton Warner in her book *Teacher*. Working with Maowri children in New Zealand, she claimed a great deal of success with difficult children by teaching them emotionally loaded words such as *love*, *kill*, and *afraid*. This type of word is usually not found in basal readers or in most stories for younger children for whom the classroom climate is kept at a lower emotional key.

It is interesting that in the nineteenth century children's readers frequently had very emotion-provoking stories of Indian massacre, heroic love, and brave deeds in face of near or actual disaster. Proponents of the language experience approach, with their emphasis on creativity as children write their own stories and with their use of a wide variety of reading material, feel that they are helpful to counteract the too-bland stories of the basal series.

CONCLUSION

The special reading methods summarized in this chapter constitute by no means an exhaustive account of possible approaches. We have considered some of the great variety of methods and materials (other than basal series) available for the imaginative teaching of reading which can be used both in a regular classroom and in a remedial reading situation. Some teachers will prefer one method and some another. At times a teacher will not know what to do next with a particular child, and a brief review of available varieties of instruction can usually turn up a useful method that she has not yet tried. For example, I have often found the Fernald method to be an excellent ace in the hole, and I have seen tape-recorded lessons pull some otherwise harassed teacher out of a difficult situation when she has too many levels to teach. The many individualized audio-output devices and overhead projectors seem to be among the fastest growing new methods.

20

HIGHER READING SKILLS

Most of this book has had a moderately strong elementary and remedial emphasis. This chapter will be devoted to older students and to those in the average and above-average ability range.

Most secondary teachers, through no fault of their own, are not well trained in the teaching of reading. They will agree that reading is an extremely important skill, a skill that is too often lacking in their students. If a teacher has had the experience of teaching a below-average secondary class, the need for reading instruction is glaring. Hence this book has attempted to demonstrate how children learn to read at the elementary level and to present some of the special methods which, even though not all are widely used, offer some excellent ideas for the teaching of reading at the secondary level. Most of the remedial reading methods we have discussed are directly applicable to secondary pupils.

Any teacher who perceives the importance of giving reading instruction to students at the secondary level and has the patience to undertake the task should indeed be honored and sought after by his colleagues. That teacher will doubtless have broader objectives in mind than just remedial reading, for the implications of language arts skills for academic achievement in high school and college are undisputed. This chapter is devoted, therefore, to the higher reading skills for average and superior students.

However, let us return to remedial reading as a starting point for the development of reading skills at the secondary level. And at the outset let me declare without qualification that any secondary school that does not offer remedial reading instruction is not doing a good job of education. If school administrators think that they do not need a remedial reading class, then they are either sticking their heads in the sand or this is the unbelievable school which defies statistical odds of 1 million to 1 or higher against such a possibility. And the smug assumption that teaching reading is the job of the elementary schools does not relieve secondary schools of the responsibility of removing whatever stumbling blocks remain in a student's pathway toward achieving up to the level of his ability. School administrators cannot close their eyes to the abundant evidence that the number one blockade to success in all academic fields is lack of skill in the language arts.

The cold facts are that schools being what they are (having to handle hundreds and thousands of children), and teachers being what they are (beset with personal problems and training deficiencies), and children being what they are (with a motley range of intelligence, reading skills, motivation, etc.), reading is a subject that simply must be taught in the secondary schools. Teachers or administrators may argue against it in theory; but if they inspect the results of students' formal or informal reading tests, they will quickly be won over to the urgent need for reading instruction in the secondary schools.

WHY ELEMENTARY TEACHERS SHOULD KNOW ABOUT SECONDARY READING

This chapter should be beneficial to elementary teachers because it is important for them to know what the higher reading skills are. For example, one of the skills stressed for normal and superior secondary pupils is reading speed. While speed is not usually emphasized at all in the elementary school, it is important for older secondary and college pupils. Also, secondary pupils are seldom required to read aloud. Knowing these two facts, the elementary teacher might modify her instructional emphasis to prepare pupils for secondary reading. For example, she might emphasize oral reading a little less and silent reading a little more. If she has a pupil who seems to be an unusually slow reader, she might try to increase his speed by giving him more easy reading material and possibly even some timed reading drills.

A major trend of educational curriculum at present is to include some college courses in the high-school curriculum, such as psychology, sociology, and economics.

THE IMPORTANCE OF SECONDARY READING

There is now a strong trend of presenting some reading instruction in secondary schools. An evidence of this is the increasing circulation of the *Journal of Reading* which is devoted mostly to secondary reading. This journal has also presented some surveys that show trends toward an increase of reading classes in secondary schools. And finally, the various programs aimed at helping disadvantaged teenagers usually have a strong emphasis on reading improvement.

In our rapidly changing society, reading is one of the few ways of keeping abreast. A person who does not read is doomed to second-class citizenship.

The printing presses are ahead of us. They are turning out more reading material in every field than anybody can read. Hence reading skills of speed and skimming are vital. A student must be taught to skim over vast amounts of material to find what he wants or needs; then, he must be able to really understand those parts which are vital.

Let us now turn to the more practical level of determining how to teach reading at the secondary level.

METHODS USED FOR A SLIGHTLY BELOW AVERAGE JUNIOR-HIGH CLASS

The methods suggested in this section are intended to be used in a typical junior-high school reading-improvement class (possibly called a developmental reading class). The class meets every day for fifty minutes and may take the place of an English class – it may even be called "English" in the school course list, but the teacher will have a strong orientation toward the improvement of reading. The same course might also be taught in a ninth- or tenth-grade senior-high school class. Students would probably have a nonlanguage IQ average of 94, with none below 87 and only a few above 100. The average reading ability on a set of oral paragraphs would be upper fifth grade, with no students falling below 5.0 and none above 7.0. The class size is twenty-five, including six girls and nineteen boys. Students of normal IQ whose reading ability is below 5.0 would be placed in a remedial reading class with a maximum class size of ten; while students of normal IQ and reading ability above 7.0 would be enrolled in a regular section of English, even in senior-high school.

TESTING Upon receiving a class list, a teacher first obtains the students' records and makes certain that the counseling office has not sent any mentally retarded children or any children whose reading ability is above seventh-grade level. The earliest and best way to ruin the class is to include the wrong pupils. In checking over the school's test records, the teacher will be careful to look at nonverbal IQ scores or a nonreading IQ test score if there is any doubt about the student's mental ability. Group-reading achievement test scores are usually adequate for screening out students who are too high. Next, the teacher verifies the school's group reading tests by giving each child an oral-reading paragraphs test. The scanning of these tests will probably result in a few vacancies in the class; these can be filled during the year as other teachers discover children with reading problems or as reading problems are found in new students who enter late. The same screening procedure is followed by the teacher before each child is admitted.

PHYSICAL TESTS Next, the teacher goes over each student's health record to see if there have been recent (within two years) tests of hearing and vision and that all recommended corrections have been taken care of. If the students have not had recent hearing or vision tests, arrangements for testing are made with the school nurse. If the school nurse cannot test them, the teacher does it herself.

SPECIAL TESTS Early in the semester the teacher administers other tests of a less formal nature, such as the Group Phonics test suggested in Chapter 6 and an informal comprehension test, perhaps one taken from a workbook or comprehension drill book. The results of these tests are recorded in each student's folder (if it seems advisable to the teacher to keep folders in this type of class – some teachers do and some do not). In any event, results of all tests are entered into her roll book so that she has them readily available. The roll book serves as a checklist to see that all children have been tested.

PACKAGED MATERIALS A number of publishers produce workbooks or sets of materials which purport to be "everything the teacher needs" for this type of class. Experienced teachers sometimes use them as part of the program, and sometimes they prefer to put together their own system of materials. Inexperienced teachers find these packaged systems handy to lean on while they are gaining experience and learning how to plan for this type of class. Typical of the packaged systems is *Reading Improvement for Junior High Schools*, a workbook published by Scott, Foresman and company which contains a variety of exercises designed specifically for this type of class in such reading skills as comprehension and phonics. For older students with greater reading ability there is a more advanced edition of this large workbook, *Reading Improvement for Senior High Schools*. Nila Smith has developed a similar series entitled *Be a Better Reader*, published by Prentice-Hall, in which the emphasis is on comprehension. Book One is about the right level for the class just described, while Book Three is more suitable for older and a little more advanced pupils.

Other "packaged systems" suitable for this type of class include the SRA Reading Laboratory. Level IIIa is about right for this class (see Chapter 18 for further description of this series). The Macmillan Spectrum system is also suitable; it contains varied levels of programmed books in comprehension, phonics, and vocabulary. In addition, some of the graded easy reading books could be used.

AUDIO VISUAL MATERIALS While not absolutely mandatory, some audio-visual materials can add sparkle and motivation to the class work and aid greatly in student learning. Two or three short (twenty-minute) tachistoscopic drills per week, using Learning Through Seeing Tachistofilmstrips from Kit JII, is at about the right level. A thorough phonics review can be accomplished using the LTS Phonics Kit of overhead transparencies.

FIGURE 20-1 A reading class in a secondary school.

Many teachers like to use a controlled reader several times per week, keeping the stories slightly below the average ability level of the class. Some of the stories at about the fourth-grade level have a workbook containing comprehension exercises. If it becomes apparent that there is too wide a spread in abilities or rates of speed for all students to be able to use a given difficulty level of group audio-visual material, then the class can be divided into two groups. One group can look at the controlled reader, and the other can read library books or work on programmed-instruction materials.

The tape recorder might be used for an occasional project—recording a group oral-reading session and then playing it back or recording a radio play. A systematic recording of each student's oral reading for comparison on the same passage at the end of the year has been found to be motivating and satisfying for both students and teacher.

Motion picture films shown at the beginning of the year help to motivate students. Besides giving useful suggestions on reading improvement, they also nicely convey the concept that it is quite proper for older students to be working on reading improvement.

ADAPTED CLASSICS AND TRADE BOOKS Adapted classics such as *Tom Sawyer* or *David Copperfield*, rewritten or edited down to the fifth-grade reading ability level, are excellent for this type of class. They give the teacher a chance to build an introduction to classical literature, they are interesting, and they give the student a successful experience in reading. A student at this grade level needs practice in reading book-length stories. Quite frequently all of his previous reading experience has been in readers and textbooks – usually only short stories. Books are a new experience, and it is essential that his first encounter be a pleasant and successful experience. Classroom sets of adapted classics provide good group lessons and discussions.

The classically oriented teacher who fears that the use of adapted (altered) classics is a prostitution of literature may feel different about it once she comes to realize that these students are often just not able to read *Tom Sawyer* in the original, which is at an eighth-grade level of difficulty. There is nothing to prevent these students from later reading the unadapted version of any classic; but if they are not introduced to an adapted version of the classic, chances are they will never have even a brushing acquaintance with Mark Twain. Classically oriented English teachers frequently direct all of their curricular ideas to the top 10 percent of the population and show surprisingly little interest in the great mass of average children, despite their "liberal" arts background.

A number of trade books are aimed specifically at the young teenage market, and some are both easy to read and of high-interest value. Such books as *Hot Rod* by Gregor Felson combine high interest in automobiles, a teen setting, and an easy reading level. Teachers should be on the alert for such books and should talk to students about books they have liked, ask librarians what children are reading, and build book lists, especially of books which appeal to poor readers.

Scholastic Magazine (Arrow Book Club) and Penguin Books (Puffin Series) specialize in paperbound books for young readers. These series contain excellent selections and are so economical that students can afford to buy the books themselves. Some students have never owned a book of fiction, and it is a step toward maturity for them to do so.

WRITING Particularly when the reading-improvement class is being substituted for a regular English class, some writing experience is desirable. Writing and even grammar lessons (if not overused), are an excellent approach in teaching comprehension.

With the slightly below-average class that is our example, the writing experiences should favor practical situations more than literary situations. That is, getting the students to write a poem might be appropriate occasionally, but the bulk of written work for this group of children should be much more practical. A boy in this class will have to know how to write letters to friends, yes, but most of his correspondence will have to do with business situations.

He will be judged (screened) and rated by how well he can fill out job applications; he will be confronted by income tax forms and health insurance papers. He may have to write a note to a fellow worker telling him how to mix paint or operate a machine. Writing exercises that are practical will have more meaning to the student. What is more important, they will have greater transfer to his life needs.

SPELLING Again, if the reading-improvement class is being substituted for English, it may be necessary for the reading teacher to teach spelling. She might use any of several approaches. It is suggested that she use more than one, sometimes isolated and sometimes in combination:

1. *The "spelling book" approach.* A spelling workbook is provided for each member of the class. Pages are assigned in connection with some supporting group lessons and regular weekly tests. This approach, while unimaginative, is sound but often lacks interest. There are regular seventh- or eighth-grade spelling workbooks published by many of the major companies, but they are designed for classes of normal spelling development. Our hypothetical class, though, is not up to this standard of spelling development; hence, a regular seventh-grade spelling workbook would be too difficult. Worse yet, it would not teach the words that these students need most. For this class we need a special remedial spelling book, preferably with a phonic teaching emphasis. The series written by William Kottmeyer, titled *Dr. Spello* and published by Webster Division, McGraw-Hill Book Company, is useful with students who have an irregular spelling development and reading problems.

2. *The "spelling demon" word-list approach.* Taking advantage of the well-known fact that a high percentage of all spelling errors made by secondary pupils are made on a relatively finite list of words, "demon word lists" are compiled of the 100 most often misspelled words. Such lists account for at least one-half of all spelling mistakes made by high-school students. These special word lists are a useful source for spelling lessons in a remedial class. If the teacher discusses and assigns for study ten of these words each week, the spelling lessons will be highly relevant and will cut across the irregular development lines which occur in the typical English class.

3. *The phonic-family word approach.* This approach consists of teaching spelling words in connection with systematic phonics instruction. For example, the teacher might assign words like *ring*, *sing*, *bing*, *thing* or *would*, *should*, *could*. This has two advantages. First, it greatly increases the number of words that can be assigned because of the simplicity of similarity; and second, it gives practice and review of the phonics principles being taught.

This method, particularly if it is combined with the spelling demon word lists, can help the teacher to build a spelling curriculum which is not only well suited to the spelling needs of students but will also provide real amplification of reading skills as well.

Spelling workbooks, too, work well when combined with this approach.

They add specific methods of instruction for the teacher and learning procedures for the children. Interesting variations of the workbook procedure can be used: flash the words tachistoscopically, have the children try to write the word, then show them the word. Both the Instant Words and words illustrating phonics principles are available on filmstrips, or the teacher can make her own flash cards for this type of drill.

PHONICS REVIEW A below-average junior-high school reading class will often need some systematic phonics review, which can be provided in a variety of ways: SRA labs, phonics overhead transparencies, charts, or spelling lessons. While spelling and comprehension can be taught in regular English classes or in other subject-matter classes, it is probable that no other class will teach word-attack skills such as phonics. Class materials can be checked against the phonics principles mentioned in Chapter 6, and the phonics test mentioned in Chapter 7 provides a method of determining whether students are learning them.

Charts, such as those published by Webster Division, McGraw-Hill Book Company or Ginn and Company, provide an excellent and systematic way of reviewing phonics learning in minimum time. To use the charts, the teacher hangs one up in front of the room, explains it, and discusses it with the students. She may leave it hanging in front of the room for another few days. By referring to it occasionally, a maximum amount of instruction can be obtained from it, especially if amplified by drills taken from phonics workbooks or constructed by the teacher. A study of dictionary pronouncing systems is also useful.

COMPREHENSION DRILLS A type of reading improvement drill that should always be included in any reading-improvement class is comprehension drills, which usually consist of reading a passage, followed by questions on the content. Passages may vary in length from several paragraphs to several pages. The reading of the passage may be timed, but the purpose of timing is to add interest, to sharpen attention, or to encourage speed. Timing is not a necessary part of comprehension training.

One very important aspect of preparing comprehension drill material is to make certain that the questions are not a stereotype of requests for rote factual answers. Some questions should aim at the comprehension skills of inference, mood, and other subjective factors.

In addition to the packaged system materials mentioned earlier ("labs" and workbooks), some of the good, standard comprehension drill materials suitable for reading improvement are the following: (1) McCall Crabbs Standard Test Lessons in Reading, Book B, published by the Bureau of Publications, Teachers College, Columbia University, for articles of one to two paragraphs in length (2) Gulliver's *Reading for Meaning, Workbook 5,* published by J. B. Lippincott Company, for articles of about one-half page in length; and

(3) the Elizabeth Simpson's *Better Reading, Book One*, published by Science Research Associates, for articles two pages in length.

Informal comprehension drills can also be made up by the teacher on a wide variety of subjects, including the students' textbooks from other courses. The usual method for devising teacher-made comprehension drills is to use short-answer-type questions, since they take less time to construct and to administer than multiple-choice questions. A very easy type of comprehension question to make up is a "cloze" technique passage, in which every fifth or tenth word is omitted and the student must try to fill them in, either before or after reading the passage. See Figure 20-2 for other cloze variations.

These several types of cloze passages can easily be constructed by the teacher to teach comprehension of prose passages from literary or textbooks. Several short paragraphs, when filled in by the students and self-corrected, are an interesting variation of a reading comprehension drill.

Fifth word

Once all that lunch________opened and piled high________a long picnic table, ________even the Bradleys and________neighbors and relatives could________it all.

Tenth word

The Bradleys had never met those people "who might________bring enough." All of the Bradleys' friends and________brought enough.

Structure words

They always tried________no one ever tried harder________Don.

Subject words

So it had always been on________15. So it was this________this very special ________15 on which________became________years old.

Multiple Choice

Ever since Don could ________ (see – remember) the highlight of the ________ (holiday – fair) had been the ________ (auto – foot) races.

FIGURE 20-2 Cloze-technique examples.

In correcting these comprehension drills, it is best to have the student either correct his own paper or to have the class exchange papers at the end of the period and correct each other's papers. Both ways save hours of the teacher's time, and both have the advantages of improved learning, better student motivation, and immediate feedback on the correctness of students' responses.

Finally, an important type of comprehension drill not to be overlooked is the use of programmed-instruction materials. For example, California Test Bureau's "Lessons for Self-Instruction" booklets, especially those entitled

Following Directions and *Reading Interpretations*, would be excellent for this type of class. Levels CD could be used at the first of the year and Levels EF toward the end. (The reading teacher might recommend programmed-instruction supplementary drills in other subject-matter areas to other teachers as a method of increasing general reading comprehension.) Programmed-instruction mathematics, social studies, English grammar, etc., all rely heavily on the student's ability to follow written directions, and this is a major comprehension skill.

DEVELOPMENT OF THE READING HABIT At least some part of every reading course should be devoted to development of the reading habit. "Reading should include not just books, but magazines and newspapers as well. Several activities might be suggested, for starters:

1. Encourage students to subscribe to a magazine in their own name. Boys often like magazines devoted to cars, airplanes, or mechanics; girls usually prefer magazines such as *Seventeen* or *Ingenue*.
2. Encourage library-book reading by requiring each student to bring to class his own book for a planned period of free reading.
3. Start a paperback book club in class using planned group buying and exchanging plans.
4. Take advantage of special events to motivate free reading. Student attendance at a suitable movie might be recommended, and paperback copies of the book from which the movie was adapted may be added to the class library. Seasonal sports such as football and basketball also suggest book titles.
5. Devise ways of helping students to increase their knowledge by enrichment reading in magazines and reference works.
6. Bring sets of newspaper articles to class for discussion of important events. This is particularly interesting immediately following historical events such as space ship launchings, presidential elections, catastrophes, and medical breakthroughs.

RATE OF READING

Reading improvement in a secondary school should certainly not be confined to remedial or below-average students. Some of the reading skills taught to bright and able students are (1) speed, (2) study techniques, and (3) vocabulary improvement.

Superior college-bound students can certainly improve their reading skills, particularly in the area of speed. A number of colleges and private organizations have been teaching speed improvement to college students and adults, when most of this job could quite properly be done in the secondary schools. It is interesting that studies of children's reading speeds show an increase at a fairly rapid rate during the elementary years, but a slowing down during the secondary years. It is quite possible that this slowing down is simply attributable to the fact that reading is not being taught in the secondary schools.

One characteristic of a poor reader is that he has only one reading speed—slow. Conversely, a good reader has a number of reading speeds, and he can select the speed he wants to suit the situation. His reading speed will vary with such factors as:

1. Intent. Is it the purpose of the reader to memorize the passage or look for tricky clauses in a legal document? Does the reader want to find out the results of a baseball game? The intent in reading the sports pages may not be the same as the intent in reading a directive about a job.
2. Familiarity with the material. Not all topics are familiar to any one reader, but as might be expected, he can read faster in areas in which he is conversant.
3. The physical condition or environment of the reader. Sometimes the reader will be feeling good and full of energy. He may be seated in a quiet, well-lighted room. At another time he may feel groggy or have a headache. He may be trying to read in a noisy, confused situation, and the lighting may be poor. Both internal and external conditions affect his reading rate.

STUDY SPEED Quite obviously, a student reads more slowly when he is attempting to comprehend difficult material than when he is doing light recreational reading. The reading-speed problem is usually not a matter of getting the student to slow down for difficult materials – it is to get him to speed up for light and easy material. Both teacher and students should recognize at the outset that it is normal and natural to have a slower reading rate for studying than for light reading. Development of flexibility in the rate of reading is of greater value, possibly, than learning how to "speed read." The student should be aware that slow reading is not necessarily the best study technique. Ways of improving study techniques will be discussed in a later section of this chapter.

AVERAGE READING SPEED Most reading is done at an average speed. The average reading speed, of course, varies considerably from individual to individual and even in one individual from time to time. It is difficult to say exactly what a norm would be; but as a rule of thumb, the average high-school graduate in the United States reads material that is not too difficult at about 250 words per minute. With training, this speed can frequently be doubled, especially if the student is bright (say, above the average for the population).

The chief method of increasing reading speed is by timed reading drills. There are many books on the market containing prose passages which vary in length from 500 to several thousand words; these passages are meant to be read under timed conditions. After noting the time it takes to read a passage, a student consults a chart that will convert the time on any given article into speed in terms of words per minute. This speed is then plotted on a graph so that he has a week-by-week record of his reading speed. At the same time, immediately following the reading of each passage (but not timed), the student answers a set of comprehension questions without referring back to the passage. The purpose is to measure comprehension after reading the passage just once. Most drillbooks allow for self-correction by placing the answers at

FIGURE 20-3 Timing devices used to measure reading rate.

the end of the book. A comprehension score graph is also maintained so that the student can keep a constant record of his comprehension scores alongside his reading-speed scores.

It is not unusual for a student's comprehension curve to decrease when speed suddenly increases, the result, simply, of trying to read faster. This is a crucial part of the reading-improvement course; one cannot help wondering: "Well, anyone can read faster if he simply lowers his comprehension." There may be some truth in this, but there is also evidence that fast readers do not have less comprehension than slow readers. When she sees this situation of speed increase and comprehension decrease, a teacher should ask the student to level off the speed increase and try and concentrate on what he is reading. If the student slows down in order to improve his comprehension, then he is right back where he started from.

A course in speed improvement or a unit within a regular English course might typically last for ten weeks, with drills being given from one to three times a week in class and additional drills assigned as homework. Students plot their reading speed and comprehension scores for drills done in class. When homework scores are plotted, socres are usually erratic. The teacher may wish to include these scores by having the student plot weekly averages instead of in-class drills.

A number of drill books are available for use in class or for homework, for example, the SRA better Reading Books (Book 2 for younger or less mature secondary students and Book 3 for older or superior students). Passages in these books are about 2,000 words long. Shorter passages (400 to 500 words) are contained in *Faster Reading, a Drillbook* (Cambridge University Press). High-school seniors may want to try a regular college freshman reading-improvement book such as *Efficient Reading* (D. C. Heath) or *Power in Reading* (Prentice-Hall). Most of the drills in these books are to be used under timed conditions.

SKIMMING AND SCANNING Skimming and scanning are, by definition, types of very rapid reading methods which must of necessity sacrifice a considerable amount of comprehension.

Some authorities make no differentiation between skimming and scanning, but let us consider them separately here in order to clarify a particular point. Skimming is defined as that type of reading activity which, first of all, is very rapid. The student reads at about twice his normal rate. In order to do this, he must eliminate nearly one-half of the material. The material he leaves out is selective; he tries to get the main idea of each paragraph, and possibly a supporting fact or two. He intentionally does not read all of the paragraph and, also intentionally, accepts a lower comprehension. The student uses this type of reading when he is in a great hurry and when comprehension or at least high comprehension is not of great importance.

Scanning is that type of rapid reading activity which allows the student to look over the page hurriedly for something specific. He may be looking for names, dates, or answers to questions. (When he goes through the pages of a dictionary rapidly, looking for a particular word, the student is scanning.) When he is looking up information, he may scan the pages until he finds the area that he wants to read. While he is scanning, most of the information he gets from a page is a negative signal. In other words, his comprehension amounts to a selective response: "I don't want to read this; I have not come to the information I want as yet."

Both skimming and scanning are extremely valuable reading skills and should be developed consciously and deliberately. The student who does not have these skills is likely to encounter considerable difficulty in high school, and even more in college. Strange as it may sound, good comprehension is not always the most desirable goal in reading, especially when it comes at a great cost of time and effort. Nearly four centuries ago, Sir Francis Bacon wrote with great insight: "Some books are to be tasted, others to be swallowed, and some few to be chewed and digested."

There are a number of useful drills which the teacher can use to teach skimming. She might have a group of students, all of whom are reading the same book, see who is first to find a certain fact buried in a given chapter. Or she might ask the students to turn to the index and see who can first locate a name or subject-matter area, and report on which pages it can be found. Similar drills can be done with dictionaries, telephone books, and encyclopedias.

SKIMMING The fastest reading speed is known as skimming. It differs from average reading in that it is much faster and the reader intentionally accepts a lowered degree of comprehension. In average reading using the type of drill-books discussed above, an untrained reader will read about 250 words a minute with 70 to 80 percent comprehension; a trained reader maintains the same degree of comprehension while reading about 500 words per minute. In skimming, 800 to 1,000 words a minute is quite normal, and many students can do much better than this if they have some familiarity with the material and good reading ability. However, comprehension while skimming is frequently in the 50 to 60 percent range. In other words, the student intentionally accepts a lowered comprehension in order to achieve a great increase in speed. This is a rather dramatic example of "flexibility" which is a characteristic of a good reader.

Skimming also differs from average reading in that the reader intentionally leaves out hunks of material; for example, he may read just the topic sentence and then let his eyes drift down through the paragraph, picking up a name or a date. The intention is to get the main idea out of each paragraph with a few specific facts. If there are too many facts or too many names and dates in a paragraph, they must be omitted for they cannot be acquired while skimming. Careful study of Figure 20-4 illustrates what a skimmer might be expected to do.

Sometimes, when first exposed to skimming, a student may be unable to do it. The student should be asked to reskim the material, trying to go faster. The comprehension drill, of course, should be taken only after the first skimming. But students need to have the experience of having their eyes go through the material at a more rapid rate. All above-average high-school students should learn to skim at 800 words per minute or more, although it may take a number of class drills to achieve this rate. In addition to class drills, homework in skimming should be assigned; for example, "Tonight, skim an entire magazine."

Skimming is an extremely valuable skill, and it is well worth the time it takes to teach it. Students should not, of course, think that skimming is a substitute for other kinds of reading or for study activities. All above-average students who are going on to college, however, should learn this technique. Without it, it is doubtful whether they will be able to keep up with the many and broad areas of interest that are required—not only in college but also in the modern world. Oftentimes, students surprise themselves at the high degree of comprehension they attain while skimming at 1,000 words a minute. It may take considerable practice before a student attains a feeling of comfort and

Usually the first paragraph will be read at average speed all the way through. It often contains an introduction or overview of what will be talked about.

Sometimes, however, the second paragraph contains the introduction or overview. In the first paragraph the author might just be 'warming up' or saying something clever to attract attention.

Reading a third paragraph completely might be unnecessary but ... ...
... ...
... ...
... ...
... ...
... ...
... ...
the main idea is usually contained in the opening sentence
... ...
... ... topic sentence ... ...
... ...
... ...
... ...
... ...
... ...
... ...

Besides the first sentence the reader should get some but not all the detail from the rest of the paragraph ... ...
... ...
... ...
... ...
... ...
... ...
... ...
... ...
... ...
... ...
... ...
... ... names ...
... ...
... ... date ... ...
... ...
... ...
... ...

This tells you nothing ...
... ...
... ...
... ...
hence sometimes the main idea is in the middle or at the end of the paragraph.

Some paragraphs merely repeat ideas ... ...
... ...
... ...
... ...

Occasionally the main idea can't be found in the opening sentence. The whole paragraph must then be read.

Then leave out a lot of the next paragraph ... ...
... ...
... ...
... ...
... ... to make up time
... ...
... ...
... ...
... ...
... ...

FIGURE 20-4 What a student might see in skimming. (From Fry, *Teaching Faster Reading*, Cambridge University Press, 1963.) [Continued on page 428.]

Remember to keep up a very fast rate

... ...
... ...
... ...
... ... 800 w.p.m.
... ...
... ...
... ...

Don't be afraid to leave out half or more of each paragraph

... ...
... ...
... ...
... ...
... ...
... ...

Don't get interested and start to read everything ... ...

... ...
... ...
... ...
... ...
... ...
... ...
... ...
skimming is work ... ...
... ...
... ...
... ...
... ...
... ...

Lowered comprehension is expected ... ...

... ...
... ... 50% ... ...
... ...
... ...
... ... not too low
... ...
... ...

Skimming practice makes it easier ... ...

... ...
... ...
... ...
... ...
... ...
... ... gain confidence ...
... ...
... ...
... ...
... ...

Perhaps you won't get anything at all from a few paragraphs ... ...

... ...
... ...
... ...
... ...
... ...
... ... don't worry
... ...
... ...

Skimming has many uses ...

... ...
... ... reports ...
... ...
... ... newspapers ... ...
... ...
... ... supplementary
... ... text ... ...

The ending paragraphs might be read more fully as often they contain a summary.

Remember that the importance of skimming is to get only the author's main ideas at a very fast speed.

(**FIGURE 20-4** *Continued from page 427.*)

ease while skimming, but this work-type reading skill is invaluable when time is short and a great deal of material must be covered. Needless to say, for recreational reading a student may proceed at any speed he chooses. Good readers will find that the choice is theirs whether they wish to skim or read intensively.

---

1. In teaching skimming, a teacher should set a goal to be reached that is approximately four times faster than the student's beginning w.p.m. rate.

Hence, if the class averages 250 w.p.m., a goal of 1,000 w.p.m. might be set.

2. When students first try to skim at 1000 w.p.m., many of them will go much slower.

They should then be told to reskim the sample article until they reach the goal of 1,000 w.p.m. (taking the comprehension test only after the first skimming).

A student's paper might look like this:

	1st drill	*2nd drill*	*3rd drill*
1st skimming	310 w.p.m.	490 w.p.m.	715 w.p.m.
2nd skimming	450 w.p.m.	630 w.p.m.	1025 w.p.m.
3rd skimming	675 w.p.m.	1100 w.p.m.	
4th skimming	1050 w.p.m.	1100 w.p.m.	

Note the improvement on the first skimming on each successive drill.

Source: Fry, *Teaching Faster Reading,* Cambridge University Press, 1963.

FIGURE 20-5 Reskimming drill.

Speed		*Poor reader*	*Good reader*
Slow	*Study reading speed* is used when material is difficult and/or high comprehension is desired.	100–200 w.p.m. 80–90% comp.	200–300 w.p.m. 80–90% comp.
Average	*Average reading speed* is used for everyday reading of magazines, newspapers and easier textbooks.	150–250 w.p.m. 70% comp.	300–600 w.p.m. 70% comp.
Fast	*Skimming* is used when the highest rate is desired. Comprehension is intentionally lower.	Cannot skim	1,000 + w.p.m.

Source: Fry, *Teaching Faster Reading,* Cambridge University Press, 1963.

FIGURE 20-6 The three speeds of reading.

Commercial courses that claim to teach people to "read" at several thousand words per minute are usually teaching them merely to do a very rapid and light skimming activity. At such high speeds, it is very doubtful that much new information can be obtained; in other words if a person does not already know a good deal about the topic he is skimming, he will not be able to answer very many comprehension questions about it. Tricks have sometimes been played on people who claim to be able to read several thousand words per minute by having them read a page of material in which the typist has left out every other line—they often report nothing wrong with the passage.

IMPROVEMENT CURVES Not all students will make the same improvement in reading speed. While it is normal for a class average speed to double without any loss in comprehension during a ten-week series of timed speed and comprehension drills, some students will do considerably better and others worse. For students who do not make significant gains, increased practice with skimming drills will sometimes help; this may even improve their normal reading rate. A few students may need to continue the timed reading drills beyond the ten-week period or to be given drills which are on an easier readability level.

Some students may reach a high level of reading speed very early in the ten-week period; they will make rapid gains for the first two, three, or four weeks and then level off. Others will seem to make no gains at all for the first few weeks; but after they attain some feeling of comfort in trying to read against a stopwatch, they suddenly display a marked increase in speed. Still a third type of student will exhibit an erratic pattern, going up one week and down the next and back up again. These erratic students often make excellent gains in the end, the breaking of old reading habits accounting for the pattern of seemingly inconsistent highs and lows. The overall trend, though, will be upward.

Another important thing can be learned from looking at a student's reading-rate improvement curve and his comprehension curve. Many drill books make provision for a student to plot his reading rate in words per minute on one graph and his comprehension score in percent of questions answered correctly. See Figure 20-7. It is important for the teacher and student to watch the relationship between speed and comprehension. If speed is increasing and comprehension remains within the normal range (70 to 90 percent), all is well. But if speed increases and comprehension drops (see the problem in Figure 20-7), then the correct solution is to level off speed and concentrate on comprehension until it returns to normal. Do not lower speed to regain comprehension, or the student will be right back where he started—having gained in neither speed nor comprehension.

If the comprehension curve remains too high, 90 to 100 percent, then probably a great price is being paid for speed. In other words, a student having very high comprehension could read faster, in fact should read faster for average reading. There are times when 100 percent comprehension or very high comprehension is desirable, but for average reading tasks a very high comprehension rate takes much time. Flexibility is the important concept to be mastered, and the mature reader adjusts his speed to his comprehension

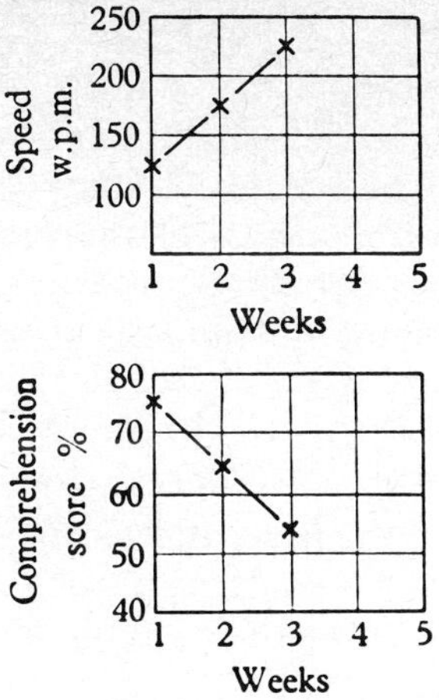

THE PROBLEM: Student makes rapid speed increase but loses comprehension.

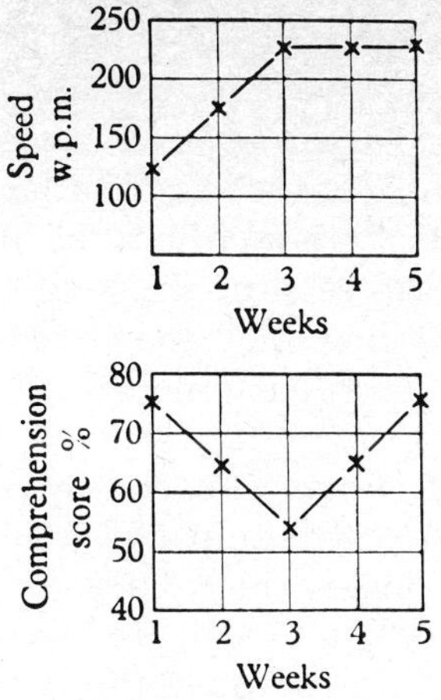

THE CORRECT SOLUTION: Level off speed increase and concentrate on improving comprehension.

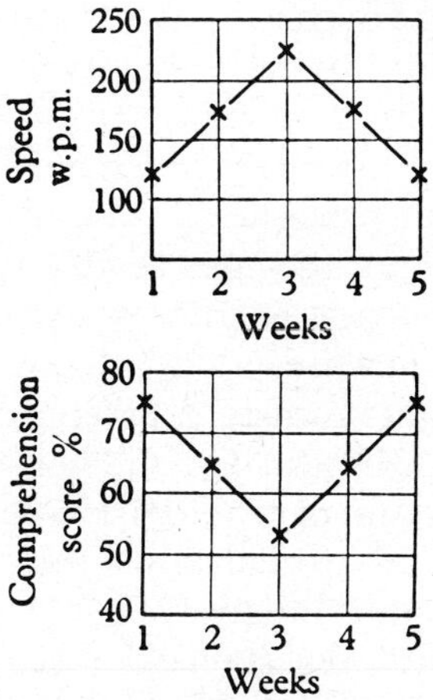

THE WRONG SOLUTION: It is wrong to lower speed (lose the gain) in order to raise comprehension.

Note: In the wrong solution the student has exactly the same speed and comprehension at the fifth week as he did at the first week; hence no improvement has taken place.

FIGURE 20-7 Graphs showing the right and wrong way to get comprehension back to normal. (From Fry, *Teaching Faster Reading*, Cambridge University Press, 1963.)

needs. Poor readers do not adjust their speed, regardless of the importance of the material.

COMMON FAULTS There are a few common faults (seen mostly in slow or poor readers) that the teacher can readily detect and help students to avoid.

Some of the most common faults are these:

1. *Head movement.* When trying to read faster, some students think that it improves their speed or comprehension to turn their head from side to side while reading a book. This is fallacious. The eye muscles are quite capable of doing the job of aiming the fovea at the print—the neck muscles accomplish nothing in the reading process. Students are often unaware of doing this; if the teacher will simply step up to the student and hold his head still, this is usually warning and admonition enough.

2. *Finger pointing.* Students may feel that reading speed can be increased if they point a finger at each word or hold a card underneath the line. While this gimmick might help a few readers on the first- and second-grade level to keep from losing their place, older readers' pointing at the words or using cards is not only unnecessary but usually slows the reading and offers a distraction which detracts from comprehension.

3. *Vocalization.* Some poor readers are so tied to saying words orally that their lips actually move when they are attempting to read. This greatly slows down the reading rate because speech normally occurs at about 125 words a minute, while even average high-school readers read at 250 words a minute. If vocalization is so bad that lips actually move, usually the students can be made aware of this by teachers' warnings. In remedial cases, vocalization may be a sign of reading at the frustration level, but in superior students it is usually a bad habit which should be broken.

A more common and more serious reading problem is subvocalization, which occurs when a reader says each word to himself as he reads "internally." He does not actually say the words aloud (this would be "vocalization"); but, even though he is "reading to himself," all the muscles involved in speech come into play as he subvocalizes quietly. There is considerable argument among reading specialists and psychologists about whether thought is of a verbal nature. Many claim that in all thinking some type of verbalization occurs in the mind. Some experimentations have even attempted to show tiny traces of physiological correlates, such as movement of the tongue while reading. No matter whether there are or are not slight physiological correlates or vocalization in all reading, we do know that the greater the amount of subvocalization (the closer it approaches actual vocalization), the lower the speed of reading. Students should be enjoined to read faster and to concentrate on the author's ideas and not to go through the motions of having an "internal radio announcer reading each word."

STUDY-TYPE READING If we follow Sir Francis Bacon's dictum, there are few books which should be "chewed and digested" or (perhaps with less lofty motives) studied well so that the student can pass an examination. Studying, almost by definition, requires maximum comprehension. Furthermore, in this case, the student probably wants maximum retention; he wishes to remember all, or at least a high percentage, of what he has read for a long period of time.

Study-type reading is usually quite slow, since the student needs time to think about what he is reading, to reflect, and to relate it to other known material. Quite frequently, the student will wish to engage in some additional activity, such as taking notes or underlining important passages. Both of these devices are good, and when done conscientiously and not mechanically, they aid in both reading comprehension and retention. The teacher can promote this type of activity by giving specific exercises in which the student is encouraged to stop and think about the material as he reads it, to take notes on it, to underline key passages, or to combine any of these three activities. If a group of students is study-reading the same passage, the teacher might then lead a discussion about which notes were taken and which passages were underlined. Figures 20-8 and 20-9 should be studied carefully to see examples

Outlining	*Notes*

Activity important for learning
a. Mental activity
  1. stop and think
b. Physical activity
  1. outlining
  2. underlining
  3. note-taking
  4. personal index
  5. SQ3R
	Activity, both physical and mental, are necessary for learning. Student may stop and think, outline chapter, underline book, take notes on reading, make a personal index, or use the SQ3R technique.

Practice important for learning
a. Both physical and mental skills
b. Mere repetition not enough
  1. try to improve each time
c. Space out practice
d. Use things learned
  1. new vocabulary in speaking
  2. reading skills on newspaper
	Practice is also important for learning both physical and mental skills. Student should try to improve each time; mere repetition not enough. Practice should be spaced out and use should be made of things learned.

Note the similarity between outlining, notes, and underlining (Fig. 20-10). All strive for main ideas. Outlining and note-taking are possibly more active than underlining. Outlining gives a better visual picture (gestalt) and shows system more clearly. Outlines or notes taken on reading are most often kept in notebooks, but sometimes they are kept on file cards for handy reference or study.

Source: Fry, *Teaching Faster Reading*, Cambridge University Press, 1963.

FIGURE 20-8 Examples of outlining and note-taking for study.

of outlining, note-taking, and underlining. All three of these techniques are excellent reading-study methods, which can be taught to students by having them practice the techniques and then discuss their activities.

Good underlining picks out main idea and important points.

Activity is an important factor in learning. Most tasks require at least some type of mental activity in order for them to be mastered by the student. Because it is difficult for mental activity to be seen by the teacher, some type of physical activity such as writing is often required. Students might also find it helpful to ensure mental activity if they force themselves to do some sort of physically active task.

Bad underlining has too much material underlined.

Activity is an important factor in learning. Most tasks require at least some type of mental activity in order for them to be mastered by the student. Because it is difficult for mental activity to be seen by the teacher, some sort of physical activity such as writing is often required. Students might also find it helpful to ensure mental activity if they force themselves to do some sort of physically active task.

Bad underlining has the wrong parts underlined.

Activity is an important factor in learning. Most tasks require at least some type of mental activity in order for them to be mastered by the student. Because it is difficult for mental activity to be seen by the teacher, some type of physical activity such as writing is often required. Students also might find it helpful to ensure mental activity if they force themselves to do some sort of physically active task.

Source: Fry, *Teaching Faster Reading*, Cambridge University Press, 1963.

FIGURE 20-9 Good and bad underlining as a study technique.

SQ3R READING-STUDY TECHNIQUE Another interesting "package" study technique is the SQ3R. In using this method, students are encouraged to follow these definite steps:

1. *Survey.* The first step is for the student simply to turn the pages to get a very broad idea of the extent of the reading material. If, for example, it is a chapter, the student should check the number of pages in the chapter to ascertain its length. He should also get a general idea of the subject matter. If it is a chapter on history, he should know whether it covers the next ten years or the next 500 years, etc.

2. *Questions.* The student next turns the pages and jots down questions on reading material in a notebook. If there are adequate subheads, the student can sometimes change the subhead into a question. In a chapter on electricity, the student might take the subhead "Direct Current" and write in his notebook, "What is direct current?"—or, more briefly, simply write, "D.C.?" The questions will be as sophisticated as the student and the book. In a more advanced text, the student's question might be, "How is direct current used in this process?" In any event, it is a sound learning principle to approach a lesson, in this case a passage to be read, with specific questions in mind.

What does SQ3R *mean?*	Survey, Question, Read, Recite and Review
What does 'Survey' mean?	Turn all the pages in the chapter being studied, see how long it is, and get a general idea of the content.
What is meant by 'Question'?	Write down questions on each main point in the chapter (as in the column on the left here). Base the questions on the main points, which can be deduced from the subheadings or extracted by skimming.
What does 'Read' mean?	Read the chapter completely to answer the questions. Note that reading is not done first.
What is meant by 'Recite'?	Answer the questions completely, either orally to another person or in writing, putting answers in your own words (as in this column).
What does 'Review' mean?	Some days later the material should be revised, possibly by quickly re-reading the chapter, and/or trying to answer the questions, looking up all wrong or partial answers.

FIGURE 20-10 Sample questions and recitation (answers) using the SQ3R study technique.

3. *Read.* The student now reads the chapter in such a manner that he can answer his own questions. This occurs after he has read all the pages twice, once to survey and another time to make questions. This is one of the ways in which the SQ3R method differs from simple study-reading in which the student simply reads the chapter slowly one or more times.

4. *Recite.* After the student has completed the reading of the chapter, he then goes back to his notes and attempts to answer his questions. He may do this mentally or by writing them out. If two or more students are studying the same lesson, they could get together and ask each other questions based upon the chapter. As every teacher knows, having to explain a subject is a good way to learn it. Rewording the studied material is a good means of measuring the reading comprehension.

5. *Review.* At a later time, the student should review the material. After he has been through it for a survey, making questions, reading, and answering his questions, he has probably absorbed all he can at the moment. Review, in this case, means coming back for a second look after a lapse of time. Interestingly enough, review can sometimes contribute as much to comprehension as it can to retention. The next day or several days later, after rereading the chapter and his notes, a student will often gain new insights into the material. Review is an excellent aid to retention. As most students are already well aware, it is an excellent idea to review on the night before a test.

Study-type reading and special methods such as the SQ3R are usually thought of as skills, especially for secondary and college readers, but some teachers on the upper-elementary level also find it useful to introduce their students to these skills. It is probably safe to say that students will usually *not learn* study-type reading and methods such as the SQ3R by *lecture* alone. If a teacher wishes to help students acquire these skills, she must prepare specific exercises and supervise them to see that students follow the proper procedures. An occasional comprehension test administered after the students have been advised to use these methods will tell the teacher whether more instruction is necessary.

The SQ3R system may appear deceptively simple. On analysis, however, a number of learning factors have been built into it. The first is the use of the "mnemonics device." Then, with the survey we step into a Gestalt-like activity of getting an "overview, or cognitive map" to be filled in.

The making of questions brings in both "physical and mental activity." Here, also, a "multisensory" approach occurs as a student is forced to write the material. The two acts of formulating questions and reading to answer them bring into play the important learning factor of "attention." A student tends to learn when he pays attention. Closely allied to this is the development of "purpose," an important factor in motivation. Many a reading text points out the close relationship between purpose and comprehension.

The stage of review again brings different multisensory factors into play. It also follows another general learning principle, that of "guidance to trial and error." This means that when learning something new it is helpful to be guided to the steps so that it is impossible to make any mistakes at first. In other words, the best way to learn is simply to be shown the correct procedure. This is followed by a trial-and-error stage in which the learner manipulates the material. At this time, immediate feedback is important to tell the student whether his response was correct. Besides correcting wrong impressions and confirming right ones, feedback furnishes a needed reward.

Overall, the SQ3R method has a good deal of practice and repetition built into it. The student first sees the material when he surveys; he sees it once more when he formulates his questions; he sees it for a third time when he reads more deliberately; and a fourth time when he answers his questions. Finally, a fifth reinforcement occurs in the review. The review stage, coming as it does at a later time, involves the principle of "spaced practice."

"Systematization" occurs when the questions are formulated, since they form in essence an outline of the chapter. Systematization is further strengthened when mnemonic devices are used in all or part of the material learned. Further systematization may occur if the student actually outlines the chapter or underlines significant parts of it; both steps are excellent and well-recognized study techniques.

This discussion has illustrated how learning principles may be applied to the teaching of other facets of reading skills.

READING IN THE SUBJECT-MATTER AREAS

Some secondary schools have staged campaigns to stress the need for, and value of, training in reading. One such campaign was entitled: "Every teacher a teacher of reading." This noble thought may encounter an obstacle or two—it might be difficult to interest a shop teacher or a music teacher in improving the reading ability of students. On the other hand, almost all subject-matter teachers are concerned because student achievement is handicapped by inability to read properly, and teachers know how closely reading is related to their subjects. This relationship is especially close in two reading areas: (1) the area of vocabulary and (2) the area of comprehension.

With respect to the first area, each subject has its own unique vocabulary, and a teacher can facilitate learning by calling attention to new words as they are introduced in lectures and in textbooks. She should explain their meanings and origins, possibly following this up by placing these words in quizzes. With respect to the second area, teachers will find that when they improve reading comprehension, they thereby improve comprehension of all that is unique to their subject. A quiz on the textbook is, in itself, really a kind of reading-comprehension drill. It should not be avoided, but neither should it be worked to the point of boredom.

VOCABULARY IMPROVEMENT

Students improve their vocabularies in many ways. Let us consider three of these ways: (1) from the environment, (2) through direct study, and (3) through an intensive skills improvement course.

1. Most words are acquired by the natural-use method, that is, by living in an environment of words. Children learn to speak because they hear words being spoken. It is no accident that Chinese children speak Chinese and English children English—that is all that they hear. Conversely, a deaf child does not speak because he hears no speech. Once a degree of literacy is attained and a child begins to read, he adds to his stock of words through seeing them in books. By simply seeing a new word used in a number of different contexts, children soon acquire the word and their reading vocabulary is thereby expanded. Brighter children, of course, acquire more words and with fewer repetitions than are needed by dull children. But even for bright children it takes exposure (namely, hours of reading) for significant vocabulary improvement.

School is one of the environments in which children experience a great deal of language. One of the most important tasks that a teacher performs is to use a large variety of words and use them precisely, both in speaking and in writing.

2. The second major way in which children improve their vocabularies is through direct study of a subject. To learn about a "neutron" or a "declining balance" frequently takes direct study of the concept. It has been said that the real way to improve vocabulary is simply to get an education. Hence in

one very real sense, the whole purpose of education may be said to be to improve the student's vocabulary. I have always liked the statement "An educated man can state a simple thing in a complicated way or a complicated thing in a simple way." This direct study of a subject method is the second main way that all teachers can improve vocabulary.

3. The third method of vocabulary improvement, while a valid method, is often a kind of intensive, or short-cut, method which is taught in a vocabulary-improvement course. This method frequently involves the study of roots and prefixes and suffixes (see Figure 20-10). It works particularly well in learning longer words, most of which tend to have Latin and Greek roots and prefixes. For example, in explaining the word *psychology*, a teacher would point out that the root *psyche* means "mind" while *ology* means "study of." She would then point out that we see *ology* in such words as *geology*, *sociology*, etc., and that *psyche* is seen in *psychiatry*, *psychometrist*, etc.

Words	*Prefix*	*Root*
1. Precept	pre- (*before*)	capere (*take, seize*)
2. Detain	de- (*away, from*)	tenere (*hold, have*)
3. Intermittent	inter- (*between*)	mittere (*send*)
4. Offer	ob- (*against*)	ferre (*bear, carry*)
5. Insist	in- (*into*)	stare (*stand*)
6. Monograph	mono- (*alone, one*)	graphein (*write*)
7. Epilogue	epi- (*upon*)	legein (*say, study*)
8. Aspect	ad- (*to, towards*)	spicere (*see*)
9. Uncomplicated	un- (*not*) com- (*together with*)	plicare (*fold*)
10. Nonextended	non- (*not*) ex- (*out of*)	tendere (*stretch*)
11. Reproduction	re- (*back, again*) pro- (*forward*)	ducere (*lead*)
12. Indisposed	in- (*not*) dis- (*apart from*)	ponere (*put, place*)
13. Oversufficient	over- (*above*) sub- (*under*)	facere (*make, do*)
14. Mistranscribe	mis- (*wrong*) trans- (*across, beyond*)	scribere (*write*)

FIGURE 20-11 Brown's 14 'master words' with common prefixes and roots for vocabulary study. (From James Brown, *Efficient Reading*. D. C. Heath, Boston.)

This direct study of vocabulary improvement is often included as part of an English course or a study skills-course but may be found in some reading improvement courses as well. There are numerous workbooks and study materials which use these word root and prefix principles.

CONCLUSION

In this chapter some of the higher reading skills that are involved in the improvement of reading at the secondary level have been considered. They are not ordinarily included as remedial reading considerations. Rather, they represent some of the goals toward which remedial reading is aimed.

A good reader is one who reads critically and with good comprehension, has the flexibility to more from a slow (study) type of reading to fast skimming, and has a large and ever-increasing vocabulary.

It is, however, impossible to be a good reader if one does not read. Hence the establishment of lifelong reading habits is a worthy goal for all school reading instruction. This goal can be aided as much by the subject-matter teachers as by the reading teacher.

It should be apparent after the discussion of skimming, scanning, and study techniques that different levels of comprehension are suitable for different purposes. Sometimes all a student wants to glean from a reading passage is the general idea. At other times he will want to learn every detail in addition to the main idea. Or, he may merely seek enjoyment. Comprehension is not important if the purpose is amusement or a refreshing change in environment.

Good readers do not always seek maximum comprehension. If they did, they could not cover much reading matter; their horizons and the breadth of their reading experiences would be sorely limited.

As a final suggestion, teachers should tell students that there are different purposes in reading and should reinforce this advice with a wide variety of reading activities.

21

FOR FURTHER INFORMATION

The teaching of reading is an ever-growing and ceaselessly changing field. For those who wish to keep abreast of ideas and new developments, the International Reading Association publishes three excellent journals: (1) *The Reading Teacher*, which carries articles aimed chiefly at elementary-school teachers; (2) *The Journal of Reading*, which is focused more at the secondary and adult-level teacher; and (3) *The Reading Research Quarterly*, which carries longer and more scholarly research reports. Teachers who subscribe for a "comprehensive membership" in the International Reading Association (P.O. Box 119, Newark, Delaware) receive all three journals; in addition, special monographs and bibliographies are sent as they are issued throughout the year. These special monographs, the reports of annual conference proceedings, and the *Perspectives in Reading* series of monographs carry a wide variety of information on reading, and cover the entire grade range from preschool to adult.

Many other educational publishers and organizations publish excellent articles in the field of reading. For example, the May issue of *Education* is devoted each year to the topic of reading. Every several years the *Review of Educational Research* carries a fairly complete summary of reading research studies. The *Journal of Elementary English*, published by the National Council of Teachers of English, frequently also carries top quality reading articles, in addition to articles on related information, such as children's literature and reading interests of special groups and an annual review of language arts research studies.

Two national organizations devote thier efforts more or less to secondary and adult reading: the National Reading Conference issues an excellent series of yearbooks and the *Journal of Reading Behavior*, while the College Reading Association publishes a small journal, *The Journal of the Reading Specialist.*

In addition to these national organizations there are a number of colleges and state and local organizations which have publications in the field of reading. Two of the better known are (1) the reading monographs published by the University of Chicago School of Education, the *Supplementary Education Monograph* series; and (2) the *Claremont Reading Conference Yearbooks.*

Two other organizations that publish excellent monographs devoted to reading are the Educational Records Bureau that publishes monographs on reading research and the National Society for the Study of Education that periodically issues a yearbook devoted to elementary, secondary, or adult reading.

Summaries of reading research appear annually in the *Reading Research Quarterly, Elementary English,* the yearbooks of the National Reading Conference, and the *Journal of Educational Research.* Reading research summaries covering longer periods appear in the *Encyclopedia of Educational Research* and the *Handbook of Research on Teaching.*

A major source of the more current, unpublished, and government-sponsored research is the ERIC Center which is operated jointly by the International Reading Association and the University of Indiana at Bloomington, Indiana. In addition to making available all government research and numerous private research papers on both microfiche (a 4-by-6-inch sheet of microfilm containing fifty to seventy pages) and regular "printed-out" copies, the ERIC Center also provides bibliographies of reading research at various levels and in various areas to those who request them.

For those interested in reading research in specific areas, both ERIC/CRIER(the specific name of the reading ERIC center; there are other ERIC centers in different subjects such as testing, disadvantaged students, etc.) and the International Reading Association publish annotated bibliographies in specific subjects. Figure 21-1 gives a sample of the type of annotated bibliographies published by the IRA.

Reading, however, is the province of no single field. Excellent reading articles occasionally appear in such journals as the *Phi Delta Kappan* and the *Elementary School Journal.* However, articles which have a direct bearing on reading might appear anywhere from the *Journal of Experimental Psychology* to the *Harvard Educational Review.* Since it is one of the major subjects taught in elementary schools, and is becoming increasingly important at upper levels, it is wise to sample a wide variety of interests and a broad assortment of sources – administrators, researchers, publishers, and the general public.

A great aid in finding articles devoted to the subject of reading are these

Junior-Community College Reading/Study Skills	Gene Kerstiens
Reading and the Denied Learner	Leif Fearn and Amelia Martucci
Critical Reading: A Broader View	William Eller and Judity G. Wolf
Issues in Language and Reading Instruction of Spanish-Speaking Children	Carl L. Rosen and Philip D. Ortego
Bibliotherapy	Corrine W. Riggs
Adult Basic Reading Instruction	David Ford and Eunice Nicholson
Speed Reading	Allen Berger
Language-Experience Approach to Reading Instruction	Lillian K. Spitzer
Linguistics and the Teaching of Reading	Yetta M. and Kenneth S. Goodman
Visual Perception and Its Relation to Reading	Magdalen D. Vernon
Readability and Reading	Edgar Dale and Barbara Seels
Sources of Reading Research	Gus P. Plessas
High School Reading Programs	Walter Hill
Sources of Good Books and Magazines for Children	Winifred C. Ladley
Classroom Organization for Reading Instruction	George D. Spache
Providing Clinical Services in Reading	Roy A. Kress and Marjorie S. Johnson
Sources of Good Books for Poor Readers	George D. Spache
Reading and the Kindergarten	Dolores Durkin
Reading in the content Fields	Leo Fay
Individualized Reading	Harry W. Sartain

FIGURE 21-1 Some titles in IRA Annotated Bibliography Series.

standard library tools: *Education Index* and *Psychological Abstracts*. Many books on reading, particularly those intended for teachers are listed in *The Subject Matter Guide to Books in Print*. And if teachers are interested primarily in curriculum materials, a fairly large listing is found in *Textbooks in Print*.

A serious search for books and articles on reading can keep one busy for a lifetime; it can also be a source of continuing education. However, most teachers learn about reading from (1) teaching and (2) attending university courses. Attending conferences and meetings of professional organizations can also provide significant additional education.

The International Reading Association (IRA) has recommended that the professional training of a reading specialist consist of a master's degree or a thirty-graduate-credit program with at least twelve hours in the field of reading, the latter to include a clinical laboratory practicum and at least twelve hours in educational psychology, part of which is a measurement and evaluation course. A complete description of the IRA standard appears in Appendix 21-A.

The bibliography at the end of the book lists many additional textbooks and reference works that appeal to both special interests and general interests in this vast and interesting field of reading.

APPENDIX 21-A IRA MINIMUM STANDARDS FOR PROFESSIONAL TRAINING OF READING SPECIALISTS

I. A minimum of three years of successful teaching and/or clinical experience.

II. A master's degree or its equivalent, or a bachelor's degree plus thirty graduate hours in reading and related areas as indicated below:

A. A minimum of twelve semester hours in graduate-level reading courses, with at least one course in 1 and 2, and 3 or 4:

1. Foundations or survey of reading.
   A basic course whose content is related exclusively to reading instruction or the psychology of reading. Such a course ordinarily would be the first in a sequence of reading courses.
2. Diagnosis and correction of reading disabilities.
   The content of this course or courses includes the following: causes of reading disabilities; observation and interview procedures; diagnostic instruments; standard and informal tests; report writing; materials and methods of instruction.
3. Clinical or laboratory practicum in reading.
   A clinical or laboratory course which might be an integral part of a course or courses in the diagnosis and correction of reading disabilities. Students diagnose and treat reading disability cases under supervision.
4. Supervision and curriculum in reading.
   A study of selected curricula and the planning of a sound school curriculum in reading; an understanding of the functions and duties of the reading supervisor or consultant and the effective ways of implementing them.

B. At least one graduate-level course in each of the following content areas:

1. A course which includes one or more of the following: principles and practices of test construction and the selection, administration, scoring, and interpreting of group standardized tests; nature, theory, function, and use of individual intelligence tests; theory, function, and use of tests of personality.
2. Child and/or adolescent psychology or development.
   A course which stresses how children and/or adolescents mature and develop, with emphasis upon school activities and their relation to normal healthy development.
3. Personality and/or mental hygiene.
   A course which includes one or more of the following: the nature, development, and patterns of the personality and methods of change; personality theories and their contributions to understanding the dynamics of personality; integration of psychological knowledge and principles and their relation to mental health; etiological factors, differential diagnosis, and methods used in the correction of behavior problems.
4. Educational psychology.
   A course which includes one or more of the following: study of behavior, development, school environment; conditions for learning and methods of assessment; theories of learning and their implications for classroom practices.

C. The remainder of semester hours in reading and/or related areas. Courses recommended might include one or more of the following:
   1. Literature for children and/or adolescents.
   2. Organization and supervision of reading programs.
   3. Research and the literature in reading.
   4. Foundations of education.
   5. Principles of guidance.
   6. Nature of language.
   7. Communications.
   8. Speech and hearing.
   9. Exceptional child.
   10. Any additional courses under IIA and IIB.

APPENDIX 21-B IRA ETHICAL STANDARDS IN READING SERVICES

1. Reading specialists must possess suitable qualifications (see Minimum Standards for Professional Training of Reading Specialists) for engaging in consulting, clinical, or remedial work. Unqualified persons should not engage in such activities except under direct supervision of one who is properly qualified. Professional intent and the welfare of the person seeking the services of the reading specialist should govern all consulting and clinical activities such as counseling, administering diagnostic tests, or providing remediation. It is the duty of the reading specialist to keep relationships with the clients and interested persons on a professional level.
2. Information derived from consulting and/or clinical services should be regarded as confidential. Expressed consent of persons involved should be secured before releasing information to outside agencies.
3. Reading specialists should realize the boundaries of their competence and should not offer services which fail to meet professional standards established by their disciplines. They should be free, however, to give assistance in other areas in which they are qualified.
4. Referral should be made to specialists in all fields as needed. When such referral is made, pertinent information should be made available to consulting specialists.
5. Reading clinics and/or reading specialists offering professional services should refrain from guaranteeing easy solutions or favorable outcomes as a result of their work, and their advertising should be consistent with that of allied professions. They should not accept for remediation any persons who are unlikely to benefit from their instruction, and they should work to accomplish the greatest possible improvement in the shortest time. Fees, if charged, should be agreed on in advance and should be charged in accordance with an established set of rates commensurate with that of other professions.

BIBLIOGRAPHY

Ablewhite, R. C., *Slow reader: A problem in two parts*. Verry, Lawrence, Inc., 1967.

Adler, N.J., *How to read a book*. New York: Clarion, 1967.

Agranowitz, A., & McKeown, M. R., *Aphasia handbook: For adults and children*. Springfield, Illinois: Charles C. Thomas, 1966.

Anderson, I. H., & Deaborn, W. F., *The psychology of teaching reading*. New York: The Ronald Press Company, 1952.

Anderson, P. S., *Linguistics in the elementary school classroom*. New York: The Macmillan Company, 1971.

Anderson, V. D., *Reading and young children*. New York: The Macmillan Company, 1968.

Arbuthnot, M. H., *The Arbuthnot anthology*. Chicago: Scott, Foresman and Company, 1953.

Artley, S. A., *Your child learns to read*. Chicago: Scott, Foresman and Company, 1953.

Artley, A. S., *Trends and practices in secondary school reading* (Eric/Crier/IRA Reading Review Series). Newark, Del.: International Reading Association, 1968.

Ashlock, P., *Teaching reading to individuals with learning difficulties*. Springfield, Illinois: Charles C. Thomas, 1968.

Austin, D. E., Clark, V. B., & Fitchett, G. W., *Reading rights for boys: sex role and development in language experiences*. New York: Appleton Century Crofts, 1970.

Austin, M. C., *The torch lighters*. Cambridge, Mass.: Harvard University Press, 1961.

Austin, M. C., *The first R*. New York: The Macmillan Company, 1963.

Bagford, J., *Phonics: It's role in teaching reading*. Iowa City, Iowa: Sernoll, Inc., 1967.

Bamman, H. A., & Dawson, M. A., *Teaching reading*. San Francisco: Howard Chandler, 1958.

Bamman, H. A., Hogan, Ursula, & Greene, C. E., *Reading instruction in the secondary school*. New York: Longmans, Green & Co., 1961.

Baratz, J. C., & Shuy, R. W., *Teaching black children to read*. Washington, D. C.: Center for Applied Linguistics, 1969.

Barbe, W. B., *Teaching reading: Selected materials*. New York: Oxford University Press, 1965.

Barbc, W. B., *Educator's guide to personalized reading instruction*. Englewood Cliffs, N. J.: Prentice-Hall, Inc., 1966.

Barnette, G. C., *Tachistoscopic teaching techniques*. Dubuque, Iowa: Wm. C. Brown Company, 1951.

Barrett, T. C. (Ed.), *The evaluation of children's reading achievement* (perspectives). Newark, Del.: International Reading Association, 1967.

Beery, A., Barrett, T. C., & Powell, W. R., *Elementary reading instruction, selected materials*. Boston: Allyn and Bacon, 1969.

Bereiter, C., & Engelmann, S., *Teaching disadvantaged children in the preschool*. Englewood Cliffs, N. J.: Prentice-Hall, Inc., 1966.

Berger, A. (Ed), *Speed reading* (annotated bibliography). Newark, Del.: International Reading Association, 1970.

Berger, A., & Hartig, H., *Reading materials handbook: A guide to materials and sources for secondary college reading improvement*. Oshkosh, Wis.: Academia, 1969.

Betts, E. A., *Foundation of reading instruction.* New York: American Book Company, 1957.

Blair, G. M., *Diagnostic and remedial teaching.* New York: The Macmillan Company, 1956.

Bloom, B. S., (Ed.), *Taxonomy of educational objectives.* New York: David McKay Company, 1956.

Bloomer, R. H., *Reading comprehension for scientists.* Springfield, Ill.: Charles Thomas, 1963.

Bloomfield, L., *Language.* New York: Henry Holt and Company, 1933.

Bloomfield, L., & Barnhart, C. L., *Let's read.* Detroit: Wayne State University Press, 1961.

Bond, A. C., & Wagner, E. B., *Teaching the child to read.* New York: The Macmillan Company, 1966.

Bond, G. L., & Bond, E., *Developmental reading in high school.* New York: The Macmillan Company, 1941.

Bond, G. L., *The auditory and speech characteristics of poor readers.* New York: Teacher's College Press, Columbia University, 1935.

Bond, G. L., & Bond, E. W., *Teaching the child to read.* New York: The Macmillan Company, 1966.

Bond, G. L., Tinker, M. A., *Reading difficulties: Their diagnosis and correction.* New York: Appleton Century Crofts, 1965.

Botel, M., *How to teach reading.* Chicago: Follett Publishing Company, 1962.

Brogan, P., & Fox, L. K., *Helping children read.* New York: Holt, Rinehart and Winston, 1961.

Brown, J. I., *Efficient reading.* Boston: D. C. Heath and Company, 1962.

Brueckner, L. J., & Bond, G. L., *The diagnosis and treatment of learning difficulties.* New York: Appleton Century Crofts, 1955.

Bullock, H., *Helping the non-reading pupil in the secondary school.* New York: Bureau of Publications, Columbia University, 1956, 1957.

Buros, O. K. (Ed.), *Reading tests and reviews.* Highland Park, N.J.: The Gryphon Press, 1968.

Burrows, A. T., *Teaching children in the middle grades.* Boston: D. C. Heath and Company, 1952.

Bush, C., & Heubner, M., *Strategies for reading in the elementary school.* New York: The Macmillan Company, 1970.

Canavan, P. J., & Heckman, W. O., *Way to reading improvement.* Boston: Allyn and Bacon, 1966.

Canavan, P. J., & King, M. L., *Developing reading skills.* Boston: Allyn and Bacon, 1968.

Carlin, R., *Teaching elementary reading principles and strategies.* New York: Harcourt Brace Jovanovich, 1971.

Carpenter, C., *History of American schoolbooks.* Philadelphia: University of Pennsylvania Press, 1963.

Carter, H. L. J., & McGinnis, D., *Teaching individuals to read.* Boston: D. C. Heath and Company, 1962.

Carter, H. G., & McGinnis, D. J., *Diagnosis and treatment of the disabled reader.* New York: The Macmillan Company, 1970.

Catterson, J. (Ed), *Children and literature.* Newark, Del.: International Reading Association, 1970.
Causey, O. S., *The reading teacher's reader.* New York: The Ronald Press Company, 1958.
Center, S. S., *The art of reading.* New York: Charles Scribner's Sons, 1952.
Chall, J. S., *Readability – an appraisal of research and application.* Columbus, Ohio: Ohio State University Press, 1958.
Chall, J. S., *Learning to read: The great debate.* New York: McGraw-Hill Book Company, 1967.
Chasnoff, R. E., *Elementary curriculum.* New York: Pitman Publishing Corporation, 1964.
Claremont College Reading Conference Yearbooks. Claremont, Calif: Claremont College.
Cohen, S. A., *Teach them all to read.* New York: Random House, Inc., 1969.
Cohn, S., & Cohn, J., *Teaching the retarded reader.* New York: The Odyssey Press, Inc., 1967.
Cole, L. W., *The improvement of reading.* New York: Farrar & Rinehart, Inc., 1938.
Conference On Reading, University of Chicago, *Reading: Seventy-five years of progress.* Chicago: The University of Chicago Press, 1966.
Conroy, S. P., *Specifics for you: A corrective reading handbook.* Brooklyn, N.Y.: Book-Lab.
Cordts, A. D., *Phonics for the reading teacher.* New York: Holt, Rinehart and Winston, Inc., 1965.
Critchley, M., *Developmental dyslexia.* Springfield, Ill.: Charles C Thomas, 1965.
Cruickshank, W. A., *A teaching method for brain injured and hyperactive children.* New York: Syracuse University Press, 1961.
Curry, R. L., & Rigby, T. W., *Reading independence through word analysis.* Columbus, Ohio: Charles E. Merrill Books, Inc., 1969.
Cushenberry, D., *Reading improvement in the elementary school.* Englewood Cliffs, N. J.: Prentice-Hall, Inc., 1969.
Cutts, W. G., *Teaching young children to read.* Washington, D. C.: U. S. Dept of Health, Education, and Welfare, 1964.
Dale, E., *How to read a newspaper.* Chicago: Scott, Foresman and Company, 1941.
Dale, E., & Reichert, D., *Bibliography of vocabulary studies.* Columbus, Ohio: Bureau of Educational Research, Ohio State University Press, 1957.
Dale, E., & Eichholz, G., *Children's knowledge of words.* Columbus, Ohio: Bureau of Educational Research and Service, Ohio State University Press, 1960.
Dallman, M., *Teaching the language arts in the elementary school.* Dubuque, Iowa: Wm. C. Brown Company, 1966.
Dallman, M., *Reading and the language arts.* Dubuque, Iowa: Wm. C. Brown Company, 1966.
Darrow, H. F., & Howes, V. M., *Approaches to individualized reading.* New York: Appleton Century Crofts, 1969.
Davis, F. B., *Educational measurements.* Belmont, California: Wadsworth Publishing Company, Inc., 1965.
Dawson, M. A., & Bamman, H. A., *Fundamentals of basic reading instruction.* New York: Longmans, Green & Company, 1960.

Dawson, M. A. (Ed.), *Children, books, and reading* (perspectives). Newark, Del.: International Reading Association, 1964.
Dawson, M. A. (Ed.), *Combining research results and good practice*. Newark, Del.: International Reading Association, 1966.
Dawson, M. A. (Ed.), *Developing comprehension/critical reading* (selected IRA reprints). Newark, Del.: International Reading Association, 1968.
Dawson, M. A. (Ed.), *Teaching word recognition skills*. Newark, Del.: International Reading Association, 1970.
De Boer, D. (Ed.), *Reading diagnosis and evaluation*. Newark, Del.: International Reading Association, 1970.
DeBoer, J., & Dallmann, M., *The teaching of reading*. New York: Holt, Rinehart and Winston, Inc., 1970.
Dechant, E. V., *Improving the teaching of reading*. Englewood Cliffs, N.J.: Prentice-Hall, Inc., 1964.
Dechant, E., *Phonics and the teaching of reading*. Springfield, Ill.: Charles Thomas, 1969.
Dechant, E., *Detection and correction of reading difficulties: readings with commentary*. New York: Appleton Century Crofts, 1970.
DeHirsch, K., et al., *Predicting reading failure*. New York: Harper & Row, 1966.
Delacato, C. H., *The diagnosis and treatment of speech and reading problems*. Springfield, Ill.: Charles C Thomas, 1970.
Delacato, C. H., *The treatment and prevention of reading problems: The neuropsychological approach*. Springfield, Ill.: Charles C Thomas, 1965.
Delacato, C., *New start for the child who can't read*. New York: David McKay Company, Inc., 1970.
Della-Piana, G. M., *Reading diagnosis and prescription*. New York: Holt, Rinehart and Winston, Inc., 1968.
Dever, K. I., *Positions in the field of reading*. New York: Bureau of Publications, Teachers College, Columbia University, 1956.
Dewey, G., *Relative frequency of English Speech sounds*. Cambridge, Mass.: Harvard University Press, 1923.
Dietrich, D. M., & Mathews, V. H. (Eds.), *Development of lifetime reading habits*. Newark, Del.: International Reading Association, 1968.
Dietrich, D., & Mathews, V. H. (Eds.), *Reading and revolution: The role of reading in today's society* (perspectives). Newark, Del.: International Reading Association, 1970.
Doehring, D., *Patterns of impairment in specific reading ability*. Bloomington, Ind.: Indiana University Press, 1968.
Dolch, E. W., *Psychology and teaching of reading*. Champaign, Ill.: The Garrard Press, 1951.
Dolch, E. W., *A manual for remedial reading*. Champaign, Ill.: The Garrard Press, 1945, 1955.
Dolch, E. W., *Methods in reading*. Champaign, Ill.: The Garrard Press, 1955.
Dolch, E. W., *Problems in reading*. Champaign, Ill.: The Garrard Press, 1958.
Dolman, G., *How to teach your baby to read*. New York: Random House, Inc., 1964.
Downing, J., *Evaluating the Initial Teaching Alphabet*. London: Cassell & Co., Ltd., 1967.
Duker, S., *Individualized reading: Readings*. Metuchen, N.J.: Scarecrow Press, Inc., 1969.

Durkin, D. (Ed.) Miel, A., *Phonics and the teaching of reading.* New York: Bureau of Publications, Columbia University, 1962.
Durkin, D., *Children who read early.* New York: Teachers College Press, Columbia University, 1966.
Durkin, D., *Teaching them to read.* Boston: Allyn and Bacon, Inc., 1970.
Durr, W. K., *Reading instruction: Dimensions and issues.* Boston: Allyn and Bacon, Inc., 1967.
Durr, W. K. (Ed.), *Reading difficulties: Diagnosis, correction, and remediation.* Newark, Del. International Reading Association, 1970.
Durrell, D. D., *Improving reading instruction.* Tarrytown-on-Hudson, N. Y.: World Book Company, 1956.
Eakin, M. K., *Good books for children.* Chicago: University of Chicago Press, 1962.
Early, M. J. (Ed.), *Reading instruction in secondary schools* (perspectives). Newark, Del.: International Reading Association, 1964.
Edwards, J. L., & Silvaroli, N. J., *Reading improvement program.* Dubuque, Iowa: Wm. C. Brown Company, Publishers, 1969.
Ekwall, E., *Locating and correcting reading difficulties.* Columbus, Ohio: Charles E. Merrill Publishing Company, 1970.
Elkins, D., *Reading improvement in the junior high school.* New York: Teachers College Press, Columbia University, 1963.
Ephron, B. K., *Emotional difficulties in reading.* New York: Julian Press, 1953.
Erickson, A. G., *A handbook for teachers of disabled readers.* Iowa City, Iowa: Sernoll, Inc., 1967.
Fader, D. N., & McNeil, E. B., *Hooked on books: Programs and proof.* New York: G. P. Putnams Sons, 1968.
Farr, R., *Measurement and evaluation of reading.* New York: Harcourt Brace Jovanovich, 1970.
Farr, R., *Reading: What can be measured?* (Eric/Crier/IRA Review Series). Newark, Del.: International Reading Association, 1970.
Farr, R., & Anastasiow, N., *Tests of reading readiness and achievement: A review and evaluation* (Reading Aids Series). Newark, Del.: International Reading Association, 1969.
Fay, L. C., *Reading in the high school.* Washington: National Education Association, 1956.
Fay, L. C., Horn, T., & McCullough, C., *Improving reading in elementary social studies.* Washington: National Council for Social Studies, 1961.
Fernald, G. M., *Remedial techniques in basic school subjects.* New York: McGraw-Hill Book Company, 1943.
Figurel, J. A. (Ed.), *Reading for effective living.* Newark, Del.: International Reading Association, 1958.
Figurel, J. A. (Ed.), *Forging ahead in reading.* Newark, Del.: International Reading Association, 1967.
Figurel, J. A. (Ed.), *Reading and realism.* Newark, Del.: International Reading Association, 1968.
Figurel, J. A. (Ed.), *Reading goals for the disadvantaged.* Newark, Del.: International Reading Association, 1969.
Fitzgerald, J. A., *A basic life spelling vocabulary.* Milwaukee: The Bruce Publishing Company, 1951.

Fitzgerald, J. A., *Teaching reading and the language arts.* New York: The Bruce Publishing Company, 1965.
Fitzgerald, J. A., & Fitzgerald, P. G., *Fundamentals of reading instruction.* Milwaukee: The Bruce Publishing Company, 1967.
Flesch, R., *The art of plain talk.* New York: Harper & Brothers, 1946.
Flesch, R., *Why Johnny can't read.* New York: Harper & Brothers, 1955.
Flower, R. M., et al., *Reading disorders.* Philadelphia: F. A. Davis Company, 1965.
Fox, L. K., & Brogan, P., *Helping children to read.* New York: Holt, Rinehart and Winston, Inc., 1961.
Frierson, E. C., & Barbe, W. B., *Educating children with learning disabilities: Selected readings.* New York: Appleton Century Crofts, 1967.
Fries, C. C., *Linguistics and reading.* New York: Holt, Rinehart and Winston, Inc., 1962.
Frost, J. L., *Issues and innovations in the teaching of reading.* Glenview, Ill.: Scott, Foresman and Company, 1967.
Frost, J. L. Hawkes, G. R., *The disadvantaged child.* Boston: Houghton Mifflin Company, 1966.
Fry, E. B. *Reading faster: A drill book.* New York: Cambridge University Press, 1963.
Fry, E. B., *Teaching faster reading.* New York: Cambridge University Press, 1963.
Fry, E. B. *Teaching machines and programmed instruction, an introduction.* New York: McGraw-Hill Book Company, 1963.
Fry, E. B. *Emergency reading teachers manual.* Highland Park, N.J.: Dreier Educational Systems, 1969.
Gage, N. L. (Ed.), *Handbook of Research on teaching.* Chicago: Rand McNally & Company, 1963.
Gallant, R., *Handbook in corrective reading.* Columbus, Ohio: Charles E. Merrill Publishing Company, 1970.
Gans, R., *Common sense in teaching reading.* Indianapolis: The Bobbs-Merrill Company, 1963.
Gates, A. I., & Pritchard, M. C., *Teaching reading to slow-learning pupils.* New York: Bureau of Publications, Columbia University, 1942.
Gates, A. I., *Teaching reading.* Washington: National Education Association, 1953.
Gates, A. I., *Reading attainment in elementary schools.* New York: Bureau of Publications, Columbia University, 1961.
George, M., *Language arts: An idea book.* San Francisco: Chandler Publishing Company, 1970.
Getman, G. N., & Kane, E. R., *The Physiology of readiness.* Minneapolis: P.A.S.S., Inc., 1964.
Gilliland, H., *Materials for remedial reading and their use.* Billings, Mont.: Eastern Montana College, 1965.
Goodman, K. S., *Choosing materials to teach reading.* Detroit: Wayne State University Press, 1968.
Goodman, K. S., *Psycholinguistic nature of the reading process.* Detroit: Wayne State University Press, 1968.
Goodman, K. S., & Fleming, J. T. (Eds.), *Psycholinguistics and the teaching of reading.* Newark, Del.: International Reading Association, 1968.
Gray, L., & Reese, D., *Teaching children to read.* New York: The Ronald Press Company, 1963.

Gray, S. W., Klaus, R. A., Miller, J. O., & Forrester, B. J., *Before first grade.* New York: Teachers College Press, Columbia University, 1966.
Gray, W. S., *Improving reading in all curriculum areas.* Chicago: The University of Chicago Press, 1952.
Gray, W. S., *The teaching of reading and writing.* Chicago: Scott, Foresman and Company, 1956.
Gray, W. S., *On their own in reading.* Chicago: Scott, Foresman and Company, 1960.
Greene, F. D., & Palmatier, R. A., *Reading: The third level.* Syracuse, N.Y.: Syracuse University Press, 1968.
Greene, H. A., & Petty, W. T., *Developing language skills in the elementary schools.* Boston: Allyn and Bacon, Inc., 1967.
Gunn, M. A., *What we know about high school reading.* Champaign, Ill., 1964.
Hafner, L. E., *Improving reading in secondary school: Selected readings.* New York: The Macmillan Company, 1967.
Hall, Mary Ann, *Teaching reading as language experience.* Columbus, Ohio: Charles E. Merrill Publishing Company, 1970.
Harris, A. J. (Ed.), *Readings on reading instruction.* New York: David McKay Company, Inc., 1963.
Harris, A. J., *A casebook on reading disability.* New York: David McKay Company, Inc., 1970.
Harris, A. J., *How to increase reading ability.* New York: David McKay Company, Inc., 1970.
Harris, A. J., & Sipay, E. R., *effective teaching of reading.* New York: David McKay Company, Inc. 1971.
Harrison, M., *The story of the initial teaching alphabet.* New York: Pitman Publishing Corporation, 1965.
Hay, J., & Wingo, C. E., *Reading with phonics.* Chicago: J. B. Lippincott Company., 1948, 1954.
Heilman, A. W., *Phonics in proper perspective.* Columbus, Ohio: Charles E. Merrill Publishing Company, 1969.
Heilman, A. W., *Principles and practices of teaching reading.* Columbus, Ohio: Charles E. Merrill Publishing Company, 1967.
Hellmuth, J., *Annual progress in reading.* New York: Basic Books, Inc., 1971.
Henderson, E. C., *Phonics in learning to read.* Jericho, New York: Exposition Press, 1967.
Henderson, E. C., & Henderson, T. L., *Learning to read and write.* New York: Holt, Rinehart and Winston, Inc., 1965.
Henderson, R. L., & Green, D. R., *Reading for meaning in the elementary school.* Englewood Cliffs, N.J.: Prentice-Hall, Inc., 1969.
Herber, H. L. (Ed.), *Developing study skills in secondary schools* (perspectives). Newark, Del.: International Reading Association, 1965.
Herber, H. L., *Teaching reading in content areas.* Englewood Cliffs, N.J.: Prentice-Hall, Inc., 1970.
Hermann, K., *Reading disability: A medical study of word blindness and related handicaps.* Springfield, Ill.: Charles C Thomas, 1959.
Herr, S. E., *Diagnostic and corrective procedure in teaching reading.* Columbus, Missouri: Lucas Brothers Publishers, 1966.
Herr, S. E., *Learning activities for reading.* Dubuque, Iowa: Wm. Brown Company, 1967.

Hester, K. B., *Teaching every child to read (2nd ed.)*. New York: Harper & Row, 1964.
Hicks, H. G., *The reading chorus*. New York: Noble and Noble, Publishers, Inc., 1939.
Hildreth, G., *Teaching reading*. New York: Henry Holt and Company, 1958.
Holt, J., *How children fail*. New York: Pitman Publishing Corporation, 1964.
Holt, J., *How children learn*. New York: Pitman Publishing Corporation, 1967.
Horn, T. D. (Ed.), *Reading for the disadvantaged: Problems of linguistically different learners*. Newark, Del.: International Reading Association, 1970.
Howes, Virgil, & Darrow, H. F., *Reading and the elementary school child*. New York: The Macmillan Company, 1968.
Huey, E. B., *Psychology and pedagogy of reading*. Cambridge, Mass.: The M.I.T. Press, 1968.
Hull, M., *Phonics for the teacher of reading*. Columbus, Ohio: Charles E. Merrill Publishing Company, 1969.
Humphrey, G., & Coxon, R. V., *The chemistry of thinking*. Springfield, Ill.: Charles C Thomas, 1963.
Hunnicutt, C. W., & Iverson, W. J., *Research in the three r's*. New York: Harper Brothers, 1958.
Hunt, L. C. (Ed.), *The individualized reading program*. Newark, Del.: International Reading Association, 1966.
Huss, H. (Ed.), *Evaluating books for children and young people* (perspectives). Newark, Del.: International Reading Association, 1968.
Jacobs, L. R., *Individualizing reading practices*. New York: Teachers College Press, Columbia University, 1958.
Jenkinson, M. D. (Ed.), *Reading instruction: An international forum* (First World Congress Proceedings). Newark, Del: International Reading Association, 1966.
Jennings, F. C., *This is reading*. New York: Teachers College Press, Columbia University, 1965.
Johnson, D. J., & Myklebust, H. R., *Learning disabilities: Educational principles and practices*. New York: Grune & Stratton, 1967.
Johnson, G. L., *Certain psychological characteristics of retarded readers and reading achievers*. New York: Vantage Press, Inc., 1968.
Johnson, M. S., & Kress, R. A., *Informal reading inventories* (Reading Aids Series). Newark, Del.: International Reading Association, 1965.
Johnson, M. S., & Kress, R. A. (Eds.), *Corrective reading in the elementary classroom* (perspectives). Newark, Del.: International Reading Association, 1967.
Kaluger, G., & Kolson, C., *Reading and learning disabilities*. Columbus, Ohio: Charles E. Merrill Books, Inc., 1969.
Karlin, R., *Teaching reading in high school*. Indianapolis, Ind: The Bobbs-Merrill Company, Inc., 1963.
Kephart, N., *The slow learner in the classroom*. Columbus, Ohio: Charles E. Merrill Books, Inc., 1961.
Kerfoot, J. F. (Ed.), *First grade reading programs* (perspectives). Newark, Del.: International Reading Association, 1965.
Kirk, S. A., & Monroe, M., *Teaching reading to slow-learning children*. Boston: Houghton Mifflin Company, 1940.
Klare, G. R., *The measurement of readability*. Ames: The Iowa State University Press, 1963.
Knud, H., *Reading disability*. Springfield, Ill.: Charles C Thomas, 1959.

Kolson, C. J., & Kaluger, G., *Clinical aspects of remedial reading*. Springfield, Ill.: Charles C Thomas, 1963.

Kottmeyer, W., *Teacher's guide for remedial reading*. St. Louis; Webster Division, McGraw-Hill Book Company: 1959.

Kress, R., & Johnson, M. (Eds.), *Corrective reading in the elementary classroom, perspectives in reading series*. Newark, Del: International Reading Association, 1967.

Lanning, F. W., & Many, W. A., *Basic education for the disadvantaged adult*. Boston: Houghton Mifflin Company, 1966.

Larrick, N., *A teacher's guide to children's books*. Columbus, Ohio: Charles E. Merrill, 1960.

Larrick, N., *Parent's guide to children's reading*. Champaign. Ill.: National Council of Teachers of English, 1964.

Larrick, N., & Stoops, J. A., *What is reading doing to the child?* Danville, Ill.: The Interstate Printers and Publishers, Inc., 1967.

Lee, D. M., Allen, R. V., *Learning to read through experience*. New York: Appleton Century Crofts, 1965.

Lee, D., Bingham, A., & Weelfel, S., *Critical reading develops early* (Reading Aids Series). Newark, Del.: International Reading Association, 1968.

Leedy, P. D. (Ed.), *College-adult reading instruction* (perspectives). Newark, Del: International Reading Association, 1964.

Lefevre, C. A., *Linguistics and the teacher of reading*. New York: McGraw-Hill Book Company, 1964.

Levin, H., & Williams, J., *Basic studies in reading*. New York: Basic Books, Inc., 1970.

Lewis, N., *How to read better and faster*. New York: Thomas Y. Crowell Company, 1958.

Love, H. D., *Parents diagnose and correct reading disabilities*. Springfield, Ill.: Charles C Thomas, 1970.

Malmquist, E., *Factors related to reading disability in the first grade*. Stockholm: Almquist & Wiksell, 1957.

Mangano, J. A. (Ed.), *Strategies for adult basic education* (perspectives). Newark, Del.: International Reading Association, 1969.

Marksheffel, N. D., *Better reading in the secondary school: Principales and procedures for teachers*. New York: The Ronald Press Company, 1966.

Massey, W. J., & Moore, V. D., *Helping high school students to read better*. New York: Holt, Rinehart and Winston, 1965.

Mathews, M. M., *Teaching to read, historically considered*. Chicago: University of Chicago Press, 1966.

Mazurkiewicz, A. J., *New perspectives in reading instruction*. New York: Pitman Publishing Corporation, 1964.

McCullough, C. M., *Preparation of textbooks in the mother tongue*. Newark, Del.: International Reading Association, 1968.

McCullough, C., *Handbook for teaching language arts*. San Francisco: Chandler Publishing Co., 1969.

McDonald, A. S. & Zimny, G., *The art of good reading*. Indianapolis, Ind.: The Bobbs-Merrill Company, 1963.

McKee, P., & Durr, W. K., *A Program of instruction for the elementary school*. Boston: Houghton Mifflin Company, 1966.

McKim, M. G., & Caskey, H., *Guiding growth in reading*. New York: The Macmillan Company, 1963.

McLeod, P. H., *Underdeveloped learner—a developmental-corrective reading program for classroom teachers*. Springfield, Ill.: Charles C Thomas, 1968.

Miel, A. (Ed.), *Individualizing reading practices.* New York: Bureau of Publications, Columbia University, 1958.

Money, J. (Ed.), *Reading disability: Progress and research needs in dyslexia.* Baltimore: Johns Hopkins Press, 1962.

Mooney, J., *Disabled reader: Education of the dyslexic child.* Baltimore: Johns Hopkins Press, 1966.

Monroe, M., & Rogers, B., *Foundations for reading.* Chicago: Scott, Foreman and Company, 1964.

Morris, J. M., *Standards and progress in reading.* New York: New York University Press, 1968.

Morrison, I. E., *Teaching reading in the elementary school.* New York: The Ronald Press Company, 1968.

Mountain, L. H., *How to teach reading before first grade.* Highland Park, N.J.: Dreier Educational Systems, 1970.

Nachez, G. (Ed.), *Children with reading problems.* New York: Basic Books, Inc., 1968.

National Education Association, Professional rights and responsibilities commission. *As the child reads.* Washington, D. C.: National Education Association, 1967.

National Reading Conference Yearbooks. (There are about nineteen yearbooks which deal with many areas of reading, with emphasis on secondary and adult. They are available in most university libraries or can be purchased from Marquette University, Milwaukee, Wis.)

National Society for the Study of Education., forty-seventh yearbook, 1948, *Reading in the high school and college.* Forty-eighth yearbook, 1948, *Reading in the elementary school.* Sixtieth yearbook, 1961, *Development in and through reading.* Sixty-seventh yearbook, 1968, *Innovation and change in reading instruction.* Fifty-fifth yearbook, *Adult reading.* Chicago: University of Chicago Press.

Newman, H. *Reading disabilities.* New York: The Odyssey Press, 1969.

Newton, J., Ray, *Reading in your school.* New York: McGraw-Hill Book Company, 1960.

Olson, A. V., & Ames, W. G., *Teaching reading in secondary schools: Readings.* New York: Intext Educational Publishers, 1970.

Otto, W., & Ford, D. H., *Teaching adults to read.* Boston: Houghton Mifflin Company, 1967.

Otto, W. & Koenke, K. (Eds.), *Remedial teaching.* Boston: Houghton Mifflin Company, 1969.

Otto, W., & McMenemy, R. A., *Corrective and remedial teaching.* Boston: Houghton Mifflin Company, 1966.

Otto, W., & Smith, R. J., *Administering the school reading program.* Boston: Houghton Mifflin Company, 1970.

Painter, H. W., *Poetry and children.* Newark, Del.: International Reading Association, 1970.

Pilgrim, G. H., & McAllister, M. K., *Books, young people, and reading guidance.* New York: Harper & Row, 1968.

Pitman, J., & St. John, J. *Alphabets & Reading.* New York: Pitman Publishing Corporation, 1969.

Pollack, M. F. W., & Piekarz, J., *Reading problems and problem readers.* New York: David McKay Company, 1963.

Pope, L., *Guidelines to teaching remedial reading.* Brooklyn, N. Y.: Book-Lab, Inc., 1967.

Preston, R. (Ed.), *A new look at reading in the social studies* (perspectives). Newark, Del.: International Reading Association, 1969.
Ramsey, W. Z. (Ed.), *Organizing for individual differences* (perspectives). Newark, Del.: International Reading Association, 1967.
Raubicheck, L., *Choral speaking is fun*. New York: Noble and Noble, 1958.
Rauch, S. J. (Ed.), *Handbook for the volunteer tutor*. Newark, Del.: International Reading Association, 1969.
Richards, C. G. (Ed.), *The provision of popular reading materials*. Paris: UNESCO, 1959.
Rinsland, H. D., *A basic vocabulary of elementary school children*. New York: The Macmillan Company, 1950.
Roberts, C., *Word attack: Teacher's guide to*. New York: Harcourt, Brace and Company, 1956.
Roberts, G., *Reading in primary schools*. New York: Humanities Press, 1970.
Robinson, F. P., *Effective reading*. New York: Harper & Brothers, 1962.
Robinson, H. A., & Rauch, S. J., *Guiding the reading program, a reading consultants handbook*. Chicago: Science Research Associates, 1965.
Robinson, H. A., & Rauch, S. (Eds.), *Corrective reading in the high school classroom, perspectives in reading series*. Newark, Del: International Reading Association, 1966.
Robinson, H. A., & Thomas, E. L. (Eds.), *Fusing reading skills and content*. Newark, Del.: International Reading Association, 1969.
Robinson, H. M., *Why pupils fail in reading*, Chicago: University of Chicago Press, 1946.
Robinson, H. M. (Ed.), *Corrective reading in classroom and clinic*. Chicago: The University of Chicago Press, 1953.
Robinson, H. M., & Smith, H. K., *Clinical studies in reading* (supplementary educational monograph). Chicago: University of Chicago Press, 1968.
Roswell, F., & Natchez, G., *Reading disability*. New York: Basic Books, Inc., 1964.
Russell, D. H., *Children learn to read*. Boston: Ginn and Company, 1961.
Russell, D. H., *Children's thinking*. Boston: Ginn and Company, 1961.
Russell, D. H., *Dynamics of reading*. Boston: Ginn and Company, 1970.
Russell, D. H., & Russell, E. F., *Listening aids through the grades*. New York: Bureau of Publications, Columbia University, 1959.
Russell, D. H., & Karp, E. E., *Reading aids through the grades*. New York: Columbia University Press, 1961.
Sargent, E. E., Huus, H., & Andresen, O., *How to read a book* (Reading Aids Series). Newark, Del.: International Reading Association, 1970.
Schell, L. M., & Burns, P. C., *Remedial reading, an anthology of sources*. Boston: Allyn and Bacon, 1968.
Schonell, F. J., *Backwardness in the basic subjects*. Edinburgh: Oliver and Boyd, 1942.
Schonell, F. J., *Psychology and teaching of reading*. Edinburgh: Oliver and Boyd, 1961.
Schubert, D. G., *The doctor eyes the poor reader*. Springfield, Ill.: Charles C Thomas, 1957.
Schubert, D. G., & Torgerson, T. L., *Improving reading in the elementary school*. Dubuque, Iowa: Wm. C. Brown Company, 1963.
Schubert, D. G., & Torgerson, T. L. (Eds.), *Readings in reading: Practice, theory, and research*. New York: Thomas Y. Crowell Company, 1968.

Schubert, D. G., & Torgerson, T. L., *Dictionary of terms and concepts in reading.* Springfield, Ill.: Charles E. Thomas, Publisher, 1969.
Scott, L. B., & J. J. Thompson, *Talking time.* St. Louis: Webster Division, McGraw-Hill Book Company, 1951.
Sebesta, S. L. (Ed.), *Ivory, apes, and peacocks: The literature point of view.* Newark, Del.: International Reading Association, 1967.
Shankman, F., *Successful practices in reading.* New York: Teachers Practical Press, Inc., 1960.
Shankman, F. V., *Successful practices in remedial reading.* Englewood Cliffs, N. J.: Prentice-Hall, Inc., 1963.
Sheperd, D. L. (Ed.), *Reading and the elementary school curriculum.* Newark, Del.: International Reading Association 1968.
Silvaroli, N. J., *Classroom reading inventory.* Dubuque, Iowa: Wm. C. Brown, 1969.
Simpson, E. A., *Helping high school students read better.* Chicago: Science Research Associates, 1954.
Singer, H., & Ruddell, R. (Eds.), *Theoretical models and processes of reading.* Newark, Del.: International Reading Association, 1969.
Sleisenger, L., *Guidebook for the volunteer reading teacher.* New York: Teachers College Press, Columbia University, 1965.
Smith, D. E. P., & Carrigan, P. M., *The nature of reading disability.* New York: Harcourt, Brace and Company, 1959.
Smith, F., *Understanding reading: A psycholinguistic analysis of reading and learning to read.* New York: Holt, Rinehart and Winston, 1971.
Smith, H. K. (Ed.), *Perception and reading.* Newark, Del.: International Reading Association, 1967.
Smith, H. P., & Dechant, E., *Psychology of teaching reading.* Englewood Cliffs, N. J.: Prentice-Hall, Inc., 1961.
Smith, H. P., *Psychology in teaching.* Englewood Cliffs, N.J.: Prentice-Hall, Inc., 1962.
Smith, J. A., *Creative teaching of reading and literature in the elementary school.* Boston: Allyn and Bacon, 1967.
Smith, N. B., *Reading instruction for today's children.* Englewood Cliffs, N. J.: Prentice-Hall, Inc., 1963.
Smith, N. B., *American reading instruction.* Newark, Del.: International Reading Association, 1965.
Smith, N. B. (Ed.), *Current issues in reading.* Newark, Del.: International Reading Association, 1968.
Sochor, E. E., *Critical reading.* Champaign, Ill.: National Council of Teachers of English, 1964.
Southgate, V., & Roberts, G. R., *Reading which approach.* Mystic, Conn.: Verry, Lawrence, Inc., 1970.
Spache, G. D., *Toward better reading.* Champaign, Ill.: The Garrard Press, 1963.
Spache, G. D. (Ed.), *Reading disability and perception.* Newark, Del.: International Reading Association, 1968.
Spache, G. D., *Good reading for the disadvantaged reader: Multi-ethnic resources.* Champaign, Ill.: Garrard Publishing Co., 1970.
Spache, G. D., *Good reading for poor readers.* Champaign, Ill.: The Garrard Press, 1970.
Spache, G. D. and Spache, E., *Reading in the elementary school.* Boston Mass.: Allyn and Bacon, 1969.

Spalding, R. B., & Spalding, W. T., *The writing road to reading*. New York: Whiteside, Inc., & William Morrow & Company, 1957.
Staats, A. M., *Learning, language and cognition*. New York: Holt, Rinehart and Winston, 1968.
Stahl, S. S., *Teaching of reading in the intermediate grades*. Dubuque, Iowa: Wm. C. Brown, Co., 1965.
Staiger, R. C., & Andresen, O. (Eds.), *Reading: A human right and a human problem* (Second World Congress Proceedings). Newark, Del.: International Reading Association, 1968.
Stauffer, R. G. (Ed.), *The first grade reading studies: Findings of individual investigations*. Newark, Del.: International Reading Association, 1967.
Stauffer, R. G., *Directing reading maturity as a cognitive process*. Evanston, Ill.: Harper & Row, Publishers, 1968.
Stauffer, R. G., *Teaching reading as thinking process*. New York: Harper & Row, Publishers, 1968.
Stauffer, R. G., *Language experience approach to the teaching of reading*. New York: Harper & Row, Publishers, 1970.
Stauffer, R., & Cramer, R., *Teaching critical reading at the primary level* (Reading Aids Series). Newark, Del.: International Reading Association, 1968.
Stern, C., & Gould, T. S., *Children discover reading*. New York: Random House, Inc., 1965.
Strang, R., *Reading diagnosis and remediation* (Eric/Crier IRA Reading Review Series). Newark, Del.: International Reading Association, 1968.
Strang, R., *Diagnostic teaching of reading*. New York: McGraw-Hill Book Company, 1969.
Strang, R., & Bracken, P., *Making better readers*. Boston: D. C. Heath and Company, 1957.
Strang, R., & Lindquist, D. M., *The administrator and the improvement of reading*. New York: Appleton Century Crofts, 1965.
Strang, R., McCullough, C. M., & Traxler, A. E., *The improvement of reading*. New York: McGraw-Hill Book Company, 1967.
Strang, R. (Ed.), *Understanding and helping the retarded reader*. Tucson: University of Arizona Press, 1965.
Supplementary Educational Monographs, *Proceedings of the annual conference on reading* (at the University of Chicago). Chicago: University of Chicago Press.
Tansley, A. E., *Reading and remedial reading*. New York: Humanities Press, 1967.
Terman, S., & Walcutt, C. C., *Reading: Chaos and cure*. New York: McGraw-Hill Book Company, 1958.
Thomas, J. K., *Teaching reading to the mentally retarded*. Minneapolis, Minn.: T. S. Dennison & Company, 1967.
Thonis, E., *Teaching reading to non-English speakers*. New York: The Macmillan Company, 1969.
Thorndike, E. L., & Lorge, I., *The teacher's word book of 30,000 words*. New York: Teachers College, Columbia University, 1944.
Tinker, M. A., *Legibility of print*. Ames: Iowa State University Press, 1963.
Tinker, M. A., *Bases for effective reading*. Minneapolis: University of Minnesota Press, 1965.
Tinker, M. A., McCullough, C. M., *Teaching elementary reading*. New York: Appleton Century Crofts, 1968.

Trela, T. M., *Fourteen remedial reading methods.* Palo Alto, Calif.: Fearon Publishers, Inc., 1969.

Triggs, F. O., *Reading: Its creative teaching and testing.* Mountain Home, N.C.: Triggs 1960.

Triggs, F. O., *Remedial reading.* Minneapolis: University of Minnesota Press, 1943.

Umans, S., *New trends in reading instruction.* New York: Teachers College Press, Columbia University, 1963.

Umans, S., *New trends in reading instruction.* New York: Bureau of Publications, Columbia University, 1963.

Umans, S., *Design for reading programs.* New York: Teachers College Press, Columbia University, 1964.

Vail, Esther, *Tools of teaching: Techniques for stubborn cases of reading, spelling, and behavior.* Springfield, Ill.: Charles C Thomas, 1967.

Veatch, J., *Individualizing your reading program.* New York: G. P. Putnam's Sons, 1959.

Veatch, J., *How to teach reading with children's books.* New York: Teachers College Press, Columbia University, 1964.

Veatch, J., *Reading in the elementary school.* New York: The Ronald Press Company, 1966.

Vernon, M. D., *Backwardness in reading: A study of its nature and origin.* Cambridge, Mass.: Howard University Press, 1960.

Verracci, C., & Larrick, N. (Eds.), *Reading—isn't it really the teacher?* Danville, Ill.: The Interstate Printers and Publishers, Inc., 1968.

Vilscek, E. C. (Ed.), *A decade of innovations: Approaches to beginning reading.* Newark, Del.: International Reading Association, 1967.

Viox, R. G., *Evaluating reading and study skills in the secondary classroom* (Reading Aids Series). Newark, Del.: International Reading Association, 1968.

Vogts, C. F., *Successful techniques for teaching reading in the elementary schools.* Englewood Cliffs, N. J.: Prentice-Hall, Inc., 1961.

Walcott, C., *Tomorrow's illiterates: The state of reading instruction today.* Boston: Little, Brown and Company, 1961.

Wall, W. D., Schonell, F. J., & Olsen, W., *Failure in school.* Hamburg: UNESCO Institute for Education, 1962.

Warburton, F. W., & Southgate, V., *i.t.a.: an independent evaluation.* London: John Murray, & W. & R. Chambers, 1969.

Wardhaugh, R., *Reading: a linguistic perspective.* New York: Harcourt Brace Jovanovich, 1969.

Webster, J., *Practical reading: Some new remedial techniques.* New York: Humanities Press, Inc., 1965.

Webster, J., *Practical reading: Some new remedial techniques.* New York: International Publications Serivce, 1970.

Weiss, M. J., *Reading in the secondary schools.* New York: The Odyssey Press, Inc., 1961.

West, R. (Ed.), *Childhood, aphasia.* Stanford, Calif.: Stanford University Press, 1960.

West, R., *Individualized reading instruction.* Port Washington, N.Y.: Kennikat Press, Inc., 1964.

Wheeler, A., *How to double your child's power to read.* New York: Frederick Fell, Inc., 1966.

Whipple, G., & Black, M. H. (Eds.), *Reading for children without—our disadvantaged youth.* Newark, Del.: International Reading Association, 1966.

Willey, R. D., *Child centered reading.* New York: Pitman Publishing Comporation, 1970.

Willson, M. F., & Schneyer, J. W., *Developmental reading in the junior high school.* Danville, Ill.: Interstate Printers and Publishers, 1959.

Wilson, R. M., *Diagnostic and remedial reading.* Columbus, Ohio: Charles E. Merrill Books, Inc., 1967.

Wilson, R. M., & Hall, M., *Programmed word attack for teachers.* Columbus, Ohio: Charles E. Merrill Books, Inc., 1968.

Witty, P. A., *Reading instruction—a forward look.* Champaign, Ill.: National Council of Teachers of English, 1964.

Witty, P. A., *Teaching of reading: A developmental process.* Boston: D. C. Heath and Company, 1966.

Witty, P. A., & Kopel, D., *Reading and the educative process.* Boston: Ginn and Company, 1939.

Witty, P. A., Freeland, A. M., & Grotberg, E. H., *The teacher of reading: A developmental process.* Boston: D. C. Heath and Company, 1966.

Woolf, M. D., (Ed.), & Woolf, M. A., *Remedial reading.* New York: McGraw-Hill Book Company, 1957.

Woolf, M. D., & Woolf, J. A., *Remedial reading: Teaching and treatment.* New York: McGraw-Hill Book Company, 1957.

Yoakam, G. A., *Basal reading instruction.* New York: McGraw-Hill Book Company, 1955.

Young, F. A., Lindsley, D. B., *Early experience and visual information processing in perceptual and reading disorders.* Washington, D.C.: National Academy of Sciences, 1970.

Zintz, M. V., *Corrective reading.* Dubuque, Iowa: Wm. C. Brown Company, 1971.

Zintz, M. V., *Reading process: The teacher and the learner.* Dubuque, Iowa: Wm. C. Brown Company, 1970.

NAME INDEX

SUBJECT INDEX